Fo

COMPARATIVE LABOR LAW

RESEARCH HANDBOOKS IN COMPARATIVE LAW

Series Editors: Francesco Parisi, *Oppenheimer Wolff and Donnelly Professor of Law, University of Minnesota, USA and Professor of Economics, University of Bologna, Italy* and Tom Ginsburg, *Professor of Law, University of Chicago, USA*

The volumes in this series offer high-level discussion and analysis on particular aspects of legal systems and the law. Well-known scholars edit each handbook and bring together accessible yet sophisticated contributions from an international cast of top researchers. The first series of its kind to cover a wide range of comparative issues so comprehensively, this is an indispensable resource for students and scholars alike.

Titles in this series include:

Comparative Administrative Law
Edited by Susan Rose-Ackerman and Peter L. Lindseth

Comparative Constitutional Law
Edited by Tom Ginsburg and Rosalind Dixon

Methods of Comparative Law
Edited by Pier Giuseppe Monateri

Comparative Law and Society
Edited by David S. Clark

Comparative Labor Law
Edited by Matthew W. Finkin and Guy Mundlak

Comparative Labor Law

Edited by

Matthew W. Finkin

University of Illinois, USA

Guy Mundlak

Tel Aviv University, Israel

RESEARCH HANDBOOKS IN COMPARATIVE LAW

Edward Elgar Publishing

Cheltenham, UK • Northampton, MA, USA

Published by
Edward Elgar Publishing Limited
The Lypiatts
15 Lansdown Road
Cheltenham
Glos GL50 2JA
UK

Edward Elgar Publishing, Inc.
William Pratt House
9 Dewey Court
Northampton
Massachusetts 01060
USA

A catalogue record for this book
is available from the British Library

Library of Congress Control Number: 2015933356

This book is available electronically in the Elgaronline
Law subject collection
DOI 10.4337/9781781000137

MIX
Paper from
responsible sources
FSC® C013056

ISBN 978 1 78100 012 0 (cased)
ISBN 978 1 78100 013 7 (eBook)

Typeset by Columns Design XML Ltd, Reading
Printed and bound in Great Britain by T.J. International Ltd, Padstow

To Ruth Ben-Israel,
A pioneer in the many paths she has taken

Guy Mundlak

To Sanford M. Jacoby
Economist, historian, policy analyst, and comparativist without compare

Matthew W. Finkin

Contents

PART III REGIONAL COMPARISONS

Contributors

Kevin Banks, Associate Professor of Law, Queens University, Canada

Alan Bogg, Professor of Labour Law, Fellow and Tutor in Law, Hertford College, Oxford, UK

Silvia Bonfanti, PhD in Labour Law, University of Milano-Bicocca, Italy

Stuart Butterworth, Research Assistant, Faculty of Law, Monash University, Australia

Sean Cooney, Professor of Law, Melbourne Law School, University of Melbourne, Australia

Luisa Corazza, Professor of Labor and Employment Law, Università del Molise, Italy

Guy Davidov, Elias Lieberman Chair in Labour Law, Hebrew University of Jerusalem, Israel,

Darcy du Toit, Emeritus Professor of Law, University of the Western Cape, Republic of South Africa

Cynthia Estlund, Catherine A. Rein Professor, New York University School of Law, USA

Keith D. Ewing, Professor of Public Law, King's College London, UK

Matthew W. Finkin, Professor of Law, University of Illinois, USA

Roberto Fragale, Labor Judge, Rio De Janeiro Labor Court, Professor of Law, Universidade Federal Fluminense, Brazil

Mark Freedland, University of Oxford, UK

Nuno Garoupa, Professor of Law, University of Illinois, USA

Stefano Giubboni, Professor of Labor Law, University of Perugia, Italy

Frank Hendrickx, Professor of Labour Law, University of Leuven, Belgium

Joanna Howe, Lecturer in Law, University of Adelaide, Australia

Alan Hyde, Distinguished Professor and Sidney Reitman Scholar, Rutgers University School of Law, USA

Nicola Kountouris, University College London, UK

Erika Kovács, Assistant Professor, Vienna University of Economics and Business, Austria

Rüdiger Krause, Professor of Law, Georg-August-Universität, Göttingen, Germany

Nikita Lyutov, Professor, Kutafin Moscow State Law University, National Research University Higher School of Economics, Russia

Emanuele Menegatti, Professor of Labour Law, University of Bologna, Italy

Leszek Mitrus, Chair of Labour Law and Social Policy, Jagiellonian University, Kraków, Poland

Guy Mundlak, Faculty of Law and the Department of Labor Studies, Tel-Aviv University, Israel

Roberta Nunin, Professor of Labour Law, Università di Trieste, Italy

Marilyn J. Pittard, Professor of Law and Associate Dean, International and Engagement, Monash University, Australia

Orsola Razzolini, Associate Professor in Labour Law, University of Genova, Italy

Kerry Rittich, Professor of Law, Public Policy, and Governance and Women and Gender, Studies, University of Toronto, Canada

Roger Ronnie, Research Associate, Social Law Project, University of the Western Cape, Republic of South Africa

Esther Sánchez, Professor of Labor Law, ESADE-Ramon Llull University, Barcelona, Spain

Kamala Sankaran, Professor Faculty of Law, University of Delhi, India

Monika Schlachter, Director, Institute for Labor Law and Industrial Relations in the EU, Professor of Law, Trier University, Germany

Achim Seifert, Professor of Law, Friedrich-Schiller-University of Jena, Germany

Andrew Stewart, John Bray Professor of Law, University of Adelaide, Australia

Hisashi Takeuchi-Okuno, Professor of Law, Waseda University, Japan

Adriana Topo, Professor of Employment Law, Law School, University of Padova, Italy

Introduction to the Comparative Labor Law Handbook

Guy Mundlak and Matthew W. Finkin

1. THE CHALLENGE OF COMPARATIVE WORK AND THE HANDBOOK'S OBJECTIVES

We begin with a rumination on the organic nature of law. Law has a shelf life. As the society in which law is embedded changes, parts of the law wither away or become vestigial; parts are extended or renewed in novel application; new law is fashioned whole, to commence the life cycle afresh. Consequently, the study of law, when not totally fixated on the here and now, is inherently comparative. Students of the law look to the before and the after – to discern change, to explore reasons for change, to ask whether there is need for change, and to see how it all fares.

But some look beyond their borders; for counterpoints, parallels, or counterfactuals. This adds another dimension. It confronts differences in legal systems and cultures – sometimes superficial, sometimes not – sometimes couched in vernaculars that lack equivalents or are so steeped in the unspoken that the meaning can and often does elude even the astute non-native. But the non-native, in open-eyed wonder, may give voice and form to that which has become so ingrained in a foreign system, is so much a matter of second nature to those who live in the system that those who live in it fail to appreciate its significance. These are the challenges and rewards of studying law comparatively.

Unlike ancient institutions long subject to comparative legal study – real property, the family, the use of violence – labor law is a young discipline. At its core, it concerns the institution of wage labor and the situation of the waged worker, which did not emerge as a major focal point for the law's concern until well into the nineteenth century, and was not a subject of systemic legal academic study until the twentieth. Labor law arose as a consequence of the rise of capitalism and industrialization – both global phenomena. In that sense, labor law from the outset was a comparative enterprise insofar as it developed in separate nation states, but in reaction to common methods of production and common means for the deployment and administration of labor on a global scale. Efforts to produce manufactured goods with interchangeable parts in the mid-nineteenth century evolved into mass industrial production,[1] accelerating the extreme division of labor characterized by the assembly line, which took on the sobriquet of "Fordism" worldwide. Meanwhile, the growth of large and complex organizations entailed the development of bureaucratic means for the administration of

[1] David Hounshell, FROM THE AMERICAN SYSTEM TO MASS PRODUCTION 1800–1932 (1984); *cf.* A.E. Musson, *British Origins* in YANKEE ENTERPRISE: THE RISE OF THE AMERICAN SYSTEM OF MANUFACTURES 25 (Otto Mayr & Robert Post eds 1981).

people and not only in manufacture. Railroading was an early mover in that regard.[2] So, too, the department store.[3] The comparative perspective was important already at the evolution of the field, accounting for different legal arrangements in what seemed to be similar organizational settings, with ideas such as 'Fordism' crossing borders, maintaining the unique features of its origin and changing with the culture of many national orders.

As solutions to the 'labor problem' developed, they continued to draw on the interplay of common ideas and different methods of implementation. In the 20s and 30s, Frederick W. Taylor's 'scientific management' drew an enthusiastic following in Western Europe and the Soviet Union.[4] In the post-war period, 'human relations'[5] eclipsed scientific management, succeeded in turn by the 'industrial relations' school that was thought at the time to bid fair for global convergence.[6] In the 80s and 90s, the work of Edward Demming[7] and Douglas McGregor[8] in the U.S. bore fruit in Japan, becoming *kaizen*[9] and *Theory Z*,[10] which rippled across the seas. Today, the call to the return to 'core competencies'[11] has spurred the growth of alternative business models – subcontracting, franchising[12] – echoes internationally.

The deployment of common ways to treat those who made the goods and supplied services in nation states with very different legal regimes, histories and shared assumptions about how people should be treated makes the comparative project both difficult and, if done well, insightful. Economic imperatives confront social values. Ideologies of management meet ideologies of law – if by ideology we mean assumptions, express or implied, about how the existence of a set of facts or legal results simultaneously explain and justify why they are or what they should be. The latter injects a normative component to the comparative enterprise that will be touched upon below.

A necessary predicate for comparative analysis is an accurate depiction of the law. Given difficulties of translation, and the fact that some concepts have no good cognates

---

2 *See e.g.* Walter Licht, WORKING FOR THE RAILROAD: THE ORGANIZATION OF WORK IN THE NINETEENTH CENTURY (1983) *with* P.W. Kingsford, VICTORIAN RAILWAYMEN: THE EMERGENCE AND GROWTH OF RAILWAY LABOUR 1830–1870 (1970); F. Jacqmin, RAILROAD EMPLOYEES IN FRANCE (1877).

3 *See e.g.* Michael Miller, THE BON MARCHÉ: BOURGEOIS CULTURE AND THE DEPARTMENT STORE, 1869–1920 (1981); Ralph Hower, HISTORY OF MACY'S OF NEW YORK 1858–1919 (1943).

4 Judith Merkle, MANAGEMENT AND IDEOLOGY: THE LEGACY OF THE INTERNATIONAL SCIENTIFIC MANAGEMENT MOVEMENT (1980).

5 Reinhard Bendix, WORK AND AUTHORITY IN INDUSTRY (1956).

6 Clark Kerr *et al*, INDUSTRIALISM AND INDUSTRIAL MAN (2d ed. 1964).

7 W. Edward Demming, OUT OF CRISIS (1986).

8 Douglas McGregor, THE HUMAN SIDE OF ENTERPRISE (Annot. by Joel Cutcher-Gershenfeld, ed. 2006).

9 Maasaki Inai, KAIZEN: THE KEY TO JAPAN'S COMPETITIVE SUCCESS (1986).

10 William Ouchi, THEORY Z: HOW AMERICAN BUSINESS CAN MEET THE JAPANESE CHALLENGE (1981).

11 David Weil, THE FISSURED WORKPLACE (2014).

12 Tony Royle, WORKING FOR MCDONALD'S IN EUROPE (2000).

in other legal vernaculars, the ability to achieve goodness of descriptive fit is a professional skill of no small dimension. There is much good depiction in what follows.

The chapters in this Research Handbook mingle subjects of long-standing comparative concern – freedom of association, representation outside collective bargaining, discrimination, the very forms of law[13] – with matters that have pressed to the fore in recent years because of the expansion of modes of entrepreneurial control and knowledge-based employment (e.g., covenants not to compete); or, because of the ever-growing fracturing of responsibilities in chains of contracting (e.g., the determination of what the subject of the law is). Even traditional subjects of comparative treatment are placed in a new light by economic and managerial change: a generation ago, scant notice would have been paid to what we now call 'soft law' as a player on the global stage; attention must now be given to emerging geographic zones – to Europe as a whole, to the former members of the Soviet bloc, and to rapidly developing economies.

In substance, these chapters speak for themselves. No introduction to what they say under their various heads is needed. We focus here on what runs through these chapters that is largely unspoken: the methodological assumptions and practical difficulties of doing labor law comparatively. These conundrums our authors tend not to confront head-on. But we believe it pays to lay them out.

Good description is a necessary, but it is not a sufficient condition for good comparative work which confronts not only the practical barriers to full comprehension, but also the unarticulated values the law embraces. Trending between the two, this volume suggests the various forms comparative work can take. These themes are strongly interrelated. They also intersect with the dialectics of shared scholarly values.

2. WHY ENGAGE IN A COMPARATIVE STUDY?

It may seem obvious that comparisons are useful, but upon probing more deeply into the literature different reasons emerge. At the one end of the spectrum, comparisons can be viewed as a way of identifying 'best practices', diffusing them ('transplantation') and improving the legal system. This in fact was an important trigger for Otto Kahn-Freund's famous warning, suggesting that simply transplanting a legal (or industrial) institution from one country into another may be a fool's errand, as institutions cannot be so easily detached from their social context.[14]

A stronger normative purpose can be found in policy making – in legislatures, at think tanks and the like, although at present, perhaps following Kahn-Freund's warning, it is less pervasive in scholarly work. The normative objective can have a stronger or a weaker version. The stronger assumes some kind of legal Darwinism, according to which the best legal arrangements hold sway and become more common. This

---

13 *See XV* INTERNATIONAL ENCYCLOPEDIA OF COMPARATIVE LAW (Bob Hepple ed. 2014) ["Labour Law"], INTERNATIONAL ENCYCLOPEDIA FOR LABOUR LAW AND INDUSTRIAL RELATIONS (Roger Blanpain ed. 2007) (with supplementation).

14 Otto Kahn-Freund, *On Uses and Misuses of Comparative Law*, 37 MOD. L. REV. 1 (1974).

assumption should be distinguished from the discussion on convergence to which we will refer later in this chapter. Identifying convergence, in itself, does not assume the positive normative assessment that Darwinism makes. For example, many findings in this volume identify convergences that evolve from the fragmentation of the standard employment relationship. This may reflect a form of Gresham's Law instead of Darwinian development. However, the authors that identify such convergence do not necessarily assume that the corresponding legal fragmentation (or attempts to counter such fragmentation) are necessarily 'good' or 'bad'. There are further 'labor values' that need to serve as the normative benchmark, and the prevalence of a particular legal arrangement is not enough in itself.

A weaker version of the normative objective may be to identify diverse solutions that are then assessed and measured according to relevant 'labor values'. The objective of the comparative study is to advance a normative claim, but the comparison is only a first step, and not an end in itself.

The normative objective is not a purpose of this volume, but it appears in several of the chapters. For example, Alan Bogg and Keith D. Ewing (**Freedom of Association**) implicitly draw on the comparative approach for normative purposes. They claim that Kahn-Freund's warning against transplantation, though warranted in particular instances, should not have a chilling effect on the venture. Comparative labor law should progress from the comparison of nation states to observe global trends and patterns. The normative claim the authors make is unique and should be carefully read. In their words, 'the fetish with difference in the modern world is a deviant activity that causes us to lose sight of major developments of convergence that threaten the very existence of labor law traditionally understood, and the need from labor lawyers for a credible response.' This claim resonates more with the weaker version of the normative claim. Identifying convergence is but a step towards assessment of global trends, but not an indication, in itself, of what the law *should be*. In fact, their normative comment contradicts the assumptions of Darwinism. Convergence of major developments are identified to indicate processes that need to be reconsidered, rather than entrenched and held to be the inevitable outcome of legal evolution.

The relative absence of the normative objective of this volume may be the result of its scholarly emphasis. Perhaps a different image would be obtained from a survey of the comparative method in case-law and policy reports. A different explanation may also suggest that at least the strong (Darwinist) normative claim is usually market-driven and in tension with the epistemic community of labor scholars, who despite differences of views among them, adhere to the importance of labor market institutions. Finally, the strength of Kahn-Freund's warning is at present a staple of academic scholarship that avoids black-letter comparisons and emphasizes instead the social context and implementation of labor law. Not only in this Handbook, but also more generally, it is rare to see recommendations to simply copy and paste arrangements of one country on to the legal system of another.

What then can be the purpose of the comparative study? Unlike the normative objectives, comparative methodology is often suggested as way of understanding solutions developed at one place or at one point of time, by identifying alternative options; i.e., it is an analytical tool. For example, Guy Davidov, Mark Freedland and Nicola Kountouris (**Employees**) discuss the question of who is viewed as an 'employee', suggesting that such a study can take a historical perspective (how did the current doctrine develop over time), or a normative perspective (who should be considered as an employee). The comparative approach supplements such studies by helping identify important moments in the development of doctrines, revealing which steps in the historical development are more universal and which are embedded in local circumstances, and revealing various options that can clarify normative choices. In this, the comparative approach aids in questioning what sometimes is presented as a matter of truism or an inevitable development of the law. Developments in other countries are not suggested as a normative recommendation, but merely as expanding the legal imagination and the range of possibilities.

Another reason given for the comparative task is that it can add depth to the study of law. Precisely for the reason that legal institutions are socially embedded, the comparative project can help in identifying how the social context matters. Demonstrating this claim, Matthew Finkin, Rüdiger Krause and Hisashi Takeuchi-Okuno (**Privacy**) view the engagement in the comparison of legal solutions to employment problems as a looking-glass through which fundamental cultural and legal differences between countries can be realized. This ambitious objective is essential to the study of employment and labor relations. Work is central to individual and communal values alike. It therefore rests on a host of values that extend beyond the daily relationship between an employer and employee. The focus of this chapter on matters related to privacy, dignity and autonomy, encompassing ideas of far broader context than that of employment, is particularly suitable to such an extended objective for the comparative task.

Kevin Banks, Roberta Nunin and Adriana Topo (**Workplace Discrimination**) pursue a similar objective, displaying the relationship between legal developments and deep cultural differences. Their study of the law on equality and workplace discrimination explains differences on the basis of the distinct social problems that triggered legal developments in the legal regimes they study. Although the authors' objective is similar to that of '**Privacy**', the direction of their inquiry is the opposite. '**Workplace Discrimination**' seeks to draw on legal comparisons as an instrument to reveal differences in legal and social cultures. By contrast, '**Privacy**' seeks to explain legal diversity by historical and cultural processes that shaped the law. Together the two chapters suggest complementary ways of drawing on comparisons for revealing the dialectical relationship between law and culture.

While normative and descriptive objectives have been set out as different ends, there is a spectrum of objectives between them. For example, Sean Cooney, Darcy Du Toit, Roberto Fragale, Roger Ronnie and Kamala Sankaran (**BRICS**) use comparative methodology to understand whether BRICS countries, which in many respects are very different, have some kind of a special recipe for economic success that can be traced in regulatory solutions in the field of labor law. The study does not end in a clear prescriptive answer, particularly given the data that indicates that some developments may have contested outcomes on matters such as inequality. At the same time, the framing of the question bids fair to continue various studies that tie policy measures with variable indicators of the nations' social and economic performance, and reveal the tradeoffs. The comparison, in itself, cannot suffice for normative prescriptions, but it can aid in identifying policy measures that should be analyzed on the basis of separate normative criteria.

3. THE COMPARATIVE METHODOLOGY

Sequencing Concepts and Findings

At first glance, the methodology of comparison can be described rather simply as 'country *a* does X, and country *b* does Y.' Easier said than done, and not always very productive. Several chapters point to the need for a broader set of options and strategic choices.

Sometimes the comparative task commences with a comparison between several countries, from which different models are identified. The sequence is first a descriptive analysis of the state of the law in the chosen countries, and then a stylized amalgamation of similar legal prescriptions into categories that distinguish some countries from others. The authors encounter a rich world of primary sources and seek to 'simplify' by categorizing solutions. For example, the chapter by Alan Hyde and Emanuele Menegatti (**Employee Mobility**) surveys the law of many countries and splits the countries into three tiers of enforcement levels with respect to covenants not to compete.

In others we see a reverse sequence. The authors reach the comparative table with an idea about stylized differences and seek evidence in various countries that fit one category or the other. For example, Luisa Corazza and Orsola Razzolini (**Employer**) bring at the outset a distinction between two rival conceptions – that of the 'single employer' and the 'plural employer', and then identify countries that resonate with one or the other. In turn they identify how the differences are gradually being blurred and particularly how the single-employer pattern is being relaxed to accommodate the notion of multiple employers. Similarly, the chapter on **Privacy** approaches the comparative project with a conceptual framework that views issues, such as monitoring in the workplace, at the junction of three concepts – privacy, autonomy and dignity. The comparative task commences with a general description of the legal status accorded to each of the three concepts in the countries they study. Only after establishing this broad basis for the study, can they provide the particular legal responses in each country.

Monika Schlachter and Achim Seifert (**Employee Voice**) pay particular attention to this approach. They organize their comparison of non-union collective voice institutions according to a list of common institutions, such as – works councils and representation on the board of directors. They view these as 'ideal types' for which they seek appearances in various countries. However, they appropriately caution that such ideal types are a 'heuristic device' or a 'hypothetical concept'. These help in organizing the discussion, but they do not suggest that each identification of a works council, for example, in one country or another, denotes the replication of the ideal type. Using ideal types requires movement beyond the mere designation to portray the actual institutional design. Moreover, the appearances of ideal types in each country require identifying the institution's relationship to other institutions. Finally, a study of the ideal type's national appearance also requires studying how it functions 'in action' and not only 'de jure'. Despite all the steps that are required over and above the identification of ideal types in each country, it is a useful strategy. Ideal types help in making the comparison clearer, more manageable for the readers. They give the clarity at the outset and accommodate a more precise account of differences as analysis proceeds.

Apples and Oranges – Comparison Between Whom?

Another challenge for comparatists is to decide what and who to compare. Comparisons involve a tradeoff. It is easier to compare when (a) many factors are controlled for, as is the case in the comparison of relatively similar countries, or (b) when the subject of comparison is very focused. It is more difficult to compare across numerous and distinct jurisdictions and across a broad spectrum of topics. There are however no strict rules and the question of what and who to compare is strongly related to the purpose of comparison. Here we observe several strategies.

Perhaps, the most difficult task was entrusted to Marilyn Pittard and Stuart Butterworth (**Sources**), who were asked to use the comparative method to present the sources of labor law. Given that labor law is well known to be polycentric, at the junction of various legal fields, and the differences in the legal systems of many countries, wholly unrelated to the problematics of labor law in particular, render a comparison difficult to manage. While the authors could have adopted a strategy of contrasting a few countries (perhaps very similar – such as commonwealth countries), or focusing on particular dilemmas that crystalize the problem of polycentric sources (such as the hierarchy of norms in labor law), the authors decided to take a plunge. They chose to create an inventory of sources and forms, demonstrated by examples from various countries. They cherry pick examples, with no prior commitment to any legal system, in which the central guideline navigating their choice is to display institutional diversity. Such a task cannot be accommodated by a preliminary selection of countries or topics, as both types of selection are likely to produce a relatively limited inventory. At the same time, such a strategy also carries a price, as it is difficult to grasp the systemic nature of any particular country, or to identify functional legal substitutes that govern the same problem, but in different bodies of law. There is no 'right' or 'wrong' in this selection, as it depends wholly on the definition of objectives. A descriptive display of diversity requires a different methodology than a prescriptive or critical study of functional alternatives.

In contrast to the broad strategy that was adopted in **Sources**, other authors opted for more focused alternatives. One is to delimit the list of countries studied. However, the actual choice of countries to compare is itself a challenge. A pragmatic constraint often requires comparing countries with which the researcher has a sound basis and familiarity with the details and nuance of the legal doctrine. Researchers are generally at home in some systems, while for others they rely on secondary sources and can easily miss important developments, misinterpret the significance of legal change, under- and over-estimate the importance of a particular case, or fail to see the systemic effect in which one rule maybe compensated by another in a different area of the law.

The choice of countries must therefore rely first and foremost on the countries with which the authors have a sound sense of legal developments. For example, the chapter on **Employees** chose to focus its attention 'on legal systems we feel reasonably familiar with.' The importance of this decision is revealed in the analysis, whereby the authors demonstrate that although the legal formulations for identifying an 'employee' are often very similar, the differences are revealed in implementation. Similarly, in the chapter on **Employee Voice,** the authors explain that one of the reasons for the European thrust of their comparison is that the authors are European. This, however, is not merely a matter of convenience. For those seeking to compare non-union employees' voice, institutionalized forms exist most readily in Europe.

Beyond the preliminary constraints of familiarity and deep understanding, the choice of countries may rest on different logics. It is possible to compare very similar legal systems to identify how small differences matter. Other times it is more effective to choose very different countries to amplify differences in the law. Again, there is no 'right' or 'wrong' in this decision, but it is important to be aware that the set of countries compared may bias the findings and conclusions. Consequently, various chapters have adopted diverse approaches.

Most notably, the third section of this volume commences with countries that share a common trait, but in other respects are marked by significant differences. Erika Kovács, Nikita Lyutov and Leszek Mitrus (**Eastern Europe**) compare the similar origins of the countries influenced by the Soviet Union, and the paths they have taken since 1991, with the collapse of the U.S.S.R. and its dominant position in the region. These three countries scarcely reflect the full panoply of possibilities in labor law, and therefore the chapter does not attempt to provide an inventory; but it is the only strategy that can accommodate the understanding of institutional change and the circumstances that affect the focus of the common theme. The choice provides a high resolution of comparison as the authors demonstrate that while the countries started in analogous positions and moved in similar trajectories, considerable difference in the paths of transition emerged.

The **BRICS** chapter starts with a predefined set of countries that have little commonality except their state of economic development, their exceptional growth levels, and the loose institutional clustering of these countries.[15] To foster a meaningful comparison, the authors had to give up the attempt to compare their labor law's systems wholesale. While some bird's-eye view could have been conducted, the outcome was assumed to be irrelevant for any kind of theoretical or policy-oriented objective. The authors therefore focused their comparison on the area of atypical/informal/precarious arrangements – a choice reflecting the common effort to move from an informal to a formal labor market – with a particular focus on the regulation of temporary work agencies. It is not argued that this is the pivotal regulatory arrangement that can explain the respective national systems' relative success (or difficulties). Instead, the choice of topic was one that could best demonstrate both common underlying tensions that are

[15] Russia was not included in this comparison of the five-nations BRICS and was studied instead in the chapter on **Eastern Europe**. It is rather clear that the portrayal of Russia would have taken a different trajectory if it was included in the BRICS comparison, instead of the chapter on Eastern Europe. These different perspectives are merely different 'parts of the elephant', although they may still give different impressions of the Russian system as a whole.

repeated in political arguments in all four countries, as well as the divergence of institutional solutions and balances.

When comparing the two regional chapters, the chapter on the countries influenced by the former Soviet Union start with shared origins and similar paths of change, while the **BRICS** faced a more difficult challenge. The legal origins of the four countries, as well as their political and social structures, are remarkably different. Consequently, the interplay of similarity and difference in the choice of countries appears in both chapters, but their weights are very different.

The selection of countries to compare is also discussed in chapters of the Handbook's first and second sections, which are coordinated on a thematic basis. One strategy is to pre-select countries that are characterized by a specific difference. The chapter on **Privacy** chooses three countries that are distinguished from each other on the basis of two axes: the importance of the individual in law and culture (demarcating Japan from Germany and the U.S.), and the extent of state intervention in the employment relationship (demarcating Germany from the U.S., with Japan being qualitatively different from the others in this respect as well). The study emphasizes the interaction between cultural norms and legal arrangements, and therefore the choice of countries aids in trumpeting differences that crystalize the comparison. We can only speculate on the findings of a similar thematic comparison in countries that are more similar on both axes (for example – Germany, Netherlands and Belgium), and ask whether a similar comparative methodology and framing of questions could have been used.

The authors of **Workplace Discrimination** chose three regimes that do not nest comfortably within the classification of comparing similarities *or* differences. Their choice of the U.S. and Canada (usually identified as 'similar') and the EU (usually suggested as a comparator for North America) reveals that in the context of discrimination in the workplace, the three countries pose three distinct historical tracks. Although they allude to the legal origins in the title and the analysis, their discussion contests fixed and often-used distinctions. Rather than comparing within the common law regimes, or between the common law and civil law regimes (as will be discussed in the following section of the Introduction), their choice of countries is based on a different criterion for selection, one that touches on the social history of the three regimes.

Frank Hendrickx and Stefano Giubboni (**European Social Model**) describe the development of a European social model and suggest a different form of comparison altogether; one that is diachronic in nature. They emphasize that the quest for understanding what can be a *European* social model requires seeking the particular features of a unitary concept developed at the European level. When defined as such, the topic may seem to be in tension with the nature of the comparative task, because the European unitary concept is unmatched by similar regional arrangements, and is distinct from an attempt to conglomerate or compare the various member states' position on what makes the 'European' model distinct. It is therefore best to characterize the comparative nature of the chapter as a comparison among the ever-changing institutional and substantive arrangements that constitute the Union. At the same time, the chapter depicts a dialogue between developments at the European Union level and changes in the member states, offering a synchronic difference in the ways member states affect, and are effected by, developments at the European level.

A diachronic approach within states also appears in other chapters. For example, the chapter on **Eastern Europe** provides a dual comparison – between the communist and post-communist periods, and between three countries that experienced a similar transition. While all countries undergo change over time, the significant rift that marks the transition away from communism merits the view that a comparison of two eras within one state is part of the comparative project as well as a comparison between separate states at a single point of time in which similar political, social and cultural conditions prevail.

Admittedly, this inclusion of the diachronic dimensions as part of the comparative project might appear unduly to extend its task and functions; it runs the risk of becoming an omnium gatherum for all of labor law. Is the comparison of the decisions of different federal Circuit Courts in the U.S. a 'comparative study'? Is the treatment of conflicting decisions between labor courts in the same jurisdiction – Germany, for example – a 'comparative study'? Does the comparative method refer to just *any* kind of comparison? On one level, these questions would seem to place an undue weight on terminology: it really does not matter how we label a study as long as the study makes sense. But these are significant questions for the epistemic community of comparatists, because, traditionally, comparative study brings with it an emphasis on national, social, or cultural differences. This is the sphere of inquiry in which researchers or policy makers must look beyond their own system.

Apples and Oranges: Comparison of What?

Side by side with the need to select the legal and industrial systems for comparison, researchers also seek methods to limit the scope of the field of comparison. Like the tradeoffs in selecting countries for comparison, there are vices and virtues in selecting either a narrowly focused comparison or a broad one. A high degree of specificity can accommodate a more accurate comparison, but avoids the systemic context and may also miss some functional alternatives. A general framing of the subject for comparison may correct these problems, but at the same time can bring too much information that defeats a hoped-for clarity. The chapters in this Handbook take different approaches to this dilemma.

The utility of specific focus is demonstrated by the authors of **Employee Mobility**. They were originally assigned the general topic of information-driven economies but decided to concentrate on contractual covenants not to compete. This focus enabled them to compare legal responses in diverse countries, and to forge a typology that distinguishes between various models. The focus – covenants not to compete – renders it difficult to illuminate general systemic difference between the countries discussed, but it allows a closer examination of the rationales given for the legal approaches taken in the various models, and even allows some attention to the question of implementation ('law in action').

Similarly, the authors of **Privacy** opted to operationalize the comparison of privacy in the workplace by looking into three specific questions: employer access to employee (or candidates') correspondence in social media, the use of geographic tracing devices, and biometric identification. While the road for comparison loops through a study of very broad concepts, the final comparison pinpoints with relative precision the legal responses to these three questions. Using the three questions provides a closure to the comparative journey, although it seems that the main lessons to be learned from the chapter are learned from the journey itself.

A similar strategy we see in the chapter by Joanna Howe, Esther Sanchez and Andrew Steward (**Job Loss**), where the authors seek to display the diversity of arrangements regarding protection from job loss. The authors refer to Kahn-Freund, noting that 'in comparing labor laws, the comparatist is faced with a multiplicity of choices in order to select which jurisdiction to study and upon which aspects of the law to focus.' The authors' focused topic for comparison allows them to choose several countries. They establish a list of countries that is a result of a priori screening, with the intention of showing both the common influences of international law and the diversity of national arrangements. Hence, there is a potential tradeoff between the range of countries chosen and the scope of the topic studied. Focusing on one dimension enables expansion on the other.

4. LEGAL ORIGINS

Framing the comparison by selecting the countries and themes for the study, can lead even seemingly similar comparative projects in very different directions and it can be used for different purposes. However, in this fluid scheme, there is always a quest for identifying the genetic code of law, or more particularly of labor law. Is there one overreaching explanation, which trumps all others, that can account for most legal differences and similarities? This is the Genome project of labor law. None of the chapters in this volume endorse such a view, but several address at different levels of specificity such attempts, and most notably, the work on **Legal Origins**. The idea of legal family – civil law, common law – as having a powerful explanatory role has long been a feature of comparative law.[16] It has been applied more recently to labor law. Drawing on a quantitative method, adherents of the theory pinpoint the civil law/ common law distinction as the animating difference that can account for divergent paths and outcomes.[17]

Silvia Bonfanti, Cynthia Estlund and Nuno Garoupa (**Market Efficiencies and Failures**) address the Legal Origins theory most directly, noting its important contribution, but also underscoring the common critique – that the distinction between two predominant forms of legal origins is too crude for both descriptive and predictive purposes. A similar critique is made by other authors, for example in the chapter on **Job Loss**. These lines of argument, however, do not lead the authors to establish a wholly idiosyncratic path determined account of legal developments in each and every country. Such a claim, in its extreme form, would basically undermine the usefulness of the comparative project. Instead, the authors of **Market Efficiencies and Failures** prefer to rely on the more sophisticated literature that distinguishes between liberal

---

16 Jaako Husa, *Legal Families* in ELGAR ENCYCLOPEDIA OF COMPARATIVE LAW 491 (Jan Smits ed., 2d ed. 2012); LEGAL ORIGIN THEORY (Simon Deakin & Katharina Pisto eds, 2012).

17 Bottero et al, *The Regulation of Labor*, 119 Q. J. ECON. 1139 (2004).

decentralized economies and centrally managed economies ('Varieties of Capitalism'[18]). The authors aptly note that while there is a strong correlation between the claim of Legal Origins and the discussion of the multiple forms of capitalism, their emphases are different. The neo-institutional literature on the varieties of capitalism facilitates a better conceptual framework for seeking incremental change, unlike the literature on origins that traces back processes to historical roots. In a sense, the difference between the two types of studies resonates with the distinction between *nature* (origins) and *nurture* (institutional change). In a similar vein, the authors of **Employees** acknowledge the importance of legal tradition in accounting for judicial decisions, but demonstrate that legal tradition is not dispositive. Path dependence is not determinative and there are examples in the study that suggest what the authors designate as 'path departures'.

As an approach the Legal Origins theory is also taken in the chapter on **Workplace Discrimination**. It accounts for differences between three legal regimes on the basis of legal origins; but the origins they highlight are not those that distinguish the civil and the common law systems. Instead, the historical roots the authors reveal are concerned with cultural differences and the social problems each country faced at the time the law on employment discrimination developed (race, religion, ethnicity and gender). Hence, the common interest in historical origins that brings the two approaches together masks the fact that actually they are quite apart in their view of history. Historical artifacts are many, and there is a need to identify those with the best explanatory power in the context of the comparison.

Even so, the hypothesis about Legal Origins and how they demarcate differences between legal systems runs throughout the volume. No chapter claims to endorse it in full, but it is interesting to note that also no chapter fully refutes the role of legal origins either, or of significant difference between civil law and common law countries. It has become generally recognized that a rigid adherence to the common law/civil law dichotomy rather over-emphasizes one distinction at the expense of other important differences; even, perhaps, that the civil law/common law diverts attention away from other valuable differences.

For example, the chapter on **Employer** identifies a distinction between civil law systems that adhere to a single-employer framework in triangular employment relations, while common law systems are more receptive to a plural-employer framework. However, a closer inspection reveals differences *within* and *between* the two clusters, and, moreover, a gradual process of partial convergence. The convergence is partial because it does not suggest that all systems develop a single framework, but that differences are less marked and the original split between the two clusters lends itself to different types of similarities and differences that cannot be accounted merely by legal origins.

Finally, it is important to note that the debate over the significance of legal origins is totally absent from some chapters. This may be simply a matter of emphases and

---

[18] *See generally*, Simon Deakin & Beth Ahlering, Labour Relgulation, Corporate Governance, and Legal Origin: A Case of Institutional Complementarity? EGI-Law Working Paper No. 72/2006. Kathleen Thelen has pointed out, just as there are varieties of capitalism, so, too, are there varieties of liberalism. Kathleen Thelen, VARITIES OF LIBERALISM AND THE NEW POLITICS OF SOCIAL SOLIDARITY (2014).

choices of reference points; the Legal Origins theory is not a canonical form or a truism that demands address. Indeed, its absence may also indicate its limits. For example, the study of **Eastern Europe**, with its illustration of difference in countries undergoing seemingly similar processes of transformation, cannot benefit from the Legal Origins theory, although it is clearly concerned with origins in general. It commences with a rather particular origin, and like other chapters here underscores the importance of institutional change rather than merely the origin. Similarly, Legal Origins is also missing from the **BRICS** contribution, where origins are tremendously different even as the economic performance of these countries converge.

Seeking where the theory of Legal Origins appears and where it has no relevance, raises the question of whether the theory is primarily applicable to a relatively short list of (the more developed) countries that resonate with the theory's a priori assumptions. To the extent that it aids in demonstrating an important, albeit not the sole, cleavage, it tends to be confirmed by some chapters and contested in others, but not really refuted. To the extent that it is intended to provide a key to unlatching the secret Genome code of labor law, it is for the most part rejected, implicitly or explicitly, throughout the volume.

5. CONVERGENCE/DIVERGENCE

One of the most important themes the Handbook seeks to identify is whether there is a growing convergence between different legal systems. As noted at the outset, this is perhaps one of the central questions that motivate comparative studies, as well as a basic question in the literature on industrial relations. This debate is in part theoretical and in part also strongly associated with ideology. Findings of convergence are often presented as evidence of an essentialist process; that is, similar pressures on different legal and industrial systems are likely to end in outcomes that are sustainable and economically feasible, leading to convergence. By contrast, findings of divergence are applauded by those who seek the continuity of labor market institutions. Consequently, there is much passion in this debate, but it is difficult to assert the facts. Empirical studies can easily display convergence or divergence, depending on the resolution of the study. Low-resolution studies, such as 'changes in the employment contract', can easily portray convergence. Many countries are facing the growth of the 'atypical' form of employment. But high-resolution studies may seek to demonstrate that the pattern of allegedly atypical contracts is very different in the countries compared. In some there is a growth in temp-work, in another in part-time work, work-sharing, outsourcing and other forms of flexibilization. Do these represent divergence or convergence? How do we decide? Most chapters in this volume reach these questions at one stage or another. Often times the framing of the comparison's objectives and the comparative methodology affect the interpretation of the findings.

One end of the spectrum, the chapter on **Sources**, celebrates diversity. This is not a verdict in the convergence-divergence debate, but an outcome of the chapter's objective. The authors launched an expedition the very objective of which was to demonstrate the 'richness of the panoply of labor laws.' To enrich the findings, the authors chose examples from different countries. The objective colors the conclusion that 'we will continue to see great divergences in the details of the laws and the degree of intervention.' This finding does not undermine signs of convergence that are revealed throughout the chapter, for example, with regard to problems in the prescription of who is an 'employee' or the pervasive difficulty in identifying the precise nature of the standard employment relationship at times when 'atypical' forms of employment are gradually becoming the standard itself. However, these similarities are mentioned in passing, because the authors are looking to satisfy a wholly different objective.

At the opposite end, perhaps the strongest argument on convergence is made by the authors of **Freedom of Association**, who realize that there are differences between systems, but emphasize the importance of convergence processes. They claim that, 'in the field of freedom of association, it is only the most willful who will fail to detect a global pressure in the direction of de-unionization and worker dis-empowerment.' However, convergence in their description extends beyond the general complaint of (or, for economic neo-liberals, applaud for) declining unionism. They observe counter-forces of increasing use of human rights instruments, at the global and national levels, that seek to secure the right to associate and its derivatives. It is in a sense a 'convergence of contradictions' that play against each other at different levels, and not a simple claim of institutional convergence. The authors admit, and in fact clearly describe, that different models of collective bargaining persist, different judicial decisions on the scope of the right to associate remain on the global table, and different institutions are applied in different countries. However, they direct the readers' attention towards processes that affect this diversity in a similar direction. The convergence of effects leads to their juxtaposition of 'convergence' with 'consistency' and 'adaptation', unlike more superficial – political and theoretical – attempts at convergence that are associated with 'transplantations.'

A similar view is demonstrated in the chapter on **Employees**, which identifies convergence in the legal indicia for determining who is an 'employee.' The authors explain that the problems the courts confront are very similar, employers' attempts to evade the law are similar, and hence solutions become markedly similar, concluding that it is 'hardly surprising that courts in different countries are experimenting with similar solutions.' The authors' conclusion seems to indicate a strong belief in convergence of overall trends. However, they acknowledge divergences with regard to the particular legal formulations, especially with regard to the way in which legal formulations are being applied in fact.

The authors of **Employee Mobility** provide at the outset an interesting portrayal of the question of convergence or divergence. The authors first present what may seem to be a paradigmatic formula for balancing between the different values that affect the law on employees' mobility. This formula is derived from the American Law Institute's *Restatement of Employment Law*. However, they are quick to dismiss the appearance of a universal formulation, noting that it 'masks considerable conflict and diversity in the potential application of these rules.' Differences are found in the industrial reality that renders the problem of covenants not to compete more relevant in some regime than in others. Other differences are found in the concrete specifications of very broad balancing tests. Finally, the authors also draw on personal communications and secondary literature that illustrate the implementation of legal formulas in practice. A balancing test that allows the prevention of competition, but is never used to that extent, cannot be considered identical to a similar formulation that is being constantly practiced towards restrictions on mobility as a matter of course. Consequently, the introductory presentation of what may seem to be a convergence around the *Restatement*, quickly becomes a heuristic device to highlight difference.

Most chapters follow suit and maintain a position that intentionally avoids clear statements on convergence and divergence. For example, the authors of **Employer** identify a 'growing global trend towards a plural employer pattern.' This is not the result of doctrinal replication across borders, but a result of a global eradication of the notion that there can be a single employer, which can, and should bear the liability for the employees' rights. Legal solutions tilt between signs of persisting divergence (with reference to the Legal Origins theory) and emerging convergence. Similarly, the authors of **Market Efficiencies and Failures** draw on quantitative studies to demonstrate divergence, but then adopt a qualitative framework that rests on incremental path-determined change and find that '[a] nuanced exploration of labor laws turns out to reveal similarities across legal families as well as significant differences within them.' Both chapters suggest that placing a pin on the continuum between convergence and divergence is highly sensitive to the comparative methodology and the adopted conceptual framework.

The chapters on **Privacy** and **Workplace Discrimination** identify strong differences between the regimes they compare. In both studies the findings of divergence are not surprising because the authors selected countries that would underscore such differences. In both there is a strong connection between differences in the general legal and social cultures that account for the findings of difference. These findings, although predicted by the methodology at the outset, are not trivial. Issues of privacy and discrimination are currently on the forefront of the legal agenda in the field of labor law everywhere. Technological advances trumpet the former, and social dynamics that forge exclusion, differentiation and segregation entrench the latter. While the problems are universal and persistent, the legal responses remain different. In both chapters we also see the authors find developing patterns of similarity that are derived from mutual learning, as well as predictions for potential convergence in the future. These however are at the margins of difference they identify.

The chapter on **Job Loss** follows the chapter on **Sources** in its search for divergence. The list of countries they compare is chosen to display different models and national solutions. At the same time their emphasis on divergence is offset by several factors – their historical interest in the effect of the ILO's convention 158, as well as the interest in the theoretical debates on the justifications for protections from dismissals that overlap national distinctions. Their depiction of the topic therefore spans two directions – differences between nations and a sense of unity with regard to basic choices, as voiced by scholars and international institutions.

6. EFFECTS OF GLOBALIZATION

Does comparative labor retain vitality or should it be replaced by international labor law as a focus of research? At the extreme, if the International Labour Organization's (ILO) vision of the past, according to which there will be one grand legal labor codex that all member states will join, would have materialized, differences would, perhaps, have been abolished and study would concern itself with the dull task of comparing identical, or cloned national legal codes. Needless to say, that this is not the case at present, nor does anyone assume that the future of international labor law lies in that direction.

Kerry Rittich and Guy Mundlak (**Globalization**) claim that globalization does not undermine the importance of the comparative project, but it does require a reconsideration of some of its methods. Globalization is first unpacked, indicating three distinct phenomena: a social and economic force; the emergence of institutions beyond the boundaries of the nation state (international, transnational, regional, contractual) and a set of values that highlight both economic neo-liberalization and universal human rights. The manifold meanings of globalization require reconsidering the common method in which comparative labor law compares the legal arrangements of one nation state with that of another. Comparisons must take into account the many levels in which labor law is authored; the influence of the nation state on new institutions, and vice versa; and the relocation of labor law into legal fields that are becoming more important for establishing the rights of workers in a global village, such as trade law and migration law. In fact, globalization percolates throughout the Handbook, indicating that its implications are seeping into the comparative nest, unsettling its inhabitants.

Resonating with the claim of **Globalization,** the chapter on the **European Social Model** provides what perhaps may be the strongest challenge to the traditional comparative project. As previously noted, the study of the European Social Model cannot be conducted by comparison to other similar institutions and requires an internal comparison. This requires looking at both the influence of discrete states on the transnational level, as well as the reverse – the influence of the transnational on single countries. Some countries in the study appear more frequently as having 'influence over,' while other countries tend to appear more commonly in the list of 'being influenced by,' designating that inter-state power relations mold the development of global institutions and therefore affect each other's domestic law on a transnational basis.

As a social force, globalization is often presented as an important factor, affecting firms 'restructuring and delocalization', as aptly demonstrated in the chapter on **Employers**. The options available for the movement and the reorganization of capital are increasingly growing, but workers enjoy a much smaller range of choice.

Supra-national institutions have an impact on changes that are described in various chapters. Some global institutions appear to have more influence and appear throughout the Handbook; but the role of others remains more tentative. The former include the EU and the ILO. The latter may be viewed in the study of **BRICS**, a loosely clustered set of countries still lacking coherent political vision and with little infiltration into national politics. In the middle, the OECD, WTO, or human rights instruments that are authored by various international organizations, as well as corporate codes and soft forms of international coordination, appear from time to time (and are clearly part of the inventory presented in the chapter on **Sources**), but their importance throughout the volume remains often time speculative.

The effects of the European Union, perhaps the most rigorous institutional arrangement beyond the single nation state, are emphasized in different chapters, but they are not uniform. The chapter on **Employers** discusses EU directives that have a converging effect on the member states. At the same time, the relatively strong impact the European Union has on its members states is also the source of divergence described in the chapter on **East Europe,** where the borders of the European Union differentiate the course of change experienced by countries with similar origins, some of which joined the Union while others remained outside.

Despite the weakness sometimes attributed to more encompassing global institutions, their impact is found to be significant as well. The chapter on the **Freedom of Association** emphasizes that globalization extends beyond the common reference to global economic pressures. It also includes international instruments on human rights, including ILO Conventions 87 and 98. Hence, globalization has a dialectic effect. On the one hand, it accounts for the growing pressure for the de-centralization of collective bargaining. On the other hand, it provides support for claims regarding the importance of unionization.

Globalization as a vehicle of new ideas: The chapter on **Job Loss** discusses the evolution of national protections against dismissals as the outcome of the ILO's Convention 158. But the authors also emphasize that globalization serves as vehicle for the transmission of ideas; in this context, for example, the concept of flexicurity. Globalization is, inter alia, a process that diffuses ideas to different nation states; and a driving force of convergence that diminishes differences rooted in the legal origins and traditions of different countries. This is not a wholesale claim about the homogenization of law throughout the global village, but rather an explanation on how converging effects come to pass.

These examples suggest that the study of globalization's effects intertwine, and are perhaps inseparable, from the quest to identifying patterns of divergence and convergence. The chapter on **Employees** identifies globalization as an important factor in favor of growing convergence, emphasizing both the role of international agents (such as international courts) and international instruments (such as ILO conventions). Why, then, do global agents and instruments not lead to complete convergence? Their answer speculates on several options that point to locally embedded traditions and habits of mind that find expression in the decisions of labor courts and legislatures. Should this lead to a dichotomy between the pairing of globalization and convergence vis-à-vis sustained national focus and divergence? The various chapters in this volume resist this dichotomy. Neither legal origins, nor globalization, justify a simple verdict on when – or whether – convergence or divergence will predominate.

PART I

COMPARING LABOR LAWS

1. The rich panoply of sources of labor law: National, regional and international

Marilyn J. Pittard and Stuart Butterworth

INTRODUCTION

To say that labor rights, obligations and entitlements as between employer and employee are many and varied is an understatement. The content and nature of these rights and duties may differ dramatically between countries and regions, public and private sectors, industry and firm, contemporary times and bygone centuries, to name just a few. The sources of labor law, though, can be corralled more readily into categories – collective and individual agreements, statutes, constitutions, international laws, custom and policy, codes and guidelines. These sources are addressed in this chapter, which focuses on the interventions of legislative and other kinds; into the unconstrained operation of the relationship of employee and employer in the market.

Very few countries today have a totally unregulated employment relationship. Indeed the spectrum of the regulation ranges from minimal – perhaps enough to satisfy health and safety and other essentials – to very prescriptive. Within countries the place on the spectrum may have fluctuated, sometimes considerably, over the years with changes in thinking, such as free market or neo-liberal ideologies or modern socialist approaches.

As with any market, and in a simplified model of the complexities of reality, if labor markets were to be entirely free of regulation, the outcomes would clearly vary considerably according to a range of factors. An individual worker might have a substantial degree of bargaining power if her or his skills were relatively rare, if she or he had knowledge of market opportunities, if the costs of obtaining that information were low, if travel to the source of work was financially viable and so on. But likewise the individual worker may have very little power to negotiate terms and conditions (including as to safe systems of work), and would have to accept what an employer in the market offered, if he or she were just one of a large number of workers with similar skills, job mobility, location mobility and so on.

By way of contrast, on the other hand, it could be postulated that a system may provide high degrees of regulation of the actual terms and conditions of employment, directing where workers could work, what occupations particular people could pursue, conditions in which people worked, and so on. This system would produce a very different outcome for a particular worker than the other extreme, however that outcome is measured.

These shorthand descriptions of aspects of systems embody, in a somewhat caricatured way, very different conceptions of the role of the individual in their capacity as a worker in an economic activity and the role of an employer requiring labor services in its business.

It is a reasonable generalisation that in economic systems, within which persons supply labor services in a market framework, the state provides a legal framework for the dealings, as between employer and worker, which is somewhere on a spectrum between these two rigidly-sketched extremes. Moreover, when considering comparisons between countries as to sources of law in labor matters, the position of a particular country is more readily characterised as being at a point on a multi-dimensional matrix, rather than being at a point along the simple linear scale, which is implied by the use of the spectrum concept.

The enormous variability in sources of labor law, and in their combination in particular countries, is illustrated by the dimensions under consideration in this chapter. All countries have much the same implements in their legal toolkits: the law of obligations as it operates on private market behavior vindicated by private action for injunctive or monetary relief; statutory actions; administrative interventions by the state including systems of licensure, or permits beforehand or prohibitive action subsequent; and more. The choice of one or another, to act, to react, or not to act at all is governed by numerous forces, some historical or intrinsic to the country's system. On that, observers have long discerned distinctions rooted in the legal family from which the state draws,[1] but, as the chapter 'Fostering market efficiencies or repairing market failure' by Silvia Bonfanti, Cynthia Estlund, and Nuno Garoupa in this volume attests, that traditional view has become subject to probing reassessment.

This chapter will examine first a primary and significant source of enshrining labor rights, the nation's constitution. It will examine statutory laws, collective and individual agreements, and codes of practice and soft laws. The role of other laws and policies that are not specifically labor laws but influence the labor and anti-discrimination legislation will be examined. The influence of international laws and conventions will be addressed. Finally the European region as an example of another layer of regulation over member states will be examined.

1. CONSTITUTIONS AS A DIRECT SOURCE OF LABOR LAW

The national constitutions of many countries enshrine labor rights and are direct sources of labor law. (Constitutions may also contain broad statements of rights, which apply in the employment context.) Other jurisdictions do not provide for labor rights at

---

1 Sean Cooney, Peter Gahan and Richard Mitchell, 'Legal origins, labor law and the regulation of employment relations' in Michael Barry and Adrian Atkinson (eds), *Research Handbook on Comparative Employment Relations*, Edward Elgar 2011, Ch 4:

> [C]ommon law countries have a weaker level of protection than other legal families. This is particularly evident in relation to the level of protection afforded to most worker entitlements. Moreover, common law countries are typically less likely than each of the civil law groups of countries to provide universal coverage of entitlements, notably through the extension of collective agreements to non-union workers. Compared with countries from other legal families, common-law countries are, on average, significantly less likely to place limits on managerial prerogatives through, for example, restrictions on the use of fixed term contracts or requirements to notify a third party (such as a government agency or union) of intentions to make workers redundant.

all – either as applications of general rights or as specific labor rights. Examples of these approaches are considered below.

Specific Labor Rights

The constitutions of some countries make specific provision for rights which are directed to labor or employment. The Thirteenth Amendment to the United States Constitution, a document otherwise directed exclusively to government, forbids slavery and involuntary servitude. The Japanese Constitution guarantees 'the right of workers to organise and to bargain and act collectively'.[2] This provision guarantees the rights of workers to organise and join an organisation for the purpose of bargaining with an employer, to collective bargaining and to collective action.[3]

The German Constitution grants all Germans the 'right freely to choose their trade or profession, their place of work and their place of training'.[4] In addition, German workers have rights which link to their work and conditions: the Constitution provides that 'the right to form associations to safeguard and improve working and economic conditions is guaranteed to everyone and to all trades and professions'.[5] This right to free association has been interpreted by the courts to guarantee the right to collective bargaining and the right to strike.[6] Both trade unions and individuals may enforce the right. Other values set out in the Constitution have been assimilated into private law via provisions in the Civil Code. The Swedish Constitution, as an interesting contrast, guarantees the right of association and right to strike but not the right to bargain collectively. Thus examining these three countries (Japan, Germany and Sweden) as examples reveals different approaches to what are and what are not included as labor rights. As the Bill of Rights in the United States Constitution applies only to government it has been held to reach public, but not private, employment.

In addition to more general rights in the Bill of Rights in the Constitution of South Africa (including the right to life,[7] the right to privacy,[8] and the right to human dignity),[9] rights which address or encompass broad labor rights include: the right to be free from slavery servitude or forced labor;[10] the right of freedom of association;[11] and the right to carry on a trade or profession.[12] More specifically too, particular labor rights are identified in section 23 as the right to 'fair labor practices' – the right to form

---

2 Japanese Constitution, Article 28. This provision is in fact based on the Constitution of the Weimar Republic, the former legal structure for government of Germany.

3 Roger Blanpain (ed.), *Comparative Labor Law and Industrial Relations in Industrialized Market Economies*, Wolters Kluwer, The Netherlands, 2007, p 140.

4 German Constitution, Article 12.

5 Ibid., Article 9.

6 Blanpain (n 3 above).

7 South African Constitution, Section 11 provides 'Everyone has the right to life'.

8 Ibid., Section 14.

9 Ibid., Section 10 provides 'everyone has inherent dignity and the right to have their dignity respected and protected'.

10 Ibid., Section 13.

11 Ibid., Section 18.

12 Ibid., Section 22.

and join a trade union and to join in union activities; and the right to strike. Significantly, rights are not limited to unions or employees but extend to rights of employers to form and join employers' associations and to participate in the association's activities. The right to collective bargaining is also expressly conferred on every trade union, employers' organisation and employee in section 23(5). Collective bargaining is also addressed in section 23(5) by the provision that national legislation 'be enacted to regulate collective bargaining'.[13]

Whilst the Indian Constitution[14] includes an extensive part on Fundamental Rights, Part III, embracing such rights as freedom of religion for every citizen in India[15] and the right to life,[16] these Fundamental Rights relate less to labor law than in some constitutions (and certainly the South African Constitution). The more limited but express labor law rights are:

- right to equality, a broad right but which includes in Article 16 that the State, in employment matters, cannot discriminate against a citizen of India;
- right to be free of exploitation, which extends to no employment of children who are less than 14 years of age in 'any factory or mine or engaged in any other hazardous employment'[17] and abolishes forced labor and human trafficking;[18]
- right of freedom of association: to form unions or associations.

The Constitution of the People's Republic of Bangladesh takes a similar approach to that of India. It also incorporates in Part III, fundamental rights to embrace rights to equality of opportunity in public employment,[19] prohibition of forced labor,[20] freedom of association to grant the right to form associations or unions[21] and the right to carry on a trade or profession.[22] Further prohibitions against discrimination in Article 28 extend not only to the grounds of sex, religion and race, but also of caste and place of birth.[23]

No Constitutional Provision for Labor Rights

The constitutions of some countries are notable for the absence of any express labor rights, hence these constitutions cannot be looked to as a source of labor rights. This is the case in Australia, where the Constitution neither provides for a Bill of Rights nor

---

13 Ibid., Section 23(5).
14 This is a federal Constitution.
15 See Indian Constitution, Articles 25, 26, 27 and 28.
16 Ibid., see Articles 20 and 21.
17 Ibid., Article 24.
18 Ibid., Article 2.
19 People's Republic of Bangladesh Constitution, Article 29.
20 Ibid., Article 34.
21 Ibid., Article 38.
22 Ibid., Article 40.
23 See generally paper presented to Labor Law Research Network Inaugural Conference, Barcelona, June 2013, Jakir Houssain, 'Standards-Rights Nexus in Action in Bangladesh: Transforming Labor Standards into Workers' Rights'.

does it attempt to enshrine either general rights that might apply to employment or specific labor rights. Amongst the few express rights provided, none translate or apply to labor rights. Some rights have been implied into the Constitution by the High Court of Australia but freedom of association, for example, whilst receiving some judicial support, is not implied. In some countries, notably Israel, New Zealand and the United Kingdom, there are no written constitutions and hence no constitution as a source of written labor rights.

Absolute Rights?

Even where countries' constitutions provide for labor rights, the rights may not be absolute or they may be subject to limits which could be placed on them by the parliament. In South Africa, for example, there is built-in provision for the possibility of clauses to restrict or limit those rights. Section 36 contains a general limitation clause enabling limits to be imposed in general law application where they are 'reasonable and justifiable in an open and democratic society based on human dignity, equality and freedom'. In India, whilst freedom of association with the right to form union or associations is conferred, restrictions can be imposed. Hence when considering the constitution as a source of rights, some caution must be expressed about the strength ultimately of some of the constitutional 'guarantees'.

Constitutional Approaches: Making Sense of Various Approaches

As the brief survey set out above demonstrates, there is an array of approaches to enshrining labor rights in the Constitution. Some of the core rights addressed in Constitutions are the right not to be discriminated against; freedom from slavery; freedom of association; the right to strike; and the right to bargain collectively.

(a) Right not to be discriminated against

A right which seems to be enshrined in many Constitutions which have incorporated rights is the right not to be the subject of discrimination. This embraces the labor right not to be discriminated against in the field of employment but of course it is a much broader right, including the right to equal treatment in a wide range of contexts – education, housing, and the provision of services. Thus the right of equal treatment in the employment context is but one aspect of the right of equal treatment more generally.

(b) Freedom from slavery

The right not to be held in slavery or servitude, however, is a more basic but important labor right. It is provided in the Constitutions of many countries – see, for example, the Constitutions of Ghana, South Africa, India, Bangladesh, and the United States. The expression of this right – and therefore its content – also varies, with some countries using a simple statement, as in Ghana whose Constitution provides that no person shall be held in forced labor or servitude or required to perform forced labor; whilst other Constitutions are more expansive and include a right to be free of exploitation and prohibit engagement of child labor, as in the Indian Constitution.

(c) Freedom of association

The freedom to form and join trade unions is seen by many countries as so fundamental that it should be enshrined in the Constitution. While it may be expressed in general terms as freedom of association,[24] it is often detailed more fully as the right to form and join trade unions and the right to join in union activities, as in the South African Constitution, or the right to join associations to improve working conditions, as in the case of Germany. The Constitution may also enshrine the ability to limit the freedom. The Indian Constitution, for example, enables the state to limit this freedom to impose 'reasonable restrictions on the examination of the right … in the interests of the sovereignty and integrity of India, the security of the State, friendly relations with foreign States, public order, decency or morality … .'[25]

Whilst the freedom may be granted in the Constitution, court decisions may flesh out its content – the extent of true conferral of freedom to form and join associations may depend on the combination of constitutional expression and its interpretation by the courts which in turn may be influenced by other sources of law, such as ILO Conventions or European Directives.

(d) Right to bargain collectively

The right to bargain collectively is expressed in some countries' constitutions, as in the case of some European Union member countries, for example Belgium,[26] and in South Africa. In other cases it may be read from the right to form trade unions and engage in union activities, as in the case of France, Germany and Italy. Canadian courts have recently read freedom of association as embracing the right to collectively bargain (see later section).

(e) Right to strike

This right is expressly conferred in the constitutions of such European countries as France, Italy, Spain, Portugal, Greece and Sweden, but strangely not in the Netherlands. It has been commented that, 'Perhaps curiously, the *right to strike* appears to be more widely recognized in European social democracies than the process of collective bargaining of which it is an essential feature.'[27] It may be, of course, that collective bargaining is no less entrenched in labor law systems because of its constitutional absence, as in the case of Sweden where it is self-regulated and given legislative backing.

Rationale for Enshrining Labor Rights in Constitutions

Enshrining the rights in Constitutions makes for more inviolable rights in the sense that Constitutions are generally more difficult to change than ordinary laws passed by the legislature – so a decision of a country to adopt rights in their Constitutions is an

---

[24] See, eg. The Irish Constitution

[25] Indian Constitution, Article 19(2).

[26] Constitution of Belgium, Article 23.

[27] Michael Rosenfelt and Andras Sajo (eds) *The Oxford Handbook of Comparative Constitutional Law*, Oxford University Press, 2012, p 1046.

indication of the seriousness with which those countries hold or regard the rights. They want these rights neither to be at the whim of Parliament, that is, not to be easily changed by the usual processes adopted by parliaments to enact laws (but in some cases the right can be constrained but not eliminated).

The underlying question, though, why some countries decided to enshrine labor rights in their Constitutions and others chose other avenues is not easily explained. The influence of other countries' approaches and the origins of a country's Constitution in colonial history may go some way to providing an adequate explanation. For other countries, the tradition of a Constitution based on convention, rather than the written law, would explain this – as in the United Kingdom. Elsewhere, the battleground of the Constitution was fought on other issues. In Australia, for example, the issues besetting the 'Constitutional forefathers' had, as a fundamental concern, the balance between powers to be held by the proposed new federation of states (the Commonwealth) as against the new states themselves (former individual colonies). In the labor-relations area, the energies in these Constitutional debates focused on the precise nature, if any, of the power to make laws with respect to labor relations to be conferred on the new Federal Parliament.[28] Perhaps no generalisation for present purposes can be made, as each country's own history will provide at least a large part of any answer there may be – although the general adoption of international conventions in the twentieth century may have encouraged some countries to include rights derived from those conventions, if their constitutions were developed in the context of the increasing frequency of conventions dealing with such matters, as occurred in India.

Quasi-Constitutional Rights Instrument: Bills or Charters of Rights

One of the problems in coming to grips with the diversity of constitutional and quasi-constitutional arrangements in various nations is that a term such as a 'bill of rights' and 'charter of rights' can represent concepts with different content and status in different countries. Whilst the constitutions of some countries include a part incorporating fundamental rights, another approach taken in recent years by a number of jurisdictions is to enact 'quasi-constitutional' rights instruments which form part of the content of domestic labor law. Essentially these laws are Acts of Parliament which provide for fundamental human and other rights (and may encompass a range of labor rights) and may be labelled as a Charter of Rights or a Bill of Rights.

This approach was adopted in New Zealand, with the New Zealand Bill of Rights Act 1990 (NZ Bill of Rights) setting out a series of fundamental rights, including the rights to free association and free assembly.[29] These rights may be subject only to such 'reasonable limits prescribed by law as can be demonstrably justified in a free society'.[30] The NZ Bill of Rights requires that any enactment must be interpreted in a way that is consistent with the rights contained in the Bill. In addition, all new

---

[28] See generally Marilyn Pittard and Richard Naughton, *Australian Labour Law: Text, Cases and Commentary,* 10th ed, LexisNexis, 2010; and Marilyn Pittard and Richard Naughton, *Australian Labour and Employment Law*, LexisNexis, 2015.

[29] New Zealand Bill of Rights Act 1990, Sections 16, 17.

[30] Ibid., Section 5.

legislation must be examined to determine its consistency with the NZ Bill of Rights. If not, the government is required to provide a justification for the inconsistency.[31] The rights contained in the NZ Bill of Rights may be exercised by legal persons, which include unions, as well as natural persons.[32] The few rights relevant to labor law are expressed succinctly – section 17 simply provides: 'Everyone has the right to freedom of association' and it does not flesh out the application to unions; and section 16 provides: 'Everyone has the right to freedom of peaceful assembly.' There is further a right to freedom from discrimination.[33]

Similarly, rights in Canada are guaranteed under the Canadian Bill of Rights. The Canadian Bill of Rights, a federal statute enacted in 1960, establishes 'fundamental freedoms', including the rights to free speech, free assembly and free association.[34] Laws of Canada are to be 'construed and applied so as not to abrogate, abridge or infringe … any of the rights or freedoms' contained in the Bill.[35] There was dissatisfaction with the Canadian Bill of Rights and, ultimately in 1982, the enactment of the Charter of Rights and Freedoms as part of the Canadian Constitution occurred.[36] The Bill of Rights remains in existence but it is not part of the Constitution of Canada and therefore, not being subject to restrictions and requirements for amending the Constitution, could be readily amended by Act of Parliament. Similar to the NZ Bill of Rights, these Canadian rights are not specific to labor relations but they are applicable to labor matters.

The major limitation of these approaches, however, is that whilst the Charters or the Bills of Rights, which are not entrenched constitutionally, endeavor to enshrine various rights, their application is limited. They do not compel the enactment of particular laws. Rather, they provide a mechanism for reviewing Acts of Parliament to ensure that these Acts are consistent with the rights which are the subject of the domestic law in the Charter or Bill and may apply, as in the case of the NZ Bill of Rights, to actions of persons or bodies performing public functions, powers or duties, but do not extend beyond this legislative check or accountability. Generally, if the court determines that the legislation is not consistent with the Charter, the legislation is not void or unenforceable but may be reviewed again by the Parliament. However, despite this limitation, in Canada, the Charter (which is now constitutionally enshrined) has lead to a significant Supreme Court decision which acknowledges the right to collective bargaining, derived from the express right to freedom of association.[37] Following challenges to the validity of British Columbia government action – in introducing legislation which repealed rights to bargain collectively without consulting those trade unions who represented affected employee members and effectively introducing the legislation without public debate – the Supreme Court of Canada, in upholding the

---

31 Ibid.

32 Ibid., Section 29.

33 Ibid., Section 19.

34 Canadian Bill of Rights Part 1, Section 1.

35 Ibid., Section 2.

36 Constitution Act 1982.

37 *Health Services and Support-Facilities Subsector Bargaining Association v. British Colombia* [2007] SCJ No 27; 2 SCR 391.

challenges, effectively overturned previous court decisions by ruling that the right to bargain collectively is part of freedom of association.[38]

2. CONSTITUTIONS SHAPING THE NATURE OF LABOR LEGISLATION

National Constitutions govern both the formation and making of domestic labor law, and the extent to which international or regional labor law is applicable in the jurisdiction. In addition to (perhaps) conferring directly labor rights they govern the ability of Parliament to legislate with respect to those labor rights.

Formation and Operation of Labor Law

Constitutions generally mandate a process by which laws are made in the jurisdiction. In most jurisdictions with developed legal systems this includes the separation of the power to make law between the legislature, the executive and the judiciary. In addition, in federal jurisdictions, the Constitution will divide the power to make law between levels of government (commonly, the national level and another level based on a region of the country).

The power to make labor law is granted to the separate institutions of government – the legislature, judiciary and executive. The legislature, empowered by the national Constitution, passes legislation which forms the content of labor law. The legislature may also delegate some legislative power to the executive, empowering it to create regulations and make administrative decisions on labor law matters. Finally, the judiciary is charged with resolving labor disputes, and in doing so interprets the law formulated by the legislature. The proportion of power that each arm of government has in the process of formulating and implementing labor law differs in each jurisdiction, and will be discussed below.

The power to make labor law will be granted to one or more levels of government. In unitary jurisdictions, such as New Zealand and the United Kingdom, there is a single, national government. Clearly, in these jurisdictions, the power to make labor law is reserved to the national government. However, in federal jurisdictions, the constitution will often divide this responsibility between the federal and state or provincial governments, but not always cleanly, thus adding to the complexity of operation and application of interacting labor laws.

In certain federal states, labor law-making power is reserved to federal governments. For example, in Germany, only the federal legislature ('Bundestag') is competent to legislate on industrial relations. Labor law can only be made by state legislatures upon a specific grant of power by the Bundestag, such as that established by the Federal Act

[38] See Judy Fudge, 'Conceptualizing collective bargaining under the Charter: The enduring problem of substantive equality' (2008) 42 *Supreme Court Law Review* (2d); Judy Fudge, 'The Supreme Court of Canada and the right to bargain collectively: The implications of the *Health Services and Support* Case in Canada and beyond' (2008) 37(1) *Industrial Law Journal* 25.

on Staff Representation. This has contributed to general homogeneity of labor law throughout Germany.

In Canada, the power to make labor law is 'divided between the two levels of government on the basis of the nature of activity involved'.[39] Under the Canadian Constitution, the federal government has the power to regulate transportation and communications, interprovincial and international trade, defence-related industries and the federal public service'.[40] This power has been interpreted to extend to the making of labor law governing employment relationships in these sectors. However, the labor law-making power in all other sectors is granted to provincial governments. Hence there is a public-private sector divide due to the federal and provincial divisions of power.

The US Constitution limits the legislative power of the Congress to certain matters, and reserves all other law-making to the states. Most of US federal labor law is based on the power to regulate interstate commerce, which since 1937 has been read quite expansively. Most employment law in the US is state law; but when federal law steps in the common question is whether it preempts the field. For the most part, federal law is not preemptive. A major exception is law of unionisation and collective bargaining.

Successive constitutional court decisions have expanded the power of the federal government to make labor law in Australia. The Australian Constitution grants legislative power to the federal Parliament only if a 'head of power' exists in the Constitution to support the legislation. The 'labor power' set out in the Constitution gives the federal Parliament the power to legislate on labor matters in a particularly constrained way, at least on the form of wording used: the federal Parliament has power to make laws with respect to 'conciliation and arbitration for the prevention and settlement of industrial disputes extending beyond the limits of any one State', thereby prescribing the method of dispute settlement and restricting it to *interstate* industrial disputes.[41] It also means the Parliament cannot directly legislate for industrial relations, for example prescribe minimum wages and conditions, unlike Brazil where the Federal Constitution establishes national minimum wages, and the Constitution and the Labor Code lay down the working week (44 hours; eight hours each day).

The Australian Constitution left intrastate labor disputes and other labor matters within the legislative power of each state. As the power to enact labor laws is held concurrently by state and federal governments and each state took the opportunity to establish its own industrial relations system, the very real possibility of clashes in laws at different levels always eventuated. However, despite the apparent limit in the federal power to legislating for interstate disputes, the High Court of Australia's broad interpretation ensured that this component of an 'interstate dispute' was easily created and easily satisfied. In reality, legislation at federal level resulted in coverage of industrial awards of approximately 80 per cent of the Australian workforce until the 1990s.[42]

---

[39] Harry Arthurs et. al. *Labor Law and Industrial Relations in Canada*, Kluwers, The Netherlands, 1981.

[40] Ibid.

[41] Australian Constitution, Section 51(xxxv).

[42] Pittard and Naughton, *Australian Labour Law*, (n 28 above), Chs 7 and 10.

However, the Australian federal legislature also has the power to make laws with respect to 'foreign corporations, and trading or financial corporations formed within the limits of the Commonwealth' (frequently referred to as 'constitutional corporations').[43] This power was used cautiously initially to outlaw trade union secondary boycotts against corporations;[44] to enable incorporated employers to enter into collective agreements *without* trade unions;[45] and to allow statutory agreements between incorporated employers and individual employees, a form of individual bargaining.[46] In 2006, Australia's constitutional court again broadened its interpretation of the corporations' power, by holding that the federal legislature's power to make labor law extends to:

> The regulation of the activities, functions, relationships and the business of a [constitutional corporation], the creation of rights, and privileges belonging to such a corporation [and] the regulation of the conduct of those through whom it acts, its employees and shareholders and, also, the regulation of those whose conduct is or is capable of affecting its activities, functions, relationships or businesses.[47]

This decision clearly confers on the federal legislature the power to regulate 'the industrial rights and obligations of corporations and their employees and the means by which they are to conduct their industrial relations'.[48] And has virtually made the express provision relating to making labor laws, section 51(35), redundant. It enabled a national system of industrial regulation to operate, with the states referring some of their law-making powers to cover non-corporate employers and leaving the states operating only in a limited sphere of government level employees.

Sources of labor then can be federal laws and state or provincial laws, with the constitution providing relevant powers and courts ruling on the validity or otherwise of the laws. The very nature of the power granted in the constitutions can shape the labor laws enacted, and the court interpretations over time are another influential source.

3. LEGISLATING THE FRAMEWORK FOR COLLECTIVE BARGAINING

Collective bargaining can generally be described as 'the process by which terms and conditions of employment are determined by negotiations between employers and trade

---

43 Australian Constitution, Section 51(xx).

44 Trade Practices Act 1974 (Cth) (now Competition and Consumer Act 2010 (Cth)).

45 Workplace Relations Act 1996 (Cth).

46 These were known as Australian Workplace Agreements. Pittard and Naughton, *Australian Labour Law* (n 28 above), Ch 12, and Pittard and Naughton, *Australian Labour and Employment Law*, (n 28 above), Ch 13.

47 *New South Wales v. The Commonwealth* [2006] HCA 52 (Work Choices Case).

48 *New South Wales v. Commonwealth* [2006] HCA 52, para 178.

unions'.[49] Having said that, some systems permit negotiations between employers and groups of employees, without union involvement.[50]

Legal frameworks are usually enacted in which collective bargaining operates. There are a wide range of schemes with differing degrees of complexity and regulation. The issues usually canvassed in these schemes relate to, on the one hand, procedural matters, such as the recognition of bargaining agents and right to use particular bargaining agents, and the requirement to bargain in good faith, and, on the other hand, the substantive matters which are the matters of the subject of bargaining. Jurisdictions differ as to what is emphasised in the regulatory framework. In the United States, for example, procedural matters loom large.[51] Important too in collective bargaining systems are issues of the enforceability of collective agreements; the extent to which the agreements are underpinned by safety nets; the extent to which there is third-party approval of the agreement necessary for its operation and enforcement and the nature of the right to undertake strike action or lockouts in support of bargaining or more generally.

On the procedural matters, frequently the parties themselves determine and agree on process for bargaining, as in the case of the United Kingdom; while in others process is laid down in statutes, sometimes in detail, for example about the appointment of bargaining representatives in Australia. Some jurisdictions leave little room for the parties themselves to decide on matters to be included in the agreement, and prescribe matters which cannot be included (eg, bargaining fees to be charged by unions for representing non-unionists in negotiations); matters which must be included (eg, dispute resolution processes) and matters which may be included (eg, matters pertaining to the relationship of employer and employee only). Thus some systems are highly regulated and shaped by legislation and therefore are at risk of legislative change with successive governments of different political persuasions. Often the rhetoric in policy is that parties freely negotiate their own agreements (deregulation) but in reality the systems can be highly regulated.

Other systems feature self-regulation. Sweden has no government intervention in bargaining, but the 1977 Codetermination Act provides a framework and does regulate some matters relating to recognition of unions, and bargaining process aspects. However, maximum working hours and minimum paid annual leave, for example, are the subject of legislation, and the system underwent changes in the 1980s.[52] Collective agreements would govern terms and conditions of work in most Swedish workplaces. The terms set are minimal which can be improved upon by employers. The content of collective agreements commonly covers wages, hours of work, sick leave, sickness and accident insurance.

---

[49] Bob Simpson in Peter Cane and Joanne Conaghan (eds), *The New Oxford Companion to Law*, Oxford University Press, 2008, p 153.

[50] For example, Australia had a non-union stream of collective bargaining between an employer and two or more employees under the Workplace Relations Act 1996 (Cth).

[51] Robert Gorman and Matthew Finkin, *Labor Law: Analysis and Advocacy*, Juris Publishing, Inc, 2013.

[52] Kristina Ahlén, 'Swedish collective bargaining under pressure: Inter-union rivalry and incomes policies' (1989) 27(3) *British Journal of Industrial Relations* 330.

Level of Bargaining

Bargaining may occur at industry or sectoral levels or at enterprise or plant levels. In the United States, Canada, Australia, Japan, many Eastern European countries and South American countries, for example, enterprise or more localised bargaining is the norm (and indeed may be prescribed). In Western Europe, as well as such countries as Brazil and Argentina, the bargaining level is industry or sectoral. Thus one collective agreement might apply to, say, the metalworking industry across the whole of Spain. Greater uniformity of employment conditions between businesses occurs where the collective agreement is negotiated at broader levels. In some jurisdictions multi-employer agreements are not permitted.

To further add to the variety of arrangements, multi-level agreements may exist where a plant, for example, is covered by one agreement at that very local level and also by an industry or sectoral level agreement. At peak or umbrella employer organisation and union confederation levels, particularly in some professions, agreements too may be concluded about specific matters, such as training. Framework agreements may be negotiated to provide a basis for the negotiation of agreements at a more local or enterprise level.[53]

Public or Private Enforcement and Administration of Collective Bargaining

Enforcement mechanisms vary considerably. Some jurisdictions have relatively little intervention and the collective agreement is binding and enforceable upon signing, as in the United States, with no third-party supervision.[54] Interpretation and enforcement of agreements in the United States reflects a private enforcement approach. Collective agreements commonly provide for resort to arbitration for disputes arising under them – there are no civil remedies for breach.[55]

Even in systems where third-party approval is not required, enforcement differs. Collective agreements are generally not enforceable in the courts in the United Kingdom, being regarded as 'gentlemen's agreements' or private arrangements at common law, with no intention to enter into legal relations.[56] However there might be ability to incorporate the terms of a collective agreement into a contract of employment to make it part of the contract and thereby enforceable as terms of that individual contract. While the Trade Union and Labor Relations (Consolidation) Act 1992 (UK) now provides for enforcement in section 179, it is limited to circumstances where the parties expressly state that it is their intention that the agreement be enforceable and the collective agreement is in writing. Hence, the matter still remains in the realm of

---

53 There might also be differences between private and public sector employees. See, eg, Marilyn Pittard and Philippa Weeks (eds) *Public Sector Employment in the Twenty-First Century*, ANU EPress, 2007.

54 Gorman and Finkin (n 51 above).

55 Craig Becker, 'The continuity of collective action and the isolation of collective bargaining: Enforcing Federal Labor Law in the Obama Administration' (2012) 33 *Berkeley Journal of Employment and Labor Law* 401.

56 *Ford Motor Co v. AUEFW* (1969) 2 QB 302. See generally, Hugh Collins, Keith D Ewing and Aileen McColgan, *Labour Law*, Cambridge University Press 2012, pp 123–30, 535.

the parties to decide on enforceability. In the United Kingdom, there is relatively little publicly funded or third-party intervention in collective bargaining – the legislation sets out processes for recognition of bargaining agents but the agreements themselves are negotiated between the parties with no requirement for third-party approval. Patterns and length of strikes are influenced by the degree of state intervention.

In other jurisdictions, third-party supervision may be considerable – the collective agreement must be approved by a tribunal or body and 'registration' of the agreement is required as a precondition of that agreement being binding and enforceable. Many jurisdictions provide publicly funded schemes to enforce collective bargaining and its requirements. In Australia, for example, there is a government funded authority (currently the Fair Work Ombudsman) which can investigate breaches of enterprise agreements and institute proceedings in the courts for enforcement – through the imposition of financial penalty and award of monies owing or other relevant orders. As an enforcement arm, it has promulgated a 'prosecution policy', inter alia, governing decisions about which cases are eligible for publicly funded prosecution. Unions or the employees themselves can also institute proceedings for breach. The enforcement, however, is in the courts of law, not specialist courts. In terms of administration, the independent, publicly funded tribunal (Fair Work Commission) is the body which approves collective agreements (necessary for enforcement) in accordance with the legislative requirements, makes orders in relation to breaches of good faith bargaining requirements and orders about coverage of agreements or where an employer is refusing to bargain.[57]

The process of bargaining and good faith bargaining are commonly matters of importance in bargaining systems and these are often prescribed, even where the degree of intervention by the state is relatively low. Good faith bargaining requirements apply through legislation in such countries as the Philippines, Korea, New Zealand, Australia, Canada, and the United States.

4. STATUTORY PROVISIONS

Collective Rights

The statutory law might also regulate collective rights, in addition to providing a collective bargaining framework, but could be a force 'for good or ill', conferring rights positively or restricting them. Trade union status, procedures for mass redundancies and the right to strike and lockout would be among these collective rights positively conferred. Freedom of association, trade union recognition and the conferral of legal status on unions are usual and significant legislative interventions in many jurisdictions. Australia, for example, conferred legal status akin to corporate status on unions in the first federal labor law legislation,[58] thereby avoiding the struggle for recognition that historically occurred in many countries. In Sweden, the Employment

[57] Pittard and Naughton, *Australian Labour Law* (n 28 above), Ch 13; and Marilyn Pittard and Richard Naughton, *Australian Labour and Employment Law* (n 28 above), Ch 14.

[58] Conciliation and Arbitration Act 1904 (Cth).

(Co-Determination in the Workplace) Act regulates employer and trade union relations and establishes rules. Notably, the employer must keep unions informed about matters such as the employer's financial position, any policies at work, and proposals for restructuring or downsizing.

In some countries unions are, or have been, institutionalised, akin to an arm of the state and carrying out policies of the state, as was the case in Mexico. Further the legislation might be a source of anti-union rights, as historically in the United Kingdom and Japan, for example, or might water down freedom of association to include a notion of freedom *from* association (Australia).

The extent of support for strikes and industrial action to create pressure on employers in the course of negotiations is often regulated by the countries' governing legislation. This has ranged from complete bans on strikes and lockouts to liberal strike laws, but commonly industrial action will be permitted in limited and specific circumstances.

Individual Rights and Entitlements

The laws may also directly provide for employment conditions, as a minimum, and in effect confer individual rights. These statutes are a significant source of labor rights in the vast majority of jurisdictions. Labor law plays a significant role in ameliorating the harsh effects of the market and protects weaker groups and more vulnerable employees. The protections range from standard labor matters, such as minimum wages, hours of work, paid holidays and sick leave to unfair dismissal protection and provisions for flexible work.

The extent of the legislated safety net or minimum standards is largely a reflection of the prevailing ideology. Neo-liberals seek to minimise interference in the free labor market; they argue that minimum wages can be set artificially above market rates, thereby discouraging hiring and altering competitiveness, including globally. The controversy of unfair dismissal laws arises from clashes of the neo-liberal view against those of left wing or labor movements. The neo-liberal view espouses that such laws prevent justifiable terminations of employment, add to labor costs, diminish productivity, impact detrimentally on competitiveness and so on. Labor or left-wing movements on the other hand propound that unfair dismissal protection prevents the worst of capricious and arbitrary employer actions, promotes job security, enables workers to have a 'voice' in resisting unfair changes in work or unsafe workplaces without threat of job loss and creates fairer workplaces. Many jurisdictions without unfair dismissal protection may nonetheless protect against terminations of employment for union activities and provide for redundancy pay or procedures. The ability of small businesses to comply with such unfair dismissal laws has also been in issue.

Thus countries may have minimal safety nets, as in the United States; a core of safety net conditions in legislation which cannot be altered by agreement, as in Australia; a core of minimum provisions, some of which may opted out of, as in the case of maximum working hours in the United Kingdom; or a considerable array of minimum rights as in Brazil where the Labor Act, Consolidacao das Leis do Trabolho, is an important source of employment rights. Standards too may be fluid and fluctuate over time, with changes in philosophy and governments, government's response to global financial crises, globalisation, privatisation and so on. Different systems reflect different values or the weighting of values.

There are additionally other forms of minimum entitlements, for example in industrial awards which might be made by tribunals and binding on the parties setting out minimum rights and conditions. These are not statues but are made pursuant to statutory processes and procedures (in Australia).

5. THE EMPLOYMENT RELATIONSHIP[59]

This relationship which arises when the parties enter into an individual agreement between employer and employee has traditionally been at the heart of labor law. It not only defines entitlements and obligations in the contract, but significantly will also determine the application of other laws (statutes) which grant rights and obligations to employers and employees.

In common law jurisdictions the modern form arose out of the relationship of master and servant which was very much a relationship of one party being subservient to the other, with the master giving the servant orders as to the tasks and the methods of completing the tasks. Frequently the servant worked alongside the master and was subject to his direction and control in a real sense. This mode of small-scale production working changed and over time the master-servant relationship as one of status was replaced by the employer-employee relationship in modern form.[60] Now, express terms are agreed upon and the courts imply terms either in fact (depending on the particular negotiated circumstances) or in law, where terms are implied in all contracts of a particular type, in this case the employment contract, as necessary to facilitate the operation of the contract. Terms implied in law have been the greatest source of change in the contract over the years – not only have terms such as the duty to obey reasonable and lawful orders been part and parcel of the contract but also terms relating to matters such as health and safety obligations and the duty of mutual trust and confidence.

The contract is now no longer subject to the free, unimpeded bargaining of the individual parties. Labor laws step in to rectify imbalances in power between the parties and to ensure that basic conditions are met. However the extent of legal intervention differs according to the jurisdictions, very often as a result of historical circumstance and political and ideological views of the extent to which the inequities of free markets should be controlled or diminished by intervention. Even where jurisdictions have minimum wage legislation, the minimum wage level may not be a 'living' wage, a wage to ensure that workers and their families are not living below the poverty line.[61]

---

59 This is addressed in detail by Guy Davidov, Nicola Countouris and Mark Freedland, 'The subjects of labor law: "Employees" and other workers', Ch 4 in this volume.

60 Peter Cappelli and J R Keller, 'Classifying work in the new economy' *Academy of Management Review* July 24, 2012.

61 Robert Pollin, 'Economic prospects: Making the federal minimum wage a living wage', (2007) 16(2) *New Labor Forum* 103.

Contractor/Entrepreneur or Employee?

One of the vexed questions is whether a contract is in law a contract of employment, that is, a contract *of* service; or a relationship of principal and contractor, that is, a contract *for* services. Commonly there is a spectrum (of facts and circumstances of the arrangements) where the true employer-employee relationship is evident at one end of the spectrum and the true principal-contractor relationship is evident at the other end, but in between are contracts for the provision of labor services which might have features of both types of arrangements as contractor or employee. In this grey area the courts have been called on to make rulings – common law courts have devised various tests to work out which is the true legal position, while the European approach is to focus on 'subordination' of the worker to the principal. Even so, the tests are not always easy to apply and the litigation that still occurs in common law countries indicates that this terrain is fraught with uncertainties.[62] In some instances legislatures have intervened to deem workers 'employees' even where the common law might regard them as 'independent contractors'.

The distinction has been subject to much criticism and, even self-employed or contractors may be dependent workers, dependent on one principal for work and remuneration.[63] However the distinction is significant because rights, entitlements and duties largely depend on, and flow from, that categorisation – duties implied in law in employment contracts, obligations and entitlements in Acts and regulations, workplace policies and codes are usually predicated on the concept of 'employee'.

Role of the Contract

On the role of the contract in various jurisdictions, Professor Mark Freedland observed, particularly in comparing the United Kingdom and the United States:

---

62 See, eg, in the United Kingdom, Mark Freedland, *The Personal Contract of Employment*, Oxford University Press, 2006; in the United States, eg, see Jeffrey M Hirsch, 'Employee or entrepreneur' (2011) 68(1) *Washington and Lee Law Review* 353–68; Noah D Zatz, 'Beyond misclassification: Tackling the independent contractor problem without redefining employment' (2011) 26(2) *ABA Journal of Labor & Employment Law* 27–994; Micah Prieb Stolzfus Jost, 'Independent contractors, employees, and entrepreneaurialism under the National Labor Relations Act: A worker-by-worker approach' (2011) 68(1) *Washington and Lee Law Review* 311–52; in Australia, see eg Pittard and Naughton, *Australian Labour Law*, (n 28 above) Ch 3 and Pittard and Naughton, *Australian Labour and Employment Law*, (n 28 above), Ch 4; in South Africa, see eg, Rochelle Le Roux, 'The evolution of the employment contract in South Africa' (2010) 39(2) *Industrial Law Journal* 139–63. Also generally Guy Davidov, 'Who is a worker?' (2005) 34 *Industrial Law Journal* 57–71; Guy Davidov, 'The reports of my death are greatly exaggerated: 'Employee' as a viable (though overly-used) legal concept', in Guy Davidov and Brian Langille eds, *Boundaries and Frontiers of Labor Law: Goals and Means in the Regulation of Work*, Hart Publishing, 2006, pp 133–52.

63 See, eg, Esther Sánchez Torres, 'The Spanish law on dependent self-employed workers: A new evolution in labor law'; Stefanie Sorge, 'German law on dependent self-employed workers: A comparison to the current situation under Spanish law'; Judy Fudge, 'A Canadian perspective on the scope of employment standards, labor rights, and social protection: The good, the bad, and the ugly' all in 31(2) *Comparative Labor Law & Policy Journal* 101.

> In English law, and the laws of the United Kingdom more generally, the contract of employment is a central organizing concept, many would say *the* central organizing concept, for labor and employment law, and indeed for the legal representation and regulation of the individual employment relationship more generally. It is easy for English common lawyers to imagine that this is a universal proposition for all legal systems, but that would be something of a misconception; for example, the US labor law system analyzes the basic employment relationship in the absence of an express contract as 'employment at will'; the contractual status of which is very debatable, at least according to the way in which the contract of employment is constructed in English law.[64]

Thus even within common law countries there is variation in the role and importance of the contract. Employment relationships in Japan too are in stark contrast to the United States:

> Above all, however, the concept of Japanese management has entailed duties towards employees, notably in avoiding dismissals, together with the participation of employees in many decisions reserved in United States to discretionary managerial rights. In these important respects Japan deviated from the Fordist, free-market employment model, enjoying decades of success.[65]

In the United States, contracts may be written or oral, although they are more likely to be written for senior executives. At common law, contracts are 'at will', meaning that an employer or an employee can terminate the contract at any time during the contract and without cause. Nonetheless, parties can negotiate terms in the employment contract which limit the ability of either party to terminate 'at will', setting out causes for termination of the contract. Alternatively, contracts may be entered into for a specified duration without ability of either party to terminate early. An employee whose contract has been breached by the employer may seek damages to compensate – to put the employee back in the position they would have been under the contract as if it had been performed. As with many other jurisdictions, the employee has a duty to mitigate financial loss by seeking another job. Workplace policies play a role in setting employment conditions and minimising employer liability. Frequently, for example, employees will be required to sign confidentiality agreements and trade secret agreements.[66]

Notably, Brazil has a principle of 'acquired rights'. Once a right has been acquired under law, any contract or amendment to that law cannot diminish the right. Even where an employee may agree to a reduction in wages (the entitlement of which has

---

[64] Peter Cane and Joanne Conaghan (eds), *The New Oxford Companion to Law,* Oxford University Press, 2008, p 221.

[65] David Kettler and Charles T Tackney, 'Light from a dead sun: the Japanese lifetime employment system and Weimar labor law' volume 1997 19(1) C*omparative Labor Law Journal* 1.

[66] For the range of approaches to confidentiality and restraining competition post employment see Marilyn Pittard, Ann Monotti and John and Duns (eds) *Business Innovation and The Law: Perspectives from Intellectual Property, Labor, Competition and Corporate Law*, Edward Elgar Publishing, 2013. See generally, Alan Hyde and Emanuele Menegatti, 'Legal Protection for Employee Mobility', Ch 7 in this volume.

been established), the reduction will be null and of no effect. Hence this concept is a way of enshrining rights and the role of contract is apparent.

A Standard Employment Relationship?

> [The] notion of what constitutes employment must … be revisited because the model of permanent, full-time employment was largely predicated on the archetype of a job – working permanently at the same workplace – and on the archetype of the person doing that job – a white male. Clearly, neither archetype is now predominant.[67]

The standard employment relationship described above is undergoing massive change, as 'the employment relationship in companies is increasingly situated in complex network-based forms of organization, which are part of international chains of production and services. The relationship between time, place, and space of action has thus been changed in profound ways'.[68] There is now frequently a triangular relationship where agencies are interposed between employer and worker casting doubt on the status of workers and employees and their rights, and also raises the fundamental question as which entity (or entities) is the employer.[69] Telecommuting is a new way of working enabled by technology. Short-term contracts, casual, temporary or at call work, and homeworking aggravate uncertainty of working hours and income. 'Precarious work', embracing non-standard employment, is as an accepted term and the subject of policy and academic debate, including at ILO level.[70] 'Flexible work' may in some cases be a euphemism for work with no job security, resulting in work that is not 'decent work'.

The burgeoning of precarious work has produced responses and legislative interventions from some countries to increase protection of non-typical workers. For example:

> Some countries, like Argentina, Uruguay, and Brazil, have sought to strengthen labor market oversight (inspection) and universalize social policy in order to include workers who do not have standard employment in the coverage offered labor legislation. These countries have even sought to expand the scope of their labor coverage, so as to guarantee fundamental

---

67 Marie-Ange Moreau, 'The reconceptualization of the employment relationship and labor rights through transnationality' 34 *Comparative Labor Law & Policy Journal* 697, 697–698.

68 Ibid.

69 Guy Davidov, 'Joint employers status in triangular employment relationships' (2004) 42 *British Journal of Industrial Relations* 727.

70 ILO Conventions have been directed to this field – eg, conventions relating to part-time work, homework and decent work for domestic workers; and the ILO has a focus on decent work, see Sangheon Lee and Deirdre McCann (eds) *Regulating for Decent Work. New Directions in Labor Market Regulation* (ILO, 2011). Academic writings on decent work is vast; see, eg, Nicola Kountouris, 'The legal determinants of precariousness in personal work relations: A European perspective' 22 *Comparative Labor law & Policy Journal* 21 and issue addressing precarious work: *Comparative Labor Law and Policy Journal,* Vol. 34(1) (Fall 2012) and Guy Standing, *The Precariat: The New Dangerous Class,* London and New York, Bloomsbury Academic, 2011.

> rights, such as access to protection in justice and family benefits. It is still timid and insufficient progress, because large contingents of workers subsist without effective protection.[71]

Intervention in some jurisdictions aims to limit the types of non-standard contracts that can be entered into. For example Sweden, under its Employment Protection Act (EPA), in addition to *Indefinite or permanent employment* (the contract of employment which continues until further notice)[72] provides for:

1. *Contract for probationary employment*: EPA's section 6 permits such contracts, where the probationary period does not exceed six months.
2. *Fixed term contract*: section 5 of the EPA permits fixed term contracts for 'general fixed term employment'; temporary substitute employment; seasonal employment; or for an employee who has reached 67 years of age.

The legislature has intervened to compel compliance with certain matters – whilst the contract may be reduced to writing or be oral, the EPA provides that the employer must provide written information about certain matters essential to the relationship. These include the place of work, commencing date, job description and title, period of notice, pay and benefits, annual leave entitlements, working day or week, and any collective agreements which might relevant. There is also provision under the Swedish Contracts Act for declaration or amendment of unreasonable terms.

As in the case of Sweden, contracts in Brazil are usually of indefinite duration. Temporary employment and fixed term contracts are permitted in certain circumstances. In Brazil, the multi-layer of regulation is evident. The contract of employment, which need not be written, sets down minimum rights under the law. Under law, the following are set out as minimum rights: 30 vacation days per year of employment are required; in December, a 13th month of salary is payable; and contributions to the Fundo de Garantia por Tempo de Servico (unemployment guarantee fund) must be made. Additional rights may be conferred by collective bargaining agreements, which might include topics such as meal vouchers and health insurance.

Implied Duty of Good Faith and Duty of Mutual Trust and Confidence

Factors such as misrepresentation and deceit at the hiring stage may be relevant to contractual remedies, for example where a person has misrepresented his or her qualifications or falsely claimed to have a clean criminal record, in order to secure the contract. Occasionally, statutes may govern misleading and deceptive conduct in entering into employment relationships.[73]

---

[71] Graciela Bensusán, 'Legislation and labor policy in Latin America: Crisis, renovation, or restoration' 34 *Comparative Labor Law & Policy Journal* 655, p 676.

[72] See Jonas Malmberg 'Employment and other long-term contracts, between unequal parties in Sweden', Arbetslivsrapport, 'National Report for the 16th World Congress of the International Society for Labor Law and Social Security', Jerusalem, 2000.

[73] See, eg, Australian Competition and Consumer Act 2010 (Cth).

Some jurisdictions require parties to act or perform in good faith *during* the employment relationship. This may be couched in different ways as a covenant of good faith or fair dealing (as in the United States) or a duty of mutual trust and confidence (as in the United Kingdom), although it is argued that while these two concepts are related they may not be the same or identical.[74] In the United States almost no state has recognised a duty of good faith and fair dealing owed to an at-will employee.[75] United Kingdom courts, by way of contrast, have embraced the implied duty of mutual trust and confidence.[76] In Australia, however, the status of this duty remained uncertain,[77] until the High Court of Australia ruled definitively in 2014 that there was not such duty of mutual trust and confidence implied by law into the contract of employment, but left open the question of any implication of the duty of good faith.[78]

Enforcing the Employment Contract

Jurisdictions commonly have their own rules and laws for enforcing contracts. In the common law jurisdictions the courts of law are the enforcement bodies with individuals bringing claims for breach of contract. Private enforcement is the main approach. However it is a matter between the two contractual parties and the courts do not generally impose penalties or fines for contract breach, as would occur for breach of a legislative provision. Rather provision for payment of monetary 'damages' or compensation for loss is the norm.

Many jurisdictions have a reluctance to enforce contracts of a personal nature by orders of specific performance or injunctions and will do so only in limited and special circumstances. The court's reluctance to oversee whether the order has been fulfilled also operates against specific performance – and forcing the contracting parties back into a personal relationship is not one favored by the courts. These arguments are increasingly irrelevant where large corporations are the employers and, where countries or jurisdictions have unfair dismissal jurisdictions, tribunals have been given power to overcome the 'continual supervision' argument by legislative provisions providing for reinstatement in employment.

Actions in tort may occur if another party has induced or interfered with the contractual relationship – although these actions are more likely in the context of industrial action which is not otherwise lawful or permitted under statute (see further section 9 below).

---

[74] See, for example, Joellen Riley, 'Siblings but not twins: Making sense of "mutual trust" and "good faith" in employment contracts' (2012) 36 *Melbourne University Law Review* 521.

[75] James J Brudney, 'Reluctance and remorse; The covenant of good faith and fair dealing in American Employment Law'; (2010–2011) 32 *Comparative Labor Law and Policy Journal* pp 773–774.

[76] Alan L Bogg, 'Good faith in the contract of employment: A case of English reserve?' (2011) 32 *Comparative Labor Law & Policy Journal* 729.

[77] See Pittard and Naughton, *Australian Labour Law* (n 42 above) Ch 4, and Mark Irving, *The Contract of Employment*, LexisNexis, 2012.

[78] See Pittard and Naughton, *Australian Labour and Employment Law*, (n 28 above), Ch 6 and *Commonwealth Bank of Australia v. Barker* [2014] HCA 32.

6. CUSTOM, POLICY AND 'SOFT LAW'

Custom at the workplace or in an industry, such as practices of paying bonuses at the end of year or the basis of selecting persons for retrenchment, may influence employment relations. Whether these are enforceable rights may depend largely on whether they are terms of the contract or there is a legal basis to regard these as rights. The common law courts have traditionally shown reluctance to find contractual terms based on custom and practice.

Policies at the workplace are more likely to be binding on the parties. Employees may be engaged on the basis that they must abide by employer policies, or the contracts may require them to sign up to the policies in force from time to time. Continuing to work for the employer after a newly promulgated policy may be taken as affirmation of the employee's agreement to be bound by the policy. The employee's duty to obey orders may be used to compel adherence to policy. In the United States where managerial discretion is more pronounced, there may be less disputation over their application to the workplace.

'Soft law' is an increasing phenomenon in the workplace. It may embrace norms of behavior, such as corporate social responsibility,[79] global compacts, guidelines or codes of conduct, ranging from the global to workplace level. A specific global example is the UN Global Compact. Based on the ILO Declaration on Fundamental Principles and Rights at Work, it enshrines ten principles which businesses can voluntarily adopt.[80] Four labor principles are included: freedom of association and the right of collective bargaining; the elimination of forced and compulsory labor; the abolition of child labor; and the elimination of discrimination in respect of employment and occupations. In the ordinary case these 'soft laws' may not be legally binding as they are voluntary and consensual; rather they may be the basis for moral suasion or 'shaming' the employer into compliance. The idea is that the good corporate citizen (employer) should 'do the right thing' by employees and sign up to or embrace fair standards. Reputation as a 'good employer' may affect employee attraction and retention and so be incentives for employers to voluntarily agree.

7. IMMIGRATION, CRIMINAL, TAX, SUPERANNUATION, EDUCATION LAWS: IMPACT OF OTHER LAWS AND POLICIES

Labor law, as we have seen, may be based on contract law as well as statutory law, and tort law can also play a role. Other laws play, or have played, a part, commonly by operating on the labor market (affecting the supply and demand for labor) or by altering or prohibiting certain behavior through criminal or quasi-criminal sanctions. Criminal laws have played a part in labor relations matters in different jurisdictions and

[79] Bryan Horrigan, *Corporate Social Responsibility in The 21st Century: Debates, Models and Practices Across Government, Law and Business*, Edward Elgar Publishing, 2010.

[80] Lisa Whitehouse, 'Corporate social responsibility, corporate citizenship and the global compact: A New approach to regulating corporate social power?' (2003) 3 *Global Social Policy* 299.

at different times. Trade unions themselves were regarded as criminal or unlawful combinations in the United Kingdom, with workers being subject to imprisonment for joining,[81] until laws were passed to declare them lawful associations.[82] Some breaches of labor laws or codes are regarded as quasi-criminal offences; and some jurisdictions impose the 'criminal' sanction of imprisonment for industrial manslaughter or criminal negligence for workplace deaths. Criminal offences (e.g., assault, battery, property damage, besetting) may be committed in the course of industrial action. Criminal laws relating to bullying are contemporary examples of the potential application of criminal law in the workplace.

Immigration laws and policy themselves directly affect the freedom of movement and mobility of workers and therefore the supply of labor, and indirectly affect the wages and conditions of domestic workers. The ease (or not) of the entry of workers to countries on temporary work visas and as guest workers has long been an issue for domestic policy makers. Incentives may operate to encourage short-term immigration to relieve particular shortages, as in the case of seasonal workers in fruit picking. A worldwide problem is the engagement of 'illegal immigrants' or undocumented labor on exploitative terms, beyond the reach of protective of labor laws. Exploitation by unscrupulous employers can occur, because these immigrants, with no legal right to work in the country, could be deported if they complain.

Incentives and barriers to employment can be imposed through tax laws, thereby affecting the supply and demand for labor. Education policies and incentives directly affect the level of, and opportunity for, training of workers and educating the workforce. Barriers to entry to work may be imposed by professional registration requirements, as in the case of doctors, dentists and lawyers; and by the need to have a clean criminal record, in the case of working with children.[83]

Superannuation laws may require employers to contribute to superannuation funds for their employees' retirement and govern portability of superannuation. Social security laws are often directly coupled with labor laws: the buffer of social security may operate to influence a person's decision to undertake paid work while there are commonly limits on social security payments for striking workers.

Corporate laws may affect business structures, and therefore employment and insolvency laws may in turn affect employee entitlements. Directors' duties may be proscribed.

---

[81] The Combination Acts 1799 (full title, eg: An Act to prevent unlawful combination amongst journeymen to raise wages).

[82] In 1825 the Combination Acts were repealed. The Trade Union Act 1871 UK then ensured that unions were not unlawful as being in restraint of trade.

[83] For example, the Criminal Records Review Act [RSBC 1996] ch. 86, and the Working With Children (Criminal Record Checking) Act of 2004 in Western Australia.

8. HUMAN RIGHTS AND/OR DISCRIMINATION LAWS: SOURCE OF PROTECTION OF LABOR RIGHTS?[84]

In addition to the impact of other laws, human rights and anti-discrimination laws may provide employment rights and obligations, although the scope of these laws is general and not limited to employment situations. These laws usually provide the following:

1. Grounds of discrimination that are unlawful or prohibited – for example, race, sex, pregnancy marital status, age, disability, physical appearance;
2. Areas of discrimination – relevant to labor law, these are employment including in hiring, during employment and in the termination of employment;
3. A tribunal to deal with complaints via designated processes, such as mediation, arbitration or referral to courts of law;
4. A mechanism for individual enforcement and remedy – for example reinstatement in the person's former job and/or monetary compensation.

How far do equal opportunity laws protect fundamental labor rights, such as freedom of association? These laws may not expressly protect union activities; such protection may have to be sought by resting the discriminatory ground on 'political opinion' which frequently is not defined in the legislation.[85] Some legislatures though have chosen to protect trade union activities via anti-discrimination laws. The Australian Human Rights Act, for example, expressly identifies trade union activity as a ground of unlawful discrimination;[86] other Acts use the terminology 'industrial activity';[87] while others may identify membership or non-membership of associations of employers or employees as a ground for discrimination.[88] Thus these laws, utilising an individual rights approach, preserve the rights of individual workers to engage in industrial activity and provide a statutory remedy. There is potential overlap with unlawful termination and its governing rules, which adds to complexity and potentially provides different remedies.[89]

Freedom of association is protected in the United Kingdom Human Rights Act 1998 as is the prohibition on discrimination. Essentially this Act gives force and effect to the Convention for the Protection of Human Rights and Fundamental Freedoms. The Australian Capital Territory's Human Rights Act 2004 protects freedom of association[90]

---

[84] See Kevin Banks, Roberta Nunin and Adriana Topo, 'The Lasting Influence of Legal Origins: Workplace Discrimination, Social Inclusion and the Law in Canada, the United States and the European Union', Ch 8 in this volume.

[85] See, eg, Human Rights Act 1993 (NZ) where some grounds are defined or fleshed out but political opinion is not.

[86] Other Acts which identify trade union activity as an express ground of discrimination include Anti-Discrimination Act (Qld), the Northern Territory Anti-Discrimination Act 1996.

[87] See, eg, Anti-Discrimination Act 1998 (Tas).

[88] See, eg, the Australian Capital Territory Discrimination Act 1991.

[89] See, eg, Fair Work Act 2009 (Cth).

[90] Section 15(2) provides 'Everyone has the right to freedom of association'.

and freedom from forced labor or being held in slavery,[91] as does the Victorian Charter of Human Rights and Responsibilities Act 2006.[92]

Discrimination or equal opportunity laws may be used to challenge employer policies because they are indirectly discriminatory, meaning that they impact disproportionately on a particular group. Examples may include the case of 'last-in or first-out' policy of retrenchment which might impact heavily on more recently employed workers who are women;[93] or policies that applicants must not have a criminal history, which might fall disproportionately on particular racial groups.[94] Class actions, too, are permissible in some jurisdictions but in the United States these have met with some judicial hostility.[95]

9. 'INDUSTRIAL TORTS' AND THE PROTECTION OF PROPERTY AND ECONOMIC RIGHTS: COMMON LAW JURISDICTIONS

In common law systems, the role played by the law of torts (or 'civil wrongs') in regulating industrial action cannot be underestimated. Laws developed by the judges to effectively promote rights to carry on business unimpeded by trade union industrial activities crushed the ability of unions to support demands with direct industrial action. The 'business torts', 'economic torts' or 'industrial torts', as they have been variously described, extend to enabling employers and businesses affected by strikes to seek injunctions to restrain the activity and/or at damages as monetary compensation. The following are the main industrial torts:

1. *Inducing breach of contract or interfering with contractual relations*
   In this tort, a third party, C, which induces a person, A, to breach a contract with another party, B, would commit the tort where there is intention to effect breach and the terms of the contract are known. In industrial relations strikes, C might be the union which persuades the employee A to breach his or her contract of employment with the employer B.

   An indirect form of that tort developed so that the union C, as a result of persuading A to breach the contract might interfere with B's contract of supply to another business D. The indirect action on the employer where unlawful means

[91] Section 26.

[92] Section 11 of the Victorian Charter provides freedom from forced work; and section 16 provides for freedom of association, which includes the right to form and join trade unions.

[93] *Australian Iron and Steel Pty Ltd v. Banovic* (1989) 168 CLR 165.

[94] See eg, for the United States, Steven Raphael, *The New Scarlet Letter? Negotiating the U.S. Labor Market with a Criminal Record*, W. E. Upjohn Institute for Employment Research, 2014 and eg. for Australia, Bronwyn Naylor, Moira Paterson, and Marilyn Pittard, 'In the Shadow of a Criminal Record: Proposing a Just Model of Criminal Record Employment Checks' (2008) 32 *Melbourne University Law Review* 171 and Marilyn Pittard, 'Discrimination Law: Constraints on Criminal Record Checks in Recruitment' (2012) 18 (8) *Employment Law Bulletin* 124.

[95] Judith Resnick, 'Fairness in numbers: Comment on *AT&T v. Concepcion, Wal-Mart v. Dukes, and Turner v. Rogers*', 125 *Harv. L. Rev.* 79 (2011).

are used, such as breach of the employees' contract of employment, might mean that the tort was made out.

Over time, the courts relaxed the element of breach of contract, ruling that a technical breach was not needed, simply interference in the contractual relations between the parties. The broad tort of causing economic loss by unlawful means is recognized in some jurisdictions.

2. *Conspiracy to injure*

   A combination of two or more persons, for example union and members, to inflict injury on an employer by taking direct industrial action are essential elements of this tort. Where the overwhelming purpose was to injure the employer, the tort would be made out.

   In the development of the tort, however, the courts acknowledged that where a trade union purpose, for example improvement of wages and conditions of its members, was the real purpose of the combination, then the tort would not be made out.

3. *Conspiracy to injure by unlawful means*

   The tort of conspiracy by unlawful means nevertheless might be committed where the combination used unlawful means (for example breach of employment contract, breach of industrial award governing the employment relationship, breach of statute) to inflict damage. The predominant purpose of the combination to promote a union purpose did not save the conspirators from liability where unlawful means were involved. While conspiracy to injure is unlikely to be made out today in industrial relations disputes, conspiracy by unlawful means is often readily committed.

4. *Intimidation*

   Developed from a tort involving two parties, the tort of intimidation applies to industrial disputes whereby an employee, whose employment is lawfully terminated by an employer – at the behest of, and under unlawful industrial strike threats made by, unions – can claim intimidation by the unions and/or other employees. No industrial action need actually occur for the tort to be made out – the threat of industrial action which involves unlawful means, for example, interference with contractual relations is sufficient.

The full impact of these torts has been ameliorated in many jurisdictions by legislation which permits industrial action to take place in certain circumstances or which grants immunity from tort action in the course of bargaining for an enterprise agreement. However, the torts have been used in notable cases to require unions to pay not inconsiderable damages to compensate for the economic loss caused by industrial action. Jurisdictions which require strict compliance with strike notices and the support by ballot of strike action find that industrial torts are still very relevant today – it is easy for a strike to become unlawful through failure to comply strictly with the legal requirements preceding strike action.[96]

[96] Hazel Carty, *An Analysis of the Economic Torts*, Oxford University Press, 2010; Pittard and Naughton *Australian Labour Law* (n 28 above), Chs 13 and 17; and Pittard and Naughton, Australian *Labour and Employment Law* (n 28 above), Chs 14 and 18.

Other torts, such as nuisance and trespass to property or goods, may also occur in the course of an industrial dispute. Picketing, for example, may set up a public nuisance, or involve acts of trespass to the property of the employer. Frequently, informational picketing, handing out leaflets about strike action and claims being advanced, is not caught by tort law.

10. INTERNATIONAL LABOR LAW INFLUENCES

Most labor law is contained in the domestic law of individual states. Differing political systems, legal traditions and national ideologies have given rise to innumerable methods of regulating the employment relationship. However, states have recognised a role for international law in formulating universal minimum labor standards.

International law is 'the law of the society of states or nations'.[97] International labor law forms part of international law, and is defined as 'the substantive rules of law established at the international level and the procedural rules relating to their adoption and implementation'.[98] The key institutions which create international law are the International Labor Organisation (ILO) and, to a lesser extent, the United Nations (UN). These institutions are constantly creating new international labor law.

(a) International Labor Organisation

The ILO is a specialised UN agency with the mandate to 'promote social justice and internationally recognised human and labor rights',[99] with the main aims 'to promote rights at work, encourage decent employment opportunities, enhance social protection and strengthen dialogue on work-related issues'.[100]

The ILO's time of formation – shortly after the First World War – is reflected in its aims. First, the creation of an international organisation to encourage higher labor standards was viewed as essential to the maintenance of 'universal and lasting peace'.[101] Secondly, the improvement of labor standards in capitalist countries was linked to containing communism, recognising that 'conditions of labor exist involving such injustice, hardship and privation to large numbers of people as to produce unrest' in capitalist nations.[102] Finally, it was noted that 'the failure of any nation to adopt humane conditions of labor is an obstacle in the way of other nations'[103] doing so, due to international competition. Therefore common standards were a method of preventing labor standards from decreasing to control costs of production. At present there is a

---

97 John Westlake, *International Law*, Cambridge University Press, (1904) p 1.

98 Blanpain (n 3 above).

99 International Labor Organisation, 'About the ILO' <http://www.ilo.org/global/about-th ilo/mission-and-objectives/lang–en/index.htm>.

100 Ibid.

101 ILO Constitution.

102 Ibid.

103 Ibid.

persisting pressure for common standards, resulting from an increasingly global environment, with reduced barriers to trade and ease of telecommunications.

Specifically, according to the ILO website, the ILO's functions relating to labor standards, policies, training and education expressly include:

1. Formulation of international policies and programs to promote basic human rights, improve working and living conditions, and enhance employment opportunities;
2. Creation of international labor standards backed by a unique system to supervise their application;
3. An extensive program of international technical cooperation formulated and implemented in an active partnership with constituents, to help countries put these policies into practice in an effective manner; and
4. Training, education and research activities to help advance all these efforts.

The 'international labor standards' created by the ILO form the bulk of the sources of international labor law.

ILO sources of labor law

The ILO Constitution lists a number of areas for improvement of employment conditions. Although not a direct source of law, these form the basis for the formation of the international labor standards. The key areas for improvement are:

1. Regulation of the hours of work including the establishment of a maximum working day and week;
2. Regulation of labor supply, prevention of unemployment and provision of an adequate living wage;
3. Protection of the worker against sickness, disease and injury arising out of his employment;
4. Protection of children, young persons and women;
5. Provision for old age and injury, protection of the interests of workers when employed in countries other than their own;
6. Recognition of the principle of equal remuneration for work of equal value;
7. Recognition of the principle of freedom of association;
8. Organization of vocational and technical education, and other measures.

Declaration on Fundamental Principles and Rights at Work

The Declaration on Fundamental Principles and Rights at Work, adopted by the ILO in 1998, 'codifies the ILO's understanding of the fundamental human rights contained in its Constitution and standards'.[104] It is binding on all ILO member states. The Declaration states that all ILO member states have:[105]

---

[104] Roger Blanpain (ed.), *Comparative Labor Law and Industrial Relations in Industrialized Market Economies*, Wolters Kluwer, The Netherlands, 2007, 141.

[105] ILO, Declaration of Fundamental Principles and Rights at Work, Art 2; the 'fundamental' conventions are C87: Freedom of Association and Protection of the Right to Organise

> An obligation, arising from the very fact of membership in the Organisation, to respect, to promote and to realise, in good faith and in accordance with the Constitution, the fundamental rights which are the subjects of those [fundamental] Conventions, namely:
>
> (a) freedom of association and the effective recognition of the right to collective bargaining;
> (b) the elimination of all forms of forced or compulsory labor;
> (c) the effective abolition of child labor; and
> (d) the elimination of discrimination in respect of employment and occupation.

Many of these fundamental labor matters (a)–(d), as we have seen, are reflected in Constitutions of the countries.

The Declaration requires that member states that have not ratified all of the fundamental Conventions must submit annual reports to the ILO, 'commenting on the status of the relevant rights and principles within their borders, noting impediments to ratification'.[106] The reports are then reviewed by the Committee of Independent Expert Advisers. In turn, the Committee's observations are considered by the ILO's governing body. The ILO then provides assistance to member states to implement the rights contained in the Declaration.[107]

Conventions and Recommendations: Real or illusory sources of law?

The Conventions and Recommendations of the ILO collectively form the international labor standards. There are 189 Conventions and 202 Recommendations currently in force. The international labor standards establish basic workers' rights, aiming to improve working conditions on a global scale. However, although it is generally agreed that the formulation of international labor standards has had a positive effect on working conditions in ILO member states, the standards are subject to a number of key limitations.

After drafting by the International Labor Office, Conventions and Recommendations are adopted by the International Labor Conference, the key decision-making organ of the ILO. The Conference, made up of delegations from member states, includes representatives of the government, employers and workers. To be adopted by the Conference, a Convention or Recommendation must be passed by a two-thirds majority of all delegates present; hence a simple majority in favor will not suffice.

The ILO Constitution requires that once a Convention or Recommendation has been accepted by the Conference, it must be submitted to the competent authority of each member state within 12 or 18 months respectively. However, the competent authority only needs to *consider* how the standard should be ratified or implemented. It may determine that the Convention or Recommendation should not be ratified or implemented. In that case, no further obligation applies except to report to the International Labor Office on the difficulties which prevent or delay ratification or implementation of

Convention (1948), C98: Right to Organise and Collective Bargaining Convention (1949), C29: Forced Labor Convention (1930), C105: Abolition of Forced Labor Convention (1957), C138: Minimum Age Convention (1973), C182: Worst Forms of Child Labor Convention (1999), C100: Equal Remuneration Convention (1951), C111: Discrimination (Employment and Occupation) Convention (1958).

106 http://www.ilo.org/declaration/thedeclaration/lang–en/index.htm.

107 Ibid.

the instrument.[108] The ILO may be criticised for the fact that insufficient pressure is placed on member states to ratify international labor standards; and there is of course no mechanism to compel countries to adopt the standards. Even where the country has ratified the convention, there is no compelling mechanism to force adoption of it into municipal law.

The international labor standards include both fundamental human rights standards, and more technical instruments. Some Conventions 'can be called promotional – some or all of the obligations they create on ratification are oriented more towards adopting and pursuing a policy than toward precise obligations to be carried out in specified ways'.[109]

Recommendations 'are used mainly to supplement Conventions, in order to indicate in greater detail the manner of giving effect to their provisions or to advocate the establishment of higher standards'.[110] However, the capacity for international labor standards to impact practice in member states can be limited by the flexibility of the standards. Flexibility is required to ensure that the standards are universally applicable. However, flexibility clauses may allow states to conform to less exacting standards. For example, some instruments allow states to lay down 'temporary standards that are lower than those normally prescribed, to exclude certain categories of workers from the application of a convention, or to apply only certain parts of the instrument'.[111] Alternatively, Conventions may require that states establish the means to set standards within their own jurisdictions, rather than containing specific requirements. For example, standards on minimum wages do not establish a set figure, but require that states establish the machinery to set an appropriate minimum wage themselves.[112]

Conventions and Recommendations are intended to be applicable in all ILO member states, while 'significantly advancing on existing practice'[113] across members. In drafting a Convention or Recommendation, the International Labor Office reviews the law and practice on the subject of the relevant standard in each member state. However, the vast differences in practice across ILO member states means that formulating universally acceptable standards can be difficult. Developing nations have consistently criticised the ILO for this reason, claiming that economic underdevelopment hampers the implementation of international labor standards.[114]

Some academic commentators have been critical of the role of the ILO. Professor Standing has been voluble in considering 'how the ILO has failed to come to terms with the Global Transformation, seeing it as trying to play three roles – a standard-setter, a technical assistance agency and a knowledge generator – without developing

---

108 ILO Constitution, Articles 5, 6.

109 Blanpain (n 3 above), p 147.

110 Ibid., p 140.

111 International Labour Organisation, 'Rules of the Game: A brief introduction to International Labour Standards', p 18. [http://www.ilo.org/wcmsp5/groups/public/ – ed_norm/ – normes/documents/publication/wcms_108393.pdf.]

112 Ibid.

113 Blanpain (n 3 above), p 140.

114 Victor-Yves Ghebali, *The International Labor Organisation: A Case Study on the Evolution of UN Specialised Agencies*, International Organization and the Evolution of World Society, Martinus Nijhoff Publishers, The Netherlands, 1989.

the professional capacity to do so'.[115] The significant question, he poses, is 'whether the ILO could become an effective development agency given the changing character of work and labor in globalizing labor markets and its antiquated governance structure'.[116]

Case law

Governments often request that various international judicial organs adjudicate labor disputes or offer interpretations of the international labor standards. These decisions form a body of 'case law' which gives content to the obligations imposed by Conventions and Recommendations.

Various ILO organs offer interpretations of Conventions, which are treated as authoritative by member states. Member states often consult the International Labor Office, either formally or informally, as to the meaning of a Convention. If a member state requests a formal interpretation of a Convention, the decision will be published in the ILO's Official Bulletin and circulated to all member states. For example, although the Right to Organise Convention[117] does not expressly deal with the right to strike, 'the case law of the ILO supervisory bodies is that this right is inherent in the right to take action to defend workers' interests'.[118]

In addition, various ILO Committees have developed 'case law' interpreting the ILO Conventions and Recommendations. The Committee of Experts on the Application of Conventions and Recommendations examines reports from member states on the implementation of ILO Conventions. Reports on the deliberations of the Committee of Experts are then submitted to the Committee on the Application of Conventions and Recommendations, which engages in dialogue with each member state on the content of each report. In evaluating the implementation of Conventions, the Committee of Experts 'has to consider and express its views on the meaning of certain provisions of Conventions'.[119]

Supervisory machinery

The supervisory machinery of the ILO is intended to encourage member states to transform the rights and obligations contained in international labor standards into domestic law obligations. The supervisory procedures rely on the examination of periodic reports and the consideration of complaints against member states.[120] It should be reiterated that the ILO cannot compel states to ratify standards, or to give effect to

---

[115] Guy Standing, 'The ILO: An agency for globalization?' (2008) 39(3) *Development and Change* 355–84. See also Standing, 'The International Labor Organization' (2010) 15(2) *New Political Economy* 307.

[116] Ibid.

[117] Freedom of Association and Protection of the Right to Organise Convention (1949) No 87.

[118] See Report III(4B), International Labor Conference, 81st Session, 194 paras 61–78 cited in Blanpain (n 3 above), p 147.

[119] See Report III(4A), International Labor Conference, 73rd Session, 1987 para 12 cited in Blanpain ibid., p 143.

[120] Blanpain (n 3 above), p 157.

the standards that they have ratified. Instead, the ILO can only 'name and shame' non-conforming states in the hope that they comply with standards.[121]

Examination of periodic reports

States are obligated to report on Conventions, both ratified and unratified, and on Recommendations. Each member state is required to 'make an annual report to the International Labor Office on the measures which it has taken to give effect to the provisions of Conventions to which it is a party'.[122] In respect of unratified Conventions and all Recommendations, each member state must make reports to the International Labor Office regarding:

> the position of the law and practice in their country in regard to matters dealt with in the [Convention or Recommendation], showing the extent to which effect has been given or is proposed to be given, to the provisions of the [Convention or Recommendation].[123]

The two ILO committees with responsibility for the application of Conventions and Recommendations examine these reports. Representatives of the ILO also conduct meetings with individual member state governments to 'discuss difficulties in the implementation of ILO standards'.[124] Although these procedures are not a formal source of international labor law, and do not bind member states, there are over 2,500 examples of governments having taken measures in direct response to comments by supervisory bodies.[125]

Consideration of complaints

Article 26 of the ILO Constitution provides that any member state may file a complaint against any other member state regarding the application of a Convention to which they are both party. After receiving a complaint, the International Labor Conference may appoint a Commission of Inquiry to investigate and report on the issue.[126]

All these various processes – including negotiation of the terms of the obligations initially and the subsequent mechanisms to have potential non-compliance with standards referred to international bodies for review – are means of encouraging individual nations to take steps to ensure that laws are adopted by them to give effect to the ILO Conventions and Recommendations. But, as they depend upon the individual nation's legislative processes, the various ILO mechanisms are at most 'best practice' influences on what a particular country does in domestic law, rather than being determinative of what it does.

Nonetheless, as the data referred to above suggest, the processes can have an effect on domestic law – albeit as a matter of choice on a case-by-case basis rather than a legally-binding consequence of a country having acknowledged being bound by the international convention.

---

121 http://www.lse.ac.uk/government/research/resgroups/PSPE/pdf/PSPE_WP1_11.pdf.
122 ILO Constitution, Article 22.
123 Ibid., Article 19(5e), 19(6d).
124 Blanpain (n 3 above), p 158.
125 Ibid.
126 ILO Constitution, Article 26.

(b) United Nations

The United Nations (UN) does not have a specific mandate for labor matters. However, in adopting international instruments concerning human rights, the UN does create international labor law. UN instruments also form part of international law, but no rights are conferred on individuals until the instrument has been transformed into the state's domestic law.

UN sources of labor law

A number of UN Conventions create international labor law. Many of the rights and obligations conferred by UN Treaties include some that are intended to be exercised specifically in the context of employment, such as the rights to equal pay and to join and form trade unions. In addition, UN instruments confer rights that are intended to be exercised generally, but also affect the employment relationship. For example, instruments that guarantee free association require that 'individual workers should have the right to form and join trade unions, and that they should have adequate protection against victimization on account of having done so'.[127]

A broad range of UN Declarations, Covenants and Conventions form part of international labor law, including:

- The Universal Declaration of Human Rights, 1948 (UDHR);
- The International Convention on the Elimination of All Forms of Racial Discrimination, 1965 (CERD);
- The International Covenant on Civil and Political Rights, 1966 (ICCPR);
- The International Covenant on Economic, Social and Cultural Rights, 1966 (ICESCR);
- The Convention on the Elimination of All Forms of Discrimination Against Women, 1979 (CEDAW);
- The Convention on the Rights of the Child, 1989 (CROC);
- The International Convention on the Protection of the Rights of All Migrant Workers and Members of their Families, 2003 (ICRMW).

The UDHR, commonly regarded as the foundation of international human rights law,[128] establishes a number of rights in respect of employment. For example, Article 23 establishes the right to work, to equal and fair remuneration and the right to form and join trade unions. Article 23 states:

(1) Everyone has the right to work, to free choice of employment, to just and favourable conditions of work and to protection against unemployment.
(2) Everyone, without any discrimination, has the right to equal pay for equal work.

---

[127] Blanpain (n 3 above), p 311.

[128] See Jochen von Bernstorff, 'The changing fortunes of the Universal Declaration of Human Rights: Genesis and symbolic dimensions of the turn of rights in international law' (2008) 19(5) *The European Journal of International Law* 903.

(3) Everyone who works has the right to just and favourable remuneration ensuring for himself and his family an existence worthy of human dignity, and supplemented, if necessary, by other means of social protection.
(4) Everyone has the right to form and to join trade unions for the protection of his interests.

UN Conventions also provide robust protection against discrimination on the grounds of gender and race. CEDAW provides that: 'States Parties shall take all appropriate measures to eliminate all forms of discrimination against women in the field of employment in order to ensure, on a basis of equality of men and women, the same rights.'[129] Similarly, CERD provides that: 'States Parties undertake to … guarantee the right of everyone, without distinction as to race, colour, or national or ethnic origin … the right to work, to free choice of employment, to just and favourable conditions of work.'[130]

In addition, the more recent ICRMW confers various rights specifically on migrant workers.[131] The ICRMW 'specifies human rights articled in the [ICESCR and ICCPR] and expresses explicitly how different rights apply to different categories of working migrants'.[132] Key rights guaranteed by the ICRMW include the right to leave and return to the state of origin, prohibition of slavery or servitude and of forced or compulsory labor and the necessity to ensure an equitable procedure of recourse to migrant workers and members of their family.[133] The ICRMW is supervised by a UN Treaty body in collaboration with the ILO.[134]

As with ILO instruments, the processes for negotiating, creating and in various ways considering non-compliance with these international conventions – which have potential to be applied in domestic law – can have the effect of encouraging individual nations to take steps to ensure that laws are adopted by that nation to give effect to those conventions as part of the domestic law of the nation.

However, as with the ILO Conventions, these processes are at best influences in what a particular country does in domestic law, rather than being determinative of what it does. Domestic law remains controlled by the legislature of the nation and nothing is ceded by the country in terms of legislative power or authority to any entity outside the country.

---

[129] Convention on the Elimination of All Forms of Discrimination Against Women, Article 11.

[130] Ibid., Article 5(e)(i).

[131] See International Convention on the Protection of the Rights of All Migrant Workers and Members of Their Families, Article 2(1). The term 'migrant worker' refers to 'a person who is to be engaged, is engaged or has been engaged in a remunerated activity in a State of which he or she is not a national'.

[132] http://www.humanrights.ch/en/Standards/UN-Treaties/Migrant-Workers/index.html.

[133] ICRMW.

[134] Blanpain (n 3 above), p 144.

11. EUROPEAN LABOR LAW: REGIONAL REGULATORY INFLUENCES

The European region has a highly developed, normative set of labor laws. Key bodies that formulate Euro-area labor law are the EU and the Council of Europe. The European regional law is worthy of study as an example of another layer of laws covering the region and above those laws of the sovereign states.

The legal position in the EU – as an economic and political union of 28 member states (as of 2014) located in Europe – is highly distinct from that which has been summarised in relation to the ILO and the UN, as they represent the usual example of general international instruments. Consequences for sources of labor law flow from the fundamentally different legal character of the international arrangements within the EU, which bear resemblance in some ways to nations which have federal governments including powers being ceded by the member entities to a central source of authority.

The European Union: Formation of European Union Labor Law

The countries of the EU have established a *sui generis* legal order with characteristics of both international and domestic law.[135] EU law operates directly on individuals within EU member states. In this respect it is distinguished from international law, which only covers states themselves. The European Court of Justice (ECJ) has held that 'the Community constitutes a new legal order of international law for the benefit of which the States have limited their sovereign rights'.[136] The consequence of this is that the subjects of EU law 'comprise not only Member States but also their nationals'.[137] However, the direct effect of EU law is limited to provisions which are 'self-executing', meaning that they are intended to confer rights on individuals, sufficiently clear and precise, and unconditional.[138]

In addition, where the domestic labor law of EU member states is inconsistent or incompatible with EU law, EU law prevails. This is because the transfer of EU member states' sovereignty to EU institutions 'carries with it a permanent limitation of their sovereign rights, against which a subsequent unilateral act incompatible with the concept of the Community cannot prevail'.[139]

---

135 Timothy Moorhead, 'European Union Law as International Law' (2012) 5(1) *European Journal of Legal Studies* 126.

136 *NV Algemene Transport en Expeditie Onderneming van Gend & Loos v. Netherlands Inland Revenue Administration* 26/62 [1963] ECR 1.

137 Ibid.

138 See Case 8/81 *Becker v. Finanzamt Munster-Innenstadt* [1982] ECR 53 para 25 where the ECJ said: that the EU provisions must be 'sufficiently precise and unconditional' in order for them to give rise to individual enforcement. See also Moorhead (n 135 above), p 143.

139 *Costa v. ENEL Case* 1964 Case 6/64 [1964] ECR 585.

The power to formulate EU labor law is shared between the European Parliament,[140] the Council of the European Union[141] and the European Commission.[142] The Council has the power to finalise EU legislation.[143] The 'European Parliament, acting jointly with the Council, the Council and the European Commission' are empowered to 'make regulations, issue directives, take decisions, make recommendations or deliver opinions'.[144] Article 189 of the Treaty Establishing the European Community (as amended by subsequent treaties) further details the effect of each action (italics added):

> A *regulation* shall have general application. It shall be binding in its entirety and directly applicable in all Member States.
>
> A *directive* shall be binding, as to the result to be achieved, upon each Member State to which it is addressed, but shall leave to the national authorities the choice of form and methods.
>
> A *decision* shall be binding in its entirety upon those to whom it is addressed.
>
> *Recommendations and opinions* shall have no binding force.

The EU organs are empowered to legislate with respect to a reasonably broad range of labor law matters set out in the Treaty on the Functioning of the EU (TFEU). These include – health and safety, working conditions; information and consultation in the workplace; equal treatment between men and women regarding labor market opportunities and work; integration of excluded persons; representation and collective defence of the interests of workers and employers; and financial contributions to promote employment.[145]

In addition, a number of labor matters are excluded from the legislative competence of the EU, including pay, and the rights to free association, to strike and to impose lockouts.[146]

Notably though, the power of the EU to legislate is limited by the principles of subsidiarity and proportionality. Subsidiarity provides that the EU organs can only legislate where the objectives of the legislation cannot be better achieved by member states acting alone, and can be better achieved by the Community by reason of the scale

---

140 The European Parliament is composed of 786 directly elected delegates who represent the people of Europe: see Eve Landau and Yves Beigbeder, *From ILO Standards to EU Law: The Case of Equality between Men and Women at Work*, Martinus Nijhoff, Leiden, 2008, 39.

141 This is not be confused with the European Council which is the body defining 'the general political direction and priorities of the European Union': http://www.european-council.europa.eu/the-institution?lang=en. The European Council includes a minister representing each member state.

142 The European Commission is composed of one Commissioner from each EU member state, chosen to represent the interests of the European community as a whole.

143 Landau and Beigbeder (n 140 above), p 39.

144 Article 189, Treaty Establishing the European Community as Amended by Subsequent Treaties, *Rome*, 25 March 1957 (the Treaty of Rome).

145 TFEU, Article 153(1).

146 Ibid., Article 153(5). For how some of these limitations may be avoided in reality, see A C L Davies, *EU Labour Law*, Edward Elgar, 2012, p 32.

and effects of the legislation. Legislation must also be proportional, meaning that it must have no greater effect than is necessary to achieve the intended objective.[147]

Content of EU labor law

Professor Blanpain outlines the broad range of matters actually governed by EU labor law.[148] It is beyond the scope of this chapter to detail all these. However, to demonstrate the development of European labor law, the issue of discrimination will be briefly outlined and the controversial Working time Directive discussed.

Prohibition of discrimination EU labor law prohibits employment discrimination on the basis of gender, racial or ethnic origin, religion, disability, age or sexual orientation. The key EU instruments governing discrimination are: Council Directive No 76/207/EEC of 9 February 1976 (Equal Treatment Directive); Council Directive 2000/78/EC of 27 November 2000 (Framework Employment Directive); and Council Directive No 2000/43/EC of 28 June 2000 (Race Equality Directive).

The Framework Employment Directive establishes a general framework for equal treatment as regards employment and occupation, prohibiting discrimination on the basis of disability, age, sexual orientation, religion or belief, whilst the Race Equality Directive implements the principle of equal treatment between persons irrespective of racial or ethnic origin. The latter Directive establishes a framework for combating discrimination on the grounds of racial or ethnic origin, which requires that Member States implement the principle of equal treatment.[149]

Both Directives relate to access to employment, including selection criteria and recruitment conditions, access to vocational guidance and training, employment and working conditions, and membership of workers or employers organisations.

GENDER DISCRIMINATION Discrimination on the basis of gender is prohibited by a combination of Treaty law, Directives and decisions of the ECJ, the court which carries out the important role of interpreting EU law.

Article 141 of the Treaty establishing the European Economic Community (EEC Treaty) prohibits pay discrimination on the basis of gender. The Article provides that 'Each Member State shall ensure that the principle of equal pay for male and female workers for equal work or work of equal value is applied'.[150] In addition, a number of Directives prohibit gender discrimination. The most important is the Equal Treatment Directive, which requires that member states give effect to 'the principle of equal treatment of men and women as regards access to employment, including promotion, and to vocational training and as regards working conditions'.[151]

The EU anti-discrimination directives are typical of much legislation in that they require interpretation. The ECJ's jurisprudence on the issue of gender discrimination

---

147 See generally, Davies, ibid., p 12.

148 Roger Blanpain, *European Labour Law*, Kluwer Law International, 2010.

149 See Memorandum of Understanding between the Council of Europe and the European Union 2007 at http://www.coe.int/t/der/docs/MoU_EN.pdf.

150 EC Treaty, Article 141.

151 Council Directive 76/207/EEC of 9 February 1976, Article 1.

has clarified the content of the Equal Treatment Directive in a number of key cases. For example, the Court has determined that a refusal to employ, or dismissal of, a pregnant woman due to her pregnancy or maternity amounts to direct discrimination on the grounds of sex.[152] The Court may also declare national legislation to be incompatible with a Directive; the Court has held for example that national legislation permitting an employer to stand down a pregnant woman without full pay is discriminatory and therefore incompatible with the Equal Treatment Directive.

REGULATION OF WORKING HOURS One of the most significant and controversial of the set minimum labor standards in Directives is the Directive on the Organisation of Working Time (Working Time Directive),[153] which requires the member states to take measures to regulate the working hours of certain employees. The Working Time Directive is 'part of a package of social rules and health and safety standards that the EU adopted … to make the single market programme more palatable to workers and trade unions'.[154]

The key provisions of the Working Time Directive provide that every worker must enjoy:

- A minimum rest period of 11 consecutive hours per period of 24 hours;[155]
- A rest break where the working day is longer than six hours;[156]
- An average weekly working period of no more than 48 hours, inclusive of overtime;[157] and
- Paid annual leave of at least four weeks.[158]

The objective of the Working Time Directive is to protect the health and safety of workers,[159] balancing this with the needs of the modern European economy. The Working Time Directive permits derogations where there is collective agreement between the employers and unions. Derogations may be granted with 'due regard for the general principles of protecting the safety of workers, where the duration of the working time is not measured and/or predetermined by the workers themselves',[160] and also in certain occupations and industries requiring continuity of service (such as

---

152 *Hofman* C-184/83 (12/07/1984).

153 Directive 2003/88/EC of the European Parliament and of the Council of 4 November 2003 concerning certain aspects of the organisation of working time.

154 Katinka Barysch, *The Working Time Directive: What's the fuss about?*, Centre for European Reform, 2013 at <http://www.cer.org.uk/sites/default/files/publications/attachments/pdf/2013/pb_workingtimedir_kb_26april13_bl-7268.pdf>

155 Directive 2003/88/EC, Article 3.

156 Ibid., Article 4.

157 Ibid., Article 6.

158 Ibid., Article 6.

159 Ibid.s Article 1, s 1.

160 Ibid., Article 17, s 1(a).

agriculture or hospital care)[161] or foreseeable surges in activity (such as tourism or postal services).[162]

The provisions of the Working Time Directive have also been interpreted by the ECJ. In the *SIMAP case*,[163] the term 'working hours' was defined to include all time when the worker was required to be on site. This decision was affirmed in the *Jaeger* case: the court confirmed that the decision in *SIMAP* applied even if workers (in this case, on-call doctors) could sleep when their services were not required.[164]

The Working Time Directive has been one of the most controversial of the EU labor directives. Particularly in the United Kingdom, opposition has centered on the economic costs of implementing the Directive.[165] There has also been some reform of working hours in EU member states, within the parameters set by the Working Time Directive. That there are variations in the working work is well illustrated by the controversial maximum 35-hour week in France and its progressive dismantling recently.[166] There is also scope for individual workers to opt out of the provisions of the Directive.

Council of Europe: Sources of Labor Law

In addition to the EU, the other key Euro-area international organisation is the Council of Europe, composed of 47 European states. The Council of Europe[167] aims to protect human rights and the rule of law, find common solutions to the challenges facing Europe and to consolidate democratic stability in Europe.

The Council of Europe has formulated a number of international human rights instruments to be ratified by its members. The most important of these are the European Convention on Human Rights (ECHR) and the European Social Charter (ESC).

European Convention on Human Rights

The ECHR – the long title of which is the Convention for the Protection of Human Rights and Fundamental Freedoms – establishes a minimum standard of civil and political rights and freedoms that member states of the Council of Europe are obliged to guarantee. The ECHR has been ratified by all Council of Europe member states.

Two Articles apply specifically in the field of labor law. First, the ECHR prohibits slavery and certain forms of forced labor.[168] Secondly, the Convention guarantees everyone freedom of peaceful assembly and freedom of association, including the right

---

161 Ibid., s 3(c).

162 Ibid., s 3(d).

163 *Sindicato de Medicos de Asistencia Publica v. Conselleria de Sanidad y Consumo de la Generalidad Valanciana* C-303/98 [2000] ECR I-7963.

164 *Landeshauptstadt Kiel v. Jaeger* [2003] IRLR 804 ECJ.

165 Barysch (n 154 above).

166 Philippe Askenazy, 'Working Time Regulation in France from 1996 to 2012' (2013) 37(2) *Cambridge Journal of Economics* 323.

167 This should not be confused with the Council of the European Union discussed earlier. The Council of Europe is not an EU organ.

168 Convention for the Protection of Human Rights and Fundamental Freedoms, Article 4.

of every employee 'to form and to join trade unions for the protection of his interests'.[169] Moreover, there is a prohibition on discrimination in relation to the rights in the convention.[170] Alleged violations of the Convention may be referred to the European Court of Human Rights (also set up under the ECHR) by parties[171] or can entertain applications from individuals, groups or non-governmental organisations[172] once domestic remedies have been exhausted.[173] Significantly, and in a departure from ILO procedures, all member states of the Council of Europe undertake to abide by the judgments of the Court.[174]

European Social Charter

The Council of Europe Treaty, the ESC, guarantees social rights within member states of the Council of Europe. The ESC was drafted in 1965, and revised in 1996, and has been ratified by 43 member states.

The ESC establishes a large number of rights and obligations. These include prohibiting forced labor, the rights of employees to just conditions at work,[175] to organise trade union and employer associations and to bargain collectively,[176] to strike,[177] to receive vocational guidance and training,[178] to be given information about the economic and financial situation of their employer and to be consulted on decisions which could substantially affect the interests of workers.[179] Further there is the right to equality of treatment in employment[180] and the right to protection in the termination of employment, essentially so that dismissal cannot occur without a valid reason.[181] It is the European Committee of Social Rights which rules on whether national laws conform to the Charter. States parties submit annual reports about compliance with the Charter.

12. CONCLUSION

The richness of the panoply of labor laws – whether derived from private individual agreement, collective bargaining, state legislative intervention, custom, policy and 'soft laws', or the overarching influences of international sources of law – is clear. While separate sovereign states remain in existence, even within such structures as the EU, we will continue to see great divergences in the details of the laws and the degree of

---

169 Ibid., Article 11.
170 Ibid., Article 14.
171 Ibid., Article 33.
172 Ibid., Article 34.
173 Ibid., Article 35.
174 Ibid., Article 46.
175 European Social Charter, Article 2.
176 Ibid., Articles 5, 6.
177 Ibid., Article 6.
178 Ibid., Articles 9, 10.
179 Ibid., Article 21.
180 Ibid., Article 20.
181 Ibid., Article 24.

intervention. Challenges may be similar in the different sovereign states – financial crises, globalisation, economic migration, for example – but responses of governments, policy makers and legislatures are many and varied, often multi-layered, and often giving rise to considerable degrees of complexity. The role of labor law in ameliorating or adequately meeting these challenges is under stress and strain, and certainly debate. To what extent ultimately global labor laws or transnational laws will emerge as sources of law – and how strongly – to play a role, and to give a degree of uniformity and certainty to governments, employers, employees and their associations and unions, remains to be seen. We are only now at the beginning of the debate.

2. Comparative labor and employment law in developed market economies: Fostering market efficiencies or repairing market failures?

Silvia Bonfanti, Cynthia Estlund and Nuno Garoupa

Labor and employment law plays a central role in modern developed economies. In this chapter, we start by reviewing the economic approach to labor markets and their failures and the different theories explaining the role and importance of labor law. We then turn our attention to the legal origins theory by which economists claim to explain differences in labor and employment law across the world. Our critical review of the legal origins theory leads us to a discussion of specific aspects of labor law in common law and in civil law jurisdictions from the perspective of the 'varieties of capitalism' approach. We conclude by suggesting that the latter could provide a more solid explanation of distinct labor law approaches than the legal origins theory.

1. ECONOMICS OF LABOR MARKET FAILURES

On the neoclassical view of labor markets, a perfectly competitive market (for, say, machinists in a particular region) would yield a single wage level, corresponding to the marginal productivity of labor, at which the demand for labor equaled the supply. Both workers and employers would be 'price-takers' at this equilibrium wage; workers who demanded more would not find a job, and employers who offered less would not find workers. In this hypothetical perfectly competitive market, regulations that raised the price of labor above the equilibrium wage, either directly or indirectly, would result in an inefficient mismatch between demand and supply in the form of unemployment.[1]

No one, including neoclassical labor economists, believes that labor markets are actually perfectly competitive.[2] It is widely recognized that labor markets are subject to a variety of 'market failures' that might lead to inefficiencies, and that might be countered by public regulation. Generally speaking, the market equilibrium fails to achieve efficiency when there are entry or exit barriers, asymmetric information, externalities, or systematic behavioral deviations from the 'rational actor' construct. In those conditions, one side of the market (supply or demand) may act as price-maker rather than price-taker; in other words, some economic agents may have market power.

[1] Richard Posner, 'The Social Costs of Monopoly and Regulation', 83 *J. Pol. Econ.* 807, 807–27 (1975).

[2] Michael Wachter, 'Neoclassical Labor Economics: Its Implications for Labor and Employment Law', in: *Research Handbook on the Economics of Labor and Employment Law* 20 (Cynthia L. Estlund and Michael L. Wachter, eds, Edward Elgar, 2012).

In the context of labor markets, economists have identified all of these possible market failures. There is debate, however, over their extent and, relatedly, over the extent to which regulatory interventions are likely to counter or compound market failures.[3] In particular, labor economists recognize that the *internal* labor markets in which many employees live most of their working lives are pervaded by market failures that may justify certain regulatory interventions.

Entry and exit barriers correspond to labor's imperfect mobility. Workers may face barriers in securing the specific skills or human capital needed to move across sectors or jobs. Or they may face geographical restrictions such as housing and transportation costs, family and other social ties, or other transaction costs. Immigration-related restrictions on employment can also impede labor mobility. Entry and exit barriers may also confer market power on one side or the other. At the extreme, economists recognize the possibility of employer monopsony. If one or a few employers dominate a particular labor market (protected, for example, by barriers to entry by competitors and barriers to exit by workers), they will be able to pay less than competitive salaries (that is, below marginal productivity). Although pure monopsonies are rare, frictions in the labor market can give employers some of the market power associated with monopsonies. In such cases, unions – which attempt to monopolize the supply of labor – could enhance efficiency by countering employers' monopsony power. On the other hand, where employers do not enjoy monopsony power, unions might enable workers to exercise market power, and to secure higher than 'competitive' salaries (that is, above the value of marginal productivity).

Another important type of market failure is information asymmetry. Some information is more available to workers than to employers, and can give rise to problems of moral hazard and adverse selection. One kind of moral hazard results from what economists call 'hidden action'; for example, employers cannot directly observe the effort exerted by employees and thus their marginal productivity. In other words, employees might be tempted to deliver less effort than the employer believed the contract called for due to asymmetry of information. Employers might also be unable to judge the quality of employees (an example of what economists call 'hidden type'), and may thus be unwilling to pay more for more productive workers. Under some conditions, a 'lemons problem' may arise: good employees may be driven out of the market by bad ones, given the inability of employers to discern and pay for quality. Public licensing (as in the labor market for professional services) may be an efficiency-enhancing response. Adverse selection may occur due to workers' superior information about their own disabilities or their family-related needs; that may discourage employers from offering socially desirable accommodations, lest they attract more than their share of workers who need such accommodations. Mandatory accommodations may be a sensible regulatory response.[4]

---

[3] Compare Wachter, ibid, with Bruch E. Kaufman, 'Economic Analysis of Labor Markets and Labor Law: An Institutional/Industrial Relations Perspective', in: *Research Handbook on the Economics of Labor and Employment Law*, ibid., 65.

[4] Of course employers may have superior access to some important information about the job or the organization, such as non-obvious or unusual hazards, history of fair versus arbitrary treatment in discipline and discharge, plans for future contraction or expansion, or demands for

Other inefficiencies may arise from systematic and stubborn behavioral deviations from the 'rational actors' that populate the textbook neoclassical model of labor markets. For example real people, unlike 'rational actors,' may overvalue what they have – the job or amenities they currently enjoy – relative to what they might secure on the external market (even apart from the transaction costs associated with moving). Or they may fail to exercise beneficial options – like optional retirement benefits – that require moving off the 'default' or status quo position, even when it is quite easy to do so. Predictable manifestations of 'bounded rationality' like these can lead to inefficient market outcomes, but might be corrected by well-crafted regulations.

There are also several potential externalities to labor market transactions. Third parties (including co-workers or the general public) may be affected by the terms of an individual employment contract. In particular, there are many workplace-specific 'public goods,' which give rise to familiar collective action problems among workers. Job safety is a clear illustration of a public good, both within the workforce and beyond. But even fairness in discipline and dismissal is partly a 'public goods' insofar as workplaces are governed by general policies and procedures, not by individual negotiations. This is yet another set of 'market failures' that flows from the actuality of internal labor markets versus the clean textbook construct of perfectly competitive labor markets.

Where there are serious market failures, the regulation of labor market can potentially improve the efficiency of labor market outcomes. In particular, regulation might enhance efficiency by decreasing search costs, improving quality and quantity of information, reducing barriers to entry and exit, overcoming collective action problems and other externalities, counteracting decision-making biases, and potentially rebalancing market power.

Moreover, the public may also pursue legitimate goals other than economic efficiency (i.e., correcting for market failures). These goals may be grounded in a paternalistic view of the role of government, or in community values other than efficiency, such as economic solidarity and equality. Some of these values (such as confidence, honesty, solidarity and trust) may in turn facilitate cooperation, build social capital, and promote collective productivity; they may enhance social welfare and foster growth in the long run, and may even lead to a higher equilibrium wage. In any event, the social willingness to pay for these values may be above their current market or economic value, thus justifying government intervention. The many public-regarding motivations that may justify government intervention figure in a public interest theory of regulation.

In opposition to the public interest theory, many economists propound a private interest theory that goes by the paradoxical name 'public choice.' This theory points to

---

drug-testing, mandatory arbitration agreements, or covenants not to compete. See: Cynthia Estlund, *Regoverning the Workplace: From Self-Regulation to Co-Regulation* (Yale University Press, 2010). Even if these things become known to employees early in the employment relationship, they are often obscure at the point of entry, when the initial wage is set and certain frictions begin to impede employee mobility.

the ever-present risks of capture and collusion.[5] From this perspective, the regulation of labor markets is seen to arise from, and to be sustained by, the interests of particular groups rather than 'the public.' Regulation is said to facilitate cartel-like behavior on the side of employers or employees (in the latter case, by favoring unions). As a result, public choice theory predicts that regulation tends to distort salaries and other relevant terms and conditions of employment (such as the quality of the working environment, number of hours to work, labor rights) to favor the interests of particular groups rather than to promote efficiency or other public values. For example, regulation may raise salaries above marginal productivity or impede discharges or layoffs, generating rents and quasi-rents on behalf of 'insiders' – those who have jobs – to the detriment of job seekers.

A realistic view of labor market regulations fits neither the pure private interest nor the pure public interest theory. Employers and employees do have an influence on the form and content of labor market regulations; labor market interest groups will try to use regulations to generate private rents, and will sometimes succeed. On the other hand, sometimes regulation – even regulation that is partly motivated by group self-interest – does advance a broader public interest.[6] Given the plethora of 'market failures' that can infect actual labor markets, and that can vary widely from place to place, and given varying views about the magnitude of those market failures and the efficacy of regulatory intervention in correcting them, one would not be surprised to find that there is no one 'efficient' or growth-enhancing way to approach labor market regulation. A variety of institutional arrangements, responding to a variety of policy and political preferences and beliefs, may be consistent with economic prosperity; and those institutional arrangements in turn will affect what is possible and desirable at the next step of policy-making. Still, it is clear that the regulatory path that a nation follows will affect labor market outcomes. Scholars have thus continued to explore the determinants of that regulatory path.

2. THE REGULATION OF LABOR: THE LEGAL ORIGINS THEORY

In a seminal paper, Botero et al. (2004) (hereon: *Botero*) sought to test the extent to which labor law is explained by legal tradition (or 'legal origin') rather than either public or private interest theories.[7] They consider what they call efficiency theories (market regulations respond to labor market failures) and public choice theories (market regulations reflect interest group captures). But they argue that much national variation in labor market regulation can be explained by what they call 'legal origins' – that is, whether the legal system has its roots in Anglo-American 'common law,' or in

[5] See Richard Posner, 'Theories of Economic Regulation', 5(2) *Bell J. Econ. & Management Sci.* 335, 335–8 (1974).

[6] Sam Peltzman, 'Toward a More General Theory of Regulation', 19 *J.L. & Econ.* 211, 211–44 (1976).

[7] Juan Botero, Simeon Djankov, Rafael La Porta, Florencio Lopez de Silanes, and Andrei Shleifer, 'The Regulation of Labor', 2004 *Q. J. Econ.* 1339, 1339–82 (2004).

Continental European 'civil law.'[8] The general thesis is that the distinction between the common and the civil law legal families (which most non-European countries acquired through transplantation during their colonization) can explain much of the variation across national legal systems, including in labor law, across the world. More specifically, the disparity between the more market-oriented approach in Anglo-American labor law and the more heavily regulated approach in civil law countries reflects ideological options embedded in a legal family. The common law legal family is perceived as being less interventionist and more respectful of individual preferences and of market arrangements. The civil law family is understood as favoring state intervention in the economy and as less respectful of individual preferences.[9]

Botero codified the laws regulating labor markets in 85 countries (fairly distributed across the world in terms of geographical location and development stage). They consider three distinct groups of regulations, namely, employment, collective labor relations, and social security laws.

As examples to motivate the econometric analysis, the authors use New Zealand and Portugal, which have roughly the same average income level (as measured by GDP per capita). They argue that Portuguese law is much more regulated than New Zealand, such that the cost to an employer of increasing working hours is much higher in Portugal than in New Zealand. For example, New Zealand does not require notice or severance pay in dismissals, while Portugal (like the rest of Europe) does. Collective labor relations laws are constitutionalized in Portugal but not in New Zealand. Social laws (such as health and pension benefits) are generous in both, but are regulated by constitutional law in Portugal and not in New Zealand. One obvious shortcoming of their descriptive analysis is that they take formal law to be equivalent to law in action. Economists know that when a market is strongly regulated, there is a trend to generate an underground market in response. Unfortunately, the authors do not discuss the share of the labor market that is subject to formal regulations and the share of the market that is totally unregulated (or regulated by extralegal norms as in any underground market) in Portugal and New Zealand.

Table 2.1 below summarizes *Botero's* – Table III. It presents the three relevant indicators (employment, collective relations, social security), the per capita GNP (1997) in logarithms, the percentage of time a left majority has dominated the government in the period 1928–1995 (to control for any political bias) and legal origin.

[8] See Simeon Djankov, Edward Glaeser, Rafael La Porta, Florencio Lopez-de-Silanes and Andrei Shleifer, 'The New Comparative Economics', 31 *J. Comp. Econ.* 595, 595–619 (2003); Rafael La Porta, Florencio Lopez-de-Silanes and Andrei Shleifer, 'The Economic Consequences of Legal Origins', 46(2) *J. Econ. Lit.* 285, 285–332 (2008).

[9] This understanding of common law and civil law families has been disputed by legal economists; see Nuno Garoupa and Carlos Gómez Ligüerre, 'The Syndrome of the Efficiency of the Common Law', 29(2) *Boston U. Int'l L.J.* 288, 288–335 (2011). A more general critique is summarized in: Sean Cooney, Peter Gahan, and Richard Mitchell, 'Legal Origins, Labour Law and the Regulation of Employment Relations', in *Research Handbook on Comparative Employment Relations* 75, (Michael Barry and Adrian Atkinson eds, Edward Elgar, 2011). Cooney et al. discuss problems with classification of legal systems and data coding (deficiencies with ignoring functional equivalents, unsophisticated aggregation and absence of longitudinal analysis).

Table 2.1 Botero et al.'s (2004) dataset

	Employment Laws Index	Collective Relations Laws Index	Social Security Laws Index	Log GNP per capita 1997	% Time Left Dominates (1928–1995)	Legal Origin
New Zealand	0.16	0.25	0.72	9.6909	0.46	English
Portugal	0.82	0.65	0.74	9.3281	0.09	French
English common law (mean)	0.3	0.33	0.42	7.8045	0.52	
French civil law (mean)	0.55	0.49	0.55	7.9034	0.45	
German civil law (mean)	0.45	0.48	0.71	10.0557	0.27	
Scandin-avian civil law (mean)	0.68	0.48	0.83	10.3310	0.77	

First, we have New Zealand and Portugal as they are the two examples used by the authors. They have similar GNP per capita in 1997. The comparison across the indicators is largely consistent with the story defended by *Botero*.[10] Portugal has an extremely rigid set of employment and collective labor relations laws (even among the French civil law jurisdictions), whereas New Zealand seems to have few regulations (even relative to English common law jurisdictions). Both have relatively interventionist social security laws.

More broadly, we can immediately see that the Anglo-American common law is associated with lower indicators in all three relevant dimensions. Scandinavian civil law seems to be associated with more regulated labor markets. French and German civil law systems are in between, with French systems having more interventionist employment laws and German systems having more interventionist social security laws.

Table 2.2 summarizes the relationship between regulation of labor and outcomes as documented by *Botero's* Table VIII.

[10] Ironically, the authors' indicators suggest that New Zealand, despite its more liberal employment laws, has been more influenced by the left than Portugal. But this is misleading, for Portugal was ruled autocratically by the right until the non-violent revolution of 1974, and since then has been ruled mainly by the left, which produced the current legislation.

Table 2.2 Botero's outcomes

Dependent Variable	Employment Laws Index	Collective Relations Laws Index	Social Security Laws Index
Size of unofficial economy	Not statistically significant	Positive	Not statistically significant
Employment in the unofficial economy	Not statistically significant	Positive	Not statistically significant
Male participation in labor force, 1990–1994	Negative	Negative	Negative
Female participation in labor force, 1990–1994	Not statistically significant	Not statistically significant	Not statistically significant
Unemployment rate, 1991–2000	Positive	Not statistically significant	Not statistically significant
Unemployment males 20–24 years old/Active males 20–24 years old, 1991–2000	Positive	Positive	Not statistically significant
Unemployment females 20–24 years old/Active females 20–24 years old, 1991–2000	Positive	Not statistically significant	Not statistically significant
Wages of machine operators/wages of clerks and craft workers, 1990–1999	Not statistically significant	Not statistically significant	Positive

From the results detailed in Table 2.2, the authors conclude that more regulation is not associated with better labor market outcomes (though they cannot reject the hypothesis that at least some of the regulation promotes efficiency).[11] Still, the major result obtained by the authors is that legal origin explains a great deal of national variation in labor laws.[12] The most that one can conclude from *Botero* is that the legal origin theory

[11] They also find some correlation between more regulation and left governments.

[12] A result debated by Beth Ahlering and Simon Deakin, 'Labor Regulation, Corporate Governance and Legal Origin: A Case of Institutional Complementarity?', 41 *L. & Soc. Rev.* 865 (2007), and David Pozen, 'The Regulation of Labor and the Relevance of Legal Origin', 27 *Comp. Labor L. & Pol'y J.* 43, 43–56 (2007), among others. *Botero's* paper was inspired by the World Bank's Employing Workers Index (supposedly measuring how labor law impedes business), now abandoned. See Sangheon Lee, Deidre McCann and Nina Torm, 'The World Bank's "Employing Workers" Index: Findings and Critiques – A Review of Recent Evidence', 147 *Int'l Labour Rev.* 416, 416–32 (2008).

gets more empirical support than private or public interest explanations of labor regulation.[13] We now turn to explaining why *Botero's* view is not immune from critique.

3. DIVERGENT ANGLO-AMERICAN AND EUROPEAN APPROACHES TO LABOR MARKET REGULATION: SOME ILLUSTRATIONS

One of the significant limitations of the legal origins theory is the failure to reckon with diversity in the regulation of labor within each legal family (which turns into a statistical problem when such variations are significant). A more nuanced exploration of labor laws turns out to reveal similarities across legal families as well as significant differences within them. Moreover it may uncover functional synergies that reflect conscious policy choices and political dynamics more than legal origins. The 'varieties of capitalism' literature offers an alternative lens through which to view the same empirical patterns observed by the legal origins approach.[14] This chapter does not permit a full treatment of these questions; but even a brief account of varying national approaches to regulation of labor, with a primary focus on Anglo-American and European countries, will suggest why the 'varieties of capitalism' perspective on labor market regulation may be more fruitful than the 'legal origins' approach. We return to that larger question in Section 4.

3.1 Regulation of Wages, Hours, Leaves, and Vacations

Nearly all industrialized countries maintain some minimum labor standards – regulation of minimum wages, maximum hours and overtime premiums, breaks, holidays, vacations, parental leaves, workplace safety, and dismissals and redundancies, among other matters – that apply in all or nearly all workplaces and that are meant to protect workers *qua* workers.[15] In principle these are issues that might be left to collective bargaining, and to unions' majoritarian processes. But reliance on legislative regulation of labor conditions has increased, and is likely to increase even more in the future, in light of the incomplete and shrinking reach of collective bargaining. To some degree minimum standards legislation serves as a substitute for collective bargaining where the latter is inoperative for whatever reason.

---

[13] The empirical results are also debatable. More recently, Gahan et al show that labor laws have converged to two models in the period 1970–2005 (although they reject the so-called Americanization of labor law), thus showing that a mere cross-country regression in a moment of time is likely to be misleading. See: Peter Gahan, Richard Mitchell, Sean Cooney, Andrew Stewart and Brian Cooper, 'Economic Globalization and Convergence in Labor Market Regulation: An Empirical Assessment', 60 *Am. J. Comp. L.* 703, 703–41 (2012).

[14] See Peter A. Hall and David Soskice, *Varieties of Capitalism. The Institutional Foundations of Comparative Advantage* (Oxford: Oxford University Press, 2001).

[15] This subpart draws heavily on Cynthia Estlund, 'Individual Employment Rights', in *Comparative Employment Relations in the Global Political Economy* (Carola Frege and John Kelley eds, Routledge, 2013) 29–48.

Yet beneath that oversimplified assessment lie sharp differences across nations. In some countries, labor standards legislation serves as an extension of industry-level agreements reached through collective bargaining; and in others (especially in the Nordic countries in Europe), collective bargaining does in fact do much of the work that minimum standards legislation does elsewhere. Moreover, in some countries minimum standards set a low floor, and leave much to private bargaining (individual and collective) above the floor; while in others the standards are high enough to govern the bulk of the labor market in a particular industry. There are, in short, important differences across nations and regions – and to some degree between nations with a common law versus a civil law tradition – in both the nature of labor standards and the mechanisms by which they are set. We will briefly take up the regulation of wages, hours of work, and vacations and leaves, as to which the differences across the leading market economies are especially stark. Those differences correspond to differences in these countries' labor relations regimes, which will require a brief detour.

Wages. In the coordinated market economies of Northern Europe, labor standards and especially wages are relatively high and are generally set at the sectoral level – either instead of across-the-board minima or in addition to and above such minima – through some form of 'peak bargaining' between trade unions and employer associations. By contrast, in liberal market economies in the common law tradition, like the US and UK, minimum standards are lower and largely uniform across the economy. Trade unions are free to seek higher wages and to attempt to set sectoral standards; but they must do so through 'voluntarist' and decentralized collective bargaining and collective self-help, and without the aid of corporatist-style mechanisms for extension of collectively bargained wage levels throughout the sector. Trade unions' organizing and bargaining efforts in those liberal market economies thus directly confront labor market headwinds that are stiffened by increasingly transnational competition in product markets. Employers that can escape higher unionized wages and labor standards by avoiding unionization and collective bargaining at the firm level will predictably resist, perhaps aggressively, both union organizing and bargaining concessions.

These differences in labor relations systems are historically rooted, but they also reflect, in part, a crucial philosophical divide: To what degree should wages, hours of work, and other economically salient labor standards be 'taken out of competition'? In the liberal market economies, labor markets and the forces of supply and demand are relatively likely to be regarded as facts of economic life; labor market competition tends to be seen as legitimate and functional (within limits), and is understood to determine most material terms and conditions of employment for most workers. Market forces are constrained only by a legally established floor that is meant roughly to keep full-time workers out of poverty (and collective bargaining consciously reflects the parties' respective positions of economic power within labor markets).

In the coordinated market economies, by contrast, competition among firms over wages and other material conditions of employment is highly suspect, and is constrained not only by what workers need to support themselves and their families but by what employers in different sectors of the economy are capable of delivering. Traditionally, values such as social solidarity and economic equality and security carry greater weight than economic efficiency, and there is greater faith in both the efficacy and the necessity of cabining and combating labor market forces. Moreover, a high-wage policy is linked to an industrial policy of promoting higher productivity and an economy that is weighted toward more productive industries and firms.

Hours, Vacations, and Leaves. These philosophical and ideological differences are also reflected in dramatically different approaches to the regulation of hours of work. The common law (and liberal market) societies of the US and the UK have tended to impose only minimal legal constraints on the number of hours that employers can require employees to work in a given week. The law intervenes, and attempts to discourage long hours, largely by 'taxing' overtime – that is, by requiring employers to pay a premium wage rate (e.g., 150 percent of the normal wage) for hours beyond a normal work week (e.g., 40 hours). In the US, even those overtime requirements do not apply to many salaried professionals and managers. In the US and UK, 'maximum hours' laws are exceptional, and 'freedom of contract' is given wide scope. That means that employers are typically allowed to impose take-it-or-leave-it demands for overtime. Employees – especially salaried employees who are exempt from overtime requirements – may be induced to 'compete' among themselves by putting in long hours, and employers may ramp up production in market upswings initially by exacting more hours from the existing workforce rather than by hiring new (or even temporary) workers.[16] (At the same time, employers have an incentive to 'misclassify' workers as exempt from overtime laws – for example, to treat low-level store managers as exempt 'managerial' employees in spite of the law's narrow definition of the latter). Employers gain flexibility in business upswings, and that may contribute to profits and growth, as well as to the incomes of incumbent workers; yet those workers (and their families) pay a price.

By contrast, the coordinated market economies of Northern Europe regulate working hours much more tightly. Whatever labor market forces might impel employers to demand or employees to accept longer hours are social evils to be restrained by law. The notion that some individuals might choose to work longer hours is simply irrelevant, as such 'choices' are deemed to be either illusory or harmful to the promotion of the greater collective good – no more worthy of recognition than an individual's 'choice' to work at less than the minimum wage. If employers want to increase production, they must either hire more workers (perhaps temporary workers) or get more productivity out of their existing workforce. The approach of the coordinated market economies has strongly influenced that of the European Union (EU); yet the liberal market economies within the EU (especially the UK) have managed to secure considerably greater space for their own more market-oriented norms, as we will see below.

The differences that underlie varying approaches to hours of work also extend to the analogous issue of vacations and leaves (such as parental leave): Such matters are

[16] The UK approach to regulation (or non-regulation) of working hours came under some pressure from the EU and its Working Time Directive; but the UK managed to insist on a provision in that Directive that permits individual waivers of the 48-hour maximum working week. UK law thus allows employers to demand such waivers, and they have become routine in much of the economy. The UK thus remains an outlier within the EU, in keeping with its historic liberal market traditions.

largely left to the market and individual or collective bargaining in the US and UK, while they are subject to comparatively generous minimum standards in the rest of Europe. The unsurprising result of these different approaches to labor market regulation is that workers in the US and UK work significantly longer hours – both more hours per week and more weeks per year – than their counterparts in Germany and Scandinavia (and much of Europe).[17] The former look with a mix of envy and disbelief at heated public debates among the latter over whether to reduce the maximum work week to 40 hours or less, or to extend minimum vacation periods to more than four or five weeks per year. And the latter look with some alarm at the prospect that competition within and beyond Europe's enlarged boundaries – as well as controversial interpretations of the founding EU commitment to free movement of persons, establishments, goods, and services – will erode high labor standards and undermine corporatist mechanisms for maintaining those high sectoral labor standards.

Regulation of working hours in the EU: Let us return, however, to the issue of working hours within the EU and its predecessor entities. Each member state's approach to labor markets and their regulation was understood to lie close to the heart of its national identity and political make-up, and beyond the EU's core mandate to foster economic integration by promoting free movement of persons, goods, capital, and services. Yet the nature of that mandate was destined to highlight differences, and eventually create tension, among the divergent national labor policies and institutions – especially as 'Europe' expanded to include the UK and Ireland, Spain and Portugal, Scandinavian countries, and much of post-Soviet Eastern Europe. The issue of diversity in labor market policies has become more salient and more complex with the simultaneous expansion of the EU's boundaries and of its substantive reach, which includes a growing set of social issues. The EU has had to balance efforts to promote convergence based on EU-wide social commitments with a necessary tolerance for national divergence over labor market regulatory norms and structures. The complexity of this balancing act is well illustrated by the law governing hours of work.

Until the 1990s, the matter of working time was regulated separately in each member state; in fact the original Treaty of Rome did not recognize the competence of Community bodies with respect to labor standards, including hours of work, except for the Commission's power to encourage cooperation between member states on issues related to working conditions.[18] In 1990, the Commission first proposed the drafting of a directive related to working time in light of the impact of working hours and their regulation on restructuring and flexibility on the part of firms, on the health and

---

[17] In 2009, the average number of hours worked per year was 1,407 in Norway, 1,559 in Denmark, 1,602 in Sweden, and 1,390 in Germany compared to 1,768 in the US and 1,643 in the UK (OECD. StatExtracts, Average annual hours actually worked per worker. (May 22, 2012), http://stats.oecd.org/Index.aspx?DatasetCode=ANHRS# 2012). The data on average annual paid leave is similarly telling (though the UK is more similar to other European countries): in 2007, the average annual paid leave (including public holidays) was 34 days in Denmark and Sweden, 32 days in the UK, 29 days in Norway and Germany, and only ten days (all public holidays) in the US. The US is one of the few countries without a federal statutory minimum of annual paid leave (OECD. Gender Brief (2010), http://www.oecd.org/dataoecd/23/31/44720649.pdf).

[18] ECT, art 140.

well-being of workers, on the creation of new jobs, and on the conditions of competition between firms. The proposal eventually yielded directives issued in June 2000 and November 2003 that regulate the matters of weekly working hours, rest, shift work and night work in both the private and the public sectors.[19]

The current Directive establishes a maximum work week which cannot exceed 48 hours in any seven-day period, 'including overtime.' But the actual shape of this 'maximum work week' mandate accommodated demands for greater employer flexibility from employers and some member states (especially the UK). So the Directive effectively allows exceptions to the 48-hour limit by permitting hours to be averaged over 'a period not exceeding four months' (art 16, letter B); that period can be extended by national law or by collective agreement up to six months. Article 19 further provides that member states may allow collective agreements to increase the period over which hours can be averaged to as long as 12 months, provided that there are 'objective, technical or organizational reasons' to justify the extension of the reporting period. The net result in nations determined to maximize employer discretion over hours is that the 48-hour maximum may often be exceeded in any one work week, or even for several weeks running, provided that the longer hours are offset by shorter work weeks during some specified time span.

The Working Hours Directive, therefore, purports to address the appropriate ratio of rest to work without actually regulating the maximum duration of daily or even weekly work performance. Some states, including both the UK and Italy, followed this rather 'liberal' approach to the regulation of hours.[20] For example Italian legislation tracked the Directive in providing that the 48 hours per week could be averaged over four months, or up to 12 months by collective bargaining agreements where justified by 'objective reasons, technical or organizational of work specified in the same collective agreement.' But some European legislatures rejected the 'liberal' valence of the Directive's model in the process of transposing it into national law. In Germany, for example, national legislation provides that the daily work schedule may not exceed eight hours, a ceiling that may be raised to ten hours only if, in the relevant six-month period, the schedule has not exceeded an average of eight hours daily. A similar approach was followed by national legislation in Spain.[21]

So national divergence continues, both between the liberal and coordinated market economies, and among the latter, even within the increasingly integrated EU. These distinct national approaches to regulation of hours reflect broader legal categories but also varying political and social contexts.

---

19 Directives 2000/34/EC and 2003/88/EC.

20 See Article 4 of the Decree 66 of April 8th, 2003. The law also provides: "In case of exceeding the 48 hours of weekly work through overtime, for production units employing more than ten employees, the employer is obliged to inform, within thirty days from the expiry of the period referred to in paragraphs 3 and 4, the Direzione Provinciale del Lavoro (Field inspection of work jurisdiction)." (Paragraph amended by Decree n. 213, July 19, 2004).

21 Law 11/1994 of May 19th, 1994.

3.2 Occupational Safety and Health Regulation

There is considerably less variation with respect to the regulation of workplace health and safety than in the area of wages, hours, leaves, and the like. That seems to reflect a far wider consensus both about the failure or inadequacy of unregulated market forces to induce an adequate level of workplace safety and about the primacy of non-economic values of human life and health over economic efficiency. Yet the history of occupational safety and health law does indeed reveal strong differences between the liberal market economies and the coordinated economies. At least in the case of the US, it took much longer for national policy-makers to address the problem of workplace health and safety, and the law that finally did so remains more controversial than its counterparts in the rest of the developed world.

Workplace Health and Safety Legislation in the US:[22] The problem of workplace hazards and accidents was a recurring source of legal and political turmoil in the US from the mid-nineteenth century onwards.[23] The problem had two sides: how to prevent or reduce accidents and injuries, and how to compensate them after the fact. Compensation claims for workplace injuries were relegated in the nineteenth century to the common law tort system, where the law was famously inhospitable to workers' injury claims: workers were said to assume most risks of employment, and were presumed to have secured a wage premium in exchange.[24] Behind these doctrines lay a powerful commitment to contract and individual 'choice' – and to unregulated labor markets – for setting terms and conditions of employment. Some modern law and economics scholars concur.[25] For the most unyielding of these economic thinkers, even the matter of job safety could be left to the market, for the wage premiums that workers would demand for dangerous work would both compensate workers (before the fact) for injuries and induce 'efficient' levels of safety precautions. In short, workers would get as much safety as they were willing to pay for. That proposition rested on assumptions of frictionless labor markets, of full information and complete rationality about occupational risks, and full internalization by the parties of the costs of injuries, disease, and destitution. Other scholars have questioned all of those assumptions, and argued on efficiency grounds for both more reliable compensation for injuries and safety regulations.[26] They pointed to market failures – cognitive biases, information asymmetries, collective action problems, and externalities – that call for public intervention.

---

[22] This subsection draws from Estlund, 'Regoverning the Workplace', *supra* note 4.

[23] See generally John Fabian Witt, *The Accidental Republic: Crippled Workingmen, Destitute Widows, and the Remaking of American Law* (Harvard U. Press 2004).

[24] See, e.g., *Farwell v. Boston & Worcester R.R. Corp.*, 45 Mass. (4 Met.) 49, (1842), 57.

[25] For relatively sophisticated versions of the argument, see Thomas A. Lambert, Avoiding Regulatory Mismatch in the Workplace: An Informational Approach to Workplace Safety Regulation, 82 *Nebraska Law Review* 1006, (2004), 1021–3 and W. Kip Viscusi, *Risk by Choice: Regulating Health and Safety in the Workplace* (1983).

[26] See Richard L. Revesz and Michael A. Livermore, *Retaking Rationality: How Cost-Benefit Analysis Can Better Protect the Environment and Our Health* (Oxford U. Press, 2008) and Susan Rose-Ackerman, *Rethinking the Progressive Agenda: The Reform of the American Regulatory State* 85–96 (Free Press, 1992).

A monumental state-by-state reform effort in the early twentieth century channeled claims for compensation for industrial injuries out of the courts and into administrative workers' compensation systems.[27] Under the workers' compensation 'bargain,' employers gave up their formidable common law defenses to liability, and workers gave up the prospect of full tort remedies, in favor of more limited but more reliable and accessible administrative remedies. Thus did US workers belatedly gain access to the kind of administrative compensation regime that was pioneered in nineteenth century Germany, and that had come to prevail as well in Europe and the UK.

To the extent that workers' compensation schemes were meant not only to compensate injured employees but also to prevent injury and disease by encouraging employers to improve health and safety, they did not do enough by themselves.[28] Prevention of occupational hazards, and compensation, was left to the states – some of which developed strong workplace safety laws and some of which did little or nothing – until 1970, when Congress enacted the Occupational Safety and Health Act (OSHA). OSHA sought to finally take workplace safety out of competition by establishing minimum standards and a public enforcement apparatus.[29] OSHA's 'general duty clause' requires employers to keep the workplace 'free from recognized hazards that are causing or are likely to cause death or serious physical harm to his employees.'[30] OSHA also regulates specific hazards, and its efforts to regulate toxic substances that were endemic to certain industries – asbestos, cotton dust, lead, benzene, and other poisons – launched epic legal battles over the reach of the regulatory state and the meaning of administrative due process. It was in the courts, for example, that OSHA fought for and gained the power to set standards for toxics that were based on what was 'technologically feasible', not what was 'economically feasible,' thus potentially forcing the least profitable actors in an industry out of business. OSHA was a perpetual lightening rod for employers and conservatives seeking to roll back regulatory 'intrusion' on business decision-making. At the same time the minutiae of OSHA's safety rules and recordkeeping requirements generated a steady current of grumbling about its bureaucratic rigidity and intrusiveness.[31]

In its broad outlines and underlying philosophy, OSHA is not dramatically different from occupational safety and health regimes across the developed world. Some are better and some are worse, depending on resources and regulatory style. In the case of OSHA in the US, reform efforts – for example, to move away from detailed, uniform 'command-and-control' regulations toward a more collaborative and process-based approach to promoting safety – have provoked polarizing political battles between the proponents of deregulation and of stronger regulation; modernization and regulatory efficacy have suffered as a result. But as compared to the deep differences seen in the

---

27 See generally Witt, 'The Accidental Republic', *supra* note 23.

28 See Sydney A. Shapiro and Randy Rabinowitz, 'Voluntary Regulatory Compliance in Theory and Practice: The Case of OSHA', 52 *Admin. L. Rev.* 97, 132 (2000), at 132.

29 29 U.S.C. §§ 651–78. See Thomas O. McGarity, 'Reforming OSHA: Some Thoughts for the Current Legislative Agenda', 31 *Houston L. Rev.* 99 (1994), 100. See also S. Rep. No. 91-1282 (1970), at 2–5; H.R. Rep. No. 91–1291 (1970), at 14-6.

30 29 U.S.C. § 654.

31 Robert A. Kagan and Eugene Bardach, *Going by the Book: The Problem of Regulatory Unreasonableness* (Temple University Press, Philadelphia, 1982), 48, 113–16.

regulation of wages, hours, leaves, and vacations, the differences here are smaller and do not neatly track different legal traditions.

Workplace health and safety regulation in Europe: A few points of comparison: The first European Community initiative in safety and working environment began after the coal mining tragedy of Marcinelle in 1956,[32] with the creation of the Permanent Body for Safety in coal mines.[33] In 1974 the European Commission established the Committee on Safety, Hygiene and Health Protection at Work, and the EU took its first steps towards the enactment of Community legislation on occupational safety and health protection at work (art 100 of the Treaty, and current art 94 ECT). Many Directives followed.[34]

National variations persisted however. For example, the Italian legislature sparked some controversy, in transposing European Directives into national law, by requiring employers to provide the '*maximum technologically feasible safety.*' By contrast, the Health and Safety at Work Act UK (1974) set a less stringent standard of '*reasonable practicability.*' In short, UK legislation permitted consideration of economic costs while the Italian legislation meant to foreclose that. It is noteworthy that on this issue, at least on paper, US law follows the more stringent standard rather than the cost-sensitive approach followed in the UK.

The Framework Directive 89/391/CEE, enacted on 12 June, 1989, marked the beginning of the third action program on safety, hygiene and health in the workplace. This Framework Directive extends to all kinds of workplace organizations, public as well as private (with some narrow exceptions for armed forces, police, or civil protection services), and apparently includes small as well as larger businesses. The Directive consists of two parts, one relating to employers' obligations and the other to workers' obligations. The Directive reflects a basic reality that prevails across the developed economies: as the technology of production gallops along with growing speed and complexity, it becomes increasingly infeasible for the public to regulate specific workplace hazards through direct government inspections. Much regulatory activity has to take place at the workplace level under an overall public regulatory framework. So much like OSHA in the US, the Directive places much importance on general principles of prevention to be complied with by employers, rather than detailed rules covering specific machines or chemicals. Employers themselves thus become critical regulatory agents.

Along with the necessary shift of regulatory power to the workplace level, workers themselves become key regulatory players.[35] How they perform their regulatory role

---

[32] On 8 August 1956, 262 miners, nearly all Italian immigrants, were killed in a coal mine called Bois du Cazier, in Marcinelle, Belgium. While Italy was in mourning for the poor immigrants, Italy formally agreed to supply 47,000 additional coal mine workers to Belgian mines in exchange for coal.

[33] Decision of July 9th, 1957, then amended June 27th, 1974 to extend the powers of the mining and extracting industries.

[34] Directive 80/1107 was implemented by Italian law, Legislative Decree 277 of August 15th, now repealed and part of the April 9th, 2008 Legislative Decree 81 called Consolidated Law on Protection of Health and Safety in the Workplace, also amended by the Decree 106 of August 3rd, 2009.

[35] See Estlund, 'Regoverning the Workplace', *supra* note 4.

differs greatly, depending on whether unions represent most workers at the workplace level, and are given a regulatory role by safety laws. Where workers are represented in the self-regulatory process by effective, independent worker organizations, they become co-regulators. Still, individual employees also play a regulatory role. For example both the EU Directive and OSHA regulations in the US empower workers to cease work if necessary to avoid an immediate threat to their lives or health. When the new EU Directive was enacted, only Italy, Germany, and France recognized employees' right to refuse work, free from any '*harmful and unjustified consequences*' (such as disciplinary action) in case of grave and inevitable danger. Directive 89/391/CEE extended this right to all workers of other member states.

Consistent with the strategy of co-regulation of hazards at the workplace level, the Framework Directive relies heavily on the role of information in reducing workers' exposure to hazards. As with OSHA in the US, notice, instructions, and training – with content that is usually determined largely by employers based on the hazards in each specific workplace – become increasingly central regulatory tools. Also as with OSHA, the Framework Directive requires the employer to provide employees and/or their representatives with all necessary information relating to risks to safety and health and measures and activities of protection and prevention. However, the Framework Directive goes further than OSHA in a way that reflects differences in labor relations institutions: it requires that employers inform and consult with worker representatives generally. (That takes place in the US only in the tiny minority of workplaces in which workers are represented by unions.) Only the German legal system was fully prepared to comply with the Framework Directive for consultation and participation, since job safety falls within the rights of codetermination under long-established German law. But the EU-wide obligation to consult with worker representatives on safety built on a spate of other EU-level initiatives on works councils and information and consulation in other contexts. So the EU is consciously following the path of co-regulation, while the US, with its shrunken and antiquated labor relations regime, lags far behind, and relies heavily on employer self-regulation.

4. CONCLUSION

Economists have developed the legal origins theory to explain differences in law, including labor law, across countries and to test the extent to which these variations shape economic outcomes. Clearly, there is important diversity in the regulation of labor. The details show that a mere divide between common law and civil law is possibly oversimplistic and does not accommodate the differences across jurisdictions. Presumably the legal origins theory identifies trends and general patterns, but significant variations require more sophisticated explanations than merely assuming that a particular legal infrastructure determines economic performance (both in terms of overall economic growth as well as with respect to labor markets). Legal economists have thus showed that a narrow version of the legal origins theory finds little empirical support.[36] However, a broader understanding of the legal origins theory has strong appeal and provides for a robust explanation of economic trends.[37] The broader version recognizes that differences in labor market regulations and employment law are part of a legal design with significant impact on the economy, but that laws and institutions change along with political and social structures; and the changes do not follow in any simple way from the system's legal origins.

In this light, the 'varieties of capitalism' theory can be understood as a version of the broader legal origins theory. Empirically, it is consistent with the distinction between the common law and civil law families. Unlike the narrow version of the legal origins theory, it recognizes a greater role for political actors and preferences in shaping labor law in a wider context of legal infrastructures and corporate governance.[38] Where the legal origins theory sought to explain patterns of law and regulation along a relatively simplistic scale of 'more' and 'less' legal intervention, the 'varieties of capitalism' theory recognized the potential complementarities among legal institutions and regulatory interventions, such that "more" regulated labor and capital markets could produce socially and economically beneficial outcomes.

In a provocative article, Roe (2006) contested the findings of the legal origin theory in the area of corporate law and suggested that social democratic political preferences – that is, modern ideologies – would be a better explanation for the observed differences between the Anglo-American world and the different European traditions.[39] In this approach legal structures and institutions are important; but rather than being exogenously determined, they respond to political preferences and change in response to social and economic dynamics. Our discussion of labor and employment law points to a similar conclusion. The 'varieties of capitalism' literature seems to offer a more plausible framework for understanding the major differences that we have observed among the developed economies.[40] It seems that the liberal market vs. coordinated market distinction provides a more thorough identification of the relevant dimensions in labor law.

---

[36] See, among others Simon Deakin, Priya Lele and Mathias M. Siems, 'The Evolution of Labour Law: Calibrating and Comparing Regulatory Regimes', 146 *Int'l Labour Rev.* 133, 133–62 (2007); John Armour, Simon Deakin, Priya Lele, and Mathias M. Siems, 'How Do Legal Rules Evolve? Evidence from a Cross-Country Comparison of Shareholder, Creditor and Worker Protection', 57 *Am. J. Comp. L.* 579, 579–630 (2009); John Armour, Simon Deakin, Viviana Mollica, and Mathias M. Siems, 'Law and Financial Development: What We are Learning from Time Series Evidence', 2009 *BYU L.R.* 1435, 1435–1500 (2009); Simon Deakin, 'The Law and Economics of Employment Protection Legislation', in: *Research Handbook on the Economics of Labor and Employment Law* (Cynthia L. Estlund and Michael L. Wachter eds, Edward Elgar, 2013).

[37] See, generally, Ahlering and Deakin, Labor Regulation, *supra* note 12, Armour et al., 'How do Legal Rules Evolve?', ibid., and Deakin, 'The Law and Economics of Employment Protection Legislation', ibid.

[38] See Deakin, 'The Law and Economics of Employment Protection Legislation', ibid.

[39] See: Mark Roe, 'Legal Origins and Modern Stock Markets', 120 *Harv. L.R.* 460, 460–527 (2006), and the discussion by Cooney et al., 'Labour Law and the Regulation of Employment Relations', *supra* note 9.

[40] See Hall and Soskice, 'Varieties of Capitalism', *supra* note 14.

To be sure, there is some correlation between the two analytic schemes: The primary liberal market economies – including the UK and the US, as well as Australia, Canada and New Zealand – grew up with a common law tradition, whereas the leading coordinated market economies – Germany, Japan, Scandinavia, the Benelux countries, Austria and Switzerland – are civil law countries (albeit mostly of German and Scandinavian origins and not of French origin). A third group of civil law jurisdictions in the French tradition – France, Italy, Greece, Portugal, Spain (and arguably Turkey) – maintains what is known as Mediterranean capitalism, which is marked by a later transition from agriculture to industry and extensive state intervention in the economy.[41]

Still the 'varieties of capitalism' offers more theoretical traction in regard to labor relation systems, for it recognizes that national approaches to labor markets regulation have some old and deep roots (as the legal origins theory would have it), but are also shaped by more recent and varied political and cultural developments that are not necessarily determined by legal origins. Scholars have recognized, for example, that legal infrastructure and political dynamics seem to be codetermined.[42] Such a pattern is better explained by 'varieties of capitalism theory' than by the narrow version of the legal origins theory (which would suggest that legal origins and infrastructure actually cause political and economic dynamics). At the same time, 'varieties of capitalism theory' is more consistent with the empirical evidence provided by legal economists.

To a large extent the 'varieties of capitalism' explanation mirrors Roe's approach in corporate law. In this context, there is no dispute concerning the empirical findings of the legal origins approach.[43] It is the theoretical explanation that has to be reassessed. Recognizing that contemporary political preferences rather than increasingly ancient legal traditions are the main determinants of labor market policy makes it easier to incorporate an understanding of the role of public and private interest economic theories in the regulation of labor markets. For it is evident that the partisans of particular political ideologies variously embrace or promote these contemporary theories of regulation, and they do so in what are often hotly contested political climates. It would be surprising indeed if the outcomes of these political debates were somehow determined by a nation's legal origins. How these same theories relate to a legal tradition is largely unexplained.

---

[41] Ibid.

[42] See Deakin, 'The Law and Economics of Employment Protection Legislation', *supra* note 36.

[43] For a summary of the literature disputing the empirical results of the legal origins theory, see Garoupa and Gómez, 'The Syndrome of the Efficiency of the Common Law', *supra* note 9.

3. The challenge to comparative labor law in a globalized era

Kerry Rittich and Guy Mundlak

INTRODUCTION

The comparative project in labor law is extraordinarily complex. Any such analysis requires an understanding of the nature of labor law, how this law emerges from and is constituted by social, political and industrial forces, and how law, in turn, affects the organization and operation of social, economic spheres, including in ways that are neither obvious nor predicted in advance. It has long been axiomatic that industrial relations systems, and collective rights in particular, are deeply embedded in national social and economic institutions as well as legal traditions, and, for this reason, are not easily transplanted or even comprehended beyond the context out of which they emerge.[1] The field of labor law itself is defined differently in different national contexts; for example, in North America, it refers primarily to collective labor relations, while elsewhere it includes the broader field of employment rights. And if disentangling legal norms and institutions from the political, economic and social context in which they operate is always a challenge for comparative law,[2] it is especially acute when it comes to labor law. As many scholars have noted, it is difficult, if not impossible, even to understand labor market norms by reference to formal law alone, as informal norms often play at least as important a role in determining workplace practices.[3] For example, job tenure and seniority protection, the keystones of the standard employment relationship in the post-war era, may be powerfully enshrined, and also dissolved, as a matter of industry and human resource practice rather than employment or labor law, as is the case in the United States.[4]

---

1 Otto Kahn-Freund, 'On Uses and Misuses of Comparative Law', 37 *Mod. L. Rev.* 1, (1974).

2 See, for example, the Watson/LeGrand debate: Alan Watson, *Legal Transplants*, (2d ed., University of Georgia Press, 1993); Pierre Legrand, 'The Impossibility of Legal Transplants', 4 *Maastricht Journal of European and Comparative Law* 111 (1997).

3 Benjamin Aaron and Katherine V.W. Stone, 'Comparative Labor Law – Bridging the Past and the Future', 28 *Comp. Lab. L. & Pol'y J.* 377, (2007); Harry Arthurs, 'Labour Law Beyond the State', *UTLJ* 1 (1996); Harry Arthurs, 'Compared to What? The UCLA Comparative Labor Law Project and the Future of Comparative Labor Law', 28 *Comp. Lab. L. & Pol'y J.* 591 (2007).

4 Katherine V.W. Stone, 'The Decline of the Standard Contract of Employment in the United States: A Socio-Regulatory Perspective', in: *Rethinking Workplace Regulation: Beyond the Standard Contract of Employment*, Katherine V.W. Stone and Harry Arthurs (eds), (New York: Russell Sage Foundation, 2013).

On top of the general difficulties ascribed to comparative labor law are the effects of globalization, which, along with demographic changes and technological innovation, is one of the main factors currently shaping the labor market. Considering the impact of globalization on labor law in a comparative context raises fundamental questions regarding the already complex comparative venture at both the methodological and substantive levels.

Labor law, both in general and as a subject of comparison, is traditionally situated within the confines of the nation state. Scholars of labor law typically begin with the premise that markets and production are socially and politically embedded, that regulation is centrally co-ordinated by the state or by territorial entities within it, and that collective bargaining is conducted according to rules prescribed by the state that cover the spectrum of domains from the enterprise to the national level. Where the borders of the state are drawn, however, the system of labor law reaches its limits. It is the premises of the Westphalian state system that have made it possible to compare the different legal solutions that have been devised *within* nation states to deal with problems such as the 'fissuring'[5] or 'vertical disintegration'[6] of enterprises and their consequences for workers' rights and power. However, it is precisely these premises that are now eroded and unstable.

When globalization is integrated into the story, framing the interaction between law and social-economic forces engages new difficulties of scale, causality and scope. The vertical disintegration of production permits employers to exploit the possibilities of lower labor costs in other jurisdictions, including those that come about because of differences in regulatory standards. But it also produces new regulatory conundrums. To the extent that vertical disintegration results in supply chains and production that cross borders, it may no longer be clear which national laws govern the workplace. Once production crosses borders ('off-shoring'), national regulatory solutions often become elusive and inadequate, and responses to the problematics of networked production may well extend beyond labor law as we have known it. Similarly, increased 'in-shoring' of, or reliance on, migrant labor often implicates fields such as citizenship and immigration law that lie beyond the traditional scope of labor and employment law.[7] The globalization of production also imports new actors and activities into the norm generation process. Along with traditional efforts to influence the shape and content of both local and national law, employers may engage in law-shopping and regulatory arbitrage, seeking at once to identify and rely on, and, along with NGOs, to influence the laws governing their activities in ways that are congenial to their interests and objectives.[8] The effects of these interventions, moreover, can sometimes be identified in territories that are remote from where regulatory decisions are actually made. Thus, there may be little or no overlap between the labor

---

5 David Weil, *The Fissured Workplace*, (Cambridge MA: Harvard University Press, 2014).

6 Hugh Collins, 'Independent Contractors and the Challenge of Vertical Disintegration to Employment Law', 10 *Oxford J. of Legal Studies* 353 (1990).

7 Symposium, 'Working Borders: Linking Debates About Insourcing and Outsourcing of Capital and Labor', 20 *Texas Int'l Law Journal* 691 (2004–5).

8 Dan Danielsen, 'How Corporations Govern: Taking Corporate Power Seriously in Transnational Regulation and Governance', 46 *Harv. Int'l L.J.* 411 (2005).

market or community of workers and employers affected by legal and labor market norms, the actors and institutions that author such norms, and the location where their broader social effects are experienced. Under these circumstances, it is hardly surprising that it is now more difficult for the agents of labor to influence the shape and content of the law of the workplace.

How then does globalization affect our understanding of the comparative project in labor law? In what way does the comparative project, when considered against the backdrop of globalization, engage new problems of scale, scope and causality?

Observing similar difficulties, Harry Arthurs has suggested that 'comparisons amongst these diverse, semi-autonomous and often obscure systems may perhaps lead to the emergence of the new syntax, grammar and vocabulary of comparativism, which will help to make them mutually intelligible'.[9] However, it is not altogether clear how such a comparison is to be made or what the syntax or structure of this new grammar might be. Following his lead and based upon an analysis of current comparative work that touches on questions of globalization, this chapter seeks to identify some of its ingredients.

In order to draw an analytical framework for engaging in comparisons in a globalized or transnational environment, we seek to identify in the first section the multiple meanings that are attributed to globalization: globalization as a *social force and social-economic environment* that challenges, and often changes, the objectives and priorities of nation states, corporations and social organizations; globalization as a set of *norms, institutions and governance projects*, some of which lie beyond the confines of the nation state, some of which are strongly connected to particular national origins and some of which are entirely detached from them; and, finally, globalization as a set of *values and ideologies* associated with economic liberalization and market integration, many of which pose deep challenges to established conceptions of justice as well as to the criteria of democratic legitimacy.

The second section examines the way in which comparative work has classically attempted to incorporate various dimensions of globalization. As this short survey illustrates, the conventional approach involves comparing like units, usually the law of one state with that of another, by treating one or more of globalization's facets as an external or exogenous factor, and examining the manner in which it operates on, and changes, national systems of labor law. Hence, the survey points to the two main features of the current comparative efforts: (a) comparing like units; and (b) exogenizing globalization. At the same time, the survey attempts to indicate approaches that deviate from one or more of these premises, including those that consider the role of national and international law in producing and sustaining processes of globalization.

Arguing that an attempt to hold on to a sharp dichotomy between the national and the international is misconceived under conditions of globalization, the third section suggests several elements that should be added to the basic comparative model. The first is the evaluation of transnational, especially non-state, modes of governance, both as regulatory systems in themselves, and in relation to formal law. Second are analyses that endogenize both law and globalization. This requires considering the many roles of law in *constituting* globalization, as well as the effects of globalization *on* law and

---

9 Arthurs, 'Compared to What?', *supra* note 3.

policy. Following directly from this, third, are more ambitious and systematic attempts to identify, model and describe the role of rules, policies and institutions *beyond* the traditional domain of labor law on labor market dynamics, workplace norms and practices, and workers' rights. Considered together, these three elements demonstrate the vast range of opportunities to engage in comparison growing out of the multiple levels of regulation and the expansion of the field that is now designated as 'labor law'.

1. UNDERSTANDING GLOBALIZATION

Attention to global economic summits, be they the G8 or the G20 summits or the Doha rounds of WTO negotiations, for example, makes it clear how much of contemporary economic discourse is shaped by contending claims about globalization. In these fora, fundamental attributes of globalization such as greater market liberalization and integration may be simply assumed to be forces for good; globalization may also be represented as a force beyond control. In either case, the demands of globalization may be invoked to justify preferences for particular types of policy or regulatory responses. At the same time, the contested nature of such claims and assumptions is visible during these meetings as well, as demonstrators roam the streets advancing diverse agendas that range from voicing the concerns of people in poverty and raising neo-socialist objections to capitalism to anarchist resistance to the power of states.

At this point, globalization has become a signifier that covers a wide range of interlinked, and contested, transformations in processes, values, and institutions. The protean character of the term itself suggests how these various changes may be connected. By collapsing many disparate processes and events into a single phenomenon, however, globalization also risks becoming an empty shell devoid of any analytic or explanatory purchase. Any systematic attempt to uncover the role of globalization in local, national, transnational and global labor markets and legal systems must, in any event, disentangle its different layers and dimensions. In this section, we describe the processes that are most directly related to labor markets and changing workplace structures and practices, thereby attempting to make more precise their relationship to changing norms in labor markets and the workplace.

(a) Globalization as a Social Force

At the most basic level, globalization refers to the processes of economic, cultural and social contact, inter-mixing, and integration that are such a salient condition of our time, much of which is produced by the intensified movement of capital, labor, commodities, and culture across borders.[10] Although nations and territory remain deeply significant to the organization of economic activity, production and service provision increasingly traverse borders; as a result, both nations and enterprises face new competitive pressures from which they were, for the most part, formerly isolated. Workers – white collar as well as blue – who once enjoyed secure employment within

---

[10] Guy Mundlak, 'Deterritorializing Labor Law', 3 *Journal of Law and Ethics of Human Rights* 188 (2009).

national or regional territories now frequently find themselves in competition for jobs with workers in other states and regions. Those at the middle and lower ends of the labor market have declining bargaining power and, in consequence, are experiencing flat or falling real wages. High-skilled workers and workers in occupations for which there is high demand, by contrast, are often courted by national migration regimes, sometimes without regard for whether local supply is short or not, and typically experience increased bargaining power as a result, although some of these workers, too, face the upheaval of continuous transitions between jobs. The mobile and transitional character of the workforce fostered by these transnational forces and flows contributes to declining solidarity and growing inequality within national workforces, as well as to the maintenance of differences between workers of different countries.

Yet, although globalization may seem to encompass, and account for, the universe of changing workplace practices, not everything that is new at work can simply be attributed to globalization. Changes in enterprise organization and the processes of production are also part of the story. The vertically integrated, hierarchically structured firms of the Fordist era are increasingly supplanted by de-centralized and fluid networks of producers and suppliers constituted by a revolving cast of participants located in diverse, and changing, jurisdictions.[11] These structural transformations have produced cascading effects on both workers and the law of work, as well as on the workplace itself. For example, the standard employment relationship, itself enabled by the stability of the firm in which the employee worked, is in fundamental crisis and probably irretrievable decline, with long-term employment being displaced by serial contractual relationships and workers' time between contracts increasingly un-compensated or under-compensated.[12] At the same time, more employment is being transformed into self-employment, with the attendant costs and risks of market volatility imposed on workers, many of whom see few of its upside benefits.[13]

The decentralization of production and the fragmentation of the standard employment relationship are strongly related to globalization, but they cannot be derived simply from globalization, at least in any straightforward way. Similar processes of disintegration can be observed in sectors such as the public sector, which are less exposed to the direct effects of global competition among workers. Quite apart from globalization, technological changes may render the standard employment relationship ill-adapted to new modes of production and service provision. And changing demographics, such as the feminization of the labor force, and, in most developed countries, an aging workforce, along with distinct problems confronting entry-level workers, fragment the identity and interests of workers and encourage the diffusion of new forms of flexible employment relations.

---

[11] Manuel Castells, 'The Network Society: from Knowledge to Policy', in: *The Network Society: From Knowledge to Policy*, Manuel Castells and Gustavo Cardoso (eds), (Baltimore MD: Johns Hopkins University, 2005).

[12] Stone, *supra* note 4.

[13] Freedland and Kountouris describe this as a 'demutualization' of risk. See Mark Freedland and Nicola Kountouris, *The Legal Construction of Personal Work Relations*, (Oxford: Oxford University Press, 2011); see, also, Guy Standing, *Global Labour Flexibility*, (Basingstoke: Macmillan, 1999), and Guy Standing, *The Precariat: The New Dangerous Class*, (London: Bloomsbury, 2011).

Some economic analyses of labor markets do attempt to distinguish the effects of globalization from those of other processes, such as technological innovation and changing demographics; studies of income inequality often do the same.[14] While this approach might be adopted for legal comparisons as well, it is important to bear in mind a number of complications it entails. First, none of these changes is fully independent of the others. The spread of technology is made possible by globalization, just as much as it drives globalization. Similarly, changing labor market demographics are strongly connected with new patterns of labor migration. For example, some countries may seek to attract migrant workers to compensate for the problems of a feminized and/or aging workforce and the fiscal, care and pension crises with which these changes are often associated,[15] while other countries may strengthen border controls and adopt policies which aid domestic producers in an attempt to protect them against the emergence of jobless futures for their youth. Second, all of these changes are themselves shaped, to some extent, by legal institutions and regulatory decisions. If they are useful to illuminate the forces and processes at work, efforts to identify the effects of globalization on labor law must therefore avoid conflating all workplace transformation with the consequences of globalization. At the same time, they must take account of the multiple ways in which changes in the workplace are themselves connected to, and enabled by, law.

Although globalization cannot account for all the changes in labor relations and labor law, it nonetheless remains a crucial factor. In a world of more intense competition of jobs and investment, national and sub-national governments no longer make law and policy in isolation with an eye to their own priorities and constituencies alone. Instead, fearing the decline or loss of investments and jobs to other jurisdictions, they are both contemplating and making changes to law and policy in an attempt to create a more attractive climate for business investment. Although the extent to which labor costs are a significant factor in investment decisions varies considerably, the presence of workers in markets with lower costs and standards creates incentives to reduce national labor standards and/or to relax their enforcement, thus diminishing their power in jurisdictions even where they remain formally in force. Firms do not automatically re-locate in response to lower labor costs abroad, and no state has simply repealed its labor laws in response to the competitive pressures introduced or exacerbated by globalization. However, exemptions and carve-outs from national labor laws, as are typically found in export processing and special economic zones, are not difficult to find.

Some suggest that intensified competition, among firms and states as well as workers, simply leads to a regulatory 'race to the bottom'; in a more hopeful vein,

---

14 See, for example, Jacob S. Hacker and Paul Pierson, *Winner-Take-All Politics: How Washington Made the Rich Richer – and Turned its Back on the Middle Class*, (New York: Simon & Schuster, 2010), which identifies the decline of unions as a leading cause of growing inequality in the US; Tali Kristal, 'The Capitalist Machine: Computerization, Workers' Power, and the Decline in Labor's Share within US Industries', 78 *American Sociological Rev.* 361–89 (2013).

15 Isabelle Grunberg, 'Double Jeopardy: Globalization, Liberalization and the Fiscal Squeeze', 26 *World Development* 591 (1998); Reuven S. Avi-Yonah, 'Globalization, Tax Competition, and the Fiscal Crisis of the Welfare State', 113 *Harvard Law Rev.* 1573 (2000).

others suggest the possibility of a 'race to the top'.[16] Evidence suggests that neither possibility fully captures the state of contemporary labor law. Although the race to the bottom has not materialized in its most extreme form, there is little doubt that competition for work and investment often discourages efforts to improve or extend labor standards where they are weak or absent, and restrains responses to both old and emerging workplace problems that might otherwise be contemplated.[17] As the empirical debate is yet to be settled, it is clear that both options have important implications and ramifications for labor law and comparative work.

A central inquiry within comparative projects has been whether these global competitive pressures will lead to greater convergence in national labor laws. In its weak form, the question often seeks to identify common regulatory trends or the presence of common debates and policy discourse across jurisdictions. A stronger claim is that global competition will eventually, in Darwinist fashion, weed out 'losing' state strategies and promote dominant rules and institutions or regulatory and governance strategies identified as 'good' or 'best' practice in their stead. Yet the most outstanding characteristic of the contemporary law and policy of work may simply be its diversity and fragmentation: it is increasingly evident that state responses to increased international competition cannot be reduced to any single strategy. Instead, the comparative analyst would observe that states have adopted (at least) the following strategies: reducing labor costs internally;[18] increasing labor costs internally;[19] and/or co-ordinating the regulation of labor standards with other states through bilateral, regional and global agreements and treaties.[20]

---

[16] Bob Hepple, A Race to the Top? 'International Investment Guidelines and Corporate Codes of Conduct', 20 *Comp. Lab. L. & Pol'y J.* 347 (1998–99); Layna Mosley and Saika Uno, 'Racing to the Bottom or Climbing to the Top? Economic Globalization and Collective Labor Rights', 40 *Comparative Policy Studies* 923 (2007).

[17] Guy Standing calls this the 'race to the middle'. Guy Standing, 'Human Development: A Response to "Realizing Labor Standards"', 26 *Boston Rev.* (2001).

[18] Jeronim Capaldo and Alex Izurieta, 'The Imprudence of Labour Market Flexibilization in a Fiscally Austere World', 152 *International Labour Rev.* 1 (2013).

[19] Various attempts have been made to improve working conditions and wages, avoiding competition in the niche of countries that offer the lowest compensation. To offset the cost of higher wages, such attempts are complemented by measures to improve trade exposure and/or improve other factors that affect productivity, such as increasing industrial peace, improving infrastructure or offering training facilities to match workers' skills with employers' demand. An example of such coordinated measures for raising wages and working conditions is Cambodia's Better Factories programme, which was later expanded by the ILO to other countries under the heading of 'Better Work'. See: Drusilla Brown, Rajeev Dehejia and Raymond Robertson, 'Is There a Business Case for Improving Labor Standards? Some Evidence from Better Factories Cambodia', in: *Workers' Rights and Labor Compliance in Global Supply Chains: Is a Social Label the Answer?* 69–87, Jennifer Bair, Marsha A. Dickson and Doug Miller (eds), (Oxford: Routledge, 2014).

[20] For reasons of sovereignty, raising labor costs in other states to even out differences between national labor markets requires a form of co-ordination. This traditionally has been the domain of international labour conventions, although free trade and investment agreements have gained more importance as instruments of inter-state coordination. ILO, Social Dimensions of Free Trade Agreements (2013).

Comprehending these different responses engages broader questions of political economy: how regulatory objectives are identified and represented; what constituencies do, and do not, have voice and influence within regulatory debates and processes; and whose interests count, or count most, in the calculus of reform. What is important in the first instance, however, is to observe that all of these strategies require an analysis that extends beyond simply identifying interest groups within the nation state and examining the effects of their actions on the internal processes of legal reform. Instead, even when considering change *within* the nation state, the authors of labor law are looking both inside and outside state boundaries and attempting to calculate the possible interactions and effects of multiple actors and decisions on the transformation of labor law.

(b) Globalization as Institutions, Norms and Governance

Globalization is not merely a force or condition of our time, nor is it merely the automatic or inevitable effect of the interconnected processes and transformations just described.[21] Globalization itself is, in part, a product of law. Global economic, social and cultural flows operate within complex legal regimes that comprise both formal and informal norms and institutions; these regimes typically reflect an accretion of old and new political priorities and decisions, economic interests and incentives, and ideological commitments. These regimes are also multi-leveled or multi-layered: they are built out of both private and public law(s) as well as domestic, international and transnational law(s) and regulations.

As many have noted, a salient aspect of globalization and global governance, one particularly important to workers and labor markets, is the growing importance of norms and institutions that transcend the political system of any one state. Some norms and institutions come from formal international institutions and organizations that themselves are based upon nation-state representation, such as the United Nations, the ILO, the WTO, and the IOM, or regional institutions and their governing bodies, such as the EU, NAFTA, MERCOSUR, and APEC. Others come from new, or newly important, private institutions that are detached from state interests and represent transnational, often sectoral or special, interests and constituencies. Examples here include international NGOs such as the Fair Labor Association, international networks such as the Global Forum on Migration, and international trade unions and business associations such as the global union federations and the International Chamber of Commerce. Some regimes are best understood as hybrid public/private regimes. For example, the UN Global Compact is an initiative that is sponsored by the office of the UN Secretary-General but which seeks to enlist and mobilize corporate support to raise labor and social standards.

Furthermore, if labor law has traditionally encompassed formal legal instruments such as treaties and conventions, statutes, regulations, case-law and, less commonly,

---

21 Harry Arthurs has called this TINA – "there is no alternative". See Harry W. Arthurs, 'Who's Afraid of Globalization? Reflections on the Future of Labour Law', in: *Globalization and the Future of Labour Law* 51, John D.R. Craig and S. Michael Lynk (eds), (Cambridge: Cambridge University Press, 2006).

collective agreements and extension decrees, it must now include a greatly expanded range of legal norms and processes. Untethered to territory and independent of the labor laws and enforcement mechanisms of the nation state, new forms of labor market governance have emerged that are directed towards standardizing work norms and practices in transnational markets and industrial sectors or across production, value and supply chains. Many of these supranational initiatives, especially those promoted by public/private or wholly private actors and bodies, involve new forms of governance and co-ordination and arise from horizontal and other non-standard forms of norm generation.[22]

Some supranational bodies still, of course, engage in traditional public international law rule-making activities, such as the development of treaties and conventions. Yet, despite widespread concern about the neglect of workers' rights in the context of globalization expressed in a range of international instruments since the Copenhagen Declaration of 1995,[23] proposals to formalize labor standards within the multilateral trade regime continue to provoke conflict between developed and developing states, primarily due to their perceived impact on the comparative advantage of national labour forces.[24] The most prominent normative initiative at the international level in recent years remains the ILO Declaration on Fundamental Principles and Rights at Work of 1998.[25] Although the Declaration itself is expressly promotional and non-binding in its obligations, the 'core' labor standards identified in the Declaration are now routinely incorporated into regional and bilateral trade and investment treaties as well as corporate codes of conduct; sometimes they are unilaterally imposed, as in the case of the General System of Preferences.[26] At the same time, with limited, but nonetheless important, exceptions such as the Domestic Workers Convention of 2011,[27] there is declining use of traditional public law mechanisms and instruments such as the ILO Convention process to address either general questions of labor market standards or those related to globalization in particular.

Despite ongoing resistance to the legal entrenchment of labor standards at the international level, domestic labor laws *are* sometimes affected by other international agreements, although these agreements may as often lead to lower as to higher labor standards. The international financial institutions, for example, often require alterations to domestic labor standards to ensure greater labor market flexibility as a lending condition for purposes of development, debt relief or economic stabilization. Such

---

[22] Gráinne de Búrca and Joanne Scott, 'New Governance, Law and Constitutionalism', in: *Law and New Governance in the EU and the US*, Gráinne de Búrca and Joanne Scott (eds), (Oxford: Hart Publishing, 2006).

[23] United Nations, Copenhagen Declaration on Social Development, Report of the World Summit for Social Development, April 19, 1995 A/Conf. 166/9.

[24] Philip Alston, 'Facing up to the Complexities of the ILO's Core Labour Standards Agenda', 16 *European Journal of Int'l Law* 467 (2005).

[25] ILO, Declaration on the Fundamental Principles and Rights at Work, June 18, 1998, (adopted by the International Labour Conference at its Eighty-sixth Session, Geneva).

[26] Marisa Anne Pagnattar, 'U.S. Trade Policy: Increased Emphasis On Worker Rights', 40 *Ga. J. Int'l & Comp. L.* 663 (2012); Jean-Marc Siroën, 'Labour Provisions in Preferential Trade Agreements: Current Practice and Outlook', 152 *International Labour Rev.* 85 (2013).

[27] ILO, Convention 189 Concerning Decent Work for Domestic Workers, June 16, 2011.

'structural reforms' to labor markets have been standard components of the structural adjustment programs of the World Bank;[28] they also formed part of the IMF bail-out conditionality following the financial crises of East Asia in the late 1990s.[29] Along with cuts to pensions and public sector employment, reductions both to labor standards and to workers' rights have been central to the policy reforms mandated by the European Commission, the European Central Bank and the IMF in exchange for debt relief in the European periphery since the financial crises of 2008.[30]

Where international or supranational institutions have no direct competence over questions of labor market governance, they may still affect national labor laws by engaging in deliberative processes that are designed to steer reforms in a convergent direction, the best-known examples being the European Employment Strategy and the Open Method of Co-ordination adopted by the European Commission.[31] They may also develop non-enforceable guidelines concerning workers' rights and labor standards and other soft modes of governance in an effort to influence the direction in which global labor norms, be they national or transnational, evolve.[32] Finally, financial and economic institutions routinely weigh in on the advisability of labor law reform in the form of technocratic advice, research studies and policy reports, as demonstrated by the IMF's World Economic Outlook,[33] the World Bank's World Development Reports[34] and Doing Business report series,[35] the OECD's Jobs Study,[36] and the OECD Employment Outlook.[37] While such policy analyses may seem to be removed from the processes of

---

[28] Rajesh Swaminathan, 'Regulating Development: Structural Adjustment and the Case for National Enforcement of Economic and Social Rights', 37 *Colum. J. Transnat'l L.* 161 (1998).

[29] Catherine Lee, 'To Thine Ownself be True: IMF Conditionality and Erosion of Economic Sovereignty in the Asian Financial Crisis', 24 *U. Pa. J. Int'l Econ. L.* 875, 894 (2003).

[30] See Catherine Barnard, 'Financial Crisis and the Euro Plus Pact: A Labour Lawyer's Perspective', 41 *Ind. Law J.* 98 (2012).

[31] Diamond Ashiagbor, The European Employment Strategy: Labour Market Regulation and New Governance, (Oxford: Oxford University Press, 2005).

[32] See, for example: Organization for Economic Co-operation and Development, OECD Guidelines for Multinational Enterprises (2008), available at: http://www.oecd.org/investment/mne/1922428.pdf.

[33] International Monetary Fund, World Economic Outlook: Spillovers and Cycles in the Global Economy (April 2007), available at: http://www.imf.org/external/pubs/ft/weo/2007/01; World Economic Outlook: Growth and Institutions (April 2003), available at: http://www.imf.org/external/pubs/ft/weo/2003/01; World Economic Outlook: International Financial Contagion (May 1999).

[34] World Bank, World Development Report 2013: Jobs, available at: http://econ.worldbank.org/external/default/main?contentMDK=23044836&theSitePK=8258025&piPK=8258412&pagePK=8258258; World Development Report 1995: Workers in an Integrating World, available at: http://wdronline.worldbank.org/worldbank/a/c.html/world_development_report_1995/abstract/WB.0-1952-1102-2.abstract1.

[35] World Bank, Doing Business, available at: http://www.doingbusiness.org.

[36] The OECD Jobs Study: Facts, Analysis, Strategy (1994), http://www.oecd.org/els/emp/1941679.pdf; Boosting Jobs and Incomes: Policy Lessons From Reassessing the OECD Jobs Strategy (2006), available at: http://www.oecd.org/els/emp/36889821.pdf.

[37] OECD, OECD Employment Outlook 2013, available at: http://dx.doi.org/10.1787/empl_outlook-2013-6-en.

labor law reform proper, they can provide crucial insight into the political, ideational and institutional context out of which labor law norms now emerge. Above all, they warrant attention in a comparative context because of their pervasive influence on the consensus about the form and content of national and transnational labor market norms and institutions.

The contemporary reliance on benchmarks and indicators, now visible in labor law as well as virtually every other field of policy and governance, stands as one of the most prominent examples of the importance of new governance techniques and strategies in the realm of work. For example, the 'Employing Workers Indicator' of the World Bank's Doing Business project measures the comparative flexibility of national labor standards.[38] Other measures, such as the ILO's Decent Work indicators, highlight different values and aim to promote an alternative, typically wider, set of labor market goals and objectives.[39] Like the Open Method of Co-ordination and the European Employment Strategy, indicators rest on the collection, comparison and diffusion of data concerning the character of state law and the direction of law and policy reform.[40] Integral to all of these regimes is the ranking and comparison of regulatory performance among peers in relation to identified goals and objectives. The self-monitoring of standards induced by the process of comparison and benchmarking, moreover, can be a powerful means of both shifting and standardizing transnational norms,[41] even where legislative power and regulatory competence still officially reside with the nation state. Over time, states tend to internalize dominant norms; once internalized, they often modify their policies, rules and behavior in conformity with those norms and standards, a process that re-orients regulatory goals and priorities in respect of workplace and other forms of regulation, at the same time increasing the likelihood that reforms to rules and institutions will reflect external, rather than domestic, regulatory demands and policy priorities.

In tandem with the de-centering of the state in the design and enforcement of labor norms and regimes is the rise of firms as agents of transnational technocratic standardization. Multinational firms now routinely adopt, promote, and disseminate policies and practices on a wide range of workplace issues.[42] Increasingly, these policies and practices are developed and elaborated by human resource professionals who bring distinct optics and preoccupations to bear on questions of workers' rights and workplace standards. In addition, the corporate social responsibility (CSR) industry

---

[38] The Employing Workers Indicator was withdrawn following complaints that it encouraged states to violate their ILO obligations. Following consultations with employee and employer representatives as well as the ILO, the OECD and civil society groups, the report no longer ranks countries according to their flexibility; however comparative data on flexibility are included as an annex to the report. See World Bank, Doing Business 2013: Smarter Regulation for Small and Medium Enterprises (2013).

[39] ILO Decent Work Indicators: Concepts and Definitions, 2012, available at: http://www.ilo.org/stat/Publications/WCMS_183859/lang–en/index.htm.

[40] Ashiagbor, *supra* note 31.

[41] Marilyn Strathern, *The Audit Culture* (Oxford: Routledge, 2000).

[42] Matthew W. Finkin et al., *Multinational Human Resource Management and the Law: Common Workplace Problems in Different Legal Environments* (Cheltenham: Edward Elgar Publishing, 2013).

has forged a new brand of specialists who are engaged in the formation and promotion of workplace norms at different levels of formality.[43] The field also includes NGOs that advocate the adoption of social commitments by business, as well as private organizations that develop social standards and indices of social responsibility and social and economic performance; there are even conferences and prizes for best practices. Originally oriented toward the generation of broad statements on moral commitments, the field of CSR now draws on complex communicative techniques that deploy sophisticated technocratic knowledge about how to induce social change.[44]

Offsetting the enhanced engagement of transnational corporate and business agents and institutions in matters of workplace governance, there is at least fragmentary evidence of new transnational alliances among workers and unions in the form of global unions and transnational networks and activist groups.[45] The emergence of these networks and groups is enabled by greatly simplified and less expensive global communication, along with a growing consciousness that problems and predicaments at work are often connected, even if they take different forms in different places. To date, however, they have not slowed or interrupted the global trends toward more fragmented labor law and greater technocratic and professional norm generation; nor have they halted the global growth of more precarious forms of work.

And despite the growth of entities and initiatives beyond the nation state that seek to affect, and sometimes even to rationalize, labor market conditions, there remain significant regulatory gaps and conflicts. For the most part, the emergent transnational regimes are patchy in their coverage and content, contested in their values and orientation, and uncoordinated in both their operation and their relation to national systems of labor law. Above all, they lack the form and structural integration that would permit the identification and comprehensive consideration of questions of labor market justice on a global scale.[46]

Consider, for example, the range of regimes and norms that might operate on workforces and supply chains within a single firm or industry. While multinational companies and industries may display some commitment to the standardization of labor norms within their own industrial or economic territory through the development of codes or principles of conduct and practice, the actual entitlements and working conditions of workers often vary enormously. Depending on the nature of the firm (multinational or national) and the scope of commitment (covering only the workers employed directly by the company, or also the workers employed by sub-contractors

---

43 Alexander Ardichvili, 'The Role of HRD in CSR, Sustainability, and Ethics: A Relational Model', 12 *Human Resource Development Rev.* 456 (2013).

44 Guy Mundlak and Issi Rosen-Zvi, 'Signaling Virtue? A Comparison of Corporate Codes in the Fields of Labor and Environment', 12 *Theoretical Inquiries in Law* 603 (2011).

45 Kate Bronfenbrenner (ed), *Global Unions: Challenging Transnational Capital Through Cross Border Campaigns* (Ithaca NY: Cornell University Press, 2007); Mark Anner, Ian Greer, Marco Hauptmeier, Nathan Lillie and Nik Winchester, 'The Industrial Determinants of Transnational Solidarity: Global Interunion Politics in Three Sectors', 12 *European Journal of Industrial Relations* 7 (2006); Jennifer Gordon, 'Transnational Labor Citizenship', 80 *S. Cal. L. Rev.* 503 (2006).

46 Nancy Fraser, *Scales of Justice: Reimagining Political Space in a Globalizing World* (New York: Columbia University Press, 2008).

world-wide), multiple, disparate regimes may be established the result of which is that workers employed in the same industrial sector or commercial enterprise are governed by different norms. Where production crosses borders, workers inevitably will be governed by different formal labor laws as well. Yet, in many countries, the protections afforded by labor law are illusory even where they remain available in theory. As a result, some workers are protected by formal labor market rules that provide either better or worse employment standards, those at the periphery of networks or at the bottom of value and production chains may be excluded either formally or effectively from the protections of labor and employment law and/or governed by 'soft' forms of law, while still other workers may remain in an informal situation altogether.[47] In short, there are typically profound differences in the authorship and content of norms, as well as in their application and enforcement even within firms and workforces that are otherwise deeply interconnected.

To summarize, the proliferation of regimes and actors is linked to the progressive fragmentation and deconsolidation of labor law. The state, which is still, in general, expected to provide a socially stable, just and efficient regime for its labor market, is torn between competing demands from its own citizens and other insiders, and those of external agents and interests. These gaps and tensions are mediated, on the one hand, and further exacerbated, on the other, by a range of new and hybrid forms of labor law and governance. Admittedly, the polycentric nature of labor law is old, rather than new.[48] But if labor law has always been diverse and multi-layered, the social-economic fragmentation associated with globalization combined with the regulatory fragmentation associated with the multiplication of normative actors and regimes has cumulated into a qualitative departure from the past.

(c) Globalization as Values and Ideology

Globalization is associated with the diffusion of values that, although pervasive, are difficult to articulate with precision; in addition, both their sources and their links to national regulatory responses can be difficult to identify or pin down conclusively. The practical significance of these values, moreover, can only be understood in relation to ideologies about the role of markets in political and economic life, on the one hand, and theories about the consequences of, and rationales for, regulation, on the other. A loose conjunction between values, ideologies and regulatory theories has nonetheless resulted in a mainstream consensus in the international order that has given rise to a set of over-arching prescriptions concerning workplace rights and regulation, the influence of which is, first and foremost, discursive and only successively, and sometimes indirectly, manifested in policy and institutional change.

At least since the second half of the twentieth century, labor law has been a central part of the embedded liberal compromise undergirding the social contract within

---

47 For a recent overview of labor market informality, see Colin C. Williams and Mark A. Lansky, 'Informal Employment in Developed and Developing Economies: Perspectives and Policy Responses: Introduction, Informality Across the Global Economy', 152 *International Labour Rev.* 355–80 (2013).

48 Kahn-Freund, *supra* note 1.

industrialized states.[49] In addition to mediating the systemic imbalance of power between employers and workers, labor law has been understood to promote a range of general public policy considerations. Depending on the time period and national legal and constitutional as well as political traditions, labor laws have advanced positive goals such as social solidarity and inclusion, equality and distributive justice, and democracy, stability and the prevention of political unrest; admittedly, they have been instruments of racial and gender segregation, class formation, and social stratification as well. Labor laws have also supported employer interests and broader economic objectives such as higher productivity, the maintenance of uninterrupted production, and macroeconomic demand.[50]

As is now well known, globalization is associated with a deterioration in the balance of power between labor and capital, a rejection of the Keynesian logic underpinning the post-war social contract, declining weight and priority given to policy considerations such as full employment and the maintenance of demand, and rising concern for fiscal probity, debt reduction and inflation control on the part of states. This transformation has been propelled by the rise of new ideology often encapsulated by the term 'market fundamentalism',[51] central to which is an emphasis on norms and values such as competitiveness, efficiency, productivity, individualism and entrepreneurialism. The priority now given to these values, along with a correlative decline and displacement of concerns such as solidarity, equality and democracy, is sharply – indeed most clearly – visible in both labor law and labor markets.

These developments are the result of several non-exclusive factors. First, technological innovation, the vertical disintegration of production, and the fragmentation of work have all disrupted the boundaries of community, permitting new alliances with people in far-flung locales while, at the same time, expanding the distance among those who live and work in close proximity to each other. In these altered social and economic configurations, people may treat community merely as a fungible space for work or living, one, moreover, which may be substituted for another, while voice and loyalty to particular locales or organizations may give way to the forces of exit and competition. Finding themselves in dispersed and unstable work sites, working under an array of different terms and conditions, and facing calls to update and market their skills continually, workers may no longer see themselves as forming distinct communities; they may not even identify themselves as workers at all.[52] Second, rather than contingent values that form part of a broader project to promote domestic social welfare and economic growth as well as international economic and political stability, liberalized trade and greater competition for goods, capital, labor and services have

---

[49] John Gerard Ruggie, 'International Regimes, Transactions, and Change: Embedded Liberalism in the Postwar Economic Order', 36 *International Organizations* 2 (1982).

[50] For a discussion of these objectives in relation to the diffusion of economic ideas, see Sanford Jacoby, 'Economic Ideas and the Labor Market: Origins of the Anglo-American Model and Prospects for Global Diffusion', 25 *Comp. Lab. Law and Policy J.* 43 (2003–04).

[51] Joseph E. Stiglitz, *Globalization and its Discontents*, (New York: Penguin Books, 2001).

[52] Stone and Arthurs, *supra* note 4; Guy Mundlak, 'Workplace-Democracy: Reclaiming the Effort to Foster Public and Private Isomorphism', 15 *Theoretical Inquiries in Law* 159 (2014).

become ends in themselves.[53] Indeed, intensified competition is often represented as simply an intrinsic or axiomatic part of globalization, one, moreover, that compels a reduction in the regulatory and re-distributive functions of the state.

However, it would be a mistake to imagine that, however hegemonic, these values are simply the spontaneous outgrowth of globalization. Rather, they are constantly nurtured and articulated by advocates of the new competition. Sometimes, they are endorsed and promoted by private actors who seek either to side-step or to influence national politics in the hope of reforming national laws and policies in ways that are (more) congenial to their interests. But new norms and values are also the result of a new regulatory and policy consensus within international institutions and the global technocracy,[54] the product of agents who, in a seemingly uncoordinated fashion, have created the orthodoxy of globalization as unfettered competition.

Globalization, in its current form, has been achieved through the successes of a distinct ideological and regulatory project, neo-liberalism, also known as the Washington or post-Washington Consensus.[55] In addition to prioritizing norms such as efficiency, competition and enhanced private sector entrepreneurialism, its advocates have promoted legal and policy reforms to re-calibrate the relations between the state and the market, and, in some cases, between those institutions and individuals and households too, in the belief that economic growth and welfare advances are best secured through the efforts of private actors operating within 'undistorted' markets.

Despite important internal debates within neo-classical economic theory about the relationship between the advancement of values and objectives such as efficiency, equality and productivity and labor market institutions,[56] workers' rights, labor standards and other labor market institutions have been, and continue to be, central targets of neo-liberal reformers, to the profound detriment of the traditional norms and values of labor law.[57] The received presumption against regulatory 'interventions' in markets except in defined instances of market failure creates pressure and, at least at first glance, the justification for the diminution or elimination of a range of job rights and entitlements. Job security rights and minimum non-waivable contractual terms are decried for their adverse effects on the allocative efficiency of labor markets as well as the costs that they impose on employers, consumers, and labor market 'outsiders'.

---

[53] Robert Howse, 'From Politics to Technocracy … and Back Again: The Fate of the Multilateral Trade Regime', 96 *American Journal of Int'l Law* 94 (2002).

[54] See Jacoby, *supra* note 50.

[55] Joseph Stiglitz, 'Is there a post-Washington Consensus Consensus?', in: *The Washington Consensus Reconsidered: Towards a New Global Governance* 41, Joseph Stiglitz and Narcis Serra (eds), (Oxford: Oxford University Press, 2008).

[56] See Kenneth Dau-Schmidt *et al.* (eds), *Labor and Employment Law and Economics* (Cheltenham: Edward Elgar Publishing, 2009); Simon Deakin and Frank Wilkinson, 'Rights versus Efficiency? The Economic Case for Transnational Labour Standards', 23 *Industrial Law Journal*, 289 (1994).

[57] Kerry Rittich, 'Rights, Risk and Reward: Governance Norms in the International Order and the Problem of Precarious Work', in: *Precarious Work, Women, and the New Economy: The Challenge to Legal Norms* 31, Judy Fudge and Rosemary Owens (eds), Oxford: Hart Publishing, 2006); Kerry Rittich, 'Global Labour Policy as Social Policy', 14 *Canadian Labour and Employment Law Journal* 227 (2008).

Disability insurance, employment insurance and social protection receive critical scrutiny for their adverse effects on work effort and capacity to induce 'benefit dependency', while the effort to 'make work pay' translates into arguments for reduced access to work-related benefits and, where benefits still remain available, for lower levels of income replacement.[58] Rather than instruments of collective voice and a counterweight to employer power in the employment relationship, unions are (re-) imagined as cartels and collective bargaining as a source of deadweight loss to both economy and society. At the same time, labor laws that support both unions and collective bargaining are being recast as the product of regulatory capture, something at odds, rather than congruent, with the general interest. All these factors have converged to form a consensus, shared among the global political and technocratic élite and, increasingly, by parts of the broader population, too, that favors enhanced employer control of the allocation of labor resources over employment protection, collective voice and income security for workers. As a result, greater labor market flexibility – along with the reduction in labor market protections that flexibility is thought to imply – is now naturalized by many quarters as simply a touchstone of common sense and good labor market governance; rather than mere regulatory objective, it has become part of the very framework in which debates about labor policy and workers' rights are now conducted.[59]

The orthodoxy of greater flexibility is sometimes simply enforced, as can be seen where reforms to labor law become a condition of financial support in the context of debt relief.[60] On other occasions it is embedded in benchmarks and indicators, or effectively promoted through incentives. Yet for the most part, flexibility operates neither as a hard constraint on state practice, nor can it be said to be truly optional or voluntary. Moreover, operationalizing labor market flexibility can be significantly more complex in practice than it seems in theory; there is considerable doubt as to whether regimes can even be identified as flexible or not.[61] Even when flexibility is endorsed as a regulative ideal, reforms tend to be sensitive to, and variable with, local context, history, institutions and politics;[62] thus, in virtually no case does the move toward flexibility result in labor market institutions that mimic or embody the *laissez-faire* ideal. Even in the face of the common pressures of globalization and technological innovation, national labor law and social protection regimes continue to exhibit wide

---

58 The OECD Jobs Study, *supra* note 36.

59 Kerry Rittich, 'Making Natural Markets', 65 *Northern Ireland Legal Quarterly* (2014).

60 This is the case in the recent bailout programs crafted by the EU, the ECB and the IMF. See Catherine Barnard, *supra* note 30; Kerry Rittich, 'Fragmented Work and Multi-level Labour Market Governance: Informality, Crisis Policy and an Expanded "Law of Work" in: *Critical Legal Perspectives on Global Governance* 185, Gráinne de Búrca, Claire Kilpatrick and Joanne Scott (eds), (Oxford: Hart Publishing, 2013).

61 Alvaro Santos, 'Labor Flexibility, Legal Reform, and Economic Development', *50 Virginia J. of International Law*, 43 (2009).

62 For a similar argument concerning the implementation of mainstream governance norms in general, see Jamie Peck, *Constructions of Neoliberal Reason*, (Oxford: Oxford University Press, 2010).

variation.[63] There are a number of possible, likely cumulative, explanations for these differences. Despite efforts to encourage convergence of national labor market norms and institutions, the path dependence or 'stickiness' of laws and institutions prevents their being overturned easily.[64] Despite (premature) claims about the end of history popularized by Francis Fukuyama and others, it is now well-understood that capitalism, too, comes in a variety of forms, with important differences in relations among workers, unions and employers expressed through corporate law, bankruptcy law, and other forms of law.[65] And worlds of production may operate in accordance with their own logics and systemic imperatives, generating norms that collide with, and sometimes prevail over, the formal law of the workplace whatever its current state.[66]

Even though they often seem hegemonic, the dominant values associated with globalization do not, of course, completely occupy the normative universe when it comes to work. Confronting the Washington consensus are other normative and institutional projects, even other types of consensus such as the Beijing consensus or the Geneva consensus.[67] Like the ILO's Decent Work initiative, some seek to advance traditional labor law values such as greater worker voice, solidarity and equality through the global recognition of workers' rights as human rights and 'core' labor standards. Some seek to use Amartya Sen's influential idea of 'development as freedom', in particular, its central claim that development should be understood in terms of the support and advancement of human capabilities, as the basis for the re-construction of labor law and workers' rights in an era of globalization;[68] in addition to respect for core rights, an important plank of the 'capabilities-based' approach is the promotion of policies designed to support the development of workers' human capital.[69] Other projects seek to find a middle way, endorsing both values such as efficiency and greater productivity through competition *and* 'core' labor standards or the protection of individual basic rights at work; this approach is particularly visible in new transnational regimes. Thus, references to basic or core workers' rights can now be found in countless official and non-state initiatives, from the UN Global Compact[70] to industry

63 Gøsta Esping-Andersen, *Three Worlds of Welfare Capitalism*, (Cambridge: Polity Press, 1990); Gøsta Esping-Andersen, *Social Foundations of Postindustrial Economies*, (Oxford: Oxford University Press, 1999).

64 On patterns of institutional change, see Paul Pierson, *Politics in Time: History, Institutions, and Social Analysis* (Princeton NJ: Princeton University Press, 2004); James Mahoney and Kathleen Thelen, 'A Theory of Gradual Institutional Change', in: *Explaining Institutional Change: Ambiguity, Agency, and Power*, 1–37, James Mahoney and Kathleen Thelen (eds) (Cambridge: Cambridge University Press, 2010).

65 Peter Hall and David Soskice (eds), *Varieties of Capitalism: The Institutional Foundations of Comparative Advantage* (Oxford: Oxford University Press, 2001).

66 Gunther Teubner and Andreas Fischer-Lescano, 'Regime-Collisions: The Vain Search for Legal Unity in the Fragmentation of Global Law', 25 *Mich. J. Int'l L.* 999 (2004).

67 Brian Langille, 'Imagining Post "Geneva Consensus" Labor Law for Post "Washington Consensus" Development', 31 *Comp. Lab. L. & Pol'y J.* 523 (2009).

68 Amartya Sen, *Development as Freedom*, (Oxford: Oxford University Press, 1999).

69 For a special issue on the capabilities approach in labor law, see: 'Voices at Work: Legal Effects on Organization, Representation and Negotiation', 33 *Comp. Lab. L. & Pol'y J.* (2012).

70 UN Global Compact, available at: http://www.unglobalcompact.org.

standards such as the Equator Principles,[71] and corporate codes. However, these hybrid or non-state regimes are adopted upon a voluntary basis by employers and are motivated both by a desire to protect reputation and by the need to remain responsive to the competitive pressures operating within dynamic global markets. For this reason, they generally avoid commitment to, or indeed any reference to, traditional labor law preoccupations such as better job security, minimum standards, and higher wages levels.[72]

As noted in the previous section, a related trend is the growing influence of experts and technocrats in the design of labor law and workplace norms. Indeed, when considering the effect of globalization on labor standards, it may make sense to think now in terms of different transnational epistemic communities that generate labor law norms and policies independently of national traditions of labor law. Following expert debates, it is possible to track the state of dominant or mainstream values and ideologies, and, often, the rise and decline of different labor law projects as a result. As David Kennedy and others have described, experts do their work in the crucial middle territory, crafting law and policy from politically established, high-level normative commitments upon the basis of shared disciplinary practices and assumptions.[73] Depending on their status and position, these different communities of experts can be the sources of both convergence and divergence in labor law norms. Some are well resourced and institutionalized, with access to multiple channels for the dissemination of their ideas and projects; others are less powerful, and their contributions remain relatively marginal to conversations about globalization and workplace norms.

Experts from the ILO continue to provide technical assistance to states, much although not all of which is designed to advance traditional objectives such as the protection of workers' rights and higher labor standards. However, technocratic advice on labor law increasingly comes from other institutions such as the OECD, the World Bank and the IMF, institutions that are among the principal authors of mainstream governance norms like the Washington Consensus as well. This shift in the institutional *locus* and power of labor law expertise has resulted in profound changes in the tenor of the regulatory advice, destabilizing, rather than re-enforcing, the post-war bargain. One reason for this is a shift in disciplinary training and values. While pressure from unions, states, institutions and others concerned about the status of workers has induced them to give some attention to, and recognition of, workers' rights, the experts and technocrats within the international economic and financial institutions are primarily economists whose foremost concern tends to be furthering allocative efficiency within labor markets.

To the values of competition, flexibility, and technocratic measurement and management, the growing juridification of labor law should be added as a third component.

---

[71] The Equator Principles (July 2006), available at: http://www.equator-principles.com; Freshfields Bruckhaus Deringer, Equator Principles Survey 2005, Part I: the Banks (February 2005).

[72] For an interesting exception, however, see the recent Bangladesh Accord on Fire and Building Safety, available at: http://www.bangladeshaccord.org.

[73] David Kennedy, 'Challenging Expert Rule: The Politics of Global Governance', 27 *Sydney Law Review* 1 (2005); Andrew Lang, *World Trade Law After Neoliberalism* (Oxford: Oxford University Press, 2011).

Workplace rules and norms are less and less frequently determined by collective bargaining between unions and employers. Instead, as labor rights are eroded by diminishing union presence and strength and/or carved back under the pressure of flexibility norms and increased competition, individual rights are supplanting collective rights in the workplace.[74] The erosion and displacement of collective rights, especially when combined with the declining reach and power of unions, leaves the juridical structure of work to be determined by the background rules of the market: constitutional rights, property and contract rights, debtor and creditor rights, and other commercial rules and norms. In many cases, the erosion of collective rights and labor market institutions also effectively (re-) installs courts in the role of arbiters of employment disputes. Here, the use of courts and reliance on individual rights masks a growing sense of anomie within industrial relations systems, as contestation over employment standards, their hard/soft nature and the determination of universally acceptable minima at work draws on legal forms and rhetoric that gradually substitute for more politically engaged forms of communication and action.

(d) The Many Meanings of Globalization and their Implication for the Comparative Project

The implications of these new actors, norms, governance mechanisms, and ideas for the comparative project are immense. First, there is no longer a single, well-defined unit of comparison; the nation state and its governance institutions are now just one of many sets of actors to consider. At the same time, the state and its domestic institutions remain crucially important; despite claims about the loss of the state's autonomy to govern, in most cases, the state still both actively authors workplace norms and co-ordinates the legal and policy responses to the changes initiated by others.

This leads to the second point. If the nation state was the subject at the core of the comparative project, it must now also be seen as an agent that affects others outside its territory and is, in turn, affected by others in complex ways. Current global governance norms are clearly not just the spontaneous outgrowth of unfettered markets. However, nor do they simply represent the aggregated preferences of states. As Santos has observed, some norms may be 'globalized localisms', that is, the norms of powerful states that have been effectively diffused and taken up by other states.[75] To complicate matters further, states are not merely the recipients or executors of international and transnational norms. Even when norms become globally dominant, states may resist them outright or in part, or merely superficially comply: here, internal power struggles, differences and disputes about the local desirability of such norms, or both, can be expected to play a role.

Whatever the causal relationship or direction of influence, neither the state and its domestic players, nor the transnational or extra-territorial agents and the norms that they author can be considered as exogenous factors to globalization or labor market conditions. Instead, comparative work must continually recognize and incorporate a

---

[74] Bob Hepple, *Labour Laws and Global Trade* (Oxford: Hart Publishing, 2005).

[75] Boaventura de Sousa Santos, *Toward a New Legal Common Sense* (Cambridge: Cambridge University Press, 2005).

sort of 'double endogeneity'. Accepting that both markets and social laws are socially embedded, it is important to bear in mind that law (partly) constitutes the phenomenon that we call globalization, while the forces associated with globalization are themselves driving the transformation of law at both the national and supranational levels.

The emergence of myriad new entities engaged in governance activities outside the formal legal, political and administrative structures of the state challenges the state-centered focus of political economy, as both politics and economy have drifted beyond the state's boundaries, albeit in very different ways. Beyond the attempt to grasp the significance of these processes descriptively, a study of the agents involved raises crucial questions of legitimacy, accountability, transparency and democracy. Given that many of their activities and initiatives are only loosely, if at all, institutionalized, they also raise basic questions of efficacy and durability.

Third, many of the traditional components of labor law remain intact, and clearly all are relevant to the various comparative projects that have been outlined. However, it is now evident that many other laws may profoundly affect both workers and labor markets; as a result the frontiers of labor law – broadly defined – have moved to incorporate legal fields whose relevance was less visible in the past, if it was even recognized at all. The most evident are trade and investment laws and citizenship and immigration laws, that is, the laws that explicitly govern the movement of people, commodities, and capital across borders. Beyond these two prominent areas, labor law has been re-located and fragmented into fields from constitutional law and welfare law to tax law and financial and credit regulation.

2. COMPARATIVE LABOR IN TIMES OF GLOBALIZATION – SURVEYING THE TERRAIN

Labor law possesses a flourishing tradition of comparative work. Despite Kahn's Freund warning, and, perhaps, at his invitation, numerous comparative projects have been pursued over the years, some of which have continued for decades. There are, in addition, dedicated journals, books, websites and working-groups that co-operate on comparative labor law research.[76] How does this comparative literature address questions of globalization? Which of the meanings that can be attributed to the term 'globalization' dominates the comparative literature? And what can we say about how globalization affects the exercise of comparison itself?

Comparison inevitably involves holding some factors or elements constant and limiting the variables under consideration, as it is difficult, if not impossible, to examine simultaneously multiple types of difference, such as differences in subject

---

[76] Key sources include the *Encyclopaedia of Comparative Labour Law and Industrial Relations* (Kluwer); the Bulletin of Comparative Labour Relations, which provides a thematic comparison on selected issues on an annual basis; and the *Journal of Comparative Labor Law and Policy*, which periodically issues volumes that are devoted to a thematic comparison. There is also an increasing number of edited collections that engage in comparative labor law, as well as websites that provide updated comparative information, most notably the European Union's EUROFOUND (http://www.eurofound.europa.eu).

matter, institutional form and external influence. For this reason, comparison is both most illuminating and most easily performed between countries, such as the US and Canada, with common patterns of industrial and economic development, similar social and economic conditions, as well as shared legal and industrial institutions such as the presence of international unions and a common industrial relations framework. However, it is possible to engage in subject matter or thematic comparison among very different countries and international institutions where the ambit of comparison is closely confined. For example, it is possible to compare overtime arrangements between countries, between international institutions, and between subjects from both groups.

Most current comparative projects center on a common theme or problem, and, through a series of articles describing the way in which the theme manifests itself in national debates, analyze the various legal approaches to the problem, usually upon the basis of one country per article. For example, they may discuss the decline of the standard employment relationship,[77] issues of working time,[78] or the legal regulation of the work/family relationship.[79] An introduction to the volume will typically indicate both similarities and differences between national approaches, sometimes highlighting or proposing 'models' or prototypes that enable the clustering of countries as either similar or different. In a similar vein, articles may address a particular controversy in labor law and compare countries representing distinct responses to, or positions within, the controversy. Usually, such comparisons seek to study countries with some shared heritage, geographical proximity, or common institutions, including legal institutions. Thus, it is implicitly assumed that comparisons such as Australia and New Zealand, the US and Canada, the Netherlands and Belgium, and Hungary and the Czech Republic will accommodate a better isolation of particular variables and factors than a comparison, say, of Germany and Niger.

Comparisons may also be made between states or national systems upon the basis of distinct models of welfare capitalism,[80] different 'varieties of capitalism' such as centrally managed *versus* liberal forms,[81] or the systemic differences between legal traditions such as the common law *versus* civil law.[82] Such comparisons generally assume that each chosen country is representative of a particular category within the

---

[77] Stone and Arthurs, *supra* note 4; Bulletin of Comparative Labour Relations, The Evolving Employment Relationship and the New Economy (Volume 41, 2001).

[78] Sangheon Lee, Deirdre McCann and Jon C. Messenger (eds), *ILO, Working Time Around the World: Trends in Working Hours, Laws and Policies in a Global Comparative Perspective* (Oxford: Routledge, 2007): EIRO Online, comparative studies of Working Time developments in the European Union (last updated 2011) (available at: http://www.eurofound.europa.eu/eiro/studies/tn1204022s/tn1204022s.htm.

[79] Joanne Conaghan and Kerry Rittich (eds), *Labour Law, Work and Family: Critical and Comparative Perspectives*, (Oxford: Oxford University Press, 2005); 'Family Friendly Policy and the Law', 27 *Comp. Lab. L. & Pol'y J.* 437, 437–532 (2005–06); Bulletin of Comparative Labour Relations, The Harmonization of Working Life and Family Life (Volume 30, 1995).

[80] Esping-Anderson, *supra* note 63.

[81] Hall and Soskice, *supra* note 65.

[82] See, for example, Simeon Djankov *et al.*, 'The Regulation of Entry', 117 *The Quarterly Journal of Economics* 1, (2002).

model, and go on to demonstrate similarities within, as well as differences between, clusters of states. In the process of comparison, the underlying models may be either confirmed or modified. Such studies can also be useful for testing claims about the convergence and divergence of legal systems.

Some studies, in addition, propose particular theories or frameworks by which to evaluate developments in different countries. For example, studies may draw on the law and finance literature and its claim that the civil law is less efficient than the common law states due to excessive state regulation in the former.[83] Projects such as the World Bank's Doing Business indicator series may then draw on such theories to assess and rank the competitiveness and efficiency of labor market institutions.[84]

These comparative projects seek to compare similar units, and, for the most part, the units are nation states. In general, these forms of comparison do not directly address issues of globalization, unless it is accepted that *any* comparative study *is* now also a study of globalization, because one aspect of globalization is the greater diffusion of legal ideas and the concomitant replication of institutional forms across legal systems.[85] Other than those that assume that 'comparative' and 'globalization' are one and the same, however, the most common approach is to treat globalization as a social condition (the first meaning of globalization as described in the previous section), something that serves as a cause or an explanation of the changes that have taken place within the basic unit – the nation state. Within these studies, national practices and problems are generally used to illustrate pervasive problems or singular achievements, not to account for similarities or differences in law or to conduct any kind of systematic analysis of national legal institutions or labor market practices.

The infiltration of globalization into the traditional model of comparative labor law can also be observed in studies of national responses to new transnational institutions, many of which are introduced to manage the processes of market integration.[86] It is, perhaps, not surprising that EU institutions are the most common object of such studies,[87] if only because they permit the most familiar and tractable forms of comparative legal analysis. The EU has the most integrated markets, including labor markets; EU Directives take the form of hard law; and the effects of EU law on the legal orders of the EU Member States are both more direct and more pronounced than those of international law. By contrast, there are far fewer attempts to conduct studies of the effects of ILO Conventions and Declarations, mechanisms of regional or international coordination, or 'soft' forms of international and transnational law,

---

83 Ibid.

84 World Bank, Doing Business, available at: http://data.worldbank.org/indicator/IC.BUS.EASE.XQ.

85 Katherine V.W. Stone, 'New Labor Law for a New World of Work: The Case for a Comparative-Transnational Approach', 28 *Comp. Lab. L. & Pol'y J.* 565 (2006).

86 Marc-Antonin Hennebert, Peter Fairbrother and Christian Levesque, 'The Mobilization of International Framework Agreements: A Source of Power for Social Actors?', 33 *Comp. Lab. L. & Pol'y J.* 691 (2010); Rüdiger Krause, 'International Framework Agreements as Instrument for the Legal Enforcement of Freedom of Association and Collective Bargaining? The German Case', 33 *Comp. Lab. L. & Pol'y* J. 749 (2010).

87 See Silvana Sciarra, 'The Evolution of Collective Bargaining: Observations on a Comparison in the Countries of the European Union', 29 *Comp. Lab. L & Pol'y J.* 1 (2009).

whether they take the form of declarations or international commitments, on the internal practices of nation states. The most prominent examples of such studies are the annual follow-up reports to the 1998 Declaration. However, while these reports typically refer to practices in different countries, they are not systematic comparative studies as such.

Many comparative articles refer to the values associated with globalization (the third meaning), usually emphasizing the orthodoxies of competitiveness and flexibility.[88] In practice however, these discussions inevitably intertwine with consideration of other factors such as technological change and the re-organization of work. For example, a common focus is the emergence of post-Fordist forms of work relations and the extent to which they permit the employer to evade labor market obligations effectively. Because of the indeterminate implications and contested content of the values associated with globalization, such articles also often intersect with a discussion of norms, institutions, and governance projects associated with globalization. They may, for example, describe how institutional changes to promote greater trade, investment and market integration privilege values such as efficiency and competitiveness, and, at the same time, undermine the achievements of national labor regulation, such as greater job security or enhanced collective voice for workers.

However, some studies have a distinct, normative thrust and, in addition to their description and analysis of the effects of globalization, seek to identify the means 'to develop transnational strategies and institutions to protect labor rights in the face of the pressures of globalization'.[89] Alternatively, they may aim to identify national strategies and responses to transnational labor market governance problems, such as supply chain regulation, which can either serve as models or be adapted for use in other national legal and industrial relations systems.[90]

These forms of comparison follow decades of comparative research attempting to identify patterns of convergence and divergence among national systems,[91] including research on common heritage to explain why some countries develop similar labor market institutions. Some studies suggest, or imply, that greater access to information and a more rapid and intense diffusion of ideas between systems can overcome the problems with transplantation identified by Kahn-Freund, thereby extending the possibilities for convergence. At the same time, others argue that the effects of mutual learning, and even of homogenizing institutions such as European Directives, are limited, and that substantial national differences can therefore be expected to remain.[92] A salient feature of contemporary comparative studies, however, is their tendency to

---

[88] These elements appear in different sequences and causal patterns. For example, Stone identifies globalization on a par with privatization and flexibilization. Stone, *supra* note 85.

[89] Aaron and Stone (2007) *supra* note 3, at 389.

[90] See, for example, Rawling and Howe's discussion of Australia's Fair Work Principles governing government procurement supply chains and its interventions in the textiles, footwear and clothing sector: Michael Rawling and John Howe, 'The Regulation of Supply Chains: An Australian Contribution to Cross-National Legal Learning', in: *Rethinking Workplace Regulation*: *supra* note 4.

[91] Aaron and Stone, *supra* note 3.

[92] Manfred Weiss, 'Convergence and/or Divergence in Labor Law Systems? A European Perspective', 28 *Comp. Lab. L. & Pol'y J.* 469 (2007).

demonstrate that different national systems respond differently to similar global pressures. Despite ongoing claims that globalization leads to convergence among national systems, much of the literature nonetheless continues to emphasize the persistence of difference. This may be an observation about the fallacy of institutional Darwinism and the hypothesis of convergence, or merely a research- or publication-bias favoring difference over similarity.[93]

Not all studies focus on the role of the nation state. An important subset of studies looks at international law proper as a response to the challenges of globalization, typically by comparing different institutional arrangements for securing workers' rights. This kind of comparison may highlight the differences between hard and soft law,[94] the distinct *modus operandi* of the ILO and the WTO when it comes to questions of workers' rights,[95] the differences between regional human rights regimes,[96] and/or the characteristic differences between transnational and regional approaches to labor law and social policy.[97] Beyond the focus on the nation state as the subject of comparison, very few examples study the labor market effects of globalization, noting how national, firm-level, sectoral and national norms intertwine. Such studies can illuminate how non-state agents may diffuse best practices across borders and may, in addition, shed light on the contested question of whose interests these agents and practices promote.[98]

Only a few studies actually abandon the nation state as the basic unit of analysis. Yet another approach is to compare the practices of multi-national firms across different jurisdictions, analyzing how those practices intersect with national, regional and international norms and observing how such practices and norms are deployed and combined to produce different results in each case.[99] It seems possible to imagine a wide range of such comparisons involving, for example, the subset of norms and practices that are applied to firms in different countries, between regions, or between regional courts and other instruments of regional coordination. Such comparisons might, of course, be performed on a range of different legal questions. These innovative

---

93 This is similar to the bias in research and publication in favor of empirical findings that are statistically significant, even though statistical insignificance is equally important.

94 Arthurs, Compared to What? *supra* note 3; Bruno Caruso, 'Changes in the Workplace and the Dialogue of Global Law in the "Global Village"', 28 *Comp. Lab. L. & Pol'y J.* 501 (2007).

95 Adelle Blackett, 'Whither Social Clause: Human Rights, Trade Theory and Treaty Interpretation', 31 *Colum. Hum. Rts. L. Rev.* (1999).

96 Chantal Thomas, 'Convergences and Divergences in International Legal Norms on Migrant Labor', 32 *Comp. Lab. L. & Pol'y J.* 101 (2011).

97 Diamond Ashiagbor, 'Embedding Trade Liberalisation in Social Policy: Social Regionalism and the Global South', 65 *Northern Ireland Legal Quarterly* 265 (2014).

98 Graciela Bensusan, 'Legislation and Labor Policy in Latin America: Crisis, Renovation or Restoration?', 34 *Comp. Lab. L. & Pol'y J.* 655 (2012–13).

99 See, for example, the comparison of the legal effects of Wal-Mart's store closing in Quebec following a successful organizing drive with rulings on its similar efforts to defeat organizing in the UK and Germany. Marie-Ange Moreau, 'The Reconceptualization of the Employment Relationship and Labor Rights Through Transnationality', 34 *Comp. Lab. L. & Pol'y J.* 697 (2013). In this study, the Wal-Mart examples are contrasted with Fujitsu Siemens' decision to close a European site in which the ECJ applied the European Works Councils Directive despite the fact that the multinational company's headquarters was not European.

studies, still relatively embryonic in the comparative legal literature, all deviate from the comparative template in which an exogenous factor affects otherwise similar and comparable subjects (states). Yet while they introduce new difficulties, within such comparisons lie the seeds for more complex, and revealing, comparisons.

In the following section, we attempt to extend such attempts and to sketch the direction of research for future comparative projects on labor law and globalization.

3. GLOBALIZATION AND THE COMPARATIVE LABOR LAW PROJECT: NEW HORIZONS

(a) Comparative Method in Times of Globalization

The transnationalization of production and service provision has produced an acute disjuncture or mismatch between labor law and its intended objects. Much comparative work in the future will undoubtedly continue to focus on the novel forms of regulation introduced by states as they attempt to respond to the challenges introduced by transnationally organized work, as well as the fragmentation of the employment relationship. However, in addition to creating new pressures on domestic law, the forces of globalization and the features of the new economy are producing new forms of law. Nothing like a comprehensive transnational regime of workplace regulation is now on the horizon, and there are few reasons to think that one will soon emerge. Nonetheless, efforts to respond to the limits of state-based workplace regulation and the new forms and conditions of work are visible, and growing. At this point, these new regimes remain fragmentary and interstitial. However, some are important sites of innovation and experimentation, and many pose implicit, if not explicit, challenges to the ambitions of national labor law; for this reason, they are highly significant to the project of comparative labor law in virtually any shape or form.

All of these changes have, in addition, implications for the methods of comparative analysis. Whether considering labor law or simply legal comparison in general, comparatists are increasingly inclined to note the limits of the traditional comparative method, observing, for example, the diminishing returns that can be expected from such traditional comparative activities as taxonomizing formal systemic differences.[100] As the forgoing discussion has suggested, tracing the implications of globalization for the project of comparison in labor law reveals not simply the increasing difficulty of engaging in such activities, but also the growing disutility in attempting to do so. It is increasingly clear that more than simply typologies and evolutionary trajectories are needed,[101] and that we need more than simply the actions and responses of the nation state as the object of analysis. Rather than merely the sources and character of labor market norms, it could be that the processes of norm generation are now an important, independent focus of attention. For example, when it comes to identifying the drivers of

---

[100] Arthurs, 'Compared to What?', *supra* note 3, 594.

[101] Annelise Riles, 'Comparative Law and Socio-legal Studies', in *The Oxford Handbook of Comparative Law*, 776, Mathias Reimann and Reinhard Zimmerman (eds) (Oxford: Oxford University Press, 2006).

change, perhaps the object of study might move from nation states to knowledge practices and epistemic communities.[102]

What might these expanded comparative law projects encompass? How should we identify the range and role of legal and other norms in the work practices of contemporary labor markets? How do diverse norms and practices relate to each other? While there is no single way to engage these issues, we suggest that the comparative project in labor law must now come to grips with the intertwined questions of *scale, causality and scope*. *Scale*: At what level are the norms that need to be compared now located? How do comparisons adapt to the fact that the units of analysis are no longer necessarily, or solely, nation states? *Causality*: How can comparisons endogenize or incorporate globalization, viewing it both as a factor that affects norms at multiple levels as well as an outcome of ongoing interaction between those norms? And finally – *Scope*: What is the range of norms that should be compared, if labor law is now displaced and dispersed into other bodies of law? The following examples illustrate such possibilities, but clearly do not exhaust them.

(i) Scale

The study of comparative labor law under conditions of globalization requires the consideration of norms operating at different levels. As we have described, global transformations have provoked the emergence of many new forms of transnational law that are distinct from both national law and traditional forms of international labor law such as ILO Conventions. These include new regional norms and practices, sub-national norms, as well as norms that apply to non-territorial units such as multi-national companies, sectors and industries. To complicate things further, these norms may be both formal and informal, and they may be promulgated or supported by a wide range of actors and institutions. The impact of the manifold sources and levels of labor law is immense and far-reaching, and, we suggest, raises (at least) two sets of questions at the meta-level.

One set of questions concerns how these norms interrelate. A classic function of labor law is to order the relationship between different types of norms. In traditional state-centered regimes, labor law prescribes when contract, regulatory standards and collectively-bargained norms apply, and to whom they apply. Drawing on doctrines and principles such as preemption, the hierarchy of norms, derogation and the like, labor law sorts out the relationship among competing norms. When the scale or level of labor law changes, however, and the sources of norms become more diverse, dispersed and, oft-times, less-formal, new sorting instruments may be required. Indeed, a comparative study of the various sorting instruments themselves may be required. Moreover, when seeking to model and analyze the relationship among different norms and regimes, we may need to resort not only to public international law but to techniques and templates for regulatory co-ordination and interface drawn from private international law as well.[103]

---

102 Horatia Muir Watt, 'Globalization and Comparative Law', in ibid.

103 For arguments that private international law provides important conceptual devices in the context of globalization and the transnationalization of legal relations, see Robert Wai, 'The Interlegality of Private International Law', 71 *Law and Contemporary Legal Problems* 107

The second set of questions concerns processes of change in labor law. We have described a variety of ways in which labor law norms are subject to pressure under conditions of globalization. While there are a variety of means by which these processes may be modeled or captured, the neo-institutional economics literature provides one way to formalize these processes, indicating four potential paths by which norms and institutions might be transformed: displacement, layering, drift, and conversion.[104] Displacement and layering refer to more formal processes of change, the former suggesting that some norms supplant others, and the latter indicating situations in which norms accumulate to create new ones. Drift and conversion address less formal processes of change, in which different norms affect one another and undergo incremental stages of latent transformation as a result. This heuristic is particularly useful as it permits the diachronic study of institutional change in addition to the synchronic study of the sorting and interaction of rules within different systems and levels of labor law.

These sets of questions signal two complementary paths for further comparative investigation, one that emphasizes form and process, the other substance. More concretely, studies of process might look into how the *locus* or site of norm generation affects the development and substance of norms at work. For example, in comparing industry norms or corporate codes to state-centered labor law, a study of process could ask: Which actors participate in determining the substantive norms? Who are they accountable to? Which interests motivate them? Who can intervene in the process? How are conflicting interests settled? To what extent is the process visible and transparent? Can the process itself be amended to be more inclusive? Who is affected by the norms but remains outside the norm-generating process? How are power relations constituted by different processes, and what consequences ensue for the affected workers and for other actors as well? In brief, rather than merely comparing different end-norms in a global setting, a comparative study, we suggest, can usefully focus on the different types of process through which these end norms are produced.[105] While questions of process may have been of lesser significance as long as the comparison took place between statutes of comparable states or between cases of comparable national courts, once norms emerge from distinct political and social processes with very different bases of legitimacy, accountability and participation, questions of process become ever more important; indeed they may become central to the comparative exercise.

Studies of substance, by contrast, might focus on the character of the emerging norms. Here, the following questions might arise. Do these new regimes reflect the classic concerns of labor law to re-balance the bargaining power of workers against capital? Are they oriented toward co-operative engagement in the workplace? To what

(2008); Karen Knop, Ralf Michaels and Annelise Riles, 'Forward: Transdisciplinary Conflict of Laws', 71 *Law and Contemporary Legal Problems* 1 (2008).

104 Mahoney and Thelen, *supra* note 64.

105 Judy Fudge and Guy Mundlak, 'Justice in a Globalizing World: Resolving Conflicts Involving Workers Rights Beyond the Nation State', in: *Global Justice and International Labour Rights*, Yosi Dahan, Hanna Lerner and Faina Milman (eds) (Cambridge: Cambridge University Press, forthcoming 2015).

extent do they invest unions or worker associations with significant governance power with regard to the terms and conditions of work or the direction of the enterprise more broadly? Or do they primarily advance norms of flexibility and competition? In short, what vision of work and industrial relations informs these regimes? And what can we say about their likely impact on the status and concerns of workers?

There is an almost limitless number of comparative projects rendered possible, even necessary, by the emerging, often transnational, forms of labor market and workplace governance. They include: comparisons of corporate codes; studies of regional trade and human rights arrangements; and interrogation of internal firm or industry labor practices, including their similarities and differences in different locales. Common to all of these projects is the fact that they transcend the traditional practice of comparing the law of one state to that of the other, as well as the seemingly more global comparison of norms at similar levels (one region to another, one corporate code to another). Instead, these projects allow – and may require – the comparison of regimes and norms that operate at different scales or levels and that, for that reason, appear to be distinct.

(ii) Causality

A second set of comparative questions seeks to understand how global norms affect national norms, and *vice versa*. Among the questions here are: when and how states adopt global norms, the extent to which such adoption provokes real change in domestic or municipal law, and in what direction labor market and workplace norms are shifting as a result. For example, what are the processes by which global norms enter the domestic realm? What incentives do particular states face to adopt, modify, or reject such norms? At the same time, the dual endogeneity to which we alluded earlier suggests that such an inquiry should also look at the influence of state norms on the development of global norms. Are there instances in which the domestic norms of particular states come to predominate transnationally, effectively becoming 'global' in their reach? More generally, how do transnational norms and ideologies such as the Washington/Geneva consensus reflect or absorb the norms of specific localities?

Both inquiries are indicated in studies of convergence among national systems, as well those that consider the range of divergence in the implementation of universal norms. Because global norms are often affected by political interaction among states, as well as the engagement of non-state actors in processes of regulation and governance, this type of comparative project might involve empirical research into the determinants of the positions and actions of states with regard to global labor norms. Such studies might consider, for example, what drives or impedes the support for new labor conventions or what motivates the inclusion of labor rights and new mechanisms of dispute resolution in bilateral and regional trade and investment regimes. Similarly, they may seek to account for the highly varied approaches to compliance, enforcement and the exercise of discretion in the implementation of trade-related protective arrangements that can be observed among the participants in such regimes. Here, it seems important to note that nation states typically do not act alone: at the same time as states may be implementing transnational or international norms, they are very likely to be subject to protest and pressure by INGOs, industry lobbyists and other actors in the economic, social and political spheres who, in furtherance of projects and interests of their own, seek alternatively to encourage or to discourage them from adopting or implementing those norms at the domestic level.

An additional set of questions that pertains to causality seeks to understand how states attempt to position themselves within the emerging global economic order. We might ask, for example, why some states attempt to accommodate, facilitate or take advantage of global economic processes and pressures on their labor forces while others seek to inhibit, diminish or block their effects, considering as well as the strategies they adopt in furtherance of their perceived interests. Such a comparison might look in the first instance at: different state approaches to structural unemployment caused by global changes; the use of income transfers, skills and training programs and other mechanisms to mitigate the effects of trade- or technology-induced labor market disruptions; or the regulatory and policy instruments, including trade barriers, by which states attempt to maintain market share and prevent the undercutting of production costs by other states. Further questions will doubtless emerge as important subjects of comparative study in the future.

It might be observed that these types of inquiries still serve to sustain the nation state as the primary unit of analysis; in the former, for example, the state acts *vis-à-vis* international agents. Yet, such approaches can be equally useful when thinking of institutions and actors beyond the nation state. Similar forms of analysis can be conducted on non-state actors and hybrid public/private initiatives in order to illuminate the ways in which they affect, and are affected by, different global forces and arrangements. Just as with states, it is possible to compare the way that firms, industries and other private actors create, influence and adopt, global norms. To put it differently, questions of scale and causality are not matters of exclusive interest to states; rather, they are relevant to comparative analysis in all of its forms.

(iii) Scope

Even if national units and national law remain the subjects of the comparative study, the scope of inquiry must change: under conditions of globalization, the study of the law of the workplace, comparative or not, must now take account of a much wider range of legal rules and institutions. The traditional core of labor law includes the panoply of norms found in employment standards and negotiated in both collective agreements and deliberative *fora* such as works councils. While it might be assumed that legal rules and institutions beyond this core have only peripheral or tangential relations to the field of labor law, given their effects upon work and labor markets, we suggest that some such norms and institutions are now properly thought of simply as an integral part of the law of work.[106] This is a claim perhaps best made, and illustrated, in reverse: if the law beyond the conventional subjects of collective bargaining law, employment standards, and discrimination law does *not* form part of the law of work, then we are at risking of excluding from view and analysis many of the legal rules, norms and institutions that are most important to work and to labor markets in an era of

---

[106] Kerry Rittich, 'Fragmented Work and Multi-level Labour Market Governance: Informality, Crisis Policy and an Expanded "Law of Work"', in: *Critical Approaches to Global Governance*, (Gráinne de Búrca, Claire Kilpatrick and Joanne Scott (eds) (Oxford: Hart Publishing, 2014).

globalization. As one scholar put it, '[f]iscal, monetary, social welfare, education, immigration and trade policies – not labor statutes – determine structural and cyclical changes in the labor market and their consequences for workers'.[107]

Moreover, forces of globalization are themselves eroding the idea that there is a stable core to labor law. For example, the main barriers to employability for many workers may be migration and citizenship laws that constrain their ability to enter formal employment relations and/or acquire and transfer social security and pension rights across jurisdictional lines. These disabilities, important not only for high-tech nomads who move from one country to another, but also for agricultural workers employed through circular migration arrangements, exemplify the gaps created by the lack of unity between territory, employers and the location of work itself.

Because the norms, rules and practices that are relevant to workers may be located in a wide variety of legal rights and institutions, it is necessary to avoid any *a priori* lexical ordering of the elements of labor law. Rather, the form and location of labor law should itself be taken as a question for investigation. However, an initial taxonomy would likely identify the following fields as potential sites of interest and analysis. It is clear that human rights, constitutional provisions and other basic or fundamental rights have had a significant impact on the discussion and analysis of labor law, in general and comparative labor law in particular.[108] As already noted, two other legal fields – trade law and immigration law – have become particularly important at times of intense globalization because they govern the trans-border movement of commodities and human beings, respectively. Both national and international regimes and norms of corporate law, investment and banking law, and taxation also have an effect on the movement of capital and, by extension, on employment and wage levels.

Aside from the laws that govern the movement of goods, people, capital and services directly, there are other legal norms which, while local or national in nature, are significant to – and affected by – the individual, organizational, commercial and political choices made in times of increased trans-border activity. First and foremost here are social laws, broadly defined as welfare law, social insurance arrangements, pensions and other forms of public and private norms that mitigate social risks. A second, related, set of relevant norms are located in the field of industrial policy: here, global pressures and forces are visibly affecting both the supply and the demand side, from labor force education and training arrangements to strategies aimed at encouraging foreign direct investment. The import of these changes is already clear, for example, in comparative analyses that study entrepreneurship within small enterprises

---

107 Arthurs, 'Compared to What?', *supra* note 3; Rittich, ibid.

108 See, for example, Volume 34(1) of the *Comparative Labor Law and Policy Journal* that is devoted to Precarious Work and Human Rights (2013); Colin Fenwick and Tonia Novitz (eds), *Human Rights at Work*, (Oxford: Hart Publishing, 2010); James A. Gross and Lance Compa (eds), *Human Rights in Labor and Employment Relations: International and Domestic Perspectives* (Ithaca NY: Cornell University Press, 2009); Philip Alston (ed), *Labour Rights as Human Rights*, (Oxford University Press, 2005), Roger Blanpain (ed), *Labour Law, Human Rights and Social Justice: Liber Amicorum in Honour of Ruth Ben-Israel* (Leiden: Kluwer Law International, 2001).

as a way of overcoming unemployment,[109] and in theoretical contributions that point to the re-location of labor law within the domain of industrial policy.[110] In times of financial crisis – the likelihood and frequency of which may very well be affected by intensified economic integration as well as policies of capital account liberalization – fiscal and monetary policy must be added to the mix as well.

These fields and studies, however, are far from exhaustive. Even acknowledging that labor law has always been polycentric and multi-faceted, when an inventory of arrangements that now have an effect on work and labor markets is drawn up, it becomes clear that globalization has intensified the importance of a broad range of private as well as public law fields. In many contexts, contract law, property rights, tort law, and family law, for example, are newly relevant, to work opportunities, to the distribution of gains from work, and to the choices individuals make about whether, and when, to enter the labor market. At the same time, as was demonstrated in the previous section, soft law and informal institutions and practices may be just as, or even more, important to the transformation of work as formal legal arrangements. A taxonomy of labor law must, therefore, also consider the effects of myriad bureaucratic and administrative policies, managerial practices, and efforts at sectoral co-ordination both within and across national borders on the constitution of work and the operation of labour markets.

Finally, it is important to note that the expansion of labor law into numerous fields and sub-systems, as well as its imbrication in different institutions and governance projects, may portend significant changes at the level of substance and institutional design. Labor laws designed by trade or economic development ministries, for example, can be expected to reflect a different set of logics and priorities than those housed in departments or ministries devoted specifically to labor. The same dynamic is of course true at the international or transnational level: when it comes to questions of labor law and workers' rights, we should not be surprised if labor organizations have different analyses of labor issues than do institutions devoted to economic concern or human rights.

(b) Globalization and Labor Market Governance: Reflections on Comparative Method

These proposed trajectories for projects in comparative labor law are designed to indicate the complexity of the enterprise at a time when globalization has profoundly altered the place, significance, and authority of national labor law. We have attempted to identify the multiplicity of venues in which labor norms are now authored, and the expansive set of norms that need to be taken into consideration as a result. We have

---

[109] Marc Cowling and William Bygrave, 'Entrepreneurship, Welfare Provision and Unemployment: Relationships Between Unemployment, Welfare Provision and Entrepreneurship in Thirty-Seven Nations Participating in the Global Entrepreneurship Monitor (GEM) 2002', 28 *Comp. Lab. L & Pol. J.* 617 (2007).

[110] John Howe, 'The Broad Idea of Labour Law: Industrial Policy, Labour Market Regulation, and Decent Work', in: *The Idea of Labor Law*, Guy Davidov and Brian Langille (eds) (Oxford: Oxford University Press, 2011).

also indicated the complex interactions among regimes and actors that may result from the multiplication of sources and norms of labor law. Finally, we have tried to suggest not only the manner in which globalization now affects labor law, work and labor markets, but also the fact that the very forms that globalization may take along with their different implications for workers and other actors, are themselves the product of legal rules and policy decisions both within and beyond the traditional compass of labor law.

In so doing, we hope to have illuminated why it is that comparisons can be usefully made both between and within different levels, as well as across different fields of law, be it upon the basis of procedural dimensions such as accountability and representation, the ways in which states or other agents both intervene in and respond to global processes, or upon other bases entirely. Comparative projects that depart from the task of simply finding similar units, similar institutions and unidirectional causality in favor of comparing institutional processes and common transformative impulses may reveal both similar and quite different effects and outcomes. They may, for example, illuminate complex processes in which norms that are rooted in different and non-comparable sources layer one on top of the other, displace one another, or transform each other in myriad unpredictable ways.

It is worth recalling that labor law has always been informed by distinct normative goals and assumptions. In the era of globalization, traditional concerns about worker voice, bargaining power and solidarity contend with claims about the institutional demands of competitiveness, efficiency and productivity, and the importance of protecting the individual rights of market actors. If globalization changes the norms and assumptions that animate labor law, because it diffuses new regulatory norms and ideals along with trade, products and labor, if it seems to make some forms of labor market regulation more possible and desirable while other forms become less so, and if globalization is itself built through particular epistemic and governance projects, then, in future, comparative labor law work must engage with these norms, regulatory ideals and knowledge practices in greater depth.

While these complexities compel significant deviations from the standard approach to comparative law, it is also the case that they track new trends and developments that are visible in comparative law in general. More importantly, they open up new possibilities for identifying the many forces, both common and distinct, that operate on labor law in different contemporary contexts. If comparison remains an important method for clarifying legal choices and alternatives, as well as for revealing deep seated logics and conjunctural developments that may affect the evolution of law, then grappling with more comparators and doing so in more complex and varied ways promises to be as useful – if not more useful – an exercise for labor law as the comparison between or among nation states.

PART II

THEMATIC COMPARISONS

4. The subjects of labor law: 'Employees' and other workers

Guy Davidov, Mark Freedland and Nicola Kountouris

I. INTRODUCTION

Who is an employee? Which workers ought to be covered by the protective panoply offered by labor law? These are questions with a long history. Courts all over the world have been struggling with these issues since the beginning of modern labor law, approximately a century ago, but variations of the same question had been troubling courts for several centuries beforehand. Laws regulating the labor market usually give rights to 'employees' without defining this term. Frequently confronted with the need to decide if one can claim such labor/employment rights or not, courts had to develop tests and indicia to assist in this task and provide guidance to employers and workers. Those tests have developed over the years. Occasionally, the legislature has also sought to take the lead in this area by introducing specific legislation aimed at recognizing labor rights to particularly defined categories of 'employees' or 'workers'. One useful way to approach this topic is accordingly by way of an historical analysis (Linder, 1989; Deakin and Wilkinson, 2005).

As in many other fields, the law on 'who is an employee' has not always been consistent and coherent. It is therefore extremely valuable to examine the law (especially case-law) of one legal system deeply and expose inconsistencies, shortcomings in application and hidden goals/assumptions. Such a descriptive/analytical/critical approach to study this problem has also been very useful (Freedland and Kountouris, 2011; Fudge, Tucker and Vosko, 2002).

'Who is an employee' is also a question with a heavy normative baggage. A decision on 'employee' status usually determines if one is entitled to a significant package of rights or to no protection at all. It establishes a line between a group of workers who enjoy substantial regulatory support, and a group who has to accept the dictates of market forces. Developing and applying tests to decide who is an employee is therefore equal to deciding the scope of labor law, which obviously necessitates an engagement with the normative foundations of this field. To determine the scope of labor law, one needs to have a clear view about its goals and justifications. Another useful way to approach this topic is therefore through a normative analysis (Davidov, 2002).

In the current contribution we take a different perspective – comparative – but this could prove useful for all the other perspectives mentioned above as well (Veneziani, 1986; Hepple and Veneziani, 2009). Our aim is to highlight similarities and differences between different legal systems. This cross-national analysis can in turn assist the national analyses. Understanding how others have been approaching the same problem can help us better understand our own legal system, including in terms of its historical development and in identifying shortcoming, inconsistencies and hidden assumptions.

Understanding to what extent the problem and solutions are universal can also assist us in identifying the normative foundations behind the law.

We are aware, of course, of the difficulties in comparing different labor law regimes. It seems, however, that such difficulties are not very pronounced in the specific context of determining who is an employee. Because this question is so fundamental – deciding who gets to enter through the gates of labor law – the answer is not strongly dependent on complex characteristics of the labor law system itself (at least compared with other labor law problems). Nonetheless, being sensitive to this concern, we focus our attention in this chapter on legal systems we feel reasonably familiar with: UK, USA, Canada, Italy, France, Spain and Israel – with some (more minor) references to other legal systems as well.

The chapter proceeds as follows. Part II provides a brief overview of the tests used in different countries to decide if one is an employee (and covered by labor law), showing some points of diversity but for the most part significant similarities, with a trend towards greater convergence. The chapter then examines some relatively recent developments in different legal systems through three prisms. First we discuss the response in different countries to employers' evasion attempts (Part III). We show how in some systems courts and legislatures remain inactive in the face of evasion, and the stagnation of the law leaves room to massive misclassification of employees as independent contractors. In other countries, on the other hand, creative solutions have been used to contain or minimize this problem. Next we consider the dialogue between the judiciary and the legislature in determining who is an employee (Part IV). We show how in some countries, judicial approaches to the problem have triggered a legislative response, while in others the legislature remains silent, possibly to signal approval or simply out of disinterest. Finally, we examine the breaking of the binary divide between employees and independent contractors (Part V). We show that a third (intermediate) category has been added in an increasing number of countries, as a response to similar problems in classifying workers who share only *some* of the characteristics of employees. In the conclusion (Part VI) we return to reflect on the issues of diversity vs. convergence, in light of the developments discussed in the previous parts.

II. BETWEEN DIVERSITY AND CONVERGENCE

The basic structure of the 'employee' category is similar across the different legal systems we have surveyed, and includes three pillars. First, the term appears in legislation but its definition (if there is one at all) leaves broad room for judicial discretion.[1] Courts have accordingly stepped in and developed tests and indicia – which they apply to decide if one is an 'employee' or not (for a comparative overview see

[1] Cf. e.g. the UK Employment Rights Act, 1996, c. 18, § 230(1)–(2); the Italian Civil Code, Codice civile [C.c.], art. 2094; the French Labor Code, CODE DU TRAVAIL [C. TRAV.] art. L. 1211-1; the Indian Industrial Disputes Act, 1947, s. 2(s); and the Japanese Labor Standards Law, art. 9; though compare the broader definition contained in the South African Labor Relations Act 66 of 1995 § 213, or in the Irish Industrial Relations Act 1990 (Act No. 19/1990), s. 23.

Casale, 2011, especially Ch. 2). Second, although the employment relationship is contractual, the agreement of the parties concerning the status of 'employee' is not determinative (ILO, 2005, at 7). Sometimes courts do show a degree of deference to contractual stipulations – and there are important differences between legal systems in this respect, which we discuss shortly – but it is generally understood that the mere agreement of an employee to be considered an independent contractor cannot be sufficient reason to deprive her of employment rights. Third, courts use multi-factor tests, which include a number of components neither of which is determinative in itself (Casale, 2011, at 54–57). The idea is to consider all the factors together and make a decision based on the picture emerging from the cumulative evidence. Sometimes the examination is formulated as a two-stage test, the first stage including some *necessary* preliminary requirements, for example an agreement of work for pay, and the performance of work personally. However even those requirements are understood to have exceptions in most countries (for example, getting occasional help from someone does not preclude the possibility of a contract to perform the work personally;[2] and the fact that one was not paid still leaves open the possibility that one was *supposed* to get paid[3]).

As far as this general structure is concerned, the main area of divergence concerns the weight attributed to the contract. In some countries the contractual terms – almost always drafted by the employer – play no role in determining the status of 'employee'. If the facts of the relationship appear to contradict what is written in the contract, then the contract is simply ignored (ILO, 2005, at 24–5). This approach is based on the understanding that there is inequality of bargaining power between the parties, or at least market failures that systematically favor the employer, coupled with the fact that employment regulations are costly for employers, creating a strong incentive to try to evade them. Under these circumstances, deference to the contract means that employers are given the power to unilaterally escape their legal responsibilities. In other legal systems an employer enjoys a presumption in favor of the status agreed in the contract, however this can be rebutted if the facts suggest otherwise. In practice, in Israel for example, such presumptions have not been very meaningful; courts tend to examine the facts and usually ignore the written contract.[4]

The UK is notable for taking a different route, at least until recently, with courts showing significant degree of deference to the written contract. Although it has been long recognized that 'sham' arrangements will not be enforced, the burden of proving a 'sham' has been traditionally extremely high (Davies, 2009; Bogg, 2012). In many cases over the years, British courts have tended to favor contractual stipulations over the true nature of the relationship, which even from the judgments themselves can be seen to be entirely different.[5] Notably, the specialized employment tribunals have been

---

2 See, e.g., *James v. Redcats (Brands) Ltd*, [2007] UKEAT 296 (I.R.L.R.).

3 See, e.g., *Sarugi v. The National Insurance Institute* 39 PDA 686 [2001] (Isr.).

4 See, e.g., *Issac v. Tahal* 36 PDA 817 [1998] (Isr.).

5 For a recent example, see *Stringfellows Restaurants Ltd v. Quashie* [2012] EWCA Civ. 1735, [2007] UKEAT 296 (I.R.L.R.).

more sensitive to the discrepancy between contract and reality,[6] but this approach has been consistently rejected by the higher courts for many years.[7] Very recently, however, there seems to be a positive change of heart among British judges. In a recent case the Court of Appeal noted that 'the focus of the enquiry must be to discover the *actual* legal obligations of the parties. To carry out that exercise, the tribunal will have to examine … evidence of how the parties conducted themselves in practice',[8] and the Supreme Court concluded that '[t]he question in every case is … what was the *true agreement* between the parties'[9] and even added that 'the relative bargaining power of the parties must be taken into account in deciding whether the terms of any written agreement in truth represent what was agreed and the true agreement will often have to be gleaned from all the circumstances of the case, of which the written agreement is only a part'.[10] It remains to be seen whether this trend will continue, but there are certainly signs that the UK is heading towards greater convergence with other countries in this respect.

In terms of the tests themselves, there is some variation in the number of tests (factors, indicia) used in different countries and their exact articulation. For example, in Canada courts sometime refer to a 'fourfold test',[11] while in the US courts prefer a 13-factor test or even a 20-factor test.[12] The ILO Recommendation concerning the

---

6 The President of the Employment Appeal Tribunal, Elias J., noted in *Consistent Group Ltd v. Kalwak* [2007] UKEAT 560 (I.R.L.R.) [57]–[58]:

> The concern to which tribunals must be alive is that armies of lawyers will simply place substitution clauses, or clauses denying any obligation to accept or provide work in employment contracts, as a matter of form, even where such terms do not begin to reflect the real relationship. … In other words, if the reality of the situation is that no-one seriously expects that a worker will seek to provide a substitute, or refuse the work offered, the fact that the contract expressly provides for these unrealistic possibilities will not alter the true nature of the relationship.

7 See, e.g., *Consistent Group Ltd v. Kalwak* [2008] EWCA Civ. 430, 505 (I.R.L.R.).

8 *Protectacoat Firthglow Ltd v. Szilagyi* [2009] 835 (I.C.R.), [2009] 365 (I.R.L.R.) [53] (emphasis added).

9 *Autoclenz Ltd v. Belcher* [2011] 4 745 (All ER), [2011] 820 (I.R.L.R.) [29] (emphasis added).

10 Ibid., at [35].

11 Following the Privy Council decision in *Montreal v. Montreal Locomotive Works Ltd* [1947] 1 (D.L.R.) 161. The four factors are control; ownership of the tools; chance of profit; risk of loss.

12 *Nationwide Mutual Insurance Co. v. Darden*, 503 U.S. 318 (1992) (quoting *Community for Creative Non-Violence v. Reid*, 490 U.S. 730 (1989), for the 13-factor test, and mentioning the IRS 20-factor test). The 13 factors are:

> In determining whether a hired party is an employee under the general common law of agency, we consider the hiring party's right to control the manner and means by which the product is accomplished. Among the other factors relevant to this inquiry are the skill required; the source of the instrumentalities and tools; the location of the work; the duration of the relationship between the parties; whether the hiring party has the right to assign additional projects to the hired party; the extent of the hired party's discretion over when and how long to work; the method of payment; the hired party's role in hiring and paying

employment relationship lists 14 factors.[13] Some countries put most emphasis on 'control', while others refer to 'integration' and yet others to 'subordination'. But notwithstanding such variations, the tests are surprisingly similar across jurisdictions (for longer comparative reviews, see Davidov, 2002; Countouris, 2007, at 57–83). Courts in different countries ultimately ask two general questions. First, to what extent is the worker under the control of the employer (or: subordinated to the employer; or: integrated into the business of the employer). The stronger the signs of control/subordination/integration, the more one is likely to be considered an employee. Second, to what extent is there evidence that the worker operates through an independent business (or, conversely, is dependent on the specific employer). The stronger the signs of independence, the less likely is one to fall within the coverage of labor law. The various factors seem to be directed – even if usually not explicitly – at assisting these two general investigations. Most courts give more emphasis to the issue of control (integration, subordination). But the degree of economic dependence is also usually examined – if not explicitly, then at least implicitly. Indeed, over the years there has been some movement, in many countries, towards greater emphasis on this second test – at the very least in the sense of examining the investment in tools, the risk of loss and chance of profit, and similar indicia of economic independence.

But these commonalities aside, judiciaries in different legal systems will tend to assign to particular tests or indicia a greater weight. The tests themselves leave broad room for judicial discretion, so it is hardly surprising that there are significant variations in the way these tests have been applied in different countries. As recently noted by the Labor Court of Johannesburg, these tests are, perhaps inevitably, 'qualitative rather than quantitative. [T]he nature of the relationship cannot be determined simply by comparing the number of indicators for and against the existence of an employment relationship [...] some indicators necessarily tell us far more about

---

assistants; whether the work is part of the regular business of the hiring party; whether the hiring party is in business; the provision of employee benefits; and the tax treatment of the hired party.

[13] Employment Relationship Recommendation (2006), Article 11(b):

Members should consider the possibility of defining in their laws and regulations, or by other means, specific indicators of the existence of an employment relationship. Those indicators might include: (a) the fact that the work: is carried out according to the instructions and under the control of another party; involves the integration of the worker in the organization of the enterprise; is performed solely or mainly for the benefit of another person; must be carried out personally by the worker; is carried out within specific working hours or at a workplace specified or agreed by the party requesting the work; is of a particular duration and has a certain continuity; requires the worker's availability; or involves the provision of tools, materials and machinery by the party requesting the work; (b) periodic payment of remuneration to the worker; the fact that such remuneration constitutes the worker's sole or principal source of income; provision of payment in kind, such as food, lodging or transport; recognition of entitlements such as weekly rest and annual holidays; payment by the party requesting the work for travel undertaken by the worker in order to carry out the work; or absence of financial risk for the worker.

the substance of the relationship than others'.[14] So for instance in recent years UK courts have somewhat favored the tests of 'mutuality of obligations' and control over other tests such as the 'integration test' or the 'economic reality test'. In *Stephenson v. Delphi Diesel Systems*, Elias J (as he then was) opined that:

> The significance of mutuality is that it determines whether there is a contract in existence at all. The significance of control is that it determines whether, if there is a contract in place, it can properly be classified as a contract of service, rather than some other kind of contract [...] The only question then is whether there is sufficient control to give rise to a conclusion that the contractual relationship which does exist is one of a contract of service or not.[15]

These judicial attitudes are often the consequence of different legal and jurisprudential traditions, but this does not mean that the various legal systems are irremediably tied to a process of path dependence, and legal and doctrinal changes can often lead to significant path departures. For instance in 2012 Elias LJ (as he had now become), elaborated on his opinion in *Stephenson*, quoted above, noting that:

> on reflection, it is clear that the [last sentence quoted above] is too sweeping. Control is not the only issue. Even where the work-wage relationship is established and there is substantial control, there may be other features of the relationship which will entitle a tribunal to conclude that there is no contract of employment in place even during an individual engagement. *O'Kelly* and *Ready Mixed* provide examples.[16]

A further powerful example of both the 'path-dependence' and 'path-departure' dynamic, and the occasional influence of doctrinal developments, can be provided by a string of South African judgments. In 2004, Benjamin noted that a 'seminal article written by Sir Otto Kahn-Freund', indirectly contributed to persuading South African courts to reject the 'control' test as the main or sole defining element of the contract of employment (Benjamin, 2004). As a consequence of this, ever since *Smit v. Workmen's Compensation Commissioners*, South African jurisprudence in this area of labor law had been effectively gravitated around the so-called 'dominant impression' test.[17] The test invited adjudicators to consider all aspects of the contract, without limiting themselves to ascertaining the existence of a right of supervision or control, that was not seen as the conclusive element of the employee relationship. This test was strongly criticized by a number of academic authors, including Benjamin (2004, at 791) and Brassey (1990, at 919) for being too imprecise. More recent court decisions engaged with this line of scholarship, with the Labor Court of Appeal expressly endorsing Benjamin's critical analysis[18] and suggesting that control, integration, and economic

---

14 *Kambule v. Commission for Conciliation Mediation and Arbitration and Others* 2013 (721/10) ZALCJHB 11 (JR).

15 [2003] 471 (I.C.R.) [11]-[14].

16 *Stringfellows Restaurants Ltd v. Quashie*, above note 5, [14].

17 *Smit v. Workmen's Comp.*, App. Bd., 69 Cal.2d 814 (1979); more recently considered in SA *Broadcasting Corporation v. McKenzie* 1999 (20) ILJ 585 (LAC) and *Somerset West Society for the Aged v. Democratic Nursing Organisation of SA & others* 2001 (22) ILJ 919 (LC).

18 *State Information Technology Agency (Pty) Ltd v. Commission for Conciliation, Mediation & Arbitration & others* 2008 (7) BLLR 611 (LAC) at paras 10–11.

dependence, ought to play a role in identifying the existence of a contract of employment:

> [12] … when a court determines the question of an employment relationship, it must work with three primary criteria:
>
> 1. An employer's right to supervision and control;
> 2. Whether the employee forms an integral part of the organisation with the employer; and
> 3. The extent to which the employee was economically dependent upon the employer.[19]

As noted above though, these national variations do not result from any major distinctions in the tests themselves. It is mostly a difference of practice, not a difference in theory.

It is interesting to note that most courts usually refrain from direct reference to the law in other countries, and appear to develop the law independently of concurrent developments elsewhere. There is however a certain degree of explicit cross-fertilization between various common law jurisdictions with strong historical and legal links to the law of England and Wales.[20] Also small countries may be more open to learning from the experience of other jurisdictions.[21] When reference to the law of other countries is made explicitly, the trend towards convergence is obviously expected.[22] But, to a certain extent, this trend appears to be strong even in the absence of direct references. In some cases, the adoption of lessons from other countries is mediated through academics: the South African Court, for example, relied on Benjamin when shifting emphasis to economic dependency; Benjamin himself relied to some extent on the laws of other jurisdictions.

III. BETWEEN STAGNATION AND CREATIVITY: RESPONDING TO EVASION ATTEMPTS

Employers often try to evade the costs associated with labor laws. One common method of doing so is by misclassifying employees as independent contractors (or some other group that does not enjoy labor laws). This is a global problem (on misclassification in the US, for example, see the various reports cited in Rubinstein, 2012). However the extent of the problem – its severity – depends on the reaction from courts and legislatures. If the response is swift and decisive, the practice of misclassification will wither. Employers might turn to other methods in further attempting to evade costs

---

[19] *Ibid.*, para. 12.

[20] See, e.g., the Indian Supreme Court judgment in *Workmen of Nilgiri Coop Mkt Society Ltd v. State of Tamil Nadu & Ors* (2002) 101 F.L.R. S.C 137 (2004); the Federal Court of Australia judgment in *Wilton & Cumberland v. Coal & Allied Operations Pty Ltd* (2007) 161 FCR 300; and the New Zealand Employment Court judgment in *McDonald v Ontrack Infrastructure Limited* [2010] NZEMPC 132.

[21] In Israel, the seminal National Labour Court case setting the tests for 'who is an employee' relied on a broad comparative survey; see *Netanya Municipality v. Birger* 3 PDA 177 [2001] (Isr.).

[22] Cf. *Wilton & Cumberland v. Coal & Allied Operations Pty Ltd* (2007) 161 FCR 300.

(for example, employment through temporary employment agencies), but closing the specific route is surely meaningful. Arguably, it sends a strong message to employers and lowers the level of evasion.

The first line of defense when a new practice of evasion comes to light is usually the judiciary. In Israel, for example, labor courts have been quite successful in their efforts to curtail massive misclassification during the 1990s. Arguably they have been slow to realize the severity of the problem – the extent of the phenomenon. But once realized, some clear signals were sent to employers. It was made plain that the tests will not be applied formalistically and not much weight will be given to the written contract. In borderline cases the courts gave preference to the workers. And they gave remedies that made the price of misclassification (when averted) high.[23] French courts have policed extremely effectively the boundary of their domestic 'binary divide' between employment and self-employment, often expressly reclassifying work arrangements that all parties involved had long accepted as being of an autonomous and self-employed nature.[24]

Italian courts have also refined their jurisprudence on the concept of subordination in order to render it more inclusive and contrast some of the centrifugal tendencies produced by what Hugh Collins famously described as the vertical disintegration of employment (Collins, 1990). An example is the introduction of the notion of '*subordinazione attenuata*', developed to contrast:

> the evolution of the systems of organization of labor, increasingly characterized by the tendency to outsource or tertiarize whole sectors of the cycle of production or series of specific professional skills [where] subordination becomes less and less significant, because of the impossibility of exercising full and direct control over the different phases of the activity performed.[25]

The Italian Court of Cassation, in a more recent decision, noted that:

> every human activity is susceptible of being subsumed into both an autonomous employment relationship and a subordinate one … some relationships present by their very nature an attenuated subordination [and] that subordination … is not always visible with the same intensity or the same modality in all relationships,

eventually re-qualifying a freelance translator into a dependent employee.[26]

---

[23] Specifically, Israeli courts award back wages and benefits and usually refuse to subtract benefits enjoyed because of the independent contractor status (for example tax benefits, sometime also higher wages). See, e.g., *Issac* case, above note 4. Admittedly, employers were quick to resort to alternative evasion methods, and this time the courts were, unfortunately, much slower in responding.

[24] A good example is offered by the 'Ile de la Tentation' litigation, Cour de Cassation (Soc.), Arrêt n° 1159 du 3 juin 2009 (08-40.981 à 08-40.983 / 08-41.712 à 08-41.714). It should be noted that French law allows for a 'requalification' of a contract for work even in the absence of the employer's intention to 'dissimulate' a contract of employment under the French Labor Code, CODE DU TRAVAIL [C. TRAV.] art. L. 8221-3 et L. 8221-5 (Fr.).

[25] Cf. for instance Cour de Cassation, July 6, 2001, No. 9167 (Fr.), introducing the concept of 'attenuated subordination' to include within the scope of labor law a journalist.

[26] Cour de Cassation (Soc.), Mar. 3, 2009, Bull. civ. V, No. 5080 (Fr.).

In a parallel trend, the Court of Justice of the European Union (CJEU) has become increasingly active in ensuring that the labor law protections bestowed to EU Member States' workers by European Directives were actually enjoyed by their addressees. Where it perceived that some national legal systems were in effect depriving some of their workers of these rights by misclassifying them as 'self-employed' persons, or as workers employed under *sui generis* work relations, it has boldly asserted that 'the formal classification of a self-employed person under national law does not exclude the possibility that a person must be classified as a worker within the meaning of [EU law] if his independence is merely notional, thereby disguising an employment relationship',[27] and that 'the sui generis legal nature of the employment relationship under national law cannot have any consequence in regard to whether or not the person is a worker for the purposes of European Union law'.[28] In effect, in these cases, the CJEU, while refraining from labeling these domestic arrangements as 'shams', has superimposed an EU reclassification resulting in their falling within the protective coverage of EU employment protection laws. In some more recent judgments it went even further by suggesting that, even in those cases where it is ultimately for national referring courts to determine whether a domestic worker is also a worker for the purposes of EU law, 'The Court may, however, mention to the referring court a number of principles and criteria which it *must take into account* in the course of its examination'.[29]

In other jurisdictions, courts have not acted decisively enough to curtail misclassification, though occasionally the legislature has stepped in. In the UK, the introduction of the 'worker' category in labor laws since the 1990s – and most notably in the National Minimum Wage Act 1998 – was partly designed to extend the coverage of a number of employment laws beyond the traditional 'employee' category, which courts had construed narrowly and in a way that excluded 'for example, those working under certain agency arrangements, or individuals who, while not having a contract of employment with an employer, work exclusively for that employer over a period of time without the freedom to select another 'customer' for their services – as they would be able to do if they were genuinely self-employed' (Department of Trade and Industry, 1998). The goal of this new category was to bring the numerous excluded workers back into the scope of protection. It is not clear, however, whether this can be seen as a success, given the fact that courts have interpreted the new category quite narrowly as well. We discuss this further in the next part.

In other countries, however, both courts and legislatures have failed to respond to misclassification. Such stagnation of the law leads to further exacerbation of the

---

27 Case C-256/01 *Allonby v. Accrington & Rossendale College* [2004] E.C.J. I-873, para. [71].

28 Case C-428/09 *Union Syndicale Solidaires Isère v. Premier Ministre and others* [2010] E.C.J. I-9961, para. [30].

29 Case C-393/10 *O'Brien v Ministry of Justice* [2012] 2 C.M.L.R. 25, para. [43] (our emphasis). The application of these criteria resulted in the UK Supreme Court declaring that a UK part-time judge had to be considered a worker for the purposes of the UK Part-time Workers (Prevention of Less Favourable Treatment) Regulations, 2000, S.I 2000/1551, (U.K)., implementing EU Framework Agreement on Part-Time Work Directive 1997/81, 1997 O.J. (L 14) 9 (EC). Cf. *O'Brien v. Ministry of Justice* [2013] UKSC 6, [2008] EWCA Civ. 1448.

problem. The law in the US varies across States, but overall it appears that response has been quite muted (Rubinstein, 2012).

An important element associated with creative response to evasion appears to be the reliance on a purposive approach to interpreting the term 'employee'. Some courts have explicitly mentioned the need to be mindful to the purpose of the law in this context. Interestingly, the US Supreme Court was perhaps the pioneer when adopting a purposive approach in this context in the 1940s, which lead to the adoption of an 'economic reality of dependence' test.[30] This test is still being used in the US in some contexts,[31] but the Supreme Court curiously backed away from the purposive approach, noting in the early 1990s that without contradictory direction it should be presumed that Congress intended to adopt the traditional 'common law' test.[32] This makes it difficult to respond to evasion attempts. In contrast, courts in other countries are increasingly turning to the purposive approach, explaining that the term 'employee' should be given a meaning that will best advance the goals of the law(s) using this term.[33] So far this has not led to any changes in the tests themselves, but it can certainly have an impact on the way they are being applied – generally in the direction of including more workers within the category of 'employees'. For example, in Israel people holding elected office and receiving a salary from the State have been considered in the past not to be employees – but more recently as a result of purposive analysis courts have granted them at least *some* employment-related rights.[34] And in the UK, Clarke LJ of the Supreme Court recently rejected the position that denied workers their rights because of the written contract terms, adding that '[t]his may be described as a purposive approach to the problem. If so, I am content with that description.'[35]

The purposive approach appears to be helpful for courts interested in developing the law in light of new evasion techniques. It assists courts in realizing when the purpose of the legislation is frustrated and new solutions are needed, thus fostering creativity and preventing stagnation.

---

[30] The 'economic reality' test includes the following factors: (1) control as to the manner in which the work is to be performed; (2) opportunity for profit or loss; (3) investment in equipment or materials; (4) whether the service rendered requires a special skill; (5) the degree of permanency and duration of the working relationship; and (6) the extent to which the service rendered is an integral part of the employer's business. See *United States v. Silk*, 331 U.S. 704, (1947); *Secretary of Labor v. Lauritzen*, 835 F.2d 1529, (7th Cir., 1988).

[31] The US courts use the 'economic reality' test in the context of the Fair Labor Standards Act, 29 U.S.C § 201 (1938); the 'common law' (13-factor) test in interpreting the National Labor Relations Act, 29 U.S.C. § 152(3) (1935), as well as Title VII (workplace equality) cases; and sometime a 'hybrid' test.

[32] *Nationwide Mutual Insurance*, above note 12.

[33] See, e.g., *Pointe-Claire (City) v Quebec* [1997] 1 S.C.R. 1015 (Can.) (Supreme Court of Canada); *Sarusi v. National Labor Court*, 52(4) PD 817 [1995] (Isr.) (Supreme Court of Israel); *Konrad v Victoria Police* (1999) 165 ALR 23 (Federal Court of Australia); *Autoclenz Ltd v. Belcher* [2011] 4 745 (All ER), [2011] 820 (I.R.L.R.) (Supreme Court of the UK).

[34] *Sarusi*, above note 33.

[35] *Autoclenz Ltd v. Belcher*, above note 9, at [35].

IV. THE COURTS-LEGISLATURE DIALOGUE

When legislatures use open-ended terms, designed to give courts broad room for discretion, it is hardly surprising that sometimes they will not like the result. In such cases it is perfectly legitimate for the legislature to amend the legislation in a way that will steer the courts in what is considered to be the right direction.

A dramatic example can be found in the Taft-Hartley Act of 1947, in which the US legislature reacted to a series of Supreme Court judgments from 1944 through 1947.[36] The judgments adopted an 'economic reality of dependence' test instead of the 'common-law agency' (control) test to ascertain employee status. The Republican-controlled Congress was not happy with this interpretation, which it considered an unwarranted expansion of the scope of labor laws.[37] The definition of 'employee' in the National Labor Relations Act was amended to explicitly exclude 'independent contractors'.[38] This was somewhat peculiar because the judgments in question clearly maintained the exclusion of independent contractors (Linder, 1989, at 191–2); however the obvious intention was to create a narrower scope for the concept of 'employee', and restore the emphasis on control, as opposed to economic dependence.[39] Marc Linder has argued that the main reason for this amendment was to 'confine the scope and power of unions', quite apart from the specific issue at hand (Linder, 1989, at 201). Importantly, the same legislation also excluded 'supervisors' from the definition of 'employee', thus further narrowing the protected group. Similar amendments were made during the same period in social security regulations (overriding a presidential veto) (Ibid., at 203–8).

In principle, it has been legitimate for Congress to direct the Court at the time by amending the legislation. However this does not mean that the dialogue cannot continue. As times change, judges should rethink old interpretations, in light of new realities. Moreover, the intentions of some members of Congress during the 1940s do not say anything about the intentions of current members of Congress who choose to keep the law as it is. Courts would be wise to interpret the law in light of its general purpose, not in accordance with specific intentions of the historic legislature. It is unfortunate, therefore, that the US Supreme Court neglects to continue this dialogue. Instead of rethinking old interpretations and adapting the law – something which Congress always has the ability to respond to – the Court expressed preference for a stagnant interpretation. Dramatic changes in labor markets and employment practices notwithstanding, the 'common law of agency test' – in the same conservative form – remains the controlling test in the US for setting the boundaries of protection.[40] This unfortunate conclusion ignores the fact that the legislation does not set specific detailed tests, but rather leaves broad room for discretion for the judiciary to develop tests – and implicitly, change them from time to time.

---

36 Most notably see *NLRB v. Heart Publications Inc.*, 322 U.S. 111 (1944); *United States v. Silk*, 331 U.S. 704 (1947); *Rutherford Food Corp. v. McComb*, 331 U.S. 722 (1947).

37 For a detailed and useful discussion see Linder, 1989, at 185–211.

38 National Labor Relations Act, 29 U.S.C. § 152(3).

39 *NLRB v. United Insurance Co.*, 390 U.S. 246, 254 (1968).

40 *Nationwide Mutual Insurance*, above note 12. And see Linder, 1999.

The clash between a progressive court and a conservative legislature described above is not very common. In the last few decades the US Supreme Court has a much more conservative tilt. But legislatures can certainly be unhappy with judicial interpretations from the other direction as well. In the UK, for example, when New Labor came to power during the 1990s, it sought to introduce a limited number of new labor laws, such as the National Minimum Wage Act 1998 or the Working Time Regulations 1998, which were extended to all 'workers', a concept explicitly defined to be broader than 'employee'. No less importantly, the personal scope of application of important areas of labor regulation such as anti-discrimination law has traditionally been broader than the one defined by reference to the subordinate 'employee' concept. Reflecting a practice that dates back to the 1970s UK equality laws,[41] the Equality Act 2010 applies to 'employment under a contract of employment, a contract of apprenticeship *or a contract personally to do work*' suggesting that equal-treatment protection ought to apply beyond the narrow confines of the 'contract of employment'.[42] This is no doubt equally well reflected by supranational instruments such as EU Directive 2000/78, prohibiting discrimination in relation to 'conditions for access to employment, *to self-employment or to occupation*, including selection criteria and recruitment conditions, whatever the branch of activity and at all levels of the professional hierarchy, including promotion'.[43] Arguably, the reference to such broader concepts represents at least to some extent discontent with judicial interpretations setting a relatively narrow scope of protection.

A more radical attempt to predetermine the scope of labor legislation involves setting specific detailed criteria – in effect, replacing the open-ended 'standard' with a 'rule'. This means that judicial discretion is significantly narrowed, and the problem of indeterminacy is minimized. The price, however, could be high, because a strict rule is easier to work around, and does not take into account new forms of employment that might emerge. This can perhaps explain why such attempts are not common. In Germany, between 1999 and 2002, there was an attempt to create a clear-cut list of indicia for the term employee in the social security context.[44] In Spain, a similarly prescriptive definition was introduced by Ley 20/2007, of 11 July 2007 for the newly introduced intermediate group of '*trabajadores autónomos económicamente dependientes*' (self-employed but economically dependent workers, often referred to as 'TRADEs'). Article 11 of the Law defines these workers by reference to a number of fairly detailed and prescriptive criteria, including, that of receiving from a single 'client' at least 75 per cent of their income (Fudge, 2010; Sanchez Torres, 2010). However, according to the Spanish organization *Unión de Asociaciones de Trabajadores Autónomos y Emprendedores,* in 2012 only 2.5 per cent of all Spanish

---

[41] Cf. For instance Equal Pay Act, 1970, c. 41, § 1(6) (U.K); Sex Discrimination Act, 1975, c. 65, § 82 (U.K).

[42] Though this initial ambition may have been diminished by the UK Supreme Court judgment in *Jivraj v. Hashwani*, [2011] UKSC 40, [2010] EWCA Civ. 712.

[43] Council Directive 2000/78, art. 3(1)(a), Establishing a General Framework for Equal Treatment in Employment and Occupation, 2000 O.J. (L 303) 16 (EC) (our emphasis).

[44] Initiated with the adoption of Law N. 3843 of 28 December 1998. See the analysis by Däubler, 1999. On the changes of this definition, see the critical commentary in Wank, 2005.

'TRADEs' were covered by the fairly extensive protections afforded by the Law of 2007 (UATAE 2012).

Another way for legislatures to limit the discretion enjoyed by the judiciary in classifying employment relations is by laying down a number of – typically rebuttable – legislative presumptions for classifying as dependent workers (or anyway subject to the scope of application of employment law) a number of typologies of workers or work relations that may otherwise struggle to satisfy the standard indicia of subordination employed by judges. The best example of this strategy is arguably provided by the various '*présomption de salariat*' contained in the French Labor Code in respect of, for instance, journalists (Article L7112-1), performing artists (Article L7121-3), models (Article L7123-3), or door-to-door salespersons (Article L7313-1).[45] Another system that has experimented with legal presumptions is the Dutch one. The Flexibility and Security Act of 1998 modified Article 7:610a of the Dutch Civil Code and introduced the legal presumption whereby if a worker has worked on a regular basis for his or her employer for a period of three months (or at least 20 hours a month), then a contract of employment is automatically presumed (Frans, 2011). It should be noted that this highly effective method of dealing with the intricacies of classification has been endorsed and encouraged by the International Labor Organization,[46] though few systems appear to have embraced it (International Labor Organization, 2007, at 27–29).

Another way for legislatures to correct judicial mistakes – or respond to the problems of misclassification and indeterminacy concerning 'employee' status – is by granting the government the power to make 'corrections' in regulations. A number of countries have added such powers into labor laws. Usually the Minister in charge of the law is allowed to issue an order determining that a specific group of workers shall be *deemed* to be 'employees', even if they do not appear to share the regular characteristics. An example of this approach could be found in the Dutch regulation produced after the recent liberalization of postal services, which provides that the post companies must make use of a contract of employment for their workers, with some exceptions (Frans, 2011, at 96). Unfortunately, however, it appears that such orders are rarely issued. In theory section 23 of the UK Employment Relations Act 1999 confers a similar, and if anything broader, power on the Secretary of State to provide by order 'that individuals are to be treated as parties to workers' contracts or contracts of employment'. But after a short consultation in 2002 (Department of Trade and Industry, 2002) the Labor Government decided not to avail itself of these powers.

V. BREAKING THE BINARY DIVIDE: INTERMEDIATE GROUPS

A final important development which we wish to discuss here concerns the introduction of intermediate groups, in-between 'employees' and 'independent contractors'. In some countries – notably Germany, Italy, Sweden and Canada – an intermediate category has been in existence for decades (for comparative reviews see Langille & Davidov, 1999;

[45] But see the adverse reading of these provisions given by the CJEU in Case C-255/04 *Commission v France* [2006] E.C.J. I-5251 para. [222].

[46] Employment Relationship Recommendation 2006.

Casale, 2011). Whether it is called 'dependent contractor' (as in Sweden and Canada) or 'employee-like' (as in Germany), or 'para-subordinate' (as in Italy) the idea is very similar: to allow for better refinement in the application of labor laws. Instead of an 'all or nothing' approach, it is acknowledged in these legal systems that some workers present only *some* characteristics of 'employees' but not others, and that it is justified to apply only *some* labor laws to them.

The need for such an intermediate category has perhaps been greater in some countries, given local labor market practices. In Canada, for example, there is a large sector of trucking, and a significant number of truck drivers are owner-operators. These people do not fall into the definition of 'employees' according to existing tests. However they often have only one client/employer, so they suffer from many of the same vulnerabilities as employees. Most Canadian jurisdictions have added 'dependent contractor' provisions to allow such workers access to collective bargaining mechanisms (although they do not enjoy other labor rights) (Langille & Davidov, 1999). In more recent years the need for such a category has grown in other jurisdictions as well, resulting from the proliferation of new work arrangements. A growing number of people are not employees in the traditional sense but do not have an independent business in the traditional sense either. So it is hardly surprising that additional countries have added an intermediate category in recent years – most notably Spain – and this trend can be expected to continue.

Currently the intermediate groups are quite narrow in most countries, in two respects. First, in terms of the scope of the group, it is usually based mostly on economic dependence, but for some reason there is often insistence on a degree of subordination/control. Second, in terms of the rights enjoyed by this group, those are usually very minimal, mostly limited to collective bargaining, health and safety, social security and tax treatment (at most). Most employment standards do not apply. In both respects intermediate groups can be expected to further expand, at least from a purposive view. Indeed, an important report invited by the Canadian government has advocated the granting of some additional rights to this group (Arthurs, 2006).[47]

The UK and, most notably, Spain appear to be an exception in this context. In the UK, the intermediate group introduced in the 1990s (the 'worker' category) already allows access to various employment rights, including the minimum wage (Davidov, 2005). It seems, therefore, as if British law is more advanced and more progressive compared to the law in other countries in this respect. However, as already noted, the 'employee' category in the UK has been narrowly construed by UK courts, and it could be argued that the 'worker' category barely fills the gap left by an exceedingly tight notion of 'contract of service'. As a result, the definition of the 'worker' category resembles what in other countries is the definition of 'employee' – and not the intermediate group. In Spain, TRADEs enjoy an extremely wide range of labor rights, including anti-discrimination rights[48] and even some protection against 'contractual

[47] Arthurs suggests a different name – 'autonomous workers' – to assist in distinguishing between their (full) employment rights in the collective bargaining context (as 'dependent contractors') and their (partial) rights in the employment standard context.

[48] Article 6 of Ley 20/2007, de 11 de julio, del Estatuto del trabajo autónomo.

termination'.[49] However, as noted above, the practical impact of these accrued protections has been minimal.

It should also be pointed out that the idea of an intermediate category is not without its detractors. When the Luxembourg Government was prompted by the 2006 Commission Green Paper to take a stance in respect of the concept of '*economically dependent work*' (Commission of the European Communities, 2006, at 11), it forcefully argued that it found it artificial to suggest that there is a group of economically dependent workers that are neither employees nor self-employed. This was seen as a mere means for reducing the protection enjoyed by employees; the real problem being, in their view, the existence of sham self-employed that should be recognized as salaried workers.[50] There have been similar, and equally forceful critiques to the suggestion of introducing intermediate groups in countries like France, as well as in the other existing European regulatory regimes already recognizing 'quasi-subordinate workers' (Garofalo, 2003; Hascöet, 2007; Pedrazzoli, 2006; Dalmasso, 2009). Surely when an intermediate category is considered, it should not be seen as a solution to misclassification (sham self-employment); rather, the goal should be to add some (partial) protection to people who are not (even without any sham) within the group of 'employees'.

VI. CONCLUSION

The fundamental, age-old problem of labor law is how to set the scope of the field – how to define who are (or should be) the subjects of labor law. In the current chapter we examine this problem from a comparative perspective. We started by showing that the tests and indicia used to identify 'employees' are quite similar around the world, and the trend appears to be towards greater convergence. Nonetheless, there are some differences in the way these tests are being applied. We then considered three major issues which we feel are crucial to understanding the problem of setting labor law's scope and how this problem has been addressed: the response to evasion attempts; the courts-legislature dialogue; and the introduction of intermediate categories. On all three fronts, a comparative review reveals similarities but at the same time differences. At the end of the day, the problems of evasion that drives a lot of the attempts to address the topic are similar across jurisdictions. So it is hardly surprising that courts in different countries are experimenting with similar solutions; that this is not always done at a satisfactory pace, which brings reaction from the legislature; and that similar difficulties with the binary divide often lead different legislatures to similar conclusions about the need to add a third, intermediate group.

There are still variations between the countries, and some take longer to reach the same conclusions, while others may exhibit a certain degree of aversion to particular solutions, as the example discussed in the final paragraphs of the last section suggests.

---

[49] Article 15.

[50] Contribution du Gouvernement du Grand-Duché de Luxembourg au LIVRE VERT «Moderniser le droit du travail pour relever les défis du XXIe siècle» (30 March 2007), 10. Available at http://ec.europa.eu/employment_social/labour_law/answers/documents/1_2_fr.pdf.

But the trend towards convergence is assisted by international courts (such as the CJEU) and perhaps also international instruments (such as the ILO Recommendation), and by academics exposing their courts to insights from other countries.

What can explain the greater convergence among some countries, but not others? Answering this question requires further research. We can speculate that perhaps the existence of an independent, specialized labor court leads to stronger efforts in fighting evasion attempts (including by way of adapting old tests). Also, legislative intervention – whether by way of adding an intermediate category or otherwise by legislating to change the results of judicial interpretation – requires political will and ability that are not always available (perhaps even rarely available). It would be interesting to examine in future research what are the political conditions needed to allow reform in this area. Either way, when there is willingness to address the problem – whether among judges or at the legislature – a comparative analysis should prove useful to such efforts.

REFERENCES

Arthurs, Harry. 2006. *Fairness at Work: Federal Labor Standards for the 21st Century*. Canada: Federal Labor Standard Review, 61–6.

Bogg, Alan. 2012. 'Sham Self-Employment in the Supreme Court,' 41 *Industrial Law Journal* 328–45.

Benjamin, Paul. 2004. 'An accident of history: Who is (and who should be) an employee under South African Labor Law' 25 *Industrial Law Journal (South Africa)* 787–804.

Brassey, Martin. 1990. 'The nature of employment,' 5 *Industrial Law Journal* 889.

Casale, Giuseppe (ed.). 2011. *The Employment Relationship – A Comparative Overview,* Oxford: Hart Publishing, Chapter 2.

Collins, Hugh. 1990. 'Independent contractors and the challenge of vertical disintegration to employment protection laws,' 10 *Oxford Journal of Legal Studies* 353–80.

Commission of the European Communities, *Modernising Labour Law to Meet the Challenges of the 21st Century: Green Paper*, COM (2006) 708 final (Nov. 22, 2006).

Countouris, Nicola. 2007. *The Changing Law of the Employment Relationship: Comparative Analyses in the European Context*, Burlington: Ashgate Publishing Company, 57–83.

Dalmasso, Raphaël. 2009. 'Salariés, travailleurs indépendants et travailleurs économiquement dépendants: vers une troisième catégorie juridique régissant la relation de travail?,' at http://gree.univ-nancy2.fr/digitalAssets/51826_DALMASSO.pdf.

Däubler, W. 1999. 'Working people in Germany' 21 *Comparative Labor Law & Policy Journal* 77.

Davidov, Guy. 2005. 'Who is a worker,' 34 *Industrial Law Journal* 57.

Davidov, Guy. 2002. 'The three axes of employment relationships: A Characterization of workers in need of protection,' 52 *University of Toronto Law Journal* 357.

Davies, A.C.L. 2009. 'Sensible thinking about sham transactions: Protectacoat Firthglow Ltd v Szilagyi,' 38 *Industrial Law Journal* 318–28.

Deakin, Simon, and Frank Wilkinson. 2005. *The Law of the Labour Market: Industrialization, Employment and Legal Evolution*. Oxford: Oxford University Press.

Department of Trade and Industry. 2002. *Discussion Document on Employment Status in Relation to Statutory Employment Rights*, at http://www.delni.gov.uk/employment_status_consultation_document.pdf.

Department of Trade and Industry. 1998. *Draft National Minimum Wage Regulations: Public Consultation, Annex 4*, at http://webarchive.nationalarchives.gov.uk/20031221001108/http://dti.gov.uk/er/nmwr/annex4.htm.

Freedland, Mark, and Nicola Kountouris. 2011. *The Legal Construction of Personal Work Relations*. Oxford: Oxford University Press.

Fudge, Judy. 2010. 'A Canadian perspective on the scope of employment standards, labor rights, and social protection: The good, the bad, and the ugly', 31 *Comparative Labor Law & Policy Journal* 101.

Fudge, Judy, Eric Tucker, and Leah Vosko. 2002. *The Legal Concept of Employment: Marginalizing Workers: Report for the Law Commission of Canada*.

Garofalo, M.G. 2003. 'La legge delega sul mercato del lavoro: prime osservazioni,' *RGL*, 362.

Hascöet, M. 2007. 'Le contrat de projet: le nouveau visage de la parasubordination en Italie,' *Droit Social*, 879.

Hepple, Bob and Bruno Veneziani. 2009. *The Transformation of Labour Law in Europe: A Comparative Study of 15 Countries 1945–2004*, Oxford: Hart Publishing.

International Labour Conference. 2005. *The Employment Relationship: Report V(1)*. Geneva: International Labor Office Publications, 7, 24–5.

International Labor Office. 2005. *The Employment Relationship: Report V(1)*. Geneva: ILO Publications, 7.

International Labor Organization. 2007. *The Employment Relationship: An annotated guide to ILO Recommendation No. 198*. At http://www.ilo.org/ifpdial/areas-of-work/labour-law/WCMS_172417/lang–en/index.htm, 27–9.

International Labor Organization. 2006. *The Employment Relationship: An annotated guide to ILO Recommendation No. 198*. At http://www.ilo.org/ifpdial/areas-of-work/labour-law/WCMS_172417/lang–en/index.htm, 27–9.

Langille, Brian and Guy Davidov. 1999. 'Beyond Employees and Independent Contractors: A View from Canada', 21 *Comparative Labor Law and Policy Journal* 7.

Linder, Marc. 1999. 'Dependent and independent contractors in recent U.S. labor law: An Ambiguous Dichotomy rooted in simulated statutory purposelessness', 21 *Comparative Labor Law and Policy Journal* 187.

Linder, Marc. 1989. *The Employment Relationship in Anglo-American Law: A Historical Perspective*. New York, Greenwood Press, 185–211.

Pedrazzoli, M. 2006. 'Le complicazioni dell'inutilità: note critiche sul lavoro a progetto,' in L. Mariucci, ed., *Dopo la flessibilità, cosa? Le nuove politiche del lavoro*. Mulino: Bologn, 119.

Pennings, Frans. 2011. 'The protection of working relationships in the Netherlands,' in Frans Pennings and Claire Bosse eds, *The Protection of Working Relationships: A Comparative Study*. Leiden: Kluwer Law International, 91–6.

Rubinstein, Mitchell H. 2012. 'Employees, employers, and quasi-employers: An analysis of employees and employers who operate in the borderline between an employer-and-employee relationship,' 14 *University of Pennsylvania Journal of Business Law* 605.

Sanchez Torres, Esther. 2010. 'The Spanish law on dependent self-employed workers: A new evolution in labor law', 31 *Comparative Labor Law & Policy Journal* 231.

UATAE, 2012. 'Autónomos TRADE, los nuevos esclavos del autoempleo' (Madrid, 25 Julio 2012).

Veneziani, Bruno. 1986. 'The evolution of the contract of employment,' in Bob Hepple ed., *The Making of Labour Law in Europe: A Comparative Study of Nine Countries up to 1945*. London: Mansell Publishing, 31.

Wank, Rolf. 2005. 'Labor Law in Motion: Germany,' in Roger Blanpain (ed.), *Bulletin of Comparative Labor Relations*, 53.

5. Who is an employer?

*Luisa Corazza and Orsola Razzolini**

1. INTRODUCTION

The question '*Who is an employee?*' and the problematic distinction between employees and independent contractors can be regarded as a cornerstone of labor and employment law. By contrast, the question '*Who is an employer?*' is usually neglected in labor and employment law. However, in the last decades, the profound transformations economic organizations have been experiencing have led lawyers to face new problems relating to the 'employing entity'.[1] As a consequence, the concept of employer has played an increasingly dominant role on both theoretical and practical levels.

The meaning of 'employer' can vary in different contexts. The answer to the question '*Who is an employer?*' is particularly sensitive to the different scopes of statutory protections. From a collective labor law perspective, for instance, the problem of who is the employer deals with the scope of collective bargaining and the definition of bargaining unit, thereby involving issues such as the boundaries of the economic activity, the business sector where the firm operates and the effective control of the firm on entrepreneurial strategies. In employment law, the question '*Who is the employer?*' affects the distribution of employer liabilities and obligations such as the duty to pay wages, the breach of minimum labor standards (e.g. health and safety protection), the prohibition of discrimination.

Furthermore, the concept of employer also needs to be discussed in a diachronic perspective. The employer is not a 'static entity', but rather an entity that can experience a number of transformations through mergers, acquisitions, outsourcing or insourcing strategies.

The problem of defining who is an employer involves crucial economic issues, such as the financial reliability of the firm, the economic independence of businesses, the boundaries of the firm, entrepreneurial strategies, national and international investments. Being employed by one firm or the other can make a significant difference to the status and the perspectives of the employee.

Moreover, by observing labor and employment law through the lens of the employer, several crucial issues concerning the role of labor and employment regulation arise, such as the freedom of contract, competitiveness, and productivity. The question '*Who*

* Luisa Corazza is the author of sections 3 and 4.1; Orsola Razzolini is the author of sections 2 and 4.2. The introductory and the concluding parts are the result of a joint effort of both authors.

[1] The concept of 'employing entity' has been used by MARK FREEDLAND, *The Personal Employment Contract*, Oxford University Press, 2003, at 26 ff.

is the employer?' then leads to other questions; what is the role of labor and employment law with respect to economic development or whether employer's competitiveness should be a concern for labor lawyers.

The global perspective has further complicated the debate on the employer issue. Among the factors leading to firms' restructuring, delocalization has played an increasingly dominant role in recent years. Firms are increasingly organized in transnational structures, and employment seems to be a factor of production that is subject to contingent changes and replacement.

However, as the governments of nations and even firms are under global economic pressure, national labor laws can hardly keep up with economic transformation. Corporations make strategic choices on how to acquire and deploy their human resources, turning to 'law shopping' across borders, while avoiding national laws they deem unfavorable. In the new transnational value chains, the identification of the employer entity plays a pivotal role.

Variations in the legal identification of the 'employer' can be usefully explored through the lens of two legal doctrines: the single employer model, which has played an important role in Continental Europe for several decades, and the plural employer one, mainly reflected in the common law. Indeed, most of regulatory techniques used by different countries can be connected to one or the other.

This chapter focuses on the distinction between the single and plural employer model. Its aim is to demonstrate and describe the main characters of these two models, highlighting differences between and within each model, and point at indications for processes of convergence between the two models.

The first part (sections 2 and 3) examines the single and plural employer models by analysing their historical roots and rationales. The second part (section 4) considers the convergence of the two models by taking into account the two cases of subcontracting and the grouping of companies. The conclusion (section 5) observes a general global trend toward a plural employer model. We suggest that legal systems are evolving from the traditional connection of the employment relationship to the Fordist firm and its owner toward the connection of the employment relationship with network forms of organizations.

2. THE SINGLE EMPLOYER MODEL

The idea of the employer as a 'single indivisible entity' is commonly accepted in Europe and in the U.S.[2] This idea appears to be rooted both in the economic phenomenon of the vertical Fordist firm and in the legal development of the bilateral employment contract of the days of master and servant.

After the advent of the vertical employment firm, in several legal systems the boundaries of the legal concept of employer have been drawn as to coincide with the

[2] *See*, among others, SIMON DEAKIN, 'The Complexities of the Employing Enterprise', in GUY DAVIDOV, BRIAN LAGILLE (eds), *Boundaries and Frontiers of Labour Law*, Hart Publishing, Oxford and Portland Oregon, 2006, at 275; JEREMIAS PRASSL, 'The Notion of the Employer', (2013) 129 *L.Q.R.*, 380

boundaries of the economic organization within which the work is performed.[3] Insofar as the Fordist vertical firm consisted of expensive material infrastructures and other means of production, it represented the ideal 'virtual place' for the allocation of employment costs and liabilities. The owner of the firm was then regarded as the most reliable employer, capable to bear and to fulfill employment costs and liabilities. In the U.S., the Supreme Court held that, for the purpose of national wage and hour law, the employer is 'the person or group of person who own and manage the enterprise'.[4]

It is worth noting that it is not the identity of the employer/entrepreneur that matters, but rather the link of the employee to the impersonal employing entity.[5] The so-called principle of the 'de-personalization of the employment relation' particularly emerges in the transfer of undertaking regulation: the changes in the employer's identity do not affect the continuity of the employment contract strictly linked to the employing entity.[6]

As a consequence, it is not surprising that one of the main tests used to identify the employer is the ownership of the firm, together with the exercise of the entrepreneurial powers of control, direction and coordination over the working activity. As Ronald Coase suggested in 1937, relying on Francis Batt's *The Law of the Master and Servant*,

---

[3] *See* for the U.K. perspective, HUGH COLLINS, 'Ascription of Legal Responsibility to Groups in Complex Patterns of Economic Integration', (1990) *Modern Law Review*, 53(6), 731 ff.; for the French perspective, ISABELLE VACARIE, *L'Employeur*, Sirey, 1979; FRANÇOIS GAUDU, *Entre concentration économique et externalisation: les nouvelles frontiers de l'entreprise*, *Droit Social*, 2001, no. 5, 471 ff.; MARIE-LAURE MORIN, *Le frontiers de l'etreprise et la responsabilité de l'emploi*, in ibid., 478 where the A. observes that the employer and the firm are the two sides of the same coin; ELSA PESKINE, *L'imputation en droit du travail*, *Revue de droit du travail*, 2012, 347; for the Spanish perspective, *see*, more recently, MARIA FERNANDA FERNÁNDEZ LÓPEZ (ed. by), *Empresario, contrato de trabajo y cooperación entre empresas*, Editorial Trotta, Madrid, 2004; for the Italian perspective, *see* ORONZO MAZZOTTA, *Rapporti interpositori e contratto di lavoro*, Giuffrè, Milano, 1979; more recently PIETRO ICHINO, *Il diritto del lavoro e i confini dell'impresa*, in *Diritto del lavoro e nuove forme di decentramento produttivo*, Atti delle giornate di studio A.i.d.la.s.s., Trento 4-5 giugno 1999, Giuffrè, Milano, 2000; MARZIA BARBERA, *Trasformazioni della figura del datore di lavoro e flessibilizzazione delle regole del diritto* in *La figura del datore di lavoro. Articolazioni e trasformazioni. Atti del convegno nazionale A.i.d.la.s.s.*, Catania, 21–23 maggio 2009, Giuffrè, Milano, 2010, 5; VALERIO SPEZIALE, *Il datore di lavoro nell'impresa integrata*, in ibid., 77.

[4] *See Clackamas Gastroenterology Assoc. v. Wells*, 538US440, 450 [2003], quoted by MITCHELL H. RUBINSTEIN, 'Employees, Employers and Quasi-Employers: an Analysis of Employees and Employers Who Operate in the Borderland Between Employer and Employee Relationship', (2012) *U. of Pennsylvania Journal of Business Law*, 14, 633.

[5] *See*, among others, MIGUEL RODRIGUEZ PIÑERO Y BRAVO-FERRER, 'Descentralización productiva y sucesión de empresas', in MARIA FERNANDA FERNÁNDEZ LÓPEZ note 3 above, 211 ff.

[6] The transfer of undertaking European Directive no. 2001/23/EC is a forceful instance of this approach. The at-will employment rule in the US renders the delegation of the employment contract a non-issue; but, whether an employee with a contract of fixed duration can be delegated – or her contract 'assigned' to – the acquiring entity has received rather little legal attention. HOWARD SPECTER, MATTHEW FINKIN, *Individual Employment Law and Litigation*, vol 1, § 3.12 (1989).

the 'fact of direction' is the essence of the economic concept of firm as well as the essence of both legal and economic concepts of employer and employee.[7]

Particularly in the Continental European legal systems the following general principle obtains: if the legal entity that exercises the entrepreneurial power of control and direction over the working activity is different from the legal entity that is formally part of the employment contract, then it is the former and not the latter that must be regarded as the employer for the scope of the employment protection.

On the one hand, this principle is rooted in the rules governing contract interpretation based on the idea that substance prevails over form, whereas in common law countries form usually prevails over substance.[8] On the other hand, in Continental European legal systems the prohibition of separation between the formal employer, who bears the employment risks and liabilities, and the employer who effectively owns the firm and exercises control and direction over the working activities, derives from the traditional hostility toward any form of labor intermediation (*merchandeur*, *meister*, *caporale*) whereas 'a general acceptance of this phenomenon took place in the United Kingdom'.[9]

This hostility is clearly stated by Article 43 of the Spanish *Estatuto de los Trabajadores* (Statute of Workers) which prohibits any labor intermediary, except for that provided through state licensed agencies (intermediaries). According to Article 43, there is an illicit form of labor supply whenever the object of the contract is a mere labor supply and/or the supplier is not accredited by the State, is not the owner of a firm and of the means of production and does not exercise any 'entrepreneurial power'. In this case, the 'supplied' worker can be held to be the employee of the end-user. Broadly speaking, the labor supply is illegal if the provider is neither a State accredited agency nor a genuine entrepreneur/subcontractor. In turn, the *subcontratación* (or contract for provision of services) represents a licit form of outsourcing (art. 42 ET) that turns out to be illegal whenever the subcontractor (the service provider) appears to be neither a 'genuine' entrepreneur nor a 'real' employer and, at the same time, is not a licensed intermediary agency (art. 43 ET).[10]

Similarly, in Italy, labor supply can take place only through State accredited intermediaries. Agency work (*somministrazione di lavoro*), on the one hand, and contract for provision of services (*contratto di appalto*), on the other, represent the two sides of the licit outsourcing (arts 21–29 of the legislative decree no. 276/2003, the so-called 'Biagi reform'). According to Article 29, there is a prohibited form of labor supply or labor outsourcing whenever the service provider (the formal employer) is not a State accredited intermediary agency (art. 21 ff.) nor the owner of a genuine and real business organization. This has to be ascertained (particularly in knowledge intensive

---

7 *See* RONALD COASE, 'The Nature of the Firm', (1937) *Economica*, 4(16), 403 ff.

8 K.W. WEDDERBURN LORD OF CHARLETON, *The Worker and the Law*, Penguin Books, Harmondsworth, 1971, at 58. However, for a new trend in the U.K. *see Protectacoat Firthglow Ltd v. Szilagyi* [2009] IRLR 365 (CA).

9 *See* LUCA RATTI, 'Agency Work and the Idea of Dual Employership: a Comparative Perspective', (2009) *Comp. Labor Law & Pol'y J.*, 835.

10 *See* MIGUEL RODRIGUEZ PIÑERO-ROYO, 'Temporary Work and Employment Agencies in Spain', (2001) *Comp. Lab. Law and Pol'y J.*, 23, 129.

sectors) by taking into consideration factors such as the absence of both a real control and direction over the employees and the entrepreneurial risks.[11]

In France, the so-called *fourniture de main d'œvre à but non lucratif* (art. L. 8241-1, art. L. 1253-1 ff., Code du Travail) and the *travail temporaire* (art. L. 1251-1 ff., art. L. 8241-1 Code du Travail), two forms of labor supply, are admitted only within strict limits, as exceptions to the general prohibition of separation between the formal employer, who bears employment risks and liabilities, and the substantial employer (user) who effectively directs and controls the working activities. As in Italy and Spain, the boundary between licit and illicit outsourcing coincides with the boundary between the (licit) contract for provision of services (*contrat de soustraitance*) and the (illicit) *fourniture de main d'œvre lucratif* (labor supply) that falls outside the strict boundaries of the *fourniture de main d'œvre non lucratif* (non profit labour supply) and *travail temporaire* (agency work).[12] Mainly, the *sous-traitance* is 'genuine' whenever the subcontractor carries out a specific task by relying on its own business organization and workforce, bearing the risks and the responsibilities and exercising the employer's powers of control and direction.[13] If this is not the case, then the *soustraitance* turns out to be a mere form of labor supply for profit that is classified in terms of *délit de marchandage de main d'oeuvre*, a criminal offence. Exceptions are allowed only in case the subcontractor is an accredited intermediary (an *entreprise de travail temporaire*) or the economic operation as a whole is a non-profit form of labor supply (particularly admitted in the case of '*Goupement d'employeurs*').

Finally, in Germany, according to the first section of the *Arbeitnehmerüberlassungsgesetz* – AÜG of August 7, 1972 – labor intermediation is permitted only by licensed employment agencies (*Verleiher*); otherwise the worker is classified as an employee of the end-user.[14] In the meantime, German judges, like other Continental European judges, generally hold that the employment costs and responsibilities must remain with the one who exercises entrepreneurial powers of control and direction (doctrine of *Mittelbares Arbeitsverhältnis*).[15]

Consequently, the question emerges of whether the entrepreneurial powers of control and direction can be exercised by two or more distinct employing entities? The doctrine of the employer as a 'single indivisible entity' clearly rejects this idea. The traditional link between the atomistic vertical Fordist firm and the legal concepts of employer and employee has rendered it difficult to accept the idea that the entrepreneurial powers of control and direction could lie outside the boundaries of a discrete legal entity.[16]

---

[11] For a detailed recent description of the Italian legal framework, *see*, in English language, LUCA RATTI, quoted above note 9; MARIA TERESA CARINCI, 'Agency Work in Italy.' Working Paper 'Massimo D'Antona'. Int., 2011.

[12] *See* recently Cass. Soc., June 21, 2011, no. 10-14.362.

[13] *See* JEAN PÉLISSIER, GILLES AUZERO, EMMANUEL DOCKÈS, *Droit du travail*, Dalloz, 2013, 314.

[14] *See* MANFRED WEISS, *Labour Law and Industrial Relations in Germany*, Wolters Kluwer, 2008, 64 ff.

[15] *See* LUCA NOGLER, *The concept of 'subordination' in European and comparative law*, University of Trento, 2009, 60 ff.

[16] *See* the Italian decision of Cass., S.U., No. 22910/2006.

The idea of the employer as a 'single indivisible entity' is traditionally well established also in the British legal system. Notwithstanding, this perspective does not appear to be related to 'hostility' towards any form of labor intermediation, which is largely accepted in the U.K. It rather seems to come from the master and servant doctrine, i.e. to be rooted in the antecedent law of domestic service, of the analogy between the 'master' – a male human employer – and the modern corporate 'employer'.[17] After the abandonment of the master and servant perspective,[18] the employment's characterization in terms of personal and bilateral contract has continued to support the identification of the employer as a single individual employing entity.[19]

In this context, the 'mutuality of obligation test', according to which the finding in favor of an employment contract requires the existence of an exchange between the employer's contractual duty to continuously provide the work and the employee's duty to work when requested, has played an important role but has led to contradictory results.[20] For instance, under the mutuality of obligation test, agency workers, involved in a triangular relationship, can be found to have a contract of employment with neither the agency nor with the end-user.[21] This clearly shows the problems posed by the individual and bilateral construction of the contract of employment in situations where the employment is organized between employing entities.[22]

At the same time, this explains why the idea of dual employership can be founded not on contract law, but rather on the tort law of vicarious liability governed by the *respondeat superior* rule.[23] In *Viasystem (Tyneside) Ltd v. Thermal Transfer (Northern) Ltd*,[24] the Court of Appeal, relying on the 'borrowed servant' rule,[25] observed that 'it is

---

[17] *See* DEAKIN, above note. 2, 274 ff. The A. observes that this metaphor is so powerful that 'the employer is still usually designated as "he" in legislation and in case law, although that attribution of single male human personality is usually as fictitious as is John Doe, the non-existent actor in common law litigation'; *see* also JUDY FUDGE, 'The Legal Boundaries of the Employer, Precarious Workers, and Labour Protection', in *ibid.*, at 298 ff.; MARK FREEDLAND, NICOLA KOUNTOURIS, *The Legal Construction of Personal Work Relations*, Oxford University Press, 162 ff.

[18] *See*, with regard to this evolution, SIMON DEAKIN, FRANK WILKINSON, *The Law of the Labour Market. Industrialization, Employment and Legal Evolution*, Oxford University Press, 2005, Ch. 2.

[19] SIMON DEAKIN, 'The Changing Concept of the Employer in Labour Law' (2001) *Ind. L.J.*, 30(1), 72 ff. who stresses the need to go beyond a mere contractual analysis to identify who is the employer.

[20] *See* MICHAEL WYNN, PATRICIA LEIGHTON, 'Will the Real Employer Please Stand Up? Agencies, Client Companies and The Employment Status of Temporary Agency Worker', (2006) *Ind. L. J.*, 35, 301 ff.

[21] *See*, for instance, *Montgomery v. Johnson Underwood* [2001] I.R.L.R. 264, analyzed by LUCA RATTI, above note 9, 851.

[22] *See* FREEDLAND, above note 1, 40 ff. See also PRASSL, above note 2, who suggests a multi-functional classification of the employer's rights and duties.

[23] *See* RATTI, above note 9; ID., *Il datore di lavoro e le sue trasformazioni*, forthcoming in *Scritti in onore di Marcello Pedrazzoli*, Franco Angeli, 2012.

[24] *Viasystem (Tyneside) Ltd v. Thermal Transfer (Northern) Ltd* [2005] IRLR 983. *See* also *Biffa Waste Services Ltd v. Maschinenfabrik Ernst Hese GmbH* [2008] EWCA Civ 1257; [2009] B.L.R. 1; 122 Con. L.R. 1; [2009] P.N.L.R. 12; (2008) 152(45) S.J.L.B. 25.

[25] *See* P.S. ATIYAH, *Vicarious Liability in the Law of Torts*, Butterworths, 1967, Ch. 3.

strange that the courts have never countenanced what might be an obvious solution in some cases, namely holding both the general and the temporary employer vicariously liable for an employee's negligence'.[26] It would appear that in British tort law, a dual vicarious liability is a legal possibility when the right to control the working activity is shared by two legal entities. Moreover, insofar as it is possible and conceivable that the right to control is shared by two or more legal entities, dual vicarious liability must be a legal possibility. As we will see, this insight plays an interesting role today even in Continental Europe, in the context of group of companies.

3. THE PLURAL EMPLOYER MODEL

As opposed to the single employer model, some common law countries have developed a different approach to the regulation of employer's responsibilities. We may refer to this approach in terms of a 'plural-employer model'. A leading example of this conception can be found in the U.S. which countenances a 'joint employment' relationship. This allows judges to consider as the employer two or more firms that share or co-determine those matters governing the essential terms and condition of employment.

The joint employment doctrine is rooted, first, in the common-law. It allows judges to determine that more than one employing entity must be recognized as jointly liable toward the employee by applying one of four tests to each of the entities: the common law right-of-control test, the economic reality test, the interference test, and the hybrid tests. The common law right-of-control test can be defined by the agency principles focused on the right to control the manner and method in which work is performed. The economic realities test takes into account the totality of the economic circumstances of the employment. The interference test examines the company's ability to interfere with or to affect access to employment opportunities of workers. And the hybrid test combines elements of both the right-to-control and the economic realities tests.[27] It is worth noting that, as observed by a number of scholars, the tests used to identify the employer or the joint-employers significantly converge with the tests used to identify who is an employee.[28]

Whether two or more entities are joint employers depends on the purpose for which the question is asked. In the U.S. the answer to the question 'Who is the employer?' largely depends either on the scope of the particular statute under which the question is raised. This is consistent with the so-called 'targeted approach' to the problem of defining either who is the employee or who is the employer.[29]

If a joint-employment relationship is found to exist, both employers are jointly liable with respect to minimum wages and overtime pay under the Fair Labor Standard

---

26 *Viasystem (Tyneside) Ltd v. Thermal Transfer (Northern) Ltd*, above note 24, para. 12.

27 *Vernon v. State*, 116 Cal. App. 4th 114, 125 n.7 (2004).

28 *See* Deakin, above note 2.

29 *See* Silvana Sciarra, *The Evolution of Labour Law (1992–2003)*, 30–34 (European Communities General Report, 2005) I.

Act,[30] or for adherence to the Occupational Safety and Health Act,[31] the Family and Medical Leave Act,[32] and non-discrimination laws.[33]

The National Labor Relations Board (NLRB) has used a similar approach in finding indicia of a joint management of the firm. When both employers co-determine working condition, meaningfully affecting matters relating to the employment relationship, such as hiring, firing, discipline, supervision and direction, they are defined as joint-employers for the purpose of collective bargaining.[34]

There is a related but more complicated question under U.S. law involving the employment of agency workers. One has to understand the law of union representation of employees who work for separate employers in a common service or industry. In that case, a union may wish to bargain with all those employers together. Such multi-employer bargaining can be agreed to by the employers, but it cannot be imposed by the Labor Board. When employees who work for an agency are seconded to a variety of employers – janitorial staff assigned by an agency to work for a number of buildings each operated by a separate company or nurses assigned by an agency to work for a variety of hospitals – each separate group of employees can be in a joint employment relationship with the agency and each of these employers. Consequently, they cannot require the agency to bargain with them as a whole as each joint employer would have to consent; nor could they bargain separately with their joint employers as part of these employers' complements of employees.[35]

At one point the Labor Board, then under Democratic control, tried to allow them to bargain with their joint employers alone, as part of those employers' workforces.[36] But the Labor Board, then under Republican control, later reversed that decision.[37] As a result, it is now virtually impossible for agency workers who are seconded into joint employment relationships to bargain collectively with the employing agency.

With respect to different business sectors, the increase of service contracts within the public sector has led to an extensive application of the joint employment doctrine to government service contracts.[38] Since the mid-1990s, the joint-employment doctrine involves also the public administration.[39]

---

[30] *Falk v. Brennan*, 414 U.S. 190, 195 (1973); *Antenor v. D & S Farms*, 88 F.3d 925 (11th Cir. 1996).

[31] *Sam Hall & Sons, Inc.*, 8 OSHC (BNA) 2176, 1980 OSHD (CCH) P 24, 927 (No. 76-4988, 1980); *Baker Tank Co./Altech*, 17 OSHC (BNA) 1177, 1995 OSHD (CCH) P 30,734 (No. 90-1786-S, 1995).

[32] *Harbert v. Healthcare Servs. Group, Inc.,* 391 F.3d 1140, 1148 (10th Cir. 2004).

[33] *Baker Tank Co./Altech*, above note 31.

[34] *Boire v. Greyhound Corp.*, 376 U.S. 473 (1964); *NLRB v. Browning-Ferries Indus.,* 691 F.2d 1117 (3d Cir.1982). As this goes to press the NLRB has called for public comment on whether it should adhere to its current standard to terminate joint employment or adopt a different one. *Browning Ferris Indus.*, Case No. 32-RC-109684 (May 12, 2014).

[35] *Lee Hospital*, 300 N.L.R.B. 947 (1990).

[36] *M.B. Sturgis, Inc.*, 331 N.L.R.B. 1298 (2000).

[37] *H.S. Care L.L.C.*, 334 N.L.R.B. 659 (2004).

[38] For a recent survey, see Steven L. Schooner, Collin D. Swan, 'Suing the Government as a 'Joint Employer' – Evolving Pathologies of the Blended Workforce,' (2010) *Government Contractor* 52, 341.

[39] *King v. Dalton*, 895 F.Supp. 831, 834-35 (E.D. Va. 1995).

In a comparative perspective, it is important to stress that the U.S. 'plural-employer model' has grown in response to the variety in the form of labor organization. Due, possibly, to the absence of a prohibition on agencies for the supply of labor, in contrast to European law discussed above, in the U.S., the organization of employment between various legal entities has not distinguished between agency work, labor supply, or subcontracting. The general and common principle is that whenever two or more firms influence an employment relationship, both can be involved in employer liabilities.[40] Agency work, employee leasing, subcontracting, service contracts, and business outsourcing are only some examples of the different organizational environment where the joint employment doctrine has been implemented.[41]

Whilst this issue is not developed as extensively in Canada as it is in the U.S., a similar doctrine, the so-called 'related employer', is spreading in Canadian jurisdictions. When two or more employers can be considered as 'related', they can be treated as one single employer for different purposes.[42] Originally rooted in the 'piercing the corporate veil' doctrine, this doctrine is now assuming a 'regulatory' rather than a 'sanctioning' content. Particularly, this technique is becoming a tool which measures the degree of integration among firms. In a 2001 decision of the Ontario Court of Appeal, *Downtown Eatery (1993) Ltd. v. Ontario*, the Court focused on integration of the companies themselves and on the existence of a single control, rather than on the role each of the four corporations played in relation to the employment.[43]

Interestingly, the British concept of 'associated employer' can echo the American doctrine of joint employment. As noted previously, English law is strictly based on the principle of formal separation of legal personality and responsibility between distinct legal entities. In recent times, this has led to the so-called 'capital boundary problem'.[44] Broadly speaking, since firms enjoy considerable discretion in manipulating their boundaries, they also enjoy a considerable discretion in manipulating the boundaries of their legal responsibilities.[45] This explains why it has been recently stressed that there is a need to focus on economic activities rather than on discrete legal entities.[46]

In the U.K., the principle of formal separation of legal personality and responsibility can be usually overcome only in the event of the allegation of a fraud, through the common law doctrine of piercing the corporate veil.[47] In addition, statutory law provides for a limited lifting of the corporate veil in a number of cases, the most

---

40 CRAIG BECKER, 'Labor Law Outside the Employment Relation,' (1996) *Texas Law Review* 74, 1527.

41 KATHERINE V.W. STONE, 'Legal Protections for Atypical Employees: Employment Law for Workers without Workplaces and Employees without Employers,' (2006) *Berkeley J. Emp. & Lab. L.* 27, 251.

42 JUDY FUDGE, KATE ZAVITZ, 'Vertical Disintegration and Related Employers: Attributing Employment-Related Obligations in Ontario,' (2007) *C.LE.L.J,* 13, 107.

43 [2001] O.J. No. 1879 (Ont.C.A.).

44 *See* COLLINS, above note 3, 736.

45 Ibid.

46 *See* DOUGLAS BAIRD, 'In Coase's Footsteps,' Chicago John M. Olin Law & Economics Working Paper No. 175, 2003.

47 COLLINS, above note 3, 740 ff.

important of which relates to continuity of employment.[48] According to the Employment Rights Act (ERA) 1996, section 231, two or more employers are to be treated as 'associated': 'if – (a) one is a company of which the other (directly or indirectly) has control, or (b) both are companies of which a third person (directly or indirectly) has control …'. The control is usually exercised through the ownership of shares (usually at least the 51 per cent), although a 'contractual control' is also possible.

As said above, the doctrine of associated employer is usually invoked to ascertain the continuity of employment for the scope of dismissal protection. According to section 108 of ERA, after one and, since 2012, two years of a qualifying period of continuous employment an employee may bring a claim for unfair dismissal. However, according to the doctrine of associated employment, a qualifying period of employer is recognized to exist even in cases in which the employee has worked less than two years for two different employers who can be classified as 'associated' within the meaning of statutory and common law.[49]

4. CONVERGENCES AND DIVERGENCES BETWEEN THE SINGLE AND THE PLURAL EMPLOYER MODELS

Since the 1990s, after the advent of the so-called 'vertical disintegration',[50] the doctrine of the employer as a 'single indivisible entity' and the reluctance towards the idea that the entrepreneurial powers of control and direction could lie outside the boundaries of a discrete legal entity seem to be in tension. In the past two decades, global competition and the information-technology revolution have led to firms' restructuring. Particularly, there has been a movement from centralized decision-making toward decentralized structures and production networks. Either in the manufacturing or in the service sector, vertical disintegration and outsourcing have enabled firms to make their operations leaner and more flexible.[51] Outsourcing and subcontracting activities, as market forms of governance which replace hierarchy, have increased in North America and in Europe.[52]

In the face of multi-polar and multi-segmented economic organizations, it has become more and more clear that the boundaries of the economic activity and

---

48 *See*, for instance, SIMON DEAKIN, *Labour Law.* 4th Edition, Hart Publishing, 2005, 213 ff.

49 *Pickney v. Sandpiper Drilling Ltd and other trading in partnership as KCA Offshore Drilling Services* [1989] I.R.L.R., 425; *Hancill v. Marcon Engineering Ltd* [1990] I.R.L.R., 51.

50 HUGH COLLINS, 'Independent Contractors and the Challenge of Vertical Disintegration to Employment Protection Laws,' (1990) *Oxford Journal of Legal Studies*, 10, 353 ff.; more recently, *see* RAFFAELE DE LUCA-TAMAJO, ADALBERTO PERULLI. 'Productive Decentralisation and Labour Law (Individual and Collective Dimensions).' World Congress of the ISLLSS, Paris, 5–8 September 2006, General Report.

51 BENNETT HARRISON, *Lean and mean: the Changing Landscape of Corporate Power in the Age of Flexibility,* New York, 1994; WALTER W. POWELL, 'Neither Market nor Hierarchy: Network Forms of Organisation,' (1990) *Research in Organisational Behavior*, 12, 295.

52 For a comparative study, see ULRIKE MUEHLBERGER, 'Hierarchies, Relational Contracts and New Forms of Outsourcing, (September 2005).' ICER Working Paper No. 22/2005.

entrepreneurial powers no longer coincide with the boundaries of the firm. In this context, by retracing Coase's footsteps, Douglas Baird has warned us about the need to resist the general idea that:

> the locus of economic activity rests with a discrete legal entity (...) In a world in which the boundaries of the firm become less clear and the identity of those who control the firm becomes more fluid, regulations that focus on the conduct of specific firms is at best incomplete and often misguided.[53]

In this respect, legal rules should be focused in the future on regulating economic activity, 'rather than on regulating discrete legal entities'.[54]

Together with the trend toward decentralization, other changes have occurred in employment practices so that the portrait of the employer has been shaped differently. Firms have increased temporary and contingent employment. Contracting-out has become a common practice, either to staff agencies or to smaller supplying firms. Work has become even more contingent.[55]

In this framework, the line drawn between the single employer and the plural employer model has been evolving. Particularly, the concept of 'joint employer' and 'associated employer', which traditionally did not have a counterpart in Continental Europe, have been gradually accepted in Continental European legal systems. Broadly speaking, the shift from a single towards a plural employer model in countries such as France, Spain, Italy and Germany is clearly shown by the progressive erosion of the prohibition of labor supply, on the one hand, and the admittance of triangular employment relations, on the other.

The next two sections are designed to illustrate as, together with agency work, the case of subcontracting (*see infra* section 4.1) and the one of group of companies (*see infra* section 4.2) may be regarded as paradigmatic examples of a convergence towards a plural employer pattern.

4.1 The Case of Subcontracting

Subcontracting challenged the legal doctrine of employer as a single indivisible entity. In several legal systems, the idea of employer as the one who exercises the entrepreneurial powers of control, direction and coordination over the working activity has been questioned by new forms of governance that seem to replace hierarchical structures by market ones, through an increasing recourse to outsourcing and subcontracting activities. New forms of organization, based on different techniques, have been used to keep a direct or indirect control over contractual relationships.[56] 'Hybrid' forms of organization challenge the legal paradigm of employment relationship. As a

---

53 BAIRD, above note 46, 14.

54 Ibid.

55 GILIAN LESTER, 'Careers and Contingency,' (1998) *Stanford Law Review*, 51, 73.

56 OLIVER E. WILLIAMSON, *Markets and Hierarchies: Analysis and Antitrust Implications. A Study in the Economics of Internal Organization*, New York: The Free Press, 1975; OLIVER E. WILLIAMSON, *The Economic Institutions of Capitalism: Firms, Markets, Relational Contracting*, New York: The Free Press, 1985.

consequence, the nature of the employer's power needs to be reassessed in order to align the legal framework to the changes worked by economic reality.[57]

Moreover, the practice of outsourcing and subcontracting engages firms not only within national borders, but also with foreign firms. Transnational contracting-out leads to complex legal issues concerning private international law, international labor standards, the supranational role of trade unions, international regulatory competition, and, more generally, the enforcement of labor law outside the national context.[58]

Subcontracting weakens the capacity for collective action. From France to Venezuela, unions are ill prepared to deal with it,[59] to identify a common union strategy. Transnational collective action is still far from playing any role.[60]

At the national level, the approach toward subcontracting varies among different legal systems. One difference concerns the sources of law. On the one hand, we may find countries – such as the U.S.[61] – where subcontracting has been traditionally left to collective bargaining, with relevant consequences due to the near disappearance of unionized workplaces.[62] On the other hand, there are countries – such as most of continental European legal systems – where outsourcing has been mainly tackled by statutory law.[63]

A second important issue relates to the ideological approach adopted with regard to the new forms of economic organization. The law can either facilitate or regulate – indeed, obstruct – outsourcing and contracting-out. Even within one single legal system, one can find conflicting approaches to outsourcing processes; some regulations can facilitate a firm's recourse to decentralization, while others seem to have been introduced to inhibit or restrain de-verticalization processes. A clear example of the different impact of employment policies on firm strategies is provided by the European debate on the regulation of undertaking transfer (European Directive 2001/123/CE),

---

57 COLLINS, above note 50, 353–80; ALAIN SUPIOT, *Au-delà de l'emploi. Transformations du travail et devenir du droit du travail en Europe,* Flammarion, Paris, 1999; Ibid., *Les nouveaux visages de la subordination, Droit Social*, 2000, 2, 131 ff.

58 BOB A. HEPPLE, *Labour Laws and Global Trade*, Hart Publishing, 2005.

59 DE LUCA-TAMAJO and PERULLI, above note 50.

60 See, for the experience of International Framework agreements and its impact on subcontracting, KOSTANTINOS PAPADAKIS, GIUSEPPE CASALE, KATERINA TSOTROUDI (2008), 'International Framework Agreement as Elements of Cross-Border Industrial Relations Framework,' in KOSTANTINOS PAPADAKIS, ed., *Cross-Border Social Dialogue and Agreements: an Emerging Global Industrial Relations Framework*?, Ilo-Iils, Geneva, 1; DIMITRIS STEVIS (2010), *International Framework Agreements and Global Social Dialogue: Parameters and Prospects*, ILO, Geneva.

61 DAVID ALLEN LARSON, 'Subcontracting and the duty to bargain,' (1989–1990) *N.Y.U. Rev. L. & Soc. Change,* 17, 255.

62 According to recent Bureau of Labor Statistic's data, union density in the private sector in the U.S. is below 7 per cent. *See*, recently, JOEL CUTCHER GERSHENFELD, 'Prospects for Collective Bargaining in a Post-Crisis, Global, Knowledge-Driven Economy'. Paper presented at the Annual Meeting of the International Association of Labor Law Journals held in Sidney on August 30–31, 2009.

63 For Spain, see FERNANDO VALDÉS DAL-RÉ, 'LA EXTERNALIZACIÓN DE ACTIVIDAEDS LABORALES: UN FENOMENO COMPLEX,' IN AA. VV, *LA EXTERNALIZACIÓN DE ACTIVIDAEDS LABORALES (OUTSOURCING): UNA VISIÓN INTERDISCIPLINAR,* LEX NOVA, VALLADOLID, 2002.

where legal approaches to the transfer of enterprise can either facilitate or introduce obstacles to business outsourcing.[64]

However, these choices have not yet been carved in stone. An evolution from the single to the plural employer model, and vice versa, is frequent. An example of the swinging movement from one to the other is provided by Italy. Here, the firms' increasing recourse to subcontracting strategies has led the Italian legislature to rely more and more on the joint-liabilities model as a tool to protect employees from negative externalities associated with de-verticalization processes.[65]

A forceful instance of this trend is also provided by the European Commission's recent investigations about the new role played by labor and employment law in 'advancing a 'flexicurity' agenda in support of a labour market which is fairer, more responsive, more inclusive, and which contributes to make Europe more competitive'.[66] On the one hand, the European Commission considers outsourcing, subcontracting and the de-verticalization of production as new licit and even fundamental forms of economic organization which allow firms to achieve new needs of flexibility. On the other hand, the system of joint and several liabilities among business contractors and subcontractors is regarded as the most efficient technique of protection of workers involved in outsourcing, subcontracting and agency work.

The idea that a 'plurality of employers' may enhance and improve employment opportunities and that joint and several liabilities may effectively protect workers has been embraced by European Institutions in two more recent occasions. The first one is the European Directive 2008/104/EC, where agency work is regarded as an instrument to enhance occupational opportunities. In this perspective, the plural employer pattern is considered a chance to revitalize the labor market.[67] The second one is the European Commission communication of March 21, 2012 about the amendment of the posting of Workers Directive 96/71/EC.[68] Here the introduction of a system of joint and several liabilities in the field of subcontracting in the construction sector is considered to be fundamental to ensure the compliance of subcontractors with legal and contractual obligations.[69]

---

[64] Paul Davies, 'Taken to the cleaners? Contracting out of services yet again,' (1997) *Industrial Law Journal*, 26, 193.

[65] Luisa Corazza, *'Contractual integration' e rapporti di lavoro. Uno studio sulle tecniche di tutela del lavoratore,* Cedam, Padova, 2004.

[66] Green Paper 2006 '*Modernising Labour Law to Meet the Challenges of the 21st Century*', at 4; see also Communication of the EU Commission 'Towards Common Principles of Flexicurity', (24/10/2007 COM (2007), 627). With regard to the concept of *flexicurity*, see Ton Wilthagen, Frank Tros, 'The Concept of 'Flexicurity': A New Approach to Regulating Employment and Labour Markets,' (2004) *Transfer*, 2, 169.

[67] For a critical perspective, see Nicola Countouris, Rachel Horton, 'The Temporary Agency Work Directive: Another Broken Promise?,' (2009) *Industrial Law Journal*, 38, 329.

[68] Brussels, 21.3.2012, COM (2012) 131 final.

[69] See, for instance, ECJ, *Wolff & Müller GmbH & Co. KG v. José Filipe Pereira Félix*, October 12, 2004, C-60/03 concerning the national mechanism of joint liability with regard to the obligation to pay the minimum rate of wage in the construction sector. The mechanism is regarded as pursuing at the same time the "objective of upholding fair competition on the one hand and ensuring worker protection, on the other" (para. 42).

A third distinguishing line can be drawn by taking into consideration the regulation of agency work and, particularly, the prescription of temporariness. Countries where only temporary agency work is admitted – such as France – tend to conceive joint-employer responsibilities as an exception to the doctrine of privity of employment contract. For example, according to the French Labor Code (art. L. 1251-39 Cd. Tr.), a worker is considered an employee of the user firm, on the basis of an indefinite employment contract from the first day of assignment, if she/he continues to work for the user firm even after the end of the assignment, which usually cannot last for more 18 months. Other countries that admit long-term staff leasing – such as the U.S. and, since 2003, Italy – are more open to the idea of multilateral employer liability.

However, not even this distinction can be taken as irreversible or *in rerum natura*. It has been noted that temporary work tends to evolve towards a more complex provision of services, where the supplying of temporary labor is followed by additional and longer services.[70]

Last, since the idea of control lies at the core of both the single and the plural employer patterns, it is possible to conclude that the caesura between these two regulatory approaches particularly emerges by focusing on remedies rather than on the theoretical construction of the concept of employer. In fact, in both models, judges tend to investigate how the entrepreneurial powers have been exercised by contracting firms. What is profoundly different is that, according to the single employer model, the firm which turns out to be *the* employer is the only one that bears all the employment risks and liabilities. On the other hand, according to a plural employer model, the involvement of both employers in a joint-liability scheme leads to the creation of a system of incentives for employers to contract out the economic activities only to reliable partners.

4.2 The Case of a Group of Companies

In recent years, a plural employer perspective has been particularly developed in the context of a group of companies. While outsourcing processes and vertical disintegration reflect a process of 'de-composition' or 'dissolution' of the firm the grouping of companies reflect its 're-composition'.[71] In fact, a group of companies usually refers to a situation in which several companies, although formally separated, are managed under the unified direction and coordination of the holding as a single economic entity. A multiplicity of companies thus coexist with the unity of the group.[72]

From a labor law perspective, in the case of subcontracting there is the need to re-draw the boundaries of the legal concept of employer and of employment responsibilities by focusing on the economic activity rather than on discrete legal entities.[73] In

[70] For a focus on risks of 'long-term temps', GUY DAVIDOV, 'Joint Employment Status in Triangular Employment Relationships,' (2004) *British Journal of Industrial Relations*, 42(4), 727–46.

[71] *See* GAUDU, above note 3, 474.

[72] *See* GUNTHER TEUBNER, *Unitas Multiplex: Corporate Governance in Group Enterprises*, Bremen/Firenze, 1988, 67.

[73] *See supra* section 4.1.

the case of a group of companies, the link between the concept of employer and the firm can be maintained, but the boundaries of the firm have to be redrawn so as to represent the situation in which the firm and the employment are shared by a number of separate legal entities. Here, the separate personalities of companies do not coincide with the real boundaries of the firm as an individual employer. The group overcomes the boundaries of the legal person as well as the boundaries of the unitary concept of employer.

According to German (§ 18 AktG) and Italian corporate law (art. 2497 Codice civile) a group of companies requires an 'effective unified direction' to exist.[74] The direct or indirect control of a corporation over other corporations by means of a number of shares so as to achieve the right to a majority of votes (*de jure* control) or by means of contracts so as to achieve a 'dominant influence' (*de facto* or contractual control) is a *condicio sine qua non* for the existence of a group of company. However, in addition, the subsidiaries must be managed under the unified direction of the holding company. Spanish judges consider the *dirección unitaria* an essential element of group of companies,[75] while French judges usually require the existence of a condition of 'economic and juridical dependence' between the companies.[76]

The unified direction usually denotes the existence of a group of companies that is significant from a corporate law perspective, but not necessarily from a labor law perspective.[77] Spanish, Italian and French judges carry out a fact-intensive inquiry by placing weight on the following factors: (a) the existence of unified direction; (b) the existence of common goals and strategy; and (c) the joint-exercise of a unified economic activity.[78] A common establishment or business undertaking is also considered of great significance. The abovementioned factors are used to ascertain that a single business undertaking, a single economic activity and business strategy are shared by a number of companies. In France and in Luxembourg these factors are relevant to assess the existence of a *unité* or *entité économique et sociale* (single economic and social entity) for the scope of collective bargaining or workers' representation at plant level.[79] With regard to the question of who is the employer for the scope of other

---

[74] *See*, for instance, PATRICK REMY, *Le groupe, l'entreprise et l'établissement: une approche en droit compare*, *Droit Social*, 2001, 509.

[75] TS (Sala de la Social), December 26, 2001, RJ/2002/5292; TS (Sala de lo Social), January 20, 2003, RJ/2004/1825; TS, Setpember 16, 2010, RJ 2010/8441.

[76] *See* Cour d'Appel Rouen, Chambre Social, May 4 2010, no. 09/00946, 09/00975, 09/01450.

[77] *See* TS (Sala de la Social), December 26, 2001, RJ/2002/5292.

[78] *See*, with regard to France, BERNARD TEYSSIÉ, *LES GROUPES DE SOCIÉTÉS ET LE DROIT DU TRAVAIL*, *DROIT SOCIAL*, 2010, 735 FF.; FRANÇOISE FAVENNEC-HÉNRY, *L'extinction de la relation de travail dans les groupes*, in *Droit Social*, 2010, 762 ff.; with regard to Spain, *see* JESÚS BAZ-RODRÍGUEZ, *Las relaciones de trabajo en la empresa de grupo*, Granada, Editorial Comares, 2002, at 64 ff.; MARÍA FERNANDA FERNÁNDEZ LÓPEZ, 'El empresario como parte del contrato de trabajo: una aproximación preliminar,' in FERNÁNDEZ LÓPEZ, above note 3, 30 ff.; with regard to Italy, *see* GISELLA DE SIMONE, *Titolarità dei rapporti di lavoro e regole di trasparenza*, Franco Angeli, 1995; more recently see the contributions published in the journal *Rivista giuridica del lavoro*, 2013, no 1, 1 ff

[79] See, for instance, Article L. 161-2 of the Code du Travail of the Grand Duchy of Luxembourg for the identification of the subjects for the purpose of determining the scope of the

employment protections (e.g. protection against unfair dismissal or collective redundancies, protection of wages and so on) there is usually a last factor which is regarded as the most relevant from a labor law perspective; namely, the fact that the employee, despite having a formal employment contract with only one corporation, works under the direct or indirect control and direction of the other subsidiaries. It is worth emphasizing that to the extent a link of juridical subordination can be established with both the formal employer and the other subsidiaries, this situation differs from the (illicit) case of labor supply, where the formal employer is only an apparent one, deprived of any control and direction over the working activity.

In presence of all the abovementioned factors, French judges ascertain the existence of *co-employeurs* (joint-employers) who become jointly liable for the employment obligations and, particularly, for the *obligation de reclassement.*[80] Under the *obligation de reclassement* the employer is bound to verify, before dismissing the employee on the ground of economic reasons, the possibility to redeploy the worker within the economic organization. In the case of an employee working for a number of subsidiaries, the obligation of redeployment is extended to the group as a whole. An economic dismissal is considered unfair if possibilities of redeployment in the holding or in the other subsidiaries have not been taken into account.[81]

Spanish judges rule similarly in favor of the existence of a joint liability and solidarity between all the companies.[82] In a recent judgment, the Audiencia Nacional, Sala de lo Social, Madrid held that the group can be regarded as a single employing entity for the scope of collective dismissal.[83] Consequently, and importantly, the existence of a crisis or of a negative economic situation that justifies economic dismissals must be ascertained with regard to the group as a whole.[84]

German and Italian judges can also ascertain the existence of a single business undertaking (rather than of a single employer) for the scope of individual and collective dismissal protection, but they tend to be hostile to the extension of employment liabilities which lead to infringe the 'sanctity' of formal separation between the

---

collective bargaining process. In France, a definition of unité économique et sociale is provided by Article L. 2322-4 Cd. Tr. for the scope of the establishment of a comité d'entreprise. For the United States, *see supra* section 3.

80 *See*, recently, Cass. Soc., September 9, 2012, no. 11-12.845; Cass. Soc., September 28, 2011, no. 10-12.278; Cour d'appel Rouen, Chambre Social, May 4 2010, no. 09/00946, 09/00975, 09/01450. *See* TEYSSIÉ, above note 78, 736.

81 *See* art. L-1233.4, Code du Travail, according to which 'the economic dismissal is possible only after the employer has done everything possible with regard to the requalification and the training of the employee as well as with regard to his redeployment within the company or within the group of companies'. See also Cour d'appel Rouen, Chambre Social, May 4 2010, no. 09/00946, 09/00975, 09/01450. Here, the holding was a Finnish corporation. A similar statutory provision is provided in Germany by § 1.2 KSchG. *See* recently LUCA NOGLER, *La nuova disciplina dei licenziamenti ingiustificati alla prova del diritto comparato*, in *Giornale di diritto del lavoro e delle relazioni industriali*, 2012, 661, 677.

82 *See*, TS (Sala de la Social), December 26, 2001, RJ/2002/5292; TS (Sala de lo Social), March 6, 2002, RJ/2002/4659; TS (Sala de lo Social), January 20, 2003, RJ/2004/1825; TS, September 16, 2010, RJ 2010/8441.

83 Audiencia Nacional, Sala de lo Social, Madrid, No. 106/2012.

84 Ibid.

corporations.[85] However, in recent Italian judgments, a co-employership situation has been recognized to exist also for the purpose of joint-liability.[86] Likewise, German judges have occasionally admitted the *Verdoppelung auf Arbeitgeberseite* (the double employer) where an employee has worked for a number of firms integrated to such an extent that it is possible to consider the existence of a single employment relationship, rather than a number of separated employment relationships, with a plural employing entity (*Einheitliches Arbeitsverhältnis*).[87]

Despite these developments there is scant evidence that judges are willing broadly to redefine the boundaries of the employment protection and of the concept of employer so as to coincide with the actual economic boundaries. In most cases, judges continue to place weight on the '*utilización abusive de la personalidad juridica en prejudicio de los trabajadores*' (an abuse of the corporate veil to the detriment of the employees),[88] on the '*confusion d'activité, d'intérêt et de direction*' (a confusion of activity, interests and direction),[89] on the holding's interference in the human resources management (*immixtion dans la gestion du personnel*) at such point and at such level as to determine a 'contractual confusion' or a mixed and indistinct use of the workforce within the group.[90]

Insofar as judges found the joint-liability regime on the piercing of the corporate veil,[91] these novel judicial approaches may be seen as an application of the *fraus legis – of a fraud upon the law* – as a response to a phenomenon that justifies the infringement of the principle of formal separation between different legal entities. Furthermore, these judicial approaches remain wedded to a 'single-employer' perspective by considering the group as a whole as the 'real single employer' upon which employment costs and liabilities should be allocated.

Only on a few occasions, have judges started to regard joint-liability and joint-employership as a 'regulatory' response to the situation in which the firm, the economic activity, the employment are *physiologically* shared by a number of corporations belonging to the same group. French judges, for instance, appear to be open to the possibility of recognizing a single employment contract between one employee and a

---

[85] *See*, for instance, REMY, above note 74; for Italy, GISELLA DE SIMONE, 'Gruppi di imprese', in M. BROLLO (ed.), *Il mercato del lavoro. Trattato di diritto del lavoro diretto da Mattia Persiani e Franco Carinci*, vol. VI, Cedam, Padova, 2012, 1509 ff.

[86] *See* Cass., March 24, 2003, no. 4274, *Rivista italiana di diritto del lavoro*, 2003, II, 746; Tribunale di Monza, April 28, 2004, *Rivista italiana di diritto del lavoro*, 2004, II, 540; Cass., November 29, 2011, no. 25270, *Rivista italiana di diritto del lavoro*, 2012, II, 375.

[87] *See* LUCA NOGLER, *Gruppo di imprese e diritto del lavoro*, *Lavoro e diritto*, 1992, 304 ff.

[88] *See* BAZ-RODRÍGUEZ, above note 78, 64 ff.; TS (Sala de lo Social), January 20, 2003, RJ/2004/1825.

[89] *See* Cass. Soc., September 9, 2012, no. 11-12.845 and, for Spain, *see* TS, September 16, 2010, RJ 2010/8441.

[90] *See* Cass., November 29, 2011, no. 25270; Cass., September 28, 2011, no. 10-12.278; *see* also, in Spain, TS (Sala de la Social), December 26, 2001, RJ/2002/5292; TS (Sala de lo Social), January 20, 2003, RJ/2004/1825 where judges place weight on the fact that the work is simultaneously performed by the employee on the behalf of all the parent companies.

[91] This clearly emerges in TS (Sala de la Social), December 26, 2001, RJ/2002/5292; TS (Sala de lo Social), January 20, 2003, RJ/2004/1825.

number of *co-employeurs* to exist whenever, despite the words used in the formal arrangement, in substance a situation of *subordination juridique* can be ascertained with more than one single employer.[92] Here, piercing the corporate veil plays no role.

The same result could be achieved in Italy, Spain, Germany and in other Continental European legal systems where the prevailing of substance over form is a dominant principle in contractual interpretation. Particularly, Continental European legal systems, where the concept of 'contract of long term duration' as well as that one of 'contractual relationship' have been analysed for a long time, assess that in long-term contract the day-to-day facts of the relationship and the parties' behavior reflect what the parties have stated to be its nature much more than the *nomen iuris* and the written document.[93]

The European Court of Justice has recently upheld the idea of multi-employership as a legal possibility. In the *Heineken* case, an employee, formally hired by one company, had been assigned on a permanent basis to another company that had then transferred its business undertaking to a third company. The question was whether the second and the third companies could be respectively regarded as 'transferor' and 'transferee' for the scope of the Transfer of Undertaking Directive. The ECJ ruled that 'within a group of companies, there are two employers, one having contractual relations with the employees of that group and the other non-contractual relations with them'.[94] In this perspective, it is possible to regard as a 'transferor', within the meaning of the Transfer of Undertaking Directive 2001/23, 'the employer responsible for the economic activity of the entity transferred which, in that capacity, establishes working relations with the staff of that entity, despite the absence of contractual relations with those staff'.[95]

By stressing the legal possibility for an employee to have a contractual relation with a formal employer and a non-contractual relation with a substantial employer to which the employee is permanently assigned, the ECJ's approach comes closer to the British perspective, rather than to the Continental European perspective. In fact, beside the statutory concept of 'associated-employer', in the U.K. a multi-employership has been recently recognized to exist by combining contract law with common law. Yet we have seen that British judges hold that a dual vicarious liability is a legal possibility when the right to control the working activity is shared by two legal entities.[96] Here, the bilateral construction of the employment contract is combined with the tort law of vicarious liability.

---

92 Cass. Soc., January 22, 1997, no. 93-43742 and 93-43743. In this respect, see also the proposal of De Simone, quoted above, note 85.

93 Consider the Italian Civil Code, art. 1362, 2, which establishes that, after that the written agreement has been concluded between the parties, in order to understand what the parties have stated to be its real nature, it is also necessary to take into consideration the *ex post* facts of the relationships. For French legislation, consider the Code du Travail (Fr.), art. L. 781-2, 2° and art. L. 120-3. For a recent interpretative reconstruction of regulatory co-employership in the context of strong contractual integration between business undertakings constituting a single economic entity (rather than in the context of the group of companies) *see* VALERIO SPEZIALE above, note 3.

94 ECJ, *Albron Catering BV v. FNV Bondgenoten, John Roest*, October 21, 2010, C-242/09.

95 Ibid.

96 *See supra* section 2.

In this context, a similar conclusion has been reached with regard to the common law duty of care. In *Newton-Sealey v. Armor Group Services Ltd*, a worker, formally hired by one company belonging to the Armor Group, was seriously injured while he was working in Iraq under the control and the direction of a subsidiary. The question was 'whether, despite a person having contractual relations with only one member of a corporate group, other corporate members have acted in such a way as to be under a duty of care to him'.[97] According to the High Court of Justice, Queen's Bench Division, notwithstanding the employee had an employment contract with one corporation, the other parts of the Armor Group had behaved in such a way as to voluntarily enter into a special 'non-contractual' relation of 'proximity' with the employee whereby they owe to the employee a duty of care.[98]

5. THE NEW CONCEPT OF THE EMPLOYER IN A FLEXICURITY PERSPECTIVE

In the previous sections we have tried to underline recent convergences towards more general acceptance of a plural employer model. In a broader perspective, it is worth noting that the rationale underpinning these new legal trends appears to be that the best protection for workers is no longer to remain 'attached' to a single business undertaking, as it was in the past.[99] Rather, the best protection for workers derives from splitting the employment risks and costs among different employing entities. In this respect, different employing entities, strongly integrated via contracts or shares ownership, can be regarded as 'internal labor markets'[100] which increase and safeguard the employee's expectations about security in income.

Since a labor market perspective is nowadays at the core of employment protection, the interaction between the employee and multiple employers can be regarded as an opportunity, rather than as a risk. An example of this different approach is offered by the recent Italian case of the 'interfirm network agreement' (art. 3, comma 4 *ter* d.l. no. 5/2009), whereby two or more firms are connected in a contract, in order to improve integration and share the challenge of global competitiveness.[101] In 2013, a law (Legislative Decree no. 76) was passed with the aim of increasing workers' mobility within the interfirm network, as to meet the firm's special needs for flexibility. First, Article 30, Legislative Decree 276/2003 has been amended, freeing the undertaking

---

[97] *Newton-Sealey v. ArmorGroup Services Ltd.* [2008] EWHC 233 (QB).

[98] In Italian private law, a similar perspective has been developed by Carlo Castronovo, *La nuova responsabilità civile*, Giuffrè, now 2006, at 122 ff. who outlines the concept of 'responsabilità da contatto sociale' (liability deriving by social contact) later employed, in the specific context of group of companies, by RAIMONDI, *Il datore di lavoro nei gruppi imprenditoriali, in Giorn. dir. lav. rel. ind.*, 2012, 307 ff.

[99] *See supra* section 2.

[100] *See* MARZIA BARBERA, above note 3, at 55 ff.; *see* also TIZIANO TREU, *Trasformazioni delle imprese: reti di imprese e regolazione del lavoro*, in *Merc. Conc. Reg.*, 2012, at 20.

[101] Generally, see ILARIO ALVINO (2014), *Il lavoro nelle reti di imprese: profili giuridici*, Milano, Giuffrè.

making the posting from the burden to prove that it has an own specific interest in the posting. Second, Article 30, as amended by the law 76/2013, sets forth, for the first time, the possibility of 'joint-employership' in the interfirm network agreement. The legal provisions leave to the contracting undertakings a broad margin of discretion in the identification of the 'jointly-employed' employees and in the regulation of the legal effects.[102] By adopting a plural employer approach, the interfirm network can be conceived as a net of protection, which offers to employees a number of employment opportunities. The same idea is at the basis of the French experiment of the '*contract d'activité*', suggested by the Boissonnat Commission, where the employment contract is organized between a number of employers, each one sharing the need for the same employee's job and tasks.

From a law and economics perspective, the option for a plural employer model testifies to the need to fit legal techniques to the changing use of relational contracts among firms. While the single employer model reflects an idea of employment relationship relying on the ownership of the firm, the plural employer pattern enables us to conceive of the employer as a network of relational contracts.[103]

The case of a group of companies is another example of how the plural employer model can turn out to be a labor market outcome for the employee. In fact, in the case of group of companies, where the integration is so deep as to give rise to a single economic entity, the 'securization' of employee's expectations can be even stronger. Particularly, the employee could be safeguarded not only about income, but also about the job – or a job opportunity.

The French and the Italian trend towards the enlargement of the boundaries of the duty of redeployment (*obligation de reclassement* or *dovere di ripescaggio*) to the group of companies as a whole should be taken as such a work in progress. This new approach can be explained in terms of counterbalance to the intensification of work and the flexibility required for a 'flexible employee',[104] working within a group of companies. In other words, to the extent that a greater degree of flexibility is demanded of employees to perform different tasks and jobs, in favor of the group as a whole, formal and substantial employers may be required to guarantee the employee her job, by providing her with requalification, training and redeployment within the group.

From this perspective, the group of companies can be regarded itself as an 'internal labor market' or as a 'market of flexicurity' capable of supplying flexible labor, on the

---

102 However, labor law is mainly based on *ius cogen* arrangements that restrict contractual freedom. The real margin of discretion enjoyed by the contracting undertakings in the definition of joint-employership and its legal effects therefore remain contested. The main risk is that in the context of labor, the regulation of the interfirm network will be left to the entrepreneurs' discretion, without the participation of workers' representatives. Otherwise stated, to what extent is the freedom of contract accorded to the interfirm network bounded by mandatory norms that normally constrain employers? See ADALBERTO PERULLI (2014), 'Contratto di rete, distacco, codatorialità, assunzioni in agricoltura.', in FIORILLO-PERULLI (eds.), La riforma del mercato del lavoro, Torino, Giappichelli, 463 ff.

103 GEORGE BAKER, ROBERT GIBBONS, KEVIN J. MURPHY, 'Relational contracts and the theory of the firm,' (2001) *Quarterly Journal of Economics*, 117, 39–84.

104 For this concept, *see* HUGH COLLINS, 'Regulating the Employment Relation for Competitiveness,' (2001) *Ind. L. J.*, 30, 17 ff.

one hand, and safeguarding employee's expectations about stability in income and job, on the other. This is the 'modern' balance struck between the business need to enhance competitiveness and the employee's need for employment security and income.

6. Employee autonomy, privacy, and dignity under technological oversight

Matthew W. Finkin, Rüdiger Krause and Hisashi Takeuchi-Okuno

I. INTRODUCTION

The Industrial Revolution established the factory as the site of waged work, eclipsing the household workshop as a center of production. Private life was thus placed at a remove from managerial oversight as the factory became a place of strict control, of punctuality and performance. Even so, management's incessant drive to reduce uncertainty in its business environment, to anticipate risk and to plan for contingencies drives it to maximize what it knows or could know about applicants and employees. The exponential growth of information technology today abets this desire: it can render the employee accessible and transparent anywhere, collapsing the distinction between life at and life away from work. To Alain Supiot, the law's anthropological function is to intervene between the human and the machine – to humanize technology.[1] The question explored in this chapter is whether that anthropological function is so; whether the laws of industrialized nations conduce toward that common end.

This examination will move along two axes: First, by specific reference to three nation-states; and, second, by reference to a set of human interests which the deployment of technology confronts and which find expression, or not, in these nations' laws. In other words, this chapter is as much an exercise in comparative legal culture as it is of comparative law alone.[2]

A. The Nation-States

Three countries have been chosen for exposition. They represent ideal types around which other states can be understood to orbit, albeit at a greater or lesser remove. The United States and Germany have been chosen for the priority of place the Western tradition gives to the individual; but, equally, because they diverge significantly on the role of the state (and so of law) and of the market respectively as the means of

---

[1] Alain Supiot, HOMO JURIDICUS: ON THE ANTHROPOLOGICAL FUNCTIONS OF THE LAW 117 (Saskia Brown trans. 2007). 'The problems raised today by the "new information and communication technologies" prove that the anthropological function of the law does not simply disappear when one moves from one type of technology to another.'

[2] *See generally*, David Nelkin, *Legal Cultures* in COMPARATIVE LAW AND SOCIETY Ch. 15 (David Clark ed. 2012); Roger Cotterell, *Comparative Law and Legal Culture* in OXFORD HANDBOOK OF COMPARATIVE LAW Ch. 21 (Mathias Reimann and Reinhard Zimmermann eds. 2006).

mediating the balance between management prerogative and individual liberty.[3] In other words, they represent distinct, perhaps antipodal strands in Western thought and law, and in political economy as well.[4] In contrast, Japan proceeds historically from assumptions of communal norms and obligations, rather than of individual rights, on which terrain individual claims of the sort explored here map uneasily. It raises the question of whether legal systems so culturally rooted might nevertheless move toward greater protection for the individual from hierarchical (or communal) oversight.

B. The Technologies: Social Media, Biometric Monitoring, Spatial Location

The introduction of technology to supplement or supplant direct human interaction as a means of monitoring employees and controlling their performance has often been met with protest by those subject to it. Time clocks, for example, when substituted for human record keeping, were protested at as being instruments of degradation.[5] The deployment of such technologies were defended as an aid of efficiency, reducing human error and obviating the possibility of favoritism; and defended as well as being no more intrusive than having the human supervisor substituted-for actually present. If one why not the other? As a federal court observed of a company's use of computerized global positioning technology to monitor its drivers, it permits the company 'to see a truck's exact location, speed, direction, and engine RPM's on a second-by-second basis. *The on-board computer system allows managers to virtually ride with every driver at all times*.'[6]

This reasoning has been persuasive to the American judiciary;[7] but the emphasis given to the word 'virtually' illuminates the difference technology makes. It would be

---

[3] *See generally*, Matthew Finkin, *Menschenbild: The Conception of the Employee as a Person in Western Law*, 23 COMP. LAB. L. & POL'Y J. 557 (2002).

[4] Beth Ahlering and Simon Deakin, *Labor Regulation, Corporate Governance, and Legal Origin: A Case of Institutional Complementarity?*, 41 LAW & SOCIETY REV. 865 (2007).

[5] As early as the 1840s, federal armory workers protested the installation of time clocks as a manifestation of 'military oppression.' Merritt Roe Smith, *Military Entrepreneurship* in YANKEE ENTERPRISE 63, 93 (Otto Mayr & Robert Post, eds. 1981). Department store saleswomen in 1920s complained that time clocks likened them to prisoners. Susan Banson, COUNTER CULTURES: SALESMEN, MANAGERS, AND CUSTOMERS IN AMERICAN DEPARTMENT STORES 1890–1940, 231–2 (1986).

[6] *Reinhardt v. Gemini Motor Transport*, 869 F. Supp. 2d 1158, 1162 (E.D. Cal. 2012) (emphasis added).

[7] Employees subject to continuous video surveillance at their work stations at a public sector worksite claimed the monitoring to violate the constitutional prohibition of unreasonable search applicable to public employees. The court opined that the workers:

> concede that, as a general matter, employees should expect to be under supervisors' watchful eyes while at work. But at some point, they argue, surveillance becomes unreasonable. In their estimation, when surveillance is electronic and, therefore, unremitting – the camera, unlike the human eye, never blinks – the die is cast. In constitutional terms, their theory reduces to the contention that the Fourth Amendment precludes management from observing electronically what it lawfully can see with the naked eye.

Vega-Rodriguez v. Puerto Rico Tel. Co., 110 F. 3d 174, 180 (1st Cir. 1997). The court rejected the claim. For private sector employees to whom the Fourth Amendment does not apply, but a

economically out of the question for an employer to post a supervisor in every work situation or in the cab of every delivery truck to observe and record an employee's every utterance, glance, and motor movement. It is the technology that makes feasible what would have been infeasible – and more.[8] It is the growth in the sophistication of the technology and the fact that some, perhaps much of it, does not merely substitute a machine for that which a supervisor had been doing that gives the issues of dehumanization its salience.

Three technologies will be addressed: May an employer require an applicant or an incumbent employee to supply the employer with a password to her social media sites to which she has otherwise restricted access? May an employer require an employee to carry on her person a chip – in a badge or cell phone – that will enable the employer to locate the employee with geographic precision in real time? May an employer require an employee to log in certain biometric data – fingerprint, handprint, iris, or facial identification – to control and record access to its facility? May an employer combine these technologies to monitor the course of an employee's total interactions?

The analysis of these questions under U.S., German, and Japanese law will tell us something about the value these countries attach to the anthropological function Supiot would have the law perform – of how their laws conceive of the human values at stake – and whether there appears to be any prospect of legal convergence despite the rather different cultural starting points.

C. Values and the Law

1. Autonomy

In both English and German the word derives from the Greek: a conjunction of the self (*autos*) and law (*nomos*); of the person as possessed of the capacity to be a self-governing or 'law-giving' agency. (Kant was to develop a moral philosophy based upon that notion.) The concept in Western usage carries a strong connotation of independence, of freedom from control:

> Autonomy has been variously conceived of as (1) personhood and acting as a person; (ii) taking one's own decisions, at least in the important affairs of his life, and directing one's own life; (iii) constructing or building a life of value for oneself; and (iv) adopting or living out a life plan: each conception is individualist and involves agency.[9]

---

common law of wrongful invasion of privacy might apply, they, too, could have no claim of a 'reasonable expectation' of electronic non-observance in an area open to human supervisory inspection.

[8] It is possible electronically to monitor the cabs of a company's vehicles including continuous video and audio recording of the drivers. The technology allows the recording to a 'G-force' event, not only a collision but a bump or a sharp swerve. These data can be transmitted by a contractor performing this service to the employer, including the video and audio monitoring for the seconds before and after the event. Was the driver using a cell phone? Drowsing? These can be used for training and disciplinary purposes. *See e.g.*, http://www.drivecam.com.

[9] R.G. Frey, *Privacy, Control, and Talk of Rights* in THE RIGHT TO PRIVACY 45, 55 (Ellen Paul, Fred Miller, Jr., and Jeffrey Paul, eds, 2000).

How does the power to direct one's own life, to be free of external control, square with the employment relationship? Wage labor existed as a modest institution in the ancient world alongside independent contractorship, patronal relations, various forms of bondage and slavery, but came to flourish in Europe and Japan in the eighteenth century. The free wage laborer had the capacity to enter into a contract of employment, surely an act of self-direction. But the conundrum is that the employment relationship is one of subordination: by entering into employment the employee placed himself under the control of another, often under legal regimes forbidding the employee to terminate the relationship before its contractual end, absent good reason so to do. Ancient Greek and Roman elites found wage labor distasteful: to work under the power of another was, to them, a mark of servility.

To philosophers of natural law of the early eighteenth century the circle could not be squared. True freedom of contract, as an expression of autonomy, could only exist where the bargaining parties stood in a relationship of equality. The fact of employment, into which the employee entered as a result of extreme want (why else would one give up her autonomy?) was inherently reflective of inequality. Thus, a persistent question in the law of employment is whether it should accede to a formal freedom of contract, as 'consent,' here to a loss of privacy or, possibly, of dignity, or should intervene either to limit the scope of agreement or to assure that consent is something more than formal.

a. The United States In the U.S., a legacy of the nineteenth century's embrace of laissez-faire, of a notion of freedom of contract so robust as to have been for a time constitutionalized and used as a bulwark against social legislation, persists. The constitutional barrier was taken down in the late 1930s; but, laissez-faire's common law cousin, the at-will employment rule, survives, save insofar as legislation or public policy might constrain it. The legislative address to the specific issues of privacy and dignity of concern here will be treated below. But the common law of the U.S. attaches little other than formalistic value to employee autonomy. The courts do have available doctrines of unconscionability, economic duress, or good faith to constrain a condition an employer might impose; but, overwhelmingly, the courts decline to apply them in this setting. Absent a specific statutory prohibition or some other well-defined public policy the employee is taken to have consented to any constraint the employer would impose no matter how constrictive of individual autonomy: that men must be clean shaven; that women must wear make-up; that no worker may date a co-worker, *any* co-worker; that the employee not oppose laws supported by the employer; that the employee live in a specific locale, or eject a roommate, or not befriend another.[10]

In sum, freedom of contract in the U.S. is most often the employer's freedom to set the terms and conditions of employment. Absent unionization – and absent some insulating legislation or public policy – the employee's autonomy is nearly exhausted by the act of acceptance or rejection of employment, to stay on or to quit. Indeed, the very interposition of an individual objection, an exercise of agency to express a desire

---

[10] These are collected in Matthew Finkin, PRIVACY IN EMPLOYMENT LAW (4th ed. 2013).

for something more or something else, could subject the employee to discharge, such being the at-will rule.[11]

b. Germany German law gives a different answer to the question of employee autonomy by establishing a legal system in which the employer's power is substantially limited and thus the employee has the real chance to act autonomously as regards his employment relationship. Generally speaking, German law grants to the employee side the voice-option and not only the exit-option. The current legal situation can be understood best against the background of the general development of employment law in Germany showing the bias of German social policy to intervene in the market in order to achieve a fair compromise between employers' and employees' interests.

Basically, the legal orders of Germany and the U.S. rest on the same values including self-determination of the individual and the decision in favor of a market-based economy with private control over means of production. Accordingly, from a conceptual point of view, in Germany, whose legal order does not distinguish between the branches of statutory law and common law, freedom of contract as a core element of private autonomy is undisputedly deemed to belong to the basic principles of private law in general and employment law in particular. Freedom of contract had been established on the level of plain law at the beginning of the nineteenth century before industrialization swept over the Channel,[12] was confirmed in the German Civil Code (*Bürgerliches Gesetzbuch*) of 1900[13] and reaffirmed once more in the field of employment law as recently as ten years ago.[14] Moreover, freedom of contract is guaranteed by constitutional law; expressly in the Weimar Constitution of 1919[15] and implicitly in the Basic Law (*Grundgesetz*) of 1949 as part of the right to free development of the personality[16] and – as regards employment contracts – of the right to occupational freedom.[17]

However, this is only one side of the coin. From the very beginning a considerable number of German economists and lawyers highlighted the phenomenon that in the working world freedom of contract, which in theory should enable both parties to the contract to express and coordinate their will, leads in practice to contracts which mirror only the will of the employer due to his prevailing bargaining power.[18] When Max

---

11 This is discussed in greater detail in Matthew Finkin, *Employee Self-Representation and the Law in the United States*, 50 OSGOOD HALL L.J. 937 (2013).

12 Freedom of contract was part of the fundamental modernization of Prussia after 1807 (so called Stein-Hardenbergian reforms), afterwards generalized in s. 134 Prussian Common Industrial Code (*Preußische Allgemeine Gewerbeordnung*) of 1845.

13 Freedom of contract is assumed but (in contrast e.g. to art. 19 of the Swiss Code of Obligations (*Obligationenrecht*) of 1911) not expressly provided in the German Civil Code.

14 Section 105 Industrial Code (*Gewerbeordnung*), revised version of 2002. Explanatory statement for the amendment in Bundestags Drucksache 14/8796 (2002), p. 23.

15 Article 152, para. 1 Weimar Constitution.

16 Article 2, para. 1 Basic Law; cf. BVerfG 12.11.1958, BVerfGE 8, 274 (at 328).

17 Article 12, para, 1 Basis Law; cf. BVerfG 23.11.2006, NZA 2007, 85 (at 86).

18 The discussion is depicted in detail by Martin Becker, Arbeitsvertrag und Arbeitsverhältnis in Deutschland. Vom Beginn der Industrialisierung bis zum Ende des Kaiserreichs (1995); Andreas Kaiser, Zum Verhältnis von Vertragsfreiheit und Gesellschaftsordnung während des 19.

Weber wrote that the formal freedom of contract granted to the employee assures not the least real freedom for him to influence his working conditions,[19] this statement echoed a common understanding not only by socialist authors but also by many conservative reformers like the so-called 'academic socialists' (*Kathedersozialisten*). Economic liberalism as a weapon against feudalism and as an ideology of the upcoming civil society – in the words of Hegel, the battlefield of individual private interests of all against all[20] – which had some committed followers in Germany in the first half of the nineteenth century, was quick to be discredited and a distrust against the idea of self-regulation of economy only by market forces spread. It was in the last decades of the nineteenth century that the short story of a largely liberal economy in Germany concluded and the state began to intervene increasingly in the economic sphere. This turn to a more activist state at the formative stage can be explained by the fact that economic liberalism was not hard won by a self-confident middle-class but granted by the state for the purpose of modernizing Germany. Thus, economic liberalism was qualified primarily as a means to an end and it could be confined without major resistance when the most influential forces in the state assessed that the unleashing of market forces jeopardized public welfare.[21] Furthermore, the rigid attitude of German employers, in particular in the heavy industry (*Herr im Haus*), provoked the employee side, and the state, traditionally conceptualized as antipode to the society, realized the necessity to take action in favor of the employees in order to maintain its own precarious legitimacy and to stabilize the social system.

However, the road to pursue employees' autonomy with the tool of employment law was long and intricate. In the first instance the focus of the state was on the repair of markets results (most prominent by way of the Bismarckian reforms in the 1880s) and not on direct market intervention.[22] Accordingly, in the nineteenth and early twentieth century private law did very little to reduce the employer's power. The prevailing approach in that period was to tackle the social problems of the working world by particular pieces of public law and not by private law, which was regarded mainly as a formal instrument of legally free and equal people for the pursuit of their own selfish interests.[23] Thus, the Civil Code of 1900 contained only 'one drop of socialist oil'.[24]

Jahrhunderts (1972); Joachim Rückert, *'Frei' und 'sozial': Arbeitsvertrags-Konzeptionen um 1900 zwischen Liberalismen und Sozialismen*, Zeitschrift für Arbeitsrecht (ZfA) 1992, pp. 225–94.

[19] Max Weber, *Wirtschaft und Gesellschaft* (1921/22, 5th ed. 1972), p. 439.

[20] Georg Wilhelm Friedrich Hegel, *Grundlinien der Philosophie des Rechts* (1821, 2nd ed. 1989), § 289.

[21] Dieter Grimm, *Die sozialgeschichtliche und verfassungsrechtliche Entwicklung zum Sozialstaat*, in: idem, Recht und Staat der bürgerlichen Gesellschaft (1987), pp. 138–61 (at pp. 152–3).

[22] Cf. Bob Hepple, Welfare legislation and Wage-Labour, in: Bop Hepple (ed.), *The Making of Labour Law in Europe* (1986), pp. 114–53 (at pp. 133–7).

[23] Cf. Gottlieb Planck, *Die soziale Tendenz des Bürgerlichen Gesetzbuches*, Deutsche Juristen-Zeitung (DJZ) 1899, pp. 181–4 (at 181); from a current perspective Joachim Rückert, *Das Bürgerliche Gesetzbuch – ein Gesetzbuch ohne Chance?*, Juristenzeitung (JZ) 2003, pp. 749–60.

[24] Cf. Otto von Gierke, *Die soziale Aufgabe des Privatrechts* (1889), p. 13. More details to the lack of notice concerning employment contracts in private law in the run-up to the Civil

Beginning with the 'new course' of 1890,[25] the following decades of German employment law were characterized by a growing number of protective acts which demonstrated that the working world had become a matter of public interest, culminating in the Weimar Constitution of 1919, which provided that labor stands under the special protection of the Reich.[26] Sure enough, in that period the mainstream favored a paternalistic protection of the employee and not a strengthening of employees' autonomy.[27] An expression of this thinking was the blurred conception of the employment relationship as a 'personal communitarian relationship' (*personenrechtliches Gemeinschaftsverhältnis*).[28] This non-liberal conception, which obligated the employer to take care of the employee (*Fürsorge*) and in turn demanded that the employee be faithful (*Treue*),[29] was long the dominant approach[30] and remained so until the 1960s.[31] Nevertheless, the historical development clarifies the deeply rooted persuasion in German social policy that the state is called upon to establish a suitable framework for employment relations and that the embodiment of labor regimes cannot be left only to market forces.

The most important steps towards a more autonomy-biased conception of employment law were made in the period after World War II. Multiple developments converged, which should be mentioned to get a full picture.

First, the compensation of unequal bargaining power and other deficits of the parity of contract became one of the great topics in German private law in general.[32] Both in

---

Code in Tilman Repgen, *Die soziale Aufgabe des Privatrechts* (2001), pp. 215–31; Alfred Söllner, Der industrielle Arbeitsvertrag in der deutschen Rechtswissenschaft des 19. Jahrhunderts, in: Walter Wilhelm (ed.), Studien zur europäischen Rechtsgeschichte (1972), pp. 288–303.

25 Hermann Reichold, *Der 'Neue Kurs' von 1890 und das Recht der Arbeit: Gewerbegerichte, Arbeitsschutz, Arbeitsordnung*, Zeitschrift für Arbeitsrecht (ZfA) 1990, pp. 5–41.

26 Article 157 of the Weimar Constitution '*Die Arbeitskraft steht unter dem besonderen Schutz des Reiches*'.

27 'Left' approaches to enhance collective autonomy (first and foremost Hugo Sinzheimer) were at that time less influential in jurisdiction and academia.

28 This conception can be traced back to Otto von Gierke, *Die Wurzeln des Dienstvertrages*, in: Juristenfakultät der Universität Berlin (ed.), Festschrift für Heinrich Brunner (1914), pp. 37–68.

29 Classical analysis in Otto Kahn-Freund, *Das soziale Ideal des Reichsarbeitsgerichts* (1931).

30 E. g. BAG 10.11.1955, BAGE 2, 221 (at 224); Herbert Wiedemann, *Das Arbeitsverhältnis als Austausch -und Gemeinschaftsverhältnis* (1966). See also (the later president of the Federal Constitutional Court) Ernst Benda, Industrielle Herrschaft und sozialer Staat (1966), pp. 411–583, in particular pp. 439–53, arguing against 'labor as commodity' and at least to a certain extent in favor of enhancing employee's autonomy.

31 Reinhard Richardi, *Arbeitsrecht als Teil freiheitlicher Ordnung* (2002), pp. 247–9.

32 See cf. Ludwig Raiser, *Vertragsfreiheit heute*, Juristenzeitung (JZ) 1958, pp. 1–8; Hans Merz, *Privatautonomie heute – Grundsatz und Rechtswirklichkeit* (1970); Ernst A. Kramer, *Die 'Krise' des liberalen Vertragsdenkens* (1974); Hermann Weitnauer, *Der Schutz des Schwächeren im Zivilrecht* (1975); Günther Hönn, *Kompensation gestörter Vertragsparität* (1982); Lorenz *Fastrich, Richterliche Inhaltskontrolle im Vertragsrecht* (1992); Christian Heinrich, *Formale Freiheit und materiale Gerechtigkeit* (2000).

legislation and before the courts,[33] the formalistic view of contract law was replaced increasingly by an extensive 'materialization'.[34] The Federal Constitutional Court (*Bundesverfassungsgericht*) even decided that the Basic Law, more precisely the fundamental right to free development of personality[35] in combination with the social state principle, which is proclaimed in the constitution as well,[36] does not only allow but prescribes a judicial review of a contract in favor of the weaker party, regarding the question as to whether or not the contract contains unacceptable conditions.[37] According to this general tendency in German private law, the Federal Labor Court (*Bundesarbeitsgericht*) reviewed the appropriateness of burdensome clauses in employment contracts for decades by case law, arguing predominantly to the weak position of the employee.[38] The same spirit is reflected in the Federal Constitutional Court's iterations, that the employee typically finds himself in a situation of 'structural inferiority'.[39] In 2002, the German legislature affirmed this approach by revising the Civil Code and giving the courts the power to scrutinize the appropriateness of every standard clause (with the exception of so-called 'main conditions') in an employment contract.[40] Consequently, the Federal Labor Court ruled that a contract clause imposing the duty on a posted employee to draw up his tax account by a tax consulting firm chosen by the employer is invalid.[41] The same is true in regard to unilateral decisions of the employer concerning the performance or the conduct of the employee; these are

[33] Cf. the plea for a limitation of freedom of contract in order to ensure real self-determination of the weaker party by the previous president of the Federal Supreme Court (*Bundesgerichtshof*) Robert Fischer, *Vertragsfreiheit und Sozialbindung*, Deutsche Richterzeitung (DRiZ) 1974, pp. 209–13.

[34] Depicted in detail by Claus-Wilhelm Canaris, Wandlungen des Schuldrechts. Tendenzen zu seiner 'Materialisierung', Archiv für die civilistische Praxis (AcP) 200 (2000), pp. 273–364; see also Jürgen Habermas, Faktizität und Geltung (1992), pp. 472–93. However, the 'master tale' of an extreme liberal German private law in the nineteenth century as an antipode for a social private law in the twentieth century seems to be an oversimplification cf. Sibylle Hofer, Freiheit ohne Grenzen? (2001).

[35] Article 2, para. 1 of the Basic Law.

[36] Article 20, para. 1 and art. 28, para. 1 of the Basic Law: 'The Federal Republic of Germany is a democratic and *social* federal state.'

[37] BVerfG 19.10.1993, BVerfGE 89, 214 (at 231–4); affirmed in BVerfG 6.2.2001, BVerfGE 103, 89 (at 100–1); BVerfG 26.7.2005, BVerfGE 114, 1 (at 34–5) and BVerfGE 114, 73 (at 89–90); BVerfG 6.12.2005, BVerfGE 115, 51 (at 67–8); BVerfG 7.9.2010, NJW 2011, 1339 (at 1340). The Federal Labor Court quickly adopted that aproach, cf. BAG 16.3.1994, BAGE 76, 155 (at 166–9). The whole issue is discussed in detail in Matthias Ruffert, Vorrang der Verfassung und Eigenständigkeit des Privatrechts. Eine verfassungsrechtliche Untersuchung zur Privatrechtswirkung des Grundgesetzes (2001).

[38] In detail described in Rüdiger Krause, in: Susanne Clemenz/Burghard Kreft/Rüdiger Krause, AGB-Arbeitsrecht (2013), Einführung, at no. 14.

[39] BVerfG 26.6.1991, BVerfGE 84, 212 (at 229); BVerfG 28.1.1992, BVerfGE 85, 191 (at 213); BVerfG 4.7.1995, BVerfGE 92, 365 (at 395); BVerfG 29.12.2004, NZA 2005, 153 (at 155); BVerfG 23.11.2006, NZA 2007, 85 (at 87); BVerfG 1.12.2010, NZA 2011, 60 (at 61).

[40] Sections 305 et seq Civil Code. Individually bargained clauses are very rare in employment contracts. Hence the less strict judicial review of this kind of clause is irrelevant.

[41] BAG 23.8.2012, BAGE 143, 62 (at 67–76).

valid only if discretion is reasonably exercised.[42] Though these legal developments lead directly only to a domestication of employer's power they enlarge employee's autonomy automatically.

Second, since 1951[43] employees who come within the scope of the Employment Termination Protection Act (*Kündigungsschutzgesetz*)[44] are protected against arbitrary dismissals by the employer: dismissal requires just cause, it must be socially justified. This voice-approach instead of an exit-approach flanks the autonomy of the worker and the exercise of rights because the level of freedom within the employment relationship correlates with the power of the employer to fire the employee,[45] although the protection against dismissals cannot be reduced to only that function. Thus, the question whether or not a conduct of the employee constitutes a just cause is crucial for the extent of employee's autonomy. However, the tendency is towards more freedom for the employee. This can be shown by the way the courts decide in cases regarding dismissals on the grounds of statements critical of the employer on intra-plant issues or on political issues. By now, the Federal Labor Court requires a concrete violation of contractual duties for the justification of a dismissal,[46] whereas older decisions held it to be sufficient that the employee disregarded unspecified 'basic rules of employment relationships.'[47] Accordingly, criticizing the employer would ordinarily not constitute just cause, even if the employee's utterance is polemical or strident.[48] Whistleblowing also does not justify a termination as long as the employee is acting in good faith.[49] This is also (on the grounds of the European Human Rights Convention which is applicable in Germany) emphasized by the European Court for Human Rights, which rejected a rather rigid approach of a German regional labor court.[50]

Last but not least, the existence of a system of tripartite labor courts – foreshadowed in 1890, expanded in 1926 and fully completed since 1953 – has intertwined the logic

---

[42] Section 106 Industrial Code (*Gewerbeordnung*).

[43] The Works Council Act of 1920 had already established a protection against dismissals but its level was lower than the Act of 1951 and it was dependent on the existence of a works council in the respective works.

[44] The establishment must have more than ten (full-time) employees and the employment contract must have lasted more than six months (s. 1, para. 1 and s. 23, para. 1 Employment Termination Protection Act).

[45] Cf. Eberhard Dorndorf, *Vertragsdurchsetzung als Funktion des Kündigungsschutzes*, Zeitschrift für Arbeitsrecht (ZfA) 1989, pp. 345–76; Martin Franzen, Das Persönlichkeitsrecht des Arbeitnehmers als Grundlage des arbeitsrechtlichen Kündigungsschutzes, in: Rüdiger Krause/Roland Schwarze (eds), Festschrift für Hansjörg Otto (2008), pp. 71–91 (at 84–91); more generally Harro Plander, Arbeitsrecht – Instrument zur Verwirklichung von Grundrechten des Arbeitnehmers, in: Wolfgang Däubler et al. (eds), Arbeit und Recht. Festschrift für Albert Gnade (1992), pp. 79–93.

[46] BAG 24.6.2004, NZA 2005, 158 (at 160); BAG 12.1.2006, NZA 2006, 917 (at 920).

[47] BAG 3.12.1954, BAGE 1, 185 (at 194); BAG 23.2.1959, BAGE 7, 256 (at 261); BAG 6.2.1969, BAGE 21, 340 (at 345–6).

[48] Cf. BAG 24.6.2004, NZA 2005, 158 (at 161); BAG 24.11.2005, NZA 2006, 650 (at 652); BAG 12.1.2006, NZA 2006, 917 (at 921).

[49] BAG 3.7.2003, BAGE 107, 36 (at 41); BAG 7.12.2006, NZA 2007, 502 (at 503–4); similar BVerfG 2.7.2001, NZA 2001, 888 (at 889–90) (testifying against the employer).

[50] ECHR 21.7.2011, NZA 2011, 1269 (at 1271–4).

of law and the logic of working life by the participation of lay judges from labor and management. This system of separate labor courts has contributed to the high level of 'juridification' of employment relations (and, arguably, to its de-politicization) as a characteristic feature of German employment and labor law.[51] This model has been widely emulated. It finds no counterpart in the U.S., with the exception of tripartite labor arbitration under collective bargaining agreements; but is echoed in the advisory labor tribunal system in Japan, attached to the district courts.

c. Japan In Japan, companies are regarded as paternalistic or corporatistic communities. The employment system has been characterized by long-term employment, formerly more often referred to as 'lifetime employment'. Consequently, protection for employees' autonomy *(jiritsu* in Japanese) has been considered in the context of the business necessities of the corporation.

The modern Japanese employment relationship, starting with its development after the Meiji Restoration in the mid-nineteenth century, took on a strong communal nature. Some *zaibatsu*, corporate conglomerates, in their inception as corporations around the mid-nineteenth century were organized in a way that emphasized the unity of the management and its workforce as if they were family members.[52] During the Sino-Japanese War and WWII, employer-employee cooperative associations at workplaces, called *Sangyo Houkokukai*, were established which similarly stressed the unity of labor and management and also strengthened the paternalistic nature of the employment relationship.[53] Meanwhile, in the 1920s, large Japanese companies, in order to secure their control of their workforce,[54] started systematically to hire newly graduated students to give them firm-specific skill and training and to keep them employed for a long time, or for life.[55] Although Article 627 of the Civil Code provides that employment is 'at will,' the courts after the end of the WWII limited the employer's right to dismiss relying on the doctrine of abuse of right thus conducing toward the practice of long-term employment. The introduction of this long-term (or lifetime) employment practice further entrenched the view that the employer-employee relationship was like that of a family with a leader and dependents.

Against this background, labor and employment law in Japan, whose real development started only after the end of the WWII, paid little attention to employee autonomy

[51] For a comprehensive assessment of this phenomenon Spiros Simitis, Zur Verrechtlichung der Arbeitsbeziehungen, in: Friedrich Kübler (ed.), *Verrechtlichung von Wirtschaft, Arbeit und sozialer Solidarität*, 1985, pp. 73–165.

[52] Nobuyoshi Toshitani, *Kindai Nihon no Kigyo Chitsujyo (the Corporate Order in Modern Japan)*, in Tokyo Daigaku Syakai Kagaku Kenkyusho ed., 4 Gendai Nihon Syakai (Japanese Society Today) pp. 141, 161–9, 174–5 (1991).

[53] Yutaka Nishinarita, Kindai Nihon Roshikankeishi no Kenkyu (Study on the Modern Industrial Relations in Japan) (1988), pp. 425–9.

[54] Japanese companies had difficulty taking control of their workforce before 1920s because until then they had employed their workforce only *indirectly* through 'labor bosses.' See Kazuo Okouchi, Roshi Kankei Ron no Shiteki Hatten (Historical Development of Industrial Relations Theory), pp. 186–9 (1972).

[55] Ibid., pp. 189–91.

(or to privacy and dignity).[56] For example, the Supreme Court shortly after the end of the WWII upheld the validity of an employment contract that required the employees to promise not to engage in political activities in the workplace; it was considered a matter of the freedom of contract.[57]

As the Japanese economy rapidly grew through 1960s, however, not only employee economic satisfaction but also their maturity as citizens began to attract concern.[58] Scholars started to emphasize the importance of securing the autonomy of employees in the employment relationship, pointing out that the connection's strong communal nature often led to extensive and comprehensive interference into employees' autonomy and personal rights.[59]

In 1977, the Supreme Court,[60] while confirming the employer's authority to establish corporate order (such as workplace discipline) which employees were required to observe, opined that that did not mean that employees were generally subject to their employer's plenary control.[61] The Court ruled that an employee was not obliged to cooperate with her employer's investigation where cooperation was either unnecessary or unreasonable; *e.g.*, investigation on matters that had no direct relationship with business operation or in that which the employer had already had knowledge.[62]

The Supreme Court later held that it was undue infringement of an employee's freedom to form personal relationships freely, for an employer, where there was no concrete fear of disturbance of the corporate order, to isolate and ostracize employees who support communism.[63] More recently, if there was no concrete fear of disturbance of the corporate order or no business necessity, if restrictions on autonomy of employees go too far in maintaining the corporate order or in fulfilling business necessities, the courts will hold that employers are not allowed to discharge or discipline their employees based on such reasons as: dating a co-worker;[64] moonlighting;[65] wearing well-groomed beards in workplaces even where there is a 'no-beard'

---

[56] Kunishige Sumida, *Rodosya Jinkakuken no Syatei (the Scope of the Personal Rights of Employees)*, in Syozo Yamada and Yasuo Ishii (eds), 1 Rodosya Jinkakuken no Kenkyu (the Study on the Personal Rights of Employees) pp. 3, 6 (2011).

[57] *Hara v. Tokachi Joshi Syogyo Gakko*, 6 Minshu 258 (S. Ct., Feb 22, 1952).

[58] Kunishige Sumida, *Kigyo Shakai ni Okeru Rodosya Jinkaku no Tenkai (Development of the Personal Right of Employees in Corporate Society)* 78 Nihon Rodoho Gakkaishi, pp. 5, 13–14 (1991); Satoshi Nishitani, Kisei ga Sasaeru Jiko Kettei (Regulations as Support System of Self-determination), pp. 157–8 (2004).

[59] *See, e.g.*, Kunishige Sumida, *Roshi Kankei ni Okeru Rodosya no Jinkakutekirieki no Hogo (Protection of the Personal Rights of Employees)*, 354 Rodo Hanrei 4, at 12 (1981).

[60] *Noguchi v. Fuji Jyukogyo*, 31 Minshu 1037 (S. Ct., Dec 13, 1977).

[61] Ibid., at 1042.

[62] Ibid., at 1042–3.

[63] *Kansai Denryoku v. Hayami*, 680 Rodo Hanrei 28 (S. Ct., Sep 5, 1995).

[64] *See, e.g., Kono (anonym) v. Hanki Kosetsu*, 554 Rodo Hanrei 17 (Asahikawa Dist. Ct., Dec 27, 1989); *X (anonym) v. Nihon Koloido*, 1916 Rodo Hanrei Keizai Sokuhou 23 (Tokyo Dist. Ct., Aug 12, 2005).

[65] *See, e.g., Kono (anonym) v. Jyochi Gakuin,* 1303 Hanrei Taimuzu 158 (Tokyo Dist. Ct., Dec 5, 2008).

policy;[66] or for dying one's hair against one's employer's direction.[67] Disciplinary measures for criticizing the employer's employment policy[68] or whistleblowing[69] are also invalid if the criticism is legitimate in terms of its credibility, purpose, and method.

In sum, today the case law has come to protect the autonomy of employees from employer interventions that lack a concrete fear of disturbance of the corporate order or reasonable business necessity. The question will be, therefore: what a concrete fear of disturbance of the corporate order or reasonable business necessity is? This is to be decided on a case-by-case basis. The courts, in general, carefully examine the employer's reason for restricting the employee's autonomy; they seem to recognize the threat to employee autonomy especially in communal and relatively closed workplaces under long-term employment relationship, or for employees who lack outside option ('exit') due to the state of the labor market. But, the formula the courts employ has the potential easily to legitimate employer interventions, insofar as the courts find or confirm a reasonable business necessity.[70] The autonomy of employees is, in this sense, dependent on the judicial view of business necessity and may not necessarily be freely exercised.

2. Privacy

There is an intense philosophical debate on whether privacy – a word that came into English usage only in the sixteenth century – has a core meaning, stands for a cluster of distinguishable concepts, or is merely a proxy for autonomy, the 'right to be left alone.'[71] Some see privacy as an aspect of dignity – of the right to be treated (and regarded) as a person, as an end and not a mere means. Again, by any of these routes, the concept emphasizes the individual: and in this theorists supportive of privacy in the U.S. and on the continent do not disagree that the individual must be shielded from personal inspection and revelation in order fully to flourish, to develop a 'self.'[72]

a. The United States The legal protection of privacy in American law is a late development. In 1960, William Prosser assembled 300 appellate opinions and, organizing them around four distinct categories – the two critical ones here being wrongful

---

[66] *See, e.g., Takeishi v. Eastern Airport Motors* 31 Rominshu 1202 (Tokyo Dist. Ct., Dec 15, 1980); *Kono (anonym) v. Yubin Jigyo*, 1006 Rodo Hanrei 49 (Kobe Dist. Ct., Mar 26, 2010).

[67] *Nishiura v. Higashitaniyamaya* 732 Rodo Hanrei 53 (Fukuoka Dist. Ct. Kokura Br., Dec 25, 1997).

[68] *Morisawa v. Sanwa Ginko*, 790 Rodo Hanrei 44 (Osaka Dist. Ct., Apr 17, 2000).

[69] *See, e.g., A (anonym) v. D (anonym)*, 855 Rodo Hanrei 22 (Osaka Dist. Ct., Sakai Br., Jun 18, 2003). The Whistleblower Protection Act also prevents employers from taking disadvantageous actions for employees' legitimate whistleblowing.

[70] *Compare Watanabe v. Tokyo Denryoku*, 512 Rodo Hanrei 12 (S. Ct., Feb 5, 1988), in which the Supreme Court held that inquiring whether an employee was a communist member was lawful under the specific fact of the case, *with Kansai Denryoku v. Hayami*, *supra* note 63.

[71] Barrington Moore, PRIVACY: STUDIES IN SOCIAL AND CULTURAL HISTORY (1983); Nomos XIII, PRIVACY (Pennock & Chapman eds. 1971); Elizabeth Nell, RITES OF PRIVACY AND THE PRIVACY TRADE (2001); Daniel Solove, UNDERSTANDING PRIVACY (2008).

[72] Jeffrey Reiman, *Privacy, Intimacy and Personhood*, 6 PHILOS. & PUBLIC AFFAIRS 26, 39 (1976). *See also* Beate Rössler, DER WERT DES PRIVATEN (2001); Wolfgang Sofsky, PRIVACY: A MANIFESTO (Steven Randall trans. 2008).

intrusion into seclusion and wrongful dissemination of personal information – declared the privacy puzzle solved.[73] The claim was premature. Seven years later, Alan Westin's *Privacy and Freedom* (1967), addressed the pervasive threat the encroachment of privacy posed to the individual. Nevertheless, Prosser's taxonomy bore fruit in the American Law Institute's *Restatement (Second) of Torts* (1977), which set Prosser's four categories in stone and became widely accepted by state courts. But, a decade later, David Linowes' *Privacy in America* (1987), addressed a range of employer privacy-invasive practices on which the common law had no bite at all: data collection (credit and criminal histories, background checks), testing (medical, psychological, drugs) and computer monitoring. Since then, the legal landscape has become littered with legislation – federal and state, broad and narrow – as well as a weltered body of case law.

The common law tort of wrongful intrusion requires that the employee first have a 'reasonable expectation' of non-intrusion. A positivist approach to this element would, and does, allow an employer to disclaim the existence of any such expectation in consequence of which no reasonable expectation to the contrary could be founded. The common law tort of wrongful dissemination of personal information requires widespread publicity, allowing disclosure to another or to a small group to pass without legal protection; and, in both cases, the intrusion or the publication must be 'offensive,' which points to the interest protected being less privacy per se than emotional well-being.[74] These torts have scant purchase when an employer pursues a privacy-invasive policy of which the employee has been informed or which a court determines to serve a business interest; that is, because it has either been consented to – the voluntaristic nature of which is never questioned – or because the business need is thought to be incapable of being offensive.

Consequently, the workhorses of employee privacy in the U.S. are legislative. In that, the U.S. has no concept of data protection and so no data protection law as such, nor any federal (or state) data protection agency. The statutory law is an amalgam of federal and state legislation dealing with specific subjects – sometimes sweepingly, sometimes with surgical narrowness – often with ambiguities and large gaps, almost entirely dependent on individual litigation for vindication.

b. Germany German law[75] follows a different approach as regards privacy and provides a unitary concept of a general right of personality (*Allgemeines Persönlichkeitsrecht*). This right has the character of a 'framework right' (*Rahmenrecht*) and serves as a source for the formation of a series of specified rights in order to protect the diverse facets of the human personality according to the onward technological and societal development. Though most of the cases decided by German courts could

[73] William Prosser, *Privacy*, 49 CAL. L. REV. 383 (1960).

[74] Prosser said as much. Ibid.

[75] The following is depicted in detail in Edward J. Eberle, Human Dignity, Privacy, and Personality in German and American Constitutional Law, 1997 UTAH L. REV. 963 (1997), pp. 963–1056; Paul M. Schwartz and Karl-Nikolaus Peifer, Prosser's Privacy and the German Right of Personality: Are Four Privacy Torts Better than One Unitary Concept?, 98 CAL. L. REV. 1925 (2010), pp. 1925–87.

without any problems be placed into one of the four categories of U.S. law, the German concept of an all-around protection of the personality is broader than the U.S. approach to privacy and thereby ensures a higher level of protection.[76]

The general right of personality is a creation of the courts and, even in the present day, only case law. Although several German law scholars[77] transferred the term personality (which was treated by Kant only in his works on ethics and not on law) into a legal context and suggested the acknowledgment of a general right of personality as early the nineteenth century,[78] the German Civil Code – unlike the Swiss Legislation[79] – refrained from establishing such a right; it would not fit into the legislature's policy to create only clear and restricted tort law actions and limit judicial power.[80] Until its very end, the Supreme Court of the German Reich (*Reichsgericht*) accepted this legislative intent and denied the existence of a general right of personality; however, to a certain extent, the gap was filled by a broad interpretation of the tort for intentional damages caused by offending good morals and by other provisions.[81]

The legal situation changed fundamentally after World War II. In a groundbreaking decision of 1954, the Federal Supreme Court acknowledged the existence of a general right of personality as part of private tort law.[82] The Court justified this renunciation of the previous jurisdiction by referring to basic (constitutional) rights enshrined in the Basic Law of 1949, more precisely to the protection of human dignity[83] and the right to free development of personality.[84] Thus, the decision expresses the effect of constitutional rights on the so-called ordinary law (*einfaches Recht*) including private law. This

---

[76] An early assessment thereof is given by Harry D. Krause, The Right to Privacy in Germany – Pointers for American Legislation?, 1965 DUKE L. J. 481 (1965), pp. 481–530 (at p. 488).

[77] Among others in particular Otto von Gierke, *Deutsches Privatrecht*, Vol. 1 (1895), pp. 702–17.

[78] Cf. Helmut Coing, Die Entwicklung des Persönlichkeitsrechts im 19. Jahrhundert, in: Armin Kaufmann (ed.), Rechtsstaat und Menschenwürde. Festschrift für Werner Maihofer (1988), pp. 75–86; Robert Scheyhing, *Zur Geschichte des Persönlichkeitsrechts im 19. Jahrhundert*, Archiv für die civilistische Praxis (AcP) 158 (1959/60), pp. 503–25; Jürgen Simon, *Das Allgemeine Persönlichkeitsrecht und seine gewerblichen Erscheinungsformen* (1981), pp. 169–90. The general development of personality in the history of ideas and of law is depicted in Heinrich Hubmann, *Das Persönlichkeitsrecht* (2nd ed. 1967), pp. 1–174; Karl-Nikolaus Peifer, *Individualität im Zivilrecht. Der Schutz persönlicher, gegenständlicher und wettbewerblicher Individualität im Persönlichkeitsrecht, Immaterialgüterrecht und Recht der Unternehmen* (2001), pp. 6–53.

[79] Swiss Civil Code (*Zivilgesetzbuch*) of 1907, art 28 and Swiss Code of Obligations (*Obligationenrecht*) of 1911, art 49.

[80] Cf. Protokolle der Kommission für die zweite Lesung des Entwurfs des Bürgerlichen Gesetzbuches, Vol. II (1898), p. 571.

[81] Cf. RG 29.5.1902 RGZ 51, 369 (at 373); RG 7.11.1908, RGZ 69, 401 (at 403); RG 8.6.1912, RGZ 79, 397 (at 398); RG 12.5.1926, RGZ 113, 413 (at 414–5).

[82] BGH 25.5.1954, BGHZ 13, 334 (at 338); more precisely in BGH 2.4.1957, BGHZ 24, 72 (at 76–8).

[83] Article 1, para. 1 of the Basic Law.

[84] Article 2, para. 1 of the Basic Law.

effect, often described as 'Constitutionalization' ('*Konstitutionalisierung*'),[85] can be regarded as the most important change in German legal thinking in the second half of the twentieth century and is strongly propelled by the landmark Lüth-decision of the Federal Constitutional Court of 1958 holding that basic rights establish an 'objective order of values' and give guidance for all parts of law.[86] From a political or social-psychological point of view this turn can be explained as a reaction to the horrors of the National Socialist terror regime and its total disregard of human personality. This dark history raised a renaissance of natural law and sometimes even religious appeals in German legal thinking after 1945 in order again to find solid ground,[87] which was the implied background of the acknowledgement of a general right of personality, as the then president of the Federal Supreme Court openly admitted.[88] Hence, the abrupt turn to an entire protection of personality in German private law in the post-war period was a result of the specific historical and mental situation of that time.[89] In a great number of consequent decisions the Federal Supreme Court has affirmed this approach, including its extension only a few years later by accepting contra legem the possibility of the plaintiff's ability to sue for immaterial damages.[90] Though several attempts to codify the general right of personality failed, it has since then been unanimously acknowledged as an element of German private law.[91] The Federal Constitutional Court approved the case law of the Federal Supreme Court as being in conformity with the Basic Law.[92] Furthermore, the Court has declared expressly that there is a general right of personality as a part of constitutional law as well.[93]

Even though the level of private law and the level of constitutional law have to be distinguished, the constitutional backing is important because the private right must be interpreted in the light of the constitutional right. This means that every extension of the constitutional general right of personality, developed by the Federal Constitutional Court, must also be adhered to by the ordinary courts. Beyond that, the qualification of the general right of personality as a constitutional right has the effect that the Court's general approach concerning the protective function of basic rights applies. According to this approach, fundamental rights – often in combination with the social state

---

85 From an outside view *see* Mattias Kumm, Who is Afraid of the Total Constitution? Constitutional Rights as Principles and the Constitutionalization of Private Law, 7 GERMAN LAW JOURNAL (2006), 41.

86 BVerfG 15.1.1958, BVerfG 7, 198 (at 205).

87 Cf. Ulfrid Neumann, Rechtsphilosophie in Deutschland seit 1945, in: Dieter Simon (ed.), Rechtswissenschaft in der Bonner Republik. Studien zur Wissenschaftsgeschichte der Jurisprudenz (1994), pp. 145–87 (at 145–56).

88 Hermann Weinkauff, *Der Naturrechtsgedanke in der Rechtsprechung des Bundesgerichtshofes*, Neue Juristische Wochenschrift (NJW) 1960, pp. 1689–96 (at p. 1693).

89 This is depicted in detail in Stefan Gottwald, *Das allgemeine Persönlichkeitsrecht. Ein zeitgeschichtliches Erklärungsmodell* (1996), pp. 59–197.

90 BGH 14.2.1958, BGHZ 26, 349 (at 354–7).

91 See only Heinrich Hubmann, *Das Persönlichkeitsrecht* (2nd ed. 1967).

92 BVerfG 14.2.1973, BVerfGE 34, 269 (at 281–2).

93 BVerfG 3.6.1980, BVerfGE 54, 148 (at 153).

principle[94] – have not only the function to prevent state activity but also to demand state activity in order to protect fundamental rights against private infringements and hence safeguard their full effectiveness in societal reality.[95] This is important in particular in situations of structural inferiority like the employment relationship.[96]

The structure of the general right of personality is complex.[97] The Federal Constitutional Court once drew a distinction and stated that this right calls for the – passive – respect of a protected sphere, whereas the general right to free development aims to protect the – active – unfolding of the person's own personality.[98] However, in concrete situations, such as the adoption of a dress code, these categories become blurred because, as in this example, the decision of an employee about what underwear to wear will touch both dimensions. A traditional approach, still employed by the Federal Supreme Court,[99] is to distinguish between different spheres (social, private and intimate) and to demand a greater weight of the justifying reason if the measure at stake intrudes into the inner circle. Moreover, the Court has developed over the course of time different case groups for typical cases, although this taxonomy is not exhaustive. At the end of the day a balancing approach applies. If the personality of somebody is affected the Courts will carefully balance the interests of both parties at stake in order to clarify whether the general right of personality is violated.[100]

As regards the employment relationship the general right of personality of the employee as part of private (tort) law has to be respected by the employer as a matter of course. Whereas the protection of the personality of the employee was mentioned only sporadically in the Weimar period, the Federal Labor Court immediately adopted the approach of the Federal Supreme Court mentioned above and transferred it into employment law.[101] Many other decisions followed and the principle of protecting the employee's personality is now absolutely undisputed in German employment law. This protection is completed substantially by works councils – elected by the whole staff of an establishment with at least five employees regardless of unionization – as another deeply rooted pillar of German collective labor law[102] parallel to unions. The works councils play a vital role in the protection of the personality of the employees in two

[94] Article 20, para. 1 of the Basic Law.

[95] Cf. Johannes Dietlein, *Die Lehre von den grundrechtlichen Schutzpflichten* (2nd ed. 2005).

[96] In the early phase of its jurisdiction the Federal Labor Court applied fundamental rights even directly against the employer, but with similar results. This deviation in employment law was abandoned in the 1980s.

[97] Cf. Marion Baston-Vogt, *Der sachliche Schutzbereich des zivilrechtlichen allgemeinen Persönlichkeitsrechts* (1997).

[98] BVerfG 3.6.1980, BVerfGE 54, 148 (at 153).

[99] Cf. BGH 23.6.2009, BGHZ 181, 328 (at 338); BGH 25.10.2011, NJW 2012, 767 (at 767–8); BGH 20.12.2011, NJW 2012, 771 (at 771–3).

[100] For a current overview see only Roland Rixecker, in: Münchener Kommentar zum Bürgerlichen Gesetzbuch (6th ed. 2012), Appendix to section 12: Das Allgemeine Persönlichkeitsrecht.

[101] BAG 10.11.1955, BAGE 2, 221 (at 224–5).

[102] The origins go back into the year 1891 (introduction of facultative works councils). Further important steps are the Works Council Act of 1920, the Works Constitution Acts of 1952 and of 1972 and a minor extension of that Act in 2001.

regards. First, since a fundamental reform of the Works Constitution Act (*Betriebsverfassungsgesetz*) in 1972, it is a legal duty both of the employer and the works council to protect and encourage the free development of the personality of the employees of the establishment.[103] Thus, for example, the Federal Labor Court declared an agreement between the employer and the works council that allowed permanent video surveillance null and void on the grounds that it violated the personality rights of the staff.[104]

Second, the works council has codetermination rights concerning all employer measures that aim to regulate the conduct of employees[105] and on the introduction and use of any technical equipment designed to monitor the conduct or performance of the employees.[106] Every action of the employer in that field without the consent of the works council (or a decision of the so-called conciliation committee (*Einigungsstelle*) with a neutral chairman) is unlawful; thus, an employee does not violate his contract if he refuses a measure taken by the employer who has disregarded the employees' codetermination rights. Empirical data show that, in 2013, only 43 per cent (West Germany) and 35 per cent (East Germany) of the employees were represented by works councils.[107] Nevertheless, nearly all large establishments, those with more than 500 employees (92 per cent in West and in East Germany), have works councils.[108]

Agreements on issues that are covered by the general right of personality are possible and can influence the balancing of interests. However, the consent of the worker to the employment contract is not regarded as such as legitimizing every employer policy or order that affects the personality of the employee.[109] Moreover, as mentioned above, even an explicit contract clause on privacy issues in a standard employment contract is only valid if it balances the interests of the employer and the employee in a legally appropriate manner. A restriction of the conduct of an employee that belongs to his intimate sphere is not allowed,[110] whereas a dress code requiring the wearing of standardized service clothing (in a retailer chain for office supplies)[111] or a jacket and

---

[103] Section 75, para. 2 Works Constitution Act.

[104] BAG 29.6.2004, BAGE 111, 173 (at 176–90).

[105] Section 87, para. 1 No. 1 Works Constitution Act.

[106] Ibid., No. 6 Works Constitution Act. This provision is interpreted broadly by case law. It is sufficient that the technical device is *suitable* to monitor the conduct or performance of the employees; cf. BAG 9.9.1975, BAGE 27, 256 (at 261).

[107] Peter Ellguth/Susanne Kohaut, *Tarifbindung und betriebliche Interessenvertretung: Aktuelle Ergebnisse aus dem IAB-Betriebspanel 2013*, WSI Mitteilungen 2014, pp. 286–95 (at p. 292).

[108] See ibid., p. 302.

[109] Expressly discussed by Günther Wiese, *Der Persönlichkeitsschutz des Arbeitnehmers gegenüber dem Arbeitgeber*, Zeitschrift für Arbeitsrecht (ZfA) 1971, pp. 273–317 (at 282). In the same sense BAG 29.6.2004, BAGE 111, 173 (at 181–2).

[110] Thus a dismissal (outside of the scope of the Employment Termination Protection Act) is not valid if it is motivated by the homosexuality of the employee: BAG 23.6.1994, BAGE 77, 128 (at 135–7). However, German courts sometimes fail to meet the line; cf. LAG Köln 18.8.2010, NZA-RR 2011, 85 (at 88) which accepted a works agreement, inter alia, on the color of the underwear.

[111] LAG Hamm 7.7.1993, LAGE § 611 BGB Direktionsrecht Nr. 14.

a tie (in a store for distinguished furniture)[112] is permitted. The difference between Germany and the U.S. was placed in a strong light when Wal-Mart tried to implement its code of employee conduct on its German subsidiaries, prohibiting co-workers dating one another – a 'no fraternization' rule. The rule is, apparently, unremarkable and quite lawful in the U.S..[113] It violates the general right of personality of the employee under German law.[114]

A particular aspect of the general right of personality is the right to informational self-determination (*informationelle Selbstbestimmung*).[115] Here we witness the close interrelationship of the value concepts – autonomy, privacy, dignity – that frame this chapter.

The right of informational self-determination was developed by the Federal Constitutional Court on the occasion of the 1983 census.[116] Living in the NSA-era, the amount of data sought to be collected at that time was ludicrously small. But from the very beginning, the underlying principle was clear: the gathering and processing of data about people, and not only the decision-making on the grounds of such data, affects one's personality; it affects one's behavior when someone knows that another person is surreptitiously or even openly collecting and storing personal data. As the then president of the Federal Constitutional Court put it, the very essence of the decision is not about the perception of a protected private sphere but about the idea that autonomy as core element of personality requires autonomy as regards the disclosure of personal data.[117] It is the freedom to a self-determined life and its relevance for a democratic society which stands behind the right of informational self-determination.[118] In other words, it is 'data power' and the uncertainty which personal data circulate, that creates a situation in which unselfconscious behavior is at risk and a deformation of personality is impending. From this, the latest 'invention' of the Federal Constitutional Court is the recognition – or creation – of a fundamental right to the confidentiality and integrity of technical information systems, to protect against being spied on, and the

---

112 LAG Hamm 22.10.1991, LAGE § 611 BGB Direktionsrecht Nr. 11.

113 Finkin, *supra* n. 10 at pp. 626–33.

114 Cf. LAG Düsseldorf 14.11.2005. NZA-RR 2006, 81 (at 87–8); Tina Kolle, Olaf Deinert, *Liebe ist Privatsache. Grenzen einer arbeitsvertraglichen Regelung zwischenmenschlicher Beziehungen*, Arbeit und Recht (AuR) 2006, pp. 177–84 (at 178–81).

115 This term was apparently created by Steinmüller et al., Grundfragen des Datenschutzes, 1971, Bundestagsdrucksache VI/3826 (1971), Appendix 1, p. 139.

116 BVerfG 15.12.1983, BVerfGE 65, 1 (at 42–3). An important forerunner decision was BVerfG 16.7.1969, BVerfGE 27, 1 (at 6–8). The literature on that topic is immense; see Marion Albers, *Informationelle Selbstbestimmung* (2005); Hans Peter Bull, *Informationelle Selbstbestimmung – Vision oder Illusion?* (2nd ed. 2011), pp. 22–66; Klaus Vogelsang, *Grundrecht auf informationelle Selbstbestimmung?* (1987).

117 Ernst Benda, *Das Recht auf informationelle Selbstbestimmung und die Rechtsprechung des Bundesverfassungsgerichts zum Datenschutz*, Datenschutz und Datensicherheit (DuD), 1984, pp. 86–90 (at 88–9). Very early conceptualized in Ernst Benda, Privatsphäre und 'Persönlichkeitsprofil', in: Gerhard Leibholz et al. (eds), *Menschenwürde und freiheitliche Rechtsordnung*. Festschrift für Willi Geiger (1974), pp. 23–44 (at 27–44).

118 BVerfG 15.12.1983, BVerfGE 65, 1 (at 42–3); BVerfG 22.8.2006, NJW 2007, 351 (at 354); BVerfG 13.6.2007, BVerfGE 118, 168 (at 184–5).

manipulating of personal computers and similar devices.[119] In line with general principles, the right to informational self-determination is not only directed vertically against state activity but also influences horizontally the interpretation of private law.[120] Moreover in situations of structural inferiority the state has to intervene in order to protect the informational self-determination of the weaker part.[121] Accordingly the Federal Labor Court has employed the right to informational self-determination of workers in assessing employer's measures in several decisions.[122] In that respect, there are fundamental differences in the perception of the threat data collection poses for the protection of personality between law in Germany and in the U.S.[123] No doubt, the historical experience of state surveillance in the fascist period, and also under a communist regime, has caused a special sensitivity on that issue which does not exist in American legal culture.

Data protection, the protection of people against the collecting, processing, and use of personal data, is not only a question of the general right of personality either on the private law side or on the constitutional law level. Germany was in fact the frontrunner for enacting special data protection laws, starting with the first Federal Data Protection Act (*Bundesdatenschutzgesetz*) in 1977,[124] and extended several times since. Although the Act does not refer in its wording expressly to the right to informational self-determination, it states in a comparable way that its purpose is to protect individuals against infringements of their right of personality as the result of the handling of their personal data.[125] From the very beginning, the Act covered not only public authorities, but private bodies as well, expressing the policy that the individual often stands in a situation of inferiority to enterprises.[126] Thus the employment relationship falls under the scope of the Federal Data Protection Act, although for the first of some 30 years the Act did not mention employees in terms. With an amendment of 2009, when some data scandals in large German corporations became public, the Act now addresses employment relationships explicitly and applies to all collection of employee data even without the help of automated processing systems or non-automated filing systems (which is normally the prerequisite for the application of the Federal Data Protection

---

119 BVerfG 27.2.2008, BVerfG 120, 274 (at 302–15); authentic interpretation by the previous judge at the Federal Constitutional Court Wolfgang Hoffmann-Riem, *Der grundrechtliche Schutz der Vertraulichkeit und Integrität eigengenutzter informationstechnischer Systeme*, Juristenzeitung (JZ) 2008, pp. 1009–22.

120 BVerfG 11.6.1991, BVerfGE 84, 192 (at 194–5); see also BGH 23.6.2009, BGHZ 181, 328 (at 337–8).

121 BVerfG 23.10.2006, JZ 2007, 576 (at 577).

122 E.g. BAG 6.6.1984, BAGE 46, 98 (at 105); BAG 4.4.1990, BAGE 64, 308 (at 312); BAG 29.6.2004, BAGE 111, 173 (at 180).

123 Cf. Benedikt Buchner, *Informationelle Selbstbestimmung im Privatrecht* (2006).

124 The worldwide first act on this issue at all was the Hessian Data Protection Act from 1970.

125 Section 1, para. 1 Federal Data Protection Act.

126 Bundestagsdrucksache 7/1027 (1973), p. 17. However, in its first version the Act embraced only the processing of personal data by private bodies. It was not until an amendment of 2001 that the scope of the Act was extended on the collection of personal data by private bodies as well.

Act).[127] As all forms of employee surveillance can qualify as the collection of personal data, the Act is now the main instrument governing such measures.

According to the general concept of the Federal Data Protection Act, every kind of collection of personal data is prohibited unless it is legitimized (i) by legal provision or (ii) by consent of the affected individual.[128] The consent must be based on a free decision.[129] Doctrinally, it is strongly disputed whether a decision of an employee can ever be regarded as truly 'free'.[130] At a minimum, statements of the employee in standard contracts are scrutinized carefully by the Federal Labor Court on whether they are appropriate.[131] Thus, in practice, the 'consent' of the workers plays only a minor role. Turning to legal provisions as the legitimizing factor the collection of employee personal data, the general rule requires employment-related purposes: the necessity of collecting the data for hiring or, after hiring, for carrying out or terminating the employment contract, and so forth.[132]

This policy is also pursued by European law, which should be sketched in here.[133] The European Charter of Fundamental Rights (entered into force in December 2009) provides (i) a right to respect for private life (Art. 7) and (ii) a right to the protection of personal data (Art. 8).[134] The European Court of Justice (ECJ) has decided that the right to respect for private life with regard to the processing of personal data concerns any information relating to an identified or identifiable individual.[135] Moreover, in 1995, the Directive 95/46/EC on data protection was promulgated.[136] It aims to protect the right to privacy in member states of the EU regardless of the nationality or residence of the natural persons and at the same time to establish a level playing field in order to ensure that personal data can flow freely from one member state to the

---

[127] Section 32, Federal Data Protection Act.

[128] Section 4, para. 1 Federal Data Protection Act.

[129] Section 4a, para. 1 Federal Data Protection Act.

[130] In detail (in parts controversely) discussed in Peter Gola, *Die Einwilligung als Legitimation für die Verarbeitung von Arbeitnehmerdaten*, Recht der Datenverarbeitung (RDV) 1992, pp. 109–16 (at pp. 110–11); Karl Riesenhuber, *Die Einwilligung des Arbeitnehmers im Datenschutzrecht*, Recht der Arbeit (RdA) 2011, pp. 257–65 (at p. 261).

[131] BAG 23.8.2012, BAGE 143, 62 (at 72).

[132] Section 32, Federal Data Protection Act.

[133] For the following, in detail, Gloria Gonzáles Fuster, *The Emergence of Personal Data Protection as a Fundamental Right of the EU* (2014).

[134] Also mentioned in art. 16, para. 1 of the Treaty on the Functioning of the European Union. Discussed in depth by Gabriele Britz, *Europäisierung des grundrechtlichen Datenschutzes?*, Europäische Grundrechte-Zeitschrift (EuGRZ) 2009, pp. 1–11.

[135] Joined Cases C-92/09 and C-93/09 *Volker und Markus Schecke and Eifert* [2010] ECR I-11063, para. 52, and Joined Cases C-468/10 and C-469/10 *ASNEF and FECEMD* [2011] ECR I-12181, para. 42. See also Joined Cases C-293/12 and C-594/12 *Digital Rights Ireland Ltd. and Kärntner Landesregierung* [2014], paras 26 and 37.

[136] Directive 95/46/EC of the European Parliament and of the Council of 24 October 1995 on the protection of individuals with regard to the processing of personal data and on the free movement of such data, O.J. 1995, L. 281, 31–50. See also Directive 2002/58/EC of the European Parliament and of the Council of 12 July 2002 on the concerning the processing of personal data and the protection of privacy in the electronic communication sector, O.J. 2002, L. 201, 37–47.

other.[137] This directive sets a floor of protection in all areas of law including employment matters throughout the European Union.[138] However, the ECJ held that member states are not allowed to provide a higher level of protection, in order to avoid hindrances to the free flow of data within the EU.[139] At the moment a new and very ambitious general data protection regulation is under way[140] which would preclude member state action along that line, but the deliberations are sluggish.[141] Interestingly the draft of the regulation states that consent may not serve as legal basis for data processing 'where there is a significant imbalance between the position of the data subject and the controller'.[142] Although addressed to prominent data controllers such as Google, this provision would apply to employment relationships as well.[143] Nevertheless, one criticism is that the regulation mainly follows the traditional approach of European law qualifying personal data as a commodity and data protection more as tool to build trust of consumers in the online environment in order to boost economy instead of enhancing autonomy as a value.[144] However, the ECJ tends in its jurisdiction to strengthen the interests of the individuals and thus employs the fundamental right to the protection of personal data also in legal relations between private subjects,[145] recently in the Google-case developing a 'right to be forgotten'.[146] The development of a European fundamental right to the protection of personal data in employment law is much discussed in the academic literature.[147]

---

137 Cf. Recitals No. 2 and 3 of Directive 95/46/EC.

138 A special directive on worker data protection was frequently considered by the European Commission but never came to a close.

139 Joined Cases C-468/10 and C-469/10 *ASNEF and FECEMD* [2011] ECR I-12181, paras 27–39.

140 Cf. Proposal for a Regulation of the European Parliament and of the Council on the protection of individuals with regard to the processing of personal data and on the free movement of such data (General Data Protection Regulation) of 25.1.2012, COM (2012) 11 final. For more details see Anne-Marie Zell, Data Protection in the Federal Republic of Germany and the European Union: An Unequal Playing Field, 15 GERMAN LAW JOURNAL (2014), pp. 461–94 (at pp. 486–92). For a partially critical view from the U.S. perspective see Paul Schwartz, The EU-U.S. Privacy Collision: A Turn to Institutions and Procedures, 126 HARV. L. REV. 1966 (2013).

141 At the moment a nonofficial consolidated version dates from 22.10.2013; *available at:* http://www.janalbrecht.eu/fileadmin/material/Dokumente/DPR-Regulation-inofficial-consolidated-LIBE.pdf (last visited 1.4.2015).

142 Article 7, para. 4 Proposal General Data Protection Regulation.

143 The nonofficial version (*supra* n. 140) treats this aspect in art. 82, para. 1b expressly. In the same sense the Explanatory Memorandum of Directive 95/46/EC made clear, that 'consent must be "freely given", in cases where pressure might be brought to bear on the data subject (the case of a wage-earner and his employer, for example)', cf. COM (1992) 422 final, p. 11.

144 Cf. COM (2012) 9 final, p. 2; COM (2012) 11 final, Explanatory Memorandum, pp. 1–2.

145 Case C-543/09 *Deutsche Telekom v. Bundesrepublik Deutschland* [2011] ECR I-3441, paras 49–66; Case C-70/10 *Scarlet Extended SA v. Société belge des auteurs, compositeurs et éditeurs SCRL (SABAM)* [2011] ECR I-11959, paras 50–51.

146 Case C-131/12 *Google Spain v. Agencia Espanola de Protección de Datos (AEPD)* [2014], paras 66–71.

147 Stephan Pötters, *Grundrechte und Beschäftigtendatenschutz* (2013), pp. 232–7; Rudolf Streinz and Walther Michl, *Die Drittwirkung des europäischen Datenschutzgrundrechts (Art. 8*

Last, but not least, the European Convention on Human Rights also provides a right to privacy (Art. 8). Even though this Convention primarily aims to protect human rights against state action, the European Court on Human Rights has developed state duties to protect individuals against private action as well.[148] The European Council Convention for the Protection of Individuals with regard to Automatic Processing of Personal Data of 1981,[149] which targets the public and the private sector, emphasizes once more the general sensibility in Europe as regards data protection and, as the Explanatory Report to the Convention puts it, the perception that 'information power' brings with it a corresponding social responsibility.[150]

However, the level of concerns about data privacy by organizations that hold personal data varies greatly in the European countries with citizens from Austria (70 per cent) and Germany (65 per cent) at the top and Netherlands (8 per cent) and Finland (5 per cent) at the bottom expressing their very level of concern about that issue.[151] Moreover as experiments show even in Germany there is a privacy paradox as many people when asked appreciate the protection of personal data as valuable but do not care for data protection in their daily life.[152] As regards the legal framework, the inflation of fundamental rights in the current European multi-level setting causes a number of problems in multi-polar relationships because the gain of freedom of one private actor automatically results in a loss of freedom to act by the other. Thus, one of the current pivotal problems in basic rights issues, including privacy issues, in the future will be the coordination of the several jurisdictions in the European multi-level system of fundamental rights.[153]

c. Japan The notion of privacy has been a difficult one for Japanese people to understand. The very fact that privacy has been referred to as '*puraibashi*' in Japanese, which is a simple transliteration of English word, indicates its strangeness. One of the important reasons for the difficulty is the way the Japanese society developed the concepts of public ('*ooyake*') and private ('*watakushi*') and the distinction between these notions. '*Ooyake*' and '*watakushi*', in the way understood in present Japanese

---

GRCh) im deutschen Privatrecht, Europäische Zeitschrift für Wirtschaftsrecht (EuZW) 2011, pp. 384–8 (at 385–8). As to the consequences of the 'right to be forgotten' for employment law see Gerrit Forst, *Das Recht auf 'Vergessenwerden' der Beschäftigten*, Betriebs-Berater (BB) 2014, pp. 2293–8.

[148] Discussed in detail by Christoph Grabenwarter, *European Convention on Human Rights, Commentary* (2014), Article 8 nos. 73–80; Angelika Nußberger, Die Verantwortung des Staates für das Handeln Dritter auf der Grundlage der Europäischen Konvention für Menschenrechte, in: Marten Breuer et al. (ed.), *Der Staat im Recht, Festschrift für Eckart Klein* (2013), pp. 1203–18.

[149] http://conventions.coe.int/Treaty/en/Treaties/Html/108.htm.

[150] http://conventions.coe.int/Treaty/EN/Reports/HTML/108.htm.

[151] See Gallup Organization, Data Protection in the European Union, Citizens' Perceptions, Analytical report, Flash Eurobarometer 225 (2008), p. 7, http://ec.europa.eu/public_opinion/flash/fl_225_en.pdf.

[152] Cf. Alastair R. Beresford et al., Unwillingness to Pay for Privacy: A Field Experiment (2011), SFB 649 discussion paper, No. 2011-010, http://hdl.handle.net/10419/56724.

[153] Cf. Markus Kotzur, *Der Schutz personenbezogener Daten in der europäischen Grundrechtsgemeinschaft*, Europäische Grundrechte-Zeitschrift (EuGRZ) 2011, pp. 105–15.

society, have their origin in mid-eighth century.[154] At that time, the sphere of national affairs or '*ooyake*' expanded and '*watakushi*', which had been a translated notion from the Chinese word '*si*', came to be understood to cover only peripheral matters attendant upon and dependent on '*ooyake*.'[155] To make comprehension even more difficult, the distinction between '*ooyake*' and '*watakushi*' was vague.[156] The concepts of '*ooyake*' and '*watakushi*' understood as such remained basically unchanged for centuries, and provide the basis for how Japanese understand 'public' and 'private' today. Some scholars point out that private means '"part" of public' in Japanese context.[157]

In addition to the cultural background concerning the distinction of public and private, the communal nature of the Japanese employment system and long-term employment practice have resulted in little care for privacy in workplaces until recently.[158] Analysis invariably starts with the reasoning of the Supreme Court in the 1973 decision in *Mitsubishi Jushi v. Takano*.[159] In that case, the Court held that absent 'statutory or other special restrictions,'[160] – and there are few such restrictions[161] – the employer is free to hire, and that a refusal to hire due to the applicant's thought or conscience was not necessarily unlawful. Therefore, it was not illegal for the employer to investigate an applicant's thoughts or conscience and to require applicants to provide relevant information. The Supreme Court pointed out, as one of the rationales for the holding, that 'an employment relationship, as a kind of continuing human relations, required mutual trust of an employer and an employee and that it was all the more so in Japan where lifetime employment practice prevailed.'[162] In fact, employers have been expected to collect, and have indeed collected, personal information about employees under long-term employment practices, because, on the one hand, employers are allowed the authority flexibly to change terms and conditions of employment of their employees, but, on the other hand, are obliged to take care for their employees, to ameliorate the effect of modification. Thus, for example, employers have been required: to inquire about and consider the situations of their employees and their families on ordering transfer;[163] and take care for the health and safety of their employees to

---

154 Takeshi Mizubayashi, *Nihonteki 'Kou-Shi' Gainen no Genkei to Tenkai (Origin and Development of 'Public' and 'Private' in Japan)*, in Takeshi Sasaki and Kim Tae-Chang eds., Nihon ni Okeru Kou to Shi (Public and Private in Japan) pp. 1, 12–13 (2002).

155 Ibid.

156 Ibid., at p. 13.

157 Makoto Higashijima, *Ooyake ha Paburikku Ka? (Is 'Ooyake' 'Public'?)*, in Takeshi Sasaki and Kim Tae-Chang eds., Nihon ni Okeru Kou to Shi (Public and Private in Japan) pp. 63, 66–7 (2002).

158 Takashi Araki, Personal Information and Privacy Protection of Employees and Japan's Employment System 8 Journal of the Japan-Netherlands Institute 167, pp. 167–8 (2005).

159 27 Minshu 1536 (S. Ct., Grand Bench, Dec 12, 1973).

160 Ibid., at 1545.

161 The Supreme Court denied that the art. 3 of the Labor Standards Act, which prohibited discrimination in working conditions based on nationality, thought or social status, be such a restriction, holding that it only proscribed discrimination *after* an employee was employed and did not regulate employers' decision to hire or not to hire.

162 27 Minshu 1536, at 1546.

163 *See, e.g.*, *Toa Paint v. Yoshida*, 477 Rodo Hanrei 6 (S. Ct., Jul 14, 1986).

prevent problems such as deaths from overwork.[164] To fulfill these obligations employers are expected to know a great deal of personal information about their workers the collection of which would be legally problematic in Germany.

Commencing in the 1960s, Japanese scholars of constitutional law and civil law as well as the courts began to discuss the right to privacy, especially referring to the discussion in the U.S.[165] Thought on personal rights in the workplace progressed following rapidly evolving information technology, together with the social change, and especially since the late 1990s in legal regulation for protection of personal information in (and outside) the workplaces: in Article 5-4 of the Employment Security Act, as amended in 1999, providing that employers that recruit employees and collect personal information on jobseekers can do so only to the extent necessary for recruitment purposes; in the Personal Information Protection Act of 2003, obligating large companies[166] to specify the purpose for collecting personal information, limit the use of personal information to the specified purpose, to acquire personal information in an appropriate manner and to provide notice of the purpose in acquiring personal information. Although these statutes anticipate criminal or administrative sanctions for violation and do not have direct civil effect, it is possible that violating these statutes would be a factor in deciding whether an employee can seek civil remedies, such as damages, for an infringement of privacy.

The courts compare the employer's purpose, method, and manner of collecting information or monitoring with inconveniences brought to the affected employee in deciding whether there is an infringement of the employee's privacy. Thus, the Supreme Court held that it was an infringement of employee privacy for an employer, without a concrete fear of disturbance of the corporate order, to open the employee's locker and take photographs of his notebook without his permission and that the employer was liable for damages for the employee's consequent pain and suffering.[167] The courts apply the same framework to e-mail monitoring by employers, though the courts tend to dismiss employees' claims for violation of privacy in specific cases.[168]

Protection of privacy in workplaces, as with protection for employee autonomy, depends on a balancing of the business necessity for collecting the information or monitoring against the disadvantages to employees by these measures. The framework seems to be derived, again, from long-term employment systems in which employers need to develop and maintain a 'good' personal relationship with their

---

[164] *See, e.g.*, *Dentsu v. Oshima,* 54 Minshu 1155 (S. Ct., Mar 24, 2000).

[165] Masami Ito, Puraibashi no Kenri (the Right to Privacy) (1963); Masami Ito and Michitaka Kaino eds., *Puraibashi Kenkyu* (Study on Privacy) (1962).

[166] The obligations under the Act are applied only to the business proprietor having 5000 or more items of personal information.

[167] *Kansai Denryoku v. Hayami*, *supra* note 63.

[168] *See, e.g.*, *A (anonym) v. C (anonym)*, 826 Rodo Hanrei 76 (Tokyo Dist. Ct., Dec 3, 2001); *Koyama (anonym) v. Rodo Seisaku Kenkyu Kensyu Kiko*, 882 Rodo Hanrei 50 (Tokyo Dist. Ct., Sep 13, 2004). In these cases, the employers did not specifically prohibit employees from sending and receiving private e-mails. It is not yet clear whether the courts will confirm the possibility of privacy protection where an employer expressly bans the use of e-mail for private purposes.

employees, and from the fact that employees are more prone to be subordinated to their employer.

3. Dignity

The concept of dignity – in Latin, *dignus*, means 'worth,' and in German, *Würde*, a cognate of 'worth,' (human dignity = *Menschenwürde*) – is as, or even more, philosophically contentious than privacy. One observer has discerned five different concepts;[169] another four.[170] And some see no meaning at all. Nevertheless, the word is enshrined in a host of national constitutions, subject accordingly to widely varying judicial interpretations,[171] and in numerous international declarations and conventions as well as in national laws.

The most common understanding of what dignity means proceeds from the idea that there lies in every human being a core or kernel of humanity that demands respect, else the person's very humanity be reduced or denied. This conception is reflected in Kant's injunction that each person be treated as an end and not be regarded or treated as merely a means to some other's end. That proposition, philosophically contested,[172] has been defended on existential[173] or experiential grounds: that respect for one's person is something that people need and seek from others, something employees seek from their employers.[174]

Dignity is sometimes identified with or taken to be a cognate of honor insofar as we speak of the 'dignity of office' or the like, of a higher respect due another. This usage points to a critical distinction, however. Honor rests on social differentiation, whether of wealth, age, merit, or hereditary status. Dignity, either in the Kantian or existential sense, assumes, indeed, presupposes, equality – whence the many political declarations that advert to the equality of all persons before the law. The idea that humanity, as a species, enjoys a dignity that raises it above the animals is an old precept, although, as we have seen, not one universally accepted in Western thought.[175] The idea that all persons must be regarded as equal in dignity is historically novel.[176]

a. The United States In the U.S., 'dignity' is oftentimes expressed in judicial opinions as a value.[177] Even as it might be referred to as underpinning the protection of

---

[169] Virginia Black, Dignity in THE PHILOSOPHY OF LAW: AN ENCYCLOPEDIA 208 (1999).

[170] Michael Rosen, DIGNITY: ITS HISTORY AND MEANING 114 (2012).

[171] The texture of constitutional interpretation in comparative context is explored by Erin Daly, DIGNITY RIGHTS: COURTS, CONSTITUTIONS AND THE WORTH OF THE HUMAN PERSON (2013).

[172] Rosen, *supra* note 170.

[173] George Kaleb, HUMAN DIGNITY (2011). *See also*, Muriel Fabre-Magnan, *La dignité en Droit: un axióme,* 2007 Revue Interdisciplinaire D'Études Juridiques 1.

[174] Andrew Sayer, WHY THINGS MATTER TO PEOPLE Ch. 6 (2011) and Randy Hodson, DIGNITY AT WORK (2001).

[175] Robert Fossier, THE AXE AND THE OATH: ORDINARY LIFE IN THE MIDDLE AGES 383 (Lydia Cochrane trans. 2010).

[176] Kent Flannery and Joyce Marcus, THE CREATION OF INEQUALITY (2012).

[177] The installation of a hidden video surveillance device to capture misbehavior, for example, was held excessive by an American court with these words: 'The status of being an

reputation or privacy or emotional well-being, it seems not to constitute a cognizable category of wrong in itself.[178] Perhaps the closest the law in the U.S. comes to acknowledging a specific role for dignity is in the tort of infliction of emotional distress. But the focus there is on the outrageous nature of the actor's behavior; and even there, employees in the U.S. are expected to endure insult and invective – absent discrimination against a statutorily protected class – almost as a matter of course.[179]

And so the discussion circles back to where this chapter began: whether the law sees privacy-invasive or dignity-depriving employer policies or actions as legally problematic. Whether, and to what extent, the law accedes to employee consent – and what is meant by consent – as a sufficient response. To what extent, and by what means, does the law intervene, and why.

b. Germany In German law, the fundamental value of human dignity is unquestionable. Article 1, paragraph 1, of the Basic Law declares that human dignity shall be inviolable and stipulates as a duty of all state authority that it be respected and protected. According to its rank at the top of the Basic Law the Federal Constitutional Court has qualified Article 1 as of the 'highest value',[180] as a 'supreme principle of the constitution'[181] and the like.[182] The paramount status of human dignity as a fundamental right cannot look back on a long tradition in German constitutional law. The Weimar Constitution of 1919 had ordered that the economy must be organized based on the principles of justice, with the goal of achieving life in dignity for everyone,[183] but it did not provide for a basic right. Thus Article 1 with its solemn wording was, consciously, a new start as a reaction to the atrocities of the National Socialist regime

---

employee does not carry with it the elimination of personal dignity.' *Richards v. County of Los Angeles*, 775 F. Supp. 2d 1176, 1184 (C.D. Cal. 2011). But the legal question was whether the camera intruded into an area where the employee had a reasonable expectation not to be observed.

[178] Paul Schwartz and Karl-Nikolaus Peifer, Prosser's Privacy and the German Right of Personality: Are Four Privacy Torts Better Than One Unitary Concept?, 98 CAL. L. REV. 1925, 1982 (2010) ('American jurists have proven skeptical of dignity as an organizing principle for legal relations').

[179] However, an employee who quits because she can no longer endure an employer's insults might be able to secure unemployment compensation benefits. *See generally*, *Imperial Valley Servs., Inc. v. Alvarado*, 72 A.3d 165 (D.C. 2013) (reviewing authority) (the employer habitually called the employee 'stupid' and 'a piece of crap' in front of other employees as well as other, more colorful profanities).

[180] E.g. BVerfG 17.8.1956, BVerfGE 5, 85 (at 204); BVerfG 16.7.1969, BVerfGE 27, 1 (at 6).

[181] E.g. BVerfG 16.1.1957, BVerfGE 6, 32 (at 36); BVerfG 13.5.1986, BVerfGE 72, 155 (at 170).

[182] E.g. BVerfG 12.11.1997, BVerfGE 96, 375 (at 399); BVerfG 5.2.2004, BVerfGE 109, 133 (at 149); BVerfG 15.2.2006, BVerfGE 115, 118 (at 152); BVerfG 20.6.2012, BVerfGE 131, 268 (at 286).

[183] Article 151, para. 1 Weimar Constitution.

with its totalitarian disregard of the individual.[184] The common wisdom that creating a constitution is always an attempt to master the future against the background of bad historical experience is particularly true for the German history of constitutions.[185] However, the main legal problem with human dignity is to find a clear legal definition[186] because there is rarely another word that is so intensely loaded with diverging philosophical ideas.[187] Although the Federal Constitutional Court tried to develop a specific legal approach independent from any philosophical conceptions[188] the definition the Court gives is close to the Kantian tradition. Following an influential academic statement[189] the Federal Constitutional Court often employs a (negative) approach and views Article 1, paragraph 1, Basic Law as violated if a concrete individual is debased as a mere object (so-called 'object-formula' *Objektformel*).[190] Sometimes the Court adds that human dignity is infringed only if the quality of an individual as a subject is not respected.[191] Other (positive) approaches emphasize the egalitarian dimension of human dignity and advocate for an understanding of it as a relational term for the quality of human communication in terms of a mutual recognition as equal persons. And even the Federal Constitutional Court stresses in some of its decisions the relation between human dignity and the conception of man that underlies the Basic Law (*Menschenbild des Grundgesetzes*) as a spiritual-moral

---

184 To the history of origins of art. 1 of the Basic Law cf. Jahrbuch des öffentlichen Rechts der Gegenwart (JöR), N.F., Vol. 1 (1951), pp. 48–54. See also Christian Starck, *Menschenwürde als Verfassungsgarantie im modernen Staat*, Juristenzeitung (JZ) 1981, pp. 457–64 (at p. 458).

185 As to the character of the Basic Act as a conscious opposite model to the National Socialist regime expressly BVerfG 4.11.2009, BVerfGE 124, 300 (at 328).

186 See Hans-Georg Dederer, *Die Garantie der Menschenwürde (Art. 1 Abs. 1 GG)*, Jahrbuch des öffentlichen Rechts der Gegenwart (JöR), N.F., Vol. 57 (2009), pp. 89–124; Christoph Enders, Die *Menschenwürde in der Verfassungsordnung* (1997); Tatjana Geddert-Steinacher, *Menschenwürde als Verfassungsbegriff. Aspekte der Rechtsprechung des Bundesverfassungsgerichts zu Art. 1 Abs. 1 Grundgesetz* (1990); Hasso Hofmann, *Die versprochene Menschenwürde*, Archiv des öffentlichen Rechts (AöR) 118 (1993), pp. 353–77; Nils Teifke, *Das Prinzip Menschenwürde. Zur Abwägungsfähigkeit des Höchstrangigen* (2011).

187 See Kurt Bayertz, *Die Idee der Menschenwürde: Probleme und Paradoxien*, Archiv für Rechts- und Sozialphilosophie (ARSP) 81 (1995), pp. 465–81; Carlos Ruiz Miguel, *Human Dignity: History of an Idea*, Jahrbuch des öffentlichen Rechts der Gegenwart (JöR), N.F., Vol. 50 (2002), pp. 281–99.

188 Cf. (the previous judge of the Federal Constitutional Court) Dieter Hömig, Menschenwürdeschutz in der Rechtsprechung des Bundesverfassungsgerichts, in: Ralf Gröschner and Oliver W. Lembcke (eds), *Das Dogma der Unantastbarkeit. Eine Auseinandersetzung mit dem Absolutheitsanspruch der Würde* (2009), pp. 25–52 (at pp. 37–8). Here the Court tries to differentiate between legal and moral communication; as to this distinction, see Niklas Luhmann, *Das Recht der Gesellschaft* (2nd ed. 1997), pp. 78–80.

189 Günter Dürig, *Der Grundrechtssatz von der Menschenwürde. Entwurf eines praktikablen Wertsystems der Grundrechte aus Art. 1 Abs. I in Verbindung mit Art. 19 Abs. II des Grundgesetzes*, Archiv des öffentlichen Rechts (AöR) 81 (1956), pp. 117–57 (at 127).

190 Cf. BVerfG 8.1.1959, BVerfG 9, 89 (at 95); BVerfG 16.7.1969, BVerfGE 27, 1 (at 6); BVerfG 3.3.2004, BVerfGE 109, 279 (at 312).

191 Cf. BVerfG 15.12.1970, BVerfG 30, 1 (at 26); BVerfG 12.11.1997, BVerfGE 96, 375 (at 399); BVerfG 15.2.2006, BVerfGE 115, 118 (at 153).

being with the capacity to self-fulfillment within the society,[192] here following the anthropological perceptions of the Court's first president.[193] In a decision of 2006 the Federal Constitutional Court emphasizes its absolute (nonconsequentialistical) understanding: human dignity cannot be outweighed against other values even human life.[194]

In employment issues, however, the courts rarely refer directly to Article 1, paragraph 1, Basic Law and, accordingly, to human dignity. For example, the Federal Labor Court decided that a clause in a collective agreement on excessive working hours (for physicians), hours that are beyond human capabilities, violated Article 1, paragraph 1, Basic Law.[195] In another decision, the Federal Labor Court held that the 'selling' of an employee, *i.e.,* the transfer of the employment relationship to the transferee of an undertaking ex lege, would not be in conformity with human dignity if the employee lacked the right to oppose the transfer of his contract.[196] Subsequently, however, the court denied a violation of human dignity in such cases.[197]

As regards privacy issues in employment, the courts commonly refer only to the general right of personality or to special provisions like the Federal Data Protection Act. Although the general right of personality is derived from human dignity in its aforementioned (Kantian) sense[198] and both values are intertwined,[199] to draw directly on human dignity as such is neither necessary nor helpful because solutions to practical problems need a careful balancing of employee and employer interests instead of a mere listing of highest values. Even so an express provision in the Austrian Work Constitution Act (*Arbeitsverfassungsgesetz*) that stipulates a codetermination right of the works council if the introduction of technical systems for the control of employees affects human dignity,[200] should remind us that, nowadays, the personality rights of workers are notably endangered by technical progress in surveillance measures.

---

192 BVerfG 20.7.1954, BVerfG 4, 7 (at 15–16), BVerfG 21.6.1977, BVerfGE 45, 187 (at 227); see also Karl Heinz Auer, *Das Menschenbild als rechtsethische Dimension*, Archiv für Rechts- und Sozialphilosophie (ARSP) 93 (2007), pp. 493–518; Ulrich Becker, *Das 'Menschenbild des Grundgesetzes' in der Rechtsprechung des Bundesverfassungsgerichts* (1996); Christan Bumke, *Menschenbilder des Rechts*, Jahrbuch des öffentlichen Rechts der Gegenwart (JöR), N.F., Vol. 57 (2009), pp. 125–48; Günter Dürig, *Die Menschenauffassung des Grundgesetzes*, Juristische Rundschau (JR) 1952, pp. 259–63; Wolfgang Zöllner, Menschenbild und Recht, in: Reinhard Böttcher et al. (eds), Festschrift für Walter Odersky (1996), pp. 123–40.

193 Cf. Josef M. Wintrich, *Zur Problematik der Grundrechte* (1957), pp. 5–10 (citing Kant, Heidegger and other German philosophers and theologians).

194 BVerfG 15.2.2006, BVerfGE 115, 118 (at 151–60).

195 BAG 24.2.1982, BAGE 38, 69 (at 80–81).

196 BAG 2.10.1974, BAGE 26, 301 (at 305–306); BAG 6.2.1980, AP BGB § 613a Nr. 21.

197 BAG 2.3.2006, BAGE 117, 184 (at 194–5).

198 Thus, the analysis of James Q. Whitman, The Two Western Cultures of Privacy: Dignity versus Liberty, 113 YALE L. J. (2004), pp. 1151–221 (at 1187–9), that the German general right of personality rests on the National Socialist ideology of honor is not persuasive. As to this issue see also Lawrence Friedman, A Tale of Two Cultures: Privacy and Dignity, in Matthias Mahlmann (ed.), Festschrift für Hubert Rottleuthner (2011), pp. 273–81 (at 277–81) and Matthew Finkin, Some Further Thoughts on the Usefulness of Comparativism in the Law of Employee Privacy, 14 EMP. RTS. & EMP. POL'Y J. 11 (2010).

199 Cf. Avishai Margalit, *The Decent Society* (1996), pp. 201–11.

200 Section 96, para. 1 No. 3 Work Constitution Act.

Human dignity is not only enshrined in the German Constitution, but also explicitly provided – with nearly the same wording as in the Basic Law – in the European Charter of Fundamental Rights (Art. 1).[201] The explanation emphasizes the pivotal character stating that the dignity of the human person is not only a fundamental right in itself but constitutes the real basis of all fundamental rights.[202] In contrast, the European Convention on Human Rights does not expressly contain an article on human dignity. However, the European Court of Human Rights has stated that the respect for human dignity is 'the very essence of the Convention'.[203] The protection of human dignity on different levels of German and European law can result in conflicts between them if the respective conceptions of dignity develop in diverging directions.[204] But it is more likely that conflicts will arise on the operational level, that is, if a case were to be brought to different courts and the concrete outcome of the weighing of interests by the judges differ – as has happened in a much debated case on freedom of expression (Art. 10 European Convention on Human Rights) some time ago.[205]

c. Japan Dignity ('*songen*' in Japanese) of employees, like autonomy and privacy, has not been well respected in Japanese workplaces where a communalistic nature and the long-term employment practice prevail. However, in tandem with developments in terms of protection for employee autonomy and privacy, scholars and courts have gradually come to insist on the need to protect the dignity as a part of a set of personal rights of employees.[206]

In a Japanese context, dignity of employees in workplaces has mattered mainly with regard to sexual harassment, abuse of power by superiors (often referred to as 'power harassment' in Japan) and bullying. According to the case law, employers are obliged to take care to 'maintain a pleasant working environment for their employees' as a part of their duty of care in employment relationship.[207] If an employer does not take proper measures to prevent or settle sexual harassment, 'power harassment' or bullying in their

---

201 Cf. Astrid Berlth, *Artikel 1 GRCh – Die Menschenwürde im Unionsrecht* (2012); Christian Calliess, Die Menschenwürde im Recht der Europäischen Union, in: Ralf Gröschner and Oliver W. Lembcke (eds), *Das Dogma der Unantastbarkeit. Eine Auseinandersetzung mit dem Absolutheitsanspruch der Würde* (2009), pp. 133–73; Katrin Schwarzburg, *Die Menschenwürde im Recht der Europäischen Union* (2012).

202 O.J. 2007, C. 303, 17-35 (at 17).

203 ECHR 12.6.2003 – 35968/97 – van Kück and Germany, Report of Judgments and Decisions 2003-VII, p. 1 no. 69.

204 Cf. Case 36/02 *Omega* [2004] ECR I-9609. See also Jackie Jones, 'Common Constitutional Traditions': Can the Meaning of Human Dignity under German Law Guide the European Court of Justice? [2004] PUBLIC LAW 167–87.

205 Cf. ECHR 21.7.2011 – 28274/08 – Heinisch, NZA 2011, 1269 (at 1271–4). As neither the Federal Constitutional Court nor the Federal Labor Court had decided on the case as such, a direct clash between these German Courts and the European Court of Human Rights did not occur.

206 Sumida, *supra* note 58, at 15–21.

207 *See, e.g.*, *Kono (anonym) v. Hei (anonym) Kikaku*, 607 Rodo Hanrei 6 (Fukuoka Dist. Ct., Apr 16, 1992).

workplace, he/she will be liable for these incidents as violation of that duty.[208] Employers' duty to care for their employees is derived from the personal and continuing nature of employment contracts and the danger of infringement of personal right under such nature. The dignity of employees is thus discussed in Japan in the context of dealing with negative effects of the continuing nature of employment relationship.

II. EMPLOYERS' ACCESS TO EMPLOYEE SOCIAL MEDIA

A. United States Law

In 2007, the U.S. National Research Council published a report on information technology and privacy. It pointed to employers' increasing demands for information about employees[209] and to the increasing social pressure on individuals to share information about themselves on social media,[210] but it did not envision, even those few years ago, the connection between the two: that employers would demand access to these sites.

In 2007, about 20 per cent of adult Americans who used the internet also used social networking sites. Four years later that figure rose to 65 per cent, especially young adults.[211] More than half of all Americans today have a profile on a social networking

---

208 *See, e.g., Sanyo Denki Consumer Electronics v. Teihara (anonym)*, 987 Rodo Hanrei 29 (Hiroshima High Ct., Matsue Br., May 22, 2009); *Koda (anonym) v. Seisyokai,* 883 Rodo Hanrei 38 (Saitama Dist. Ct., Sep 24, 2004).

209 ENGAGING PRIVACY AND INFORMATION TECHNOLOGY IN A DIGITAL AGE 34–5 (James Waldo, Herbert Lin and Lynette Millet, eds. 2007):

> Employers are demanding more information about employees as they seek to validate employment credentials, to better match a person to a job, and to avoid liability suits. Would-be employees submit extensive application forms documenting previous work histories and education; once hired, they are often subject to drug tests and location checks to help ensure that they are continuing to observe the conditions of their employment. On the job, intensive work monitoring has increased, particularly as individuals work with computers and or work in areas subject to video surveillance. This may go beyond monitoring of work products per se, to the monitoring of behavior unrelated to work and sometimes behavior off-duty.

210 Ibid. at 35:

> Individuals demand more information from each other in many contexts. For example, it is common that individuals – especially young people – using social networking sites post large amounts of personal information. No one forces these people to do so, and yet the social context of the sites' use provides a strong impetus for doing so.

211 Mary Madden and Kathryn Zickuhr, 65 per cent of online adults use social networking sites (Pew Research Center Report) *available at:* http://pewinternet.org/Reports/2011/Social-Networking-Sites.aspx.

site.[212] It has been reported that Facebook, MySpace, Twitter, and LinkedIn represent a combined user base worldwide of over a billion people.[213]

Managers in the U.S. and abroad routinely access applicant and employee social media. In the former, to secure background information thought to be helpful in making a hiring decision.[214] In the latter, possibly to assure that trade secrets and other confidential business information is not being disclosed or to have early warning of possible situations of sexual harassment.[215] The prevalence of applicant screening has been the subject of several surveys. The results are set out below in Table 6.1.

Table 6.1 Use of social networking websites to screen applicants (Facebook, LinkedIn, etc.)

	Use	Has disqualified applicants
SHRM (2011)	18%	15%
Career Builder (2012)	37%	–
Eurocom (2012)	40%	20%

Sources: Society of Human Resource Management (SHRM), Survey Findings: The Use of Social Networking Websites and Online Search Engines in Screening Job Applicants (April 25, 2011) (survey of 541 responding HR managers); Survey for Career Builder conducted by Harris International of 2303 human resource managers. www.careerbuilder.com; Eurocom Press Release of survey of 318 public relations agencies, 80 per cent in Europe. www.eurocompr.com.

How employers use what they learn from accessing an applicant's or employee's social media has been surveyed internationally. The results are shown in Table 6.2.

Where the employee or applicant's site is available to the public at large there is no ground of complaint when an employer accesses it.[216] However, there may be legal limits on negative employment decisions made on the basis of the information learned;

212 Edison Research, The Social Habit (June 2012).

213 Proskauer Rose LLP, 2012 Survey: Social Media in the Workplace Around the World 2.0.

214 *Grounds for rejecting* an applicant based on review of social media included: posting inappropriate photos, inappropriate comments (e.g., about drink or drugs), negative comments about prior employers, poor communication skills, discriminatory comments, lies, discussion of a previous employer's confidential information.

Grounds for hiring an applicant on the basis of social media included having a positive impression of organizational fit, professional qualifications, creativity, communication skills, well roundedness, good references posted by others and the receipt of accolades. www.reppler.com (Job Screening with Social Networks) (nd) and www.careerbuilder.com.

215 A 2010 survey by Proofpoint indicated that social networking site monitoring for those investigative purposes had risen to 20 per cent, from 17 per cent in 2009. Outbound Email and Data loss Prevention in Today's Enterprise, 2010.

216 Federal and most cognate state fair credit reporting laws regulate the conduct of background checks for employment run by third-party credit reporting agencies. This includes notice to and consent by the employee and receipt of a copy of the report. These laws (California being an exception) do not apply to the employer itself. Even if these laws reach the review of the content of social media, they are inapplicable when such review is not done by a third party.

Table 6.2 Types of online reputational information that influenced decisions to reject a candidate

	U.S.	U.K.	Ger.	France
Concerns about the candidate's lifestyle	58%	45%	42%	32%
Inappropriate comments and text written by the candidate	56%	57%	78%	58%
Unsuitable photos, videos, and information	55%	51%	44%	42%
Inappropriate comments to text written by friends and relatives	43%	35%	14%	11%
Comments criticizing previous employers, co-workers, or clients	40%	40%	28%	37%
Inappropriate comments or text written by colleagues or work acquaintances	40%	37%	17%	21%
Membership in certain groups and networks	35%	33%	36%	37%
Discovered that information the candidate shared was false	30%	36%	42%	47%
Poor communication skills displayed online	27%	41%	17%	42%
Concern about the candidate's financial background	16%	18%	11%	0%

Source: Cross-tab, Online Reputation in a Connected World (Jan. 2010), at 9.

for example, that the employee is advocating union representation or other acts for mutual aid protected by the National Labor Relations Act.[217]

Where an employer gains access to a site for which consent is required without securing it, the access might be unlawful either as a tort or as in violation of federal or cognate state law regulating access to electronically stored communications. The most likely scenario is one in which an employer requests that a co-worker, who has been given access by the target, provide the employer with the password. On the former, the tort, the employee would have to establish that she had a reasonable expectation of privacy and that the intrusion was offensive to a reasonable person. The fact of restricted access would seem to satisfy the first prong, though the employer might argue, depending on the number of people to whom the employee had given access, that disclosure of the password beyond that circle was a foreseeable risk the target

[217] Amanda Green, Using Social Networking to Discuss Work: NLRB Protection for Derogatory Employee Speech and Concerted Activity, 27 BERKELEY TECH. L.J. 837 (2012). *See e.g., Hispanics United of Buffalo, Inc.* 359 NLRB No. 37 (2012). The creation of an impression of surveillance for union activity is also forbidden, but the reach of that doctrine into this sphere is unexplored.

assumed. The second prong would present the question of whether a co-worker's faithlessness was unforeseeable; perhaps, evidence of duress or coercion brought on the co-worker, a threat of job loss, for example might render disclosure actionable.[218]

On the latter, statutory regulation, federal law governing electronically stored communications allows access by a 'user' of the service. A federal court of appeals held that although a co-worker who had been given access was a 'user,' the exception applied only if the co-worker had accessed the website before having given the employer the password.[219] All in all, there is as yet almost no texture of law on any of these questions.

But the question that has captured public attention is not surreptitious, but direct access: where the employer requests an applicant or an incumbent employee to give the employer access to her social media, failing which she will not be hired or, possibly, be discharged. In the absence of legislation, the demand would be lawful. The applicant or employee will have consented or, less strongly, no case has yet confronted the applicant or employee's right to say no or to consider what a remedy might be.

However, starting in 2012, 17 states, thus far, have legislated to prohibit employers from requiring or requesting applicants or employees to disclose a user name or password for the purpose of accessing personal social media.[220] Obviously, the issue has captured public awareness. Though Wyoming and Florida have declined to enact such a restriction so far,[221] it seems likely that more states will be added to the list. This exemplifies the ad hoc nature of the U.S. law of employee privacy as it proceeds not from a well-wrought legal conception but from public reaction to a sensed overreaching by employers.

B. German Law

According to a survey on behalf of the German Ministry for consumer protection in 2009,[222] some 28 per cent of all interviewed enterprises use the internet to gather information in the hiring process, 36 per cent of them also grasp data from social networks, which are rampant in Germany (in 2011, 91 per cent of all persons between 16 and 24 years are active users;[223] total numbers in 2013: Facebook: 25 million active users; XING: 7 million active users; LinkedIn: 4.5 million active users). A quarter of

[218] *Ehling v. Monmouth-Ocean Hosp. Serv. Corp.*, 872 F.Supp.2d 379 (D. N.J. 2012). The U.S. has no conception of 'breach of confidence' as an actionable wrong, though it is taking root elsewhere. Megan Richardson, et. al., BREACH OF CONFIDENCE: SOCIAL ORIGINS AND MODERN DEVELOPMENTS (2012).

[219] *Konop v. Hawaiian Airlines*, 302 F.3d 868 (9th Cir. 2002).

[220] These are compiled in Matthew Finkin, PRIVACY IN EMPLOYMENT LAW (4th ed. 2013) and 2014 Cumulative Supplement. To these must now be added New Hampshire. N.H. Rev. Stat. Ann. § 275:71-73 (2014).

[221] 13 PVLR 424 (March 10, 2014) (Wyoming); 13 PVLR 928 (May 30, 2014) (Florida).

[222] *Available at:* http://www.bmelv.de/SharedDocs/Downloads/Verbraucherschutz/InternetnutzungVorauswahlPersonalentscheidungen.pdf;jsessionid=D3DC11ED3F409858A50845FADF2C144B.2_cid376?__blob=publicationFile (last visited 1.4.2015).

[223] *Available at:* https://www.destatis.de/DE/PresseService/Presse/Pressemitteilungen/2012/05/PD12_172_63931.html (last visited 1.4.2015).

the enterprises using the internet declared that web information was the reason for the disqualification of applicants. The digital track becomes a career bracket.

German law does not provide special regulation of this matter. A draft for an amendment to the Federal Data Protection Act from 2010[224] had stipulated that an employer must not collect data in private social networks (like Facebook), even if the data was publicly available, unless the employee had given his consent.[225] (This restriction should not count in case of professional social networks such as XING or LinkedIn.) However, due to political opposition the draft has not entered into force so far. Thus, the existing provisions of the Federal Data Protection Act mentioned above,[226] apply. In terms of consent, as legitimizing the collecting of personal data, it is commonly acknowledged that the legal limits of collecting personal data during the hiring procedure must not be circumvented.[227] It follows that there cannot exist a duty of the applicant to disclose her password because this would inevitably lead to the unveiling of personal data beyond employment-related purposes. The problem is practical, not legal, however, as an applicant is surely aware of the fact that he will not be hired if he rejects the employer's demand. Consequently, there is no case law.

In the absence of concrete cases, are there legitimating grounds for collecting personal data in social networks? One must try to pierce the doctrinal mist.[228] It is widely acknowledged that the gathering of data on applicants via the internet is lawful, if these data are publicly available.[229] The same is true in regard to personal data in professional social networks which are determined to be available for other professionals. On the other hand, data in private social networks to which only members have access shall remain private and thus a search by the employer would not be lawful.

Even so, the enforcement of violations of the Federal Data Protection Act is problematic. In theory, an applicant who has been rejected on the basis of information the employer has unlawfully collected could sue the employer for damages on grounds of contract and/or tort, but, in practice, such claims have not been made because the applicant will ordinarily not be aware of the reason for disqualification.

C. Japanese Law

In Japan, although the number of active uses of social networking service is increasing (especially by the younger generation), use of social networking remains relatively low: in 2013, the percentage of people participating in social networking was about 15 per cent, and the percentage of companies using social networking services was about 16

[224] Bundestags-Drucksache 17/4230 (2010).

[225] Section 32, para. 6 Draft for an amendment to the Federal Data Protection Act.

[226] *Supra* n. 127.

[227] Wolfgang Däubler, *Gläserne Belegschaften?* (6th ed. 2015), at no. 161.

[228] Cf. Gerrit Forst, *Bewerberauswahl über soziale Netzwerke im Internet?*, Neue Zeitschrift für Arbeitsrecht (NZA) 2010, pp. 427–33; Christian Oberwetter, *Bewerberprofilerstellung durch das Internet – Verstoß gegen das Datenschutzrecht?*, Betriebs-Berater (BB) 2008, pp. 1562–6; Christian Rolf, Michael Rötting, *Google, Facebook & Co als Bewerberdatenbank für Arbeitgeber?*, Recht der Datenverarbeitung (RDV) 2009, pp. 263–7.

[229] In this case the employer can rely on s. 28, para. 1 sentence 1 no. 3 Federal Data Protection Act.

per cent.[230] The number of active users of Facebook in Japan was about 20 million in 2013.[231] The number of LinkedIn users in Japan was only '1 million plus' in early 2014.[232]

The percentage of companies using social networking service for recruitment purposes is also low; only about 14 per cent of companies use social media for recruitment in 2012.[233] The main purpose of using social networking service for hiring process is for public relations, and only about 10 per cent of companies using social networking service for recruitment employ it for background investigation of applicants.[234]

As previously described, Article 5-4 of the Employment Security Act requires employers conducting recruitment of employees to collect personal information of jobseekers only to the extent necessary for recruitment. An administrative guideline issued under the law[235] requires an employer conducting recruitment of employees to collect jobseeker's personal information directly from him/her and to obtain his/her consent if an employer wants to collect personal information from those other than the jobseeker. However, as it is only a guideline it has no legally binding effect.

If the applicant's social media profile is open to the public, it is considered that there is no ground for the applicant to expect privacy, since the applicant can be deemed to have given consent for his/her personal information to be to collected in an indirect manner.[236] If the applicant's social media profile is not open to the public, collecting his/her personal information from his/her social media profile without his/her consent (*e.g.*, through an employee who has access to the profile as his/her 'friend') would be an infringement of privacy.[237] However, even under that guideline, an employer could lawfully access a jobseeker's social networking profile as far as the employer would be able to secure the consent of the jobseeker. There is no statute to prohibit employers from requiring applicants to consent to accessing to their social networking profile.

Likewise, an incumbent employee's social media profile is considered to be protected from his/her employer's access if it is not open to the public. What seems to be

---

230 Ministry of Internal Affairs and Communications, *Heisei 24 Nen Tsushin Riyou Doko Chosa no Kekka (Results of Survey on Trend of Use of Information and Communication Service in 2012), available at:* http://www.soumu.go.jp/johotsusintokei/statistics/data/130614_1.pdf.

231 Nihon Keizai Shinbun, Aug 14, 2013, p. 10.

232 LinkedIn Corporate Communications Team, *LinkedIn crosses 50-million member mark in Asia Pacific, available at:* http://press.linkedin.com/News-Releases/328/LinkedIn-crosses-50-million-member-mark-in-Asia-Pacific.

233 Disco, *Saiyou Katsudou ni Kansuru Kigyo Chosa Anketo Kekka (2012 Nen 12 Gatsu) (Result of Survey on Recruiting Activities (December 2012))* 8.

234 Ibid.

235 The Guideline for Employment Agency, Recruiters, Commissioned Recruiters, Labor Supply Agency etc., to Properly Deal with Equal Treatment, Specification of Conditions of Employment, Management of Personal Information of jobseekers, Responsibility of Employment Agency, Correct Indication of Conditions of Recruitment (Nov. 17, 1999 Rodosyo Kokuji No. 141 (last amended on Sep. 10, 2012)).

236 Kiyoshi Takechi, *Web 2.0 Jidai ni Okeru Saiba Rodoho no Arata na Kadai (1) (New Challenges for Labor and Employment in the Era of Web 2.0 (1)),* 55 Tomidai Keizai Ronshu 313, 331 (2010).

237 Ibid., at 331–2.

different is that it is well anticipated that an employer could not lawfully discharge his/her employee for refusing the employer's request to allow access to the employee's social networking profile, as this would be an abuse of the right to discharge.

III. GEOLOCATION

A. United States Law

As the 2007 NRC report observed, employees have become ever more subject to 'location checks.'[238] This has been facilitated by geolocation technology – global positioning systems (GPS) and radio frequency identification (RFID). The former may be placed in company or private vehicles; all cellphones sold in the U.S. must be GPS capable. RFID chips may be placed on company badges, even inserted subcutaneously. These systems allow employers to ascertain an employee's exact location – a hospital could identify the room a nurse is in, for example, and for what period of time.[239] If an employee is on a lunch break, the employer can locate the restaurant and for how long the employee was there. If she is joined by a co-worker equally subject to geolocation, the employer can learn who her dining companion is.[240] If pictures are circulated on their social media, the employer might be able to monitor them, to see who else is present; and, under computer applications conjoined to company 'wellness' programs, the employer could learn what food and drink was consumed.

There are obvious beneficial uses of geolocation technology – should there be an accident or a medical emergency, for example, or, in the nursing example, to ascertain whether a patient's complaint of inattentiveness is well founded.[241] But some uses might be less benevolent and employees have complained of the deployment insofar as it further collapses work life and private life[242] or as an instrument of an intensification of workplace surveillance.[243]

A 2006 survey of human resource managers indicated that 23 per cent of the companies surveyed 'frequently' – and 11 per cent 'occasionally' – used RFID

---

238 *Supra,* n. 209.

239 For example, Google has announced a product – Google Map Coordinate – that couples its map product to smartphones that will allow an employer to create a real-time record of worker location inside a building as well as outside. Quentin Hardy, Google Maps Where Your Workers Are, N.Y. TIMES BITS [THE BUSINESS OF TECHNOLOGY] (June 21, 2012); Thomas Claburn, google Maps Coordinate App Connects Mobile Workers, *available at* http://www.informationweek.com/news/smb/mobile/240002512 (June 22, 2012).

240 Rachel Emma Silverman, Tracking Sensors Invade the Workplace, WALL ST. JOURNAL, March 6, 2013.

241 179 DLR A-4 (Sept. 16, 2002).

242 *See* Jean-Emmanual Ray, *De la géo-localisation à la telé-localisation,* Droit Social 61 (Jan. 2012) (discussing the decision of the Cour de Cassation (Ch. Soc.) of 3 Nov. 2011).

243 *See e.g.*, Sarah Jaffee, *Hyatt Surveils Its Workers Via iPods*, Working in These Times (Oct. 24, 2012) (reporting on Hyatt's requirement that hotel housekeepers carry an iPod on which they must record when they enter and leave a room and which assigns them the next room to clean and which a supervisor may call as he or she tracks the housekeeper's performance).

technology to monitor employees. A survey the following year indicated a much lower use of GPS technology – 8 per cent tracked vehicles, but fewer than 1 per cent used it to monitor employees at that time.

The law in the U.S. was indifferent when analogous worker claims of sweatshop conditions resulting from the computerized monitoring of work were made a generation ago,[244] and is equally indifferent today to the complained of surveillance worked by this technology. In the U.S., the pace of work, the monitoring of employees at work, are working conditions determined by market forces, absent union representation, which means, in the face of private sector union density of about 6.6 per cent, that market forces, not law, govern. The law has stepped in in only one state, Connecticut, which requires that employees be informed if they are to be made subject to electronic monitoring 'on an employer's premises.'[245] It is possible that a company vehicle would be considered an ambulatory part of the employer's premises,[246] but it is undetermined whether that provision would reach the employee herself.[247]

In any event, hidden devices are not the source of concern. It is deployment with the knowledge of the employee that makes such devices effective as instruments of control. It is possible that deployment of such devices might be met with religious objection that would bring employment discrimination law to bear,[248] but as far as the law in the U.S. has gone is that four states have legislated to forbid employees from requiring employers to have RFID chips subcutaneously implanted.[249]

B. German Law

As the Federal Constitutional Court has held, geolocation is a threat to the right to informational self-determination.[250] Hence, it is clear that an unlimited geolocation of employees by GPS or RFID technology would violate both plain law and constitutional law. Once again, the problem is the boundaries of surveillance. As only very little case

244 Office of Technology Assessment, The Electronic Supervisor (1987); Paul Attewell, Big Brother and the Sweatshop: Computer Surveillance in the Automated Office, 5 SOC. THEORY 87 (1987).

245 CONN. GEN. STAT. § 31-48d (2011).

246 *See Gerardi v. City of Bridgeport*, 985 A.2d 328 (Conn. 2010).

247 A majority of the New York Court of Appeals, the state's highest court, found no constitutional violation per se in a public employer's attaching a hidden GPS device to an employee's private vehicle to see if he was falsifying his reporting of his hours at work. *Cunningham v. New York State Dept. of Labor*, 997 N.E.2d 468 (N.Y. 2013).

248 *Cf. Hernandez v. Northside Indep. Schl. Dist.*, 916 F.Supp.2d 757 (W.D. Tex. 2013) (student objects to RFID 'smart badge' on religious grounds).

249 CAL. CIV. CODE § 52.7 (2012 Supp.); MO. REV. STAT. § 285.035 (2012 Supp.); N.D. CENT. CODE § 12.1-15-06 (2012 Supp.); WIS. STAT. § 146.25 (2012 Supp.). Interestingly, these laws would not appear to forbid voluntary compliance with a non-coercive 'request' to submit to implantation. *See* Marisa Anne Pagnattaro, Getting Under Your Skin – Literally: RFIC in the Employment Context, 2008 U. ILL. J.L. TECH. & POL'Y 237 (2008).

250 BVerfG 12.4.2005, BVerfGE 112, 304 (at 319–320); BVerfG 22.8.2006, NJW 2007, 351 (at 354–5) concerning actions by public bodies.

law exists on that issue,[251] different opinions have emerged in doctrine.[252] Some authors argue in favor of a 'stay secret' which may only be broken if the employee is suspected of misconduct. Others argue that a reasonable cause on the side of the employer is sufficient for sporadic geolocation. A minimal consensus exists that a complete local profiling of employees without a concrete necessity (*e.g.*, for safety reasons) is unlawful.

The enactment of the amendment to the Federal Data Protection Act (mentioned above) would clarify the situation. According to the draft's provision,[253] a geolocation shall only be lawful (i) for safety reasons or (ii) for the coordination of the operation of employees. The data collected for these reasons must not be used for other reasons (*e.g.*, checking working hours). Geolocation shall also be lawful to protect movable goods, but not during the time in which the worker is authorized to deal with the goods. Every kind of geolocation has to be transparent for the employee. Moreover the worker has to be informed on the extent of the records. Unfortunately there is no indication that these legal concretions will enter in force and so the uncertainty on the exact limits of geolocation remains.

C. Japanese Law

There are no statistics as to the number or percentage of companies deploying GPS or RFID technology for monitoring their employees. But, judging from the fact that several major companies in Japan provide location services using GPS or RFID technology,[254] it is estimated that these technologies are used for employee monitoring, at least to some extent.

As discussed, the Personal Information Protection Act of 2003 obliges companies having 5000 or more employees to specify the purpose for collecting personal information, limit the use of personal information within the specified purpose, acquire personal information in an appropriate manner, and notice the purpose in acquiring personal information.[255] Location and other information acquired through GPS and

---

[251] See LAG Baden-Württemberg 25.10.2002, Juris, holding that a hidden geolocation via GPS is lawful in case of a commercial agent being strongly suspicious of having committed a fraud on expenses.

[252] Cf. Peter Gola, *Datenschutz bei der Kontrolle 'mobiler' Arbeitnehmer – Zulässigkeit und Transparenz*, Neue Zeitschrift für Arbeitsrecht (NZA) 2007, pp. 1139–44 (at 1140–4); Rüdiger Krause, Die Lokalisierung und Identitätsfeststellung von (Außendienst-)Mitarbeitern, in: Klaus Vieweg and Heinz Gerhäuser (eds), *Digitale Daten in Geräten und Systemen* (2010), pp. 153–81 (at 156–63, 166–74).

[253] Section 32g Draft of an amendment to the Federal Data Protection Act.

[254] *See* Kiyoshi Takechi, *Sumaho to Tomoni Jiosureigari ga Yattekuru! (The Era of Geoslavary Is Coming with Smartphone!)*, 58 Tomidai Keizai Ronshu 234, 237–8 (2013).

[255] One of the Guidelines under the Act, namely the Guideline for Personal Information Protection in the Field of Economy, Trade and Industry (Oct. 22, 2004 Koseirodosyo and Keizaisangyosyo Kokuji No. 4 (last amended on Oct. 9, 2009)), requires employers to, among others, notice the purpose of monitoring, stipulate a policy for monitoring. The other guideline, namely the Guideline for Personal Information Protection in Telecommunication Business (Aug. 31, 2004 Somusyo Kokuji No. 695 (last amended on Jul. 29, 2010)) further requires location

RFID technology is considered to be personal information covered by the Act. Although the Act mainly anticipates administrative sanctions for violations and does not have direct civil effect, it is considered that monitoring employees in violation of the Act would be a factor for the courts to find an employer liable for damages under the current framework for examining whether there is an infringement of employee privacy. So far at least one court case has held that it was an infringement of employee privacy for an employer to monitor his employees' location through a GPS system before and after working hours and that the employer was liable for damages, relying on the framework of comparing business necessity and disadvantages on part of employees and pointing out that in that case no business necessity was provided for monitoring before and after working hours.[256]

IV. BIOMETRIC IDENTIFICATION

A. The United States

'Identification management' has become an industry unto itself, stimulated by the commercial aspects of consumer identification and all the data mining attendant to the pursuit of business opportunities, the claims of national security, and the growth of identity theft in an electronic era.[257] This has led to the creation of the International Biometric & Identification Association (IBIA).[258] As IBIA has pointed out, there are three ways a person can be identified: (1) by display of something one possesses that betokens identity, such as a driver's license or an electronic swipe card; (2) by display of something one knows that betokens identity, such as a password; or (3) by display of something that one is or how one behaves, *e.g.*, scanning patterns of a person's fingers, hand, iris, signature, skin, voice, or face, the pattern of one's use of a computer keyboard. The latter are used to create mathematical formulae that can be matched with those stored in a database. In employment, this technology has been developed thus far to control access to the workplace and to record entrance and exit.

Considerable advances in facial recognition have been made in recent years with the prospect of ever-greater sophistication. It may be possible to capture the identity of previously unidentified people by applying facial recognition technology to their profiles on a social medium such as Facebook. Given the increasing ubiquity of social media in general, and of employer access to employee social media in particular, it might be possible for an employer to identify the persons depicted in an employee's

service providers not to provide personal information unless the user (*i.e.*, employer) obtain consent of those monitored (*i.e.*, employee).

[256] *Kono (anonym) v. Azuma Kigyo,* 1056 Rodo Hanrei 19 (Tokyo Dist. Ct., May 31, 2012). Interestingly, the court denied the employer's liability for monitoring the employee's location *during* working hours, pointing that in that case it was based on rational business necessity to control the employees working outside the office.

[257] *See generally*, Lisa Nelson, AMERICA IDENTIFIED: BIOMETRIC TECHNOLOGY AND SOCIETY (2011).

[258] http://www.ibia.org.

photo posted on her or another's social media site[259] and place them in time and place.[260] *I.e.*, to reveal with whom the employee is associating – a former co-worker who now works for a competitor or a union organizer.

Turning to the legal response, a number of states have included biometric information as part of their identity theft statutes, but in terms of employment only three state laws affect what employers may do; one of which deals with employment specifically. Texas requires consent to the 'capture' of a biometric identifier, requires reasonable care in storage, and destruction of the identifier within a reasonable time.[261] Colorado requires businesses to have policies for the destruction of all paper documents carrying 'personally identifying information.'[262] Illinois' Biometric Information Privacy Act[263] requires employee consent to the release of biometric information and requires the destruction of data.

However, to the extent biometric data may contain genetic information or indicate a disability covered by antidiscrimination in employment law, these data may be regulated by other laws, for example, the Genetic Information Nondiscrimination Act, the Americans with Disabilities Act, or cognate state laws.[264] There is as yet no legal texture to this aspect of biometric identification in employment.

B. Germany

Although the use of biometric data of employees also exists in Germany, the topic is less discussed than other features of data privacy in employment matters.[265] The Federal Labor Court has dealt with biometric (fingerprint-scanner) control for access to the premises of a customer of the employer, but only in regard to the existence of a codetermination right of the works council.[266] However, there is no indication that the Court would not accept such measures as regards the Federal Data Protection Act or the

---

[259] Natasha Sinjer, *Never Forgetting a* Face, N.Y. TIMES, May 18, 2014 at p. B1 (reporting, inter alia, on NameTag which produces an 'app' that allows a glance at a stranger to match against Facebook instantly to reveal name, occupation, and Facebook profile). The U.S. Federal Trade Commission reports that in a single month in 2010, 2.5 billion photos were uploaded to Facebook. Federal Trade Commission, FACING FACTS: BEST PRACTICES FOR COMMON USES OF FACIAL RECOGNITION TECHNOLOGY 4 (Oct. 2012).

[260] Mark Bordon, Privacy Invasive Geo-Mashups: Privacy 2.0 and the Limits of First Generation Information Privacy Laws, 2010 U. ILL. J.L. TECH. & POL'Y 1 (2010).

[261] TEX. BUS. COM. CODE § 503.001 (2010). The time is no more than a year from the anniversary date of the 'purpose' for collecting it. Inasmuch as the purpose is employment is continuous while in employ the data would seem to progress accordingly.

[262] Colo. Rev. Stat. § 6-1-713 (2010).

[263] 740 ILCS 14/1-14/99 (2012 Supp.)

[264] Rachel Minter, The Informalization of the Body: What Biometric Technology Could Reveal to Employers About Current and Political Medical Conditions (remarks presented at the ABA Conference on Equal Opportunity Law, April 7, 2011).

[265] Cf. Peter Gola, *supra* n. 252, (at 1140–1); Gerrit Hornung, Roland Steidle, *Biometrie am Arbeitsplatz – sichere Kontrollverfahren versus ausuferndes Kontrollpotential*, Arbeit und Recht (AuR) 2007, pp. 201–7; Rüdiger Krause, *supra* n. 252, (at 163–6).

[266] BAG 27.1.2004, BAGE 109, 235 (at 237–43) (the Court held that the will of the customer to apply the biometric control access also to posted employees does not deprive the

general right of personality: if the employer can show a sufficient operational reason for the procedure, if the collection of biometric data is limited to a necessary extent, and if the data will be deleted when no longer required there should no expectation for these to be legal wrongs. The Austrian Supreme Court (*Oberster Gerichtshof*) has held that biometric control systems (fingerprint-scanner for the record of working hours) affects human dignity in terms of section 96 paragraph 1 no. 3 Work Constitution Act (see above) and thus the works council has a co-determination right.[267] Like its German counterpart, the Austrian Supreme Court stressed the principle of proportionality which governs the question whether such controls are lawful, but it did not declare biometric control systems as generally incompatible with human dignity.[268]

Again, the amendment of the Federal Data Protection Act (mentioned above) would clarify the legal situation. According to the draft provision,[269] biometrical data of employees may only be collected for authorization and authentication purposes. The draft also stipulates that the consent of the employee does not basically have the effect of legitimizing other employer's control goals. This policy expresses some distrust in regard to the capability of the employee to decide 'freely' which kind of control purpose the worker is willing to accept and hence limits his autonomy. However, Directive 95/46/EC provides that the 'free' consent of the affected person is sufficient for the legitimization of collection of personal data.[270] Given the view of the ECJ that Directive 95/46/EC defines not only a minimum, but also a maximum level of data protection,[271] it is at least doubtful whether German law could establish a stricter standard in regard to the legal effect of employee's consent.

C. Japan

So far, no specific labor or employment statutes regulate the acquisition or use of biometric information in Japan. However, biometric information, when stored in a database with other information, such as employee names, in order to control access to the workplace or record employee attendance and hours, is considered to be 'personal information' which the Personal Information Protection Act regulates. Therefore, an employer having 5000 or more employees is required to specify and limit the purpose for collecting biometric information, to acquire biometric information in an appropriate manner, and notice the purpose in acquiring it.

---

works council of his co-determination right). See also LAG Rheinland-Pfalz 8.3.1991, RDV 1992, 33 (at 33–4).

267 OGH 20.12.2006, DRdA 2008, 326 (at 327–30).

268 A similar test has been recently applied by the ECJ stating that the collection of fingerprints (by the state in a passport issue) constitutes a threat to the right to respect for private life (art. 7 CFR) and the right to the protection of personal data (art. 8 CFR), but that this threat can be justified by proportional aims; case C-291/12 *Michael Schwarz v. Stadt Bochum* [2013] EuGRZ 2013, 597, paras 23–64.

269 Section 32h Draft of an amendment to the Federal Data Protection Act.

270 Article 7(a) Directive 95/46/EC.

271 See *supra* n. 139.

V. DIFFERENCE AND CONVERGENCE

By the 1950s, none of these three countries had developed anything close to a set of significant protections for employee privacy. Germany had a deep wellspring of legal theory, rooted in natural law and in Enlightenment thought, but little of it had practical purchase. The U.S. drew from a legacy of laissez-faire and its catchphrase, 'freedom of contract.' This bequeathed to management the power to make the rules governing employment which, fictively, were taken to have been consented-to by those subject to them. Japan was deeply wedded to communal or familial norms as a feature of employment.

Three generations on we see that: German law was able to draw upon that wellspring to fashion a robust conception of the person protective of employee privacy; the U.S., proceeding piecemeal, has moved, or lurched, legislatively toward pockets of protection, some broad, some quite narrow, usually in reaction to the public's felt perception of managerial overreaching; and Japan has begun to come to grips with an individualism that is historically (and linguistically) alien, but with legal consequences that, at points, and surprisingly, are more protective of the individual than in the U.S. In sum, values latent in Germany have become legally realized; and insofar as law reflects societal values, in the U.S. and Japan the law would seem to reveal a growth in the value attached to privacy in the employment relationship.

There seems to be little doubt that as technology burgeons, placing in managerial hands ever-more effective means of oversight and control,[272] advanced democracies will be equally challenged to protect the individual from near total transparency and loss of autonomy, a condition that bids fair to erode the autonomous self that is a critical component of liberal democracy. Given the common trajectory these three very different states' laws reflect, the ubiquity of global managerial practice may well be met with a reciprocal convergence, not in precise outcome, but in the sensed need for legal response protective of the individual.

---

[272] American textile mill workers in company housing in the early twentieth century recalled factory bosses checking on who was up at night to ensure an alert and productive workforce the next day. If the lights were on at 9:00 p.m. the boss would 'knock on the door and tell you to cut the lights out and get into bed.' Jacquelyn David Hall et. al., LIKE A FAMILY: THE MAKING OF A SOUTHERN COTTON MILL WORLD 123 (1987). Today, developers of wearable technology are touting the benefits to productivity of having employees' sleep telemetered. The Human Cloud at Work: A Study into the Impact of Wearable Technologies in the Workplace (2014). The intrusive knock on the door is gone. Employees, now used to wearable technology for monitoring their health and habits, can seamlessly transition to continuous behavioral employer monitoring.

7. Legal protection for employee mobility

Alan Hyde and Emanuele Menegatti

INTRODUCTION

A critical function of labor law around the world is to ensure labor mobility. Every system of labor law places limits on the employer's ability to impede this mobility. Employees' promises not to move to, or start, competing businesses are not automatically enforced in any legal system.

There are several reasons that such covenants not to compete ('restrictive covenants', or 'noncompetes') are not automatically enforced. We shall refer to these as labor law values, competition values, and economic growth values. The first two are recognized in nearly every legal system, and economic growth is surely not rejected as a value. In other words, variation among jurisdictions does not reflect lack of agreement on fundamental values.

Working men and women have a right to work, to practice their skills and professions. They are free to enter into economic life, to support themselves and their families, to develop services as they are able, and to compete with others. Common law jurisdictions tend to understand this right in this economically liberal sense. Civil law jurisdictions often add an additional understanding of the right of economic participation, often in their constitutions: the right to work is also the right to the social and moral development of the person. People must be free to choose work because work is one of the chief ways in which they develop as mature, responsible, happy and satisfied adults. Systems of labor in which workers may not select their employment have been tried but are today universally rejected as incompatible with human dignity. A third, related labor law value is the protection of the weaker party. Of necessity, working men and women may enter employment contracts in which more powerful employers extract promises that are against the best interests of working people. Many jurisdictions regard the 'protection of the weaker party,' implying scrutiny of such imbalances of power, as a major function of labor law generally. We shall refer to these values of freedom to work, dignity of the worker, and protection of the weaker party, as the 'labor law values.' Most jurisdictions are more likely to enforce restrictive covenants growing out of sale of a business, than restrictive covenants in a contract of employment. This chapter deals only with restrictive covenants in contracts of employment.

Employee promises not to compete may also be disfavored in the name of free competition. Monopolies, cartels, and other restrictions on competition inevitably damage the public by interfering with markets and raising prices. A building contractor may not lawfully agree, in any legal system, with other contractors that only one of them will construct buildings in a given region. Such a covenant in restraint of trade creates a monopoly that obviously harms consumers. A similar agreement between that contractor and his employee is potentially equally injurious to the public. A jurisdiction that enforces the contractor-employee agreement is thus making a very partial exception to the general refusal to enforce agreements to restrict competition. We shall refer to values of this type as 'competition' or 'antitrust' values.

Finally, there has been much attention in recent years to the critical role of employee mobility in high-technology industry, which often clusters in particular regions,[1] where employees share information with friends and colleagues across firm lines;[2] and may themselves frequently change employers.[3] New firms are invariably founded by personnel departing established firms. If those older firms could extract and enforce promises not to compete, there could be no start-up firms.[4] Regions, such as Silicon Valley, California, and its analogs in Singapore, India, Israel, and elsewhere, that experience growth as knowledge spreads beyond the boundaries of the firm, demonstrate the 'endogenous growth' through generation and diffusion of nonrivalrous and nonexclusive information.[5] We shall refer to arguments of this type as 'economic growth' values.

---

[1] Hyde, Alan. 2003. Working in Silicon Valley: Economic and Legal Analysis of a High-Velocity Labor Market. Armonk NY: M.E. Sharpe; Langlois, Richard N. 1992. 'External Economies and Economic Progress: The Case of the Microcomputer Industry,' 66 *Business History Review* 1–50; Saxenian, AnnaLee. 1994. *Regional Advantage: Culture and Competition in Silicon Valley and Route 128*. Cambridge, MA: Harvard University Press.

[2] Agrawal, Ajay, Iain Cockburn, and John McHale. 2006. 'Gone but not Forgotten: Knowledge Flows, Labor Mobility, and Enduring Social Relationships,' 6 *Journal of Economic Geography* 571–91; Corredoira, Rafael A., and Lori Rosenkopf. 2010. 'Should Auld Acquaintance be Forgot?: The Reverse Transfer of Knowledge Through Mobility Ties,' 31 *Strategic Management Journal* 159–81; Feldman, Yuval. 2003. 'Experimental Approach to the Study of Normative Failures: Divulging of Trade Secrets by Silicon Valley Employees,' 2003 *University of Illinois Journal of Law, Technology and Policy* 105–80; Sitkin, Sim B. 1986. 'Secrecy in Organizations: Determinants of Secrecy Behavior among Engineers in Three Silicon Valley Semiconductor Firms,' Ph.D. dissertation, Graduate School of Business, Stanford University; von Hippel, Eric. 1988. *The Sources of Innovation*. New York: Oxford University Press.

[3] Fallick, Bruce, Charles A. Fleischman, and James B. Rebitzer. 2006. 'Job Hopping in Silicon Valley: Some Evidence Concerning the Micro-foundations of a High Technology Cluster,' 88 *Review of Economics and Statistics* 472–81.

[4] Paul Almeida and Bruce Kogut, 'Localization of Knowledge and the Mobility of Engineers in Regional Networks,' 45 *Management Science* 905 (1999); Chatterji, Aaron K. 2009. 'Spawned with a Silver Spoon?: Entrepreneurial Performance and Innovation in the Medical Device Industry,' 30(2) *Strategic Management Journal* 185–206; Franco, April Mitchell, and Darren Filson. 2006. 'Spin-outs: Knowledge Diffusion through Employee Mobility,' 37 *RAND Journal of Economics* 841–60.

[5] See generally: Cooper, David P. 2000. 'Innovation and Reciprocal Externalities: Information Transmission via Job Mobility,' 45 *Journal of Economic Behavior and Organization* 403–25; Romer, Paul M. 1990. 'Endogenous Technological Change,' 98 *Journal of Political Economy* S71–102; Warsh, David. 2006. *Knowledge and the Wealth of Nations: A Story of Economic Discovery*. New York: W.W. Norton.

On Singapore as a location of choice for Silicon Valley-type manufacture involving numerous networked contractors and employee mobility, see: Franco and Wilson, Spin-outs, Ibid.; McKendrick, David G., Richard F. Doner, and Stephen Haggard. 2000. *From Silicon Valley to Singapore: Location and Competitive Advantage in the Hard Disk Drive Industry*. Stanford CA: Stanford University Press.

Some jurisdictions (California, Israel, India, Malaysia, Mexico) find some or all of these values so compelling that they never enforce an employee's promise not to compete with a former employer. Most jurisdictions, however, believe that there are sometimes reasons to enforce such a promise, and in individual cases may balance such concerns against the above acknowledged harms in enforcing such promises. They may believe, for example, that contracts should normally be enforced as written unless some overreaching event occurred; or that employers will not train employees if those employees might immediately leave and compete with them; or that legal devices for enforcing property in trade secrets are so ineffectual that they must be supplemented by enforcing employee promises not to compete. Recent economic analysis casts doubt on all three of these assumptions, but they are commonly encountered as justifications for restricting employee mobility.[6] Most systems of employment law purport to balance some or all of these values, although, as we shall see, there is variation in the relative importance given to particular reasons or sets of reasons. There is also variation as to whether individual cases will have recourse to the underlying reasons, as is the case when an individual legal decision is understood as a balance, or search for proportion, among competing interests. Other jurisdictions may instead incorporate the underlying values into flat rules that do not call for individuated application of the values in particular cases, as is the case in the jurisdictions that do not enforce any contractual limits on employee mobility after employment. Cases rarely distinguish clearly among these values, although some or all are present in every legal system with which we are familiar.

In other words, it is possible to state a kind of global legal standard for the enforcement of employee promises not to compete. It is similarly possible with minor modifications to apply such a standard to other impediments to employee mobility, such as the definition of employer trade secrets. The American Law Institute, which purports to 'restate' the common law of US jurisdictions, has advanced in the Restatement of Employment Law the following summary of the US law of restrictive covenants, which, so long as it remains suitably abstract, might serve as a rough comparative law summary as well.[7]

> §8.06. Enforcement of Restrictive Covenant in Employment Agreement
>
> Except to the extent other law or applicable professional rules provide otherwise, a covenant in an employment agreement restricting a former employee's activities is enforceable if it is reasonably tailored in scope, geography, and time to further a protectable interest of the employer, as defined in §8.07, unless:
>
> (a) the employer discharges the employee on a basis other than cause that makes enforcement of the covenant inequitable; or
> (b) the employer acted in bad faith in requiring or invoking the covenant; or
> (c) the employer materially breached the underlying employment agreement; or

---

[6] Hyde, Alan. 2012. 'Intellectual Property Justifications for Restricting Employee Mobility: A Critical Appraisal in Light of the Economic Evidence,' in Cynthia L. Estlund and Michael L. Wachter, *Research Handbook on the Economics of Labor and Employment Law*, 357–84. Cheltenham, UK, Northampton, MA, USA: Edward Elgar.

[7] American Law Institute. 2010. *Restatement of the Law – Employment Law (Tentative Draft No. 3, April 8, 2010).*

(d) in the geographic region covered by the restriction a great public need for the special skills and services of the former employee outweighs any legitimate interest of the employer in enforcing the covenant.

§8.07. Protectable Interests for Restrictive Covenants

An employer has a legitimate interest in protecting, through a reasonably tailored restrictive covenant with its employee, the employer's

(a) confidential information, as defined in §8.02,
(b) customer relationships,
(c) investment in the employee's reputation in the market, or
(d) investment in the purchase of the employee's business.

Obviously, a statement of law at this level of generality masks considerable conflict and diversity. May all four listed employer interests really be protected by an enforceable restrictive covenant? If any employer could claim that its employment of an individual improved that employee's returns in the labor market, merely because the employee worked at this particular employer, then any could enforce a restrictive covenant. Start-ups are more profitable when founders worked at firms in the industry with valuable patents even if the new firm makes no use of them,[8] and employees make more on the next job if they previously worked at a firm with valuable technology.[9] If the exception does not swallow the rule, how may it be determined that a given employer has really made such protectable investments, beyond the training that any enterprise must give employees? For any protectable employer interest, how does the tribunal determine whether a given restriction is reasonable in geographic scope and duration? Since most jurisdictions independently protect an employer's confidential information, is there any difference between the confidential information independently protected as a trade secret, and the confidential information that supports the enforcement of a restrictive covenant? There is little global uniformity in approach to these questions. While this variety complicates the presentation in this chapter, it also permits empirical analysis of the consequences for various legal regimes of employee mobility.

The questions of this chapter are obviously not of equal importance in all systems of employment law, though they are probably of increasing importance in all of them. German employers, for example, rarely extract promises not to compete from employees. There is essentially no labor market for mid-career German professionals – Germany has the second-lowest mobility rate for technical and scientific personnel in the European Union (EU), next to Italy – so departure of personnel has not been either a problem for German employers, or an opportunity for those employees.[10] It is likely

---

[8] Chatterji,. Spawned with a Silver Spoon? *supra* note 4.

[9] Balsvik, Ragnhild. 2011. 'Is Labor Mobility a Channel for Spillovers from Multinationals? Evidence from Norwegian Manufacturing,' 93 *Review of Economics and Statistics* 285–97; Franco and Filson, Spin-outs, *supra* note 4; Møen, Jarle. 2005. 'Is Mobility of Technical Personnel a Source of R&D Spillovers?' 23 *Journal of Labor Economics* 81–114.

[10] Casper, Steven. 2007. *Creating Silicon Valley in Europe: Public Policy towards New Technology Industries*, Oxford, UK: Oxford University Press, at 98–101, 180–81; Vitols, Sigurt, and Lutz Engelhardt. 2005. 'National Institutions and High Tech Industries: A Varieties of Capitalism Perspective on the Failure of Germany's 'Neuer Markt.' Discussion Paper SP II 2005-03, Wissenschaftszentrum Berlin für Sozialforschung.

however that many such labor markets will increasingly experience mobility, both national and international, though most will probably fall far short of California. There is no inevitability of development here.

Space obviously does not permit a comprehensive account of global variation on these matters. Instead, this chapter will follow the following plan. Part 1 will present and contrast three ideal types of enforcement of restrictive covenants. Section 1(a), 'Nonenforcers', will discuss the legal devices that some jurisdictions use to ensure employee mobility by never enforcing restrictive covenants. California (and some other US jurisdictions), India, Israel, Malaysia, Mexico, Argentina, Chile, and several other Latin American jurisdictions are 'nonenforcers.' They never enforce restrictive covenants. In some cases, this reflects a broad view of labor law values; in others, sensitivity to competition; in others, historical accident that has become institutionalized.

Section 1(b) will discuss 'low enforcers', that is jurisdictions that rarely enforce restrictive covenants, almost never longer than one year. This group includes most of the member states of the EU, most common law jurisdictions, China, and Japan.

Section 1(c) will present a group portrait of a small number of 'high enforcers', that is – jurisdictions that normally enforce a restrictive covenant merely because the employee signed it; do not require that employers demonstrate much in the way of special protectable interest; frequently enforce for periods longer than a year; rewrite unreasonably long or broad covenants to make them reasonable; and take a correspondingly broad view of trade secret protection. These jurisdictions include Thailand, Korea, and some US states such as New Jersey and Illinois.

All these comparisons will be somewhat doctrine-bound, as there is an interesting gap in the literature. We have been unable to locate a single 'legal realist' or sociolegal study of restrictive covenants that identifies, even for a single jurisdiction, the social or economic factors that actually predict the degree of enforcement.

Part 2 will explore scholarship on these issues that permit systematic comparison among our ideal types. Part 2(a) will examine the little scholarship that assembles databases of decisions. Part 2(b) will examine recent studies that use information theory to analyze judicial classifications of information. Part 2(c) will consider historical studies of how jurisdictions develop into nonenforcers, low enforcers, or high enforcers. Part 2(d) will examine economic and sociological literature making empirical comparisons between nonenforcers and high enforcers, or between low enforcers and high enforcers. So far, every study shows all social advantage to lie with a refusal to enforce restrictive covenants. Jurisdictions that never enforce restrictive covenants, or do so only minimally, experience higher growth, more business start-ups, higher employee compensation, and attract talent from jurisdictions that enforce restrictive covenants. Part 3 will conclude by reflecting on the construction of narratives in comparative law.

1. THREE MODELS OF REGULATING EMPLOYEE COMPETITION

(a) Nonenforcers

Several important legal systems never enforce negotiated limits on employee competition. Employees are always free to leave employment and either join a rival firm or go into competition with their former employer. Such jurisdictions typically expand their nonenforcement into a broader policy of employee mobility. For example, they may have a restricted definition of the kind of trade secret or confidential information that the departing employee may not take to the new employer. There are several paths to this outcome.

Most European, Asian, and Latin American constitutions protect the worker's fundamental right to earn a livelihood. In Asia and Latin America, some of these provisions have been construed to render noncompetes unenforceable.

The largest such jurisdiction is India. India has implemented its constitutional protection of the right to earn a livelihood with the Indian Contract Act (1872), Section 27 of which provides: 'Every agreement by which any one is restrained from exercising a lawful profession, trade or business of any kind, is to that extent void.' An exception permits such restraint as part of a sale of business. The section is interpreted in just such absolute terms. Noncompetes are unenforceable after the term of employment; there is no inquiry into reasonableness. Indian courts will not enforce noncompetes valid in other jurisdictions.[11] Nor will they enjoin a former employee from adopting and using processes learned at his previous employment.[12] This absolute opposition to noncompetes has been succinctly explained: 'autonomy is a crucial ingredient in individual well-being and law should not help individuals to give up further autonomy unnecessarily'; and 'unnecessary restraints hinder the free flow of labour and resources crucial to the efficient functioning of a market economy.'[13] India combines this commitment to employee mobility with unusually weak intellectual property protection for software, and this combination arguably helps account for the growth of the Indian software industry.[14] Indian courts will, however, enforce contracts that restrict approaches by the former employee to his former employer's customers.

Malaysia is similar. The Malaysian Contracts Act 1950, Section 28, is taken verbatim from Indian section 27 and is interpreted with reference to Indian cases. Bars on competition following employment are unenforceable. As in India, restrictions on

---

[11] *Taprogge Gesellschaft MBH v. IAEC India Ltd*, AIR 1988 Bom 157.

[12] *Dessicant Rotors Int'l Pvt Ltd v. Sarkar* (New Dehli High Court 2009); *M/s Sociedade de Fomento Indl. Ltd v. Kamath*, AIR 1995 Bom 158.

[13] Pollock, Frederick, and Dinsha Fardunji Mulla. *Indian Contract and Specific Relief Acts*. 12th ed, 795, as quoted in: Kanagasabai, Siva Kumar. 2010. 'Malaysia,' in Wendi S. Lazar and Gary R. Siniscalco, 2 *Restrictive Covenants and Trade Secrets in Employment Law: An International Survey*, 75-1–75-58. Arlington VA: BNA Books.

[14] Anand, Aarthi S. 2012. '"Less is More": New Property Paradigm in the Information Age?,' 11 *Duke Law and Technology Review* 65–144.

soliciting customers or other employees, or on use of confidential information, are tested for reasonableness as in most common law jurisdictions (discussed below Part 2(b)).[15]

While Latin American countries all have labor codes that derive from European origins, they diverge in their attitudes toward employee competition. Mexico is a nonenforcer. Article 5 of the Mexican Constitution, following its prohibition of forced labor, expressly provides: 'no person can legally agree to his own proscription or exile, or to the temporary or permanent renunciation of the exercise of a given profession or industrial or commercial pursuit.' Mexican employers evade this language by entering into contracts with departing employees in which the employer pays compensation in exchange for the employee's promise not to compete. Should the employee then compete, the employer sues to enforce the contract in civil court (as opposed to the Conciliation and Arbitration Board). The civil court solemnly declares the contract null and void under Article 5, then orders restitution of any amounts paid under it. The threat of such restitution is said to be a disincentive to employee competition.[16] Presumably, however, the need for the employer actually to pay compensation during the period covered by the 'null and void' noncompete must dissuade many employers from following this procedure.

In the US, standards for enforcing noncompetes are matters of state law. There is considerable variation among the states, which creates natural experiments to which we will refer in Part 2(d). The best-known jurisdiction that never enforces noncompetes is California. An 1872 statute, now codified as California Business and Professional Code Section 16600, provides: 'Except as provided in this chapter, every contract by which anyone is restrained from engaging in a lawful profession, trade, or business of any kind is to that extent void.' Ronald Gilson has shown that the adoption of this statute reflects nineteenth century codification and no considered policy judgment.[17] Some other western states (for example Montana and Oklahoma) enacted the same or similar language, but understood it merely to codify a common law approach testing such restraints for reasonableness.[18] California courts, however, for reasons not well understood, interpreted the statute as a complete ban on restrictive covenants. At some point, possibly as early as 1909, the area around Stanford University developed a concentration of high-technology businesses characterized by venture capital, ease of starting a business, and rapid employee mobility.[19] The region's leading chronicler attributes this pattern to various demographic and geographic factors, not mentioning any legal factors.[20] Gilson claims that California law's refusal to enforce noncompetes entirely

---

15 *Wrigglesworth v. Wilson Anthony*, [1964] 30 MLJ 269 (noncompete unenforceable against departing solicitor under sec. 28; 'The distance and place in respect of the restraint are irrelevant.')

16 De la Vega Gómez, Oscar, and Monica Schiaffino. 2010. 'Mexico,' in Lazar and Siniscalco, *supra* note 13, 54-1–54-31.

17 Gilson, Ronald J., 'The Legal Infrastructure of High Technology Industrial Districts: Silicon Valley, Route 128, and Covenants Not To Compete,' 74 *NYU L. Rev*. 575 (1999).

18 Malsberger, Brian M., ed. 1996. *Covenants Not to Compete: A State-by-State Survey*. 2d ed. Washington DC: BNA Books.

19 Hyde, *Working in Silicon Valley*, *supra* note 1.

20 Saxenian, AnnaLee. 1994. *Regional Advantage*, *supra* note 1.

explains Californian dominance in high-technology.[21] Hyde documents a process in which the unenforceability of noncompetes encouraged a culture of start-ups, employee mobility, and information sharing.[22] Employers and their lawyers today share that culture and do not sue departing employees even under legal theories that might permit this, such as the law of trade secrets. Whatever the history, today courts, and the California business establishment, identify their leadership in high technology with a broad policy of employee mobility, for which Section 16600 is taken to stand. The California Supreme Court has recently emphasized that there are no exceptions to that section: all covenants not to compete are unenforceable in California.[23] Lower California courts now apply this policy of employee mobility, refusing, for example, to enforce an agreement that the departing employee will not solicit customers of the former employer. The employee is liable only if he tortiously violates an independent obligation to preserve trade secrets.[24] California courts have long refused to give independent force to agreements to preserve trade secrets; such agreements may cover only secrets that the law independently considers trade secrets, and if they go beyond, they become unenforceable noncompetes.[25]

Israel also essentially never enforces noncompetes, largely for the reasons that California now understands its statute to protect: the economic benefits of employee mobility, particularly in high technology. The path to this result is a bit complicated. Until the late 1990s, Israel followed a common law 'reasonableness' analysis, until the legal landscape was changed by two decisions.[26] As a result of those cases, Israeli employers seeking enforcement of a restrictive covenant must demonstrate a particular need for enjoining employee mobility, beyond the fact that the employee signed it and the old employer would prefer not to face competition. Formally this is little different from the formulation of the American Law Institute (Secs 8.06–8.07), purporting to restate US law, stating that US employers seeking to enforce a restrictive covenant also must demonstrate a 'protectable interest'. In practice, however, Israeli employers are almost never successful in demonstrating such a protectable interest, and thus Israeli courts almost never have occasion to evaluate restrictive covenants for reasonableness. Employer claims that departing employees will disclose trade secrets, or that they need reimbursement for training costs, are normally rejected, or, where accepted, support injunctions only for very brief periods of under a year.[27]

(b) Characteristics of Nonenforcers

Nonenforcers typically recognize that the former employer may have an independent cause of action against departing employees for theft of trade secrets or confidential

---

[21] Gilson, The Legal Infrastructure of High Technology Industrial Districts, *supra* note 17.

[22] Hyde, *Working in Silicon Valley*, *supra* note 1.

[23] *Edwards v. Arthur Andersen LLP*, 189 P3d 285 (Cal 2008)('Sec. 16600 represents a strong public policy').

[24] *The Retirement Group v. Galante*, 98 Cal Rptr 3d 585 (Ct. App 2009).

[25] *State Farm Mut.Auto Ins. Co. v. Dempster*, 344 P2d 821 (Cal App 1959).

[26] *Checkpoint and Frumer v. Redguard* (National Labor Court 1999), and *AES Systems v. Sa'ar* (Supreme Court 2000).

[27] Guy Mundlak, personal communication.

information. However, they may be careful to limit this doctrine, lest it turn into the kind of restraint on competition that they have abolished. For example, India recognizes only very limited property rights in software.[28] California does not permit employers to designate trade secrets beyond the statutory definition. It requires plaintiffs in trade secret cases to identify the precise secret taken, which is a strong disincentive to litigation in the technology sector, where firms often do not want their rivals to know even which projects are under development.

(c) Low Enforcers

A larger group of jurisdictions sometimes enjoin employees from competing with former employers. These jurisdictions value the worker's mobility, but, unlike India, Mexico, or California, balance it against supposedly legitimate employer interests in preserving confidential information or recouping training. Jurisdictions in this group often state that restrictive covenants are not preferred. Enforcement for longer than a year or 18 months is rare, and may (in the civil law world) be conditioned on the plaintiff, that is, the former employer, compensating the employee.

(i) Common law jurisdictions

Common law jurisdictions (excluding, of course, the nonenforcers: India, Malaysia, California and a few other western US states, Israel) normally analyze noncompetes along the lines of the US Restatement. There must be a clear, negotiated promise not to compete, not merely one inferred from context. The plaintiff employer must demonstrate what the American Law Institute (ALI) calls a 'protectable interest' but which nonUS common law jurisdictions are more likely to term a 'property right', and the noncompete must be reasonable in duration and geographic scope to protect that property right. It is rare for common law jurisdictions to discuss matters of policy, or, for example, to describe themselves as low enforcers. The inquiry into 'reasonableness' is normally the proxy for these policies. Some common law jurisdictions describe noncompetes as 'presumptively void' unless the above showings are made.[29] While this phrase is not commonly used in the US, the US practice of placing the burden of proof on the party seeking to enforce the noncompete, and requiring that party to demonstrate protectable interest and reasonable scope, is substantively the same as treating the noncompete as presumptively void. Many famous common law cases reinforce these generalizations. The quotations that follow are from classic English cases and have been cited in hundreds of reported cases around the common law world.[30] As in any system, it can be difficult to form a reliable picture of how they are applied in practice.

---

[28] Anand, 'Less is More': New Property Paradigm in the Information Age?, *supra* note 14.

[29] *Elsley v. JG Collins Insurance Agencies Ltd*, [1978] 2 SCR 916 (Canada); *CLAAS Medical Centre Pte. Ltd v. Ng*, [2010] SGCA 3, at para. 44 (Singapore) ('prima facie void').

[30] See generally: Goulding, Paul, Gerard Clarke, Tristan Jones, and Catherine Taylor. 2011. 'Restrictive Covenants', in Paul Goulding, ed., *Employee Competition: Covenants, Confidentiality, and Garden Leave*. 2d ed. Oxford: Oxford University Press.

Part of employment contract and conspicuous Often cited is the decision of the UK Employment Appeal Tribunal, refusing to enforce a purported contract, signed by the former employee, restricting commissions to employees still on payroll on the payment date. The Tribunal held that the employment contract was formed when the employee started work the previous week and did not include terms presented to him afterwards, at least where these were onerous and had not been sufficiently brought to his attention.[31]

Property right

> I cannot find any case in which a covenant against competition by a servant or apprentice has, as such, ever been upheld by the Court. Wherever such covenants have been upheld, it has been on the ground, not that the servant or apprentice would, by reason of his employment or training, obtain the skill and knowledge necessary to equip him as a possible competitor in the trade, but that he might obtain such personal knowledge of and influence over the customers of his employer, or such an acquaintance with his employer's trade secrets as would enable him, if competition were allowed, to take advantage of his employers' trade connection or utilise information confidentially obtained … . [T]he reason, and the only reason, for upholding … a restraint on the part of an employee is that the employer has some *proprietary right*, whether in the nature of a trade connection or in the nature of trade secrets, for the protection of which such a restraint is – having regard to the duties of the employee – reasonably necessary.[32]

> The employers' claim for protection must be based upon the identification of some advantage or asset inherent in the business which can properly be regarded as, in a general sense, his property, and which it would be unjust to allow the employee to appropriate for his own purposes, even though he, the employee, may have contributed to its creation.[33]

Property rights are least controversial when applied to patents, trade secrets, or other intellectual property. They are more controversial when applied to customer relations or stable staff, which are not employer property at all.[34]

Effect of employer's repudiation Many English cases explore the implications of the General Billposting rule that a repudiation of an employment contract by the employer releases the employee from any restrictive covenants that it contains.[35] The rule is often applied when the employee is wrongfully terminated. The ALI found for the US that, 'The case law specifically addressing the enforceability of reasonable restrictive covenants against discharged employees is quite variable.'[36] It proposes that a reasonable restriction should be enforceable against the employee discharged for cause, but

---

31 *Peninsula Business Services Ltd v. Sweeney*, [2004] IRLR 49.

32 *Herbert Morris Ltd v. Saxelby*, [1916] AC 688, (HL), 709–10.

33 *Stenhouse Ltd v. Phillips*, [1974] AC 391, 400.

34 For a critique of the broadening concept of property in Australian case law on noncompetes, see: Riley, Joellen. 2009. 'Commodifying Sheer Talent: Perverse Developments in the Law's Enforcement of Restrictive Covenants,' in Christopher Arup and William van Caenegem, eds, *Intellectual Property Policy Reform: Fostering Innovation and Development*, 267–84. Cheltenham UK, Northampton, MA, USA: Edward Elgar.

35 *General Billposting Co Ltd v. Atkinson* [1909] AC 118 (HL).

36 Restatement of Employment Law Sec. 8.06, Reporter's Note f (Tent. Draft No. 3, 2010).

not against those terminated without cause,[37] while recognizing that the US cases do not all adopt such an approach. It further suggests: 'If the employer materially breaches the employment agreement, it cannot enforce an otherwise valid restrictive covenant contained in the agreement.'[38]

Reasonableness The employer who proves a property right may enforce only a covenant that is reasonable between the parties, and not injurious to the public. Surely the most quoted statement of this rule, found in decisions in the UK, Canada, Australia, Hong Kong, and Singapore, comes from the case of *Nordenfeld v. Maxim Nordenfeld Guns & Ammunition Co.*, holding that:

> The public have an interest in every person's carrying on his trade freely; so has the individual. All interference with individual liberty of action in trading, and all restraints of trade of themselves, if there is nothing more, are contrary to public policy, and therefore void. That is the general rule.
>
> But there are exceptions: restraints of trade and interference with individual liberty of action may be justified by the special circumstances of a particular case. It is a sufficient justification, and indeed it is the only justification, if the restriction is reasonable – reasonable, that is, in reference to the interests of the parties concerned and reasonable in reference to the interests of the public, so framed and so guarded as to afford adequate protection to the party in whose favour it is imposed, while at the same time it is in no way injurious to the public.[39]

Nordenfeld's reference to 'adequate protection' has been interpreted as the outer limit of enforceability. 'I think it is clear that what is meant is that for a restraint to be reasonable in the interests of the parties it must afford *no more than* adequate protection to the party in whose favour it is imposed.'[40] It is rare in common law jurisdictions to find restraints longer than a year to be reasonable.[41] For example, in Singapore the known outlier case, with enforcement for two years, stands out.[42]

Characteristics of low-enforcing common law jurisdictions The hallmark of legal analysis in a low-enforcing jurisdiction is the requirement that the plaintiff employer demonstrate particular need for restricting employee mobility. The desire not to face competition is not such a particular need. It is rare in practice for an employer to identify successfully any such need other than the protection of its trade secrets or particularized investment in customer relations.

It is sometimes asserted that an employer may restrict the mobility of an employee who has received very specific training, beyond 'the skill, experience, know-how and general knowledge acquired by an employee as part of his job during his employment, even though that will equip him as a competitor, or potential employee of a competitor,

---

37 Ibid., Sec. 8.06, Comment f.

38 Ibid., Comment g.

39 *Nordenfeld v. Maxim Nordenfeld Guns & Ammunition Co.*, [1894] A.C. 535 (H.L.)

40 *Herbert Morris v. Saxelby*, *supra* note 32 (emphasis original).

41 However, for a critique of increased enforcement in Australia, see: Riley, Commodifying Sheer Talent, *supra* note 34.

42 (*Heller Factoring*, [1998] 3 SLR 299); Ravi Chandran, personal communication.

of the employer,'[43] but we have been unable to find any cases resting a noncompete on this ground. The ALI does not recognize an employer interest in training that will support restricting mobility, and there appear to be no US cases that recognize an employer's training of an employee, or investment in that employee's reputation, as reasons to restrict the employee's mobility. Simply hiring personnel who possess the requirements specified by a customer does not convert the employee into a 'trade secret.' In other words, 'a stable of trained and talented at-will employees does not constitute an employer's trade secret.'[44]

It is often asserted that enforcement may be denied if doing so would harm the public interest. However, very few cases actually deny enforcement on this ground. Most involve medical professionals who, if enjoined from practicing, would leave a geographic area underserved.[45] In light of the economic evidence discussed in Part 2(d) *infra*, showing how restricting employee mobility harms the public interest, greater attention by common law courts to the public interest would probably reduce further the enforcement of noncompetes.

In contrast with civil law jurisdictions, it is unusual in the common law world for enforcement of a noncompete to be conditioned on payment to the employee. Enforcement, though rare, can thus be quite cruel as the employee is unable to work in his or her area of expertise and receives nothing from the former employer.[46]

(ii) European Union countries

In all member states of the EU, it is difficult to enforce a noncompete for anything but short periods of time and limited geographic scope. This results from application of national constitutions and labour statutes, as there are not yet common EU rules dealing with covenants not to compete, apart from peculiar provisions concerning self-employed commercial agents (Directive 86/653/EEC).

The validity of noncompetition agreements under EU law Restrictive covenants are deeply incompatible with fundamental principles of EU law, specifically competition law, though development of this principle mostly lies in the future.

The European Commission has expressed concern about the compatibility of noncompetition agreements with EU law, most fully in the answer given on behalf of the Commission by Mario Monti, then European Commissioner for Competition, to a written question of June 2002. Mr. Monti wrote:

---

[43] *FSS Travel and Leisure Systems Ltd v. Johnson*, [1998] IRLR 82 (CA).

[44] *Metro Traffic Control Inc. v. Shadow Traffic Network*, 22 Cal App 4th 853, 862 (1994) ('Actors, musicians, athletes, and others are frequently trained, tutored, and coached to satisfy the requirements of their sponsors and audiences, but their talents belong to them to contract away as they please … .').

[45] See: Trebilcock, Michael J. 1986. *The Common Law of Restraint of Trade: A Legal and Economic Analysis* Toronto: Carswell Company Ltd. Restatement Sec. 8.06(d), comment i.

A rare case denying enforcement as not in the public interest is *Thomas Cowan & Co Ltd v. Orme* [1961] MLJ 41 (Singapore) (noncompete reasonable between the parties but unenforceable because it unreasonably harmed public interest by perpetuating a monopoly in fumigation).

[46] Marx, Matt. 2011. 'The Firm Strikes Back: Noncompete Agreements and the Mobility of Technical Professionals,' 76 *American Sociological Review* 695–712.

> A particular clause which has a disproportionate effect on a person's ability to seek employment may well amount to a barrier to the provision of services under Article 49 of the EC Treaty as well (e.g. in the case where a company which operates in the high-tech sector needs to recruit a highly qualified person to be able to provide its services). Any rules that may hinder or make less attractive the exercise of a fundamental freedom guaranteed by the EC Treaty, such as the freedom to provide services must, according to the established case-law of the Court of Justice, fulfil certain requirements. There are four such requirements: they must be applied in a nondiscriminatory manner; they must be justified by imperative requirements in the general interest; they must be suitable for securing the attainment of the objective which they pursue; and they must not go beyond what is necessary in order to attain it. It is for the national authorities to apply the said criteria in individual cases and the question of the compatibility or otherwise of an agreement with the said criteria is a matter for the national courts to assess in the light of Community rules and principles on free movement of workers and services.

Noncompetition agreements, if not proportional, can therefore conflict with EU law and in particular with the freedom to provide services and the free circulation of dependent workers. Proportion might be evaluated from different perspectives. The Commission, as we saw, considered the needs of the enterprise – the example given was of a company, operating in the high-tech sector, which needs to recruit a highly qualified person to be able to provide services. Presumably a given restrictive covenant by one employer might therefore be disproportionate to the hiring needs of other employers. However, it might also be disproportionate to the well-recognized needs of employees, for example an employee, prevented by a covenant not to compete, from moving to other European countries to respond to job offers. Every restrictive covenant limits both competitors' freedom to hire and employees' freedom to move. It is not yet clear what sort of interest by the employer extracting the noncompete, if any, might sustain its enforceability in the teeth of the recognized harm to competitors and employees.

EU law of competition suggests that this balance should normally tip toward not enforcing restrictive covenants, even without considering any labour law values. EU rules on competition are designed to prohibit agreements which stifle competition. In particular, Article 101 of the Treaty on the Functioning of the EU prohibits as incompatible with the internal market 'all agreements between undertakings, decisions by associations of undertakings and concerted practices which may affect trade between Member States and which have as their object or effect the prevention, restriction or distortion of competition within the internal market.' Although the rule has primary reference to agreements between enterprises, agreements restricting competition between employer and employee may be included as 'concerted practices,' that 'have as their object or effect the prevention, restriction or distortion of competition within the internal market.'

An issue that would arise, should the EU begin to regulate restrictive covenants, would be whether the covenant, in order to come under EU regulation, would have to interfere with the functioning of the European labour market as a whole, for example a 'mass' restrictive agreement by a big company in order to prevent a large number of its employees from moving anywhere in the European labour market. It is however quite possible that a breach of EU law would arise even if the limitation purportedly imposed on employees lies only within the borders of a Member State. As stated by the European Court of Justice, the prejudice of the internal common market between

Member States may also result from purely national agreement, as long as it is likely to affect the entire territory of the Member State and therefore not limited local markets.[47] Such an agreement has the effect of 'reinforcing the compartmentalization of markets on a national basis, thereby holding up the economic interpenetration which the treaty is designed.'

Combining these principles of freedom to provide services and the free movement of workers, and anti-competitive rules, suggests EU law's adversity to noncompetition agreements between employer and employee. This adversity might exist even if, as is often argued, the protection of freedom of competition brought by European law is more protection of the market system in its objective structures, rather than protection of spheres of individual freedom. However, in practice, restrictive covenants in Europe are normally evaluated under national constitutions and other legislation, to which we now turn.

Restrictive covenants under European national constitutions and statutes European countries typically regard the regulation of restrictive covenants as a question of balancing, categorically and not in the individual case, the freedom of the employer against the freedom of the worker, both sets of freedoms often regarded as constitutional.

The employer seeking to enforce a restrictive covenant can invoke its freedom of economic initiative of the employer-entrepreneur, considered as the freedom to dispose of resources (material and human) in order to produce. This principle is located at the basis of all European constitutions: in some Constitutions it is expressly provided – for example, in the Spanish (Article 38), the Italian (Article 41) and the Hungarian (Article 9) ones – in others it is only implicit. This freedom of economic initiative includes the freedom of contract. The employer, on this view, is free to agree with employees to restrict their post-contractual competition. The employer may invoke agreements that represent companies' strategies or initiatives in order to preserve their know-how (knowledge, experience, secrets), or their investments in human resources (cost of acquisition and training of certain employees). Therefore, what is freely stipulated by parties in an agreement, should be considered invalid only if in conflict with other constitutional principles. As stated by the French Constitutional Court (Constitutional Council n 2002-465 de 13 janvier 2003) the legislator cannot legally invalidate contracts concluded if there is not a sufficient reason of general interest.

This freedom of economic initiative provides not only a legal support to covenants not to compete, but also a first limitation for them. In fact freedom of economic initiative provides, as a corollary, the right to compete, granting to each person to perform the same activities already carried out by another individual and then to fight against him to conquer the market. The principle of free competition – a principle embraced by all EU countries, in accord with EU Treaties that recognize this principle widely and firmly – prohibits restrictive agreements that go beyond the legitimate initiative of the entrepreneur, encroaching into the realm of equal freedom of economic initiative of his competitors and of his employee. In other words, the very principle of freedom of economic initiative that might be thought to support restrictive covenants,

[47] *Case V.C.H.*, October 17th, 1972

simultaneously renders invalid any restrictions which have no purpose except to prevent the employee (or any other person) from competing with the former employer. We will see later how this translates into concrete limitations.

The most important counterweight, to the interests of the employer who seeks to enforce a covenant not to compete, is the protection of individual workers. The right to work, here meaning the right of citizens to free choice of employment, not only in order to satisfy their family and own needs, but also to develop their own person, is recurrently present in the European Constitutional Charters. Recurrent also is a link between employment and human personality: the work is elevated to an instrument of social, moral and political development of the citizen; a means for workers to make an improvement in their personality through the improvement of their professional position.

From the protection of the right to work as a means of livelihood and social and moral development of the citizen comes the right of the citizen-worker to accede to job opportunities offered by the labour market. Guaranteed free movement inside the labour market is the tool necessary to ensure an effective right to work to the citizen. This right finds an express recognition in many European Constitutions: Article 12 of the German Constitution provides for freedom of employment; Article 35, para. 1 of the Spanish Constitution recognizes the right to choose a profession and to improve professionalism; Article 35 of the Italian Constitution states the promotion of training and professional advancement; Section 18 of Finland's Constitution recognizes the right to receive training that promotes employability. While the recognition of the right to work is the main antagonist to the validity of noncompetition agreements, it is not an insurmountable obstacle. The Italian Constitutional Court, in a judgment quite dated, but still relevant, stated that the recognition of the right to work provided by Article 4 of the Italian Constitution can be derogated where the statutory law places restrictions for the protection of other interests and other social needs.[48]

The protection of the right to work is recognized in many European Constitutions under a second and no less important profile: the protection of human dignity, including professional dignity. In all European jurisdictions the inviolability of human dignity is configured as a limit on the choices taken by individuals exercising their freedom of contract. Therefore, the restrictions imposed on the employee through a noncompetition agreement must still allow the expression of his professionalism. The degree of compression to which the dignity of the profession may lawfully be submitted by a noncompetition agreement varies from country to country.

The translation of the constitutional values into statutory rules European legislation on restrictive covenants is normally understood as a balance among these conflicting interests. As mentioned above, the freedom of economic initiative by itself can never justify restricting free competition. There must be another purpose that justifies limiting competition, and the limit must be proportional to that purpose. In practice, this is substantially similar to the doctrine of restraint of trade of common law countries. There is little difference between 'employer protectable interest' of the common law and European civil law's 'socially and objectively appreciable interest' necessary to

48 See: Corte Costituzionale 61/1965.

justify the restriction provided by a covenant not to compete. Sometimes the need to demonstrate such an interest is expressly required by the statutory rules (i.e. Spanish Workers Statute, German Commercial Code; Hungarian Labour Code); more often it is imposed by case-law.

The employer's interest is always measured by the actual needs of the employer, compared to the subjective characteristics of the employee and the activity he can perform. Specifically, for the existence of such a legitimate interest there must be a 'competitiveness' of the activity the employer wants to inhibit in the employee. Therefore any agreement that imposes restrictions on the worker, outside the activities that can be considered competition, is considered null and void.

Spanish, German, and French case-law recognize an employer's legitimate interest only where there is a loss or potential damage that the company may suffer as a result of the passage of the worker into competition. Thus the interest of employers is restricted only to those workers who: have access to important information; have close relationships with customers (such as commercial) or are aware of the lists of clients and price lists; perform particular functions; or possess a particular experience. By contrast, the employer has no legitimate interest in restricting the mobility of employees who perform simple tasks. Belgian legislation provides strict and objective rules, which limit the employer's interest to those employees who receive a salary higher than a given amount.

In addition to the requirement of legitimate employer interest, European legal systems fairly uniformly place identical limits to the noncompetition agreement. A covenant not to compete must be in writing, must be of limited duration, specify the geographic area of validity of the agreement and the activity inhibited by the agreement, and provide for compensation to the worker. These are all conditions for the validity of the covenant, except for the indication of the duration of the agreement. It is a rule shared by the various jurisdictions that the agreements exceeding the law time limits are valid only up to the roof of the law, and ineffective for the remaining period.

What emerges from the varied European legislation is the widespread desire – consistent with the constitutional principles already highlighted – to safeguard not only the prospect of economic livelihood of the worker, but also the free development of their professionalism. What varies considerably among the different legal systems is the level of protection accorded to these values. In actual litigation, there is much more concern with labour law values, typically protection of the worker, than with competition values. For example, in Germany the prospect of economic livelihood of the worker is well protected by imposing a minimum remuneration for the covenant not to compete at least equal to half of the salary of the employee. France similarly requires financial compensation to the employee ('contrepartie') that may lie somewhere between full compensation and the derisory. In some sectors, collective negotiations have defined the minimum compensation. By contrast, in other countries, such as Italy, any payment beyond the merely symbolic is sufficient, perhaps as little as 10 or 15 percent of salary. As mentioned, there is little use in Germany of noncompetes and little litigation.[49] It is possible that German tribunals are satisfied with enforcing a non-compete so long as the employee is compensated, while in Italy, where the constitution

[49] Casper, Creating Silicon Valley in Europe, *supra* note 10.

protects the right to practice a profession, tribunals place more emphasis on the reasonableness of the restriction even if the employee is well-paid and the employer's interest legitimate.

France is a low enforcer that may be evolving towards nonenforcement. Five decisions of the Chambre Sociale de la Cour de Cassation, all issued 10 July 2002, collectively require that a noncompete meet five conditions before it may be enforced. First, it must be included in the contract of employment. Second, it must permit some employment to the affected employee. Third, it must be 'indispensable to the legitimate needs of the enterprise.' Fourth, it must be limited in time and space. Fifth, as noted, the employer must compensate the employee with a *contrepartie*. As a result, when a French employee, who has signed a clause de nonconcurrence, resigns or is dismissed, the employer has only two choices. It can 'lever la clause de nonconcurrence,' permitting the employee to take any job. Or it may seek to apply the clause, paying the employee monthly compensation, with enforcement by no means certain.[50]

It is rare in Europe for the analysis of a restrictive covenant to consider the impact of its enforcement on levels of competition. Even though competition is a constitutional value present in all European Constitutional Charters and among fundamental principles of the EU (see above), every question on the validity of noncompetition agreements is resolved by national judges considering only the 'social' aspects of the issue, that is to say the protection of workers as the weaker party to the employment relationship. As in common law jurisdictions, the need to protect competition requires that the employer identify a legitimate interest, such as protection of trade secrets or customer relations. A desire not to face competition is not such a legitimate interest. However, if the employer successfully identifies such a legitimate interest, there is no further inquiry into the effect on the particular labour or product market of enforcing the specific restrictive covenant.

(iii) Other low enforcing jurisdictions

Japanese company work rules normally purport to restrain employees who leave employment from competing with their former employer. For decades, these provisions were mainly symbolic. Under the 'lifetime employment' prevailing in large Japanese corporations, employees did not depart and there was no labor market for mid-career managers or professionals. Recently labor mobility has increased in Japan. Courts hearing cases under the work rules have determined to enforce only 'reasonable' restrictions on competition. When personnel of a bar exam preparation school departed to found a rival, the court enforced the noncompete for two years against the departing director, on the grounds that this was necessary to protect trade secrets of the old employer, but refused to enforce the noncompete against instructors or auditors. If a noncompete does not protect employer trade secrets, it is enforceable only if the employer makes 'counterpayment' to the employee.[51] In the case of Nihon Convention,

---

[50] Guillaume Maréchal, personal communication.

[51] Nihon Convention Service, 711 RODO HANREI 30, 47 (Osaka Dist. Ct., Dec. 25, 1996), rev'd in part on other grounds, aff'd in part, 745 RODO HANREI 42 (Osaka High Ct., May 29, 1998); Ogawa, Miwako. 1999. 'Noncompete Covenants in Japanese Employment Contracts: Recent Developments,' 22 *Hastings International and Comparative Law Review* 341–77.

the departing employees took no trade secrets, only good relations with customers; this was held insufficient to support enforcement of the noncompete.[52] Japanese courts consider many different factors in their inquiry into reasonableness, and the cases are somewhat unpredictable, but overall, enforcement of noncompetes is not favored.[53]

China Employment Contract Law (2008), Article 24, restricts enforcement of 'competition restrictions' to 'senior managers, senior technicians and other personnel with a confidentiality obligation'; requires compensation during the noncompete period, of at least 30 percent of average salary; and cannot exceed two years.[54]

(d) High Enforcers

Korea, Thailand, and some US jurisdictions, are more likely to enforce noncompetes. They follow a common pattern. The noncompete is treated like any contract. It is not considered presumptively or prima facie invalid. The employer will not, in practice, have to show any special need for a noncompete. In such jurisdictions, it is enough that the employee signed it. Such jurisdictions do sometimes state that the noncompete must be 'reasonable' in duration and geographic scope. However, since the purpose of the noncompete – that is, the employer's protectable property interest – is not clearly specified, the 'reasonableness' inquiry is subjective and unfocused. Moreover, in high enforcing jurisdictions, an unreasonable noncompete may be redrafted by the court and enforced as rewritten.

Thailand gets the Olympic gold medal for restricting employee mobility. Its Supreme Court recently enforced a promise by a departing low-level manager in the logistics industry not to work in the industry for five years in Thailand, Vietnam, Cambodia, Laos, or Myanmar.[55] This is the longest and broadest enforcement of a noncompete that we encountered in our research (since the laissez-faire nineteenth century when cartels and other agreements in restraint of trade were also enforceable). There are few, if any, jurisdictions that would restrain someone from working in his field for such a long period, and over five countries. The employer demonstrated no particular need for the noncompete. For example, it did not identify any trade secrets or confidential information, loss of which it feared.

Courts in Korea and Taiwan undertake a balancing process similar to common law jurisdictions, so it is difficult to say whether they are really high enforcers or not. We include them as high enforcers because they will rewrite an unreasonable covenant to one of reasonable length; they consider two years presumptively reasonable; and because other commentators have described Korea as favoring employers.[56] Taiwan, by contrast, is said increasingly to protect employees.[57] Such assessments by local counsel

[52] Tokyo Legal Mind, 894 HANREI TAIMUZU 73 (Tokyo Dist. Ct., Oct. 16, 1995); Ogawa, Miwako. 1999. 'Noncompete Covenants in Japanese Employment Contracts', ibid.

[53] Ogawa, 'Noncompete Covenants in Japanese Employment Contracts', ibid.

[54] Decision of Supreme People's Court, January 31, 2013.

[55] *JVK International Movers v. Howell*, case 1275/2543, 2007.

[56] Kim, Beomsu, Young-Seok Ki, and John Kim. 2010. 'South Korea,' in Lazar and Siniscalco, *supra* note 13, 78-1–78-45 ('current trend is towards enhanced protection for employers and their trade secrets').

[57] Yu, Lawrence. 2010. 'Taiwan,' in Lazar and Siniscalco, ibid., 79-1–79-38.

are interesting but difficult to evaluate; we return to this point in Part 2 when we discuss scholarship on these issues.

Intermediate appellate courts in two, but only two, US jurisdictions (Illinois and New Jersey) have enjoined employees from changing jobs on a theory known as 'inevitable disclosure of trade secrets.' This is the equivalent of giving every employer a noncompete without its negotiating it. As mentioned, employers in the US who sue departing employees, alleging the statutory 'actual or threatened disclosure' of trade secrets, must normally identify the precise trade secrets, loss of which they fear. This is a disincentive to litigation. In the theory of 'inevitable disclosure,' the employer alleges simply that the employee had access to trade secrets (as all employees do); that the employee proposes to join a direct competitor to work on the same sort of matters; and that the employee will thus 'inevitably disclose' something or other on the new job, though the old employer cannot demonstrate precisely what.[58] No state supreme court has adopted the theory of inevitable disclosure. A few trial courts have.[59] Following the *Pepsico* decision, which was widely noted,[60] hundreds of employers sued, all over the US, to enjoin the departure of personnel on the theory that they would 'inevitably disclose' trade secrets. Nearly all of these suits were unsuccessful, courts adhering to the traditional standard that the employer must both identify trade secrets, and show that their loss was 'actual or threatened,' usually by showing some untrustworthiness in the departing employee.[61] The ALI concluded that the doctrine of 'inevitable disclosure of trade secrets' is limited to few states and only to 'exceptional circumstances' typically requiring a 'pattern of deceit or misappropriation' by the departing employee.[62]

2. SCHOLARLY LITERATURE ON THE LAW OF EMPLOYEE MOBILITY AND SUGGESTIONS FOR FUTURE SCHOLARSHIP

The topic of legal restrictions on employee mobility has a thinner scholarly literature than some other topics in this volume. This doubtless reflects its uneven importance in different labor markets and systems of labor law. However, some very interesting scholarship is emerging. The variation among jurisdictions permits interesting comparative study, so far, however, limited to comparison among US jurisdictions.

---

58 *National Starch and Chemical Corp. v. Parker Chemical Corp.,* 530 A.2d 31 (N.J. App.Div. 1987); *Pepsico, Inc. v. Redmond*, 54 F.3d 1262 (7th Cir. 1995) (Illinois law); *Strata Mktg. v. Murphy*, 740 NE2d 1166, 1175-79 (Ill. App. 2000).

59 Interestingly, there do not appear to be any New Jersey cases applying the theory since *National Starch*, Ibid.

60 See *supra* note 58.

61 See, e.g., *Whyte v. Schlage Lock Co.*, 125 Cal.Rptr.2d 277 (Ct.App. 2002); *Northwest Bec-Corp v. Home Living Service*, 41 P3d 263 (Idaho 2002) ('An employee will naturally take with her to a new company the skills, training, and knowledge she has acquired from her time with her previous employer. This basic transfer of information cannot be stopped, unless an employee is not allowed to pursue her livelihood by changing employers.'); *LeJeune v. Coin Acceptors, Inc.,* 849 A2d 451, 467–70 (Md. 2004).

62 Restatement Sec. 8.05, comment b.

(a) Realist or Socio-legal Prediction of Outcome: A Gap in the Literature

We have been unable to locate a single article that assembles a database of decisions and examines which variable factors predict litigation outcomes. The closest is Christopher Arup, who assembles a database of over a hundred decisions from the Australian states of New South Wales and Victoria, which he then examines for their analysis of the type of information involved (see Part 2(b)).[63] One could regress such variables as the size of the old and new enterprise, type of industry, age and salary of the departing employee, and other variables, in order to determine the factors that actually predict when noncompetes will be found to be reasonable.

A New York lawyer who has litigated many cases involving noncompetes suggested to us, only partly in jest, that the law of New York is as follows. When the departing employee, against whom enforcement of a noncompete is sought, makes less money than the judge, the judge will find the noncompete to be an unreasonable interference with the working man or woman's right to make a living. However, when the departing employee makes more money than the judge, and especially if that high earner is younger than the judge, the judge will enforce the noncompete, finding it a reasonable attempt to recover the old employer's investment in the young person. While made in jest, the hypothesis is more than a little bit plausible. Belgian and Chinese law, as we have seen, specifically limit enforcement of noncompetes to employees with high salaries. As a descriptive thesis about New York law it could, in principle, easily be tested by assembling a database of reported decisions, coded for variables of this type. Scholarship of this kind would permit advance beyond the truisms, endlessly repeated in the literature, that 'reasonableness' is a vague standard and the cases unpredictable.

(b) Information Theory

As we have seen, cases in which employers successfully impede employee mobility often turn on the characterization of information. The employee's mobility may be impeded if the employee has disclosed or threatens to disclose 'confidential information' or 'trade secrets,' categories that include such common reifications as 'customer lists,' 'customer information,' 'business plans,' and so on. The employee will be permitted, by contrast, to change jobs and trade on information that is 'common knowledge' or the result of 'general training.' Some information will itself support the employer's cause of action, such as loss of trade secrets, while the same or other information may instead represent the employer's 'protectable' or 'property' interest supporting enforcement of a noncompete. As we also have seen, it is common for scholars to observe that all these legal categories are somewhat malleable.

Theorists of information have developed more refined categories of information but little use has been made of them in legal analysis. Arup classifies a set of Australian decisions by the type of information involved.[64] He invokes a six-part matrix under which knowledge may be explicit, tacit, or personal, and each of these may apply to

---

[63] Arup, Christopher. 2012. 'What/Whose Knowledge? Restraints of Trade and Concepts of Knowledge', 36 *Melbourne University Law Review* 369–414.

[64] Ibid.

knowledge about production or about customers. Arup argues that courts should protect only knowledge that is genuinely confidential, not merged into employee know-how, and in his analysis this danger is particularly acute in cases involving knowledge about customers.

Hyde identifies several employer practices in Silicon Valley that individually and collectively transmit information across firm boundaries.[65] Firms hire for short tenures with rapid employee turnover, which is positive for productivity in firms with high R&D expenditure,[66] or that employ advanced technologies.[67] They make heavy use of independent contractors and temporary employees whose loyalty is to technology rather than to organization.[68] They frequently share technical information with rivals or make such inquiries themselves, a practice facilitated by rapid mobility of personnel.[69] They do not sue departing employees and make this policy known when they recruit.[70] Hyde explains this pattern through the New Economics of Growth, in which legally nonexcludable information, shared by multiple users, is the key variable in rapid economic growth. Following this literature, Hyde does not distinguish between nonrivalrous information (codes and formulas that may be used simultaneously by many users) and rivalrous information (information in a human body that can only be in one place at one time), since both are important factors in economic growth. For example, the classic study of Harry Collins showed that no laboratory ever successfully constructed a particular type of laser without employing someone who had previously worked with it, even though all of its plans and specifications were in the public domain.[71] Collins has considerably elaborated his concept of tacit knowledge.[72] It is possible that these studies of information will someday influence legal understandings of employee intellectual property.

---

65 Hyde, Working in Silicon Valley, *supra* note 1.

66 Andersson, Fredrik, Clair Brown, Benjamin Campbell, Hyowook Chiang, and Yooki Park. 2008. 'The Effect of HRM Practices and R&D Investment on Worker Productivity,' in Stefan Bender et al., eds., *The Analysis of Firms and Employees: Quantitative and Qualitative Approaches*. Chicago: University of Chicago Press, 19–43.

67 Abowd, John M., John Haltiwanger, Julia Lane, Kevin L. McKinney, and Kristin Sandusky. 2007. 'Technology and the Demand for Skill: An Analysis of Within and Between Firm Differences.' National Bureau of Economic Research Working Paper 13043.

68 Barley, Stephen R., and Gideon Kunda. 2004. *Gurus, Hired Guns, and Warm Bodies: Itinerant Experts in a Knowledge Economy*. Princeton: Princeton University Press.

69 Feldman, Experimental Approach to the Study of Normative Failures: Divulging of Trade Secrets by Silicon Valley Employees, *supra* note 2; Saxenian, Regional Advantage, *supra* note 1; Sitkin, Secrecy in Organizations, *supra* note 2.

70 Hyde, Working in Silicon Valley, *supra* note 1.

71 Collins, Harry M. 1974. 'The TEA Set: Tacit Knowledge in Scientific Networks.' 4 *Science Studies* 165–86.

72 See also: Collins, Harry M. 2010. *Tacit and Explicit Knowledge*. Chicago: University of Chicago Press; Lucas, Robert E. 1988. 'On the Mechanics of Economic Development.' 22 *Journal of Monetary Economics* 3–42; Romer, Paul M. 1986. 'Increasing Returns and Long Run Growth,' 94 *Journal of Political Economy* 1002–37; Romer, *Endogenous Technological Change*, *supra* note 5; Warsh, *Knowledge and the Wealth of Nations*, *supra* note 5.

(c) Historical Studies

There are few historical studies of changing concepts of workplace intellectual property over time. Exemplary is Catherine Fisk, documenting gradual acquisition by US employers of rights to exploit their employees' inventions, under the flexible device of implied contract.[73] Similar studies for other jurisdictions would facilitate comparative analysis.

(d) Economic and Other Empirical Social Science Comparing Jurisdictions

A growing body of empirical social science, all in the US so far, studies the social consequences of enforcing noncompetes. Some exploit the variation among US states to make comparisons between enforcers and nonenforcers. Some study consequences of changes in the law. While this work is in its infancy, so far *all* of it suggests that all the economic advantages accrue to jurisdictions that do not enforce noncompetes.

Early work often compared California, the leading nonenforcer, with enforcers such as Massachusetts. This is a noisy measure. There are many reasons California is not Massachusetts. Sampsa Samila and Olav Sorenson compared metropolitan areas based on a more sophisticated index with varying levels of enforcement of noncompetes, depending on which of a list of relevant legal doctrines had been adopted in a given state.[74] They found that full enforcement of noncompetes reduces venture capital, business start-ups, and patenting. The finding on patenting is crucial. The usual legitimate reason for enforcing noncompetes, as we have seen, is their supposed tendency to encourage employer investment in training and information, investment that, supposedly, will never take place if employees are free to depart. If there is anything to this scenario, it is outweighed by its opposite. '[N]ot only does the enforcement of noncompete agreements limit entrepreneurship … but also it appears to *impede* innovation.'[75] Another interesting feature of the Samila-Sorenson study is that its results remain robust even if the San Francisco Bay area is entirely omitted from the comparisons. In other words, the association between employee mobility and economic growth is not limited to the specific conditions of information technology, or Silicon Valley in the 1990s. Similarly, Mark Garmaise, who studied executive compensation, shows that managers in jurisdictions that enforce noncompetes are less mobile, are paid less, and take more poorly paid jobs if they change jobs.[76] They invest less in their own human capital. As a result, employers in jurisdictions that do not enforce noncompetes are more productive and better able to attract financing. Like Samila and Sorenson,

---

[73] Fisk, Catherine L. 2009. *Working Knowledge: Employee Innovation and the Rise of Corporate Intellectual Property, 1800–1930*. Chapel Hill: University of North Carolina Press.

[74] Samila, Sampsa, and Olav Sorenson. 2011. 'Noncompete Covenants: Incentives to Innovate or Impediments to Growth,' 57 *Management Science* 425–38.

[75] Ibid, at 23; emphasis in original.

[76] Garmaise, Mark J. 2011. 'Ties that Truly Bind: Noncompetition Agreements, Executive Competition, and Firm Investment,' 27 *Journal of Law, Economics, and Organization* 376–425.

Garmaise constructed an index that permits him to classify US states by differing levels of enforcement of noncompetes, which has already proved valuable to other researchers.[77]

Michigan in 1985 repealed, apparently inadvertently, its previous California-like statutory restrictions on the enforcement of noncompetes, and began after 1985 to enforce noncompetes. This created a natural experiment analyzed by Matt Marx, Deborah Strumsky and Lee Fleming by studying patents.[78] Firm-to-firm mobility among inventors dropped 8.1 percent, with higher drops among inventors with more human capital. There was no social benefit from this decline in mobility. In particular, there was no increase in patents. Michigan employers may have gained the power to impede their employees' mobility, but they did not do anything useful with this power. The results did not change significantly if the automobile industry was completely excluded.

Matt Marx, Jasjit Singh and Lee Fleming then tracked inventor mobility nationally, through the patent database, and found a significant brain drain from states that enforce noncompetes to states that do not, controlling for general economic conditions.[79] The most productive, and most networked, patenting inventors are the most likely to move from enforcing to nonenforcing states. The result does not change if California is left out of the analysis entirely. Png found that adoption of the Uniform Trade Secrets Act also increases out-of-state mobility of scientists and engineers from states that had not previously been full noncompete enforcers, in Garmaise's typology.[80]

What happens to employees who are subjected to a covenant not to compete? The first such study is by Matt Marx, who interviewed around 60 inventors in the automatic speech recognition industry.[81] He found that the waste of human capital is enormous. A significant number were unable to use their skills again. They switched industries, or absorbed the cost of being out of work for the duration of the noncompete. Those that decided to change jobs anyway were much likelier to go to a large firm that could afford litigation with Employer 1 than to a smaller firm.

These are all studies that in principle could be adapted to make similar comparisons between enforcers and nonenforcers outside the US. Marx, studying the labor market experience of those subjected to restrictions on mobility, presents no methodological difficulties if replicated outside the US, and is long overdue everywhere.[82] Comparison between enforcers and nonenforcers could start with an adaptation of the typologies of Samila-Sorenson or Garmaise, then comparison for the outcomes they studied (patents,

---

77 Png, I.P.L. unpublished. 'Trade Secrets, NonCompetes, and Mobility of Engineers and Scientists: Empirical Evidence.' (August 21, 2012). Available at SSRN: http://ssrn.com/abstract=1986775 or http://dx.doi.org/10.2139/ssrn.1986775.

78 Marx, Matt, Deborah Strumsky, and Lee Fleming. 2009. 'Mobility, Skills, and the Michigan NonCompete Experiment,' 55 *Management Science* 879–89.

79 Marx, Matt, Jasjit Singh, and Lee Fleming. Unpublished. 'Regional Disadvantage: Noncompete Agreements and Brain Drain.' Available at SSRN: http://ssrn.com/abstract=1654719 or http://dx.doi.org/10.2139/ssrn.1654719.

80 Png, Trade Secrets, NonCompetes, and Mobility of Engineers and Scientists, *supra* note 77.

81 Marx, The Firm Strikes Back, *supra* note 46.

82 Ibid.

start-ups, economic growth, compensation, mobility of personnel), or related outcomes. The results of such comparison are not easy to predict. It is possible that other labor market factors will prevent enterprises outside the US from realizing California (or India or Israel-style) growth when employee mobility may no longer legally be impeded. For example, if German employers still make little use of noncompetes, as demonstrated by Casper,[83] it cannot matter much (except to the affected individuals) whether they are enforced or not, and if there is still no labor market for mid-career German professionals,[84] there may be few productivity gains to be had from altering the law of employee mobility. On the other hand, there are surely other jurisdictions that, like the low-growth jurisdictions in the studies by Samila and Sorenson,[85] Garmaise,[86] Marx, Strumsky and Fleming,[87] Marx Singh Fleming,[88] and Png,[89] might owe some of that low growth to the impediments their law of employer intellectual property place on employee mobility and new business formation.

3. CONCLUSION: ON NARRATIVES OF COMPARATIVE LAW

Thus, despite many differences in emphasis, all known systems of labor and employment law recognize the potential harm to the public in permitting employers to impede employee mobility or to extract 'voluntary' promises to do the same. Without legal limits, impediments to employee mobility might have devastating impact on affected employees; harm consumers by limiting competition and new business formation; and harm entire societies by restricting economic growth, particularly the kind of rapid diffusion of information that is essential to technological advances. Consequently, every system of labor law places limits on employers' ability to impede employee mobility. Every system of labor law limits the enforcement of restrictive covenants and some very large jurisdictions never enforce them at all. Every system of labor law stakes out areas of knowledge that employees may carry into the labor market and take to their next employer: general knowledge; general training; scientific facts; information not kept secret by the old employer; in some cases the employee's own market reputation and customer relations. However, many of the common legal formulations are vague and cast unnecessary shadows on employee mobility. Global technological and economic growth would be enhanced by more widespread adoption of best practices.

We stand by this story. We are well aware, however, that this is not the way that the story is usually told in the comparative law literature on restrictive covenants and trade secrets.[90] It is more common to view this problem the wrong way round, through an

---

83 Casper, Creating Silicon Valley in Europe, *supra* note 10.

84 Vitols and Engelhardt, National Institutions and High Tech Industries, *supra* note 10

85 Samila and Sorenson, Noncompete Covenants, *supra* note 74.

86 Garmaise, Ties that Truly Bind, *supra* note 76.

87 Marx, Strumsky and Fleming, Mobility, Skills, and the Michigan NonCompete Experiment, *supra* note 78.

88 Marx Singh Fleming, Regional Disadvantage, *supra* note 79.

89 Png, Trade Secrets, Non-Competes, and Mobility of Engineers and Scientists, *supra* note 77.

90 See for example: Lazar and Siniscalco, *supra* note 13.

American myth that wrongly associates economic growth with strong intellectual property rights. Propagation and enactment of this myth has taken a great deal of US diplomacy and publicity. The US government, and publicists who absorb its myths, believe that other countries should join the US in recognizing these (mythical) intellectual property rights, and, if they would prefer not to, they will be forced to, in trade negotiations. For it is no secret that, for decades, the chief US objective in any trade negotiation has been the recognition by its partners of supposed US intellectual property rights. US trade negotiators do not typically seek, for example, job growth in the US, lower prices for US consumers, let alone a fair and just world. This myth simply ignores the thousands of vital US technology companies, particularly in information technology, that hold few patents; whose products may be reverse engineered; and whose internal practices and projects are entirely in the heads of employees who, in the US, can and will walk out the door, without fear of lawsuit, at any time.[91]

> [T]he regime of intellectual property rights under which the scientific and technological platform of the digital economy was constructed in the United States was radically at odds with present standards: software was not patentable and business processes were not even subject to copyright, let alone patent; cross-licensing of patents was widespread and in some instances mandatory; and the requirements of national security forced the active creation of second sources.[92]

Like any myth, the myth of intellectual property requires suppression of alternative narratives, such as the reality of employee mobility. California's principle of employee mobility is well-known, but rare indeed is the published reference to the similar policies of such large economies as India, Mexico, or Israel. By contrast, the supposed doctrine of 'inevitable disclosure of trade secrets,' giving every employer a restrictive covenant even if it did not negotiate one, has received enormous comment, despite the fact that it has supported injunctions in appellate courts in precisely two US jurisdictions, has been rejected in nearly all of the hundreds of US cases litigated under that theory, and is not part of the law anywhere outside New Jersey and Illinois.[93]

The problem of the starting-point pervades every narrative of comparative law, no matter how scrupulous, including every narrative in this volume. There is never just one way of telling the story. There is never one obvious place to start. There is no master jurisdiction whose narratives are privileged. So we hope that our understanding of the comparative law of employee mobility, in addition to informing our readers, might also represent a kind of deconstruction of the entire enterprise of narratives of comparative law.

---

[91] Hyde, Working in Silicon Valley, *supra* note 1.

[92] Janeway, William H. 2012. *Doing Capitalism in the Innovation Economy: Markets, Speculation and the State*. Cambridge UK: Cambridge University Press.

[93] Lazar and Siniscalco, *supra* note 13, polled attorneys in every country in their international survey about the supposed doctrine of 'inevitable disclosure of trade secrets,' helpfully adding a footnote to each chapter explaining this doctrine, only to learn that it is, we are happy to say, entirely unknown outside the US.

8. The lasting influence of legal origins: Workplace discrimination, social inclusion and the law in Canada, the United States and the European Union

Kevin Banks, Roberta Nunin and Adriana Topo

1. INTRODUCTION

This chapter will compare laws in Europe and North America seeking to eliminate discrimination and to achieve greater social inclusion in the workplace. While descriptive comparisons covering these subjects have been available for some time,[1] there has been little analysis aimed at explaining international similarities and differences. We contribute to filling this gap. We show how fundamental differences in the way that different legal systems apprehend the concepts of workplace discrimination and equality emerged notwithstanding the shared influence of United States (U.S.) equality rights jurisprudence. We then consider the very different roles of law and government in fostering social inclusion in Canada, the European Union (EU) and the U.S.

We argue that the different types of discrimination addressed in precedent setting anti-discrimination cases in each jurisdiction led courts and legislators in Canada, the U.S. and Europe to develop legal principles and concepts first articulated in the U.S. in very different ways. Specifically, the focus of U.S. jurisprudence on race, Canadian jurisprudence on religion, and European jurisprudence on sex discrimination led eventually to the development of different paradigms of anti-discrimination law. In the U.S. the dominant paradigm became one of colour-blindness, whereas in Canada and the EU the paradigm was one of difference-consciousness. These paradigms shaped the ways in which discrimination was understood to arise, and how it should be remedied.

Others have made similar arguments before,[2] but we offer a new and different account of how originating context influenced legal development. In our view

[1] See for example Richard N. Block & Karen Roberts, *A Comparison of Labour Standards in the United States and Canada*, 55(2) INDUS. REL. 273, 273–306 (2000); Peter Berg, Richard N. Block & Karen Roberts, *Comparing and Quantifying Labour Standards in the United States and the European Union*, 19(4) INT'L J. OF COMP. LAB. L. & INDUS. REL. 441, 441–67 (2003); Richard N. Block et al., *The Legal and Administrative Context of Work and Family Leaves and Related Policies in the United States, Canada, and the European Union,* in MANAGING THE WORK-HOME INTERFACE: A PSYCHOLOGICAL PERSPECTIVE 39 (Ronald Burke, Fiona Jones & Mina Westman, eds., forthcoming).

[2] See Katarina Linos, *Path Dependence in Discrimination Law: Employment Cases in the United States and the European Union*, 35 YALE J. INT'L L. 115 (2010); Ravi Malhotra, *The Legal Genealogy of the Duty to Accommodate American and Canadian Workers with Disabilities: A Comparative Perspective*, 23 WASH U. J.L. & POL'Y 1 (2007). Linos shows how colour-blindness and sex-consciousness influenced the willingness and methods of courts to infer discrimination from statistical patterns in hiring and promotion, or to find it where employees experienced

international differences in anti-discrimination law most fundamentally reflect the imprint of originating context on legal doctrines of employer responsibility to further workplace equality of opportunity. Within the race-blind paradigm of the U.S., the responsibility of an employer to remove barriers that it had not intentionally or arbitrarily created proved less morally obvious and more technically difficult to implement than it did under the difference-conscious paradigms of Canada and Europe. These challenges to the extension of anti-discrimination law in the U.S. were amplified in a jurisprudential, policy and political context that both associated discrimination with moral blameworthiness and had long resisted attempts to restrict employer prerogatives. As a result redress for intentional and blameworthy discrimination remained the animating concern of the law, and U.S. law came to understand equality of opportunity as requiring no more than treatment without invidious intent or arbitrary imposition of adverse impacts. By contrast, at the time that key anti-discrimination precedents were set in Canada a jurisprudential and policy consensus had developed in support of accommodation of difference, regardless of blame, to provide equality of opportunity within a multicultural society. Canadian anti-discrimination law came to see equality of opportunity as often requiring reasonable accommodation, and to require employers to provide it where their practices adversely impacted employees on the basis of protected characteristics. The development of a sex-difference conscious analysis of discrimination led the European Court of Justice (ECJ) to insist upon objective justification of, and proportionality in, adverse impacts or differences in treatment related to protected differences.[3] This set the stage for a later EU embrace of wider policies of social inclusion based on positive action and accommodation of differences.

Thus we find beneath a surface of doctrinal similarities three fundamentally different understandings of the non-discrimination requirements of equal opportunity. These ideas of equal opportunity have in turn informed very different policy stances towards social inclusion. Courts and legislators in Canada and the EU have proven more willing to assign employer social responsibilities to remove barriers to equal opportunity arising without employer invidious intent or arbitrariness. As a result, U.S. anti-discrimination law is much less likely than its Canadian counterpart to hold employers responsible for adverse impacts of neutral practices serving legitimate business purposes, and EU Directives seeking to foster social inclusion go much further than U.S. employment statutes do.

The plan of this chapter is as follows. In Part 2 we canvass the reach and requirements of anti-discrimination laws. Here we develop our argument about the influence of originating context on doctrines of employer responsibility. This is the main argument of the chapter. In Part 3 we briefly survey laws requiring employers to foster social inclusion, namely those requiring employers to grant leave or flexibility to workers with disabilities or with family responsibilities, provide injured workers with

disparate treatment on the basis of characteristics associated with but different from characteristics expressly protected by law. Malhotra argues that that court interpretations of the First Amendment of the United States Constitution holding that government could not lend aid to any religion limited the development of concepts of accommodation in U.S. anti-discrimination law.

[3] See for example the case of 'age' discrimination. On the topic, AGE AS AN EQUALITY ISSUE (S. Fredman & S. Spencer eds., 2003).

assistance in returning to work, take affirmative steps towards equity in pay, hiring and promotion, or eliminate harassment and bullying from the workplace. This survey brings the different policy stances of the U.S., EU and Canada towards workplace equality of opportunity and social inclusion into sharper relief. We then summarize and conclude.

In order to keep the analysis manageable, our comparison is restricted to national level laws in the U.S., legal models operating in most sub-national jurisdictions in Canada, and to EU law. Within these restrictions we are nonetheless able to discuss laws directly affecting the great majority of workers and employers in each jurisdiction. We note however that there are inherent limits to what can be inferred from comparing Canada and the U.S. with the EU. The competence of EU institutions is delegated by treaty and therefore EU law represents a basic minimum acceptable to EU member states. This means that the contents of EU law do not necessarily measure the willingness of many or even most EU members to legislate to foster social inclusion.[4]

2. THE REACH AND REQUIREMENTS OF ANTI-DISCRIMINATION LAWS

The principal federal anti-discrimination laws in the U.S. are Title VII of the Civil Rights Act, the Age Discrimination in Employment Act, the Americans with Disabilities Act, the Immigration Reform and Control Act, and the Genetic Information Nondiscrimination Act, which came into force in 1964, 1967, 1990 and 2008 respectively.[5] By virtue of the jurisdiction granted to the federal government under commerce clause and the Fourteenth Amendment of the U.S. Constitution these statutes apply to the vast majority of public and private sector employers in the U.S.[6]

In Canada jurisdiction is divided differently. Provincial governments have exclusive competence with respect to 'property and civil rights' – a category that includes employment relations, except in specific industries enumerated in the Constitution as

[4] To see how any state member has implemented a given Directive go to http://eur-lex.europa.eu_law/directives_transposition_en.htm.

[5] The Civil Rights Act of 1964, Pub. L. No. 88-352, title VII 78 Stat. 241 (codifed as amended in scattered sections of 5 U.S.C., 31 U.S.C., and 42 U.S.C.); The Age Discrimination in Employment Act of 1967, 29 U.S.C. §§ 621-634 (2000); Americans with Disabilities Act of 1990, 42 U.S.C. §§ 12101–12213 (2000); The Genetic Information Nondiscrimination Act of 2008, Pub. L. No. 110-233, 122 Stat. 881 (2008).

[6] Note however that the Eleventh Amendment to the U.S. Constitution provides sovereign immunity to the states. As a result, state government employers may be regulated by federal law, but may not be subject to private lawsuits by employees seeking to enforce such laws without the state's consent unless the U.S. Congress clearly intends to make a federal law applicable to state government actors and acts within its lawmaking powers under the Constitution's Fourteenth Amendment. Thus the U.S. Supreme Court has ruled that state employers can be sued by individual employees for gender discrimination, but not for disability discrimination. See *Nevada Dept. of Human Resources v. Hibbs*, 538 U.S. 721, 724, 727 (2003); *Bd. of Trustees of Univ. of Ala. v. Garrett*, 531 U.S. 356, 363–364 (2001).

federal heads of power.[7] As a result, it falls largely to provincial governments to legislate against workplace discrimination. Every province has enacted a comprehensive human rights statute prohibiting discrimination in a range of social and economic relations, including employment.[8] The federal government has enacted similar legislation applying to federally regulated employers.[9]

The EU derives its competence to legislate in any given subject matter from treaties among member states. Those treaties in turn empower member states through the Council of the European Union to adopt Directives and other forms of legislation proposed by the European Commission. Directives generally allow member states to adapt EU disciplines to their own particular legal structures.

At the origin of the European Community the Treaty of Rome established, in 1957, the principle that men and women should be equally paid for equal work.[10] The Treaty also established non-discrimination on the basis of nationality so as to further the free movement of people. Numerous longstanding directives implement these non-discrimination principles.[11] But it was not until 1997 that the Amsterdam Treaty established a new wider EU competence to forbid discrimination on a range of other grounds, namely sex, ethnic origin, race, age, disability, sexual orientation and religion and belief. In 2000 the EU enacted laws requiring equal treatment of persons on those other grounds. Even then equal treatment of persons was linked with the 'free movement of labour forces,' a fundamental tool for building market integration.[12] The

---

[7] *Toronto Elec. Comm'rs v. Snider*, [1925] 1 W.W.R. 785 (Can.), [1925] 2 D.L.R. 5 (Can.); *Emp. of the Canadian Pac. Ry. in Empress Hotel, Victoria (City), Re*, [1950] 1 W.W.R. 220 (Can.), [1950] 1 D.L.R. 721 (Can.).

[8] Alberta: Alberta Human Rights Act, R.S.A. 2000, c A-25.5 (Can.); British Columbia: Human Rights Code, R.S.B.C. 1996, c. 210 (Can.); Manitoba: The Human Rights Code, C.CSM c H175; New Brunswick: Human Rights Act, R.S.N.B. 1973, c. H-11 (Can.); Newfoundland and Labrador: Human Rights Code, R.S.N.L. 1990, c. H-14 (Can.); Nova Scotia: Human Rights Act, R.S.N.S. 1989, c. 214 (Can.); Ontario: Human Rights Code, R.S.O. 1990 c. H.19; Prince Edward Island: Human Rights Act, R.S.P.E.I. 1988, c. H-12 (Can.); Quebec: Charter of Human Rights and Freedoms, R.S.Q. c. C-12 (Can.); Saskatchewan: Saskatchewan Human Rights Code, S.S. 1979, c. S-24.1 (Can.).

[9] Canadian Human Rights Act, R.S.C. 1985, c. H-6.

[10] Article 119.

[11] The Directives in matter of discrimination were: Directive 75/117 (1975 O.J. (L 045)), on equal pay for male and female workers; Directive 76/207 (1976 O.J. (L 039)), on equal treatment with regards to access to employment, vocational training, promotion and working conditions; Directive 79/7 (1978 O.J. (L 6)) on the implementation of equal treatment with regard to statutory social security schemes; Directive 86/378 (1986 O.J. (L 225)) on the implementation of equal treatment in occupational schemes of social security; Directive 86/613 (1986 O.J. (L 359)) on equal treatment for men and women carrying out a self employed activity; Directive 97/80 (1998 O.J. (L 014)) on the burden of proof in case of discrimination based on sex. Many of these Directives are now summarized into the 'consolidation' Directive 2006/54 (2006 O.J. (L 204/23)).

[12] See, EUROPEAN SOCIAL POLICY, BETWEEN FRAGMENTATION AND INTEGRATION, (S. Leibfried, P. Pierson eds, 1995); M. BELL), ANTI-DISCRIMINATION LAW AND THE EUROPEAN UNION, (2002); E. ELLIS, EU ANTI-DISCRIMINATION LAW, (2005).

anti-discrimination principle has nonetheless played an important role in the development of the EU's social policy, and is one of the matters on which the EU has the power to issue Directives binding upon member states.

(a) Animating Concerns of the Law: The Small Differences that Eventually Mattered

The foundation stone of employment discrimination law in the U.S. is Title VII of the Civil Rights Act. Subsequent legislation was patterned after Title VII, adopting its linguistic forms and its enforcement agency in the field of employment – the Equal Employment Opportunities Commission.[13] The Civil Rights Act was a response to post-World War II agitation, unrest and reform initiative arising out of the discrimination against and the oppression of the black minority by the white majority that continued during the century following the end of slavery in the U.S. Notwithstanding that it also protected against discrimination based on sex and religion, the political history of the Act makes it clear that race relations between whites and blacks were its principal animating concern.[14] As we will see, this central focus on race relations has left important imprints on the development of U.S. anti-discrimination law.

Canadian provinces began to enact comprehensive statutes, commonly referred to as 'human rights codes' around the same time as civil rights struggles in the U.S. bore fruit in the Civil Rights Act. Between the early 1960s and the mid 1970s all Canadian jurisdictions enacted such laws.[15] One of the first to do so was Ontario, Canada's most populous province. Ontario's legislation and the debates surrounding it were influential elsewhere in Canada. The movement for legal protection against discrimination in Ontario was led by a loose coalition of religious, labour, and ethnic community organizations.[16] At the centre of this movement were Jewish organizations aiming to change the pervasive anti-Semitic practices of post-World War II Canadian society.[17] Jewish leaders saw the protection of democracy and the elimination of discrimination against religious and racial minorities as inextricably linked. Many saw the pursuit of these aims as essential to ensuring that Canadian society would not again react with indifference to the persecution of Jews at home or abroad. They also saw that the project of eliminating anti-Semitism entailed seeking greater acceptance of all religious, racial and ethnic minority rights. Labour leaders joined the cause in part because they viewed the elimination of racial, religious and ethnic prejudice as making for a more egalitarian society in which the aims of the labour movement would find a better

---

[13] GEORGE RUTHERGLEN, EMPLOYMENT DISCRIMINATION LAW 6–10 (2d ed. 2007).

[14] See generally HUGH DAVIS GRAHAM, THE CIVIL RIGHTS ERA (1990).

[15] WALTER TARNOPOLSKY & WILLIAM PENTNEY, DISCRIMINATION AND THE LAW 2–4, 2–13 (John D. Gardner ed., Robert De Boo Publishing rev. ed. 2010).

[16] R. Brian Howe, *The Evolution of Human Rights Policy in Ontario*, 24 CAN. J. POL. SCI. 783 (1991); Irving Abella, *Jews, Human Rights and the Making of the New Canada*, 11 J. CAN. HIST. ASS'N 3 (2000); Carmela Patrias & Ruth A. Frager, *'This Is Our Country, These Are Our Rights': Minorities and the Origins of Ontario's Human Rights Campaigns*, 82 CAN. HIST. REV. 1 (2001); James St. G. Walker, *The Jewish Phase in the Movement for Racial Equality in Canada*, 34 CAN. ETHNIC STUD. 3 (2002).

[17] Abella, ibid.; Walker, ibid.

reception in local and national politics. Black-white race relations were also an important aspect of the animating concerns of Ontario reformers and legislators. Racial segregation not that different from that found in the southern U.S. was practiced in some places in Ontario.[18] But it is fair to say that such concerns were intermingled with the struggle for religious and ethnic equality and with efforts to construct what would later become known as a 'multicultural' society, rather than being overriding as they were in the U.S. The Canadian post-World War II human rights project, though sharing important common threads with its U.S. counterpart, has a distinct character, one which eventually favoured the development of a very different theory of the purposes of anti-discrimination law, and thus of the concept of discrimination itself.

Initially, the EU had competence only with respect to gender and nationality-based discrimination. The focus on gender discrimination reflected the pursuit of two different goals: avoiding market distortions produced by discrimination against women in some member states, and creating a common platform of social action for the new political project.[19] The European Community (which later became the European Union) was also eager to affirm itself on the international scene as committed to 'social progress'. The sex equality principle has therefore been at the core of the Community since its beginning in 1957, when the EC Treaty, Article 119 (now Art. 157) provided the equal pay principle with an important support.

The first Directives on gender equality were adopted in the mid 1970s.[20] The provisions of Directive 76/207 were interpreted broadly by a dynamic ECJ. By 1976 it was clear that the sex anti-discrimination principle had come to serve more than the original function of avoiding 'social dumping' between member states.[21] That year the rationale for the gender equality principle was clearly described by the ECJ:

> The aim of Article 141[22] is to avoid a situation in which undertakings established in states which have actually implemented the principle of equal pay suffer a competitive disadvantage in intra-Community competition as compared with undertakings established in states which have not yet eliminated discrimination against women workers as regards pay. Second, this provision forms part of the social objectives of the Community which is not merely an economic union, but is at the same time intended, by common action to ensure social progress and seek the constant improvement of living and working condition of their peoples.[23]

---

18 Ross Lambertson, *The Dresden Story: Racism, Human Rights and the Jewish Labour Committeee of Canada* 47 LAB./LE TRAVAIL 41 (2001).

19 C. BARNARD, EC EMPLOYMENT LAW 297 (3d ed. 2006).

20 On the development of EU gender policy and sex equality law see C. HOSKYNS, INTEGRATING GENDER. WOMEN, LAW AND POLITICS IN THE EUROPEAN UNION, (1996); T. Harvey, *Thirty Years of EU Sex Equality Law: Looking Backwards, Looking Forward*, 12 MAASTRICHT J. COMP. & EUR. L., 307 (2005). For a comparative approach see S. Burri & S. Prechal, *Comparative approaches to gender equality and non-discrimination within Europe*, *in* EUROPEAN UNION NON-DISCRIMINATION LAW. COMPARATIVE PERSPECTIVES ON MULTIDIMENSIONAL EQUALITY LAW, 215 (D. Schiek, & V. Chege eds., 2009).

21 BARNARD, *supra* note 19, at 298.

22 Now Art. 157.

23 Case 43/75 *Defrenne (no. 2) v. SABENA* [1976] E.C.R. 455.

Equality between men and women eventually came to be recognized as a fundamental principle of Community law under Article 2 of the EU Treaty [new consolidated version] and the case law of the Court of Justice.[24] This Treaty provision proclaims equality between men and woman as a 'task' and an 'aim' of the Community and imposes a positive obligation to promote it in all its activities.[25] The ECJ has repeatedly said that the economic aim pursued by the principle of equality between men and women is secondary to the social aim of human rights protection.[26] While EU law now also treats the right to be free of discrimination on a wide range of other grounds as a fundamental human right,[27] as noted above, this was much later in coming. The concern with gender equality exerted a formative influence on EU anti-discrimination law.

(b) Common Contours: Shared Organizing Concepts and Doctrines

The similarity between formative political contexts and the continuing cross-border influence of U.S. legal thought has produced striking similarities in the substantive contours of Canadian and U.S. employment discrimination law. The scope of coverage, prohibited grounds of discrimination, remedies available to complainants, defences available to defendants, and the general legal categories and elements of discrimination are quite similar under statutes on each side of the border in North America. The influence of U.S. law was less direct in Europe. Nonetheless each of these aspects of EU anti-discrimination laws is also similar to its U.S. and Canadian counterparts.[28]

(i) Aspects of employment covered

Anti-discrimination laws in Canada and the U.S. generally cover all aspects of employment relationships from pre-hiring to termination.[29] U.S. federal anti-discrimination statutes each cover applicants for employment, employees and former

---

[24] On this evolution see C. Docksey, *Equality between Man and Women as a Fundamental Right under Community Law*, 20 INDUS. L. J. 258 (1991); B. BERCUSSON, EUROPEAN LABOUR LAW 6 (2d ed. 2009).

[25] Council Directive 2006/54, Recital (2), *supra* note 11.

[26] C-234/96 *Deutsche Telekom AG v. Vick and Conze* [2000] E.C.R. I-799. See earlier Case 43/75 *Defrenne (No. 3) v. SABENA* [1978] E.C.R. 1365.

[27] 'The Treaty of Amsterdam explicitly introduced equality between man and women as one of the tasks of the Community (Article 2) and one of it Activities (Article 3). In addition it introduced a new article, Article 13 allowing the Council, to take action on various ground including sex.' BARNARD, *supra* note 19, at 306.

[28] An approach to discrimination law which gives evidence to comparable devlopments in European and non-European Laws, see S. FREDMAN, DISCRIMINATION LAW (2d ed. 2011).

[29] It should be noted that the definition of employment under anti-discrimination law is narrower in the U.S. than than it is in Canada. The U.S. Supreme Court has held that in the absence of an expression of congressional intent to the contrary, federal anti-discrimination statutes are confined to the concept of employment traditionally applied at common law. See *Clackamas Gastroenterology Associates, PC v. Wells* 538 U.S. 440 (2003) at 445 (holding that 'when Congress has used the term "employee" without defining it, we have concluded that Congress intended to describe the conventional master-servant relationship as understood by

employees. Each prohibits, in very similar general and inclusive terms, covered employers, unions and employment agencies from discriminating on specified grounds against any individual in respect of hiring, discharge, compensation and the setting of terms, conditions and privileges of employment.[30] Similarly, in matters of equal treatment between men and women European law covers all aspects of employment relationships and collective agreement terms.[31] It also covers access to employment, including promotion and vocational training, working conditions including pay and occupational social security schemes[32] (Art. 1 Directive

---

common-law agency doctrine'). This concept generally requires a high degree of control by the employer and remuneration for work done rather based on the profitability of the enterprise. Ibid. at 450, adopting the following guidelines of the Equal Employment Opportunity Commission (EEOC):

1. Whether the organization can hire or fire the individual or set the rules and regulations of the individual's work;
2. Whether and, if so, to what extent the organization supervises the individual's work;
3. Whether the individual reports to someone higher in the organization;
4. Whether and, if so, to what extent the individual is able to influence the organization.

By contrast, Canadian human rights tribunals have tended to take a purposive approach to defining the employer-employee relationship, aiming to address discrimination in relationships of economic dependence in which a non-dependent party exerts sufficient control to eliminate it. Courts and tribunals have therefore tended to treat the traditional indicia of the employment relationship at common law as instructive, but not decisive of the issue. (See generally, KEVIN D. MACNEILL, THE DUTY TO ACCOMMODATE IN EMPLOYMENT, 3-4–3-30 (rev. ed. 2003).) Evidence of economic dependency and administrative control has outweighed the conclusion at common law that the individual was an independent contractor (see for example *Sharma v. Yellow Cab Co.* (1983), 4 C.H.R.R. D/1432 (Can. B.C. Bd. Inq.)), and the absence of many of the traditional common law indicia of employment, including remuneration. Thus one human rights tribunal found that a cadet was an employee of the Canadian Armed Forces where the facts revealed an element of control by the Armed Forces over the cadet, some amount of remuneration and a benefit to the Armed Forces by the cadet's attendance at a training program. See *Rosin v. Canada (Canadian Forces)* (1989), 10 C.H.R.R. d/6236 (Can. Trib.). Similarly, another tribunal determined that the relationship between a doctor and a hospital that granted him admitting privileges, while not constituting a traditional common law employment relationship, did fall within the meaning of employment under the applicable human rights legislation, despite the fact the hospital provided no remuneration. The facts that the doctor had been obliged to apply for the admitting privileges, agreed to abide by the hospital's policies and the hospital retained the right to terminate the privileges were sufficient to ground an employment relationship. See *Sinha v. Eastern Shores Memorial Hospital* (1996), 25 C.H.R.R. D/263 (Can. N.S. Bd. Inq.). This approach has been upheld on judicial review. See for example *Canadian Pac. Ltd. v. Canada (Human Rights Comm'n) and Fontaine* (1990) 16 C.H.R.R. D/470 (F.C.A.); *Prior v. Newfoundland (Department of Health)* (1996), 31 C.H.R.R. D/405 (Can. Nfld. C.A.).

[30] Title VII, § 703(a); ADEA, § 623; ADA §12112 (a); GINA, § 202.

[31] Directive 2006/54, Art. 23 (b), *supra* note 11.

[32] Under Art. 2, Directive 2006/54/EC, Social security schemes are 'schemes not governed by Council Directive 79/7/EEC of 19 December 1978 on the progressive implementation of the principle of equal treatment for men and women in matters of social security whose purpose is to provide workers, whether employees or self employed, in an undertaking or group of undertakings, area of economic activity, occupational sector or group of sectors with benefit intended to supplement the benefits provided by statutory social security schemes or to replace

2006/54/EC).[33] Similarly the Framework Directive on factors other than sex relates to the following: a) conditions for access to employment, to self-employment or to occupation, including selection criteria and recruitment conditions, whatever the branch of activity and at all levels of the professional hierarchy, including promotion; b) access to all types and to all levels of vocational guidance, vocational training, advanced vocational training and retraining, including practical work experience; c) employment and working conditions, including dismissal and pay; and d) membership of, and involvement in an organisation of workers or employers, or any organisation whose members carry on a particular profession, including the benefits provided for by such organisation (Art. 3, Directive 2000/78/EC).

(ii) Coverage of employers

U.S. federal anti-discrimination statutes each apply broadly to private sector employers, but exclude very small employers from their ambit.[34] Each applies to federal, state and local governments, though the latter may often be immune from lawsuits to enforce employee rights. Canadian human rights statutes cover at a minimum the acts and omissions of employers and persons acting on behalf of employers, with some prohibiting discrimination by any person in respect of employment.[35] The statutes apply broadly to both public and private sector employers, but unlike U.S. federal statutes, they apply without regard to the size of the employer. EU laws apply to all employers public and private with some limited exceptions. For example, the Framework Directive on gounds other than gender allows member states to not extend the protection to the armed forces sector in relation to discrimination based on age or disability.

(iii) Prohibited grounds

There is a high degree of overlap between the grounds of discrimination prohibited in Canada and in the U.S. U.S. federal statutes identify the following prohibited grounds of discrimination in the context of employment: race, colour, religion, sex, national origin, age, physical or mental disability, and genetic information. With the exception of genetic information, all Canadian jurisdictions prohibit discrimination on each of

---

them, whether membership of such schemes is compulsory or optional'. In any case Art. 5 to 13 Directive 2006/54/EC regulate equal treatment related to occupational social security schemes. *Supra,* note 11. On this issue M. Haverland, *When the Welfare State Meets the Regulatory State: EU Occupational Pension Policy*, 6 J. EUR. PUB. POL'Y, 886, (2007).

[33] The Goods and Service Directive 2004/113 (Art. 3), 2004 O.J. (L373/37), has widened the scope of gender protection outside the employment field to cover 'all the persons who provide goods and services, which are available to the public irrespective of the person concerned as regards both the public and the private sectors. A. Masselot, *The State of Gender Equality Law in the European Union*, 2 EUR. L. J. 152, (2007).

[34] Title VII, the ADA and the GINA apply to employers with 15 or more employees. The ADEA applies to employers with 20 employees. The IRCA applies where there are four or more employees.

[35] TARNOPOLOSKY & PENTNEY, *supra* note 15, at 12-12.18–12-12.19.

those grounds.[36] In addition to the grounds covered under U.S. federal legislation, all Canadian jurisdictions prohibit discrimination in employment on the basis of marital status and sexual orientation.[37] A majority also protect against discrimination on the basis of family status, political belief, one or more of 'record of criminal conviction' and 'pardoned criminal conviction', and source of income.[38]

EU law now prohibits discrimination on the basis of gender, race, ethnicity, sexual orientation, religion, belief, disability and age. This expansion of anti-discrimination law was based on Article 13 of the Amsterdam Treaty. As Barnard notes, 'the European Council, the Council, Commission and Parliament had long been concerned about racism and xenophobia but, prior to the introduction of Article 13 into the EC Treaty at Amsterdam in 1997, doubted the Community's competence to act'.[39] Following the Amsterdam Treaty, it was the Tampere European Council in October 1999 that made the Commission act in the field of race discrimination. This was due to the rise of far right parties in some member states and due to an increasing level of discrimination against the Roma in some member states.[40] Article 13 served as the cornerstone on which Directive 2000/43 against racial discrimination and Directive 2000/78 against discrimination on grounds of religion, belief, disability, age, and sexual orientation, were based. Directive 2000/43/EC not only implemented the principle of equal treatment between persons irrespective of racial or ethnic origin, it extended EU anti-discrimination law beyond the narrow confines of employment law and 'elevat[ed] non-discrimination law towards a policy in its own right'.[41] Directive 2000/78/EC of 27 November 2000 established a general framework for equal treatment in employment. These Directives spring from the same policy sources as equality guarantees, adopted that same year, in the Charter of Fundamental Rights of the European Union.[42] On the

---

[36] While British Columbia does not list national or ethnic origin as a prohibited ground, it does list ancestry and place of origin.

[37] Lack of coverage of sexual orientation in the U.S. is probably a direct result of the higher incidence of religious conservatism or fundamentalism in that country. Compare Gerald N. Rosenberg, *Saul Alinsky and the Campaign to Win the Right to Same-Sex Marriage*, 42 J. MARSHALL L. REV. 643 (2009) with J. Scott Matthews, *The Political Foundations of Support for Same-Sex Marriage in Canada*, 38 CAN. J. POL. SCI. 841 (2005).

[38] TARNOPOLSKY & PENTNEY, *supra* note 15, at 12-3–12-7.

[39] BARNARD, *supra* note 19, at 308.

[40] See Council Directive 2000/43, Recital (7), 'The European Council in Tampere, on 15 and 16 October 1999, invited the Commission to come forward as soon as possible with proposals implementing Article 13 of the EC treaty as regards the fight against racism and xenophobia' (O.J. (L 180) (EC)).

[41] Dagmar Schiek, *From European Union Non-Discrimination Law Towards Multidimensional Equality Law for Europe, in* EUROPEAN UNION NON-DISCRIMINATION LAW. COMPARATIVE PERSPECTIVES ON MULTIDIMENSIONAL EQUALITY LAW, *supra* note 20, at 4.

[42] Article 20 of the Charter proclaims that 'everyone is equal before the law' Art. 21, para. 1, then states that 'any discrimination based on any ground such as sex, race, colour, ethnic or social origin, genetic features, language, religion or belief, political or any other opinion, membership of a national minority, property, birth, disability, age or sexual orientation shall be prohibited', while para. 2 states that 'within the scope of application of the Treaty establishing the European Community and of the Treaty on European Union, and without prejudice to the special provisions of those Treaties, any discrimination on grounds of nationality shall be

other hand, the Race Directive and the Framework Directive do not cover differential treatment based on nationality. They are without prejudice to provisions and conditions relating to the entry into and residence of third-country nationals and stateless persons on the territory of member states, and to any treatment which arises from the legal status of the third-country nationals and stateless persons concerned (Art. 3, para. 2, Directive 2000/43 and Art. 3, para. 2, Directive 2000/78).

(iv) Types of discrimination

There is also broad similarity in typologies of prohibited discriminatory action found in Canada, the U.S. and the EU, although as we will see below, there are important differences in the legal justifications available to employers in each jurisdiction.

In both Canada and the U.S., the relevant statutes prohibit both intentional and unintentional discrimination. In both countries intentional discrimination is understood broadly to include practices treating persons unequally in which a protected characteristic was a motivating factor.[43] Intent can range from overt hostility to subtle and unconscious stereotyping.[44] Prohibited conduct ranges from acts of harassment to the operation of workplace practices and rules established on the basis of implicit stereotypes. In the U.S. such intentional discrimination is referred to globally as 'disparate treatment'. In Canada intentional discrimination includes 'direct discrimination' – measures that on their face impose disadvantage on a prohibited ground, and 'systemic discrimination' – measures resulting from the influence of harmful stereotypes on the formation of employer rules, practices or cultural norms.

Anti-discrimination laws in the U.S. and Canada also forbid facially neutral measures which adversely affect employment opportunities on prohibited grounds, regardless of employer intent, if such measures cannot be legally justified as necessary. In U.S. jurisprudence, these are referred as 'disparate impact' discrimination, and in Canada as 'adverse impact' discrimination. The concept of disparate impact was recognized by the U.S. Supreme Court as a form of discrimination in the seminal 1971 case of *Griggs v. Duke Power Co.*[45] The disparate impact theory of discrimination was based on a recognition that facially neutral rules or practices with neutral or benign motives, such as standardized tests used in the hiring process, could be fair in form but discriminatory in effect if they have a disproportionate adverse impact on the employment

---

prohibited'. The Charter also particularly considers the topic of gender equality, stating that 'equality between men and women must be ensured in all areas, including employment, work and pay. The principle of equality shall not prevent the maintenance or adoption of measures providing specific advantages in favour of the under-represented sex' (Art. 23). It has been noted that Art. 21 of the Charter does not specifically address multiple discrimination 'or the many possible intersections between the many prohibited grounds of discrimination' – R. Nielsen, *Is European Union equality law capable of addressing multiple and intersectional discrimination yet? Precaution against neglecting intersectional cases, in* EUROPEAN UNION NON-DISCRIMINATION LAW. COMPARATIVE PERSPECTIVES ON MULTIDIMENSIONAL EQUALITY LAW, *supra* note 20, at 35.

[43] Civil Rights Act of 1991, Pub. L. No. 102-166, § 107, 105 Stat. 1071.; RUSSELL W. ZINN, THE LAW OF HUMAN RIGHTS IN CANADA: PRACTICE AND PROCEDURE, 1-15–1-17 (2012).

[44] RUTHERGLEN, *supra* note 13, at 32–4; ZINN, *supra* note 43, at 1-15–1-17.

[45] 401 U.S. 424 (1971).

opportunities of workers based on a protected characteristic. The *Griggs* decision was soon cited for this proposition by Canadian human rights tribunals,[46] and eventually by the Supreme Court of Canada as it endorsed the adverse impact theory of discrimination in the leading case of *O'Malley v. Simpsons Sears*.[47]

EU law similarly distinguishes 'direct' discrimination from 'indirect' discrimination. Direct discrimination is where 'a person is treated less favourably on the ground of sex than another is, has been or would be treated in a comparable situation.'[48] The law adopts a 'causation-based approach', so that direct discrimination means that the person would have been treated better but for race or other forbidden reason.[49] Indirect discrimination occurs where 'an apparently neutral provision, criterion or practice would put persons of one sex at a particular disadvantage compared with persons of the other sex, unless that provision, criterion or practice is objectively justified by a legitimate aim, and the means of achieving that aim are appropriate and necessary'.[50]

EU anti-discrimination law's prohibition of indirect discrimination aims to foster substantive equality in employment relations.[51] It is important to underline that the EU notion of indirect indiscrimination forbids not only the *existing* but also the *potential* disadvantage. For that reason, indirect discrimination can be proven not only on the basis of statistical evidence but also by different means of inference.[52] '[I]t is enough that the adverse treatment is grounded upon, or caused by, a prohibited classification'[53] to make the practice unlawful if it cannot be legally justified. The ECJ set out its approach to this issue in 1986 in its seminal *Bilka* decision,[54] which is now reflected in Directive 2006/54.

The EU concept of indirect discrimination is similar to what in the U.S. is referred as 'disparate impact' discrimination, and in Canada as 'adverse impact' discrimination, and it seems that EU law was inspired in this respect by the North American jurisprudence. In the EU, indirect discrimination jurisprudence first emerged in the

46 See for example *Singh v. Sec. & Investigation Services Ltd.* (May 31, 1977), Cumming Member (Ont. Bd. of Inquiry)

47 [1985] 2 S.C.R. 536 (Can.).

48 Directive 2006/54, Art. 2, 1 (a), *supra* note 11.

49 BARNARD, *supra* note 19, at 321.

50 Directive 2006/54, Art. 2, 1 (b), *supra* note 11.

51 In its 1998 decision in Case 136/95 *Thibault* [1998] ECR I-02011, the ECJ observed that substantive and not only formal equality was the aim pursued by Council Directive 76/207, 1976 O.J. (L 039) 40(EEC). The ban on indirect sex discrimination (such as the development of positive actions) is mainly directed to achieve substantive equality. See R. Nielsen, *supra* note 42, at 46.

52 Thus while originally EU law required statistical proof of actual disadvantage (see Case C-167/97 *R v. Sec'y of State for Employment, ex parte Nicole Seymour-Smith and Laura Perez* [1999] E.C.R. I-623; C-226/98 *Jørgensen v. Foreiningen af Speciallæger and Sygesikringens Forhandlingsuvadvalg* [2000] E.C.R. I-2447), 'the shift from actual to potential disparate impact recognizes that in some areas common sense would dictate that there may well be disparate impact but it is difficult to obtain statistical proof (particularly in those countries which prohibit the collection of data on sensitive issues such as race)'. See BARNARD, *supra* note 19, at 325.

53 BARNARD, *supra* note 19 at 321, and see Case 69/80 *Worringham v. Lloyds Bank* [1981] E.C.R. 767; AG Lenz in Case C-127/92 *Enderby* [1993] E.C.R. I-5535, 5558.

54 Case 170/84 *Bilka-Kaufhaus GmbH v. Weber von Hartz* [1986] E.C.R. 1607.

field of freedom of movement. In the seminal case of *Sotgiu v. Deutsche Bundespost*[55] the ECJ said that 'The rules regarding equality of treatment, both in the Treaty and in Article 7 of Regulation No 1612/68, forbid not only overt discrimination by reason of nationality but also all *covert* forms of discrimination which, by the application of other criteria of differentiation, lead in fact to the same result.' In the employment sector early application of the indirect discrimination doctrine took place in U.K.[56] where the law was inspired by *Griggs*.

(v) Permissibility of positive/affirmative action

Title VII of the Civil Rights Act permits employers to voluntarily adopt measures granting preferential treatment to members of a group based on race, colour, religion, sex or national origin where such programs are designed to counteract older patterns of segregation or hierarchy, provided that they do not unnecessarily affect the rights of workers not benefitting from the program.[57] Courts may also order such programs where necessary to prevent future discrimination.[58] Canadian jurisdictions permit similar measures.[59]

EU guarantees of equality in employment also permit government or private employer systems designed to offset disadvantages experienced by members of protected groups. Such measures are referred in EU legal discourse as 'positive discrimination'.[60] The EU approach to substantive gender equality treats acceptance of positive discrimination as an 'asymmetric approach' and as 'an exception [...] legitimate in defined circumstances'.[61] The ECJ has allowed employers, for example, to apply quota systems to ensure the hiring of women into occupations in which they are under-represented. In the leading case of *Marschall* the ECJ recognized both that employers may accord preference to equally meritorious female candidates, and that merit criteria themselves may reflect discriminatory standards.[62] Such preferences

---

[55] Case C-152/73 *Giovanni Maria Sotgiu v. Deutsche Bundespost*, [1974] E.C.R. 153, para. 11.

[56] FREDMAN, *supra* note 28, at 178.

[57] *United Steelworkers v. Weber*, 443 U.S. 193 (1979).

[58] *Local 28, Sheet Metal Workers' International Association v. EEOC*, 478 U.S. 421 (1986).

[59] TARNOLPOLSKY & PENTNEY, *supra* note 15, at 12-82.62–12.82.68; *Can. Nat'l Ry Co. v. Can. (Canadian Human Rights Comm'n)* (1987), 40 D.L.R. (4th) 193 (S.C.C.) (Can.).

[60] As Barnard describes it:

> Positive discrimination … consists of setting recruiting targets or quotas and discriminating in favour of women at the point of selection in order to meet these targets. Although ostensibly contravening the principle of formal equality, such discrimination can be justified in that it compensates for past discrimination, providing an immediate remedy to a long standing problem.

BARNARD, *supra* note 19 at 418.

[61] FREDMAN, *supra* note 28, at 237.

[62] The Court adopted the following approach to resolving the conflict 'between a recognition of the limits of formal equality, on the one hand, and a firm adherence to individual merit, on the other':

> A national rule which, in a case where there are fewer women than men at the level of the relevant post in a sector of the public service, and both female and male candidates for the

remain in the view of the Court a derogation from the right to equal treatment which must be assessed against proportionality requirements.[63]

(c) Fundamental Differences Beneath a Surface of Similarities and Shared Concepts

Beneath these broad structural similarities and common points of origin lie fundamental differences in the concepts of discrimination that operate in Canada, the U.S. and Europe. The root of differences lies in the varying degrees of willingness to assign responsibility to employers to address unequal access to opportunity resulting from causes outside an intention by an employer to treat people differently on the basis of specific protected personal characteristics. These differing approaches to employer responsibility show up in two key places.

The first is in how the law regards disparate treatment of employees on the basis of characteristics closely associated with but not identical to prohibited grounds. In all three jurisdictions, employers can only justify disparate treatment based on protected characteristics by demonstrating that it is a bona fide occupational requirement. Such defences are narrowly defined. Now, to the extent that intent matters to employer responsibility, one would expect anti-discrimination law to be more reluctant to require such strict justification for disparate treatment that does not fall exactly upon the legislatively protected class of people, but rather upon one closely but not perfectly overlapping with it. This is because measures affecting overlapping groups may after all reflect employer motives other than intent to discriminate on a ground specifically prohibited by legislation. Imposing strict justification requirements on employers with respect to such measures therefore risks making them responsible for effects on protected classes of people regardless of an invidious motive based on the characteristics specifically protected in legislation. In U.S. terms, it thus blurs the line between

---

> post are equally qualified (…) requires that priority be given to the promotion of female candidate unless reasons specific to an individual male candidate tilt the balance in his favor is not precluded (…), provided that:
>
> - In each individual case the rule provides male candidates who are as equally qualified as the female candidates with guarantee that the candidatures will be the subject of an objective assessment which will take in account of all criteria specific to the individual candidates and will override the priority accorded to female candidates where one or more of those criteria tilts the balance in favor of the male candidate, and
> - Such criteria are not such as to discriminate

See E.C.J., Case C-409/95, *Marschall Helmut v. Land Nordrhein-Westfalen*, [1997] E.C.R., 6363.

[63] In a recent decision the ECJ makes it clear that:

> In determining the scope of any derogation from and individual right such as the equal treatment of men and women laid down by the Directive, due regard must be had to the principle of proportionality, which requires that derogations must remain within the limits of what is appropriate and necessary in order to achieve the aim in view and that the principle of equal treatment be reconciled as far as possible with the requirement of the aim thus pursued.

C-319/03, *Briheche v. Ministre de L'Interieur, Ministre de l'Education nationale and Ministre de la Justice* [2004] E.C.R. I-8807.

disparate treatment and disparate impact discrimination. As we will see, that is what has happened to a considerable extent in Canada and the EU, but much less in the U.S.

The second place where different theories of employer responsibility make their mark is in the justifications available to employers for rules, policies or actions that unintentionally have disparate impacts. Again, to the extent that employer intent is central to the theory of employer responsibility, one would expect that the burden of justification would be relatively light. Indeed one might expect that disparate impacts would generate liability mainly where the reasons proffered by the employer are thin enough as to appear pretextual and perhaps a cover for invidious motive. On the other hand, to the extent that the law treats the employer as having social responsibilities to advance substantive equal opportunity, one might expect to see a greater burden of justification, or even positive duties to change employer practices to afford such opportunities to all workers.

The position that the law takes with respect to the issue of the extent of employer responsibility thus effectively defines the concept of discrimination that it prohibits. As we will see, in each jurisdiction the law reflects a different concept. In the U.S., the core concept of discrimination remains intent-based, and employers are generally held responsible only for adverse impacts without business justifications. One might describe the notion of equal treatment embedded in this legal model as treatment without invidious intent or arbitrary imposition of adverse impacts. In EU law, intent plays a less central role. Employers face a strict burden of justification where their policies or practices affect protected groups in direct manner, regardless of intent. On the other hand, where disparate impacts are less direct, employers have a lighter burden of justification requiring only that they demonstrate an objectively legitimate aim and proportionate means. One could roughly term this approach equal treatment as objective justification and proportionality. In Canada, little legal significance attaches to intent. Anti-discrimination law imposes a duty upon employers to reasonably accommodate the protected characteristic of an employee who can demonstrate that employer practices impose adverse impact on the basis of that characteristic. This model sees equal opportunity as often requiring reasonable accommodation.

In this part we will demonstrate how these different concepts of equality and discrimination evolved out of different originating contexts in each jurisdiction. We begin by setting out the high standard of justification in each jurisdiction for intentional discrimination. We then explore the different degrees of willingness in each jurisdiction to apply such standards to employer actions other than disparate treatment of specifically protected classes of persons. Finally we consider how each jurisdiction treats the justification of disparate impacts, what this tells us about the concept of discrimination at work in the law, and how that concept responds to its originating context.

(i) Justification of intentional discrimination based on occupational requirement

Under U.S. and Canadian law an employer can justify intentional discrimination by proving that it constitutes a bona fide occupational requirement (BFOR). The employer bears the burden of producing evidence and persuading the trier of fact of this defence. In both countries the BFOR defence is narrow. In the U.S. an employer must prove that all or substantially all the members of the protected class of persons could not perform safely and efficiently the duties of the job involved,[64] and the BFOR defence is not available at all for race discrimination. In Canada, a measure that directly discriminates on a prohibited ground may be justified as a BFOR if it was adopted in an honest and good-faith belief that it was necessary to the fulfillment of a legitimate work-related purpose, and it was in fact reasonably necessary for that purpose. In order to show that a measure was reasonably necessary the employer must demonstrate it would be impossible to accommodate employees sharing the characteristics of the claimant without imposing undue hardship on the employer.[65] In practice, as in the U.S., this most often means showing that there is no way for such persons to safely and efficiently perform the job.[66]

Though not without controversy,[67] as in Canada and the U.S., EU Directives permit derogation from the prohibition on direct discrimination on the basis of genuine occupational requirements. For example, Directive 2006/54 on equal treatment of men and women at Article 14(2) provides justifications for derogations 'where, by reason of the nature of the particular occupational activities concerned or of the context in which they are carried out, such characteristic consitutes a genuine and determining occupational requirement, provided that its objective is legitimate and the requirements are proportionate'. Similarly, as one commentator points out:

> Equal pay legislation has always permitted employers to justify differences of pay for equal work by reference to a material factor which is not itself the difference in sex. In addition, it has always been possible to justify direct race and sex discrimination where sex or race is a genuine occupational qualification. [...]
>
> Direct discrimination in relation to age is also expressly capable of justification.[68]

(ii) The scope of employer actions subject to occupational requirement justification

U.S. courts have tended to interpret the scope of prohibited grounds narrowly, refusing to treat as prohibited disparate treatment on the basis of characteristics that are strongly associated with but not necessarily coterminous with grounds listed in the statute.[69] For

---

64 *Dothard v. Rawlinson*, 433 U.S. 321, 333 (1977).

65 *British Columbia (Public Service Employee Relations Commission) v. BCGSEU* [hereinafter *Meiorin*], [1999] 3 S.C.R. 3 (Can.), ¶ 54.

66 DONALD J.M. BROWN, DAVID M. BEATTY & CHRISTINE DEACON, CANADA LABOUR ARBITRATION 7:6120 (4th ed., 2006).

67 Some commentators had taken a position against the idea of an open list of justifications because this choice would leave room to unpredictable judicial solutions and 'would have the effect of extending the range of defences open to the employer in an open-ended manner contrary to the intention of the drafters of the legislation, and would seriously undermine discrimination law as it now stands'. See E. Ellis, *The Definition of Discrimination in European Community Sex Equality Law,* 19 E. L. Rev. 563, (1994);

BARNARD, *supra* note 19, at 323, SIMON DEAKIN & GILLIAN S. MORRIS, LABOUR LAW, ¶ 6.19 (4th ed., 2005). A different point of view highlights the fact that 'the possibility of justification can make direct discrimination more context-sensitive'. See FREDMAN, *supra* note 28, at 197.

68 FREDMAN, *supra* note 28, at 198.

69 Linos, *supra* note 2, at 150–8.

example, the U.S. Supreme Court refused to treat pregnancy discrimination as sex discrimination until Congress passed legislation to that effect.[70] Similarly, a number of U.S. appeal courts do not consider 'English only' work rules to constitute discrimination on the basis of national origin.[71] This line of case law treats employer intent to discriminate on the basis of the specific characteristic prohibited by legislation as necessary to make out a disparate treatment claim. As a result, employer actions that on their face discriminate on the basis of characteristics closely associated but not coterminous with prohibited grounds often cannot be challenged as intentional discrimination. Rather, they can only be challenged on the basis of disparate impacts. This jurisprudential insistence on intent to discriminate on specified grounds is consistent with notions of employer responsibility that U.S. courts have developed within the race-blind paradigm of anti-discrimination law, discussed below.

By contrast in the EU 'it is clear from the case-law of the Court of Justice that unfavourable treatment of a woman related to pregnancy or maternity constitutes direct discrimination on grounds of sex'.[72] The ECJ played a pivotal role in the development of protections against pregnancy and maternity discrimination law.[73] In *Dekker* the ECJ treated protection against pregnancy discrimination as an aspect of providing women with substantive rather than formal equality in the workplace, ruling that pregnancy classifications constitute disparate treatment on the grounds of sex because 'only women can be refused employment on grounds of pregnancy'.[74] On the facts, the employer had decided not to appoint an applicant woman who was pregnant, even if she was the best applicant for the job. The employer's refusal was due to the fact that the employer's insurance company denied the payment of costs due to maternity leave. The Court characterized the situation of a woman not appointed because of pregnancy as direct discrimination despite the obvious impossibility of a male comparator. The ECJ did not accept such cost considerations as justifications for disparate treatment. The Court's pregnancy and maternity discrimination judgments in turn shaped its approach to defining discrimination on other grounds later added to EU law. As Linos argues, these decisions reflect a moral judgment that employers who disregard the foreseeable consequences of their policies and practices may not be all that different from those who act with the intent of harming a subset of employees.[75] The ECJ has since applied the disparate treatment framework to traits highly correlated with, or causally connected to, a protected status, accepting that discrimination on the basis of immigrant status can be discrimination on the basis of ethnic origin, and that

---

[70] *Gen. Elec. Co. v. Gilbert*, 429 U.S. 125 (1976); overturned by the Pregnancy Discrimination Act 42 U.S.C. § 2000(e)–(k) (2006).

[71] *Garcia v. Gloor*, 618 F.2d 264 (5th Cir. 1980); *Garcia v. Spun Steak Co.*, 998 F.2d 578 (9th Cir. 1993); *Long v. First Union Corp.*, 86 F.3d 1151 (4th Cir. 1996); *Gonzales v. Salvation Army*, 985 F.2d 578 (11th Cir. 1993).

[72] See Case C-13/94, *P. v. S. and Cornwall County Council* (1996) E.C.R. I-2143.

[73] See ELLIS, *supra* note 67, at 24.

[74] Case C-177/88, *Dekker v. Stichting Vormingscentrum voor Jong Volwassenen (VJV-Centrum) Plus*, [1990] E.C.R. I-3941, I-3973.

[75] Linos, *supra* note 2, at 119.

distinctions based on marital status may constitute disparate treatment on the basis of sexual orientation.[76]

Courts and tribunals in Canada have also more readily treated discrimination on the basis of characteristics associated with protected traits as discrimination on the basis of those traits.[77] In the Canadian case, however this is perhaps best understood as an aspect of an even more complete erosion of the normative and legal significance of distinguishing between measures that directly discriminate on the basis of enumerated grounds and those that adversely impact individuals on the basis of such grounds, a matter to which we now turn.

(iii) The extent of employer responsibility for disparate impacts

The theory of disparate impact discrimination originated in the U.S. However, once transplanted on to Canadian soil, it fared much better than it did in its home environment. Once it had been joined to another U.S. innovation – the duty to accommodate – it came to shape the modern meaning of discrimination in Canada today. This happened even as U.S. court jurisprudence pushed disparate impact theory back into an uncertain and at times narrow role without broadly accepted theoretical foundations. EU law was also influenced by U.S. disparate impact jurisprudence in adopting the theory of indirect discrimination. There, however, indirect discrimination was not linked to the duty to accommodate. It consequently imposes lighter burdens of justification upon employers than it does in Canada.

In this section we explore how and why unintentional discrimination met these different fates on either side of the border, and of the Atlantic. We locate the primary source of these divisions in jurisprudential and policy currents shaping legal doctrines governing employer responsibility.

To serve as a theory of discrimination, an adverse impact model must not only identify effects on the complainant that can lead to liability, it must supply principles that distinguish effects for which an employer should be held responsible from those for which it should not. The origins of disadvantages that limit the capacity of individuals to succeed in employment may lie well beyond the employer's practices – in the school system, the incidence of poverty, or lack of access to health care, for example. No judge or adjudicator would enlist employer resources to remedy all such disadvantages absent clear direction from a legislature. Such direction is nowhere to be found in North American or EU anti-discrimination statutes. Drawing the required distinction therefore requires a theory of employer responsibility and obligations to remove barriers to employment opportunity. This in turn requires a theory of the purposes of anti-discrimination law that can account for such obligations.

The North American divide Perhaps surprisingly, these elements appear to be missing from U.S. disparate impact jurisprudence more than 40 years after its inception. Careful analysts have long argued that it lacks a theory of employer responsibility and

---

76 Ibid., at 151–6.

77 ZINN, *supra* note 43, at 10-1.

obligations,[78] and that no available consensus on the purposes of anti-discrimination law in the U.S. provides a clear foundation for one.[79] In the absence of a clear articulation of the nature and limits of the employer obligations upon which it is based, courts have effectively restrained the application of disparate impact doctrine. This has sometimes been out of hostility to it, and sometimes out of caution resulting from a lack of firm doctrinal footholds upon which to review employer decision making.[80]

In *Griggs* the U.S. Supreme Court held that the employer's use of a standardized test which bore no demonstrable relationship to job performance and disproportionately screened out black applicants violated Title VII. The Court ruled that Title VII imposes an obligation on employers to '[remove] unnecessary barriers to employment when the barriers operate invidiously to discriminate on the basis of racial or other impermissible classification.'[81] The Court made it clear that this was the case regardless of the employer's intent, stating that, 'good intent or absence of discriminatory intent does not redeem employment procedures or testing mechanisms that operate as 'built-in headwinds' for minority groups and are unrelated to measuring job capability.'[82]

The touchstone defining the scope of the employer's obligation, said the Court, is 'business necessity.'[83] Responsibility to remove procedures that create 'built-in headwinds' ends where those procedures constitute a business necessity. The actual extent of the obligation in turn depends upon the latitude afforded to employers to define what is necessary to their business. If the employer remains free to justify employment practices on the basis of any legitimate business purpose, regardless of whether changing it would impose any business hardship, the obligation may leave in place many 'headwinds' for persons facing disadvantages related to their race, religion or other protected characteristic. For example, an employee whose religion forbade her to work on a Sabbath would often have no recourse against an employer with some business justification for requiring her to work on that day. On the other hand, if the test of business necessity is applied so as to require employers to eliminate barriers to employment unless doing so would affect the viability of the business, such an employee would in many or most instances be able to require an employer to accommodate her religious beliefs.

Griggs offered relatively little guidance on such questions. The application of the Court's doctrinal pronouncements to the facts shed little light. Since the standardized tests in issue had not been validated as job-related, the Court easily concluded that they could not be shown to be job-related and were therefore prohibited.[84] Nor did the Court's analysis of statutory purposes offer much guidance. In one passage the Court states that Congress intended through Title VII to remove barriers 'that have operated

---

78 Steven Willborn, *The Disparate Impact Model of Discrimination: Theory and Limits*, 34 AM. U. L. REV. 799 (1985).

79 Michael Selmi, *Was the Disparate Impact Theory a Mistake?* 53 UCLA L. Rev. 701(2006).

80 Ibid., at 768–82.

81 401 U.S. 424, 431 (1971).

82 Ibid., at 432.

83 Ibid., at 431.

84 Ibid., at 431.

in the past to favor an identifiable group of white employees over other employees.'[85] This formulation suggests that the purpose of the obligation to remove unnecessary barriers is to eliminate the effects of past discrimination upon equality of opportunity. But which past discrimination? On the facts of the case, Duke Power had overtly discriminated against blacks prior to Title VII, and the hiring tests stood to perpetuate the effects of that discrimination. Some commentators have argued that *Griggs* is best understood as requiring the removal only of barriers created by the employer itself. This is consistent with the Court's observation that '[d]iscriminatory preference for any group, minority or majority, is precisely and only what Congress has proscribed.'[86] Yet in other places the Court also notes that the disadvantage of blacks on the test in question flowed from the poor quality of education that had been provided to them in North Carolina,[87] and suggests that employers have an obligation to afford a substantive equality of opportunity that takes into account the challenges that people may face because of the race, religion or other protected ground:

> Congress has now provided that tests or criteria for employment or promotion may not provide equality of opportunity merely in the sense of the fabled offer of milk to the stork and the fox. On the contrary, Congress has now required that the posture and condition of the job-seeker be taken into account. It has – to resort again to the fable – provided that the vessel in which the milk is proffered be one all seekers can use. The Act proscribes not only overt discrimination but also practices that are fair in form, but discriminatory in operation.[88]

There is little in the judgment to assist in resolving the tension between these dicta. *Griggs* is, in the words of one leading U.S. commentator, a 'short and undertheorized' judgment.[89] Yet these tensions raise fundamental questions about the very definition of discrimination and the purposes served by prohibiting it. Without a more precise statement of the business necessity test and a more elaborated theory of the legal and policy basis for employer responsibility to eliminate barriers, the disparate impact doctrine was born inherently uncertain both in its scope of application and in its justifications.

Subsequent jurisprudence and legislation have not filled these gaps. In 1975 the U.S. Supreme Court extended disparate impact analysis to sex discrimination, in a context in which the neutral practices were not simply perpetuating previous intentional discrimination.[90] Yet soon afterwards, the Court refused to extend disparate impact analysis to constitutional law under the Fourteenth Amendment, and in *dicta* seemed to call into question the premise that disparate impacts could amount to discrimination in the absence of discriminatory intent.[91] In 1989 the Supreme Court decided *Ward's Cove Packing*, resolving differences that had arisen within U.S. federal circuit courts over the meaning of the business necessity test. The Supreme Court rejected the requirement of

---

85 Ibid., at 429–30.
86 Ibid., at 431.
87 Ibid., at 430.
88 Ibid., at 431.
89 Selmi 2006, *supra* note 79, at 721.
90 *Dothard v. Rawlinson*, *supra* note 64.
91 *Washington v. Davis*, 426 U.S. 229 (1976).

some circuits that the employer demonstrate that the practice in question was necessary to the safe and efficient conduct of its business.[92] Instead, the Court held that an employer could satisfy the test simply by showing that the practice serves 'in a significant way, the legitimate goals of the employer'.[93] This formulation did not even require that the practice be related to the requirements of the particular job employees alleging discrimination. Congress responded with the Civil Rights Act of 1991, expressly overruling *Ward's Cove*.[94] The Act provided that 'an unlawful employment practice based on disparate impact is established under this title only if –

(i) a complaining party demonstrates that a respondent uses a particular employment practice that causes a disparate impact on the basis of race, color, religion, sex, or national origin and the respondent fails to demonstrate that the challenged practice is job related for the position in question and consistent with business necessity; or
(ii) the complaining party … [demonstrates that the employer can meet its business necessity through an] alternative employment practice and the respondent refuses to adopt such alternative employment practice'.[95]

This test includes a requirement that the practice be 'job related for the position in question,'[96] but offers no direct guidance on the meaning of business necessity.[97] Nor did the preamble to and legislative history of the Act offer any discussion of purposes that could ground a theory of employer responsibility and obligations to remove barriers to equal opportunity.[98] The 1991 Act further demonstrated the ambivalence of legislators towards disparate impact doctrine by enabling successful complainants to recover compensatory and punitive damages, and attorneys fees only in cases of intentional rather than disparate impact discrimination.[99]

Faced with this definitional void, trial and appellate courts have proceeded cautiously, with most deferring to employer articulations of business needs.[100] This has most often effectively restricted the reach of disparate impact doctrines to employer practices without any proven business justification.

Selmi's extensive review of post-1991 jurisprudence shows that disparate impact doctrine has served mainly to invalidate employer hiring tests not associated with successful job performance. It has most often not helped plaintiffs where older workers sought protection against adverse impacts during layoffs, where women sought to

92 *Wards Cove Packing v. Atonio*, 490 U.S. 642 (1989).
93 Ibid., at 659.
94 Civil Rights Act of 1991, §§ 2 and 3.
95 Ibid., § 105(a), amending § 703 of the Civil Rights Act of 1964.
96 Civil Rights Act of 1964, § 703(k)(1)(A)(ii).
97 Melissa Hart *From Wards Cove to Ricci: Struggling Against the 'Built-in Headwinds' of a Skeptical Court*, 46 WAKE FOREST L. REV. 261, 271 (2011).
98 Neither the purpose and findings sections of the statute (ss 2 and 3) nor the only document in the congressional record sanctioned by the Act as a source of interpretive guidance offer any discussion of this issue. See 137 CONG. REC. S15276 (daily ed. Oct. 25, 1991).
99 Civil Rights Act of 1991, § 102.
100 Selmi, *supra* note 79, at 749–54.

balance the demands of work and family, or where employees sought to challenge subjective hiring practices.[101] He concludes that the jurisprudence reveals a reluctance on the part of the judiciary to prohibit common employer practices without a clearer statutory mandate providing a theory of why such practices should be impermissible.[102]

The fate of adverse impact doctrine in Canada has been markedly different. As noted above, adverse impact theory entered Canadian jurisprudence in the mid 1970s. By the end of that decade a number of human rights tribunals and lower courts had adopted and applied adverse impact analysis.[103] This trend was not unanimously accepted by Canadian courts however, and eventually the issue of whether human rights code prohibitions on discrimination extended to adverse impacts came before the Supreme Court of Canada. In *O'Malley v. Simpsons Sears* the Court upheld the adverse impact doctrine, defined a set of employer responsibilities and obligations flowing from the doctrine, and linked both to the purposes of anti-discrimination legislation.

In *O'Malley* a Seventh Day Adventist challenged an employer requirement that she work on Saturdays, something that her religious faith forbade her to do. The factual record made it clear that the employer requirement was for legitimate business reasons and not as a result of any intent to discriminate on the basis of religious faith. The Court accepted with relatively little discussion the proposition that the human rights code's aim of removing discrimination requires addressing the differential effects of employment rules, even those made only for sound economic or business reasons.[104] In doing so, it relied not only upon Canadian lower court and tribunals, but also upon *Griggs*.[105] The Court then considered the implications of this proposition for employers, and in particular to what extent they may be required to accept employee religious practices. The Court was again aided in these deliberations by American legal innovation – this time in the form of the duty to accommodate religion under Title VII.[106] Following another relatively concise discussion, the Court read the duty into the operation of the human rights code, notwithstanding the absence of any text in the code providing for it. In a key passage, it derived the duty from the special role of employers in relation to employees, and the need to preserve a social structure in which rights are both protected and reconciled with each other:

> The Code accords the right to be free from discrimination in employment. While no right can be regarded as absolute, a natural corollary to the recognition of a right must be the social acceptance of a general duty to respect and to act within reason to protect it. In any society the rights of one will inevitably come into conflict with the rights of others. It is obvious then that all rights must be limited in the interest of preserving a social structure in which each right may receive protection without undue interference with others. This will be especially important where special relationships exist, in the case at bar the relationship of employer and employee. In this case, consistent with the provisions and intent of the Ontario Human Rights

---

101 Ibid.
102 Ibid., at 754.
103 TARNOPOLSKY & PENTNEY, *supra* note 15, at 4-44–4-52.
104 *O'Malley, supra* note 47, ¶¶ 12, 18.
105 Ibid., ¶ 16.
106 Ibid., ¶ 20.

> Code, the employee's right requires reasonable steps towards an accommodation by the employer.[107]

Having accepted the proposition that there is an employer duty to accommodate, the court found it necessary to 'put some realistic limit upon it.'[108] Consistent with the aim of creating a social structure in which 'each right may receive protection without undue interference with others', the Court articulated those limits as follows:

> The duty in a case of adverse effect discrimination on the basis of religion or creed is to take reasonable steps to accommodate the complainant, short of undue hardship: in other words, to take such steps as may be reasonable to accommodate without undue interference in the operation of the employer's business and without undue expense to the employer.[109]

This doctrinal structure coherently ties the extent of employer responsibility to the purposes of the legislation. The court treats equality of opportunity as requiring positive steps to remove barriers by accommodating the protected differences of employees, even where those barriers arose for legitimate business reasons and the employer would have maintained them regardless of any discriminatory motivation. The limits of that responsibility are reached when an employer faces 'undue hardship.'

While based on an interpretation of the Ontario Human Rights Code, the *O'Malley* analysis was soon applied under all Canadian human rights statutes. Though it was built on concepts borrowed from the U.S., the Canadian jurisprudential structure linking the duty to accommodate to freedom from adverse impact discrimination subsequently evolved in accordance with its own logic – that equal opportunity imposes positive duties to remove barriers – and quite independently of U.S. legal developments.

In the years immediately following *O'Malley*, the Supreme Court of Canada clarified that the duty to accommodate always requires employers to take into account the individual circumstances of those to whom general rules apply unless doing so would cause undue hardship;[110] that the undue hardship threshold implies that some hardship must be accepted in the interests of furthering equal opportunity;[111] and that the duty applies to unions as well as to employers.[112] Finally, in its landmark *Meiorin* decision the Court integrated its jurisprudence on employer defences to and remedies for direct and adverse impact discrimination so as to erase the legal consequences of distinguishing between them. The Court reasoned that in practice the distinction was often artificial, and that attaching consequences to it did not serve the purposes of anti-discrimination law.[113] Under the unified approach established in *Meiorin*, once a complainant has established a prima facie case either of adverse effect or direct

---

107 Ibid., ¶ 22.
108 Ibid., ¶ 23.
109 Ibid.
110 *Central Alberta Dairy Pool v. Alberta (Human Rights Commission)*, [1990] 2 S.C.R. 489 (Can.).
111 *Central Okanagan School District No. 23 v. Renaud* [1992] S.C.J. No. 75; 2 S.C.R. 970 (Can.), ¶ 19.
112 Ibid.
113 *Meiorin*, *supra* note 65, ¶¶ 27–29, 39–49.

discrimination the employer must satisfy the following three-part test in order to justify its policy, practice or decision as a bona fide occupational requirement:

(1) that the employer adopted the standard for a purpose rationally connected to the performance of the job;
(2) that the employer adopted the particular standard in an honest and good faith belief that it was necessary to the fulfillment of that legitimate work-related purpose; and
(3) that the standard is reasonably necessary to the accomplishment of that legitimate work-related purpose. To show that the standard is reasonably necessary, it must be demonstrated that it is impossible to accommodate individual employees sharing the characteristics of the claimant without imposing undue hardship upon the employer.[114]

The court thus merged the bona fide occupational requirement defence developed under its direct discrimination jurisprudence with the duty to accommodate developed under its adverse impact jurisprudence. By this time the legal analysis under each line of jurisprudence had for practical purposes become very similar, so that maintaining different verbal formulations and structures simply created needless complexity. But the effect of this integration was not only to simplify Canadian anti-discrimination law. The Court quite consciously saw it as eliminating any suggestion in earlier jurisprudence that the duty to accommodate served simply to offset unintentional adverse impacts, once proven, of otherwise legitimate employer rules or practices. It pointedly rejected the suggestion that the law sanctioned treating certain persons as normal and others as exceptions to be accommodated.[115] In *Meiorin* the Court makes it clear that the lawfulness of employer practices depends upon meeting the duty on an ongoing and proactive basis. In this sense, accommodation is non-discrimination, and the duty is a direct correlate of the right to be free of discrimination in employment.[116]

In the contemporary Canadian social context overt discrimination is no longer common. Anti-discrimination law has come to focus on more subtle barriers to inclusion usually arising out of efforts to carry out legitimate business purposes. Many if not most cases today turn on whether the employer has in fact met the duty to accommodate. Human rights tribunals and arbitrators have developed a detailed jurisprudence that often provides for a searching review of whether employers have

---

114 Ibid., ¶ 54.

115 Ibid., ¶¶ 39–49.

116 In some recent lower court decisions, most notably *Ontario (Director, Disability Support Program) v. Tranchemontagne*, 2010 O.N.C.A. 593 (Can.), the Ontario Court of Appeal suggests that complainants need to establish that measures with disparate impacts are substantively discriminatory before an employer can be asked to meet the duty to accommodate. This is inconsistent with *O'Malley* and with the Supreme Court of Canada's most recent pronouncement in *Moore v. British Columbia (Educ.)*, 2012 SCC 61, at para. 33. For detailed arguments that the approach in *Tranchemontagne* is legally incorrect, see Denise Réaume, *Defending Human Rights Codes from the Charter*, 9 J.L. & EQUAL. 67 (2012), and Benjamin Oliphant, *Prima Facie Discrimination: Is Tranchemontagne Consistent with Supreme Court of Canada Jurisprudence?* 9 J.L. & EQUAL. 33 (2012).

sufficiently canvassed alternative means of accommodation, and been willing to undertake reasonable effort and expense to provide it.[117] The Supreme Court's jurisprudence has provided a legal environment in which the duty to accommodate grew in effect from a bare foreign transplant into the central metaphor and principal means of implementing Canadian anti-discrimination law today.

The obvious and interesting question, therefore, is why the seeds of *Griggs* flowered and spread in Canadian soil while their growth remained stunted in the U.S. This outcome was not a result of necessity or of mistake. While it was once arguable that *Griggs* itself lacked legal foundation – that in 1964 Congress had intended only to prohibit intentional discrimination in the Civil Rights Act of 1964[118] – the U.S. Supreme Court never overruled it, and the 1991 Act made it clear that Congress had accepted the *Griggs* formulation of disparate impact discrimination. Nor was it that Canadian courts and tribunals simply misconstrued *Griggs*. As discussed above, a plausible reading of that decision as requiring significant positive steps to remove barriers to equal opportunity was available. The divergence cannot either be attributed to textual differences between statutes on either side of the border. At the time that *O'Malley* arose, the wording of the relevant provisions of the Ontario Human Rights Code was substantially identical to those of Title VII.[119] The difference in the fates of disparate impact law in each country is the result of contingent but, as we shall demonstrate, non-arbitrary influences on jurisprudential development. To begin to understand it we need to grasp its most salient features and explore their underpinnings in legal thought.

The most striking aspect of the difference is the extent to which U.S. legal thought places a concept that has become increasingly irrelevant in Canada – intent – at the centre of mainstream understanding discrimination, while relegating the concept that is now central to Canadian anti-discrimination law – accommodation – to its margins or beyond, treating it as a form of preference rather than a measure of whether

---

[117] See generally MACNEILL, *supra* note 29.

[118] Michael Evan Gold, *Griggs' Folly: An Essay on the Theory, Problems, and Origin of the Adverse Impact Definition of Employment Discrimination and a Recommendation for Reform*, 7 INDUS. REL. L.J. 429, 489–577 (1985).

[119] At the time that the *O'Malley* case arose, the relevant provisions of the Ontario Human Rights Code read:

> '4.–(1) No person shall …
>
> (g) discriminate against any employee with regard to any term or condition of employment, because of race, creed, colour, age, sex, marital status, nationality, ancestry or place of origin of such person or employee.'

See Ontario Human Rights Code, R.S.O. 1980, c. 340, s.4(1)(g). In the U.S., section 703 of the Civil Rights Act provides that:

> 'It shall be an unlawful employment practice for an employer –
>
> (1) to … discriminate against any individual with respect to his compensation, terms, conditions, or privileges of employment, because of such individual's race, color, religion, sex, or national origin.'

discrimination exists.[120] In the U.S. the duty to accommodate applies only to grounds stipulated by statute, namely religion under Title VII and disability under the ADA.[121] Jurisprudence has not extended it so as to make it an aspect of non-discrimination. In fact, as Christine Jolls observes, in mainstream U.S. legal discourse anti-discrimination and accommodation are generally theorized as distinct bodies of law.[122]

At the root of this categorization lies an argument that treating people differently, in a favourable way, on the basis of their differences necessarily amounts to 'discrimination in their favour' rather than enacting equality of opportunity.[123] This proposition entails two more fundamental but often unarticulated notions that limit the idea of equality of opportunity itself. The first is that anti-discrimination law aims only to prevent employers from imposing disadvantage, on the basis of protected grounds, of which they themselves are the sole or primary authors. The second and converse proposition is that dealing with potential adverse consequences of an individual's differences from the social norm is his or her own responsibility, rather than that of his or her employer or potential employers. Mainstream U.S. theorizations of the purposes of anti-discrimination law are consistent with these ideas. Rutherglen, for example, identifies three purposes which can account for the current state of the law: (1) removing prejudice and stereotyping from employer decision making, a purpose captured in the metaphor of 'colour-blindness'; (2) promoting economic efficiency by doing the same; and (3) remedying the effects of past prejudice and stereotyping.[124] None of these purposes requires or justifies mandating changes to employment practices having adverse effects the causes of which do not lie in employer attitudes and intentions. Against these currents of thought, the duty to accommodate required specific legislative enactment, and appears as a 'new and surprising direction.'[125]

Yet these currents of thought are in tension with some basic features of U.S. disparate impact doctrine and its implementation. To be sure, the fact that the duty to accommodate was specifically enacted in a limited way suggests that it would have been questionable to extend it to other grounds by judicial interpretation. But Congress could have done this when it affirmed the disparate impact doctrine in the Civil Rights Act of 1991. At that point a duty to accommodate, or something like it, could have served to clarify the business necessity doctrine. It would also have addressed the obvious limitations on the ability of disparate treatment doctrine to ensure that, to

---

[120] Even a comment strongly supportive of a robust application of the duty under U.S. law starts from the premise that it is form preference. See for example Mark C. Weber, *Unreasonable Accommodation and Due Hardship*, 62 FLA. L. REV. 1119 (2010).

[121] The duty to accommodate an employee's religious belief was added to Title VII by amendment in 1972, and has been restrictively interpreted by the U.S. courts in light of the Establishment Clause of the U.S. Constitution, which forbids the state from favouring any religion, and thus in the analysis of the courts, from requiring employers to do so. See Malhotra, *supra* note 2. A more robust duty to reasonably accommodate disability up to the point of undue hardship was enacted by the ADA in 1990. See Weber, ibid.

[122] Christine Jolls, *Antidiscrimination and Accommodation*, 115 HARV. L.REV. 642, 643–4 (2001).

[123] Ibid.

[124] RUTHERGLEN, *supra* note 13, Ch. 2.

[125] Ibid., at 219.

paraphrase *Griggs*, the vessel of employment opportunity is one that all groups can use. Finally, it would have made sense of the fact that, as Christine Jolls has demonstrated, disparate impact doctrine has, where it has been robustly applied, in fact required accommodation of employee-protected characteristics.[126] Yet in 1991 supporters of a more robust approach to disparate impact succeeded in obtaining no more than a studied legislative silence, a silence evidencing a lack of consensus within Congress over the reach and purposes of disparate impact law.[127] The question therefore becomes why no consensus could be achieved in support of a more robust notion of equal opportunity, one that could have supported accommodation requirements within disparate impact law.

A comparative law perspective can help to shed light on this question. The political conflicts and settlements that produced anti-discrimination laws were similar on both sides of the border. In both countries adjudicators played a key role in defining legal obligations to eliminate discrimination. In both legal systems precedent leaves a lasting imprint. As a result, the causes of different national trajectories of legal development may lie as much or more in factors inherent in the operation of the legal system as in broad cultural and political tendencies. Small differences in the formative context of early legal decisions may therefore explain a great deal.[128]

In their early and influential disparate impact precedents, Canadian and U.S. case law responded to quite different facts. In the U.S, courts were confronted with barriers based on race. In Canada the cases concerned impacts based first on religion, and then on sex and national origin. These factual contexts affected both how jurisprudence constructed disparate/adverse impact discrimination, and the political discourse of anti-discrimination within which legal institutions and actors were situated. These interpretations became precedents that were later applied to other types of discrimination. Interpreting the law in the light of different facts and somewhat different policy contexts yielded very different jurisprudence, guided by different paradigms of analysis. These paradigms continue to furnish implicit theories of how discrimination generally happens, how it should be corrected, and therefore what responsibilities employers should bear.

Commentators on U.S. anti-discrimination law have long noted that it operates primarily within a paradigm of 'colour-blindness' or 'race-blindness.'[129] As noted above, race discrimination was the overriding animating concern of the Civil Rights Act of 1964, and race was the subject of key early employment discrimination jurisprudence.[130] A number of factors favoured the emergence of a paradigm in which sameness of treatment is effectively presumed non-discriminatory, discrimination is

---

[126] Jolls, *supra* note 122, at 652–67.

[127] Michael Selmi, *The Supreme Court's Surprising and Strategic Response to the Civil Rights Act of 1991*, 46 WAKE FOREST L. REV. 281, 288 (1991).

[128] Linos, *supra* note 2, at 120–32.

[129] See for example Catharine A. MacKinnon, *Reflections on Sex Equality Under Law*, 100 YALE L.J. 1281, 1289 (1991); Reva B. Siegel, *She The People: The Nineteenth Amendment, Sex Equality, Federalism, and the Family*, 115 HARV. L. REV. 948, 949 (2002); Michael Ashley Stein & Michael E. Waterstone, *Disability, Disparate Impact, and Class Actions*, 56 DUKE L.J. 861, 863–6 (2006); Kenji Yoshino, *Covering*, 111 YALE L.J. 769, 779–80 (2002).

[130] Linos, *supra* note 2, at 130–4.

understood to be primarily an intentional phenomenon, disregard for the protected characteristic (race) is the hallmark of non-discrimination, and the pursuit of legitimate business purposes is often treated in effect as immunizing employer actions from a finding of discrimination.

First, much of the thrust the civil rights movement, of early court legal victories such as *Brown v. Board of Education*,[131] and of the Civil Rights Act of 1964 was the elimination of forms of differential treatment such as segregation in services and employment that imposed enormous disadvantages on African Americans. In this context, the ideal of colour-blind treatment had great normative appeal.

Second, it is difficult to imagine legitimate business reasons for disparate impacts based on race. It is easier to attribute such impacts to intentional discrimination hiding behind pretext. Early decisions quickly rejected customer racial preferences as a justification, rightly recognizing that this simply enacted intentional prejudices of the clientele.[132] In *Griggs* and in subsequent employment testing cases, the issue is generally whether the test truly predicts work performance (a legitimate business purpose) or instead unnecessarily adversely impacts on the basis of race. As a result, it can be argued that but for the influence of factors originating outside of the workplace (such as unequal access to education), such employer practices are not themselves likely to create barriers to equal opportunity unless they are based on some form of intent to discriminate, whether overt or founded in stereotype.

Third, where social factors outside the workplace do interact with the pursuit of business purposes, separating discriminatory disparate impact from business necessity can be very complex, and assigning liability on the basis of statistical inferences can create risks of arbitrary results.[133] Consider disparate impact in hiring. Disparities in employment can arise out of a multitude of socially created disadvantages, and thus it may often be possible to show that the pattern of hiring adversely impacts African Americans. The causes of this pattern may or may not lie outside the workplace, and it may be very difficult to clearly identify those causes statistically. At the same time, it may be very difficult to prove that employer hiring practices accurately predict work performance. If the employee need only show a statistical disparity to shift the burden of proof to the employer, a risk will arise that employers will often be unable to justify their practices notwithstanding legitimate business purposes. Fears that the application of disparate impact analysis could lead employers to abandon merit-based testing in favour of race-based quotas had some basis in reason.[134]

Finally, the association of discrimination with racist intent and stereotyping, in context of the U.S. history of deep oppression of African Americans, freights it with blameworthiness. Accordingly, the concept of discrimination requires an intuitively plausible basis for assigning blame. As Selmi remarks, in the U.S. context a 'desire to

---

131 347 U.S. 483 (1953).

132 See for example *Fernandez v. Wynn Oil Co.*, 653 F.2d 1273, 1276–7 (9th Cir. 1981).

133 Gold, *supra* note 118, at 439–66.

134 Such concerns pushed the Supreme Court to adopt the specific practice requirement (of requiring the plaintiff to show that statistical disparities were caused by specific employer practices) in *Ward's Cove*, *supra* note 92. The requirement was retained in the Civil Rights Act of 1991. See Civil Rights Act of 1991, § 105(a)(i).

avoid blameworthiness misunderst[ands] the crucial role blame plays in fostering a willingness to remedy discrimination. Without an element of blameworthiness, there is no basis on which to require remedial action.'[135]

U.S. political discourse does not seem to have produced a widely accepted set of duties or obligations the breach of which would attach blame to employer decisions to pursue legitimate business interests in ways that adversely affect people on the basis of their protected personal characteristics. This lack of a national level consensus leaves room for wide regional differences in how the disparate impact provisions of the Civil Rights Act of 1991 are interpreted and applied in different judicial circuits. As noted above, many judicial circuits quite readily accept business purposes proffered by employers as meeting the business necessity test. Further, some circuits treat many employer rules and practices within the employment relationship, as not being 'practices' at all for the purposes of meeting the 'specific practice' requirement for proof of disparate impact discrimination under the Civil Rights Act of 1991.[136] This somewhat contrived interpretation effectively confines disparate impact liability to the pre-hiring stage of the employment relationship, and insulates any employer decision with a plausible business purpose from review.

This insulation, in addition to reflecting a lack of consensus on the purposes of the disparate impact model, may also be a manifestation of a deep-seated reluctance by many U.S. judges to interfere with employer prerogatives to manage their businesses as they see fit. As Weber demonstrates, even under the ADA – where Congress intended to enact a relatively robust duty to accommodate – courts have shown greater reluctance to impose positive obligations to change current practices on employers than they have on other entities like service providers covered by the Act.[137] As many before us have noted, the extent of unregulated employer prerogative under U.S. common law and statutory regimes is exceptional by industrialized country standards, and likely reflects lasting structures of thought and power within U.S. political life.[138] This reluctance to regulate employer decision-making is evident in our review of regulation for inclusion in Part 3 below.

By contrast with their U.S. counterparts, the early leading Canadian cases dealt with adverse impacts on the basis of religion, sex and national origin. In these cases employer rules clearly and directly caused disadvantage based on protected grounds: employees lost their jobs because attendance requirements conflicted with tenets of religious faith, as did women who failed physical strength and endurance tests. The

---

[135] Selmi, *supra* note 79, at 773.

[136] Linos, *supra* note 2, at 143 and cases cited therein.

[137] Weber, *supra* note 120, at 1166–1170.

[138] See for example: Clyde Summers, *Employment at Will in the United States: The Divine Right of Employers*. 3 U. PA. J. LAB. & EMP. L. 65 (2000); Saul Levmore, *Parental Leave and American Exceptionalism*, 58 CASE W. RES. L. REV. 203 (2007); Sanford M. Jacoby, *American Exceptionalism Revisited: The Importance of Management, in* MASTERS TO MANAGERS: HISTORICAL AND COMPARATIVE PERSPECTIVES ON AMERICAN EMPLOYERS 173, 174 (Sanford M. Jacoby ed., 1991); William F. Forbath, *The Shaping of the American Labor Movement*, 102 HARV. L. REV. 1109 (1988); John Godard, *The Exceptional Decline of the American Labor Movement*, 63 INDUS. & LAB. REL. REV. 82 (2009); Joel Rogers, *Divide and Conquer: Further Reflections on the Distinctive Character of American Labor Law,* 1990 WIS. L. REV. 1.

relationship between rules, practices and adverse consequences was either evident on its face, or was easily demonstrated through a rudimentary statistical analysis. Moreover, it was fairly obvious that identical treatment would not produce equal opportunity, given widely understood physiological differences between women and men, or the obvious constraints on the behaviour of people imposed by faithful observance of religious tenets. These cases forced into the open a consideration of the extent of employer obligations to treat differently people who are different in socially significant ways.

This issue arose in a legal and political context favourable to notions of accommodation. During the 1970's Canada reimagined itself as a multicultural society.[139] Governments responded towards the end of that decade and into the next with initiatives to explicitly expand the scope of anti-discrimination protections. In Ontario, the Human Rights Commission released an influential report entitled Life Together, which argued for anti-discrimination laws providing a positive right to equal opportunity in order to promote acceptance of religious, ethnic, racial, gender and other forms of diversity.[140] By the time that *O'Malley* had reached the Supreme Court of Canada, the Ontario legislature had amended the Ontario Human Rights Code so as to provide a positive right to 'equal treatment without discrimination', and to stipulate that a discrimination could arise simply from requirements that 'result in exclusion, restriction or preference.'[141] Shortly after *O'Malley*, in the *Action Travail des Femmes* case the Supreme Court of Canada more explicitly endorsed a broad notion of equal opportunity in employment, quoting from an influential 1984 Royal Commission report by Judge Rosalie Abella to the government of Ontario. Judge Abella was mandated to report on the 'the most efficient, effective and equitable means of promoting employment opportunities, eliminating systemic discrimination and assisting individuals to compete for employment opportunities on an equal basis.' The Supreme Court quoted with approval her statement that:

> Discrimination [...] means practices or attitudes that have, whether by design or impact, the effect of limiting an individual's or a group's right to the opportunities generally available because of attributed rather than actual characteristics.[142]

Legislatures and courts recognized these human rights code commitments, formally at least, as foundational to the legal and political order. Judges and legislators described human rights legislation has having 'quasi-constitutional' status.[143] By 1982 similar

---

139 See Joseph Garcea, *Provincial Multiculturalism Policies in Canada, 1974–2004: A Content Analysis*, 38 CAN. ETHNIC STUD. 1 (2006); Patricia Wood and Liette Gilbert, *Multiculturalism in Canada: Accidental Discourse, Alternative Vision, Urban Practice*, 29 INTER'L J. URB. & REG'L RES. 679 (2005).

140 ONTARIO HUMAN RIGHTS COMM'N, LIFE TOGETHER: A REPORT ON HUMAN RIGHTS IN ONTARIO (1977).

141 An Act to Revise and Extend Protection of Human Rights in Ontario, S.O. 1981, C-53, s.1, and s.10 (Can.).

142 *Canadian Nat'l Ry. v. Canada (Human Rights Comm'n)*, [1987] 1 S.C.R. 1114, at 1138 (Can.).

143 *Winnipeg Sch. Div. No.1 v. Craton,* [1985] 2 S.C.R. 150 (Can.).

commitments to equal protection and benefit of the law had been enacted in Canada's new constitutional Charter of Rights and Freedoms. By 1989 the Supreme Court of Canada had interpreted those equality commitments to include protection against adverse impacts of state action.[144]

The legal and political context was therefore hospitable to a duty to accommodate. Courts and legislatures had accepted that equal opportunity would require changes to established practices of employers and government institutions. The duty would serve to define and limit the extent of employer responsibilities. The policy direction embedded in human rights legislation permitted the assignment of responsibilities to employers without first assigning blame. The Supreme Court began its judgment in *O'Malley*, in fact, by setting aside questions of blame as irrelevant.[145] It then went on, in a single paragraph (quoted above) to simply state that employers have a social responsibility to accommodate the protected individual characteristics of workers. This opinion is especially notable in that it was unanimous and was authored by a relatively conservative judge.

O'Malley has spawned an extensive jurisprudence interpreting and applying the duty to accommodate all protected grounds in myriad contexts. The duty now reaches well into the employment relationship. Adjudicators and arbitrators have ordered employers to adapt hiring, promotion scheduling, disciplinary, and pay and benefit rules and practices, among others. The case law often requires adjudicators, and by extension employers, employees and unions, to grapple with where the ambiguous threshold of undue hardship lies.[146] While this presents difficulties for many, the days of arguing about whether it must be done have long passed.

In short, the term 'discrimination' has come to mean very different things in Canada and the U.S. These meanings reflect the different animating concerns, doctrinal challenges, and larger statutory purposes that informed their jurisprudential origins. They have propelled anti-discrimination law onto very different trajectories. In the U.S., anti-discrimination law serves a largely negative policing function, rooting out unlawful employer aims or stereotyping. Even where it addresses unintentional adverse impacts, in most cases it leaves employer prerogatives to define and pursue legitimate business purposes undisturbed. In Canada anti-discrimination law has come to impose positive obligations to accommodate grounded in legally recognized employer social responsibilities to afford opportunity structures that accept the protected characteristics of individuals. As a result, the logic of Canadian anti-discrimination law reaches much further into employer decision-making, considering whether adverse impacts resulting from the pursuit of legitimate business purposes can be avoided without undue hardship to the employer. As we will see in Part 3, this development of anti-discrimination law in turn lends a human rights policy justification to measures found in other parts of workplace law designed to foster greater social inclusion.

Differences across the Atlantic Like its Canadian and U.S. counterparts, EU anti-discrimination law requires employers to furnish objective justifications based upon

144 *Andrews v. Law Soc'y of British Columbia*, [1989] 1 S.C.R. 143 (Can.).
145 *O'Malley*, *supra* note 47, ¶¶ 12–15.
146 See generally MACNEILL, *supra* note 29.

legitimate business needs for measures that adversely impact employees on the basis of protected characteristics. For example, under Directive 2006/54 an employer can justify a neutral rule or practice that disadvantages employees on the basis of sex if it can show that the 'provision, criterion or practice is objectively justified by a legitimate aim, and the means of achieving that aim are appropriate and necessary.' Similar language can be found in the other relevant Directives.[147] The Directives adopt the test articulated by the ECJ in the seminal *Bilka* case,[148] and seek to control the reasonableness of the employer's chosen means in relation to its legitimate aims.

The ECJ has applied the requirement of objective justification by a legitimate aim in a manner more akin to the business necessity test found in U.S. jurisprudence than the duty to accommodate found in Canadian law. There is nothing in ECJ jurisprudence suggesting that an employer must seek to accommodate employee characteristics in formulating its business practices. To the contrary, ECJ decisions indicate that if an employer can articulate a legitimate business aim for a particular employment practice, the only question remaining is whether the means chosen are appropriate and necessary. Thus in *Handels* the Court ruled that an employer could justify compensation criteria giving significant weight to adaptability to variable hours and to varying places of work, despite the disparate impact of such requirements on women given their tendency to shoulder greater family responsibilities, if it could show that such requirements were 'of importance for specific tasks entrusted to the employee.'[149] The Court imposed no requirement that employers demonstrate that entrusting such tasks to the employee was necessary to the business, or that business practices could not in fact be made more accommodating to women.

Further, in later cases the ECJ appears to have granted a wider margin of discretion when the respondent is the state. Instead of requiring states to demonstrate that the means are necessary to achieve legitimate ends, the Court held that it is sufficient for a state to demonstrate that it could reasonably consider that the means were 'suitable for attaining a legitimate aim.'[150] This nevertheless does not mean exemption from ECJ scrutiny. The ECJ has held that generalizations[151] about the capacity of a policy or other chosen means to give favourable economic results are not enough to justify a

---

[147] Directive 2000/43, Art. 2, para. 2, b), 2000 O.J. (L 180) 22 (EC), on racial or ethnic discrimination; Framework Directive 2000/78, Art. 2, par. 1, b), 2000 O.J. (L 303) (EC).

[148] Case C-170/84, *Bilka-Kaufhaus GmbH v. Weber von Hartz*, [1986] E.C.R. 1607.

[149] Case C-109/88, *Handels-og Kontorfunktionaerernes Forbund I Danmark v. Dansk Arbejdsgiverforening, ex parte Danfoss*, [1989] E.C.R. 3199, at para. 21.

[150] FREDMAN, *supra* note 28, at 192, 193, referring to Case 371/93 *Nolte* [1995] E.C.R. I 4625.

[151] In matter of age direct discrimination which admit justifications, see a similar E.C.J.'s holding where the Court said that:

> Mere generalisations concerning the capacity of a specific measure to contribute to employment policy, labour market of vocational training objectives are not enough to show that the aim of that measure is capable of justifying derogation for that principle and do not constitute evidence on the basis of which it could reasonably be considered that the means chosen are suitable for achieving that aim [in *R (on the application of Age UK) v. Sec'y of State for Bus. Innovation and Skills* (*Heyday case*) [2009] E.W.H.C. 2336 (Admin).]

disparate impact.[152] But it clearly leaves room for employer practices falling short of accommodation.

Despite the fact that it defined the scope of employer responsibility for disparate impacts around the same time as the Supreme Court of Canada, and that it was influenced by U.S. legal developments in its equality jurisprudence, the ECJ did not look to the duty to accommodate to define its limits. In fact, EU law, like its U.S. counterpart, appears to treat the duty to accommodate as a conceptually separate matter from non-discrimination. Like U.S. law, EU law imposes on employers the responsibility to accommodate employees with disabilities.[153] But, as in the U.S., this duty is understood to go beyond the requirements of non-discrimination by affording a form of preferential treatment. It is considered to be a form of lawful discrimination designed to counter personal disadvantage, reflecting an 'asymmetric approach' that imposes on the employer requirements of differential treatment in favour of some employees.[154]

The EU approach likely reflects the constraints of the EU political order and consequent divisions of responsibility between the judiciary and legislatures with respect to ensuring substantive equality of opportunity. The foundational anti-discrimination decisions of the ECJ arose out of gender discrimination cases in the 1980s. At that time the ECJ was playing a leading role in advancing European integration.[155] Eliminating discrimination on the basis of gender served to create an undistorted single market while providing a foundation of human rights principle to European social integration. Yet the Court's mandate was limited in important respects. The foundations for EU action on other grounds of discrimination were laid much later. Debate continued over the extent to which delegation of social policy to EU institutions was appropriate or desirable. In such a context the duty to accommodate and its limiting threshold of undue hardship may have been a less attractive means of defining the extent of employer responsibility than it was in Canada, where the language of accommodation was tied to an ascendant policy of multiculturalism, and Canada's constitutional substantive equality rights protections had just been enacted. The ECJ was able to advance substantive equality for women by categorizing disparate treatment

---

[152] See E.C.J. Case C-167/97, *R (Seymour-Smith) v. Secretary of State for Employment*, [1999] ECR I-623; [1999] 2 A.C. 554 at para. 76 where the Court says that, 'Mere generalisations concerning the capacity of a specific measure to encourage recruitment are not enough to show that the aim of the disputed rule is unrelated to any discrimination based on sex nor to provide evidence on the basis of which it could reasonably be considered that the means chosen were suitable for achieving that aim.' As one commentator has written:

> it is hoped that courts will continue to be vigilant in resisting the temptation to accept generalizations by respondents under the guise of deference and in lieu of close scrutiny of actual evidence. It is also particularly important to mantain the emphasis on possible alternatives which are less discriminatory. Otherwise, the possibility of justification allows the status quo to be maintained without giving proper attention to whether the discriminatory practice can be adjusted better to accommodate the excluded group.

FREDMAN, *supra* note 28, at 196.

[153] FREDMAN, *supra* note 28, at 196, remembers that 'Rather than demarcating a discrete and insular minority, disability should be regarded as fluid and continuous.'

[154] Ibid., at 216.

[155] JOSEPH WEILER, THE CONSTITUTION OF EUROPE (1999).

on the basis of pregnancy as direct discrimination. Its more cautious stance to disparate impacts left more room for employer justification, perhaps reflecting the view, as Linos has argued,[156] that women's differences vis-à-vis men should be recognized not only in defining what is disparate treatment, but also in allowing employers to treat women differently for legitimate business reasons.

That more cautious approach would leave the matter of accommodation of women, and later of other protected groups, to EU policy machinery. As we will see below, that machinery has since acted so as to promote positive measures that have the effect of accommodating difference.

3. LEGAL REQUIREMENTS OF POSITIVE INCLUSION

Creating an inclusive work environment[157] – one that reduces rather than perpetuates divisions along social fault lines – can require positive steps by employers. Policy makers across jurisdictions have, to quite varying degrees, imposed legal obligations to take such steps. As discussed above, the duty to accommodate in Canadian anti-discrimination laws requires positive steps to ensure substantive equality of opportunity. As we describe below, in other instances statutes and Directives directly stipulate accommodative measures, require employers to proactively adapt their policies and practices in the interests of equality of opportunity, or require employers to enforce basic standards of civility in the workplace.

In this part we outline the broad contours of key laws in each jurisdiction imposing such obligations. We first canvass the accommodation of three sets of worker characteristics or activities particularly likely to come into conflict on a widespread basis with employer work rules and production methods: family care-giving, disability, and temporary illness. These last two categories overlap under each legal system, but not perfectly. Temporary illness merits distinct attention because, where they are in place, rigid employer attendance requirements stand to negatively affect the employment prospects of low income workers, deepening their disadvantage in the labour market.[158] Next we examine laws requiring employers to proactively implement equal pay and equal opportunity in hiring, as opposed to reactively responding to successful employee complaints of rights violations. Finally, we survey legal requirements to eliminate bullying and harassment at work.

---

156 Linos, *supra* note 2, at 159–66.

157 On the concept of social inclusion see H. Collins, *Discrimination, Equality and Social Inclusion*, 1 MOD. L. REV. 16 (2003).

158 On the interaction between rigid attendance and family responsibilities of low income workers, see Stephanie Bornstein, *Work, Family, and Discrimination at the Bottom of the Ladder*, 19 GEO. J. ON POVERTY L. & POL'Y 1 (2012). Refusal to grant leave for illness would predictably have the same effects on workers.

(a) Accommodating Pregnancy and Family Responsibilities

Here we consider the extent to which the law protects employees from adverse employment consequences resulting from pregnancy or from caring for family members. We include in such care-giving responsibilities both parenting and the care of other close family members.

In the U.S. family status is not a protected ground under federal anti-discrimination legislation. Some indirect protection against care-giver discrimination is nonetheless available to employees. Prohibitions against sex, race, ethnic origin and disability discrimination extend to disparate treatment based on stereotyped views of women's or men's roles with respect to care-giving, stereotyping about care-giving roles in different racial or ethnic communities, and stereotyping about the care-giving responsibilities of persons who care for persons with disabilities.[159] These protections do not however address the disparate impacts per se that employer policies may have on care-givers. While pregnancy discrimination is expressly prohibited, for reasons discussed above a failure to accommodate pregnant women, by allowing them greater time off or scheduling flexibility for example, is not likely to be considered discriminatory unless it is either without business purpose or reveals an invidious intent to disadvantage them. Thus, for example, a refusal to grant leave for pregnancy-related medical reasons will generally not violate Title VII if leave for other medical conditions is similarly denied.[160]

On the other hand, there are statutes in the U.S. that stipulate employer obligations and employee entitlements that can serve to accommodate care-giving, or medical needs related to pregnancy. The federal Family and Medical Leave Act entitles eligible employees of covered employers to take up to 12 weeks of unpaid leave in a 12-month period for (1) the birth of a child and to care for the newborn child within one year of birth; (2) the placement with the employee of a child for adoption or foster care and to care for the newly placed child within one year of placement; (3) to care for the employee's spouse, child, or parent who has a serious health condition; (4) a serious health condition that makes the employee unable to perform the essential functions of his or her job.[161] In addition, under section 7 of the Fair Labor Standards Act, employers must provide reasonable break time for an employee to express breast milk

---

[159] EEOC, Equal Emp't Opportunity Comm'n, Enforcement Guidance: Unlawful Disparate Treatment of Workers With Caregiving Responsibilities (2007), *available at* http://www.eeoc.gov/policy/docs/caregiving.html.

[160] *Cal. Fed. Savings and Loan Ass'n v. Guerra*, 479 U.S. 272 (1987); *Piraino v. Int'l Orientation Res.*, 137 F.3d 987 (7th. Cir. 1998); *Armindo v. Padlocker, Inc.*, 209 F.3d 1319 (11th Cir. 2000).

[161] 29 U.S.C. § 2611-2619. An employee may also take such leave in response to exigencies arising because a son, daughter, or parent is a covered military member on 'covered active duty'; and may take 26 workweeks of leave during a single 12-month period to care for a covered service member with a serious injury or illness if the eligible employee is the servicemember's spouse, son, daughter, parent, or next of kin. This is known as military care-giver leave. To be eligible, employees must among other things have worked for the employer for 12 months. Only employers with 50 employees or more are covered by the Act. See 29 U.S.C. § 2611.

for her nursing child for one year after the child's birth each time such employee has need to express the milk.[162]

Outside such statutory protections however, and in the absence of employment contract terms to the contrary, employees are subject to dismissal without compensation should the employer prove unwilling to accommodate employee caregiving responsibilities. This is because the employment-at-will doctrine in U.S. common law, which informs the interpretation of employment contracts in the absence of express contrary terms, allows employers to dismiss employees without notice and without compensation for good reason, bad reason, or no reason at all.[163] The combination of limited statutory protections and the at-will doctrine can make employment precarious for the significant number of low-wage workers who face rigid scheduling rules.[164]

In Canada, family status is a protected ground under the human rights codes of all jurisdictions except those of two provinces.[165] Family status protection has been interpreted by tribunals as covering essential care-giving responsibilities towards one's children or aging parents.[166] Pregnancy and childbirth discrimination are either explicitly prohibited or recognized as sex discrimination in all jurisdictions.[167] One influential tribunal has treated discrimination against breast feeding as sex discrimination.[168] Accordingly, employers have a duty to accommodate pregnancy and family care-giving responsibilities of employees. Meeting this duty can entail providing leaves of absence, modified schedules or modified duties up to the point of undue hardship on the employer.

In addition, legislation stipulates employee rights to leave for such purposes. Employment standards legislation in all Canadian jurisdictions entitles employees to at least 15 weeks of unpaid leave for pregnancy, 35 weeks of such leave during the first year of the life of a child by birth or following an adoption, and eight weeks of such leave to care for a family member who has a serious medical condition with a significant risk of death within 26 weeks.[169] This latter form of leave is commonly referred to as compassionate care leave. Canada's unemployment insurance system provides a basic level of income support during such periods of leave, a level to which employers may add voluntarily or by contract. In addition, employment standards statutes in most Canadian jurisdictions provide employees with entitlements to leave ranging between three and 12 days for family responsibilities including attending to the

---

162 Employers are also required to provide a place, other than a bathroom, that is shielded from view and free from intrusion from co-workers and the public, which may be used by an employee to express breast milk.

163 29 U.S.C. 207.

164 Bornstein, *supra* note 158.

165 TARNOLSKY & PENTNEY, *supra* note 15, at 12-3–12-6.

166 *Devaney v. ZRV Holdings Ltd.*, 2012 H.R.T.O. 1590 (Can.); *Hoyt v. Can. Nat'l Ry.*, [2006] C.H.R.D. No. 33, C.H.R.T.(Can.); *Canadian National Railway v. Seeley*, 2014 FCA 111 (Can.) and *Att'y General (Canada) v. Johnstone*, 2014 FCA 110, (Can.).

167 TARNOLSKY & PENTNEY, *supra* note 15, at 12-3–12-6; *Brooks v. Can. Safeway Ltd.*, [1989] 1 S.C.R. 1219.

168 *Cole v. Bell Canada*, 60 C.H.R.R. D/216 (2007) (C.H.R.T.) (Can.).

169 Richard N. Block, *Work-Family Legislation in the United States, Canada, and Western Europe: A Quantitative Comparison,* 34, Table 4, 343 PEPP. L. REV. (2007).

needs of family members purposes range between days.[170] Outside the first year of child rearing, the Canadian legislative fabric clearly leaves a gap between compassionate care leave and the relatively short periods of leave available for other family medical or other caring responsibilities. As a result employees may increasingly have recourse to the duty to accommodate in cases of conflict between work and family responsibilities.

The contemporary EU approach to discrimination is simply a part of a wider set of policies, sometimes adopted by the EU itself and sometimes adopted by member states, for the purpose of changing social behaviours and general trends that may affect social inclusion of women or of other members of protected groups.[171] EU policy makers have accepted that 'with women historically taking primary responsibility for childcare in most western societies, their flexibility to participate fully in work has often been limited. Since the first equality action program the Commission has [therefore] recognized that full equality of opportunity can be achieved only by taking measures which 'will enable men and women to reconcile their occupational and family obligations.'[172] The Charter of Fundamental Rights of the European Union, Article 33 (2) on 'Family and professional life' protects the right of everyone to reconcile family and professional life, and grants the right to paid maternity leaves and to parental leaves following the birth or adoption of a child. The Charter has been legally binding since 2009.

The EU has enacted several directives dealing with the reconciliation of work and family life. The first is Directive 96/34 on parental leave that puts into effect an agreement concluded between EU level business and labour representative organizations. This Directive, 'grants [...] men and women workers an individual right to parental leave on the ground of the birth or adoption of a child to enable them to take

---

[170] By way of exception, Saskatchewan and Quebec provide up to 12 weeks of leave without pay for family and medical purposes, while Alberta, Nunavut, the Yukon and Northwest Territories and the federal jurisdiction provide none at all. See ibid.

[171] See *Communication From the Commission to the European Parliament, The Council, The European Economic and Social Committee and the Committee of the Regions of 21 September 2010 – Strategy for Equality Between Women and Men 2010–2015*, COM (2010) 491 final (Sept. 21, 2010).

See also S. Fredman and the European Network of Legal Experts in the Field of Gender Equality, *Making equality effective: the role of proactive measures, publication commissioned by the European Commission under the framework programme PROGRESS,* Council Decision 1672, 2006 O.J. (L 315/1) (EC).

[172] BARNARD, *supra* note 19, at 445. See also European Commission, *Communication from the Commission to the European Parliament, the Council, the European Economic and Social Committee and the Committee of the Regions, Strategy for equality between women and men 2010–2015,* COM (2010) 491 final, SEC (2010) 1079, SEC (2010) 1080:

> The impact of parenthood on labour market participation is still very different for women and men in the EU today because women continue to shoulder a disproportionate part of the responsibilities involved in running a family. Many women feel that they still have to choose between a career and their children. Current demographic trends also mean that women and men increasingly have to care for dependents other than children over indefinite periods of time. Member States which have put reconciliation policies in place are seeing high numbers of both women and men in work and relatively sustainable birth rates.

care of that child for at least three months, until a given age up to eight years.'[173] Directive 2006/54 makes the link between substantive equality of women and protection in case of pregnancy and maternity in its preamble. It goes on to provide that a woman shall be entitled, after the end of her maternity leave, to return to her job or to an equivalent post on terms and conditions which are no less favorable to her and to benefit from any improvement in working conditions to which she would have been entitled during her absence. The Directive on Part Time Work,[174] the Directive on fixed term work,[175] and the Directive on working time[176] serve similar ends, even if the last Directive's aim is mainly health and safety. The Directives on part time work and on fixed term work seek to protect atypical employees, who are mainly women and statistically more frequently victims of discriminatory behaviours.[177]

(b) Integrating Disabled Workers and Accommodating Temporary Illness

The Americans with Disabilities Act imposes a duty to accommodate on employers. Since the Americans with Disabilities Act Amendment Act of 2009, disability has been defined broadly, as a physical or mental impairment that substantially limits one or more major life activities, a record of such impairment, or being regarded as having such an impairment.[178] The duty to accommodate requires that employers provide reasonable accommodations to disabled employees, subject to the stipulation that an employer need not provide an accommodation that would impose upon it undue hardship.[179] Such accommodations may include job restructuring, leave, a modified or part-time schedule, modified workplace policies, or job re-assignment.[180] The wording of the ADAAA suggests that temporary but substantially limiting impairments resulting from illness would be covered.[181] It is therefore arguable that the ADA provides rights to sick leave without pay where a temporary illness substantially impairs major life activities. In any event, the Family and Medical Leave Act, as noted above, gives

---

173 Council Directive 96/34, 1996 O.J. (L 145) (EC).

174 Council Directive 97/81, 1997 O.J. (L 14/9) (EC).

175 Council Directive 99/79, 1999 O.J. (L 175) (EC).

176 Council Directive 2003/88, 2003 O.J. (L 299) (EC).

177 Under a different point of view it should be noted that the E.C.J. had pointed out that the purpose of Directive 76/207 was not to 'settle question concerning the organization of the family or to alter the division of responsibility between parents.' See Case C-184/83 *Hofman v. Barmer Ersatzkasse*, [1984] E.C.R. 3047.

178 Americans With Disabilities Act, 42 U.S.C. Tit. 42, Ch. 126, § 12102. The Act specifies that 'major life activities include, but are not limited to, caring for oneself, performing manual tasks, seeing, hearing, eating, sleeping, walking, standing, lifting, bending, speaking, breathing, learning, reading, concentrating, thinking, communicating, and working.' Ibid. The duty to accommodate applies only to persons with an actual impairment or record of impairment, and not to persons who are simply regarded as having an impairment by the employer.

179 Ibid., § 12112(b)(5)(A) (2000).

180 EEOC, Enforcement Guidance: Reasonable Accommodation and Undue Hardship Under the Americans with Disabilities Act, (2002) available at http://www.eeoc.gov/policy/docs/accommodation.html#undue.

181 Gordon Good, *The Americans With Disabilities Act: Short-term Disabilities, Exceptions and the Meaning of Minor* 37 U. DAYTON L. REV. 99 (2011).

employees a right to up to 12 weeks of unpaid leave in the case of serious illness. Given the limits on FMLA protections, and the vulnerability of employees under the at-will rule, it would not be surprising to see a growing number of claims for accommodation of illness under the ADA.

In Canada, as noted above, the duty to accommodate applies to disability in all Canadian jurisdictions. The concept of disability in Canadian human rights law extends to injury, illness and addictions,[182] and includes at least some temporary conditions though perhaps not 'normal ailments' such as the flu or a common cold.[183] In enforcing the duty adjudicators have required employers to provide workers with accommodations such as modified duties and schedules, leaves of absence, or furniture and other equipment needed to attend work or do the essential duties of a job.[184]

In addition, in several jurisdictions workers' compensation statutes impose on employers further positive obligations to assist employees with injuries or illnesses arising out of or in the course of employment to return to work as soon as they are ready to do so.[185] These obligations are similar to those imposed by the duty to accommodate, but may also include cooperating with case workers tasked by government operated workplace safety and insurance agencies with seeking to return injured workers to active employment. From the employee's perspective these provisions have the advantage of being pro-actively administered rather than requiring a complaint to a human rights tribunal for enforcement.

In most jurisdictions employment standards legislation adds only modestly to the above protections, providing employees with access to between three and 12 days of leave without pay.[186] This leaves employees who cannot characterize their temporary illness as a disability and whose employers have rigid attendance requirements legally vulnerable to dismissal.

---

[182] Zinn, *supra* note 43, at 5-10.1–5-13.

[183] See the obiter dicta of the Supreme Court of Canada in *Montreal (Ville) v. Quebec (Commission des droits de la personne et droits de la jeunesse)*, 2000 S.C.C. 27, at para. 82.

[184] See MacNeill, *supra* note 29, at 13-77–13-78, 16-2, 17-1, 18-2 and 20-1.

[185] The federal jurisdiction, Manitoba, Ontario, Quebec, Yukon, Nova Scotia, New Brunswick, Prince Edward Island and Newfoundland and Labrador impose a statutory obligation on employers to return injured employees to work. All except Quebec exclude employees with less than a year's service with the employer from the statutory protection. Ontario, Nova Scotia, Prince Edward Island, Newfoundland and Labrador and the Yukon exempt employers employing less than 20 employees; New Brunswick exempts employers employing less than ten employees; Manitoba exempts employers employing fewer than 25 employees. For Ontario, see s. 41 of the Workplace Safety and Insurance Act; Nova Scotia see ss 89–101 of the Workers' Compensation Act; New Brunswick, see s. 42.1 of the Workers' Compensation Act; Prince Edward Island: s. 86.1–86.12 of the Workers' Compensation Act; Newfoundland and Labrador: s. 89–89.4 of the Workplace Health, Safety and Compensation Act; Manitoba: s. 49.3 of the Worker's Compensation Act; Quebec: ss 32, 234, 251 of Act Respecting Industrial Accidents and Occupational Disease; Federal Jurisdiction: s. 34 of the Canada Labour Standards Regulations and s. 239.1 of the Canada Labour Code.

[186] Notable exceptions include the federal jurisdiction, Saskatchewan, and Quebec, which provide up to 12, 12 and 26 weeks of unpaid sick leave respectively. See Block, *supra* note 169, at Table 4, 343.

EU law imposes on employers a duty to provide reasonable accommodation to disabled people. As Barnard puts it, the duty of reasonable accommodation is grounded in 'the realization that the achievement of equal treatment can only become a reality where some reasonable allowance is made for disability in order to enable the abilities of the individual concerned to be put to work.'[187] These aims lay behind the EU decision to become party to the United Nations Conventions on the Right of Persons with Disabilities (CRPD).[188] Specifically, Directive 2000/78, Article 5, requires employers to 'take appropriate measures, where needed in a particular case, to enable a person with a disability to have access to, participate in, or advance in employment, or to undergo training unless such measures would impose a disproportionate burden on the employer.' It further stipulates that '[t]his burden shall not be disproportionate when it is sufficiently remedied by measures existing within the framework of the disability policy of the Member State concerned.'

An appropriate measure within the meaning of the Directive is an 'effective' practical measure to adapt the work place to the needs of the disabled even if the measure is not the best or the ideal solution.[189] Accommodation can include, in the words of the Directive, measures such as 'adapting premises and equipment, patterns of working time, [...] distribution of tasks or the provision of training or integration resources.' The accomodation should not produce a disproportionate burden for the employer. The Directive says that 'to determine whether the measures in question give rise to a disproportionate burden, account should be taken in particular on the financial and other costs entailed, the scale and financial resources of the organisation or undertaking and the possibility of obtaining public funding or any other assistance.'[190]

This duty does not extend to accommodating short-term illness. The ECJ has ruled that disabiliy, for the purpose of the Directive is 'a limitation which results in particular from physical, mental, or psychological impairments and which hinders the participation of the person concerned in professional life.'[191] This concept is different from 'sickness' in that it would only include sickness of long duration.

(c) Proactive Steps Towards Equity

The EU approach to social inclusion recognizes the limitations of reactive enforcement of negative prohibitions on discrimination. As has been pointed out, 'litigation is stressful for those involved, particularly if the employment relationship is ongoing, it is expensive and it depends on the court's understanding, and being responsive to the

---

[187] BARNARD, *supra* note 19 at 401.

[188] Council Decision on the conclusion of the United Nations Conventions on the Rights of Persons with Disabilities, (EC) No. 2010/48. of Nov. 26, 2009, 2009 O.J. (L 23/35); G. De Burca, *The European Union in the Negotiation of the UN Disability Convention* 35 EUROPEAN LAW REVIEW (2010). Interestingly, while Directive 2000/78 does not explicitly define the denial of accommodation as discrimination, CRPD (Art. 2) includes the denial of reasonable accommodation in the category of 'discrimination on the basis of disability.' Therefore, it could be argued that the refusal of reasonable accommodation is now a 'direct discrimination.'

[189] Council Decision, *supra* note 188.

[190] Council Directive 2000/78, Recital 21, 2000 O.J. (L 303) (EC).

[191] Case C-13/05 *Sonia Chacón Navas v. Eures Colectividades*, [2006] E.C.R. I-6467.

issues involved.'[192] Moreover discrimination is not always individualized but it is the consequence of social situations for which the employee is not to blame because he or she is not responsible.[193] Attention has therefore shifted in the EU to the possibility of alternative and complementary means of addressing gender inequality[194] and other forms of inequality. Rather than leaving it to individual workers to file complaints against individual perpetrators, responsibility is placed on bodies, such as public authorities or employers, or trade unions that are in a position to bring about change, whether or not they have actually caused the problem. If effectively implemented, this stands to relieve individual victims of the burden and expense of litigation. Further, this approach aims to initiate systematic rather than random or ad hoc change, ensuring that all those with a right to equality are covered. The institutional and structural causes of inequality can be diagnosed and addressed collectively and institutionally. Moreover, in recognition of the institutional basis of discrimination, there is no need to prove discrimination or find a named perpetrator. Instead, the duty to bring about change lies with those with the power and capacity to do so. Rather than determining a breach of the law, the focus is on identifying systemic discrimination and creating institutional mechanisms for its elimination. Finally, proactive models broaden the participatory role of civil society, both in norm setting and in norm enforcing. In this sense, the citizen is characterized not as a passive recipient but rather as an active participant.[195] The idea of equality behind these initiatives is an 'equality of opportunity' concept in which policies seek to create a 'level playing field' between all groups in society.[196]

This concept has driven significant policy initiatives at the European level. As one observer has noted:

> At the EU level, mainstreaming strategies have given a powerful boost to the effectiveness of sex equality legislation. Also of increasing importance is the role of the open method of coordination (OMC) which operates in the fields of employment, social inclusion and pensions. The OMC moves deliberately away from the legal method and instead depends on reporting mechanisms and peer review under the coordinating auspices of the European Commission. Equality concerns are integrated or mainstreamed with the stated policy concern. Proactive measures are also increasingly widespread in the EU.[197]

The Revised Equal Treatment Directive imposes a duty on member states 'actively to take into account the objective of equality between men and women when formulating and implementing laws, regulations and administrative provisions, policies and activities' and to take the necessary measures to ensure that any discriminatory provisions contained in collective agreements, individual contracts of employment, staff and other

---

192 Barnard, *supra* note 19, at 258.

193 S. Fredman, *Changing the Norm: Positive Duties in Equal Treatment Legislation*, 12 Maastricht J. Eur. & Comp. Eur. L. 369, 370 (2005); Barnard, *supra* note 19.

194 Barnard, *supra* note 19.

195 See Fredman and the European Network or Legal Experts in the Field of Gender Equality, *supra* note 172. See also FREDMAN, *supra* note 28.

196 A.C.L. Davies, Perspectives on Labour Law, 126 (2d ed., 2009).

197 Fredman, *supra* note 28, at 301.

internal rules of undertakings are declared null and void or are amended.[198] As Barnard points out such duties go beyond compensating victims and aim at restructuring institutions.[199] Outside gender equality, EU law exhorts but does not require member states, employers and unions to implement proactive measures.[200]

In addition, the European Commission has produced a work program on gender equality.[201] This program can be regarded as a form of soft law. By 'soft law' we do not mean a particular legal tool but rather a wide range of measures adopted by different European institutions with the purpose of social change enhancing equality and social inclusion for persons in groups subject to discrimination.[202]

As a result of this approach member states provide specific statutory duties to take steps to achieve equality. Nothern Ireland has been at the forefront of this approach. Pioneering legislation introduced in 1989 imposed a positive duty on employers to take measures to achieve fair participation of Protestant and Roman Catholic employees among the workforce. Under this legislation, employers must periodically review the composition of the workforce and their employment practices to determine whether members of each of those two main communities are 'enjoying fair participation in employment in concern.' If this is not the case, the employer is required to institute positive action in order to make progress towards fair participation.[203] Other EU member states place a statutory duty on public bodies to generate equal opportunity policies. These bodies operate in very different ways to promote substantive equality through strategies enacted by different institutions including trade unions.[204]

---

198 See Arts 1(1a), 23(a) and (b), and 29 of the Consolidated Directive 2006/54, and Art. 3(2)(a) and (b) of Directive 76/207, *supra* note 11.

199 BARNARD, *supra* note 19, at 431. See the report 'Making Equality Effective: The Role of Practive Measures', *supra* note 172. The report has been produced by a group of experts under the direction of S. Fredman.

200 Numerous EU Directives encourage member states, employers and unions to do so. See Directive 2006/54 on equal treatment of men and women in matter of employment and occupation, at Recital (7) declares that 'employer and those responsible for vocational training should be encouraged to take measures to combat all forms of discriminaions on grounds of sex for the purposes of this Directive' (O.J. (L 204/23) (EC)). Under Art. 3 'Member States [...] may adopt measures [...] with a view of ensuring full equality in practice between men and women in working life.' Directive 2000/43 implementing the equal treatment between persons irrespective of racial or ethnic origin, at Recital (8) underlines the 'need to foster condition for a socially inclusive labour market by formulating a coherent set of policies aimed at combating discrimination against groups such ethnic minorities' (O.J. (L 180) (EC)). Directive 2000/78 on equal treatment in employment and occupation at Recital (27) cites EU acts that promote guideline framework setting out examples of positive actions to promote employment and training for disabled persons (O.J. (L 303) (EC)).

201 European Commission, *supra* note 173, at 5.

202 BARNARD, *supra* note 19, at 80, describes soft law as having the 'consequence of ... desire of flexibility in the form of legislative instruments.' 'The flexibility of soft laws allows the Community insitutions to stimulate European integration by building on and around existing Treaty objectives without directly creating legal obligations. They are a kind of informal law-making by exhortation.'

203 FREDMAN, *supra* note 28, at 301.

204 This is for example the case of a non-member state, Iceland, where 'the Gender Equality Act stipulates that trade unions must deliberately work with employers to achieve equality for

By contrast, there is little legislation in Canada systematically requiring employers to proactively change their hiring and employment practices to remove barriers to equal opportunity. Only two jurisdictions impose such requirements.[205] On the other hand, several Canadian jurisdictions have in place narrower legislation that requires employers to take positive steps towards achieving equity in pay between women and men. Manitoba, New Brunswick, Ontario, Quebec, and Prince Edward Island have pay equity statutes.[206] However, only those of Quebec and Ontario, Canada's two largest jurisdictions in terms of population, apply to the private sector. In general terms, all of these statutes require employers (except for smaller employers) to systematically evaluate within stipulated timeframes and against objective criteria the value of the jobs within female- and male-dominated job classes in their organization, and to make pay equity adjustments necessary to achieve equal pay for work of equal value between women and men. This obligation is an ongoing one, requiring that pay equity be maintained over time. Such legislation is premised on the view that systemic pay discrimination against women is endemic in Canada.[207]

There are no direct counterparts to pay and employment equity legislation at the federal level in the U.S. The closest analog is found in the Office of Federal Contract Compliance Programs regulations.[208] The regulations apply to most employers who have contracts with the U.S. federal government. Employers with 50 or more employees must prepare written affirmative action programs which include a 'work force analysis', a determination of whether any racial or ethnic minority group or

---

women and man in the labour market'. FREDMAN, *supra* note 28, at 304, whose already quoted report 'Making Equality Effective', *supra* note 172, is the source for many other examples.

[205] The Employment Equity Act in the federal jurisdiction requires employers to identify and eliminate employment barriers against persons in designated groups (women, aboriginal peoples, persons with disabilities and members of visible minorities) that result from the employer's employment systems, policies and practices. It also requires them to institute positive policies and practices and make reasonable accommodations to ensure that persons in designated groups achieve a degree of representation in each occupational group in the employer's workforce that reflects their representation in the Canadian workforce, or in those segments of the Canadian workforce that are identifiable by qualification, eligibility or geography and from which the employer may reasonably be expected to draw employees. See Employment Equity Act, S.C. 1995, c. 44, § 5. Starting in 2015 the Integrated Accessibility Standards regulation made under the Accesibility for Ontarians with Disabilities Act 2005 will, among other things, require employers to develop policies for accommodating persons with disabilities, to inform their employees of those policies, notify applicants for jobs or promotions of those policies and that accommodations are available, and to develop procedures for creating individual accommodation plans with the involvement of the employee and his or her representative. See O. Reg. 191/11, §§ 20-32, (Can.) *available at* http://www.e-laws.gov.on.ca/html/source/regs/english/2011/elaws_src_regs_r11191_e.htm.

[206] For a discussion of these statutes and their requirements see TARNOPOLSKY & PENTNEY, *supra* note 15, at 12-82.22–12.82.28(4); and PETER BARNACLE & RODERICK WOOD, EMPLOYMENT LAW IN CANADA, 8-43 – 8-435 (4th ed., 2005).

[207] *Univ. of Sask. v. Sask. (Human Rights Trib.l)*, (2007) 60 C.H.R.R. D/413 (Can. Sask. Q.B.) ¶ 82.

[208] Exec. Order No. 11246, 3 C.F.R. 339 (1964-5), reprinted as amended in 42 U.S.C. 2000e note (2000).

women have been under-utilized, and if so goals and timetables to remedy the under-utilization.[209] The regulations can be enforced through termination of contracts.

(d) Preventing and Remedying Workplace Harassment

Anti-discrimination laws in Canada and the U.S. require employers to take positive steps to eliminate harassment on the basis of prohibited grounds by making employers responsible not only for the actions of supervisors but also for ensuring that co-workers do not harass each other. In the U.S., under Title VII employers are strictly and vicariously liable for actions of supervisors directly imposing a tangible employment detriment on an employee. In addition, an employer must exercise reasonable care to prevent and correct promptly harassing behaviour, whether by supervisors or by co-workers, about which it knew or should have known. It will face liability for the creation of a hostile environment in the event that it fails to do so.[210] Human rights codes impose substantially the same obligations and liabilities on employers in Canada.[211]

Similarly, in the EU harassment and sexual harassment are declared by Directive 2006/54 Recital (6) to be 'contrary to the principle of equal treatment between men and women and constitute discrimination on grounds of sex.'[212] As a consequence they are prohibited and must be subjected to effective and dissuasive penalties. Similarly Directives 2000/78 and 2000/43 treat harassment on the basis of other grounds as discrimination, though the former Directive gives to member states the power to define the concept of harassment relating to factors as religion, belief, disability, age or sexual orientation, in accordance with their own law and practice. Cases of alleged harassment, like other forms of alleged discrimination, are subject to the special norm on the burden of proof which requires member states[213] to facilitate for the claimant the proof of the discrimination.

EU law does not address harassment outside discrimination on prohibited grounds, leaving such matters to member states. Similarly, in the U.S. neither federal statute nor the common law of contract imposes any further obligations upon employers to prevent and remedy harassment.[214]

---

[209] For a discussion, see RUTHERGLEN, *supra* note 13, at 108–11.

[210] See HAROLD S. LEWIS & ELIZABETH J. NORMAN, EMPLOYMENT DISCRIMINATION LAW AND PRACTICE 110–20 (2d ed., 2004).

[211] Ibid.

[212] Directive 2006/54 Art. 2, 1 (c), *supra* note 11, describes harassment 'where unwanted conduct related to the sex of a person occurs with the purpose or effect of violating the dignity of a person, and of creating an intimidating, hostile, degrading, humiliating or offensive environment,' and (d) 'sexual harassment' 'where any form of unwanted verbal, non- verbal or physical conduct of a sexual nature occurs with the purpose or effect of violating the dignity of a person, in particular when creating an intimidating, hostile, degrading, humiliating or offensive environment.'

[213] Directive 2006/54, Art. 19, *supra* note 11.

[214] See Susan Harthill, *The Need for a Revitalized Regulatory Scheme to Address Workplace Bullying in the United States: Harnessing the Federal Occupational Health and Safety Act* 78 U.

In the U.S. this leaves employees harassed for reasons other than their membership in a group protected by anti-discrimination law largely without recourse. While such employees may be able to sue employers in tort for intentional infliction of emotional distress, under U.S. law this tort is very difficult to prove since it requires demonstrating that: (1) the defendant acted intentionally or recklessly; (2) the conduct was extreme and outrageous; (3) the conduct caused the plaintiff emotional distress; and (4) the emotional distress was severe.[215] Employees have had little success invoking this tort in response to workplace bullying.[216]

This situation stands in growing contrast to recent legal developments in Canada. Since 2007 the Saskatchewan Occupational Health and Safety Act has expressly treated workplace harassment that constitutes a threat to the health or safety of a worker, whether or not on the basis of protected grounds under the relevant human rights code, as a hazard that employers must abate and that may trigger a work refusal by the employee.[217] One Ontario tribunal decision suggests that harassment may constitute such a hazard even in the absence of express statutory recognition as such.[218] Amendments in 2009 to the Ontario Occupational Health and Safety Act now require employers to develop a policy with respect to workplace harassment and to implement that policy through a program including procedures for workers to report incidents, and investigating and dealing with incidents and complaints.[219] In Quebec, employment standards legislation has since 2002 provided that 'every employee has a right to a work environment free from psychological harassment', and that '[e]mployers must take reasonable action to prevent psychological harassment and, whenever they become aware of such behaviour, to put a stop to it.'[220] Employees may seek before the relevant tribunal a wide range of remedies including reinstatement and compensatory and punitive damages.[221]

CIN. L. REV. 1250, 1270 (2010); Susan Harthill, *Workplace Bullying as an Occupational Safety and Health Matter: A Comparative Analysis* 34 HASTINGS INT'L & COMP. L. REV. 253, 253 (2011).

[215] Jordan F. Kaplan, *Help is on the Way: A Recent Case Sheds Light on Workplace Bullying*, 47 HOUS. L. REV. 141, 161 (2011).

[216] Ibid., at 161–4.

[217] Occupational Health and Safety Act, S.S. 1993, c. O-1.1, §. 2(1)(l) (Can.).

[218] *Au v. Lyndhurst Hosp.*, [1996] O.L.R.B. Rep. 456 (O.L.R.B.); affd. [1996] O.L.R.B. Rep. 902 (Can. Ont. Ct. Gen. Div.) For a discussion of the potential significance of this ruling on Ontario and other Canadian jurisdictions, see STACEY BALL, CANADIAN EMPLOYMENT LAW 29-4 – 29-43 (rev ed. 1996).

[219] Occupational Health and Safety Act, R.S.O. 1990, c. O.1 §§. 32.0.1, 32.0.6. The Act defines harassment in s. 1(1) as 'engaging in a course of vexatious comment or conduct against a worker in a workplace that is known or ought reasonably to be known to be unwelcome.'

[220] An Act Respecting Labour Standards, R.S.Q. c. N-1.1, §. 81.19 (Can.). Section 81.18 defines psychological harassment as 'any vexatious behaviour in the form of repeated and hostile or unwanted conduct, verbal comments, actions or gestures, that affects an employee's dignity or psychological or physical integrity and that results in a harmful work environment for the employee.' For a discussion of jurisprudence interpreting these new provisions, see Rachel Cox, *Psychological Harassment Legislation in Quebec: The First Five Years*, 32 COMP. LAB. L. & POL'Y J. 55 (2010).

[221] Act Respecting Labour Standards, § 123.15.

In the last two decades Canadian courts have also recognized that employer failures to address workplace harassment can attract liability for breach of implied contractual terms and in tort.[222] At Canadian common law, harassment by supervisors or a failure to address harassment by co-workers may amount to a breach of an employer's implied duty to provide a safe work environment.[223] It will amount to breach of the employer's implied duty of good faith and fair dealing in the manner of dismissal where it occurs in the course of dismissal or amounts to constructive dismissal.[224] Harassment by a supervisor may also constitute a breach of an employer's implied duty to treat employees with civility, decency, respect and dignity,[225] and may expose employers (at least outside Ontario)[226] to liability for negligent infliction of mental suffering.[227] Where such harassment amounts to flagrant or outrageous conduct, is calculated to produce harm, and results in a visible or probable illness, and employee will also have, as in the U.S., an action for intentional infliction of emotional distress.[228]

(e) Observations

With the exception of obligations to prevent and remedy harassment on the basis of grounds protected in anti-discrimination law, and with the possible exception of the duty to accommodate disability,[229] U.S. federal law imposes fewer and less stringent obligations on employers to positively accommodate important employee needs or to proactively address extreme incivility in the workplace than do its Canadian and EU counterparts. This leaves U.S. workers with pregnancy or family-related care-giving needs with substantially less legal protection. They also have less protection than their Canadian counterparts when facing bullying or harassment that cannot be tied to statutorily prohibited grounds.

This difference in levels of legal protection will surprise few. As noted at the end of Part 2, the exceptional scope of employer prerogative within the U.S. legal system is nothing new. It is evident in the way in which the at-will doctrine has served, as James Brudney has demonstrated, to prevent the development of implied contractual good faith doctrines which could oblige employers to address workplace abuses such as harassment, as well as to constrain the development of statutory limits on unfettered

---

222 For a discussion, see Kevin Banks, *Progress and Paradox: The Remarkable Yet Limited Advance of Employer Good Faith Duties in Canadian Common Law*, 32 Comp. Lab. L. & Pol'y J. 547 (2011).

223 Ibid., at 577–8.

224 Ibid., at 566–7.

225 Ibid., at 575–6.

226 *Piresferreira v. Ayotte*, [2008] 72 C.C.E.L.3d 23, *rev'd in part* [2010] 82 C.C.E.L.3d 14 (Can.).

227 Ibid., at 583–4.

228 Ibid., at 582–3.

229 As Weber notes, prior to the ADAAA restrictions on the scope of 'disability' under the ADA meant that few cases triggered the duty to accommodate and thus the law with respect to the scope of the duty remains somewhat undeveloped. See Weber, *supra* note 120.

employer powers to dismiss employees.[230] The continuing influence of the at-will doctrine stands in sharp contrast to the gradual recognition by Canadian courts of the vulnerability of employees in relations with their employer, and the resulting incrementalist development good faith and similar duties in Canadian common law.[231] It also contrasts with the more protective tradition of employment and labour legislation in Europe. But these differences in turn reflect very different legal and political structures, conditions and histories.

One can also see in this survey of legislation the influence of the different ideas of equal opportunity operating in Canada, the EU and the U.S. The idea that accommodation gives effect to equal opportunity is gradually working its way into the general fabric of Canadian employment law. It shows up in the purposes of the federal Employment Equity Act, in evolving interpretations of protections against discrimination on the basis of family status, and in the relatively lengthy pregnancy and parental leaves available to Canadian employees. Influential analysts of Canadian employment law have begun to view such minimum employment standards as serving in part to reinforce, implement and stipulate the general aims and requirements of anti-discrimination law.[232] EU Directives increasingly impose positive obligations in the service of a 'level playing field' idea of equality of opportunity. Meanwhile in the U.S. the duty to accommodate remains largely confined to the field of disability law, and the Family and Medical Leave Act is not understood in anti-discrimination terms. The potential transformative influence of civil rights thinking upon employment law is thus cabined by its largely negative theory of discrimination.

4. CONCLUSIONS

Beneath many structural similarities U.S., EU and Canadian workplace anti-discrimination law put into operation very different ideas of equal opportunity. In general terms, U.S. laws treats equal opportunity as the absence of invidious motivation or obstacles to participation that serve no legitimate business purpose. EU law seeks to eliminate obstacles that cannot be justified as necessary and proportionate on objective grounds. Canadian law makes reasonable accommodation the jurisprudential core of equal opportunity.

Each of these ideas of equal opportunity in turn reflects a different notion of employer responsibility to address inequality, a notion in turn heavily influenced by the type of workplace discrimination that first was the animating concern of legislatures and courts. In the U.S., the paradigm of race-blindness reflects both the dominant understanding of what workplace racism is and the moral and technical challenges of holding employers responsible for unintentional disadvantage of racialized groups. This paradigm allowed for a full development of disparate treatment doctrines, while leaving

---

230 James Brudney, *Reluctance and Remorse: The Covenant of Good Faith and Fair Dealing in American Employment Law*, 32 COMP. LAB. L. & POL'Y J. 773 (2011).

231 Banks, *supra* note 222, at 554–63.

232 FEDERAL LABOUR STANDARDS REVIEW COMMISSION, FAIRNESS AT WORK: REPORT OF THE FEDERAL LABOUR STANDARDS REVIEW COMMISSION 101–3 (2006).

disparate impact law under-theorized and tentatively applied with respect to all grounds of discrimination. In the EU the ECJ pursued, on basis of a mandate restricted to address sex discrimination, a single market with human rights social policy foundations. This led it to expand the concept of direct discrimination to protect pregnancy and maternity, and to examine disparate impacts on women as indirect discrimination requiring justification to be lawful. When the time came at the turn of the twenty-first century for the EU to advance an agenda of equal opportunity for other social groups, the Court's gender jurisprudence was codified in directives prohibiting discrimination on a wider range of prohibited grounds, and EU policy branches sought to foster, outside anti-discrimination law, positive measures in support of social inclusion. In Canada, the duty to accommodate, borrowed from the U.S., resonated with an ascendant political discourse of multiculturalism, served well to define employer obligations to religious minorities within that discursive context, and was extended with little jurisprudential controversy to other protected personal characteristics.

In each place, the jurisprudence of anti-discrimination was also influenced by and in turn influenced the wider political culture and set of power structures that generate longer term tendencies in employment regulation. In the U.S., a more limited notion of equal opportunity was consistent with an ongoing history of legislative deference to employer prerogative. EU institutions relied upon directives and member state legislation, rather than anti-discrimination jurisprudence, to impose positive obligations on employers to accommodate women and minority groups. This reflected both longstanding European approaches to workplace regulation and the division of responsibility between the executive and judicial branches at the EU level. In Canada the notion of reasonable accommodation as a human right developed by courts and tribunals has begun, not without controversy,[233] to influence wider policy thinking about regulation in the workplace and beyond.

We have thus uncovered substantial divergence between U.S., EU and Canadian law and policy. This divergence gathered momentum despite globalization and despite significant international sharing of organizing legal concepts. These comparisons throw into sharp relief alternative versions of basic ideas like discrimination, equality of opportunity and social inclusion, providing an opportunity to consider critically the particular content of notions often taken for granted within national legal systems. Nonetheless, the formative contexts in which those different ideas took hold continue to evolve in light of internal pressures and imperatives. We can see no reason for these three legal trajectories to converge any time soon.[234]

[233] The most notable flashpoint in recent years was around the accommodation of religious minorities in public institutions in Quebec. See LUC TREMBLAY, THE BOUCHARD-TAYLOR REPORT ON CULTURAL AND RELIGIOUS ACCOMMODATION: MULTICULTURALISM BY ANY OTHER NAME? (2009).

[234] For an argument that globalization need not produce convergence in the employment legislation of industrialized countries, see Kevin Banks, *Must Canada Changes its Labour and Employment Law to Compete with the United States?*, 38 QUEEN'S L.J. 419 (2013).

9. Job loss

Joanna Howe, Esther Sánchez and Andrew Stewart[*]

1. INTRODUCTION

This chapter is concerned with the evolution of legal protection for workers who lose their jobs.[1] The regulation of job loss has become one of the most contested areas of labour law. But it was not always so. At various points during the twentieth century, most developed countries introduced laws that constrained employment being terminated in certain circumstances, stipulated particular procedures to be followed, and/or mandated the payment of compensation to affected workers. As we will explain, these developments inspired the creation of international labour standards on job loss that remain in effect today. Those standards, and the domestic laws that reflect them, can apply in relation to both *personal dismissals*, where employment is terminated in response to concerns about the conduct or capacity of an individual worker; and *economic dismissals* (redundancies), where an employer determines that a particular job should no longer be performed by anyone, or reduces the number of workers hired to perform a type of work.[2]

Since the economic crisis of the 1970s, however, a fierce debate has developed over the sustainability and value of employment protection laws. Over the ensuing years, labour law has struggled to coexist with what some call the 'uncomfortable' requirements of the economy.[3] During that time, existing laws have been immobilised or 'frozen', in the sense that worker protections have not been extended or further developed. Certain rights have been cut back, generating a process which some groups (particularly those linked to trade unions) have described as increasing 'job insecurity'. The circumstances in which it is not possible to enforce certain rights, or in which they can be suspended, have been extended. And labour costs have been cut by, for example,

* We would like to thank the following people for their assistance with this chapter: Jaime Carbonell (Baker & McKenzie), Lluis Tutusaus-Zeus Villalonga (Department of Enterprise and Employment, Government of Catalonia), Rachael White and Katherine Varsos (University of Adelaide).

1 For reasons of practicality, we have opted in this chapter to concentrate on the loss of *employment*, focusing on the form of work relationship that continues to be the central concern of labour law as conventionally understood. Hence we do not, for example, examine the various ways in which efforts have or might be made to regulate the loss of work by the likes of independent contractors, franchisees, and so on.

2 We prefer this terminology to speaking of 'individual' and 'collective' dismissals. There is no reason why a single worker cannot be dismissed for economic rather than personal reasons; while, conversely, it is possible (though less common in practice) for a group of employees to lose their jobs for conduct or capacity reasons.

3 Palomeque López, Manuel Carlos. 2000. 'La Función y la Refundación del Derecho del Trabajo,' 13 *Relaciones Laborales* 21–31.

reducing compensation in the case of dismissal or considering certain cases of dismissal or unilateral amendment to working conditions as justified and not subject to financial compensation or other kinds of recompense.

Likewise, the appearance of united economic areas, the phenomena of the establishment and mergers of groups of companies and multinationals, and the transnational mobility of businesses and workers, have not only caused changes in internal legal systems,[4] but also led to pressure for the creation or reform of international or European Community regulations.[5]

At bottom here is a contest over the values and purposes of labour regulation.[6] Since modern labour law emerged in the late nineteenth and early twentieth centuries, its rules have generally been configured to protect workers. However, civil contract rules, inspired by the idea of contractual balance between the parties, have been gaining ground. The commitment to the protection of job security has been questioned, particularly in countries where state intervention in the labour market has been at its strongest, because of the 'rigidities' associated with the unconditional recognition of workers' rights. At times of economic crisis, these may make it difficult or costly to recover competitive capacity, even more so as the economy is ceasing to be local and becoming globalised.

If we analyse recent employment reforms in a range of countries with long established systems of labour law, we see that most of the reforms have been aimed at combating some of the effects of globalisation, giving the labour market more flexibility, incorporating more prerogatives for employers and allowing working conditions to be more easily adapted to the demands of an increasingly competitive and changing market. Indeed according to the OECD, from 2008 to 2013, more than one-third of OECD countries moved to relax their employment protection laws, with reforms 'concentrated in countries with the most stringent provisions at the beginning of the period'.[7]

A paradigmatic example that has attracted international attention, not only because of the deep economic crisis the country is experiencing, but also for the lack of tangible results for most of its previous employment reforms, is that of Spain.[8] Since 1984 a

---

[4] One of the reasons adduced to explain the 'crisis of labour law' is the clear, perceptible crisis of the nation-state. See: Perulli, Adalberto. 1999. 'Postfordismo, Forma Dello Stato e Diritto del Lavoro: Spunti di Riflesione,' 2 *Lavoro e Diritto* 251–70.

[5] Romagnoli, Umberto. 1998. 'Per un diritto del lavoro post industriale e sovranacioanle,' 2 *Lavoro e Diritto* 209–20.

[6] Sinzheimer, Hugo. 1984. *Crisis Económica y Derecho del Trabajo: Cinco Estudios sobre la Problemática Humana y Conceptual del Derecho del Trabajo*. Madrid: Ministerio de Trabajo y Seguridad Social; Weber, Max. 1984. *Economía y Sociedad*. Mexico: Fondo de Cultura Económica; Davidov, Guy, and Brian Langille (eds). 2011. *The Idea of Labour Law*. Oxford: OUP.

[7] OECD (Organisation for Economic Co-operation and Development). 2013. 'OECD Employment Outlook 2013.' P. 10. Available at: http://www.oecd.org/australia/employmentoutlook2013-countrynotes.htm.

[8] Baviera, Immaculada. 2013. 'Employment Stability in Spanish Labor Law: Between Regulatory Tradition and Social Reality' 34 *Comparative Labor Law and Policy Journal* 677–96; Gil, José. 2014. 'Strengthening the Power of Dismissal in Recent Labor Reforms in Spain' 35 *Comparative Labor Law and Policy Journal* 413–48.

succession of reforms have openly sought to achieve a more flexible model of labour relations. Act 32/1984 did this by promoting temporary forms of contract, a reform which succeeded in increasing participation rates, but also created one of the problems most endemic to the Spanish labour market: the duality between temporary and indefinite employment. It also made no difference to the unemployment rate, which ten years later was still over 20 per cent. Acts 10 and 11/1994 brought the abolition of a series of minimum rights and the delegation of power to collective bargaining, which increased the capacity to adapt working conditions to market dynamics. The unemployment rate did not fall significantly, there was a clear reduction in job offers, and both the use of temporary contracts and the duality of the labour market increased even more, while forms of training contracts, aimed at increasing youth employment, were not used by businesses. Meanwhile, instead of making things more flexible, collective bargaining has had quite the opposite effect over the past few decades, making it hard to adapt the working day, hours and wages to market conditions, and encouraging employers to look to dismissals to make adjustments.[9]

International demands to address the unemployment rate and the duality in the labour market prompted a debate over whether the cost of dismissal in Spain was too high, leading, in 1997, to a reform whose key measure was the creation of a form of indefinite contract with lower redundancy pay costs. This halted the increase in temporary contracts, although these still remained at very high levels, at over 35 per cent of the workforce. The desire to reduce dismissal costs was once again maintained in 2001 reforms, which abolished interim wages and recognised the concept of 'fast-track dismissal'. This allowed employers to recognise that dismissals without just cause were unfair, deposit the appropriate amount of redundancy pay with the authorities and restrict almost any possibility of legal challenge to the dismissals. Once again, there was no significant reduction in temporary contracts, but economic growth based on the building and construction sector allowed a four million increase in the number of employed people. In 2006, the labour law system was reformed again to limit temporary contracts, although the rate of temporary employment remained above 30 per cent.

The global financial crisis sent the unemployment rate soaring again, and the most important reforms since the coming into force of the Workers' Statute of 1980 were carried out during 2011 and 2012. Employers were given greater capacity to make unilateral changes to working conditions, even when governed by collective agreement. Economic dismissals were made easier to implement and severance pay was reduced. Most of these measures were adopted in a reactive fashion and in haste. Some of the new legal rules lack definition and clarity, giving the judiciary an important role and adding even more insecurity to the system.

As this example illustrates, adjustments of this kind have not been easy or free of controversy. This has been especially true in the case of erratic reform processes that have made little difference to labour market competitiveness or that have started from the erroneous premise that legal regulation is the true generator of sustainable

---

[9] An adversarial rather than 'win-win' approach to bargaining, together with poor management and leadership at most companies, perhaps help to explain this situation and provide some clues about how to solve it in the medium to long term.

development, as opposed to the way such regulation is applied in the context of collective bargaining, employment contracts and human resources management.[10] Worse still is an unthinking approach that focuses on legal regulation without considering the stability of production systems, size of businesses or the nature of production activity (especially in relation to seasonality and market fluctuations).

The experience of Spain is emblematic of broader debates over how to marry the need for business to achieve flexibility and the rights of workers to job security. What seems clear is that, in the most recent labour reforms around the developed world, a 'business' view has gradually been incorporated, as well as a strictly 'labour' view. One approach that has emerged has been the European idea of 'flexicurity', which attempts to combine benefits for businesses and for workers. The European Commission's Green Paper on 'Modernising Labour Law to Meet the Challenges of the 21st Century' declares in its introduction that the great challenge for European markets is 'combining greater flexibility with the need to maximise security for all'.[11]

The aim of flexicurity is to have fewer and shorter periods of unemployment for each employee despite major economic upheavals such as restructuring, the introduction of new technologies or plant closures. The model assumes that reforms are needed in the regulation of dismissal, to make it easier and cheaper for employers to shed staff, while at the same time providing new 'transition rights' for employees. These latter should ideally include continuous, permanent training, as well as active employment policies focused on an individual's entire professional life (including transitions both into and between occupations, as well as education, childcare and so on), rather than looking in isolation at their current employment contract.[12] This in turn is intended to make the workforce more adaptable to the changing demands of the labour market, increase productivity, reduce the costs associated with arbitrary or badly designed outsourcing policies, encourage the attraction and retention of good workers and, not least, reduce the financial and social costs associated with unemployment.

On the other hand, some authors are openly sceptical of this approach. They argue that it is not possible to establish a common European model of flexicurity, whether because of the significant differences between countries,[13] because it requires a

---

10 After the Spanish employment reform of 1994 that stated that:

> at origin, the means of making the job market more flexible are presented and used as mere tools to combat unemployment; means to preserve an acceptable volume of employment in the economy as a whole. Nowadays, however, flexibility has lost the characteristics of a tool and become an end in itself. There has been a move from system flexibility to a flexible system.

Valdés Dal-Ré, Fernando. 2000. 'Poder Normativo del Estado y Sistema de Relaciones Laborales,' 2 *Relaciones Laborales: Revista Crítica de Teoría y Práctica* 33–44.

11 European Commission. 'Modernising Labour Law to Meet the Challenges of the 21st Century', Green Paper, COM (2006) 708 final. Brussels: European Commission, at p. 3.

12 Rodríguez-Piñero, Miguel. 2007. 'Flexiseguridad el Debate Europeo en Curso,' 2 *Relaciones Laborales* 113–137.

13 Miguélez, Faustino. 2007. 'Flexiseguridad, Bienestar y Cohesión Social,' 1 *Revista del Ministerio de Trabajo y Asuntos Sociales* 145–60.

long-term perspective which is simply not there at present,[14] or because of the obvious risk, especially in the current climate of economic crisis, that most legal efforts will focus on flexibility at the expense of security. This last is something that has been an obvious feature of recent reform processes in Southern Europe.[15]

Against this backdrop of the growing controversy of unfair dismissal and redundancy laws, amidst the growth and consolidation of the 'economic globalisation process',[16] this chapter seeks to trace the evolution of legal regulation of termination at the initiative of the employer. We look first at the growth and nature of legal standards relating to personal dismissal, then turn to economic dismissals. We conclude by reviewing some of the debates concerning the justification for employment protection laws and their economic effects.

2. THE DEVELOPMENT OF NATIONAL AND INTERNATIONAL STANDARDS ON PERSONAL DISMISSAL

The principle of protecting employees against arbitrary or unreasonable dismissal emerged during the twentieth century in legislation or collective agreements in a number of countries; and it was these provisions that served as the precedents for the standards later developed in international law. Edward Yemin suggests that the earliest forms of unfair dismissal law can be found in the Mexican Constitution of 1917 and in the Russian SFSR Labour Code adopted in 1922. Germany too, was an early innovator in developing statutory safeguards.[17] The German Work Councils Law of 1920 rendered invalid any 'anti-social' notice to terminate. This was later expanded in 1951 by the Law on Statutory Safeguards in respect of the Notice to Terminate which was drafted on a tripartite basis and strictly regulated the termination of employment.[18]

1963 was a watershed year, with the development by the International Labour Organisation (ILO) of Recommendation 119 concerning Termination of Employment at the Initiative of the Employer. Over 40 countries subsequently reformed their labour laws to develop some protection against arbitrary dismissal. In cases such as Cambodia, Rwanda, Cyprus and Zaire, governments directly requested ILO technical cooperation experts to assist in the drawing up of national legislation; whereas in India pre-existing limitations under the Industrial Disputes Act restraining the independent examination of

---

14 Klammer, Ute. 2007. 'Flexiseguridad: Perspectiva Europea', 1 *Revista del Ministerio de Trabajo y Asuntos Sociales*, 117–43.

15 Valdés Dal-Ré, Fernando. 2010. 'Flexiseguridad y Mercado de Trabajo,' 1 *Relaciones Laborales: Revista Crítica de Teoría y Práctica* 125–36; Gorelli, Juan. 2013. 'Crítica a la Flexiseguridad,' 16 *Revista Latinoamericana de Derecho Social* 51–82.

16 According to Manuel Castells, the global economy is 'the economy whose nuclear components have the institutional, organisational and technological capacity to operate as a unit on a global scale in real time or in an established time'. Castells, Manuel. 1996. *La Era de la Información, Vol I: La Sociedad Red*. Madrid: Alianza Editoriai., p. 136.

17 Yemin, Edward. 1976. 'Job Security: Influence of ILO Standards and Recent Trends,' 113 *International Labour Review* 17–34, at p. 20.

18 Cronin, J.B. 1968. 'I.L.O. Recommendation 119: Job Security in Cyprus,' 17 *International and Comparative Law Quarterly* 760–72, at p. 761.

an employer's dismissal decision were removed in 1971.[19] In response to Recommendation 119 the British Government asked both the National Joint Advisory Council, made up of union and employer representatives, as well as the Royal Commission on Trade Unions and Employers' Associations, to investigate whether Britain should introduce statutory protection against unfair dismissal.[20] In Finland the Recommendation prompted the central organisations of employers and workers to conclude a General Agreement on Protection against Dismissal in 1966, while in Sweden it led in 1964 to amendment of the Basic Agreement between the relevant peak bodies).[21] In many countries, ILO Recommendation 119 either directly inspired unfair dismissal legislation or acted as a catalyst to the development of national laws protecting against arbitrary dismissal.

A decade after its adoption by the ILO, a request that countries supply reports on the extent to which the Recommendation was being domestically applied received the largest response ever to a request of that kind, with 100 countries handing in a report.[22] This, among other developments, led to the impetus for ILO Convention 158 on Termination of Employment at the Initiative of the Employer, which was created in 1982 after serious wrangling between national governments, employers and unions as to its content. Its central provision is Article 4, which stipulates that employment 'shall not be terminated unless there is a valid reason for such termination connected with the capacity or conduct of the worker or based on the operational requirements of the undertaking, establishment or service'. Certain reasons are not to be regarded as 'valid' for this purpose, such as those based on trade union membership or activities, race or gender (Arts 5–6); while a worker should not be dismissed for conduct or performance reasons without a reasonable opportunity to be heard in their own defence (Art. 7). Article 8 goes on to provide that workers should be able to challenge their dismissal before an impartial body; while Article 11 insists that dismissed workers be given reasonable notice of their dismissal (or compensation in lieu), except where they are guilty of serious misconduct. The Convention is complemented by Recommendation No 166, also adopted in 1982, which suggests additional safeguards in relation to both substantive and procedural matters.

According to Brian Napier, the adoption of ILO Convention 158 was only achieved by 'a compromise which took the form of consigning to the Recommendation some of the more radical (and, to the employers, more objectionable) proposals first designated for Convention status'.[23] In particular, the British Government led by Prime Minister Thatcher mounted strong resistance to the proposal that standards previously contained in the form of a Recommendation should be replaced by a Convention, as the latter is conceived to directly influence national legislation while the former acts more as a guideline influencing national policy over time. Britain also tried, albeit unsuccessfully,

---

[19] Yemin, Job Security, *supra* note 17, p. 21.

[20] United Kingdom Ministry of Labour. 1967. Dismissal Procedures. Report of a Committee of the National Joint Advisory Council; Donovan, Lord. 1969. Report of the Royal Commission on Trade Unions and Employers' Associations, Cmnd 3888.

[21] Yemin, Job Security, *supra* note 17, p. 22.

[22] Ibid., p. 23.

[23] Napier, Brian. 1983. 'Dismissals – The New I.L.O. Standards,' 12 *Industrial Law Journal* 17–27, p. 18.

to convince the ILO that the new provisions on burden of proof would be more appropriate in the Recommendation than the Convention, in an attempt to dilute the influence these provisions would have on British unfair dismissal law.[24] Consistent with its approach of resistance during negotiations, Britain rejected the final Convention and Recommendation when the ILO adopted them in 1982.

Even though only 34 countries have ratified ILO Convention 158, the labour laws in many more countries give effect to its basic principles.[25] Indeed in the three decades since its promulgation, laws protecting against arbitrary dismissal have generally remained in place around the developed world. In some countries (including Belgium, Greece, Spain, France, Italy, Luxembourg, Denmark and Sweden) unfair dismissal laws have been promulgated as a consequence of the constitutional recognition of a 'right to work', which is considered to oblige public policies (and as a consequence also the law) to be oriented to the protection of employment.[26] Other countries have gone further and dealt with the matter explicitly in their constitution. For example, Article 18 of Finland's Constitution provides that '[n]o one shall be dismissed from employment without a lawful reason.' Such provisions embody a principle of employment stability under which dismissal can only be justified for cause, and as a *last resort* – that is, when the reason for termination is real and serious and no other business measure is reasonably possible.

On the other hand, the job security protection afforded by national unfair dismissal laws has been consistently pared back in response to economic arguments that conceive of unfair dismissal law as too burdensome upon business. Prominent recent examples include the French legislature's attempt to exclude some young workers from 'just cause' laws – an attempt thwarted by public opposition;[27] the Australian exclusion of employees from 'small' businesses with 100 or fewer employees, a bar which (as explained later) operated between 2006 and 2009;[28] and the doubling of the qualifying period that must be served in Britain before an unfair dismissal claim can be lodged, from one to two years.[29] Reforms such as these have highlighted the ongoing debate over the value and costs of unfair dismissal laws – a subject to which we return at the end of the chapter. First, however, we endeavour to provide some sense of the nature and variety of contemporary unjust dismissal laws around the world, at least as they stood in 2012 when the research for this chapter was originally undertaken.

---

[24] CEACR (Committee of Experts on the Application of Conventions and Recommendations). 1982. 'Termination at the Initiative of the Employer,' International Labour Conference, 68th Session. Geneva: ILO.

[25] CEACR. 2009. Report III (Pt 1A), International Labour Conference, 98th Session. Geneva: ILO, p. 537.

[26] Nogler, Luca. 2007. 'La Disciplina dei Licenziamenti Individuali Nell'epoca del Bilanciamento tra i 'Principi' Costituzionali,' 116 *Giornale di Diritto del Lavoro e di Relazioni Industriali* 593–694.

[27] Davidov, Guy. 2007. 'In Defence of (Efficiently Administered) 'Just Cause' Dismissal Laws,' 23 *International Journal of Comparative Labour Law and Industrial Relations* 117–38.

[28] Chapman, Anna. 2009. 'Protections in Relation to Dismissal: From the Workplace Relations Act to the Fair Work Act,' 32 *University of New South Wales Law Journal* 746–71.

[29] Unfair Dismissal and Statement of Reasons for Dismissal (Variation of Qualifying Period) Order 2012 (UK), art 3.

3. CONSTRAINTS ON PERSONAL DISMISSAL: A COUNTRY COMPARISON

As Otto Kahn-Freund notes, upon the comparatist 'the gods have bestowed the most dangerous of all their gifts, the gift of freedom', because in comparing labour laws, the comparatist is faced with a multiplicity of choices in order to select which jurisdictions to study and upon which aspects of the law to focus.[30] For reasons of convenience, we have limited our analysis of personal dismissal laws to ten selected countries from around the developed world: Australia, Chile, France, Germany, Israel, Japan, Spain, Sweden, the United Kingdom and the United States. Between them, these countries afford a representation of unfair dismissal laws in developed economies that are spread across four different continents.[31]

Of these, the last is easily dealt with. In terms of legal protection for job security, the US is a clear 'outlier' among developed countries. There is statutory protection against dismissal for certain reasons, notably those which are based on discriminatory factors such as gender, race or age, or which relate to the exercise of collective bargaining rights. Collective agreements also typically provide that an employee may only be dismissed for 'just cause', a matter on which an independent arbitrator can be asked to rule. But Montana is the only State to have adopted a Wrongful Discharge from Employment Act that extends similar protection to non-unionised workers. At common law, employment is generally treated as being 'at will', terminable at any time for any reason, whether good or bad. While State courts have been prepared to impose liability for discharging employees in retaliation for seeking to exercise their legal rights, or in breach of a clear commitment to provide secure employment, few jurisdictions have been prepared to adopt a more general requirement of good faith and fair dealing.[32]

Leaving aside the US, of the remaining nine countries, only Australia, France, Spain and Sweden have ratified ILO Convention 158. Nonetheless, they each have provisions in force at the national level which are consistent with some, or all, of the core requirements of ILO Convention 158. For example, all provide some protections against wrongful and unfair dismissals by requiring that any termination be based on a valid reason or on objectively reasonable grounds. Almost all these countries exclude one or more categories of workers from the scope of application of provisions related to termination of employment under their domestic legislation, while a few have sought to exclude certain types of enterprises. We will now explore some of these variations in more detail.[33]

---

30 Kahn-Freund, Otto. 1966. 'Comparative Law as an Academic Subject,' 82 *Law Quarterly Review* 40–61, at p. 41.

31 In the following section on economic dismissals we expand our sample group of countries to include countries such as Austria, Denmark and Greece because of their particular experiences of law reform in that area.

32 Brudney, James J. 2011. 'Reluctance and Remorse: The Covenant of Good Faith and Fair Dealing in American Employment Law,' 32 *Comparative Labor Law & Policy Journal* 773–808.

33 Most of the information that follows is drawn from: International Labour Organisation, 2011. Termination of Employment Instruments. Background Paper for the Tripartite Meeting of Experts to Examine the Termination of Employment Convention, 1982 (No. 158), and the Termination of Employment Recommendation, 1982 (No. 166), ILO, Geneva ILO 2011a. For an

It is an accepted principle, recognised in Article 2(b) of ILO Convention 158, that workers can be excluded from unjust dismissal law during their initial period of employment. A legitimate period of probation enables an employer to have the time to see if the decision made to recruit a worker is supported by their actual job performance. The qualifying period ranges from two weeks to two years for our selected group of countries, with Chile the only jurisdiction to possess no such period for unjust dismissal laws, except for a two-week period for domestic workers. The UK is the most restrictive in this regard, with the Cameron Government doubling the previous qualifying period of one year from April 2012.[34] Both Australia and Germany impose a qualifying period of six months, although in the former jurisdiction small businesses are permitted a 12-month period before they are exposed to an unfair dismissal claim. Japanese law provides that the requirement to give 30 days' notice of dismissal does not apply to workers during a probationary period, but the Act does not fix that period. The notice requirement also does not apply to workers who have been employed for 14 days or less. In Sweden probationary periods are generally established by collective agreement and are not to exceed six months. In Israel a permitted period of probation is not prescribed by legislation, although most collective agreements have trial periods ranging from six months to three years. In Spain this period is generally established by collective agreement, although in the absence of any such provision it may not exceed six months for skilled technicians or two months for other workers. But a legal reform came into force in 2011, allowing small companies with less than 50 employees to hire young people and to fix a probationary period of one year.

Article 8 of ILO Convention 158 requires that a worker be permitted to appeal the employer's dismissal decision to an impartial body. This requirement of an independent and external adjudicative mechanism is aimed to safeguard the worker's right to query the fairness of the employer's decision to dismiss. All of our selected countries except for Japan, Sweden and the US permit this appeal to a specialised labour court or tribunal. In Chile workers can go to the labour inspectorate to challenge an unjustified, unfair or improper dismissal. The inspectorate is obliged to mediate the dispute. If mediation does not result in any agreement the worker may elect to proceed to arbitration. In Spain, Australia and France conciliation is a mandatory precursor to a final decision by a labour tribunal or court. In the UK a person claiming unjust dismissal can use arbitration, which precludes the possibility of proceeding to the tribunal. In the alternative, a person can choose conciliation. If this fails, a person can then proceed to the employment tribunal. In Israel the Labour Court resolves unjust

older but still useful study, see: Wheeler, Hoyt N., and Jacques Rojot. 1992. *Workplace Justice: Employment Obligations in International Perspective*. Columbia: University of South Carolina Press.

[34] The UK's period of qualification has been amended many times since the introduction of unfair dismissal laws in 1971. Claire Kilpatrick observes that the rationales for limiting access to the unfair dismissal jurisdiction in the early period were 'very different' to those raised after 1979, when the Thatcher Conservative Government reinstated a two-year qualifying period, first for small firms and then (in 1985) on a general basis. Upon forming the government, in 1997 Labour amended the qualifying period to be of one-year duration, which remained consistent during its time in office. Kilpatrick, Claire. 2003. 'Has New Labour Reconfigured Employment Legislation?' 32 *Industrial Law Journal* 135–63, p. 147.

dismissal disputes, whereas in Japan there is no specialist labour tribunal as disputes that cannot be resolved through conciliation must be litigated in the ordinary civil courts. Relatively few cases are actually litigated, between 2000 and 3000 per year.[35]

All nine of our selected jurisdictions limit how much time a worker is given to mount an unjust dismissal application. Article 8(3) of Convention 158 stipulates that a worker is deemed to have waived any right to appeal against the termination of their employment if they do not exercise that right within a reasonable period. Australia has a very strict time limit, as claims must be lodged within 21 days of dismissal (recently increased from 14 days), although this can be extended under exceptional circumstances. In Sweden, there is a general time limit of two weeks, although this is one month if the employee was not informed of the procedures for challenging the employer's dismissal decision. If the employee is seeking only damages and not reinstatement, then the time limit is extended to four months. In Spain complaints against dismissal must be lodged within 20 days, whilst in Germany the time limit is one of three weeks. In the UK claims must be lodged within three months from when dismissal occurred, while in Chile if mediation is unsuccessful a worker has 60 days from their termination to take the employer before the employment tribunal.

The ability of the independent adjudicator to award a remedy of reinstatement and/or compensation is an essential component of the law of unjust dismissal. Each of the selected countries provides for one or both of these remedies. In Australia, Germany, Israel and the UK, compensation may be awarded where reinstatement is impracticable, although there are caps on the amount. In Sweden the compensation amount includes pay and other employment benefits to which the employee may be entitled, although damages are capped by reference to an employee's total period of employment at the time of dissolution of the employment relationship. In Chile there is no general right to reinstatement following unfair dismissal. Reinstatement is available only in cases of termination based on discriminatory grounds and in those cases related to the termination of workers who benefit from special status-based protection. In Spain, by contrast, reinstatement with back pay is mandatory if the dismissal is deemed a nullity. If the termination is judged invalid or where the requirements applicable for objective dismissal have not been observed, the employer can choose between reinstatement plus back pay or compensation according to a prescribed formula. If the terminated employee is a workers' representative, the employee makes the choice between reinstatement and compensation. Collective agreements can allocate to the unfairly dismissed worker the right to choose between these remedies. In Japan, if the reason for dismissal is considered invalid, the employer is compelled to continue the

[35] Tsuneki, Atsushi, and Manabu Matsunaka. 2011. 'Labor Relations and Labor Law in Japan,' 20 Pacific Rim Law and Policy Journal 529–662.

Matthew Finkin et al. note that in 2008 only 719 court actions were filed in Japan seeking a formal 'declaration of status'. This represented just 0.01 applications per 1000 workers. By contrast, the rate of 'individual discharge complaints' was higher in the other countries covered in the study, ranging from 0.13 per 1000 workers in the US to 1.24 in Australia, 4.23 in Germany and 20.09 in Brazil. See: Finkin, Matthew W., Joel Cutcher-Gershenfeld, Takashi Araki, Philipp Fischinger, Roberto Fragale Filho, Andrew Stewart and Bernd Waas. 2013. *Multinational Human Resource Management and the Law*. Cheltenham and Northampton, Mass.: Edward Elgar, at p. 228.

employment relationship. This does not always mean the worker is restored to the position they held before but the employer must pay wages as long as the labour contract is in effect. If dismissal for a valid reason occurs without 30 days notice, the employee is entitled to wages for the notice period.

In some jurisdictions there has been a growing desire to exclude small businesses from unjust dismissal laws. There is some provision for this in Convention 158, as Article 2(5) allows countries to exclude from the application of the Convention workers 'in respect of which special problems of a substantial nature arise in the light of … the size or nature of the undertaking that employs them'; although strictly speaking such exclusions can only be made prior to the country in question submitting its first report to the ILO under Article 22 of the ILO Constitution. The threshold of the number of workers employed tends to vary between countries. In Germany businesses with less than five workers are excluded, whereas in Australia the figure has been as high as 100 – an exemption that can scarcely be justified as protecting 'small' enterprises!

The Australian exclusion was introduced in 2005 by the conservative Howard government as part of its controversial 'Work Choices' reforms. It followed a decade of unsuccessful attempts to secure parliamentary support for a small business exemption aimed at firms with less than 15 or (under later proposals) 20 employees.[36] The eventual cut-off figure of 100, implemented after the government finally gained control of the Australian Senate, was apparently a compromise between those in the governing Liberal/National Coalition who wished to implement the previous proposals (which has been part of the policy platform taken to the 2004 election) and those who wanted to take the opportunity to abolish unfair dismissal protection entirely. In the result, the Coalition was thrown out of office in 2007, in large part because of public disquiet over this and other aspects of the Work Choices laws. The 'Fair Work' laws introduced by the Australian Labor Party in 2009 have now restored unfair dismissal access to employees at smaller businesses, although as noted above those at firms with less than 15 workers must still serve a longer qualifying period (12 months as opposed to six months).[37]

In France, new legislation was passed in 2005 enabling enterprises with fewer than 20 employees to employ workers without providing the protection required under ILO Convention 158 during their first two years of employment. However a union challenge to the legitimacy of this law under the Convention led to a finding by the Court of Cassation that the Convention was directly applicable and that two years could not be considered a reasonable period under Article 2(b). The legislation was abrogated in 2008. More recently, in the UK the Cameron Government considered, and then

[36] It was repeatedly claimed, without any support from the available evidence, that such a reform would increase job creation in the small business sector. See: Robbins, W. and G. Voll. 2005. 'The Case for Unfair Dismissal Reform: A Review of the Evidence,' 31 *Australian Bulletin of Labour* 237–54. More recent research for the OECD has confirmed that changes in the unfair dismissal threshold in Australia have had 'no impact on hiring, firing or working hours'. See OECD, Employment Outlook 2013, *supra* note 7, at p. 72.

[37] Chapman, Protections in Relation to Dismissal, *supra* note 28.

rejected, a compensated no-fault dismissal system that would effectively exempt businesses with less than ten employees from the unfair dismissal system.[38]

By way of conclusion, this comparison has revealed the significant extent to which many countries possess laws protecting employees from unjust dismissal. While these laws have been subject to continuous reform since their inception, all of the selected countries except the US provide that an employee can query the fairness of their dismissal through an independent adjudicative mechanism. Notwithstanding the fact that there are some differences in the protective quality of the selected countries' unfair dismissal laws and the attempts in many of these countries to impose exclusions limiting access to the unfair dismissal jurisdictions, it remains true that of the ten countries, only the US makes no attempt to comply with the spirit and letter of ILO Convention 158. Aside from the US, the norm in our selected group is still the availability of unfair dismissal protection.

4. ECONOMIC DISMISSALS

Turning now to economic dismissals, contemporary efforts to regulate the termination of employment on the ground of redundancy largely reflect the philosophy of 'flexicurity' identified earlier in this chapter. This idea recognises that employers should be free to structure their workforces for economic reasons. However, this is not an unconditional or absolute power, not only because the desire to enjoy a sustainable economic system with potential for growth requires the employer to have good organisational models which, in decision-making, are governed by criteria of rationality and proportionality, but also because a lack of control over labour market exit flows unquestionably generates social costs. Given that economic dismissals impact on both the pension system and the capacity for consumption and investment, a collective viewpoint is essential. Thus, redundancy is typically treated not just as a private contractual matter, but an action with social consequences.

So much is recognised by ILO Convention 158. Articles 13 and 14 apply in cases where an employer is contemplating the termination of employment 'for reasons of an economic, technological, structural or similar nature'. In such a case, the employer must notify both the workers' representatives and a 'competent authority', explaining the reasons for the terminations, and identifying 'the number and categories of workers likely to be affected and the period over which the terminations are intended to be carried out'. The employer must also afford those representatives an opportunity for consultation over measures that might be taken to avert or minimise the terminations or to mitigate their adverse effects, such as finding alternative employment for those concerned. Similar obligations are imposed by EU Directive 98/59/EC concerning collective redundancies for business reasons. The aim of this Directive was to establish

---

[38] UK Department for Business Innovation and Skills, 2012. Dealing with Dismissal and 'Compensated No Fault Dismissal' for Micro Businesses. Government Response; Howe, Joanna. 2013. 'Poles Apart? The Contestation between the Ideas of No Fault Dismissal and Unfair Dismissal for Protecting Job Security,' 42 *Industrial Law Journal* 122–51.

a common procedure, through which to warrant more contractual flexibility and adjustment capacity and to avoid social dumping inside the EU.

Countries have approached the question as to whether to regulate economic dismissals in different ways.[39] Some countries have little or no regulation of such dismissals, leaving any protection for workers to individual or collective bargaining. In the US, for example, the federal Worker Adjustment and Retraining Notification Act requires firms with at least 100 workers to give 60 days' notice of a plant closure, or of a 'mass layoff' involving more than a prescribed number of employees. But nothing is said about any requirement to consult with the affected workers, or about how any resulting dismissals should be handled.

Another model involves the specific recognition of redundancy for economic reasons as a good cause for terminating an employment contract. This is the case in all the EU Member States, but also in the Philippines, where an authorised reason for dismissal includes the installation of labour-saving devices, cutbacks to prevent losses, and the closure of the business. The same is true in China, where Article 41 of the Employment Contract Act allows dismissals for various reasons pertaining to the economic situation of the business. Australian law likewise protects employers against any claim for unfair dismissal by an employee who has 'genuinely' been made redundant, provided the employer has discharged any consultation obligations of the type discussed below and explored options for redeploying the employee elsewhere in its business. In Mexico too, the causes for contract termination without penalty include a lack of profitable production and the legal declaration of insolvency or bankruptcy.

As these examples demonstrate, in most regions of the world there are express references to economic dismissals and specific legal provisions to regulate how they are effected, most of them different from or adapting the rules applicable to ordinary (personal) dismissals.

Some legal systems expressly exclude protection against economic dismissals for certain types of business. For example in Austria, Germany, Denmark, Greece, France, Italy and Luxemburg, public administration workers are exempt from the general law on economic dismissals, as it is understood that governments do not operate under market criteria. But it should be noted that this rule has been changed in some countries particularly affected by both the economic and public deficit crisis, as for example in Spain, where the most recent labour reform allows public servants with labour contracts to be made redundant.

Another increasingly important exception concerns the size of the business employing the workers who are dismissed for economic reasons. In the EU both Community and national standards typically differentiate between individual and collective agreements, not only from the perspective of the affected employees, but also from the point of view of the company's size. In Germany the general regulations do not apply to companies with fewer than ten workers, while in Austria the limit is set at five workers. In Italy and Australia in the case of businesses with fewer than 15 workers, some exemptions from general redundancy laws exist, while in Luxembourg businesses with

---

39 As with the section on personal dismissals, information about each country's laws on economic dismissals has largely been sourced from ILO, Termination of Employment Instruments, *supra* note 33.

fewer than 150 workers have to consult the affected worker about the dismissal and, in the case of businesses with fewer than 20 workers, the employer can choose between redundancy pay and extending the notice period. In Sweden for businesses with fewer than ten workers the selection measures for workers affected by dismissal are relaxed. These attempts to minimise the impact of regulations concerning economic dismissals on small- and medium-sized businesses mirror reforms to unfair dismissal laws discussed earlier in this chapter. The aim of such laws is to offer some guarantees in the event that dismissals have a major socio-economic impact, while at the same time trying not to burden SMEs (small or medium enterprises) with legal requirements that might deter economic activity.

In some countries too, there are special protections for workers with particular attributes. For example Argentina establishes an increase in compensation costs for workers who are pregnant, have just given birth or are on maternity leave, workers who have just got married or workers who are on sick leave. In Austria, further protection exists for workers' representatives, as well as those on a compulsory leave of absence because they hold a public post, are on military service or are carrying out mediation activities. Other countries such as Germany, Belgium, Greece, Denmark, Finland, France, the Netherlands and Portugal all provide additional protection for certain types of workers based on their personal attributes. In the UK workers' representatives, workers under effective judicial protection, whistleblowers, workers who refuse to work on Sundays and workers on jury service are among those singled out for protection from economic dismissals.

Some legal systems even go further, demanding that prior authorisation should be obtained from the relevant administrative authority. In Germany this approval must occur in the case of pregnant and disabled workers and workers on parental leave, whereas in Greece it is required for workers with disabilities. In Austria and the Netherlands this approval must be sought from the courts or, in the case of Germany where the dismissal is of a workers' representative, from workers' representative bodies. Some of these guarantees also apply to personal dismissals, but the previous intervention of a public authority means that they can be more easily controlled. It is also relevant to consider that in the case of collective dismissals that can affect such types of worker, the aim of these kinds of measure is to protect their employability and make it easier to get a new job. So in the EU, for example, a list of the people affected and their positions in the organisation must sometimes be attached to the documentation given to the public authority and employee representative.

In the case of economic dismissals for certain groups, some countries go further and recognise periods of legal protection when dismissal is entirely prohibited. This again applies to groups who, if dismissed, would probably suffer an increase in job insecurity or who would find it difficult to return to the labour market. Normally, these are factors associated with age. In Brazil collective bargaining normally establishes special protection for workers who are within two years of retirement. In China, workers with more than 15 years' seniority at the company who have less than five years to retirement enjoy this protection. A new obligation recently introduced in Spain stipulates that in the case of collective dismissals affecting employees over 50-years-old in businesses with over 100 employees and under certain conditions,[40] the employer must refund any unemployment benefits provided to the worker by the relevant government agency.

Once particular workers are selected for redundancy, the law seeks to regulate the procedure to be followed by businesses seeking to make redundancies for economic reasons. As a general rule, notice of any kind of dismissal has to be given in writing in order to preserve the worker's right to object. This means the reason and the effective date of the termination of the contract must be made clear. The requirement of notice has multiple aims: first, to ensure that workers can prepare their defence and challenge the decision; secondly, so that they have enough time to look for another job without losing their current one; thirdly, to give employers an opportunity to undertake any retraining or skilling measures that may be required either by law, by the terms of a collective agreement or by their own policies; and finally, to allow negotiations over alternative solutions or measures that will reduce the impact of the dismissal. The duration of notice periods may range from one or two weeks up to several months, and generally depend on the duration of the worker's service. For example, in Ireland the minimum notice period is one week, rising to eight weeks for relationships lasting more than 15 years. In the Netherlands, the equivalent range is one to four months. The required period of notice is usually longer than that mandated for personal dismissals.

Another procedural requirement is for information to be provided to workers' representatives and for consultation to occur, or even for redundancies to be agreed with them. In EU countries, this intervention is normal in the case of redundancies based on economic reasons, both when their impact is individual (when the intervention is basically for information) and in the case of group redundancies (when a period of consultation with employee representatives is required). Such intervention is rooted in the idea that workers' representation within the business is a democratic guarantee of protection for workers' interests. By participating in a redundancy process, representatives can put forward proposals of their own, oversee proper compliance with procedural regulations or even immunise the terminations against a legal challenge. Under recent legal reforms in Spain, for instance, an agreement between an employer and an employee representative may have the effect of waiving some (though not all) rights to appeal the validity of the dismissals.

It is normal in these cases for legislators to limit the duration of any consultation process to prevent any delay that might worsen the commercial position of the business, and to accelerate the outplacement process or the employees' participation in active employment policies. In Austria, the employer has to discuss the redundancy with the workers' representatives for at least three days. If the company gives notice of the redundancy before five days have elapsed or before they have given their opinion, the dismissal will be null and void. In Denmark, the dismissal of a workers' representative requires an eight-day period of negotiation with the trade union. In France, in the case of redundancies of fewer than ten workers, the employer has to call the workers' representatives to meetings at least twice. The first meeting is to give them the information its decision is based on and the second is consultative but not binding.

[40] These include that the proportion of dismissed employees over 50 is greater than the general proportion of such employees in the business.

In the case of redundancies affecting more than ten workers, Article 1233-34 of the Labour Code establishes an obligation to meet at least three times and the procedure can last between two and six months. In Luxembourg, in the case of companies with more than 150 workers, the worker has to be invited to discuss the redundancy. The employer has to send a copy of the invitation to the workers' representatives or, failing that, to the Employment Inspectorate. The meeting must be held within two days of the written notification.

The information the employer has to provide during this period is usually the same in all EU countries mandating such a procedure: documentary proof of the alleged reasons for dismissal; how the workforce has changed in the months immediately prior to the redundancies; the criteria by which the affected workers have been selected; the benefits or support they will be given; and an outline of actions to be taken during the dismissal process.

In legal systems where consultation with workers' representatives is required, it is critical that the employer gives them enough information about the reasons for its decision and sets aside sufficient time between meetings so that the representatives can study this and properly evaluate their response, in some cases with the help of experts. For example, Article L.2323-78 of the French Labour Code can require the involvement of a chartered accountant, whose fees will be paid by the company. The accountant will have access to the relevant information and documentation on the restructuring contemplated and will prepare a report for the works council's attention, which will then be presented by the council to the company management. French regulations do not limit the period during which the chartered accountant can be involved, so that if the workers' representatives demand an accountant's involvement and ask to wait for the report before giving their opinion, the process can be slowed down by around two months. Any breach of these obligations can cause a dismissal to be declared void. This is the case in Spain, where the law specifies a duty to bargain in good faith and there have been several court decisions to that effect.

Economic dismissals ordinarily result in redundancy pay being given to the worker, although this is not mandated by ILO Convention 158.[41] It is interesting to observe, however, that in countries such as Germany, Denmark and Greece, the consequence of a dismissal being declared null and void or unfair may be compulsory reinstatement instead of redundancy pay. Even in these cases, the redundancy pay option may be an alternative solution to reinstatement, such as in Italy for businesses with more than 60 workers, or merely a subsidiary one which can depend on the wishes of the worker, as in the Netherlands, Portugal and France. The German system stipulates that it is up to a judge to determine whether there has been an irreconcilable breakdown in trust and confidence, such that it is impossible to re-establish the employment relationship. It is similar in France and Ireland, where a commissioner or tribunal has the discretion to order reinstatement or redundancy pay.

---

[41] Article 12 of the Convention merely requires that a worker terminated for economic or personal reasons (other than serious misconduct) *either* receive 'a severance allowance or other separation benefits … based inter alia on length of service and the level of wages', to be paid by the employer or a fund to which the employer has contributed, *or* have access to unemployment or other social security benefits.

As with notice of termination, the amount of redundancy pay that must be provided is typically linked to the employee's length of service, but it may also depend on the age of the employee, the sector or profession in which they work, or the size of the employer's business. The maximum amounts payable vary dramatically. In Sweden, for example, a worker who is made redundant over the age of 60 with more than ten years' service may be entitled up to four years' pay. By contrast, in Australia the maximum severance pay mandated by federal law is just 16 weeks' pay – although it is common for higher amounts to be required by collective agreements. In some countries, additional redundancy pay can be imposed where procedural rules are breached, or where the dismissed worker remains unemployed for a particular period after dismissal. The latter is the case in Azerbaijan, which obliges the employer to pay two extra months' wages if the public employment service certifies that the worker has been unable over that period to find another job. Other nations, such as Luxembourg, have opted for a system of redundancy pay that can be replaced with long notice periods to make it easier for the worker to find a new job.

It is precisely the fact that redundancy pay has become a labour cost – and a large one as workers gain seniority and levels of qualification – that explains why countries such as Spain have sought to reduce the amounts involved in order to promote hiring, reduce unemployment rates and activate the economy. This is not an uncontroversial matter, as shown by the fierce debate in Italy over the abolition of Article 18 of the Workers' Statute, which guarantees a minimum of five months' wages. Some countries have established capitalisation funds that are activated at the time of redundancies. In Austria, for example, the employer must set up a 'Bietrebliche Vorsorgekasse' (contribution fund), paid for by monthly contributions deducted from the worker's wages which can be accessed in the case of redundancy. In Brazil, the employer is obliged to establish a capitalisation fund into which it pays 8 per cent of the workers' wages every month and which can be accessed upon retirement or in the case of dismissal without just cause.

There has also been an open debate in the EU around the idea that the focus should not be on quantitative aspects (amounts of redundancy pay), but on active employment policies that improve the quality of outcomes for retrenched workers. The paradigmatic example has been France, which has recently adopted a series of legislative changes to strengthen protection for workers and guarantee them support to prevent their exclusion from the labour market. In the case of an individual redundancy, a business with fewer than 1000 workers must offer the worker a 'contrat de sécurisation professionnelle' (professional employability agreement), under which the employer will provide psychological assistance, professional counselling and coaching, professional ability evaluation and training to facilitate the employee's redeployment after their dismissal. Larger employers must offer a period of 'redeployment leave' which may last between four and nine months and during which the employee is not obliged to come to work but still receives 65 per cent of their former wage. In the case of redundancies affecting more than ten workers, the employer must present an Employment Safeguard Plan, with information about the measures proposed to limit the number of dismissals or avoid them (part-time jobs, professional training, outplacement, financial or organisational support to help the employees to find new jobs, etc).

This type of regulation is inspired by the principle of 'transversality' which, in practice, means, first, a reform and modernisation of employment services and, secondly, a reform of workers' training and adaptation based on the arc of their professional career. Provisions such as those just described introduce a new element to the debate about workers' rights, one that is concerned not so much with the promotion of wage or job stability, as with meeting new needs for outplacement and reassignment.

5. THE DEBATE OVER EMPLOYMENT PROTECTION LAWS

In this chapter thus far, we have explored how different countries approach the challenges arising from personal and economic dismissals. As we have seen, the desire to protect job security has been increasingly juxtaposed against an emerging agenda of achieving favourable economic outcomes for businesses and national economies. In this second part of the chapter, we now seek to unpack the normative underpinnings of recent reforms to the regulation of job loss, first in terms of theories of justification of employment protection, second, economic effects of these laws and third, in relation to broader debates over legal origins.

(a) Theoretical Perspectives

All of our selected countries, other than the US, have accepted the case for protection of job loss to varying degrees. Commentators who support the idea of protecting employees from unjust dismissal commonly stress the importance of the job to the individual, to the broader community and even to the economy. Other theorists, however, criticise laws requiring just cause in dismissal as unduly interfering with the contract of employment. Trying to marry these opposing views are a number of writers who support the concept of unfair dismissal protection but seek to advocate its efficient operation. Each of these perspectives will now be discussed in turn.

Frederic Meyers' concept of job property provides one basis for building a legal framework against arbitrary dismissal.[42] It rests upon the discernment of a proprietary interest acquired during a period in employment. The tangible asset being taken away by dismissal is the employee's labour services, causing the deprivation not just of income but potentially of an employee's dignity, autonomy, livelihood, sense of self-worth, membership of a union and place in the community. This notion has been recently developed by Wanjiru Njoya in her influential work on job security and job property.[43] While Meyers advocated reinstatement as the remedy for unfair dismissal, Njoya proposes a more nuanced version of job property which accepts the contemporary dominance of compensation payments as the primary remedy in many national unfair dismissal systems. She states that the idea of job property is 'not simply on trying to keep one's job at all costs, but on drawing attention to the true value involved

---

[42] Meyers, Frederic, 1964. *Ownership of Jobs: A comparative Study*. Berkeley: University of California.

[43] Njoya, Wanjiru. 2007. *Property in Work*. Aldershot: Ashgate.

when the job was lost'.[44] By contrast, Bob Hepple canvasses the more limited possibility of unfair dismissal law being used to achieve a 'right to remain continuously employed including the right to re-employment in the event of unjustified termination'.[45] Unlike theories of job property, which recognise the power of employees to have relative control and autonomy over their jobs, this 'right to work' perspective focuses upon the extent to which an employee who is arbitrarily dismissed can insist upon returning to their job.

'Industrial justice' is another concept that provides justification for laws protecting against arbitrary dismissal. As developed by Hugh Collins, this notion hinges on two principles: first, that there needs to be a restraint on absolute managerial prerogative to terminate the employment contract; and second, that the 'interest' being protected by legislative intervention is the individual employee's self-worth, which goes beyond the remuneration they receive for their work. These two strands justify legislative intervention on the basis that management power needs to be regulated so as to enhance the 'opportunities for people to bring meaning to their lives through work'.[46] Collins draws upon the writings of Joseph Raz to develop a justification for unfair dismissal law based on the principle of autonomy, arguing that a liberal society should foster worthwhile opportunities for people to pursue their personal goals and become 'the author of his or her own life'.[47] The earlier work of Selznick on industrial justice likewise advocated the use of state regulation to reduce arbitrariness in managerial decision-making.[48] In his view, while the application of the rule of law to industrial relations initially acts as a constraint upon managerial prerogative, its end result is transformative, because it achieves more than the correct exercise of power. He argues:

> The 'progressive reduction of arbitrariness' knows no near stopping-place. The closer we look at that process, the more we realise that it calls for an affirmative view of what it means to participate in a legal order, whether as citizens, judge or executive. In its richest connotation, legality evokes the Greek view of a social order founded in reason, whose constitutive principle is justice.[49]

Closely linked to the notion of 'justice', as this quote would suggest, is that of 'citizenship'. Ron McCallum and Judy Fudge have each drawn upon ideas of industrial citizenship to provide a theoretical basis for protecting against arbitrary dismissal.[50] Citizenship theory can also be deployed to support a floor of minimum wages and

---

44 Ibid., at p. 63.

45 Hepple, Bob. 1981. 'A Right to Work,' 10 *Industrial Law Journal* 65–83, at p. 76.

46 Collins, Hugh. 1992. *Justice in Dismissal: The Law of Termination of Employment*. Oxford: Clarendon Press, p. 19.

47 Raz, Joseph. 1986. *The Morality of Freedom*. Oxford: Clarendon Press, pp. 369–73, p. 417.

48 Selznick, Philip, Philippe Nonet and Howard M. Vollmer. 1969. *Law, Society and Industrial Justice*. New York: Russell Sage Foundation. pp. 12–13.

49 Ibid., at p. 18.

50 McCallum, Ronald C. 1996. 'The New Millennium and the Higgins Heritage: Industrial Relations in the 21st Century,' 38 *Journal of Industrial Relations* 294–312; Fudge, Judy. 2005. 'After Industrial Citizenship: Market Citizenship or Citizenship at Work?,' 60 *Relations Industrielles* 631–56.

conditions to protect labour, participatory institutions where worker representation is uncontested and a right to collectively bargain.[51] But already in the second edition of his influential work *Contemporary Political Philosophy*, Will Kymlicka penned an additional chapter on citizenship because of its increasing popularity amongst theorists and policy-makers.[52] His conclusion was that notions of 'justice' are merely being repackaged into notions of 'citizenship' and that it may simply be a 'matter of putting old wine into new bottles'.[53] His argument is that 'what used to be rejected as intrinsically wrong (unjust), is now said to be instrumentally wrong (as eroding the virtues needed to sustain a liberal-democratic order)'.[54] He does not think that merely because citizenship arguments are invoked strategically that they are invalid, but suggests that more work needs to be done to differentiate citizenship theory from theories of justice.

Some scholars raise ideas of 'employability' or 'employment security' as justifications for protective regimes which go beyond traditional unfair dismissal law as conceived by ILO Convention 158. They argue that the contract of employment could include a positive duty upon employers to invest in the consistent and meaningful training of their staff. This translates into making their employees more secure in their current job but also with a better chance of securing future employment should they be made redundant. The substantial work by Katherine Stone on what she calls the 'new psychological contract' has led her to argue that long-term employment with a single employer and advancement up a single job ladder is no longer the norm in the 'new economy'.[55] In her view job security protected through unfair dismissal law is of no help to the contemporary worker embarking on a 'boundaryless career'. She defines this as 'a career which unfolds unconstrained by clear boundaries around job activities by fixed sequences of such activities, or by attachment to one organisation'.[56] Stone says that there is now a new 'job insecurity reality' which can only be addressed through the promise of employability security. In her view this security is not just created by governments promoting robust labour markets but involves the imposition of positive obligations upon employers to promise their employees that they will provide opportunities to develop their human capital through an investment in training and skills development. Even if there are no promotional opportunities available or if their job becomes redundant, then the employee is in a better place to become 'an entrepreneur marketing their own human capital in a market place'.[57] Stone advocates the development of a 'model employability contract' by which the firm promises to upgrade worker skills and to help provide new job opportunities should those at the

---

51 These are a few of the commonly regarded aspects of an industrial citizenship model. For a more detailed discussion, see: Ronald McCallum, 1997, 'Crafting a New Collective Labour Law for Australia' *Journal of Industrial Relations* 405.

52 Kymlicka, Will. 2002. *Contemporary Political Philosophy: An Introduction* (2nd ed.). Oxford: Oxford University Press.

53 Ibid., at p. 319.

54 Ibid., at p. 318.

55 Stone, Katherine V. W. 2001. 'The New Psychological Contract: Implications of the Changing Workplace for Labor and Employment Law,' 48 *UCLA Law Review* 519–662.

56 Ibid., at p. 554.

57 Ibid., at p. 570.

business disappear.[58] In this way, she views the contract of employment, and not the statutory law of unfair dismissal, as a vehicle for providing protection for the worker. Her idea is that the contract of employment could be used to apply positive duties of investment and training upon the employer which would correspond with the employee's duty to become their very best in order to add value to their employer, or to subsequent employers down the track.

Another scholar to weigh into the employability debate is Hugh Collins.[59] He addresses the challenge of low skilled workers by arguing that the labour force can be divided into three types of employees: the compliant employee, the good faith employee and the flexible employee. For the compliant employee who is unskilled or low skilled, job security protection is needed as there is little avenue for improving their employability. In particular, there may be a case for a minimal level of protection against arbitrary dismissal through a statutory right not to be dismissed without just cause. However, for the other two categories of employees, the aim should be to achieve employment security. He argues that the 'good faith employee' – an employee who is generally cooperative with her employer and performs her job according to what is expected under the contract – should seek to become the ideal type, that is, the 'flexible employee'. He notes that 'the flexible employee does not simply work hard at her job but uses all her skills and knowledge to contribute to the process of continuous improvements in quality, efficiency and technological and product innovation'.[60] Like Stone, Collins advocates the contract of employment as the best vehicle for enforcing employability or employment security. As he observes, 'the contract of employment guards against abuse of managerial discretion by constituting and enforcing a job specification, thereby achieving institutional stability in employment relations'.[61] He goes on to write that 'the common law reinforces this institutional arrangement both by enforcing job specifications as express terms of the contract and by placing weak limits on the exercise of managerial discretion through implied terms'.[62] Given this basis, Collins argues that the common law contract of employment could be strengthened in what it requires of employers and employees.

Unlike Stone, Collins draws a distinction between employment security and employability. He disregards the latter as too speculative because it is unlikely to provide the assurance needed to the employee to establish stable institutional structures for the flexible employee relation. He says that the employee needs to acquiesce in becoming flexible, that is, the ideal type. The promise of employability due to a higher level of skill, meaning that the dismissed worker has a better chance of obtaining a good job with another employer, is too speculative and insubstantial in the present to be a sufficient motivation for the employee to become the ideal type. Thus, Collins argues that labour law should seek to achieve 'employment security' which is the idea that 'the employment relation will continue indefinitely, but the employee will have to perform

---

58 Ibid., at p. 569.

59 Collins, Hugh. 2001. 'Regulating the Employment Relation for Competitiveness,' 30 *Industrial Law Journal* 17–48.

60 Ibid., at p. 24.

61 Ibid., at p. 27.

62 Ibid.

different kinds of work, for which training will be required.'[63] Unlike unfair dismissal law, which is conceived as employment protection for the employee but at a cost to the employer, the concept of employment security offers a win/win to both parties to the employment contract. He argues:

> For the employer, this commitment is a crucial long-term strategy for improving competitiveness by means of investment in human capital. For the employee, the commitment to training is an essential component to the promise of employment security and employability that replaces the earlier commitment to job security. Default rules that reflected such an economic model would require the employer to provide worthwhile training opportunities, including training in general skills, and require the employee to take up those opportunities.[64]

Collins acknowledges that the weakness of his proposals lies in the 'normal defect of private law regulation: its weak sanction'.[65] He suggests that this could be overcome through a mandatory legal right, similar to the right to paid leave, that would enable the employee to take a certain number of days as paid leave to participate in employer-initiated training. According to Collins 'the reason why a mandatory legal right serves effectively to strengthen the commitment in this case is that the right is self-enforcing: the employee takes the time off work. It does not suffer from the weakness that the exercise of the right requires the threat to take an employer to court'.[66]

For some writers, by contrast, the very concept of state regulation of employment termination is unacceptable. Richard Epstein argues that such intervention alters the entire fabric of contract law by creating an environment that makes it difficult for the vast majority of good employers and good employees to structure their relationships efficiently.[67] He says that the whole purpose of the unfair dismissal system is to target the less likely occurrence of a bad employer and thus it is inefficient as 'it exposes every decision in labour markets to second guessing by either a court or an administrative agency'. In defending the concept of at-will employment, he argues that market forces alone can be relied upon to dissuade or punish arbitrary or unreasonable behaviour, since employers who treat their workforce poorly will be unable to attract or retain good staff and thus will lose ground on their competitors.

There are many who would challenge this idealistic vision of the labour market – not least the assumption that the average employee (as opposed, for instance, to the average executive) has the necessary bargaining power, information and/or mobility to allow them to pick and choose between employers.[68] Nevertheless, what unites the otherwise very disparate views offered by scholars such as Epstein and Collins is a concern with the potential *economic effects* of employment protection laws – and to that we now turn.

---

[63] Ibid., at p. 24.
[64] Ibid., at p. 40.
[65] Ibid., at p. 44.
[66] Ibid., at p. 45.
[67] Epstein, Richard A. 2001. 'The Common Law and the Labour Market,' HR Nicholls Society. Available at http://www.hrnicholls.com.au/articles/hrn-epstein.php.
[68] See for example; Weiler, Paul C. 1990. *Governing the Workplace: The Future of Labor and Employment Law*. Cambridge: Harvard University Press, at pp. 56–78.

(b) Economic Effects

In each of our selected countries there have been some attempts to reform laws regulating job loss, predicated on a belief that these laws impede a country's economic prosperity. Indeed it has become an article of faith for many that employment protection laws must be wound back in order to promote productivity and economic growth.[69] This is particularly true of business groups. For example, at a Tripartite Meeting of Experts convened in April 2011 to examine the ILO's standards on termination of employment, the spokesperson for the employer representatives present noted that 'strict employment protection regulation [of the type] encouraged by Convention No 158 increases the costs of hiring workers, and also hits hardest the weakest groups in the labour market'.[70] While acknowledging the need for constraints on 'abusive and arbitrary dismissal', and for workers to be afforded notice of termination, he stressed the need to ensure that any protections 'do not unduly burden employers and hence their ability and willingness to hire'.[71]

Views of this kind find support in a neoclassical approach to labour economics that treats such laws as an interference with the efficient operation of the labour market. At the microeconomic level, unfair dismissal regulation of the type conceived by ILO Convention 158 is said to create a disincentive for employees to work productively. In part, this is because it is difficult for an employer who wishes to replace a capable but relatively unproductive employee to establish inadequacy of performance as a good reason for dismissal.[72] More commonly, however, critics of employment protection laws focus on their macro effects. For example, it is asserted that by making job shedding more costly, unfair dismissal laws reduce the overall demand for labour.[73] For example, earlier in this chapter we discussed the case of Australia's controversial Work Choices reforms, which removed unfair dismissal protection for workers in businesses with less than 100 employees. One justification for these reforms was that they would stimulate job creation.[74] In addition, it is commonly asserted that employment

---

[69] See: Beecroft, Adam. 2011. Report on Employment Law, Department for Business Innovation and Skills, United Kingdom. The report, which was commissioned by the UK Coalition Government, proposed the replacement of unfair dismissal law with a system of compensated no fault dismissal.

[70] ILO. 2011. Final Report. Tripartite Meeting of Experts to Examine the Termination of Employment Convention, 1982 (No. 158), and the Termination of Employment Recommendation, 1982 (No. 166), ILO, Geneva, at p. 10.

[71] Ibid. The meeting concluded without any consensus on the future of the ILO termination of employment standards, with the government and worker representatives' support for them being countered by employer demands that they be abrogated and substantially reviewed.

[72] Vandenberghe, Ann-Sophie. 2009. 'Employment Contracts' in Kenneth G. Dau-Schmidt, Seth D. Harris and Orly Lobel, eds., *Labor and Employment Law and Economics*. Cheltenham: Edward Elgar, at p. 70. Davidov, In Defence of (Efficiently Administered) 'Just Cause' Dismissal Laws, *supra* note 27, at p. 129, argues that an efficient unfair dismissal law could mitigate this potential inefficiency by mandating a standard of 'incapability' that would allow employers to discharge employees who are less productive than what is reasonably expected.

[73] See for example: Posner, Richard A. 1989. 'Hegel and Employment at Will: A Comment,' 10 *Cardozo Law Review* 1625–36, at p. 1634.

[74] Chapman, Protections in Relation to Dismissal, *supra* note 28.

protection laws may encourage employers to prefer contingent work relationships that are not covered by labour regulations.[75]

The assumption that dismissal regulation is essentially onerous in nature is supported by the World Economic Forum, which ranks countries according to their 'global competitiveness'.[76] Countries with greater statutory protection against arbitrary dismissal are deemed less competitive on the index, indicating a belief that the laws are prohibitive to job creation and business efficiency. Similar assumptions underlie both the OECD's Employment Protection Index and the much-debated Employing Workers index that appears in the World Bank's Doing Business Reports.[77]

However, it is far from clear that the available evidence fully bears out this assessment of employment protection laws. Few would argue with studies showing the negative impact of extreme restrictions on job shedding, such as laws that forbid workers to be laid off without the government's permission.[78] But beyond that, claims of a detrimental effect have been hotly disputed. This is particularly true of the suggestion that there is a causal link between employment protection measures and rates of unemployment. For every study that has claimed to establish such a link,[79] others have challenged that view.[80]

In a helpful survey of what has become a substantial body of economic research on employment protection legislation, Per Skedinger presents the following findings:[81]

- There is relatively weak evidence for any impact (negative *or* positive) on employment or unemployment levels. Indeed to the contrary, 'there is a great deal of evidence which indicates that both dismissals and hirings decrease at approximately the same rate'.
- There is rather stronger evidence of regressive distributional effects, in that more stringent protection tends to stengthen the employment prospects of those already secure in the labour market, while doing the opposite for young workers and other 'vulnerable groups'.

---

75 See for example: Autor, David H. 2003. 'Outsourcing at Will: The Contribution of Unjust Dismissal Doctrine to the Growth of Employment Outsourcing,' 21 *Journal of Labour Economics* 1–42.

76 World Economic Forum. 2012. The Global Competitiveness Report 2012–2013. World Economic Forum, Geneva.

77 Available, respectively, at http://stats.oecd.org/ and http://www.doingbusiness.org/data/exploretopics/employing-workers.

78 See for example: Fallon, Peter R., and Robert E.B. Lucas. 1993. 'Job Security Regulations and the Dynamic Demand for Industrial Labor in India and Zimbabwe,' 40 *Journal of Development Economics* 241–75.

79 For a paradigmatic example, see: Lazear, Edward P. 1990. 'Job Security Provisions and Employment,' 105 *Quarterly Journal of Economics* 699–726.

80 See for example: Baccaro, Lucio, and Diego Rei. 2007. 'Institutional Determinants of Unemployment in OECD Countries: Does the Deregulatory View Hold Water?,' 61 *International Organization* 527–69; Deakin, Simon, Malmberg, Jonas and Sarkar, Prabirjit. 2014. 'How Do Labour Laws Affect Unemployment and the Labour Share of National Income? The Experience of Six OECD Countries, 1970–2010', 153 *International Labour Review* 1–27.

81 Skedinger, Per. 2011. *Employment Protection Legislation: Evolution, Effects, Winners and Losers.* Cheltenham and Northampton, Mass.: Edward Elgar, at pp. 7–8.

- Many studies reveal a decrease in productivity as a result of strong employment protection, 'probably due to slower structural change and decreased work intensity among the employed'. Conversely, there is only weak support for the proposition that enhanced job security will encourage higher productivity.
- It is 'difficult to prove that employees in countries with stricter employment protection actually perceive greater job security or psychological well-being'.

Overall, Skedinger concludes that 'the evidence is not all that strong regarding many of the cherished and most visible notions in the public discourse surrounding employment protection'.[82]

By contrast, in 2013 the OECD was continuing to insist – quoting rather selectively, it must be said, from the available literature – that 'research on the labour market impact of employment protection has found that overly strict regulations can reduce job flows, have a negative impact on employment of outsiders, encourage labour market duality and hinder productivity and economic growth'.[83] Unsurprisingly then, it expected that the recent wave of reforms would 'increase labour reallocation and [yield] dividends in terms of job creation as well as efficiency and productivity growth in the near future'.[84] At the same time, however, it recognised that there were social costs to labour turnover that would likely be heightened under present economic conditions. It called for a 'comprehensive policy mix' to mitigate the impact on workers, including 'adequate unemployment-benefit schemes' and 'effective re-employment services for jobseekers'.[85]

(c) Legal Origins and Convergence

A similar contest of assumptions and values is evident in the recent literature on the effect of 'legal origins' on economic performance. As part of what David Pozen describes as 'arguably the most important social science research' of recent years,[86] Juan Botero et al explored the link between the strength of labour regulation in a country and the nature of its legal system.[87] Using a 'leximetric' approach that attached a numerical value to statutory rules according to the extent to which they imposed constraints in relation to a standardised employment relationship, they evaluated the

---

[82] Ibid.

[83] OECD Employment Outlook 2013, *supra* note 7, at p. 68.

[84] Ibid., at p. 107.

[85] Ibid.

[86] Pozen, David E. 2006. 'The Regulation of Labor and the Relevance of Legal Origin,' 28 *Comparative Labor Law and Policy Journal* 43–55, at p. 43.

[87] Botero, Juan C., Simeon Djankov, Rafael La Porta, Florencio Lopez-de-Silanes, and Andrei Shleifer. 2004. 'The Regulation of Labor,' 119 *Quarterly Journal of Economics* 1339–82. The study is part of a much broader body of work in comparative law and economics. For helpful overviews, see: Deakin, Simon, and Katharina Pistor (eds.). 2012. *Legal Origin Theory*. Cheltenham: Edward Elgar; Garoupa, Nuno and Mariana Pargendler. 2012. 'A Law and Economics Perspective on Legal Families,' Illinois Program in Law, Behavior and Social Science Paper No. LBSS13-01; Illinois Public Law Research Paper No. 13-11, University of Illinois College of Law.

employment, collective labour relations and social security laws in 85 countries, as those laws stood in 1997. As part of the first of these categories, they tested for the cost of firing workers on both personal and economic grounds, expressed as a proportion of the employer's wages bill; and for the effect of other dismissal procedures, including requirements as to notifying or seeking approval from third parties, requirements to re-train or re-employ, and so on. On the basis of their results, Botero et al posited both that common law countries tended to have lower levels of labour regulation than nations from other 'legal families' (notably French or German-style civil law systems), and that heavier regulation of labour was associated with lower labour force participation and higher unemployment.

Although very influential on certain policy-makers, notably at the World Bank, the methodology adopted in this study has been widely criticised, not least for presenting a static view of labour regulation as it stood at a particular point in time; and for concentrating on the strict letter of the law, as opposed to application and variation in practice.[88] A richer and more dynamic picture is revealed by an alternative coding framework, the Longitudinal Labour Regulation Index (LLRI), which was used by Simon Deakin et al to chart the evolution of labour law regulation in five selected countries (France, Germany, India, the UK and the US) over the period 1970–2005.[89] Although still limited in important respects, the LLRI seeks to capture not just change over time, but standards that emerge from sources other than legislation (such as collective bargaining). The LLRI includes a sub-index on the regulation of dismissal that involves asking seven different questions about a country's approach to notice of termination, redundancy pay, qualifying periods for unfair dismissal protection, and various other procedural or substantive constraints on termination.

The results of this study reveal some support for the hypothesis that the protective strength of labour law is greater in civil law than common law countries. But this is not uniformly true – for example, in relation to dismissal, India (a common law country) comes close to France and has a much higher level of protection for workers than Germany for most of the period in question. Importantly too, Deakin et al note that the legal origins theory seems unable to explain many of the changes observed within the various systems. At best, their data supports the existence of a 'weak' legal origins effect that varies over time, with nothing like the obvious 'path dependence' that legal origins theories might suggest.

This conclusion is strengthened by later work by researchers in Australia and New Zealand, two common law countries that have experienced successive rounds of radical change to labour regulation in the past three decades. Using the LLRI to code Australian and New Zealand laws on the same basis as the five countries in Deakin et al's study, Anderson et al note that the two countries have at various times been much closer to France and Germany than the US in the strength of their protection

---

88 See for example: Pozen, The Regulation of Labor and the Relevance of Legal Origin, *supra* note 86; Deakin, Simon, and Beth Ahlering. 2007. 'Labour Regulation, Corporate Governance and Legal Origin: A Case of Institutional Complementarity?' 41 *Law and Society Review* 865–908.

89 Deakin, Simon, Priya Lele, and Mathias Siems. 2007. 'The Evolution of Labour Law: Calibrating and Comparing Regulatory Regimes,' 146 *International Labour Review* 133–62.

for workers.[90] Although there has been some recent evidence of convergence with the UK, this seems to have had more to do with the introduction of neoliberal policies, and then their progressive dismantling by labour-friendly governments, in all three countries. The shifts in protection since 1970 in all seven countries are shown in Figure 9.1.

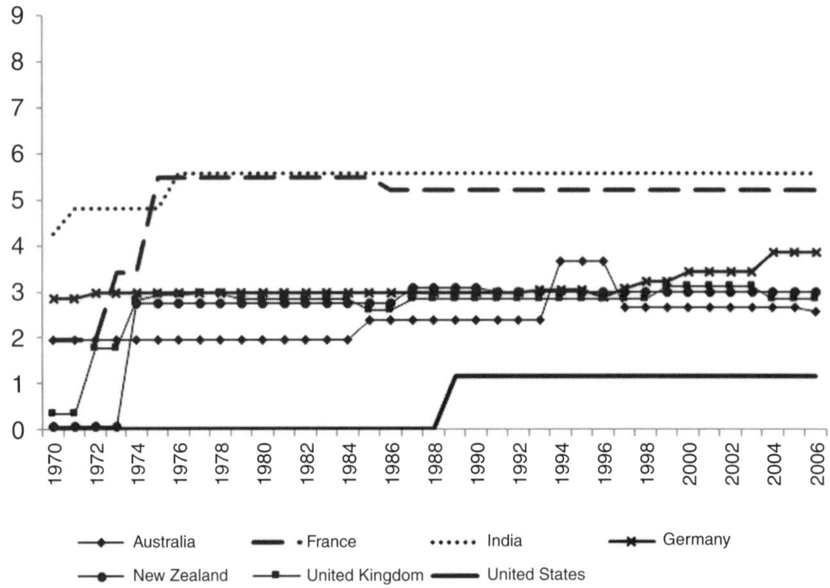

Note: The dismissal index consists of nine items and takes, and was developed by Sean Cooney, Peter G. Gahan, Shelley D Marshall, Richard James Mitchell, and Andrew Stewart. For definitions, see Cooney, Sean, Gahan, Peter G, Marshall, Shelley D, Mitchell, Richard James and Stewart, Andrew, *The Labour Market Regulation Index, Australia 197–02010: Variable Definitions and Description of the Data* (22 March 2010), http://ssrn.com/abstract=1576907.

Source: LLRI data, as detailed in Anderson, Gordon, Peter Gahan, Richard Mitchell, and Andrew Stewart. 2011. 'The Evolution of Labor Law in New Zealand: A Comparative Study of New Zealand, Australia and Five Other Countries,' 33 *Comparative Labor Law and Policy Journal* 137–70.

Figure 9.1 Dismissal protection, 1970–2006, seven countries compared

Further analysis by Peter Gahan et al of the LLRI data for Australia and the five countries from the Deakin et al study confirms that while there is some evidence of 'bipolar' convergence, with the common law countries moving towards a general level of protection that is lower than in the civil law systems, the effect is a weak one at best – and there is little support for the suggestion that labour laws around the world are

[90] Anderson, Gordon, Peter Gahan, Richard Mitchell, and Andrew Stewart. 2011. 'The Evolution of Labor Law in New Zealand: A Comparative Study of New Zealand, Australia and Five Other Countries,' 33 *Comparative Labor Law and Policy Journal* 137–70.

gradually becoming 'Americanised'.[91] Instead, the pattern remains one of divergence, both within and between legal families.

Of course these studies were undertaken before the recent round of changes inspired by the Global Financial Crisis and the Eurozone crisis. It should be evident from what has been said about some of those measures in the first part of this chapter that they have reduced the level of employment protection in many countries. The extent to which either the nature or outcomes of the reforms can be explained by reference to the origins of each country's legal system remains to be tested – just as their full social and economic effects are yet to be assessed.

It is clear then that if there is no broad agreement that employment protection laws necessarily deter job creation and create economic inefficiencies, then neither can it be asserted with confidence that common law countries are more likely than civil countries to find an appropriate balance between flexibility for employers and protection for employees. In any event, as Simon Deakin and Prabirjit Sarkar note in their study of the long run impact of labour law regulation, the truth is that 'legal rules do not operate in a straightforwardly instrumental way to reshape economic outcomes'.[92] The story is inevitably a more complex one that defies 'silver bullet' solutions to complex social and economic problems.

---

[91] Gahan, Peter, Richard Mitchell, Sean Cooney, Andrew Stewart, and Brian Cooper. 2012. 'Economic Globalization and Convergence in Labor Market Regulation: An Empirical Assessment,' 60 *American Journal of Comparative Law*, 703–42.

[92] Deakin, Simon, and Prabirjit Sarkar. 2008. 'Assessing the Long-Run Economic Impact of Labour Law Systems: A Theoretical Reappraisal and Analysis of New Time Series Data,' 39 *Industrial Relations Journal* 453–87; and see also Deakin et al, *supra* note 80.

10. Freedom of association

Alan Bogg and Keith D. Ewing

1. INTRODUCTION

This chapter is concerned with freedom of association, and in particular the right of individuals to form and join trade unions for the protection of their interests. Much of the debate and scholarship in this area has been dominated by the pioneering work of Sir Otto Kahn-Freund, who writing about a particular experience of the United Kingdom, warned against the dangers of legal transplants in the field of labour law, where he identified problems in relation to collective labour law in particular.[1] The transplant in this case was based on the Wagner and Taft Hartley Acts, brought from the US to the UK by the Industrial Relations Act 1971. Taft Hartley may well have come to Great Britain,[2] but it did not last long, wilting mercilessly in what appeared to be an inhospitable terrain, before being repealed within only three years. Of course, the element of the Industrial Relations Act 1971 that was most repugnant to the trade unions was its system of trade union registration, which constituted a profound breach in the principle of industrial autonomy. That particular element had no counterpart in the US system, which meant that the lessons to be drawn for comparative lawyers from the failed transplantation are somewhat complex. The Industrial Relations Act 1971 was replaced by something more recognisably consistent with the labour law traditions and practices of the UK, with a new blend of laws promoting collective bargaining, permitting closed shop arrangements, and re-introducing legal immunity for industrial action of a wide and varied nature. But although leading to triumphant scholarship about industrial relations and the limits of the law,[3] these liberating replacement measures were themselves short-lived, being replaced in turn by legal controls that bequeathed to a generation Taft-Hartley without Wagner. In retrospect, it is striking how much argumentative weight was being carried in Kahn-Freund's work by the then recent experience of the Industrial Relations Act 1971 without the benefit of very much hindsight on the political dynamics of that particular episode in British legislative history. The derivation of general propositions from specific legal events such as this is fraught with difficulties.

From this single experience of the Industrial Relations Act 1971 has developed a most remarkable theory about the transplanting of legal rules, a theory that is now

[1] O Kahn-Freund, 'On Uses and Misuses of Comparative Law' (1974) 37 *Modern Law Review* 1.

[2] William B Gould, 'Taft-Hartley comes to Britain: Observations on the Industrial Relations Act of 1971' (1972) 81 *Yale LJ* 1421.

[3] B Weekes, M Mellish, L Dickens and J Lloyd, *Industrial Relations and the Limits of Law* (Blackwell, Oxford 1975).

uncritically acclaimed as the received wisdom in the field of labour law scholarship.[4] If correct, however, the theory is surely a suicide note for a discipline, fatal to the very survival of the utility of comparative labour law. What is the point of comparative enquiry if comparative application is bound to fail? One implication of this categorical position on transplantation is that comparative scholarship is doomed to a dry scholasticism. The comparative method enables us to understand why labour law systems are essentially closed and largely static regulatory systems by virtue of unique constitutional and political configurations. For those who believe that the point of scholarship is to make the world better, then comparative enquiry would likely be a depressing pursuit. It is true that Kahn-Freund claims that his concerns are addressed principally to collective labour law and that his concerns about transplantation do not apply to individual employment law, the success of which is vindicated by the work of the International Labour Organisation (ILO), which in his terms is 'a gigantic enterprise of transplantation'.[5] Although something of a distraction for present purposes, it is nevertheless not clear to us that such a distinction between collective and individual labour law can so easily be drawn, not least because some core issues (such as protection of the right to organise) reveal the false division that such a distinction presumes. Nor is it necessary to consider whether – even if that distinction can be sustained – it can plausibly be claimed that individual employment rights are any more susceptible to 'transplantation' than collective labour rights. We have in mind here the law of unfair dismissal in relation to which the civilian model has been impossible to transplant successfully in a common law system that is unable to overcome the rule against specific performance of personal contracts.

Our starting point in this chapter as labour lawyers with an interest in comparative labour law thus is not whether it is possible to 'transplant' collective labour laws in the field of freedom of association (the matter about which Kahn-Freund was principally writing, and the matter about which his work has had the greatest influence). Our position is that 'transplantation' is a false starting point for comparative study in labour law, and for this reason we would also suggest that it misrepresents the role of the ILO and ILO Conventions to see these as part of 'a gigantic enterprise of transplantation'. For the most part law is not transplanted, but is rather adopted and adapted for the national conditions to which it is to apply, there being no ambiguity about this at least so far as international standards are concerned, the nature of the exercise being found in the language used. International law sets *binding standards* with which nation states are expected to comply,[6] and even where these standards are prescriptive, they generally

---

4 See B Langille and B Oliphant, 'From the Frying Pan to the Fire: Fraser and the Shift from International Law to International "Thought" in Charter Cases': labour law systems 'are intricate, multifaceted systems with countless parts, both core and peripheral ... tinkering with one part will have consequences elsewhere, and transplanting one aspect without the support of the rest of the system is a recipe for failure', accessed at http://www.labourlawresearch.net/sites/default/files/papers/Langille.pdf.

5 Kahn-Freund, above n 1, 21.

6 See ILO Convention 87, Freedom of Association and Protection of the Right to Organise Convention 1948, Arts 2 and 3.

take the form of *principles* rather than rules,[7] with a great deal of flexibility permitted as to the manner of their implementation in national law. This is true at regional level as well, most notably in relation to the EU, where even within a much more closely integrated economic and fiscal union, considerable scope was left to member states to implement social rights, before the idea of a Social Europe began seriously to disintegrate.[8] The spectre of judges drafting labour codes when enforcing these labour standards in constitutional fora is likewise implausible, and disappears under close scrutiny.[9]

But not only does the focus on the perils of transplantation distort the *nature* of the comparative exercise, it also distorts the modern *purpose* of the comparative exercise. In a different epoch in the development of labour law it may well have been appropriate to emphasise the differences between national labour law systems. In a changed and changing world, however, the comparative exercise may have a new and different function, which in part is to identify trends and patterns in the regulation of labour globally. This is undertaken with a view to respond to these global trends, particularly where the latter are thought to challenge the values that underpin the study of labour law. These values are reflected in part in core ILO Conventions and the ILO Constitution, and provide the normative spine of the discipline with even greater urgency today than at any time in the past. Such an exercise thus requires not a celebration of differences in treatment between systems, or an analysis of the barriers to transplantation; it rather requires an awareness of consistency and convergence of outcomes across systems, and an understanding of movements and their consequences. We appreciate that this will be inconvenient for those who have invested great intellectual effort in the study of difference and in the process have published impressive papers. Nevertheless, in the field of freedom of association (as that term is widely defined), it is only the most wilful who will fail to detect a global convergence in the direction of de-unionisation and worker dis-empowerment, reflected in various forms of trade union exclusion, collective bargaining decentralisation or denial, and tighter restrictions on the right to strike. Nor is this pressure attributable to natural forces, like the movement of the tides or the orbit of the moon. On the contrary, it is a regulatory pattern that is being deliberately orchestrated to very great effect by important international actors such as the IMF and transnational blocs such as the EU.

Whether or not these latter developments represent what appears sometimes to be referred to pejoratively as an 'Americanisation' of labour law on a global scale is neither here nor there, though in an era of globalisation dominated by US multinationals, it would be hardly surprising if such an epithet were apt. But globalisation is only one of the forces nudging in the direction of a global approach to trade unions, collective bargaining and the right to strike. In this chapter we seek to show how two

[7] As in the case of ILO Convention 98, Right to Organise and Collective Bargaining, 1949, Arts 1 and 2.

[8] Legal formalism cannot be used as an excuse for the lack of greater integration on matters relating to freedom of association, collective bargaining and the right to strike: this reflects political judgments, not legal ones.

[9] Compare B Langille, 'Why are Canadian Judges Drafting Labour Codes – and Constitutionalizing the Wagner Act Model?' (2010) 15 *Canadian Journal of Labour and Employment Law* 101.

other – apparently contradictory – forces are creating a greater convergence in national laws relating to freedom of association, the first being the growing significance of international human rights, which could not have been anticipated by Kahn-Freund, but without fully acknowledging which no modern comparative account of freedom of association would now be complete. If nothing else, recent developments in the jurisprudence of the European Court of Human Rights (ECtHR) under Article 11 demolishes the asserted distinction between 'individual' and 'collective' labour law in Kahn-Freund's comparative theory.[10] The other is economic, and in particular the global financial crisis and the related crisis in the Eurozone, which have created an opportunity/obligation for hitherto social democratic regimes to initiate a range of de-unionising measures. In this respect, perhaps we are seeing another iteration of Polanyi's 'double movement' thesis.[11] In making these claims we are not denying that there are important differences between systems on a range of matters. But we are suggesting that the fetish with difference in the modern world is a deviant activity that causes us to lose sight of major developments of convergence that threatens the very existence of labour law as traditionally understood, and the need from labour lawyers for a credible response.

2. THE NATURE OF FREEDOM OF ASSOCIATION

Before developing these arguments, it is first necessary to give an account of the scale of freedom of association, a legal principle which is not limited to the right to form and join trade unions. People join organisations for a wide range of social, religious, charitable, economic or political purposes, and the principle of freedom of association is one that must thus adapt to a wide range of purposes and a wide range of organisations. But quite apart from the range of purposes and the nature of the organisations that gather beneath its shelter, the right to freedom of association is a multi-dimensional right that includes not just the right to join an association and take part in its activities, but also the right of the association to administer its own affairs and determine its own organisation and structure, as well as determine how best to promote the interests of its members. The last of these will not normally give rise to any difficulty: the football club exists to play football in accordance with the rules of the Scottish Football Association, the religious body to worship its idol, and the political party to secure the election of its candidates to Parliament. It would, however, be a curious principle that declared that people are free to form and join football clubs and to administer the affairs of the club, but have no right to play the game for which they have associated as individuals in the first place. Such a liberty would be formal

---

[10] The beginning of this process can be identified in *Wilson v United Kingdom* [2002] ECHR 552, where the ECtHR identified both individual and group rights as simultaneously arising under Article 11's protection of freedom of association.

[11] K Polanyi, *The Great Transformation: The Political and Economic Origins of Our Time* (Beacon Press, Boston, 2nd ed, 2002). For an application to the development of social rights in an era of globalisation, see J Fudge, 'The New Discourse of Labour Rights: From Social to Fundamental Rights?' (2007) 29 *Comparative Labor Law and Policy Journal* 1.

and hollow. Perhaps that is why the ECtHR has seen fit to recognise a fundamental *right* (and not merely a liberty) to bargain collectively as an essential element in freedom of association, for a *right* encompasses correlative *duties* on the part of the State and other actors.

(a) Freedom of Association and Trade Unions

Consistently with the foregoing, in the field of labour law, freedom of association is a principle that contains a number of elements. These may be said to be as follows:

- freedom to associate with others, which in a trade union context means the right of the individual (usually a worker) to be a member of a trade union;
- freedom in the association of others, which means the freedom of the members of an organisation (in this context the trade union) to organise their own affairs free from state control, thereby establishing a principle of trade union autonomy; and
- freedom to act in association with others, which in turn raises questions about who decides what trade union members may do when acting collectively and who may decide the conditions under which they may act together. It also encompasses questions about the *duties* that others are subject to, such as governments and employers, in relation to those actions undertaken by trade unions and their members.

These three aspects of the principle of freedom of association are embodied in ILO Convention 87, which is the cornerstone of the right to freedom of association in international law. This provides by Article 2 that workers (and employers) 'without distinction whatsoever', have 'the right to establish and, subject only to the rules of the organisation concerned, to join organisations of their own choosing without previous authorisation'. Also important is Article 3, which covers the second of these three principles by providing that 'Workers' and employers' organisations shall have the right to draw up their constitutions and rules, and to elect their representatives in full freedom'. Article 3 also sustains the third of these principles by recognising the right of organisations 'to organise their administration and activities and to formulate their programmes'.

ILO Convention 87 is important for not specifying the protected means by which trade unions may organise their activities or formulate their programmes. But apart from being organisations of workers, ILO Convention 87 is significant for the fact that it does not define a trade union by reference to its objects and activities, leaving it to workers' organisations to determine how best to promote their members' interests. Presumably, this could be by the provision of services to members; representing members in their dealings with employers; or engaging in political action whether by supporting a sympathetic political party or its candidates at an election or in lobbying for new laws. Most importantly, of course, ILO Convention 87 protects the right to strike as an essential element in the trade union's pursuit of its objectives through concerted action. This is a well-established principle of the committee jurisprudence dealing with ILO Convention No 87,[12] to which we return below. In the meantime, ILO Convention 87 is accompanied by ILO Convention 98 which at least recognises what many would regard as the core functions of a trade union: to organise in the workplace and to engage in collective bargaining with employers. Thus, Article 1 provides that workers should enjoy protection from acts of anti-union discrimination by their employer, with Article 2 providing that employers should not seek to interfere with workers' organisations. But ILO Convention 98 is principally about collective bargaining, with Article 4 providing that:

> Measures appropriate to national conditions shall be taken, where necessary, to encourage and promote the full development and utilisation of machinery for voluntary negotiation between employers or employers' organisations and workers' organisations, with a view to the regulation of terms and conditions of employment by means of collective agreement.

(b) From Collective Bargaining to the Right to Strike

Some of these features of the right to freedom of association are beginning to unfold in jurisprudence now emerging in different parts of the world. It is accepted – for example – that the right to freedom of association must include the right to bargain collectively, which at least one court has said is an 'essential element' in the principle of freedom of association.[13] But what about the right to strike, unusually described in a common law context as an 'essential element in the principle of collective bargaining'?[14] There is no reference to the right to strike in ILO Convention 98, nor indeed in any other ILO instrument. It does not follow, however, that the right to strike is not a crucial feature of the right to freedom of association, having been read into ILO Convention 87 as one of the means by which trade unions 'organise their administration and activities' and 'formulate their programmes'.[15] As a result, both the ILO Committee of Experts and the ILO Freedom of Association Committee have developed a detailed body of jurisprudence, to determine the scope and content of the right to strike,[16] albeit to the great irritation and inconvenience of the international employers' lobby.[17] But because the right to strike is thus berthed in a freedom of association rather than a collective bargaining convention, it means that the right to strike can be developed in ways that do not confine its use to the securing of a collective agreement.

But although the scope of protected action is wide (political protest strikes, strikes by public sector workers as well as private sector workers, and solidarity and sympathy

---

[12] A Bogg, 'Viking and Laval: The International Labour Law Perspective' in M Freedland and J Prassl (eds), *EU Law in the Member States:* Viking, Laval *and Beyond* (Hart, Oxford 2014). On *Viking* and *Laval*, see below.

[13] *Demir and Baycara v Turkey* [2008] ECHR 1345.

[14] *Crofter Hand Woven Harris Tweed v Veitch* 1942 SC (HL) 1, per Lord Wright.

[15] See, generally, T Novitz, *International and European Protection of the Right to Strike* (OUP, Oxford 2003).

[16] B Gernignon, A Odero, and H Guido, 'ILO Principles Concerning the Right to Strike' (1998) 137 *International Labour Review* 441.

[17] K D Ewing, 'Myth and Reality of the Right to Strike as a "Fundamental Labour Right"' 29 (2013) *International Journal of Comparative Labour Law and Industrial Relations* 145.

strikes), the scope of international protection of the right to strike is in fact quite limited, notwithstanding implausible employer claims to the contrary.[18] A key limitation (curiously submerged in a leading ILO publication on the right to strike) is that strikes may be forbidden during the lifetime of a collective agreement.[19] Given that collective agreements may now extend for two, three or even five years, this is a major limitation, which is not easily reconcilable with the idea that freedom of association generally and the right to strike in particular is a fundamental human right.[20] This may be an unfortunate side effect of ILO Convention No 87 Article 3's focus on the *workers' organisation* as the relevant right-holder, rather than the individual worker himself or herself. This makes it less straightforward to deploy a human rights perspective, unimpeded by the legal form of the protections. It diminishes the special qualities of a human right if it can be waived by contract, particularly if the contract is one negotiated by a third party (as in this case if we view the right as being the right vested in the individual, and the third party being the trade union of which he or she is a member). But although this is the main limitation, others are also permitted, including (i) restrictions on strikes in essential services, (ii) the requirement of minimum service provision in the case of strike in the public services; (iii) restrictions on some political strikes (iv) the requirement of a vote of the workers before the action is taken, as well as (v) strike notice to the employer. We return to some of these matters below.

3. A NEW LEGAL ORTHODOXY?

Supranational organisations have assumed an importance in the sphere of collective labour rights that was not anticipated at all in Kahn-Freund's work. For example, in his seminal article on comparative labour law, Kahn-Freund draws a sharp distinction between 'freedom of organisation' and collective labour relations such as collective bargaining and the right to strike, with only 'freedom of organisation' (which Kahn-Freund seems to take as meaning freedom of association in its narrow sense as a civil and political right) capable of being 'expressed in strict legal terms'.[21] This distinction has now been superseded in the international law governing 'freedom of association' under Article 11 of the European Convention on Human Rights (ECHR), given the ECtHR's full recognition of fundamental rights to bargain collectively and to strike under Article 11, which we consider in this section. These remarkable developments have been driven by an 'integrated' approach to human rights adjudication at the international level, with the ECtHR drawing upon norms from the ILO, the European Social Charter, the EU Charter of Fundamental Rights, and convergent normative

---

[18] Ibid.

[19] Above n 16.

[20] For discussion, see K D Ewing, 'Laws Against Strikes Revisited', in C Barnard, S Deakin and G Morris (eds), *The Future of Labour Law* (Hart, Oxford 2004) 41.

[21] Kahn-Freund above n 1, 22.

practices in European states.[22] The dissolution of the membrane between 'freedom of organisation' and collective bargaining and action could not have been predicted by Kahn-Freund. That this has occurred, however, indicates how significant supranational bodies such as the ILO Committees and the ECtHR have now become in articulating international standards governing collective labour rights in national labour law systems.[23] This degree of penetration of international labour standards into national systems is likely to grow rather than diminish, and is reflected in the growing practice of constitutional courts invoking binding international standards to interpret national constitutional provisions or labour statutes.[24] It would also be enhanced were the EU ever to accede to the ECHR.

(a) International Human Rights Law

Although there are regional human rights treaties in various parts of the world, the most active of these is in the Council of Europe, an international organisation of 47 member states (a jurisdiction of some 800 million people, representing about a quarter of the member states of the ILO). By Article 11, the ECHR provides that:

(1) Everyone has the right to freedom of peaceful assembly and to freedom of association with others, including the right to form and to join trade unions for the protection of his interests.
(2) No restrictions shall be placed on the exercise of these rights other than such as are prescribed by law and are necessary in a democratic society in the interests of national security or public safety, for the prevention of disorder or crime, for the protection of health or morals or for the protection of the rights and freedoms of others. This article shall not prevent the imposition of lawful restrictions on the exercise of these rights by members of the armed forces, of the police or of the administration of the State.

Article 11(1) was read by the ECtHR in a 'trilogy' of cases in the 1970s as not guaranteeing to trade unions the protection of any particular form of trade union action: no protection of the right to be consulted, the right to bargain, or the right to strike.[25] To the dismay of trade unionists, however, it was also read to mean that a worker could not be required as a condition of employment (in an expanding range of circumstances)

---

22 V Mantouvalou, 'Labour Rights in the European Convention on Human Rights: An Intellectual Justification for an Integrated Approach to Interpretation' (2013) 13 *Human Rights Law Review* 529.

23 A theory of comparative collective labour law that does not accord a prominent position to international labour standards as an instrument of dynamic change, and as a strategic tool for resisting attacks on workers' collective rights in national labour law systems, would be seriously deficient as an explanatory account.

24 This has been especially prominent, and particularly controversial, in respect of Canadian constitutional litigation on the constitutional right to freedom of association.

25 M. Forde, 'The European Convention on Human Rights and Labor Law' (1983) 31 *American Journal of Comparative Law* 301.

to become a member of a trade union to which he or she objected.[26] In these latter cases, the 'original intent' theory of construction evident in the 'trilogy' was displaced by the 'living instrument' theory of construction, which appears to have prevailed ever since.

The 'living instrument' approach to construction was deployed by the ECtHR in *Demir and Baycara v Turkey*,[27] where the ECtHR held that the annulment of a collective agreement by a Turkish court was a violation of Article 11 of the ECHR. In reversing its earlier jurisprudence to hold that the right to freedom of association in Article 11 must now be read to include the right to bargain collectively, it was not suggested that there should be a common approach to collective bargaining throughout the Council of Europe, the Court accepting that 'States remain free to organise their system so as, if appropriate, to grant special status to representative trade unions'.[28] But reinforcing the importance of the ILO Conventions referred to above (as well as other treaties), the Court appeared to suggest that for the purposes of Article 11(1), there was an obligation on Member States to have in place 'legislation necessary to give effect to the provisions of international labour conventions already ratified by Turkey',[29] thereby resolving the knotty problem of the normative standard by which the otherwise opaque principle of collective bargaining was to be set: the minimum standard for the Council of Europe is the standard set by the ILO and its supervisory bodies. It is true that in this case the collective agreement annulled was one to which a local authority was a party, leading the Turkish Government to argue that the government was protected by the second sentence of Article 11(2) above, the dispute relating to workers involved in the 'administration of the State'. But in another extraordinary turn, the Court appeared to hold that the term in parenthesis should be read consistently with the same term in ILO Convention 98, Article 6, which had been read narrowly by the ILO supervisory bodies so as not to exclude local government workers from the scope of the latter Convention. The Court thus confirmed the influence of ILO Convention 98 in the construction of both Article 11(1) AND Article 11(2).[30]

(b) Constitutional Protection

Developments such as these are not only dissolving the membrane between freedom of association and the right to bargain collectively, but also between international and national law. The carriage of international standards into domestic law is helped also by what some anticipate as the increasing 'constitutionalisation' of labour rights, though this is a process that is by no means novel, with a remarkably large number of states –

---

[26] M. Forde, 'The 'Closed Shop' Case' (1982) 11 *Industrial Law Journal* 1.

[27] [2008] ECHR 1345.

[28] Ibid., paragraph 154.

[29] Ibid., paragraph 157.

[30] It may be that the *Demir and Baycara* approach to international labour standards under Art. 11 requires some reappraisal as regards the right to strike in the light of the ECtHR's recent decision in *RMT v United Kingdom*, Application No 31045/10 judgment of 8 April 2014, on which see A Bogg and K D Ewing, 'The Implications of the *RMT* Case' (2014) 43 *Industrial Law Journal* 221. It should be noted, however, that this is not a Grand Chamber decision, and that subsequent decisions of the Court have not suggested any equivocation.

especially in the era after the Second World War – including labour rights in their national constitutions.[31] A good and topical example is Italy where the constitution – which purports to be that of a 'democratic republic based on labour' – provides that 'being represented in proportion to their registered members', trade unions 'may jointly enter into collective labour contracts which are mandatory for all who belong to the respective industry of these contracts'. Although the first of the post-war democracies to include provisions of this kind in its redrafted constitution, this is a formula that was repeated in the 1970s when Greece, Spain and Portugal adopted social democratic constitutional models. In Spain, the modern constitution provides that 'the law shall guarantee the right to collective labour negotiations between the representatives of workers and employers, as well as the binding force of agreements', while in Greece it is provided that 'the general conditions of work shall be determined by law and supplemented by collective agreements arrived at by free collective bargaining and, in the event of their having failed, by the regulations fixed by arbitration'. It is a great irony that these are the very countries where rights in relation to freedom of association in general – and collective bargaining in particular – are under greatest challenge in the age of austerity. This is a matter to which we return below.

In the meantime, it is noteworthy that recognition of the constitutional logic of core labour rights is expanding, with such rights being included in most of the constitutional texts of the so-called 'new democracies' established in Europe since 1989, as well as in South Africa, where the Constitutional Court also has a constitutional mandate to have regard to ILO Conventions.[32] But not only is there express reference to these core labour rights in national constitutions, even the generic right to freedom of association in common law systems is being developed – albeit tentatively in some cases – to recognise not just a freedom to be in association with others, but also to act in association with others, and to do so with reference to ILO standards. The most controversial example of this in recent years relates to Canada where in a process almost identical to that in the ECtHR, the Supreme Court (SCC) has repudiated a body of jurisprudence developed in the 1980s, and gradually expanded the meaning of the right to freedom of association to include a right to bargain collectively.[33] This is all the more impressive for the fact that while Article 11 of the ECHR expressly refers to the right to form and join trade unions for the protection of one's interests, there is no equivalent reference in the express acknowledgement of the right to freedom of association in the Canadian Charter of Rights and Freedoms. But like the ECtHR, the SCC has been influenced (albeit unlike the ECtHR controversially) by Canada's ILO obligations in what has become a new orthodoxy of informing international treaties and constitutions by reference to international law.[34] It is noteworthy that the ECtHR has

---

[31] K D Ewing, 'Economic Rights', in M Rosenfeld and A Sajo (eds), *Oxford Handbook of Comparative Constitutional Law* (OUP, Oxford 2012), Ch 50.

[32] 'When interpreting any legislation, every court must prefer any reasonable interpretation of the legislation that is consistent with international law over any alternative interpretation that is inconsistent with international law' (Constitution of the Republic of South Africa, Art 233).

[33] *Fraser v Ontario (Attorney General)* [2011] 2 SCR 3.

[34] Even though in this case the SCC embarked on a frolic of its own, defining collective bargaining for these purposes in a manner that falls short of setting a standard that meets the full extent of these obligations: for discussion, see A Bogg and K D Ewing, 'A (Muted) Voice at

now also constitutionalised a fundamental right to strike as an element in the Convention's protection of freedom of association,[35] and that the same critical step was taken by the SCC, recognising the right to strike as a corollary of the right to bargain collectively.[36]

4. FREEDOM OF ASSOCIATION AND THE RIGHT TO ORGANISE

One of the great contradictions of modern labour law is that the expansion of international and constitutional protection of labour rights is matched only by the contraction of such rights in practice. De-unionisation is taking place in the shadow of legality, beginning with the right to organise. Here we are concerned with the right of the worker to join a trade union without previous authorisation, an essential building block of effective trade unionism, which is recognised by most labour law systems in the world. There are few – if any – advanced countries that put serious legal obstacles in the way of membership of a trade union, although it remains the case that in many countries trade unionists are the subject of reprisals of various kinds, from murder at one end of the scale to workplace discipline at the other.[37] But although protection for the right to organise is widely recognised, such recognition nevertheless masks important differences between systems about the nature and extent of the protection, the burden of proof when allegations are made that the right to organise has been violated, and even more fundamentally the right of carriage of the complaint. Is it the right of the state in bringing criminal proceedings? Or is the right of the individual victim, the right of the union, or both? The approach in European systems would tend to favour the individual, while the North American systems would tend to favour the union. The ECtHR suggests both, in the sense that adverse action against a worker for reasons related to trade union activities is a violation of the rights of the worker and the trade union, each of which is protected by the ECHR. The ECtHR has also suggested that criminal laws alone do not provide sufficient protection for freedom of association, affirming the need for protection under civil law without the extensive procedural and evidential protections for the criminally accused.

Work? Collective Bargaining in the Supreme Court of Canada' (2012) 33 *Comparative Labor Law and Policy Journal* 379, 384–8. This is of course very different to the fidelity displayed to ILO standards in *Demir*.

35 In its most recent decision in *RMT*, above n 30, the ECtHR has confirmed that the right to strike is protected under Art. 11.

36 On the right to strike in Canada, see *Saskatchewan Federation of Labour v. Saskatchewan*, 2015 SCC 4. Brian Langille has been particularly critical of what he sees as the SCC's misuse of international law: B Langille, 'The Freedom of Association Mess: How we got into it and how we can get out of it' (2009) 54 *McGill Law Journal* 177. These arguments were not influential in the *Saskatchewan* case.

37 ITUC, *Report on Violations of Trade Union Rights* (ITUC, Brussels, 2013).

(a) A Right of Non-Association?

An issue that divides freedom of association in the US and freedom of association in Europe is whether the right to associate implies a duty to associate. Most member states of the Council of Europe have traditionally prohibited closed shop arrangements whereby workers were required as a condition of employment to be a member of a particular trade union. Partly this was because of the principle of trade union pluralism, with trade unions being organised on religious and political lines in some countries. But such pluralism was not a feature of the industrial relations systems of all countries where closed shop arrangements were prohibited, and in relation to which other explanations need to be found. And although closed shop arrangements were not universally prohibited (with the UK, Sweden and Denmark being among the exceptions), following the intervention by the ECtHR referred to above, it appears now to be the case that closed shop arrangements are prima facie forbidden (subject to the narrow possibility of justification under Art. 11(2)) throughout the Council of Europe.[38] A similar approach to that of the ECtHR has also been taken by the Social Rights Committee of the Council of Europe (responsible for administering the European Social Charters of 1961 and 1996), which appears also to disapprove forms of trade union security other than trade union membership. So although it was held that non-union workers may be required to pay a wage monitoring fee to a trade union, it was also held that if the fee was used for any other purpose, it would be unlawful, as violating the right to organise in the European Social Charter, Article 5.[39]

The position in Europe contrasts with the default position in North America, where the right of the individual is much more clearly subordinated to the interests of the majority.[40] This is perhaps a reversal of what might be expected, with the liberal democracy of the US being thought more likely to take a more trenchant approach to individual rights than the erstwhile social democracies of the Council of Europe. Paradoxically, this may reflect (or at least perhaps be justified by virtue of) the different role that collective bargaining plays in North American labour law systems (a point to which we return below, though it would not explain or justify the difference with the UK where collective bargaining increasingly performs a role similar to that in the US). As will be discussed more fully below, in the North American systems, the trade union is formally a 'bargaining agent', elected by a group of workers in a 'bargaining unit', to represent them collectively in negotiations with their employer. In these systems it is logical – albeit surprising – that the individual worker should be required either to join

---

38 Some scholars are critical of the ECtHR's approach, mounting a credible argument that some forms of closed shop should be regarded as permitted under Art 11: see V Mantouvalou, 'Is There a Human Right not to Be a Trade Union Member?' in T Novitz and C Fenwick (eds), *Human Rights at Work: Perspectives on Law and Regulation* (Hart, Oxford 2010) 439.

39 *Confederation of Swedish Enterprise v Sweden*, Complaint No 12/2002. In this way it appears that only a limited form of agency fee arrangement is thought to be consistent with the Social Charter, again despite the clear intention of its authors that union security measures should not be prohibited.

40 The states are allowed to legislate for individual opt out of fee payment in so-called 'right to work' laws and half the states have done so, most recently, and surprisingly, Michigan.

the trade union where it has majority support as a result of a process in which the individual has had full rights of participation (as upheld by the SCC), or to pay an agency fee to the union in lieu of membership. Since 1947, however, it has been possible for individual US states to prohibit such practices, and a large number of so-called 'right to work' states have done so.

(b) A Right of Limited Association?

Apart from the right not to join a trade union, the other question to arise here is whether workers can be required to accept all the obligations of membership or whether they can insist on a form of membership on their own terms. The issue arises most sensitively, however, where union security arrangements of the kind discussed above are in place, and most acutely in the context of trade union political action. As already explained, trade unions seek to promote their members' interests not by collective bargaining alone, but also by political action: perhaps to create or sustain or improve a legal framework within which collective bargaining can operate; perhaps to deal with matters that collective bargaining traditionally has been unable to deliver; and/or perhaps to deal with a wider range of social or economic questions for the benefit of their members. Although they may benefit from such regulatory initiatives, just as they may benefit from the fruits of collective bargaining, there is nevertheless a concern by some that workers should not be required by their union dues to support financially a political party to which they may be opposed, particularly in circumstances where failure to do so could lead to expulsion from the union and consequently the loss of employment. One option here is to say that trade unions are democratic bodies in which all members are free to participate and that the individual must be bound by the democratic decision of the majority. Another option would be to say that the right of the individual must prevail and that as a result either no one should be required to join a trade union or support it financially, or that if such an obligation does arise, then it should be qualified or limited in some way to protect the individual from having to support causes of which he or she disapproves.

This is not a problem in all systems, not least because union security arrangements of the kind to be found mainly in common law countries are by no means widespread. But in dealing with this problem, courts have responded in very different ways: in Australia and Canada on the one hand, the response was to protect the trade union by permitting the union to use general funds for political purposes (including political party affiliations), in the latter case despite strong constitutional protection of the right to freedom of expression and association on which the complainants sought unsuccessfully to rely. In the UK on the other hand, the response was to protect the individual by prohibiting trade unions from imposing a parliamentary levy on anyone, though the problem was addressed by legislation introduced in 1913 that sought to reconcile the interests of the majority with those of the minority. It remains the case that trade unions can pursue certain prescribed political objects only by first establishing a separate political fund from which such payments are to be made, the fund to be financed only by a separate political contribution paid by the members, from the payment of which all members have a right to claim exemption.[41] This model was adopted by the US Supreme Court, which appended the Trade Union Act 1913 (UK) to an important decision,[42] at a time when foreign law was not treated with the disdain that it is today. That decision – applied initially to workers covered by the Railway Labor Act but extended since to workers covered by other statutes – had the effect of requiring unions to reimburse agency fee payers of that portion of their agency fee that was used for purposes other than collective bargaining.[43]

5. RIGHT TO ORGANISE AND COLLECTIVE BARGAINING – REGULATORY BARGAINING MODELS

It is strongly arguable that there is a measure of convergence between the US and the Council of Europe states on this question of trade union security, due in part to human rights (in the case of Europe) and constitutional litigation (in the case of the US), though in these cases not informed by ILO standards. It is, however, a convergence in the direction of trade union weakness and dis-empowerment, both industrial and political,[44] as most recently underlined by the adoption of right to work laws by another three US states. Another area where for different reasons a measure of convergence is taking place is in relation to collective bargaining and workplace representation procedures, which have always been thought to operate very differently in different countries, given Kahn-Freund's categorical pronouncements on the matter. This too may be seen to be a development in the direction of trade union weakness if indeed not in the direction of de-unionisation, and it is here that the talk of the 'Americanisation' of labour law appears to resonate most loudly. Certainly, there has been a most palpable shift towards decentralised models of collective bargaining, even in those jurisdictions that had been associated historically with strongly centralised or even corporatist bargaining systems. As we will see, it is possible in broad terms to identify two different collective bargaining models, which we refer to here as the 'regulatory' and 'representation' models, the latter which we associate particularly with the US and Canada, though its normative influence has extended throughout the English-speaking common law world. While in recent years several jurisdictions have adopted legal instruments to underpin collective bargaining regimes of this latter kind, we are unaware of any that has adopted the former 'regulatory' model.

---

41 These arrangements remain in place despite the fact that the closed shop that provides their principal justification is now unenforceable in English law, as is any other form of union security device.

42 *Brotherhood of Railway Clerks v Allen* 373 US 113 (1963).

43 The history since *Allen* has been one of gradually tighter procedural restraints on trade unions, of which *Knox v SEIU, Local 100*, 567 US (2012) is the most recent development at the time of writing.

44 In terms of political restraints, these arise also collaterally as a result of campaign finance laws, so that although there may be no labour law restraints on the political activities of trade unions in Canada under federal law, there is now a prohibition on trade union contributions to political parties as well as tight controls on election expenditure in support of a political party. Similar (though not identical) measures exist at State level in Australia, though not yet at federal level.

(a) Regulatory Bargaining Models

There is a sharp and well-known difference in collective bargaining procedures between the social democracies of the EU and the liberal democracies of North America, though even within the European countries there are differences that are as great (if not greater) as those between the US and Canada. These differences are illustrated by Directive 96/71/EC on the posting of workers, under the terms of which member states are required to ensure that workers in one country (the home state) posted by their employer to work in another country (the host state) are paid the minimum terms and conditions provided for in the host country. In determining what are the minimum terms and conditions for these purposes, it is provided expressly that for some purposes set out in the Directive they are the relevant terms and conditions laid down by:

- law, regulation or administrative provision, and/or
- collective agreements or arbitration awards which have been declared universally applicable within the meaning of paragraph 8, insofar as they concern the activities referred to in the Annex.[45]

In order to be universally applicable for these purposes, a collective agreement must be 'observed by all undertakings in the geographical area and in the profession or industry concerned'. That is to say, the collective agreement must have regulatory (or quasi-legislative) effect, reflecting the status of collective agreements in a number of member states. Where collective agreements do not quite enjoy the status of being declared 'universally applicable', they may nevertheless be treated as the normative base for the national application of the Directive where they are 'generally applicable to all similar undertakings in the geographical area and in the profession or industry concerned', and/or 'have been concluded by the most representative employers' and labour organizations at national level and which are applied throughout national territory'.[46]

The Posted Workers Directive, Directive 96/71/EC, is a remarkable instrument for a number of reasons, not least because it illustrates the nature of the collective bargaining process in most EU member states. As reflected by the terms of the Directive, collective bargaining will traditionally take place at the level of the branch or sector (or even higher) between trade unions and employers' federations, in some cases provided the union is able to demonstrate its 'representativeness' (a concept also acknowledged by the Directive). As also reflected by the Posted Workers Directive, by engaging in this kind of activity the trade union may be said to be participating in a regulatory (and perhaps even quasi-legislative) process, in which it establishes norms to be applied sector-wide (or even nationally), a process that may be reinforced in some – but not all – cases by legislation extending the scope of collective agreements to cover employers

---

[45] The annex deals mainly with construction work and building services, though there is also a power in Art. 3(10) to extend the application of collective agreements to other sectors: see *C-319/06, European Commission v Luxembourg* [2008] ECR I-04323.

[46] The latter would apply to systems such as the Greek, where until the austerity crisis terms and conditions of employment were governed by national agreements between the social partners.

who were not party to the agreement in question (so-called extension mechanisms, whereby the agreement is said to have an *erga omnes* effect).[47] In some cases (such as Finland), the *erga omnes* application of collective agreements applies as a matter of routine, in other cases (such as Italy) it applies indirectly as a result of the prevailing collective agreement being the reference point for the constitutional guarantee of a decent wage,[48] and in other cases still (such as Germany) it is discretionary and more limited in scope (with the result that the agreement in question may not be said to be universally applicable for the purposes of the Posted Workers Directive).

As recognised by the OECD, this system of collective bargaining has traditionally been associated with high levels of collective bargaining coverage, and it is indeed the case that levels of collective bargaining density in some Council of Europe States may be as high as 98 per cent.[49] This is not surprising. Since 'regulatory' models conceive of collective bargaining as a public regulatory activity, a form of public governance at national or sectoral levels, trade unions themselves enjoy a form of public legitimacy as regulatory actors in these democratic structures. In many of the countries characterised by 'regulatory' modes of bargaining, however, recent years have seen a steadily growing role for decentralised company level agreements to supplement or derogate from industry collective agreements. Sometimes (as in Belgium) lower level agreements are only permitted to improve upon the norms specified in higher level agreements. In Germany pressures have grown on regulatory bargaining structures through the negotiation of 'opening clauses' giving negotiators some flexibility at the level of individual companies but more particularly through growing numbers of employers disassociating from employers' federations.[50] Nevertheless, while the pressures on centralised regulatory bargaining are real enough, the model continues to be resilient in those countries that have avoided the need for financial assistance from the IMF and the European Central Bank in the wake of economic crisis.

(b) Regulatory Bargaining and Workplace Representation

Regulatory bargaining is associated with bargaining taking place at the level of the sector or industrial branch, covering large swathes of workers. Although effective in terms of coverage, it does nevertheless raise questions about the representation of workers in the enterprise. In other words, sectoral bargaining applies horizontally across enterprises, leaving a need to deal vertically with representation within enterprises. Whether by conscious design or otherwise, it is a feature of systems that have adopted this form of collective bargaining that they typically supplement collective bargaining at the sector level with works councils or equivalent bodies at the level of the enterprise. This is a system most famously developed by German labour law, where

47 OECD, *Economic Outlook* (OECD, Paris 1994).

48 The Italian Constitution provides by Art. 36(1) that 'Workers are entitled to remuneration commensurate with the quantity and quality of their work, and in any case sufficient to ensure to them and their families a free and honourable existence'.

49 OECD, above n 47.

50 L Fulton, 'Worker Representation in Europe' (ETUI, Brussels 2013), accessed at http://www.worker-participation.eu/National-Industrial-Relations.

the collective agreement will deal with the so-called economic questions (such as hours, pay and holidays), while the works council will deal with the so-called social questions (such as occupational health and safety, collective redundancy and dismissal). This model – or a variation thereof – has been adopted by labour law systems throughout the EU, the arrangements usually to be triggered by a request from a prescribed number of workers, leading to the election of representatives from the existing workforce, who will have rights to be informed and consulted on a wide range of prescribed questions (including the dismissal of employees), the employer in some cases having a duty to negotiate with the works council. Works council members will generally have the right to facilities provided by the employer to enable them to carry out their duties and to protection from dismissal or other forms of disadvantage during their tenure.

The influence of this model within most EU member states is reflected in Directive 2002/14/EC, the Information and Consultation Directive, which requires the adoption of at least a diluted version of this model by all member states. The information and consultation requirements of the Directive thus fall some way short of the best practice already in place, although several countries have had to make minor adjustments to their national laws to accommodate various features of the Directive. While for most countries with the regulatory bargaining model this would be a simple process, it was more difficult to adapt this model of workplace representation to the realities of enterprise-based 'representative' collective bargaining model in those jurisdictions – notably the UK – where the latter prevailed, and where mandatory information and consultation procedures continue to be viewed with some suspicion. Nevertheless, these arrangements at EU level are complemented by Directive 2009/38/EC, the Recast European Works Council Directive, which applies to companies with at least 1,000 employees in the EU and at least 150 employees in at least two member states. Either at their own initiative or at the request of employees, the central management of these companies is responsible under national laws which have transposed the terms of the Directive to initiate procedures to establish a European Works Council (EWC) for the purposes of informing and consulting worker representatives about transnational matters. The latter obligation applies to all such companies, even though the parent company may be based outside the EU, in which case it is the responsibility of the 'central management's representative agent' to initiate the relevant procedures.[51]

Workplace representation through the medium of works councils or information and consultation procedures does not sit comfortably with representational bargaining models discussed below. These forms of workplace representation operate alongside and overlap with collective bargaining structures in ways that are potentially awkward and clumsy. They create what is sometimes referred to as a 'twin-track' approach to representation in the same enterprise, with potentially different representatives representing what are potentially different constituencies. While such arrangements are

[51] As a result, there are a number of US-based companies to whom this obligation applies, and indeed only Germany has more companies with an EWC than does the US. According to ETUI, the US companies in question include General Electric, Johnson & Johnson, Kellogg, Levi Strauss and McDonalds, a nice irony perhaps in an era of the 'Americanisation' of labour law.

unlikely to be functional from an employer's perspective they are typically unwelcome from a trade union perspective, if only because most trade unions are unwilling to take part in representative structures that require them to sit down with non-trade unionists. It is for this latter reason in particular that British trade unionists have been lukewarm in principle and hostile in practice to EU information and consultation procedures, and have tried to integrate them into collective bargaining arrangements in order to continue to operate what might be referred to as a 'single-track' approach to workplace representation. These concerns do not apply to European Works Councils, largely because trade unions have a more clearly defined role in the operation of the procedure. Whether the hostility to works council or information and consultation procedures operating at a national level below the level of European Works Councils can always be justified is controversial. These procedures typically have low thresholds to trigger their establishment, and certainly would not require majority support. Although they typically have limited powers, such procedures nevertheless create an institutional framework that trade unions could infiltrate and adapt for the purposes of collective bargaining.

6. RIGHT TO ORGANISE AND COLLECTIVE BARGAINING – REPRESENTATIONAL BARGAINING MODELS

As already explained, we view the nature of collective bargaining in the former social democracies of the EU as being of a qualitatively different nature, from the collective bargaining that we find in what happen – coincidentally or not – to be common law jurisdictions. If nothing else, this should give us some serious pause for thought before joining in an emerging academic orthodoxy that the 'common law' genotype is of limited explanatory significance in elucidating patterns of labour law change over time.[52] We have painted a picture of horizontal regulation by collective bargaining and vertical representation through works councils (or similar) and EWCs. It should be added of course that the foregoing is something of a caricature – an attempt to distil the essential features from a number of different systems. So we should not be taken to say that the model of horizontal regulation by collective bargaining and vertical representation by works councils mean that there is no trade union representation at enterprise level in such systems. Structures are never so tidy, and even in the German system where there is representation through the works council, it is widely acknowledged that the works councillors are generally union members and that trade unions play an essential role in supporting and sustaining the system. In Italy, moreover, the main piece of labour law – the Workers' Statute of 1970 – helps to embed trade union representation at plant level. Italy is one of a minority of major EU member states where there are no statutory works councils, and where workplace representation is conducted principally by trade unions.[53] But just as there are deviations from what we characterise as the norm in relation to regulatory bargaining models, so there are

[52] S Deakin, P Lele and M Siems, 'The Evolution of Labour Law: Calibrating and Comparing Regulatory Regimes' (2007) 146 *International Labour Review* 133.

[53] See generally, M Carley and M Hall, *Impact of the Information and Consultation Directive on Industrial Relations* (Eurofound 2009).

deviations from what we characterise as the norm in relation to the representational bargaining models which we now address. This does not, however, detract from the fact that in the representational bargaining systems in question the impact is very different from that relating to regulatory bargaining described above.

(a) Adopting the Model

The classic example of representational bargaining is the US National Labor Relations Act of 1935 (NLRA), the preamble to which reveals its intellectual origins in a different economic orthodoxy to the one prevailing today:

> The inequality of bargaining power between employees who do not possess full freedom of association or actual liberty of contract, and employers who are organized in the corporate or other forms of ownership association substantially burdens and affects the flow of commerce, and tends to aggravate recurrent business depressions, by depressing wage rates and the purchasing power of wage earners in industry and by preventing the stabilization of competitive wage rates and working conditions within and between industries.

This is pure Keynesianism, adherence to which we find in steps to promote collective bargaining in other industrialised economies in the non-fascist world of the time. However, the choice made by the US policy-maker was different from that made in the UK, the former choosing by legislative means to cement a system of enterprise-based bargaining, the latter choosing by administrative means to develop a system of sector wide bargaining, which has now been largely abandoned.[54]

In affirming this choice, Congress nevertheless offered labor unions the promise of certification as an exclusive bargaining agent for workers in a defined bargaining unit if the union could show that it had majority support of the employees in the bargaining unit. On crossing what might superficially seem to be an easy hurdle, the union would acquire the right to bargain ‘in respect to rates of pay, wages, hours of employment, or other conditions of employment’, the employer being under a corresponding duty to bargain in good faith with a view to concluding a collective agreement, which as already explained above would apply to all relevant employees, union members or not. The collective agreement would be legally binding, and it would be unlawful for the employer to pay any worker more or less than stipulated in the agreement. In this way the labor union is given the authority to act as bargaining agent by those workers who have chosen to be represented by it. But it was not so simple: what was designed in principle as an opportunity to facilitate collective bargaining has become in practice an obstacle to frustrate, with collective bargaining density in the US being the lowest in the developed world, barely scratching double figures. In a culture where employers are

[54] It has to be pointed out, however, that the National Industrial Recovery Act of 1933 made provision for a form of sector-wide regulation of the US economy through ‘codes’ in which it was anticipated that labor unions would play a part in negotiating. Although there were 546 such codes (which dealt with prices as well as wages), a number of problems were identified with America’s attempt at sectoral regulation before the NRA was declared unconstitutional in 1934. The provisions of the Wagner Act re-enact right to organise provisions first contained in the NRA. See A J Badger, *FDR: The First Hundred Days* (Hill and Wang, New York 2008).

generally hostile to unions (such hostility at least in some quarters to be presumed from the very existence of measures like the NLRA), legal instruments designed to facilitate collective bargaining on an enterprise-by-enterprise basis in which a union must secure and maintain majority support presents what are proving to be insuperable obstacles for trade unions.

So although it is an unfair labor practice to 'interfere with, restrain, or coerce employees in the exercise of [their rights]', hostile employers have many advantages which enable them successfully to resist union organising and certification campaigns, and to deny the promise of the NLRA to restore 'equality of bargaining power' between workers and employers. The problems encountered by what ought to be a simple procedure are well known, not the least of which is that the employer has a captive audience which he or she may seek to persuade to resist the union by fair means or foul. Even if the union achieves certification, the substantive requirements of 'good faith' are so insipid, and the remedies so weak, it is sometimes unlikely that a certified union will manage to deliver anything of substance to its supporters to make collective organisation enduring in the workplace. For its part the union will have no legal right of access to the workplace to counteract the employer's hostile conduct, and may indeed find that its activists are disciplined or fired, in circumstances where they are unlikely to be reinstated even if the discharge is found at some much later date to be unjustified. The failure of the very modest proposals in the AFL-CIO's Employee Free Choice Act 2009 (card check, first contract arbitration and enhanced remedies) to gain any legislative traction confirms the characterisation of the US system as 'ossified',[55] beyond the effective reach of political reform. But whether these reforms would have made much difference in practice is unclear, for part of the problem may lie with the design of a system that no amount of legislative revision will significantly change.

(b) Adapting the Model

This model has been adopted and adapted – if not transplanted – by labour law systems throughout the common law world. Each adaptation has involved a revision and an improvement of the original, with some US scholars attracted by what they see as the benefits of some of the Canadian jurisdictions (with labour law in Canada being a provincial rather than a federal matter), which have adopted the Wagner model but with important modifications. Variations that have been highlighted as particularly important include the right to secure certification on the showing of majority support by a system of card authorisation, which avoids the need for a ballot.[56] More recently, however, the movement in Canadian jurisdictions has been away from card check and back towards US-style mandatory representation ballots, albeit with those ballots subject to strict statutory time limits. It is now the case that card check does not reflect the position in the majority of Canadian provincial jurisdictions.[57] Critics of the US model have also

---

[55] C Estlund, 'The Ossification of American Labor Law' (2002) 102 *Columbia LR* 1527.

[56] P Weiler, *Governing the Workplace* (Harvard UP, Boston 1990).

[57] S Slinn, 'The Canadian Conception of Collective Representation and Bargaining', in B Creighton and A Forsyth (eds), *Rediscovering Collective Bargaining: Australia's Fair Work Act in International Perspective* (Abingdon, Routledge 2012) 246.

commented favourably on the system of 'first contract arbitration' that operated in a number of Canadian jurisdictions, reinforcing the point that the union's problems are not resolved even where certification is secured. One variant in Canada, which – in contrast – has attracted little attention beyond its borders, is the system for the extension of collective agreements operating in Quebec. Although it seems counter-intuitive that collective agreements could have an *erga omnes* effect in a system of predominantly enterprise-based bargaining, since 1934 the Quebec Government has had the power by decree to extend the terms of a collective agreement that has 'acquired a preponderant significance and importance for establishing conditions of employment', without causing 'serious inconvenience for enterprises competing with enterprises established outside Quebec'.[58] But like many other collective bargaining arrangements, this procedure is said now to be in decline and to apply mainly to the service sector jobs – such as security guards and building maintenance – which are sheltered from foreign competition. It is nevertheless a fascinating precedent.

Still other adaptations to the representation bargaining system have been adopted in the UK and, more recently, Australia.[59] Though neither can be said to be true adherents of the Wagner model, the statutory frameworks nevertheless reflect the deeper values of a decentralised model of collective bargaining that is legitimised by explicit worker consent. In the UK, the current statutory recognition procedure operates not only in a regime where there is a mixed system of sectoral (mainly public sector) and enterprise-based (mainly private sector) bargaining, but also in a system where there is a long tradition of recognition arrangements being established on a voluntary basis, without reliance on the law and without any legal obligation on the part of the employer (though often voluntary arrangements would be agreed 'in the shadow' of legal compulsion).[60] Introduced in 2000, the legislation was designed to support the voluntary system by encouraging employers to recognise a union under the shadow of the statute if not as a direct result of any formal obligation imposed as a result of resort to the statute. Where, however, the union has no option but to use the statutory procedure, there are a number of improvements on the Wagner Act, including the right to recognition (albeit subject to statutory exceptions) without a vote on demonstrating majority membership in the bargaining unit.[61] In addition, the union has a right of access to the workplace, and also the right to hold mass meetings and 'surgeries' with small groups of interested workers, it being unlawful since 2004 for employers by various means to disrupt this activity. Nevertheless the same type of anti-union conduct reported in the US is prevalent in the UK, where use is also made of 'labour consultants' and the methods they employ. Dogged by its complexity, this procedure

[58] An Act Respecting Collective Bargaining Decrees, RSQ 1964 (as subsequently amended on several occasions), s. 6.

[59] See generally Creighton and Forsyth (eds), above n 57.

[60] In Australia, the system is underpinned by the award system that sets minimum standards across a range of workplace issues.

[61] The British equivalent of the NLRB (the Central Arbitration Committee or CAC) has a discretion to require a ballot to be held in defined circumstance even where the union has majority support. Though the numbers of cases are very small, it is fair to say that the CAC has been sparing in its use of this discretion.

has proved to be too fragile when employers resort to such tactics,[62] and it has failed miserably to halt the alarming decline in collective bargaining density in the UK, which at the time of writing is estimated to stand at 23 per cent. Direct use of the statute now stands at tens rather than hundreds of applications,[63] and this has also corresponded with a significant drop in new voluntary recognition deals.[64] The 'shadow effect' has therefore all but disappeared.

The Antipodean approach is different again, but in our view it still fits naturally into the 'representative' characterisation even if on the face of it the legislative structures differ markedly from the 'Wagner Act' framework. In New Zealand, for example, procedures for measuring worker support are simply dispensed with, and there is a system of 'members-only' collective bargaining supported by good faith obligations. In many respects, this is probably the purest form of a consent-based model. Commentators have painted a somewhat pessimistic view of the state of collective bargaining in New Zealand, and the regulatory capacity of the current legal model to alter its trajectory.[65] In Australia, by contrast, unions, by statute, are given automatic bargaining representative status on behalf of any members employed in the enterprise. As such, union representatives are entitled to bargain collectively on behalf of their members. In this respect, there is a pluralism that would be absent from the Wagner Act model. In one respect, however, the Australian Fair Work Act integrates Wagner-style majoritarianism into its structure where an employer refuses to negotiate with a bargaining representative. In this situation, the representative may seek a 'majority support determination' the effect of which, if successful, is to subject the employer to a legal duty to bargain in good faith.[66] Crucially, the Australian model dispenses with mandatory ballots allowing Fair Work Australia (FWA) to deploy a range of possible methods for gauging majority support consistent with its industrial relations expertise. It would seem that the Australian rendering of 'representative' bargaining fares best out of the English-speaking common law jurisdictions, although this assessment cannot be detached from the awards system and the deeply entrenched (and therefore enduring) conception of the state as responsible guarantor of egalitarian norms in the sphere of work.[67]

---

62 A L Bogg, 'The Mouse that never Roared: Unfair Practices and Union Recognition' (2009) 38 *Industrial Law Journal* 390.

63 A L Bogg, 'The Death of Statutory Union Recognition in the UK' (2012) 54 *Journal of Industrial Relations* 409–410.

64 G Gall, 'Union Recognition in Britain: The End of Legally Induced Voluntarism?' (2012) 41 *Industrial Law Journal* 407.

65 G Anderson and P Nuttall, 'The Good-Faith Obligation: An Effective Model for Promoting Voice?' in A Bogg and T Novitz (eds), *Voices at Work* (OUP, Oxford 2014) 194.

66 For discussion, see A Forsyth, 'Comparing Purposes and Concepts in United States and Australian Collective Bargaining Law', in Creighton and Forsyth (eds), above n 57, 212–14.

67 A Bogg, A Forsyth and T Novitz, 'Voices at Work: The Role of the State Reconfigured?' (2013) 34 *Adelaide LR* 1. One of the fortunate side-effects of comparative reflection is its jarring of parochial assumptions. The model of 'regulatory' bargaining demonstrates that it is perfectly possible to experiment and innovate with collective bargaining functions, methods and supporting structures. This counteracts the tendency in Anglo-American scholarship for the debate surrounding union legitimacy to be trapped in an ever-decreasing circle of reflection on how best to measure worker consent, rather than thinking big and challenging the consent-based paradigm itself.

7. FREEDOM OF ASSOCIATION AND THE RIGHT TO STRIKE

We have argued that labour law systems have more in common than is sometimes acknowledged. This is true in relation to both the right to organise and the right to engage in collective bargaining, and, as we shall see, true also in relation to the right to strike, which is the third of the aspects of freedom of association considered here. As discussed in relation to the other two rights, there are strong global pressures nudging in the direction of convergence, a direction of travel that is invariably de-unionising in its design, decentralising in form, and deregulatory in its impact. Similar pressures are at work in relation to the right to strike, which as already explained is under tremendous political pressure internationally, with the courts at regional level, moreover, sending contradictory messages. The conflict between human rights and economics can be seen most clearly in conflict between the ECtHR on the one hand and the European Court of Justice (ECJ) on the other, with the former – as befits a human rights court – embracing the right to strike as a fundamentally important element of the principle of freedom of association, and the latter – as befits a commercial court safeguarding constitutionalised market freedoms – seeing the right to strike as an impediment to free enterprise. What is happening internationally is also occurring nationally, and here we consider two areas where there is a convergence of restraint on the exercise of a right that is defined in most countries by its restrictions rather than its substance. The message is simple: most workers are constrained by peace obligations in collective agreements; when they are not so constrained, in many cases they are likely to be restrained by the ad hoc exercise of power by institutions of government.

(a) Legality

The first of these constraints is based on legality, the principal constraint being one that it is difficult for the British labour lawyer fully to comprehend, given that the UK is such an obvious outlier amongst developed countries. It is not simply because it is only most recently that it has been recognised judicially that there is a 'right to strike' in British law (by virtue of the infusion of international treaties), but also because perhaps uniquely there is no tradition of collective agreements being legally enforceable in the British system. This means that in British law – unlike in most labour law systems – strikes during the lifetime of a collective agreement are not forbidden, at least for the fact alone that they are in breach of a procedure in a collective agreement or deal with a matter covered by the agreement. This common law rule has been replaced by a strong statutory presumption that collective agreements are intended not to be legally enforceable, a presumption that can be displaced only by an express term to the contrary in a written agreement. But not only are such terms unknown in practice, the legislation further provides that a 'no strike' provision in a collective agreement cannot be enforced against individual workers through the medium of the contract of employment, the typical vehicle for giving legal effect to the terms of the collective agreement designed to regulate the relations between the employer and his or her employees.[68] This is not to say that there are no limits on the right to strike in the British system, with the absence of temporal controls being matched by the presence of very tight procedural controls imposing notice and ballot obligations on trade unions that are unusual in their complexity and detail.

Britain is not alone in permitting industrial action to take place during the lifetime of a collective agreement. But the absence of such a restraint is very unusual. A peace obligation during the lifetime of a collective agreement operates in both the US and Canada, as well as in at least 17 of 27 member states of the EU (most notably in Germany), as well as in Australia. It is true that in some countries it may be possible to strike during the lifetime of a collective agreement in relation to a matter that is not covered by the relevant collective agreement or that it may be possible to take solidarity action in favour of other workers involved in a dispute with their own employer (as in the case of the so-called *Lex Britannia* in Sweden). It is also true that where a dispute arises about the subject-matter or operation of a collective agreement, there will typically be procedures in the agreement for the resolution of the dispute – this much is indeed demanded by the ILO supervisory bodies. Nevertheless, when the existence of this constraint is conceded, it seems to us that everything is almost peripheral, for the fact is that the effect of the peace obligation (however it is described and whatever its origin in different systems) is to create a situation where most workers in most countries are forbidden to take strike action for most of the time, indeed for most of their working lives. The restraint is all the more significant given the tendency in some countries to negotiate collective agreements to operate for several years before expiry, as workers are constrained to provide concessions for a measure of security in uncertain times.

(b) Proportionality

The other ground for restraint that appears to us to be significant relates to controls introduced on the ground of proportionality in those circumstances where the right to strike is not prohibited on temporal or procedural grounds. This issue came to prominence most recently in the *Viking* case in which the ECJ acknowledged that the right to take collective action was recognised as part of the general principles of EU law, even though at the time the right to strike had no base in the EU treaties, and even though at the time the EU Charter of Fundamental Rights (in which it is recognised albeit with equivocation) had an uncertain legal status.[69] However, before the exercise of the right to strike could be accepted as a permissible restraint on the right of businesses to freedom of establishment, the exercise of the right to strike in any particular case would not only have to be objectively justified, but would also have to be 'necessary to achieve the objective pursued'. For this latter purpose, it would be

[68] We should note, however, that where industrial action in the UK is characterised as 'unofficial' because it is not authorised or endorsed by the trade union, individual strikers forfeit unfair dismissal protection for the duration of the industrial dispute. The effect of this is, indirectly at least, to entrench the union's authority in the conduct of industrial disputes: see Trade Union and Labour Relations (Consolidation) Act 1992 (UK), s. 237(2).

[69] *Case C-438/05, International Transport Workers' Federation (ITF) and Finnish Seamen's Union (FSU) v Viking Line* [2007] ECR I-10779. Also *Case C-341/05, Laval Un Partneri Ltd v Svenska Byggnadsarbetareförbundet* [2007] ECR 1-11767.

necessary to examine whether the union had 'other means at its disposal which were less restrictive of [the employer's] freedom of establishment in order to bring to a successful conclusion the collective negotiations', and whether the trade union had 'exhausted those means before initiating such action'. It is true that these qualifications introduced by the ECJ apply only in the context of transnational disputes affecting freedom of movement between EU member states, and that they do not affect the legality of disputes confined to matters within the territory of each member state. Their impact is nevertheless not to be diminished, the ILO Committee of Experts referring to:

> the likelihood of such issues becoming more frequent within the current context of globalization, particularly in certain sectors of employment, like the airline sector and considered that the doctrine being articulated in these ECJ judgments was likely to have a significant restrictive effect on the exercise of the right to strike in practice in a manner contrary to the Convention.[70]

In this way the ECJ has prohibited the right to strike while appearing to permit it, the *Viking* doctrine being invoked by British Airways in 2008 to restrain a strike by pilots. In jurisdictions such as the UK, where procedural methods such as injunctions (administered by commercial rather than labour courts) loom large in the employer's armoury of counter-measures, the destructiveness of the *Viking* doctrine cannot be gainsaid. However, although unusual *de jure*, the requirement of proportionality is not unique to EU law or to the law of several of its member states, even if the ILO Committee of Experts 'has never included the need to assess the proportionality of interests bearing in mind a notion of freedom of establishment or freedom to provide services'.[71] An incipient and *de facto* proportionality requirement is now being developed across the world as different governmental actors intervene to ban strikes by individual groups of workers where these strikes are seen to have a significant impact on consumers. For example, although not designated by the ILO as an essential service, it now seems impossible for airline pilots to take strike action without state intervention. Thus, a dispute in 2011 involving Qantas pilots was brought to an end when the Australian Government applied to Fair Work Australia for an order to suspend 'protected industrial action'. Under the legislation the order can be made where FWA is satisfied that the action would 'cause significant damage to the Australian economy or an important part of it', it being enough in this case that there would be damage to the tourism and aviation sectors.[72] Similarly, in 2012 Air Canada pilots were met with back to work legislation,[73] a uniquely Canadian way of dealing with industrial action, and one which has been upheld by the SCC as not violating the Charter of Rights and Freedoms.[74] The effect of such legislation is to prevent a strike starting (or bringing it to an end if it has started), by ordering (i) workers to remain at work (or go back to

---

70 ILO Committee of Experts, Observation 2010 (ILO, Geneva 2011) (referring to ILO Committee of Experts, Observation 2009 (ILO, Geneva 2010)).

71 ILO Committee of Experts, Observation 2009 (ILO, Geneva 2010).

72 See *Australian and International Pilots Association v Fair Work Australia* [2012] FCAFC 65.

73 Protecting Air Service Act 2012 (SC 2012, c 2).

74 But see now *Saskatchewan Federation of Labour v. Saskatchewan*, above n 36.

work as the case may be), (ii) the extension of an existing collective agreement, and (iii) the resolution of the dispute by arbitration. This heavy reliance on discretion and specifically tailored legislative interventions seems difficult to reconcile with basic constitutional norms such as the rule of law (a value that neo-liberal critics of trade unions are especially fond of invoking).

8. A NEW ECONOMIC ORTHODOXY – ECONOMIC PRESSURES TOWARDS DECENTRALISATION

Returning to some of the questions addressed earlier in this chapter, we saw that – despite *Viking* and other decisions of the ECJ – there was emerging a new legal orthodoxy in which human rights and constitutional standards were now being read to protect the right to organise, the right to bargain and the right to strike. These developments provide an opportunity by litigation to resist some of the erosions of labour rights that appear to be taking place across the globe. But there is another orthodoxy at work here, which we identify as the new economic orthodoxy which has gripped regional and national governments as they seek to secure a competitive base in a global economy. Whereas in the past the logic of the prevailing economic orthodoxy favoured the promotion of trade union membership and the expansion of collective bargaining coverage, the logic of the new orthodoxy appears to favour – indeed demand – the reverse. Deregulation and market freedom are now nudging in the direction of a new convergence in which labour standards are being eroded by a process of de-unionisation, with the gap to be filled in some cases by minimum standards as a floor below which people are not to be permitted to fall. This is a process that appears indifferent to political tradition or constitutional obligation, with the Eurozone crisis leading to the imposition of measures designed to dilute or remove the influence of trade unions and trade union activity in what were once social democracies. Let us be under no illusions here. This is no globalised invisible hand. It represents a very deliberate attempt by identifiable international actors to use economic leverage to bring about radical changes in national labour law systems, often in defiance of democratic and constitutional constraints in those systems. The main impact of these developments has been to decentralise collective bargaining activity and to drive a number of EU member states in the direction of representational collective bargaining activity at the expense of traditional forms of regulatory bargaining, a process made most famous by developments in Greece. This phenomenon raises serious questions over the veracity of scholarly claims denying that there is a process of comparative neo-liberal convergence underway.

(a) The Impact of the Sovereign Debt Crisis

The rising significance of international labour standards identified above has perhaps only been surpassed by the escalating role for international organisations such as the International Monetary Fund, the European Central Bank, and regional blocs such as the EU. The example of Greece in the wake of the sovereign debt crisis demonstrates how these supranational entities can bring about seismic changes in national labour law systems through the conditions in international loan agreements.[75] A central element in these reforms has been a promotion of the *decentralisation* of bargaining structures as a mechanism for removing 'rigidities' in wage setting.[76] As Koukiadaki and Kretsos have argued powerfully, 'the priority that is given to firm-level agreements over those concluded at sectoral level, in conjunction with the prohibition on extending agreements, points to significant deregulatory trends in the collective bargaining system'.[77] Both Ireland and Romania have also faced contentious deregulatory pressures in their own memoranda of understanding connected to loan arrangements. More generally and apparently quite independently of the conditions attached to the loan agreements, the new forms of economic governance in the EU 'encourage the right framework conditions for wage bargaining systems and labour cost developments consistent with price stability, productivity trends over the medium-term and the need to reduce macroeconomics imbalances'.[78] If the precise mix of steers in the new arrangements might defy a simple reduction into a deregulatory logic, decentralisation of collective bargaining mechanisms appears as an important goal, even allowing for a measured sensitivity to social partner autonomy. And while the regulatory techniques inherent in the new forms of economic governance are somewhat softer than the brutalism of the arrangements imposed on Greece and other countries, the difference is one of tone rather than ideology.

It is remarkable how supranational institutions – the IMF and the ECB – have emerged as rapacious agents of a neo-liberal ideology that identifies bargaining decentralisation as both a means and an objective in the reform of national labour law systems, especially in countries left economically vulnerable by the financial crisis. At the heart of the austerity measures, was the desire of these institutions to secure an 'internal devaluation', defined to mean 'a sharp reduction in wages and consequent living standards'.[79] In the case of Greece, for example, this was designed to enhance competitiveness in the international economy, to be achieved by 'fundamentally revising the way the collective bargaining system functioned, especially at sectoral level'.[80] The system operating in Greece was one where the national agreement set minimum terms and conditions for all workers. Sector agreements could then make specific provision in individual sectors to improve upon the national agreement, while enterprise agreements in turn could in some cases build upon the sectoral agreements in individual enterprises. Apart from imposing pay cuts by law and invalidating any provisions of collective agreements that made provision to the contrary, the austerity package – imposed by the 'Troika' of the IMF, the European Central Bank and the

---

[75] A Koukiadaki and L Kretsos, 'Opening Pandora's Box: The Sovereign Debt Crisis and Labour Market Regulation in Greece' (2012) 41 *Industrial Law Journal* 276.

[76] Ibid, 290.

[77] Ibid.

[78] For fuller details, see K D Ewing, 'The Death of Social Europe' (2015) 26 *King's Law Journal* (in press).

[79] This was being imposed as an alternative to a currency devaluation, which was not possible for Greece as part of the Eurozone.

[80] ILO, *Report of the High Level Mission to Greece* (19–23 September 2011) (ILO, Geneva 2011), para 47.

European Commission – also provided that both sector- and enterprise-based agreements could make provision less favourable than that contained in the national agreement. Under the new law, moreover, ad hoc associations of employees could negotiate these latter arrangements where there were no trade unions. This last provision was a response by the Greek Government to the concerns of the supranational institutions that enterprise-level agreements were not sufficiently widespread. This was because there were very few trade unions at enterprise level, with enterprise agreements applying only to enterprises with more than 50 workers, and with Greek law requiring a minimum of 20 persons to establish an association.

(b) Troika v ILO

The regulatory activity of the supranational entities requires particular attention in developing a coherent theory of comparative collective labour law. While the traditional focus of attention has properly been with bodies like the ILO and more recently the OECD, these other entities are now providing a countervailing source of deregulatory pressure, and they appear at the moment to be prevailing. The extent of the clash between the new and once new economic orthodoxies is to be revealed by the initial response of the ILO supervisory bodies to the afore-mentioned developments in Greece. The issue having been brought to the attention of the Committee of Experts in 2011, the latter concluded that such was the complexity of what was happening that the government of Greece should be invited to avail itself of the technical assistance of the ILO and to accept a High Level Mission 'to facilitate a comprehensive understanding of the issues', before the Committee proceeded to assess the impact of the austerity measures on a number of ratified Conventions that included but ranged well beyond those relating to freedom of association. The High Level Mission was composed of ILO officials and produced a report that made sobering reading, highlighting not only the decentralisation of pay bargaining, but also the changing nature of the employment from permanent to flexible forms of engagement, and the swingeing cuts in public and private sector wage rates. Quite apart from their implications for workers generally and freedom of association specifically, the measures were said to have a disproportionate impact on women, more likely to be bearing the brunt of the move to flexible employment arrangements, and more likely to be employed in the public sector where jobs were being cut.

On freedom of association, the Committee found that there had been a breach of both ILO Conventions 87 and 98. The latter gave rise to particular concern, here the Committee challenging the procedures for the decentralisation of collective bargaining, and in particular the procedures permitting derogation from sectoral agreements by non-union associations of workers at enterprise level. These latter provisions led the Committee to express '*deep concern*' that the changes – 'aimed at permitting deviations from higher level agreements through "negotiations" with non-unionized structures' – are '*likely to have a significant – and potentially devastating – impact on the industrial relations system in the country*'. This, however, was only the start, the Committee expressing the fear '*that the entire foundation of collective bargaining in the country may be vulnerable to collapse under this new framework'*.[81] This was because 90 per cent of the (private sector) workforce was employed in small enterprises, in a system where trade unions cannot legally be formed in enterprises with less than 20 employees. In these circumstances,

> granting collective bargaining rights to other types of workers' representation which are not afforded the guarantees of independence that apply to the structure and formation of trade unions and the protection of its officers and members is likely to seriously undermine the position of trade unions as the representative voice of the workers in the collective bargaining process.[82]

The 'risk' that 'the entire foundation of collective bargaining in the country may be vulnerable to collapse', was reinforced 'given that the abolition of the favourability principle set out [in legislation of 2010 and 2011] has the effect of nullifying the binding nature of collective agreements'. Here the Committee recalled the general principle enunciated in ILO Recommendation 91 (Collective Agreements Recommendation, 1951) that:

> collective agreements should bind the signatories thereto and those on whose behalf the agreement is concluded. Employers and workers bound by a collective agreement should not be able to include in contracts of employment stipulations contrary to those contained in the collective agreement. The Committee considers that this recognition of the principle of favourability should apply, according to the circumstances, to lower level collective agreements, unless the same parties are involved in the negotiations.[83]

9. WHEN ORTHODOXIES COLLIDE

The developments in Greece and elsewhere in the EU are notable for the fact that they are being driven through in a manner which appears to conflict with the other emerging orthodoxy, which involves a growing juridical recognition of the core freedom of association rights that have been shown to be vulnerable to erosion in the name of austerity. The question now is which will prevail in this conflict of economic and human rights? This is a question which the Greek trade unions are testing to its limits, with complaints made to the ILO (in the manner described) as well as to the Council of Europe's Social Rights Committee (though with limited effect in relation to freedom of association in view of the failure of Greece formally to accept the freedom of association provisions of the Social Charters of 1961 and 1996). Proceedings were also brought in the Greek courts claiming that the austerity measures introduced by the Greek Government at the bidding of the Troika violated both the Greek constitution and the European Convention on Human Rights. After a very long delay, judgment was not delivered until the summer of 2014, the Council of State dismissed both legal challenges in what was a high stakes initiative by the Greek trade union confederation

[81] ILO Committee of Experts, Observation 2011 (ILO, Geneva 2012).
[82] Ibid.
[83] Ibid.

(GSEE). However, the legal questions are by no means resolved, with the developments in Greece raising a serious crisis of legality, in the sense that it is difficult to see how the austerity package introduced at the demand of the Troika could be said to be consistent with the ECHR post *Demir and Baycara* (above), and how as a result it could be consistent with the requirements of EU law.

(a) EU Charter of Rights

The alacrity with which core trade union activity was sacrificed on the altar of economic liberalism is all the more surprising for following so soon in the wake of the Lisbon Treaty in which the EU renewed its vows, and in the course of doing so proclaimed in Treaty on European Union (TEU), Article 2 that the Union is 'founded on the values of respect for human dignity, freedom, democracy, equality, *the rule of law and respect for human rights*', in a society in which pluralism, non-discrimination, tolerance, justice, solidarity and equality between women and men prevail' (emphasis added). Similar values are rehearsed in Article 3 which proclaims an obligation on the part of the Union to 'combat social exclusion and discrimination', and a duty 'to promote social justice and protection, equality between women and men, solidarity between generations and protection of the rights of the child'. It is presumed that these provisions are meaningful and enforceable, and that they are not the 'beautifully worded Articles [which are] nothing but sententious platitudes, binding no one', which famously according to Kahn-Freund were said to be found in the Weimar Constitution.[84] Perhaps more important is TEU, Article 6, which provides that the Union recognises the rights, freedoms and principles set out in the EU Charter of Fundamental Rights, now said to have 'the same legal value as the Treaties'. Article 12 of the EU Charter of Fundamental Rights provides in turn that everyone has a right to freedom of association, said to imply 'the right of everyone to form and to join trade unions for the protection of his or her interests'. This is particularly important in the light of the provisions of Article 52(3), which provides that:

> In so far as this Charter contains rights which correspond to rights guaranteed by the Convention for the Protection of Human Rights and Fundamental Freedoms, the meaning and scope of those rights shall be the same as those laid down by the said Convention. This provision shall not prevent Union law providing more extensive protection.

TEU, Article 12 of course corresponds *directly* (if not word for word) with ECHR, Article 11, relevant in view of the spectacular flowering of the latter in *Demir and Baycara v Turkey*, above, where as we have seen the Court held – having regard to ILO Convention 98 as well as other instruments (including the EU Charter!) – that the right to bargain collectively was protected by ECHR, Article 11.[85] If Article 12 of the EU Charter is to be read consistently with the ECHR, Article 11, and if the ECHR, Article 11 is to be read consistently with ILO Convention 98, the implications are as enormous as they are obvious. It is true that Article 28 of the EU Charter of Fundamental Rights

---

84 O Kahn-Freund, 'The Weimar Constitution' (1944) 15 *Pol Q* 229.

85 The ECtHR in *Demir and Baycara* appeared to pay more respect to the Charter than did the ECJ in the corresponding decisions in *Viking* and *Laval*, above n 69.

provides that 'the right to negotiate and conclude collective agreements at the appropriate level', and that this applies only 'in accordance with Community law and national laws and practices'. In our view, however, this provision has been rendered largely – if not wholly – redundant by *Demir and Baycara*, to the extent that the latter now expands Article 12 of the Charter to include collective bargaining. Since Article 12 thus interpreted is a norm of Community law, and since Article 28 is subject to the requirement that the provision be 'in accordance with Community law', it would seem to follow that Article 28 must track Article 12. The right to bargain collectively is thus now separately recognised by the latter, but without the qualification in Article 28.[86] Following the report of the ILO HLM in 2011 and the ILO Committee of Experts in 2012, it is thus strongly arguable the austerity plan for Greece is utterly illegal for its failure to respect the requirements of Article 12 of the EU Charter.

(b) Social Europe

Apart from the embedding of the EU Charter of Fundamental Rights at Lisbon in 2008, the other reason why the direct assault on freedom of association is surprising is because it so obviously undermines the provisions of Title X of the Treaty on the Functioning of the European Union (TFEU), which provides both the commitment and infrastructure necessary to develop social policy, which now looks like a wretched after-thought, finished off by the euro-crisis. Title X is the legacy of another era, imposing a duty on the Commission to promote consultation between management and labour at Union level and to facilitate dialogue between them, management and labour designated for this purpose as social partners. Where it is proposed to initiate legislation on a given issue relating to social policy, the Commission must consult with the social partners, who may elect to initiate a procedure whereby the matter is resolved by an agreement between them, this agreement to be presented to the Council for a decision following a proposal from the Commission. This procedure had been used on a number of occasions, and provides the source of the authority for Directive 2010/18/EU, the Parental Leave Directive; Directive 97/81/EC, the Part-time Workers Directive; and Directive 99/70/EC, the Fixed-term Workers Directive. Under this procedure, the TFEU provides simply that the European Parliament shall be informed, giving rise inevitably to questions about the democratic legitimacy of a process in which legislative power is exercised by the representatives of capital and labour, who are unlikely to be directly accountable in any meaningful sense to those on behalf of whom they act, and in the case of the trade union official there will be no accountability to the majority of workers who are not trade union members. The potential of the social dialogue process has yet to be realised fully, its weaknesses attributable in large measure to political indifference on the part of institutions such as

---

[86] In any event, to the extent that Art. 28 provides a right to bargain collectively in accordance with 'Community law', the afore-mentioned Community law must surely include Art. 12 of the Charter, which by virtue of Art. 52(3) must also include the right to bargain collectively.

the European Commission and the diminishing threat of European social legislation enacted in the standard way.[87]

Trade union involvement in law-making in this way might be thought of as the highest form of regulatory engagement on the part of trade unions. But the TFEU did not stop there, also addressing the trade union role where legislation is made at EU level by more conventional means. Although the social partners are not the authors of any such legislation, the treaty provides that member states may entrust to management and labour the responsibility to implement Directives or Decisions by means of collective agreement, provided the member state ensures that the obligations in the instrument in question are fully met by such agreements. This is an indication not only that the European Social Model acknowledges the regulatory bargaining model (as we saw in relation to the Posted Workers Directive), but that it is in fact built upon it, a point reinforced by individual Directives such as Directive 2003/88/EC, the Working Time Directive. The latter permits derogations by collective agreement from various limits set out in the Directive, it being clear that when referring to collective bargaining the authors of the Directive had regulatory bargaining in mind as the paradigm, referring to agreements concluded at national or regional level, with express provision having to be made for those member states where there is no such bargaining to enable agreements to be made between the two sides of industry at the 'appropriate collective level'. The point of this rather lengthy exegesis is to suggest that by undermining the infrastructure of regulatory collective bargaining at national level, the Commission and the European Central Bank are succeeding also in undermining a procedure on which the European Social Model was in part constructed and fully embedded in the treaty.

10. CONCLUSION

International treaties such as ILO Conventions 87 and 98 help to define core questions with which the law should deal, and help also to constrain the normative options within which countries should operate when designing or developing labour laws relating to freedom of association specifically. This is not to deny of course that compliance with ILO standards permits wide variations in the implementation of these principles. That said, we would also argue that international supervision begins a process tending towards convergence which is reinforced by (and this is important when we contrast Europe and North America) regional supervision of freedom of association under human right norms, and by national supervision of freedom of association by constitutional norms informed by international standards. It appears to us that there is now more active supervision of labour standards on human rights grounds, and universally greater protection of labour rights in national constitutions, which in some cases are becoming more alert in their protection of these rights. By these means we detect a potential loss of autonomy on the part of those making labour laws, and a need

[87] See A Bogg and R Dukes, 'The European Social Dialogue: From Autonomy to Here', in M Freedland and N Kountouris (eds), *Resocializing Europe in a Time of Crisis* (CUP, Cambridge 2013) 466.

to defer to higher sources of law, whether it be international human rights law or constitutional law.

There are, however, other forces at work pointing in the other direction. Despite the greater recognition of the substance of the right to freedom of association, there is more and more evidence of its erosion in different countries, with three symptoms of that erosion identified in this chapter. Although there is no formal transplantation of deregulatory laws, there is a process of convergence at work, which is seeking to minimise trade union influence. On the *right to organise* we see this in the renewal of interest in 'right to work' laws, as more jurisdictions adopt regimes in which union security arrangements are forbidden. Put another way, we are unaware of any regime that in recent times has legislated to permit closed shop or other arrangements. On the *right to bargain collectively*, we have presented two models, and have suggested that the pressure is now on for a move towards more representative than regulatory systems of bargaining. This is reflected in the tolerance of non-union forms of bargaining (which we see also in jurisdictions other than those referred to here, most notoriously in Mexico), and also in the insistence that collective bargaining should be decentralised, in a manner consistent with the representative bargaining arrangements we have discussed. To that extent, it may be that we begin to see a softening of the common law/civil law divide, as more civilian countries adopt decentralised bargaining arrangements that have tended to be associated with the English-speaking common law world.

The purpose of all of this is clearly to shift the balance of power in the workplace. By undermining the regulatory role performed by trade unions, it is also about diluting the role of trade unions in liberal democracies, and about shifting the balance of power relating to the role of organised labour in society as a whole. These objectives are also reflected in the laws and practices relating to the *right to strike*, where trade unions in most systems traditionally have been tightly constrained, most commonly by a prohibition on strikes during the lifetime of a collective agreement. In the modern era, however, we find a different kind of convergence on the right to strike in circumstances where its exercise is likely to be effective, with governments operating on an ad hoc basis to stop specific strikes, or empowering employers to do the same. Not only do we find a convergence of purpose by different methods, by a curious coincidence we find strikes by the same groups of workers constrained by government intervention in different countries. As in the case of union security, it is difficult to find recent examples of governments or Parliaments in leading industrialised economies willingly introducing new laws on the right to strike to remove controls from organised labour.

This is not to deny that there are contradictions at work here, not the least of which is that human rights litigation now appears to protect trade union freedom, having earlier provided the basis for an earlier wave of attacks, notably in the Council of Europe on the question of trade union security, with the result that closed shop and other arrangements are now almost impossible to pursue. The greatest contradiction, however, is the contradiction between the two orthodoxies, between human rights and economics, a contradiction revealed most clearly for lawyers in the clash between the ECJ (the business court) and the ECtHR (the human rights court). It is difficult at this stage to see how this conflict will be resolved, though it is not necessary to be a Marxist to be pessimistic about the most likely outcome, which will see a reconciliation of the two orthodoxies in a manner most consistent with the new economic orthodoxy.

Indeed it is already the case that in its most recent report, the ILO Committee of Experts has moderated its tone in relation to Greece and appears to accept that decentralised bargaining arrangements are consistent with ILO Convention 98, provided that workers are represented by a trade union in the process. It should be evident that none of these contradictions are playing out as blind economic forces, separately from the deliberate agency of institutional actors such as courts, political institutions, financial institutions and business corporations. The outcomes at this time are impossible to predict. But there is everything to play for. Ultimately, it is only where workers exercise their social agency through collective organisation that the fate of the new 'double movement' can be assured in a way that ensures work is constituted as a decent and civilising human activity. The true significance of freedom of association is in providing the principal constitutional basis to this exercise of social agency.

11. Employee voice outside collective bargaining

Monika Schlachter and Achim Seifert

1. INTRODUCTION

a. Identifying the Meaning of 'Employee Voice Beyond Collective Bargaining'

Collective bargaining has been and still is the most relevant instrument of collective employee voice on the labor markets. Through their 'countervailing power', labor unions try to establish minimum labor standards on the labor markets and may provide their members with an appropriate level of protection guaranteed by collective agreements. There is not only historical evidence for this outstanding impact of collective bargaining on employee protection.[1] Also, the numerous guarantees of freedom of association and of the right to collective bargaining in both national laws as well as international law reveal the extraordinary relevance of collective bargaining.

Nonetheless, there is a wide range of other forms and mechanisms to give employees a voice toward the employer or the State which have been developed over the last 150 years beyond collective bargaining. Many countries have institutionalized through statutory law or collective agreements other channels of (collective) employee voice and guarantee thereby forms of employee 'representation', 'participation' or 'involvement'. Such forms of a collective voice beyond collective bargaining may be institutionalized on different levels. By far the most important level is the workplace or plant level where specific problems related to the work process can be solved in cooperation with the workforce. Some national systems have gone beyond a mere workplace representation and have additionally institutionalized an employee representation on company level (*e.g.* in the supervisory boards or boards of directors of big corporations) enabling employees to really participate in the company's decision-making. As to transnational companies, their cross-border character requires specific solutions that are not limited to the boundaries of national law. And finally, we find in many national legal orders employee representations in public institutions such as Administrative Bodies (*e.g.* social security bodies), Labor Courts, Labor Chambers or Economic and Social Councils which are involved in the legislative procedure. Many countries cumulate and interlink different levels of employee involvement, creating thereby a

[1] For a summary of the historical development of the freedom of association and collective bargaining between the nineteenth century and 1945 cf. Antoine Jacobs, Collective Self-Regulation, in: Bob Hepple (ed.), *The Making of Labour Law in Europe – A Comparative Study of Nine Countries up to 1945*, Mansell, 1986, pp. 193–241, and for the period between 1945 and 2004 cf. Antoine Jacobs, Collective Labour Relations, in: Bob Hepple & Bruno Veneziani (eds), *The Transformation of Labour Law – A Comparative Study of 15 Countries 1945–2004,* Oxford & Portland/Oregon 2009, pp. 202–31.

very complex network of relationships between the actors of the different representation levels.

The purpose of this chapter is to give a broad overview of existing institutionalized types of employee voice that have been developed outside collective bargaining, and to systematize them. Due to the limited space of this chapter, non-institutionalized forms of employee voice such as 'work centers', social protest movements, community networks and the like will not be emphasized.[2] In analyzing institutionalized forms of employee voice, we will include models of union representation (*e.g.* at the workplace) as well as those representing the whole workforce, *i.e.* unionized as well as non-unionized employees, bodies exclusively representing employees and those integrating the employers' side as well. Emphasis will be laid on employee voice at the workplace (infra 2), but also the various forms of employee participation at company level (infra 3), in transnational companies (infra 4) and in public institutions (infra 5) will be considered. But before dealing with these different levels of employee voice, some preliminary remarks on the authors' methodology (infra 1.b) as well as on the functions of the various institutionalized forms of employee voice (infra 1.c) might be useful.

b. Methodology

From a methodological point of view, three major caveats are made for this chapter.

A first point to be made concerns the typologization of existing forms of employee voice outside collective bargaining. Our aim is to analyze ideal types in the sense *Max Weber* has used the term.[3] The ideal type of a social phenomenon is a fictional construct for research purposes by which the analyzed social reality is not fully reproduced, but is accentuated and radicalized in a coherent synthesis of the various forms a social phenomenon exists in reality. It, thus, can serve as a standard or a scale for legal comparison and is an appropriate methodological tool to measure and to analyze the concrete existing forms of a social phenomenon that have been synthesized in an ideal type. This does not mean that the ideal type of a social phenomenon has the meaning of a social optimum or of a 'good' social development, serving as a 'good example', 'best practice' or a normative model for social reality; its function is not to establish a rule for a 'necessary' development (*e.g.* of labor law in the analyzed legal orders). The ideal type only has heuristic meaning: although elaborated in an empirical (inductive) way by synthesizing the different varieties of a social phenomenon, it only guides the analysis of individual social phenomena and serves as a hypothetical concept that gives the researcher a scale to measure the concrete social phenomena to be analyzed. Thus, the Weberian method of the ideal type facilitates the work of the comparative lawyer considerably: In the present context, it enables us to establish a typology of different forms and mechanisms of employee voice beyond collective

---

[2] See for example: Richard B. Freeman, Joni Hersch, and Lawrence Mishel, eds. *Emerging Labor Market Institutions for the Twenty-first Century*, University of Chicago Press, 2007.

[3] See Max Weber, Die Objektivität sozialwissenschaftlicher Erkenntnis, in: 19 Archiv für Sozialwissenschaft und Sozialpolitik 24-87 (under II.), reprinted in: Max Weber, Soziologie – Universalgeschichtliche Analysen – Politik, Eduard Baumgarten (ed.), Stuttgart 1973, pp. 186–262, at 234–50.

bargaining. However, the reader should always be aware of the Achilles' heel of this method when reading this chapter. As a matter of fact, the real existing forms ('Realtypen') of ideal types such as works councils or board-level representation may differ from one country to another even though national labor laws have made a choice for one ideal type. Even though a number of countries have 'transplanted' forms of employee representation from other countries, these 'legal transplants',[4] through their embedding in a different legal and political setting, have had their own development, disconnecting them more and more from the country of origin of the 'legal transplant'. Thus, as it will be shown later (see infra 2.b.i), the French Company Committee [*comité d'entreprise*] served as a point of reference for various national legislators (*e.g.* in Belgium, Luxembourg or Spain) that established a body bringing together the employer as well as employees' representatives. However, the composition and the competences of these 'legal transplants' as well as their embedding in a pre-existing set of industrial relations differ considerably from the French Company Committee. One should therefore always be careful in emphasizing the common points of these representative bodies.

The second methodological caveat refers to the fact that all representative bodies we will be dealing with are embedded in a (national) structure or 'system' of industrial relations. If we analyze in the following pages different representative bodies or mechanisms separated from other channels of employee voice in a given national context, it should always be borne in mind that their real power and significance only become obvious when also taking into account their complex relationship(s) with other levels and bodies of employee representation. Thus, the real power of a German works council [*Betriebsrat*] or a French company committee only becomes clear, if one takes also into consideration the role and the weight labor unions have within these representative bodies as well as other existing channels of employee representation such as the board-level representation in big German corporations. A comparative analysis that goes beyond a mere typology as suggested in this chapter, would therefore have to consider the complex relationships a given employee representation body entertains with the existing other institutions or tools of employee voice in a given national context. The different types of employee voice beyond collective bargaining, analyzed in this chapter, are consequently nothing more than a superficial orientation and only provide the reader with some raw material to go further in a concrete analysis of comparative labor law.

A third preliminary remark concerns the geographical scope of this chapter. As both authors are writing within the European context, the focus will clearly be on the various forms of employee voice outside collective bargaining that have been developed in European countries even though occasional references will be made to national systems in other parts of the world. This geographical limitation is not only justified by the authors' regional origin but also by the fact that the institutionalization of employee representation outside collective bargaining has been particularly developed in Europe since the end of the nineteenth century and still is found in its different forms and models, above all, in European countries. As far as institutionalized forms of employee

---

[4] For an in depth analysis of 'legal transplants', see Alan Watson, *Legal Transplants – An Approach to Comparative Law*, 2nd edition, University of Georgia Press, 1993.

involvement are found in other parts of the world, they are often inspired by one national law of a European country.

c. Functions

As far as the functions of these different channels of employee voice beyond collective bargaining are concerned, it is interesting to note that the starting point of this long development has been marked by individual employers who established forms of worker participation or involvement on a voluntary basis. A few examples will suffice in the present context. In France, *Léon Harmel* created a Factory Council [*Conseil d'usine*] for his spinning company at Val-des-bois in 1875 and *Eugène Schneider* established Worker Delegates [*Délégués ouvriers*] in his steel works at Le Creusot.[5] In Germany, notably *Ernst Abbe* – one of the co-founders of the Carl-Zeiss-Jena plants – institutionalized a Worker Committee [*Arbeiterausschuss*] in his company;[6] the same applies to *Heinrich Freese* who established a Worker Committee for his company in the 1880s.[7]

There are various reasons for establishing employees' representation apart from unions. Philanthropy of employers was probably the reason in some cases.[8] Nonetheless, the motives of employers to establish employee involvement on a voluntary basis were mostly far more selfish. There is no doubt that in many cases the most important reason was the employers' attempt to undermine the increasing influence of labor unions on their workforces. By means of factory councils, works councils, joint committees or other forms of collective voice, employers tried to keep labor unions out of their shops and to offer their employees peaceful cooperation within the company. This anti-union direction of worker representation bodies has been put into a nutshell by *August Bebel*, one of the founding fathers of the German Social-democratic Party (SPD) who characterized in a speech in the German Reichstag the establishing of Workers' Committees [*Arbeiterausschüsse*] in 1891 as the 'fig leaf of the crypto-constitutionalism, aiming at masking the existing factory feudalism'. It is therefore not without reason that Article 5 of ILO Convention No. 135 concerning Protection and Facilities to be afforded to Workers' Representatives in the Undertaking (1971) obliges the ratifying Member States to take appropriate measures 'to ensure that the existence of elected representatives is not used to undermine the position of the trade unions

---

5 See Jean-Pierre Le Crom, L'introuvable démocratie salariale: Le droit de la représentation du personnel dans l'entreprise (1890–2002), pp. 14 et seq; see also Norbert Olszak, Histoire du droit du travail, Paris 1999, p. 117.

6 For details see Ernst Abbe, Über die Aufgaben des Arbeiterausschusses, in: id., Gesammelte Abhandlungen III – Vorträge, Reden und Schriften sozialpolitischen und verwandten Inhalts, Hildesheim, Zürich & New York 1989, pp. 250–61.

7 An account of this experience can be found in Heinrich Freese, Die konstitutionelle Fabrik, Jena 1909.

8 At about the same time employers in the United States were setting intramural systems of worker representation; some as a matter of progressive social policy. E. Burton, *Employee Representation* (1926), C. French, *The Shop Committee in the United States* (1923), some to keep unions out. *E.g.* Jonathan Rees, *Representation and Rebellion: The Rockefeller Plan at the Colorado Fuel and Iron Company, 1914–1942*, University Press of Colorado, 2010.

concerned or their representatives and to encourage cooperation on all relevant matters between the elected representatives and the trade unions concerned and their representatives', 'where there exist in the same undertaking both trade union representatives and elected representatives'.

Finally, in some cases the institutionalization of alternative channels of employee voice replaces missing trade unions. Notably in countries where the union density is under-developed or for plants and companies where no trade unions are represented the institutionalization of other channels of employee representation (*e.g.* through works councils) may be an appropriate instrument to ensure an effective employee protection through collective action. One example is probably the role the Personnel Delegate [*délégué du personnel*] plays in various African countries:[9] even though the legal provisions are very similar to French law, to which goes back the Personnel Delegate, it has another function in industrial relation systems where a real union representation is lacking in many companies. However, the question must be raised whether this institutionalization of employee representation may have a deterring effect from future unionization.[10]

2. EMPLOYEE VOICE AT THE WORKPLACE

Historically, employee representation was institutionalized for the first time at the level of the workplace, *i.e.* in the modern plant. At the modern workplace specific problems arise which need to be addressed by labor law. A few keywords will suffice to characterize the problematic. The modern (industrial) plant essentially is characterized by an aggregation of 'means of production' and of work such as machines, other tools, raw materials, know-how and workers in one organization. Dependent on the company's size and on the complexity of the work process, the modern workplace is embedded in a wider net of work steps and is part of a division of labor between the workers. This complex working process is organized and coordinated by the employer; this remains one of his essential managerial prerogatives even though the law has limited this unilateral power of the employer. Employees are integrated in this work process in the plant, which is unilaterally determined by the employer, and experience personal subordination vis-à-vis their employer: At the workplace, they are subjected to the employers' instructions, directives and orders concerning the work performance. It is also there where they are exposed to specific health and safety risks. And as the coming together of a number of employees at one and the same workplace often is the source of conflicts within the workforce, employers need to coordinate their employees,

---

[9] The Personnel Delegate is recognized in the legal systems of most of the French-speaking African countries: cf. *e.g.* Art. L. 211 et seq Senegal Labor Code and Art. 61.1 et seq Labor Code of the Ivory Coast; see also Art. 172 et seq of the Proposal for a Uniform Act concerning Labor Law [*Avant-projet d'un Acte uniforme relatif au droit du travail*] of the Organisation pour l'Harmonisation en Afrique du Droit des Affaires (OHADA).

[10] Mark Barenberg, 'Democracy and domination in the law of workplace cooperation: from bureaucratic to flexible production.' *Columbia Law Review* (1994): 753–983.

which often is done by the establishing of work rules [*règlements intérieurs* or *Arbeitsordnungen*].

The ways in which national labor laws address these challenges, resulting from the structure of the modern workplace, differ considerably. A number of countries have institutionalized by statutory law specifically at the plant level exclusively representing employees, namely works councils (infra, 2.a.). Other models bring together employee representatives and the employer within the committee, such as the French company committee (infra, 2.b.i). However, various national legal orders have not created such representation bodies at all and trust the union representatives or provide the establishing of union representatives in addition to already existing institutionalized forms of worker representation at plant level (infra, 2.c). In a number of countries, employee representation bodies have been established, which address specific questions such as health and safety at work, or represent specific groups of employees being more in need of protection than the regular employee (infra, 2.d). Finally, there are also forms of employer driven employee voice at the workplace such as 'quality circles' (infra, 2.e).

a. Works Councils

One important model of institutionalizing employee voice at plant level is the works council. These are bodies that exclusively represent the employees of a plant and are elected by its unionized as well as the non-unionized workforce. Thus, works councils do not integrate the employer's representatives, as is the case with joint committees (see infra 2.b). One well-known example is the German *Betriebsrat* whose roots go back to an Act of 1891. But also many other countries have established works council systems, inter alia, Austria, France [*Délégué du personnel*] and the Grand-Duchy of Luxembourg with the personnel delegations [*Délégations du personnel*] and the Netherlands with its company council [*ondernemingsraad*]. Even though we subsume all these bodies under the term 'works council', it should be borne in mind that they differ considerably as to their designation, organization and to the competences statutory law has conferred to them vis-à-vis the employer. For the following comparative analysis, the main criterion will be the rights and powers accorded to the works councils. We propose to distinguish works councils with real co-determination rights, negotiating on an equal footing with the employer (infra, 2.a.i), from bodies that only have information and consultation rights vis-à-vis their counterpart (infra, 2.a.ii).

i. Works councils with co-determination rights

Works councils with co-determination rights exist in a number of States. In historical terms, they were established for the first time in Germany after the end of World War I. But countries like Austria and the Netherlands have also recognized strong works councils.

The German works councils [*Betriebsräte*] go back to late nineteenth century. In 1891, the German legislator had already provided a legal framework for voluntary worker committees [*Arbeiterausschüsse*] in industrial plants. During World War I, these worker committees became compulsory for strategic plants. After the end of the war, during the so-called November Revolution 1918, workers elected in many plants works councils without, or even against the labor unions which were disavowed for their collaboration with the government during the war. These councils were part of the wider soviet movement [*Rätebewegung*] in Germany that gained considerable influence within the working class. The German legislature rapidly understood that it was necessary to give to these works councils a legal framework restraining their (revolutionary) attitudes. As a result, the German Parliament adopted in 1920 the Works Council Act [*Betriebsrätegesetz*] and institutionalized the works councils as a second channel of employee voice with co-determination rights on certain matters. In later years, the Works Constitution Act of 1972, which is in force today[11] has preserved this model.

Section 1(1) BetrVG provides that establishments [*Betriebe*] in the private sector employing at least five workers (over the age of 18), three of whom have been employed for at least six months, can establish a works council. From the workers' perspective, to establish or not to establish this representative body is a purely voluntary decision. The employer, on the other hand, is legally forbidden to obstruct the setting up of works councils. Works councils are legally independent from the unions. However, the law gives unions represented within the establishment certain rights to intervene. Thus, they can present an electoral list for works council elections, they are entitled to give assistance to works councils and they can act on their behalf before the labor courts in order to enforce their participation rights. In contrast to the origins of the works council system in the late nineteenth century, there is no longer a strict divide between unions and works councils. One can even go further and say that works councils have become the 'extended arm of the unions at establishment-level': Almost 90 percent of the representatives on the works councils are unionized in one of the unions of the German Federation of Unions [*Deutscher Gewerkschaftsbund*] and cooperate with their unions very closely.

As a general principle, employee voice is statutorily implemented on a cooperative basis: Both the employer and works council are obliged to cooperate in good faith (Sec. 74(1) BetrVG) with the aim of furthering the successful operation of the establishment and the common interests of employees (Sec. 2(1) BetrVG). This obligation aims at enhancing mutual trust and understanding, therefore outlawing industrial action between employer and works council (Sec. 74(2) BetrVG). In case of a conflict between both sides, a special dispute settlement arrangement through an in-house arbitration committee is established (Sec. 76 BetrVG). Council members must also refrain from promoting political parties or conducting political activities within the establishment, and from all other activities jeopardizing the peace at the workplace.

Under this pattern, the statute provides works councils with far-reaching competences. They range from information and consultation rights, rights to veto certain management decisions to some specific co-determination rights. In the latter case,

---

[11] Works Constitution Act [*Betriebsverfassungsgesetz*] (BetzVG). For a detailed analysis of the Act see Reinhard Richardi (ed.): Betriebsverfassungsgesetz, 12th edition, Munich 2010. For an assessment of the Act in English see Manfred Weiss & Marlene Schmidt: *Labour Law and Industrial relations in Germany* (Kluwer 2008), pp. 222–47: Stefan Lingemann, Robert von Steinau-Steinrück & Anja Mengel: *Employment & Labor Law in Germany*, Beck, 2012, pp. 55–67.

management needs the works councils' positive consent for deciding the respective matters. Once consent is obtained, the parties conclude a 'works agreement' [*Betriebsvereinbarung*], which binds the contracting parties and produces a legal effect on the employment contracts in the plant. If consent is denied, any unilateral decision would be illegal and therefore irrelevant for the employees concerned. Management instead would have to invoke the arbitration committee to replace the councils' consent. Whichever party is not satisfied with the outcome of the arbitration can appeal to the labor court, but the courts power in such cases is limited to whether the committee exceeded its discretionary powers.

The participation rights of works councils are divided into three different areas of decision-making, namely 'social matters', 'personnel matters' and 'economic matters'. Co-determination rights are primarily assigned to 'social matters', which are enumerated in Sec. 87(1) BetrVG. They include important topics related to social consequences of economic decisions, such as:

- the establishing of work rules,
- the beginning and end of daily working hours including breaks (*i.e.* working time schedules),
- the temporary reduction or extension of the regular working hours (short time working or overtime work),
- the introduction and use of technical devices enabling the employer to keep his employees at work under surveillance,
- the prevention of industrial accidents and health and safety at the workplace,
- the administration of social facilities the employer has created and confined to the establishment, company or group (*e.g.* company kindergarten, canteens, cafeterias etc),
- questions relating to the wage structure in the company (but not the amount of wage itself).

In these cases, the employer needs the works council's consent in order to establish rules. The law even goes further when attributing to the works council the right to initiate rules in these fields. In the event that the parties cannot find a compromise, the arbitration committee can be seized which settles the dispute in the end through a compulsory arbitration award.[12]

Personnel matters, on the other hand comprise few co-determination rights, such as the content of guidelines for employee selection. Participation concerning other personnel questions is different: hiring in a company with more than 20 employees needs the works councils' consent, but this may not be denied deliberately but only on the basis of enumerated statutory grounds. Where consent is denied the employer may bring the question to the labor court to replace the negative works council decision with a positive court order. For a dismissal, consent of the works council is needed only in cases where a council member as such is to be dismissed. For other employees' dismissal, the council should only be informed and consulted prior to taking the

[12] Sec. 76, 87(2) BetrVG.

decision. If the employer fails a proper consultation containing all necessary details, the dismissal is deemed invalid and the employment contract is upheld.

As far as economic matters are concerned, participation rights normally take the form of information and consultation provided to a specialized body, the economic committee [*Wirtschaftsausschuss*], which is established in companies with more than 100 employees. However, the works council itself has participation rights in companies with more than 20 employees when the employer is planning a change of the establishment causing substantial disadvantages to the workforce [*Betriebsänderung*] such as the closing of the establishment, collective dismissals, or the introduction of new work methods.[13] In this event, management and works council should reach, on the one hand, a 'reconciliation of interests' [*Interessenausgleich*] which is an agreement on whether and how the relevant economic measures are to be carried out. The works council, though, cannot force the employer to accept such an agreement: Although the arbitration committee can be seized by each of the parties, it is not entitled to solve the dispute through a compulsory arbitration award. On the other hand, the parties are under the obligation to conclude a so-called 'social plan'; in case of disaccord between the parties, the arbitration committee is entitled to settle the dispute by a compulsory arbitration award.

Beyond the German example, there are also other countries that have institutionalized works councils with co-determination rights. A system similar to the German works council exists in Austria. The Austrian Labor Constitution Act [*Arbeitsverfassungsgesetz*] entitles the works councils to more or less the same participation rights vis-à-vis the employer.[14]

Another example is the Dutch Company Council [*ondernemingsraad*].[15] The Dutch system goes back to the Company Council Act of 1950. Since the reform of the Act on Company Councils of 1979, the Dutch company council exclusively represents the company's workforce, and does not include the employer's representatives. The company council must be established in each company employing 50 or more employees,[16] its members being elected in a secret ballot by the company's whole workforce.[17] The council is to be informed and consulted by the employer on a number of economic issues,[18] but its competences are not limited to information and consultation. The council has a number of co-determination rights [*instemmingsrechte*] concerning social matters such as regulations concerning working time and holidays, bonus systems, regulations concerning health and safety at the workplace, employees'

---

13 Cf. Art. 111 Works Constitution Act.

14 Cf. Ar. 33 to 134b Austrian Labor Constitution Act. For a detailed analysis of the Austrian model see Franz Marhold & Michael Friedrich, *Österreichisches Arbeitsrecht*, 2nd edition (2012), pp. 513 et seq.

15 The legal framework of the Company Council is provided by the Company Councils' Act [*Wet op de ondernemingsraden*]. For an in depth analysis of the Dutch Company Council cf. Antoine Jacobs, *Collectief arbeidsrecht*, 2nd edition, Deventer 2005, pp. 261 et seq (historical development) and pp. 297 et seq.

16 Art. 2 Company Councils' Act.

17 Art. 6(1), combined with Art. 9 Company Councils' Act.

18 Art. 25 Company Councils' Act.

evaluation and issues regarding employee surveillance in the company.[19] In the event that the company council does not agree to the employer's (planned) decision in one of the fields covered by the co-determination right, the employer can ask the Cantonal Tribunal to affirm the company's decision on the allegation that the council's refusal is unfair [*onredelijk*] or the employer's decision is required by serious operational reasons.[20]

ii. Works councils as information and consultation bodies

Many countries have not gone so far by way of according the works councils co-determination rights and only extend to employee representatives information and consultation rights, or the right to bring to the employer's attention the employees' grievances. It is interesting to note that this level of employee involvement was in various countries the starting point for the institutionalization of representation bodies at the workplace.[21]

Since the Agreements of *Matignon*, concluded in 1936 under the government of *Léon Blum* composed of the socialist and the communist party (*Front Populaire*), France has a system of elected employee representatives at the workplace, which conforms to this lesser model of information and consultation.[22] In France, personnel delegates [*délégués du personnel*] shall be elected in each establishment [*établissement*] employing 11 or more employees every three years by the whole workforce of the company.[23] According to the jurisprudence of the French *Cour de Cassation*, their competences are limited to communicate to the employer or to the Labor Inspectorate the employees' grievances; but these are limited to complaints about the violation of compulsory law and cannot include employees' bargaining demands.[24] However, in companies where there is no company committee [*comité d'entreprise*],[25] the personnel delegate(s) fulfills the functions of the company committee. In these cases, he or she is to be informed and consulted on the issues that are otherwise submitted to the information and consultation of the company committee (see infra 2.b.i). Furthermore, the personnel delegate(s) may fulfill the functions of the company's union delegate if the

---

19 See the exhaustive catalogue of co-determination rights in Art. 27 (1) Company Councils' Act.

20 Art. 27(4) Company Councils' Act.

21 See *e.g.* the Worker Committees [*Arbeiterausschüsse*] in Germany at the end of the nineteenth century. The historical development of the German Works Council system since the second half of nineteenth century has been aptly described by Hermann Reichold, Betriebsverfassung als Sozialprivatrecht: Historisch-dogmatische Grundlagen von 1948 bis heute, München 1995, pp. 54 et seq.

22 For an in-depth analysis of the historical context see Jean-Pierre Le Crom, L'introuvable démocratie salariale: Le droit de la representation du personnel dans l'entreprise (1890–2002), Paris 2003, pp. 22–6.

23 Cf. Article L. 2312-1 French Labor Code [*Code du travail*].

24 See François Gaudu, *Droit du travail*, 4th edition (2011), par. 429.

25 The Company Committee will be dealt with infra 2.2.

representative union appoints him or her: In this event, he or she even has the power to negotiate collective agreements at company level.[26]

A considerable number of countries have adopted the French model of personnel delegates, inter alia, the Grand-Duchy of Luxembourg,[27] Spain[28] and many of the French-speaking African countries.[29] To the same group of works councils belong also the Spanish Company Committee [*Comité de empresa*][30] and the Portuguese employees' commission [*Commissão de trabalhadores*],[31] which has only information and consultation rights, as well as the Swiss employee representation [*Arbeitnehmervertretung*].[32] Thus, the French model of personnel delegates 'inspired' other countries and has been 'transplanted' in their national contexts, but its significance in each of the countries is dependent on their general pattern of industrial relations.

b. Joint Committees

Another type of employee representation on plant or company level is the joint committee, which is composed of both the employer's and the employees' representatives. Whereas the works council model is based on the idea of a body representing the interests of workers vis-à-vis the employer, joint committees are based on a distinct idea that deliberations should take place in one body representing both sides and thereby facilitating the cooperation between workers and the employer in the undertaking. The virtue of deliberating interests of workers and management is appreciated in both models, but only joint committees do this without providing first for a representative body to establish common ground among different groups of workers, without the employer's representatives. The idea behind this mixed representation of the workforce and the employer within one and the same institution essentially is to intensify the ties between employer and the workforce. From a historical perspective,

---

[26] Cf. Art. L. 2143-6 French Labor Code. This does not mean, however, that personnel delegates have the power to conclude collective agreements that derogate from the minima of a sector level collective agreement applicable in the company.

[27] For the *délégation du personnel* under Luxembourgish Law see Art. L. 411-1 et seq Lux. Labor Code.

[28] For the Spanish *delegados del personal* see Art. 62 et seq Estatuto de los trabajadores.

[29] See the references in footnote 9. Also the Proposal for a Uniform Act concerning Labor and Employment Law [*Avant-projet d'Acte uniforme relative au droit du travail*] of the Organization for the Harmonization of Business Law in Africa [*Organisation pour l'Harmonisation en Afrique du droit des affaires* – abbr. *OHADA*] provides the election of personnel delegates in establishments occupying ten or more employees: cf. Arts 165 et seq Proposal for a Uniform Act concerning Labor and Employment Law.

[30] Cf. Art. 63 et seq Spanish Worker Statute [*Estatuto de los trabajadores*]. Even though the name of this institution suggest an influence of the French Company Committee [*comité d'entreprise*], the structure of the Spanish *comité de empresa* differs considerably from that of the French *comité d'entreprise*.

[31] Art. 415 et seq Portuguese Labor Code. For a more in-depth analysis see Antonio Monteiro Fernandes, Direito do trabalho, 16th edition (2012), paras 552 et seq.

[32] See Federal Law of December 17, 1993 on the Information and Consultation of Employees at Plant level [*Bundesgesetz über die Information und Mitsprache der Arbeitnehmerinnen und Arbeitnehmer in den Betrieben (Mitwirkungsgesetz)*].

also joint committees are reflecting a paternalist or social conservative view of the 'social question'. The prototype of such joint committees is, without doubt, the French company committee [*comité d'entreprise*]; it therefore will be analyzed more in depth (infra, 2.b.i). Over the years, a number of other (European) countries have also 'imported' the French model though with significant modifications. In embedding this institution in their national context, these have given a different face to their joint committee. Some significant examples will be presented in section 2.b.ii.

i. The French company committee as prototype

Early roots of the French Company Committee can be found in the social company committees [*comités sociaux d'entreprise*] established under the Vichy regime during World War II. The company committee, as it still exists nowadays, was established under the Government of the General *De Gaulle* after the liberation from the German occupation.[33] Its current form was established by a decree of February 22, 1945.[34] Behind this institution is the *De Gaullien* idea of an intensification of social partnership at the establishment or company level.

A company committee must be established in all companies employing 50 or more employees; in the event that a company has several establishments, there should be an establishment committee [*comité d'établissement*] for each establishment with 50 or more employees. The company committee is composed of the employer, normally represented by the director or a member of the executive staff, who chairs the committee, employee representatives elected by the company's workforce and by union representatives.[35] Thus, it has a tripartite structure. As to the union representatives in the company committee [*représentants syndicaux auprès du comité d'entreprise*], this function is fulfilled by the union representatives [*délégués syndicaux*] who are appointed by the representative unions in the company (see infra 2.c); in companies with 300 or more employees, each representative union in the company appoints one representative to the company committee. As far as the employer's position within the company committee is concerned, he or she does not participate in decisions of the committee when the latter makes decisions as a personnel delegation (*e.g.* consultation on redundancies, the choosing of a chartered accountant, the company's social and cultural activities; see infra):[36] in these areas, the character of the company committee as a joint committee slightly transforms and it becomes more similar to the works council model.

As to the general mission of the company committee, it ensures the collective expression of the employees and takes into account their interests with regard to the economic and financial development of the company, the organization of work, professional training and the production technologies to be used by the company (Art. L. 2323-1 of the French Labor Code). In addition, the committee is also involved in the administration of the company's social and cultural activities. Thus, employees have an influence on the various social activities such as occupational pension schemes,

---

33 Cf. Le Crom, L'introuvable démocratie salariale (n 5), pp. 27 et seq.
34 Ibid., pp. 45 et seq.
35 See Art. L. 2324-1 and L. 2324-2 French Labor Code.
36 See Art. L. 2325-18(2) French Labor Code.

company owned kindergartens, sporting activities, libraries, company restaurants, housing, holiday apartments, etc.[37]

In addition, the company committee has a number of information and consultation rights vis-à-vis the employer. These essentially refer to economic issues [*attributions économiques*]. Thus, Article L. 2323-6 of the French Labor Code gives the committee information and consultation rights regarding the company's organization, the general economic development of the company, working time arrangements, working conditions and occupational training. Contrary to the German works council (supra 2.a.i.) and to the Luxembourg mixed company committee (infra 2.b.ii.), the French company committee has no co-determination rights at all.

As already pointed out, the original concept of the company committee was to strengthen social partnership in the company. In particular *De Gaulle*'s social conservatism intended to establish a peaceful cooperation between labor and capital within the company. It must be doubted, however, whether this intention has been fulfilled since the company committees are embedded in a wider set of industrial relations and also integrate unionized employees defending the union position within the body.

ii. Other examples of joint committees

The French company committee inspired a number of other national legal orders. Well-known examples are the Belgian company council [*conseil d'entreprise/ondernemingsraad*], the Luxembourgish mixed company committee [*comité mixte d'entreprise*] and the Spanish company committee [*comite de empresa*]. However, their concrete design, their powers and their relationship to other representative bodies differ considerably from the French original.

In the Kingdom of Belgium, a company council must be established in every company with 50 or more employees.[38] The institution goes back to the year 1948[39] and is of course influenced to a large extent by the French company committee, which was established a few years earlier. The company council is composed of elected employees' representatives and the employer's representatives who, beside the director himself, are appointed by him, and their number must not exceed that of the employees' representatives. Thus, both sides have an equal number of representatives within the council. Unlike the French company committee, the Belgian company has effective decision rights in addition to the information and consultation rights.[40] For instance, the committee has the power to administer the company's social institutions (company restaurants, kindergarten, housing, etc.), to elaborate or to change the work rules [*règlement intérieur*], to determine the criteria to be applied to dismissals or to recruitments. These decision rights of the company council may be considered as the

[37] For a definition of company's social and cultural activities see Art. R. 2323-20 French Labor Code.

[38] Art. 14(1) Act on the Organization of the Economy [*Loi portant organisation de l'économie*] of 20 September 1948.

[39] For more details see Antoine Jacobs, Collectief arbeidsrecht (n 15), pp. 297 et seq.

[40] For the different issues covered by the information and consultation rights of the company council cf. Art. 15 a), b), c), k) and l) Act on the Organization of the Economy.

functional equivalent to the co-determination rights works council dispose of in some national systems (*e.g.* in Germany).

In the Grand-Duchy of Luxembourg, each company that employs at least 50 employees has to establish a mixed company committee. The mixed company committee is composed of an equal number of representatives of the employer and of the employees. The latter are elected by the personnel delegations existing in that company. This has the effect that by far the majority of employee representatives in mixed company committees are unionized. Thus, the Luxembourg union movements are quite influential in the mixed company committees. Similar to the French company committee, the Luxembourg mixed committee benefits from a number of information and consultation rights regarding the economic situation of the company as well as in corporate restructuring processes.[41] It is interesting to note, however, that it also has, like the Belgian company council, real decision rights regarding issues such as discipline, introduction of new work methods, health and safety issues, general criteria of evaluation, etc.[42] In cases of dissent between the two groups within the mixed committee, each side can appeal to a conciliation and arbitration body:[43] there is, however, no compulsory arbitration. Thus, in the event that the parties cannot agree on the issue at stake, the employer is not entitled to take a unilateral decision on the question submitted to the committee's decision right.

c. Union Representatives

Works councils as well as joint committees are the results of institutionalization through statutory law. In many countries, however, there are also union representatives at the plant level. In national legal orders based on a single channel system, union representatives are the only collective voice employees have to defend their interests and to enforce their rights at the workplace. The prototype of these union representatives in a single channel system is union stewards or shop stewards as they have developed in the United Kingdom and the United States. But in a number of countries, union representatives have a role at the workplace additional to institutionalized works councils or joint committees. In these cases, union representatives are also often members of a works council or a joint committee and are able to influence the decision-making of these bodies. In some countries, the legislature even has recognized the role of union representatives and conferred to them specific tasks.

In the UK, unions have traditionally represented the 'single channel' for employee participation[44] even though union strength has declined rapidly over the years. Unions are competent to represent their members in bargaining on employment terms and conditions once recognized by the employer. Recognition[45] can either follow a

---

[41] Art. L. 423-2 and L. 423-3 Lux. Labor Code.

[42] Art. L. 423-1 Lux. Labor Code.

[43] Art. L. 424-5 (2) combined with Art. L. 163-1 et seq. Lux. Labor Code.

[44] For details cf. European Commission, Directorate-General for Employment, Social Affairs and Inclusion: Industrial Relations in Europe, 2010, p. 42.

[45] Gregor Gall: Trade union recognition in Britain, 1955–2002: turning a corner?, 35 *Industrial Relations Journal* (2004) pp. 249–69.

voluntary agreement between both sides, establishing the union as representative for a particular group of workers, the bargaining unit. If no such voluntary agreement can be obtained, the union can follow a statutory recognition procedure by applying to the Central Arbitration Committee. Once 50 percent or more of the employees in the respective bargaining unit are union members, recognition will be awarded. Where fewer than 50 percent but at least 10 percent are unionized, a secret ballot must be held among all employees belonging to the bargaining unit to evaluate the support for the union. Recognition will then be awarded once 40 percent of employees take part in the vote and a majority of those taking part support the union. If fewer than 10 percent of the employees are union members, no recognition is possible.

Once recognition has been granted, the employer is required to bargain, inform and consult with the union for the next three years; afterwards, they can apply to the Central Arbitration Committee for de-recognition of the union, which can be granted after a similar procedure has been successful. Where unions are recognized union representatives ('shop stewards'[46]) are elected by the unionized employees for their local work units or bureaus. Because the union representatives count as union officials, some unions reserve the right to approve the elected persons. Shop stewards can be permitted to spend part or all of their working time on union duties, depending on the respective amount of workplace collective bargaining in the company. Representatives are responsible for the interests of rank and file in the work unit concerned; the non-unionized employees are not formally included. The main consequence of recognition is the right of the representatives to bargain collectively on terms and conditions of employment contracts in the bargaining unit. Additionally they gain the statutory right to be consulted about specific matters such as health and safety, collective redundancy and transfer of undertakings.

Union or shop stewards in the UK are established on the basis of collective agreements. They therefore essentially depend on the unions' bargaining power and do not exist in non-unionized sectors. In other countries, however, union representatives have been institutionalized through statutory law. A famous example for an institutionalization of union representatives is the French union section [*section syndicale d'entreprise*] on company level which was legally recognized in the aftermath of the revolts in May 1968, on the basis of the so-called Grenelle Agreement between the unions and the French Government.[47] Its aim was to strengthen union influence within the company. However, for some right-wing members of Parliament, the recognition of union sections within companies also had the purpose to 'tame' the union movement by integrating it into the company.

According to the French legislation, in each company or establishment where a representative union has members it is entitled to constitute its own union section,

[46] Andy Charlwood & John Forth: Employee representation in: William Brown, Alex Bryson, John Forth & Keith Whitfield (eds.): *The Evolution of the Modern Workplace*. CUP, Cambridge 2010, Chap. 4, pp. 74 et seq.

[47] Act of December 27, 1968. For the historical context of this Act see Le Crom, L'introuvable démocratie salariale, pp. 138 et seq; see also Norbert Olszak, Histoire du droit du travail, pp. 120 et seq.

which ensures the representation of the 'material and moral interests of its members'.[48] As far as the facilities are concerned, the union section in companies with 199 and less employees has no right to an office room. In companies with at least 200 employees, the employer has the duty to provide an appropriate office room for the sections of the different unions represented within the company (Art. L. 2142-8 French Labor Code), which they have to share. In companies with at least 1,000 employees, the employer has to provide an appropriate office and the equipment necessary for its functioning to each section of a representative union within the company. Thus, in big companies, each union section (*e.g.* the CGT, CFDT, CGT-FO, etc.) has its own office room.

The union section in the company has no specific rights vis-à-vis the employer. Its essential function is to provide representative unions with an anchor within the company to defend the interests of their members employed in the company.[49] However, the Labor Code concretizes various competences of the union representatives within the company. Thus, they are entitled to collect union dues from union members in the company[50] and are allowed to engage in union publicity and to distribute union leaflets or other union publications.[51] A company agreement may entitle the union to distribute its publications via the company's intranet or via email.[52] Each union section may hold meetings once every month within the company; the details to be determined by an agreement with the employer.[53] Persons who do not belong to the company can only be invited to meetings with the consent of the employer.[54] Furthermore, in many cases the union delegates are at the same time personnel delegates (supra 2.a.ii.) or employees' representatives on the company committee (see supra 2.b.i.). Their activities are therefore often linked to those of the other representative bodies within the establishment or the company.[55]

d. Representative Bodies for Specified Issues and Groups of Employees

Works councils and joint committees represent employee interests in a broad sense. They act on behalf of all employees working in a plant or company and deal with issues ranging from work rules to surveillance at the workplace, health and safety, working schedules and the co-administration of the company's social institutions. Nonetheless, some countries establish bodies that represent employees' interests in a more limited way. They are either entrusted with power to engage on a limited set of topics, or to represent a limited group of employees.

i. Representative bodies for specified issues

The best example of representative bodies whose jurisdiction is limited to specified issues is that of health and safety representatives elected by the workforce at plant

---

48 Art. L. 2142-1 French Labor Code.
49 Ibid.
50 Art. L. 2142-2 French Labor Code.
51 Art. L. 2142-3 and L. 2142-4 French Labor Code.
52 Art. L. 2142-5 French Labor Code.
53 Art. L. 2142-10 (1) French Labor Code.
54 Art. L. 2142-10 (2) and (3) French Labor Code.
55 See Le Crom, L'introuvable démocratie salariale, pp. 142–6 with further references.

level. In some countries, these health and safety representatives were the historical origin of institutionalized employee representations. Thus, in France, for instance, in 1890 the legislator had already established delegates of mining workers [*délégués mineurs*] who had to ensure that health and safety rules where respected by the employer.[56] The French Labor Code provides a committee for hygiene, safety and working conditions [*Comité d'hygiène, de sécurité et de conditions de travail*][57] to be established in each establishment with 50 or more employees. This committee is composed of the employer's representatives, personnel delegates and the workplace doctors. It is to be informed and consulted by the employer concerning health and safety issues on company level and performs a control function in this field, in cooperation with the Labor Inspectorate.

A similar arrangement was set up in the UK, where statutory health and safety committees were established on the basis of the Health and Safety at Work Act 1974.[58] Today, the representatives entrusted with the protection of employees' safety have their basis in the Health and Safety (Consultation with Employees) Regulations 1996. Another example is the Belgian Committee for prevention and protection at work [*Comité pour la prevention et la protection au travail*].[59] Since 1989, all Member States of the EU have to establish specific bodies representing the employees in questions related to health and safety.[60] Hence, there are currently employee representatives with specific responsibility for health and safety in all 28 Member States of the EU.[61]

ii. Representative bodies for specific groups of employees

A number of national systems provide specific bodies representing groups of employees with specific interests and needs. These groups' interests are considered to be particularly in need of protection, not only vis-à-vis the employer, but also toward other employees and their representatives.

One example is bodies representing apprentices and young employees. Thus, the German Works Constitution Act provides the election of a younger workers' and apprentices' representation [*Jugend- und Auszubildendenvertretung*] in each plant with at least five employees or apprentices under 18 years of age. The representatives can

[56] Act of 8 July 1890 concerning the Safety Delegates for Mining Workers [*Loi sur les délégués à la sécurité des ouvriers mineurs*]. For a more in depth analysis of this Act see Le Crom, L'introuvable démocratie salariale, pp. 14 et seq.

[57] Cf. Art. L. 4611-1 et seq. and Art. R. 4612-1 et seq. French Labor Code. For an overview on the composition, the functioning and the missions of the Committee see Pélissier, Auzero & Dockès, *Droit du travail,* 27th edition (2013), paras. 862 et seq with further references.

[58] See Simon Deaking & Gillian Morris, *Labour Law*, 4th edition, Hart Publishing, 2005, 9.46 et seq (Health and Safety).

[59] See the Royal Decree concerning the missions and the functioning of the Committee for prevention and protection at work [*Arrêté royal relative aux missions et au fonctionnement des comités pour la prevention et la protection au travail*], Moniteur belge of 10 July 1999.

[60] Article 11 Directive 89/391/EEC of 12 June 1989 on the introduction of measures to encourage improvements in the safety and health of workers at work, O.J.C.E.E. 1989 L 183/1.

[61] An overview on the existing institutions in the Member States gives the European Agency for Safety and Health at work, available at: https://osha.europa.eu/en/topics/worker-participation (last visited on 16 January 2014).

participate in the works council meetings and pursue the interests of apprentices and young workers.[62] In Luxembourg, young workers elect a delegate in each plant with at least five young workers, *i.e.* workers who are younger than 21 years.[63] Belgian law provides yet another model, where young workers are entitled to elect at least one delegate to the company council.[64]

Another example concerns the representation of people with disabilities. In Germany, for instance, a specific representative body is to be elected by employees with disabilities in plants with at least five such employees.[65] These representatives are to be involved in hiring as well as in dismissal procedures and have various other information and consultation rights.

Finally, some countries have established specific representative bodies for female employees in order to promote equality of opportunities in the company. Thus, each personnel delegation under Luxembourgish law appoints an equality delegate [*Délégué à l'égalité*] whose task is to pursue the interests of the respective under-represented gender in the company.[66] In other countries, there is a statutory obligation to elect an equality delegate in establishments of the public sector: one example is the various Regional Equal Opportunity Acts in Germany which only apply to the State Administration:[67] These equal opportunity delegates [*Gleichstellungsbeauftragte*] are to be involved in the elaboration of equal employment opportunity plans within the State Administration and in hiring procedures.

e. Employer Driven Forms

Beside the legally institutionalized forms of employee representation analyzed so far, there are also channels of employee voice that have been unilaterally established by employers. They are often established to undermine unionization or to reduce pressure on managerial control. In this sense, these forms of employees' voice for the employer represent the lesser of two evils. Depending on the relevant HR-management strategy, it can also embrace enhancing employee involvement thereby adding to the performance of the undertaking. In any case, where the legal system is associated with an undertakings' hostility to union representation, there will be little welcome for any forms of institutionalized, collective representation, whether provided by unions or other bodies; if at all, employee involvement is deemed acceptable only where the individual workers raise their voices directly.

---

62 Cf. Sec. 60 et seq German Works Constitution Act.

63 Cf. Art. L. 411-5 Lux. Labor Code.

64 Cf. Art. 16(6) of the Act on the Organization of the Economy. For more details on the Belgian Company Council see supra 2.2.2.

65 See Sec. 94 et seq. Social Security Code Part IX.

66 For details cf. Art. L. 414-3 Lux. Labor Code.

67 See e.g. Art. 14 et seq of the Equal Opportunity Act of the State of Hesse [*Hessisches Gleichberechtigungsgesetz*], and Art. 15 et seq of the Equal Opportunity Act of the State of Thuringia [*Thüringer Gleichstellungsgesetz*].

i. Non-union employee representation bodies

It has already been pointed out that the (voluntary) establishment of some kind of worker's representation may have an anti-union direction.[68] It provides an employer-driven alternative to formal representation with statutory rights thereby winning more acceptance among employers.

In the US, under Section 8(a)(2) of the National Labor Relations Act of 1935 (NLRA), it is an unfair labor practice for an employer to dominate, support, or interfere in the administration of a 'labor organization'. The term 'labor organization' in this context is not restricted to labor unions but includes all kind of employee representation bodies that 'deal with' with the employer on terms and conditions of employment. Most employer-driven non-union representation bodies are therefore prohibited. In sectors not covered by the NLRA, such as the airline industry, a remarkable exception emerged: large-scale, formally structured, representation plans establish company-wide representation councils. While they are lacking a basis in law, they are created, operated and funded by the employer. Such representation schemes tend to operate on the basis of highly formalized written rules that prescribe the function and procedure of representation, and representatives are chosen by secret ballot of the workforce. Those committees' influence can resemble formal collective bargaining expanding terms and conditions of employment contracts. From managements' perspective, such bodies can become difficult to administer and as costly and time consuming as bargaining with a union. They may additionally strengthen the emergence of a 'collective identity' among the workforce, which might even translate into forming a union once employees consider the level of influence achieved not to be satisfactory.

For most other sectors, though, such formalized representative bodies lack attraction. As the employer's primary interest in operating representation systems is not in bargaining but improving communication between both sides, the preferred instrument is not a formalized structure but more informal settings engaged in consultation and advisory functions only. This can take the form of joint or advisory committees, quality or coordination circles or staff associations. Regularly, representation bodies are not allowed to realize independent financial resources or outside professional counsel or any form of collective action. In effect, they are left with a large degree of dependency on employers' discretion whether management wants to respond to the employees' concerns. On the other hand, when creating employee representation companies raise hopes and expectations on the part of their workforce that are better not disappointed; otherwise employees could react with less cooperation and trust in management decisions.

Employer driven employee representation can also be attractive for employers aiming at factually replacing statutorily regulated representation mechanisms such as works councils. Such alternative representation bodies are emerging especially in smaller German companies[69] where the establishment of works councils is legally possible but

---

[68] D. Taras & B. Kaufman: Non-union employee representation in North America: diversity, controversy and uncertain future, 37 *Industrial Relations Journal* (2006), pp. 513 et seq, at p. 516.

[69] Peter Ellguth: Betriebe ohne Betriebsrat, in: I. Artus, S. Böhm & S. Lücking: Betriebe ohne Betriebsrat – informelle Interessenvertretung in Unternehmen (2006), pp. 43–80; O.

factually very rare, even though employee voice culturally is widely acknowledged and therefore expected by the workforce. Forms vary, but the most common forms are joint committees, round tables or staff representatives that are informed or consulted on company policies of special relevance for the workforce. Their competences do not go any further than the companies' preference to consult with employees instead of statutorily established representation bodies. This tends to be more frequent in the service sector than in industry, and in owner-led smaller companies or in special professions like information technology or the media.[70] The larger the respective company, the more influential an alternative representation tends to become, sometimes even bargaining for wage arrangements which would be even beyond the statutory competences of a German works council. It nevertheless must be borne in mind that the legality of alternative representation bodies is challenged. While there is no explicit statutory expression rendering alternative representation illegal, this can be deducted by implication from section 3 German Works Constitution Act.[71] As a result, it appears that voluntarily established alternative representation bodies under German law are considered to be non-existent;[72] agreements resulting from the consultative process lack enforceability.

ii. Issue specific representation at the workplace

Employee voice of a different kind may be implemented by alternative forms of issue specific representation.[73] They are concerned with topics of a sudden or a more regular concern for employees at the specific enterprise, so that their potential form and content depend on the specific circumstances of the workplace. This form of employee involvement represents a specific human resources management tool focusing on better-informed decisions and promoting higher commitment among the workforce. Here, we will only give an overview of some common variations of issue specific forms of representation.

The least formal method of employee involvement takes place by regular communications from management to the workforce, either in written or electronic form, which are extended to two-way communication if suggestion schemes or other means of soliciting feedback are included. However, the potential employee voice realized

---

Stettes: Betriebsräte und alternative Formen der Mitbestimmung, Ergebnisse aus dem IW-Zukunftspanel, IW-Trends (2008).

[70] Wolfgang Däubler: Privatautonome Betriebsverfassung? In: Wolfhard Kohte, Hans-Jürgen Dörner & Rudolf Anzinger (eds.) Festschrift für Hellmuth Wißmann, Munich 2005, pp. 275 et seq, at 276.

[71] Section 3 German Works Constitution Act allows for limited derogations from the organizational structure of a works council provided by the law; these derogations require a collective agreement. Thus, derogations through unilateral decision of the employer or via individual employment contract are not allowed.

[72] One early decision of the Federal Labor Court points in this direction: cf. Bundesarbeitsgericht, ruling of 19 February 1975, case No. 1 ABR 55/73, in: Arbeitsrechtliche Praxis (AP), § 5 BetrVG 1972 No 9.

[73] Daphne Taras & Bruce Kaufman: Non-union employee representation in North America, 37 *Industrial Relations Journal* (2006), pp. 513–42; Chris Brewster, Richard Croucher, Geoff Wood & Michael Brookes: Collective and individual voice-convergence in Europe? 18 *International Journal of Human Resource Management* (2007), pp. 1246–62.

through such means offers rather limited options for providing input in the managerial decision-making process.

A more formal but still ad hoc approach to communication is the establishment of team briefings or problem-solving groups. In either case, management deals directly with all the employees concerned by the problem they are supposed to react to, and not only with their representatives. The frequency of such meetings is wholly dependent on the emergence of relevant problems.

More long-term and frequent meetings are established where quality circles or health and safety committees are set up, regularly working with a predefined topic whenever it occurs. The committees are frequently small groups comprised of employees taking on the task of identifying and solving problems in their area of responsibility. Health and safety committees are among the oldest forms of employee involvement dealing with vital aspects such as hazardous working practices. The necessity of giving employees their say in this perspective is acknowledged by all systems of employee voice, either backed by statutory rights or left to voluntary management decisions.[74]

Dispute-resolution panels or employee-management advisory committees set up representation in a more formal, long-term manner for the purpose of improving communications between both sides and rectifying problems both sides identify. Advisory committees can discuss the social aspects of work or interpret unresolved questions in handbooks or manuals. Representatives can either be elected by their constituency *e.g.* through balloting or by an informal show of hands; alternatively they can be appointed or even chosen by management, which raises questions of legitimacy. Their authority for problem solving depends on the legitimacy towards their fellow employees on the one hand and the willingness of management to take into account the views of the employees' representatives. Once advisory or consultative functions provide only employee involvement but no actual influence on management decisions, representatives and employees may remain dissatisfied, and the objective of improving employees' relations with management is defied. If there is a concrete threat of immediate unionization, on the other hand, management might wish to convince their workforce that they are better off with non-union representation, and therefore offer substantial influence to representatives. Where companies have other effective methods of union avoidance at their disposal, forms of long-term employee representation might not become attractive.

3. EMPLOYEE VOICE IN THE DECISION-MAKING OF THE COMPANY

Employee voice in the decision-making of the company goes beyond the limits of the various forms of employee representation at the workplace that have been analyzed in the previous sections. The participation of works councils, personnel delegations,

---

[74] As health and safety are statutory 'working conditions' in the US, employers are legally forbidden to create such bodies by § 8(a)(2) of the Labor Act even though a number of States have mandated their creation. M. Finkin, Employee representation outside the Labor Act, 5 *U. Pa. J. Lab. & Emp. L.* 75 (2002).

personnel delegates or joint committees only refers to concrete questions which have a concrete impact on the employment relationships of the employees. By contrast, employee participation at company level, in particular through representatives in the company's boards of directors, covers corporate policy in general, including issues that are not (directly) related to employment.

Forms of employee representation on company level have been institutionalized in different ways. By far, the most discussed model of an institutionalized employee participation on company level is employee co-determination, *i.e.* employee representation within the supervisory boards or the boards of directors in the big companies. This model, going back to the German '*Mitbestimmung*', will be analyzed first (infra, 3.a). A less institutionalized channel of employee voice on company level will then be examined – employee ownership, which enables employees to participate in the company's decision-making process (infra, 3.b).

a. Employee Representation on Company Boards

Board level employee representation is essentially characterized by a representation of employees in the organs of the employer's company (supervisory board or board of directors). It therefore links labor law with corporate law.[75] Unlike the involvement of works councils or joint committees, employee representation at board level is not limited to issues related to the workplace and employment such as working time schedules, work rules or employee control. It embraces the whole strategic decision-making in the company as well as areas that are under management's control. Its strength essentially depends on the percentage of employee representatives within company bodies, but also on its interaction with other bodies of employee representation. Even though the difference between two-tier systems and one-tier systems of corporate law are diminishing under the auspices of the current corporate governance schemes, it might be useful to distinguish between board-level representation in these two models of corporate law since their legal framework differs.

i. Board level representation in two-tier systems

The two-tier board system was developed in Germany towards the end of the nineteenth century. At that time, the German legislator abolished the so-called license-system according to which a corporation only could be established with the license [*Konzession*] of the competent administrative body. Thus, (external) administrative control of a company's respect for the rules was replaced by a mechanism of internal control. The two-tier-system essentially is characterized by a separation of the company management in a board of directors [*Vorstand*] and a supervisory board

---

[75] For an overview on the different models of board level employee representation in Europe see the country reports in Peter Ulmer & Theodor Baums (eds), Die Unternehmens-Mitbestimmung der Arbeitnehmer im Recht der EU-Mitgliedstaaten – Employees' Co-determination in the Member States of the European Union, Heidelberg, 2004. See also Achim Seifert, Employee participation at board level in Europe, in: Jürgen Basedow, Chen, Matteo Fornasier & Ulla Liukkunen (eds), Employee Participation and Collective Bargaining in Europe and China, Beiträge zum Internationalen Privatrecht, Tübingen 2015 (Mohr Siebeck) (forthcoming).

[*Aufsichtsrat*] whose main task is to control management. The board of director's function is to manage the day-to-day business autonomously, *i.e.* without any directives of the shareholders' meeting,[76] whereas the supervisory board has to appoint or revoke the members of the board of directors and to control its activities. It is in the supervisory board that board-level representation of employees in the two-tier-system takes place. All board members share the same legal status.

The German 'Mitbestimmung' Board-level representation of employees was established for the first time in Germany.[77] Even though its early roots can be found in the Republic of Weimar (1918–33),[78] its formative period was in the years after World War II. At that time, the Western Allied Forces, *i.e.* the US, the UK and France planned to destroy the German 'military-industrial complex' which supported the Nazi regime and contributed to the outbreak of World War II. The key idea of the Allies was to 'de-concentrate' the German industry. Also in the German political arena (*e.g.* in the Social-Democrat Party but also in parts of the Christian-Democrat Party), there were plans to nationalize the key industries such as coal, steel and iron. In order to avoid expropriation, managers of the steel industry in the Ruhr region proposed to the unions that they involve employees' representatives in the supervisory boards of their companies. Thus, without any legal basis, the main steel companies in the British Zone elected supervisory boards composed of an equal number of shareholders' representatives and employees' representatives. Board-level participation was therefore considered to be a key element of what was called during the 1920s by the Labor Movement 'Economic Democracy' [*Wirtschaftsdemokratie*].[79] The representatives of the key industries together with unions suggested a model for Economic Democracy, to be achieved by a democratic input of stakeholders into the strategic decision-making process of companies. At first, the Federal Government refused to recognize and extend the co-determination model of the mining and steel industry. But following a serious strike threat by the unions, the governmental majority of Chancellor Konrad Adenauer sought to regularize this model and adopted in 1951 the Act on Co-Determination by Employees on the Supervisory Boards of Undertakings of the Mining, the Iron and Steel Manufacturing Industries.[80]

---

76 Cf. Sec. 76(1) Act on Public Limited Companies [*Aktiengesetz*].

77 For a brief summary of the key elements of the German system of board level representation cf. Manfred Weiss & Marlene Schmidt: *Labour Law and Industrial Relations in Germany*, Kluwer, 2008, Chap.6, pp. 248–60.

78 See sec. 70 of the Act on Works Councils [*Betriebsrätegesetz*] of 1920. For an assessment of the experiences with this first form of board-level representation see Kurt Brigl-Matthiaß, Das Betriebsräteproblem in der Weimarer Republik, Berlin 1926, pp. 216–41.

79 See Fritz Naphtali, Wirtschafsdemokratie: Ihr Wesen, Weg und Ziel, Allgemeiner Deutscher Gewerkschaftsbund (ed.), Berlin 1928.

80 Montan-Mitbestimmungsgesetz of 25 May 1951, Bundesgesetzblatt, Part I, p. 347. See Otfried Wlotzke, Hellmut Wissmann, Wolfgang Koberski & Georg Kleinsorge (eds.), *Mitbestimmungsrecht*, 4th edition 2011.

This unique[81] model represents an equal division of power between representatives of shareholders and employees on the supervisory board. The shareholders's bench, as well as that of the employees, consists of five seats. As to the employees' bench, four of its members are proposed by the company's works councils and are elected by the shareholders' meeting. It is noteworthy that a certain number of the employees' representatives are proposed by the unions represented in the company, giving the unions a strong influence on the participation in the supervisory board. The election of the supervisory board's chair person ('the eleventh man') follows a complex procedure aiming at ensuring that he or she really is a neutral person that does not belong to the shareholders' or the employees' side. Both sides must agree upon a candidate. If there is no agreement, a conciliation procedure takes place. Only the shareholders' meeting can refuse the election for a substantial reason [*wichtiger Grund*]. A shareholders' refusal may initially be reviewed by the court but a second shareholders' meeting may decide autonomously on the basis of a substantial reason confirmed by the court. Furthermore, the supervisory board elects a work director [*Arbeitsdirektor*] as a member of the board of directors in charge of personnel affairs: this member of the board cannot be elected against the majority of the votes of the employees' representatives and therefore needs their support. The work director in his capacity as a member of the board of directors allows the employee side some influence on the company's day-to-day operation.

Further attempts to extend the legislation on co-determination to other areas of the economy failed; only modest levels of employees' representation were successfully implemented. The 1952 Act (*BetrVG*), since 2004 replaced by the Act on Board-level Representation by one Third [*Drittelbeteiligungsgesetz*],[82] is applicable to companies[83] employing more than 500 persons. It allows employees to elect one-third of the members on the supervisory board. It is interesting to note that this model disregards the role of the unions that are represented in the company. Perhaps for this reason, but in particular for the reason that the Act of 1952 fell behind the model of parity representation in the mining, iron and steel manufacturing industries, the unions were not satisfied with the 1952 Act and continued the fight for extension of board-level representation.

Although the German unions' political power was never strong enough to push the political parties towards an extension of the 1951 parity model in the coal and steel industry, they enjoyed partial success. In 1976, the German Parliament passed the Act on board-level participation [*Mitbestimmungsgesetz*][84] establishing a third model of participation applying to companies organized in the legal form of a public limited company, a private limited company, a partnership limited by shares or a cooperative, and employing more than 2,000 employees. The shareholders as well as the employees

---

[81] See Kathleen Thelen & Lowell Turner, *German Codetermination in Comparative Perspective*, Verlag Bertelsmann Stiftung: Gütersloh, 1997.

[82] Drittelbeteiligungsgesetz, 18 May 2004, Bundesgesetzblatt 2004, Part I, p. 974.

[83] The application of the law is restricted to predefined legal forms of companies above a specific size, primarily public limited companies, private limited companies, cooperatives or mutual insurance companies employing at least 500 persons.

[84] Mitbestimmungsgesetz of May 4, 1976, Bundesgesetzblatt 1976, Part I, p. 1153.

have an equal number of representatives on the supervisory board. The employees' bench is composed of employees of the company and union representatives. All employees' representatives are elected by the company's workforce. At first sight, this model guarantees full equality between 'labor and capital'. However, the equal number of shareholders' and employees' representatives in the supervisory board is misleading: the board's chairperson who is elected by the majority of the shareholders' representatives has a second vote in case any ballot results in a tie. The chairpersons' casting vote allows the shareholders to make the final decision as long as they vote in unison. Nevertheless, the chairperson's second vote does not play an important role since the key decisions to be taken in the board are discussed before each board session between the chair of the supervisory board and the employees' representatives. Similar to the 1951 parity model, the 1976 Act requires the election of a work director on the board of directors. But unlike the 1951 Act, the work director can be elected against the votes of the employees' representatives, when the chairperson casts his or her second vote. Nonetheless, many companies that fall under the scope of the 1976 Act have work directors who belong to the employees' side (*e.g.* former union officials). It is obvious that the employees' influence in the supervisory board is more significant here than under the 1952 Act that remains applicable to smaller companies.[85]

The 1976 Act also allows for a special representative of the executive staff who counts as a workers' representative. In addition, it is interesting to note that many employee representatives on the board act at the same time as works council members. They tend to establish informal meetings to discuss critical aspects long before the supervisory board is officially informed. Internal members' influence seems higher through such informal channels than through formally applying their rights on the board. Also when being members of works councils, representatives tend to internalize the partnership approach that characterizes plant level councils. Effectively, most decisions on the board tend to be unanimous. Even high bonus payments awarded to the management board are usually decided with the approval of employees' representatives.

Employee representation on supervisory boards is understood by some authors as an additional tool for monitoring management's performance and reinforcing sustainable development decisions in the long-term interest of the whole company (instead of concentrating solely on maximizing short-term profits for shareholders).[86] In that sense, employee representation on supervisory boards is understood as an instrument of corporate governance.[87] The principal function of a governance system is to solve the

[85] All three German models of employee representation at supervisory boards currently exist, but with different practical applicability: the co-determination model of 1951 decreases in numbers together with the industries it is assigned to. The 1952 One-Third-Participation Act covers most of the companies that have to establish board representation, whereas the 1976 Act remains applicable to the largest companies.

[86] Klaus Hopt: New Ways in Corporate governance: European Experiments with labor representation on corporate boards, *Michigan Law Review* 82 (1983–84) pp. 1338–63.

[87] Franklin Allen & Douglas Gale: Corporate Governance and Competition, in: Xavier Vives (ed.), *Corporate Governance, Theoretical and Empirical Perspectives,* CUP, 2006, p. 23.

'agency problem'[88] by preventing managers of corporations from pursuing their individual interests rather than that of the company. Economics focusing on the shareholder-value approach require that corporate governance ensures that management decisions reflect the interests of shareholders, as they legally 'own' the company. For such a line of reasoning, including employees in the governance mechanism is counter-productive as it might allow decisions the costs of which diminish the immediate return for shareholders. Employee representation can harm shareholders' interests, because management can avoid monitoring by playing off various interests against each other. By contrast, economists following the stakeholder-value approach accept that increasing shareholders' value is a legitimate aim for management but not the exclusive aim. Corporate governance should instead ensure all stakeholders' interests,[89] including those of employees, consumers or society at large.[90] Shareholders own the company's shares, but not the company. Their legitimate interests are financial ones, not specifically protected ownerships rights,[91] placing them on equal footing with other legitimate interests.

The impact of the German system of board level employee participation on the affected corporations has been contested. Proponents emphasize that employee participation in the supervisory boards has considerably contributed to structural changes in the affected companies. They claim that cooperation between capital and labor within the company can facilitate peaceful adaptation to changing circumstances. For example, they point at the effects of co-determination in responding to the far-reaching changes in the coal and mining sector during the 50s and 60s of the last century.[92] Opponents fear, however, that employee representatives in supervisory boards prefer conservative corporate strategies to lessen adaptability.[93]

The Dutch model The Dutch model of co-determination [*Structuurregeling*] merits being analyzed separately since it differs in its structure from the German prototype. It is mainly characterized by the fact that the employees do not have the right to elect their representatives but only have the right to propose to the shareholders' meeting a

---

[88] Michael Jensen & William Meckling: Theory of the Firm: Managerial Behaviour, Agency Costs and Ownership Structure, *3 Journal of Financial Economics* (1976) pp. 305–60.

[89] Marleen O'Connor: Employees and corporate governance: United States Labor's role in the American governance structure, 22 *CLLPJ* (2000) p. 97.

[90] German Corporate Governance Codex, No.4.1.1, reads as follows: 'managing directors govern the company [...] while considering interests of shareholders, employees and other groups involved (stakeholders)'. For details see Henrik-Michael Ringleb/Thomas Kremer/ Marcus Lutter/Axel v. Werder (eds.) *Kommentar zum Deutschen Corporate Governance Kodex*, 4th edition, Beck publ., 2010, paras 601 seq.

[91] Margaret Blair: *Ownership and Control, Rethinking Corporate Governance for the Twenty-first Century*, The Brookings Institution, Washington, 1995.

[92] See in particular the Report of the 'Biedenkopf Commission': Mitbestimmung im Unternehmen – Bericht der Sachverständigenkommission zur Auswertung der bisherigen Erfahrungen bei der Mitbestimmung (Mitbestimmungskommission), 1970, in: Bundestagsdrucksachen VI/334, pp. 29 et seq.

[93] For this criticism see *e.g.* Friedrich Kübler, Aufsichtsratsmitbestimmung im Gegenwind der Globalisierung, in: Friedrich Kübler, Joachim Scherer & Joachim Treeck (eds), *The International Lawyer – Freundesgabe für Wulf H. Döser*, Baden-Baden, 1999, pp. 237 et seq.

certain number of candidates for the supervisory board. Thus, it is not a model of employee representation *stricto sensu* but only a system that guarantees employees a certain influence in designating some of the members of the supervisory boards [*raad van commissarissen*] of big companies.[94] The model goes back to an Act of 1971 and was profoundly reformed in 2004.[95]

The *Structuurregeling* in the Netherlands applies to all public limited companies [*Naamloze Vennootshap*] and to private limited companies [*Besloten Vennootschap*] whose capital exceeds a minimum of 16 million Euros, and in which a company council [*Ondernemingsraad*] has been established and has at least 100 employees.[96]

Originally, the members of the supervisory board were elected by the board itself (Co-optation); but this highly criticized system of self-reproduction of managers was abolished by the legislator in 2004. Under the reformed law, the members of the supervisory board of public and private limited companies are elected by the shareholders, who vote on the proposal of the supervisory board. The influence of the employees in this procedure essentially consists in the company council's [*Ondernemingsraad*] right to propose candidates for one-third of the board seats. The supervisory board may object to the company council's proposal, if the proposed candidate(s) do not have the necessary aptitude. In this case, the company's council and the supervisory board try to find a compromise and if necessary a representative of the Amsterdam Court's Company Chamber [*ondernemingskamer van het gerechtshof te Amsterdam*][97] will be involved in order to mediate between the parties. In the end, the Company Chamber makes a compulsory decision on whether the supervisory board's objections against one or several candidates proposed by the company council are justified. Once the candidates of the employees' side are accepted by the supervisory board, it is up to the shareholders' meeting to elect the members of the supervisory board. In the event that the shareholders' meeting does not elect the proposed candidates, the company council needs to present other candidates who can obtain the approval of the majority of the shareholders.

Thus, the candidates elected on the proposition of the company council are not directly representatives of the employees, as in the case of the German system of board-level participation. The aim of this complicated model is to avoid conflicts of interests within supervisory boards that are co-determined. As all the board members are elected upon the company council's proposition and accepted by the majority in the shareholders' meeting, the Dutch model avoids conflicts within the supervisory board resulting from a one-sided pursuit of employees' interests by their representatives.

---

[94] However, also EU-law considers that this model guarantees a form of employee participation According to Art. 2(k) Directive 2001/86/EC supplementing the Statute for a European company with regard to the involvement of employees, the term 'participation' also embraces 'the right to recommend and/or oppose the appointment of some or all of the members of the company's supervisory or administrative organ'. For a more detailed analysis of the board-level participation model of Directive 2001/86/EC see infra 4.1.2.

[95] For an analysis of the Dutch model of board-level participation cf. Antoine Jacobs, Collectief Arbeidsrecht, 2nd edition, Deventer, 2005, pp. 267 et seq.

[96] Cf. Art. 2:153(2) and 2:263(2) Civil Code [*Burgerlijk Wetboek*].

[97] The Company Chamber is part of the Court of Amsterdam and has judicial functions in the field of corporate law.

Consequently, board-level representation and trade union activity are strictly separated from each other. The Dutch model therefore relies much more on the idea of cooperation in the company than the German *Mitbestimmung* does.

ii. Employee participation in one-tier-systems

The concept of board-level participation has been adopted by a number of European countries, but in most of these countries the employee representation takes places in one-tier systems of corporate law. Thus, in one-tier-structures employees participate in the body managing the company's day-to-day business. At first sight, this might give the impression that employee participation in one-tier-systems even is more intensive than in two-tier-structures where employee participation emphasizes on the control of management. However, it may be observed a tendency toward convergence of employee participation in one-tier and two-tier systems.[98] As a matter of fact, employee representatives in boards of directors normally do not become managing directors and often are not involved in the work of the various board committees; in most cases, there role is therefore limited to management control.

In countries where corporate law gives companies the choice between the one- and two-tier systems, board-level participation is predominant in the one-tier corporate structure. It would go beyond the limits of this brief overview to analyze all national systems recognizing a form of employee representation on the company level. A few examples must therefore suffice in the present context.

In the Grand-Duchy of Luxembourg, employee participation at company level goes back to 1974. According to Article L. 426-1 combined with L. 426-3 (1) Labor Code, in the boards of directors of all public limited corporations [*sociétés anonymes*] that are established according to Luxembourg law, which have their registered office on the Luxembourg territory and employ at least 1,000 employees in the Grand-Duchy, one-third of the seats in the board of directors (or of the supervisory board in a two-tier-structure) are reserved for employee representatives. They are appointed by the company's personnel delegation(s) through secret ballot according to the principle of proportionality (Article L. 426-4 Labor Code). The employee representatives have the same rights and duties as the directors representing the shareholders. They benefit from a specific dismissal protection: they only can be dismissed with the authorization of the labor court, which requires that there is an important reason justifying a dismissal without notice (Art. L. 426-9 Labor Code). The Luxembourg participation model originally covered in particular ARBED,[99] the famous Luxembourg steel producer, which was later merged with the French Group Arcelor and in 2006 with the Indian steel producer Mittal to Arcelor Mittal. However, nowadays the participation regime of Article L. 426-1 et seq. Labor Code applies also to other public limited corporations in Luxembourg.

---

98 Cf. Seifert, "Employee participation at board level in Europe", in: Jürgen Basedow, Chen, Matteo Fornasier & Ulla Liukkunen (eds), *Employee Participation and Collective Bargaining in Europe and China*, Beiträge zum Internationalen Privatrecht, Tübingen 2015 (forthcoming).

99 Aciéries Réunies de Burbach, Esch et Dudelange.

Another example for board-level representation in the one-tier system is France.[100] Even though French corporate law allows for both models, the one-tier system is clearly predominant in practice. Under French law, a compulsory board-level representation exists for the public sector, which is very relevant in France. In corporations dominated by the State, a minimum of one-third of the members of the board of directors is elected by the employees.[101] Following the re-privatizations under the Gaullist Government of the first 'Cohabitation' (1986–88), the French Government of the second 'Cohabitation' (1993–95) adopted a law in 1994 providing the maintenance of the board-level representation in public sector companies that were privatized.[102] As far as the private sector is concerned, the French Commercial Code allows that at board-level representation up to one-third is established by corporate statute[103] and exists therefore only on a voluntary basis. The most recent reform of board-level representation in France, in the Act of 14 June 2013 on employment protection, mandates compulsory board-level representation in companies that have at least 5,000 employees in France, or in a transnational group with at least 10,000 employees.[104] Hence, despite the trade unions' fierce opposition to company level cooperation in the past, France is increasingly strengthening board-level participation.

iii. Board-level participation on a voluntary basis

Many countries do not legally recognize board-level participation of employees. The main reasons for such reticence, or even resistance, toward this model are the employers' oppposition to sharing their power in management with employee representatives and the unions' fear of getting involved in unpopular decisions of the company that may produce de-solidarizing effects and undermine the unions' collective bargaining power. A good example for this attitude is observed in the UK where the establishment of board-level employee representation by one-third was envisaged in the 1970s.[105] This does not mean, however, that these countries have not experienced board-level participation at all. As a matter of fact, even in the UK and in the US there have been, and still exist, examples for voluntary implementation of employee participation in the company's board of directors.

---

[100] For an assessment of the French case cf. the contributions in Aline Conchon & Marie-Noëlle Auberger (eds), *Les Administrateurs salaries et la gouvernance d'entreprise, La documentation française*, French Documentation, 2009. See also Achim Seifert, Mitbestimmung im Verwaltungsratsmodell: Frankreich und Luxemburg als Beispiele, in: Christoph Teichmann (ed.), Verhandelte Mitbestimmung, Baden-Baden, 2014 (*forthcoming*).

[101] See Act No 83-675 of 26 July 1983 on the democratization of the public sector [*Loi n° 83-675 relative à la démocratisation du secteur public*], J.O.R.F. 1983, p. 2267.

[102] See Art. 1 of the Act No. 94-640 of 25 July 1994 concerning the amelioration of the employees' participation in the company [*Loi n° 94-640 relative à l'amélioration de la participation des salariés dans l'entreprise*], J.O.R.F. 1994, p. 10832.

[103] See Art. L. 225-27 of the French Commercial Code [*Code de commerce*].

[104] Art. 9 de la Loi n° 2013-504 relative à la sécurisation de l'emploi.

[105] See the Report of the Committee of Inquiry on Industrial Democracy, London 1977 ('Bullock-Report'); also the Trade Union Congress (TUC) favored at that time the establishing of a board-level representation under the label of 'industrial democracy'; cf. TUC, Industrial Democracy: A Statement of Policy, London 1974.

In the UK, for instance, the British Steel Corporation experienced a negotiated board-level participation model in the 1970s which gave the unions a right to nominate some worker directors on the board of directors but which existed only for a few years.[106] The British Post Office also established an employee representation at the board level.[107] Both companies were under the dominant influence of the government. However, there have been and there still are a few companies in the private sector that have established a board-level representation model for their employees.

Similarly, in the US, examples of union representation on boards of directors can be found.[108] They often were and still are the result of negotiations between unions and management over the institution of Employee Stock Ownership Plans (ESOP). In some cases, board seats for union representatives are a quid pro quo for concessions on the employees' side in the event of a corporate restructuring process.

Nonetheless, these experiences are rather isolated and confirm the general rule that industrial relations in these two countries essentially rely on collective bargaining and not on the idea of a cooperation of unions and management within the company.

b. Workers' Ownership of the Company

One of the oldest instruments for giving employees a voice in the company is to make them owners of the company they are working for. It is assumed that by extending ownership to workers or employees the social and economic antagonism between labor and capital will be eliminated. There are in particular two types noteworthy to be analyzed here: worker cooperatives (infra, 3.b.i) and employee shareholder programs (infra, 3.b.ii.).

i. Worker cooperatives

One type of workers' ownership is the membership in a worker cooperative. By joining a worker cooperative, a worker is obliged to perform work and receives an (equitable) remuneration. As the cooperative is democratically organized, the workers participate through the general assembly of the cooperative in the determination of their working conditions, and sometimes even issues that extend working life, such as housing arrangements. Thus, the subordination of the worker, inherent to the capitalist employment relationship, is at least softened by the democratic participation of the worker members within the bodies of the worker cooperative. It is obvious that the intensity of participation largely depends on the size of the worker cooperative. In small (local) cooperatives, the participation intensity is much higher than in big cooperatives, in which hundreds or even thousands of workers are members. Namely the famous

[106] See also Bernd Atenstaedt, Mitbestimmung der Arbeitnehmer im Board britischer Kapitalgesellschaften, Frankfurt 1987.

[107] For an assessment of these worker or employee directors see E. Batstone, E. Ferner & M. Terry, *Unions on the Board: An Experiment in Industrial Democracy*, Oxford, 1983. See also Bernd Atenstaedt, Mitbestimmung der Arbeitnehmer im Board britischer Kapitalgesellschaften, Frankfurt, 1987.

[108] For an overview see Tove H. Hammer, Steven C. Currall & Robert N. Stern, Worker representation on boards of directors: A study of competing roles, 44(4) *Industrial and Labor Relations Review*, (1991), pp. 661–80.

Mondragón Cooperatives are a good example for a cooperative movement which has developed from a cooperative grass root movement in the 1950s to a multinational company employing almost 80,000 workers: under these circumstances, worker self-determination through cooperativism is considerably watered down.[109]

The movement of worker cooperatives goes back to the nineteenth century. In particular reformers such as Robert Owen and the French socialist philosopher Pierre-Joseph Proudhon saw in the cooperative movement ('mutualism') the way out of the then existing class struggles.[110] Although there are voices that favor the expansion of worker cooperatives, for example – the ILO, in its Recommendation No 193 on the Promotion of Cooperatives (2002), only a few countries have legally recognized worker cooperatives and try to promote this concept of worker self-determination in the labor market. For example, the State of Massachusetts established in the 1980s a statute for 'employee cooperatives', which is widely used.[111] Another example is the French Act of 26 April 1917 ('Loi Chéron')[112] establishing a specific type of public limited company whose shares are exclusively distributed to workers of the company [*Société anonyme à participation ouvrière*]. They contribute to the company's interest through their work. However, this type of public limited companies has not played any role in France until today.[113]

Generally speaking, the worker cooperatives' movement does not play an important role nowadays among the options of non-union institutions of voice.[114]

ii. Employees as shareholder of the employer's company

Employee shareholder programs are far more common than worker cooperatives. By becoming a shareholder of the employer's company, employees not only participate in the company's benefits as all other shareholders but are also entitled to exercise all rights shareholders have in the shareholders' meeting. In the event that employees organize a shareholders' association of the company's employees, they can exercise their voting rights in a coordinated way, *e.g.* through representatives. There are various

---

[109] For an instructive overview on the development of the Mondragón cooperatives and the tensions and antagonisms that have been arisen cf. Amanda Latinne, Workplace Democracy and Globalization: The Mondragón Cooperatives, Cambridge – Antwerp – Portland 2014 (Intersentia).

[110] See *e.g.* Pierre Joseph Proudhon, *Idée générale de la révolution au XIXe siècle*, 2nd edition, Paris, 1851, pp. 255 et seq.

[111] See e.g. Massachusetts General Law Chapter 157A, A Statute for Employee Cooperative Corporations; Maine Revised Statute Title 13, Chapter 85, Subchapter 3; Worker Cooperative Corporations Statute Vermont. For an in-depth analysis of the Massachusetts Model cf. David Ellermann & Peter Pitegoff, The democratic corporation: The new worker cooperative statute in Massachussetts, 11 *N.Y.U Review of Law & Social Change* (1982–83) 441.

[112] Loi Adjonction des art. 72 à 80 (Sociétés Anonymes à participation ouvrière) et modification de l'art. 64 (émission d'actions) de la loi du 27 juillet 1867 (J.O.R.F. 1917 du 28 avril 1917, 3386). Today, Art. L.225-258 et seq French Commercial Code are dealing with the joint stock company with worker participation.

[113] Cf. Le Vey, Jurisclasseur Sociétés Traités (2008), fascicule 173-50 – Société Anonyme à Participation Ouvrière, para. 3 with further references.

[114] For further information see the Website of the Canadian Worker Co-op Federation 'Tenacity works' under: http://www.canadianworker.coop/.

examples for such a bundled exercise of employee-shareholder rights in shareholders' meetings.[115] Employee shareholder programs may therefore be a tool to exert influence on the business administration of the employer's company. Many employers consider employee shareholder programs to be an instrument to increase the employees' motivation to the company goals; additionally, they sometimes also intend to further social partnership in the company and to avoid conflicts with the workforce (in particular strikes). These advantages for employers are, however, often contested by unions. They warn about the potential accumulation of risks on the employees' side, namely their risk of losing their job as well as their capital invested in the employer's company in case of the employer's insolvency. Despite these objections, employee ownership has increasingly become important in many countries and merits therefore being analyzed in the present context. Of particular interest are countries in which employee shareholder status has been, or is still, promoted by statutory law. Two European examples – France and the UK – illustrate two different policy approaches.

In France, the participation of the employee stock owners in the company's decision-making was institutionalized in the 1990s. Even though employee stock ownership [*actionnariat salarié*] has a long tradition going back to the Presidency of *de Gaulle* in the late 50s and 60s – it was considered to be a core element of the Gaullist politics of reconciliation between labor and capital – those early reforms provided no specific participation rights of the employee stock owners.[116]

The position of the employee shareholders changed after the Act of July 24, 1994 on the improvement of employee involvement in the company.[117] Article L. 225-23 Commercial Code, introduced by this Act, provided that an extraordinary shareholders' meeting should be convoked where the employee shareholders own more than 5 percent of the corporate capital. The stockholder meeting then has to take a decision on whether the company bylaws should be modified in order to allow the election of one or two representatives of the employee shareholders on to the board of directors or – in the event of a two-tier-structure of the corporation – on to the supervisory board. This representation was only on a voluntary basis. In case of a negative decision, the shareholders' meeting would only be obliged to take a decision on the same question five years later. In practice, the impact of the reform was not significant.[118]

---

115 In the case of the famous German steel company Krupp, for instance, that established an employee shareholder program in the early 1920s the company even transferred the shares to a trust organizing the employees who were supposed to benefit from the dividends. For more details see Th. Fabri, Die Kleinaktie, Berlin 1959, pp. 85 et seq.

116 For an analysis of the development of financial participation of employees in France see Guiol, La participation à la gestion de l'entreprise: une lecture historico-politique, in: Aline Conchon & Marie-Noelle Auberger (eds): Les administrateurs salariés et la gouvernance d'entreprise, p. 35, at 41 et seq. See also the so-called Sudreau Report which has been important for the political debate in France: La réforme de l'entreprise – Rapport du comité présidé par Pierre Sudreau, Paris 1975, pp. 143 et seq.

117 Loi relative à l'amélioration de la participation des salariés dans l'entreprise (J.O.R.F. 1994, p. 10832).

118 That is the opinion of Gilles Auzero, JurisClasseur Sociétés Traité, Fascicule 130-60: Représentation des salariés dans les organes de gestion de la société anonyme (2002), § 92.

Several changes in law sought to increase the importance of employee ownership. The Act of February 19, 2001 on Employee Financial Participation reduced the threshold for the extraordinary shareholders meeting, from 5 to 3 percent of the employees' ownership of the corporate capital.[119] The Act of January 17, 2001 on Social Modernization mandated representation of the employee stockholders on the board of directors or the supervisory board of the company when the employees retain at least 3 percent of the corporate capital.[120] This right does not exist, however, when there are already employee representatives on the board of directors or the supervisory board.[121] Thus, co-determination and participation through employee shares cannot be cumulated. Despite these attempts to juridify and strengthen the participation of employee shareholders in the company boards, its impact remains rather modest.[122]

Another recent example for legislative intervention and promotion of the Employee Shareholder status is the Employee Shareholder Status introduced by the Growth and Infrastructure Act in 2013 in the UK.[123] The policy behind this act differs considerably from the French policy approach.

This highly controversial Act established, in section 205A of the Employment Relations Act (ERA), a new arrangement that makes it possible for the employer and employee entitled to contract away a number of statutory employee rights in exchange for the employee's entitlement for shares in the company. By way of such an agreement, the parties may contract away, inter alia, the right under section 94 ERA not to be unfairly dismissed and the right under section 135 to a redundancy payment (sec. 205A(2) ERA). Thus, the employee shareholder status, in particular the voting rights as well as the right to a dividend linked with that status, are considered to be an appropriate compensation for the loss of statutory rights the employee is entitled to. The purpose of this trade-off between statutory employee rights and employee shareholder status is to stimulate growth in times of an economic and financial crisis. Consequently, the legislator's aim is not to establish a solid channel for employee voice in the company's decision-making process. Whether this policy of a contracting away of the statutory employee protection in exchange for a shareholder status will stimulate growth and grant effective voice to employees remains to be seen.

c. Employee Voice in Shareholders' Meetings

A weaker mechanism of employee voice at company level is to give employee representatives a voice in the shareholders' meetings of public limited companies. By

---

[119] Loi n°2001-152 sur l'épargne salariale (J.O.R.F. 2001, p. 2774).

[120] Loi de modernisation sociale n° 2002-73 of January 17, 2001 (J.O.R.F. 2002, pp. 2851 et seq).

[121] Art. L. 225-23 and Art. L. 225-71 (3) Commercial Code.

[122] As to the impact of employee shareholder programs in France cf. Cornut-Gentille & Godfrain, Une ambition: la participation pour tous – Rapport au Premier Ministre de la mission parlementaire confiée à MM. François Cornut-Gentille et Jacques Godfrain, députés, Paris, 29 September 1995, pp. 54 et seq.

[123] For a critical assessment of this new Act, see Jeremias Prassl, Dismantling the contract of employment? The new employee shareholder status in the United Kingdom, in: European Labour Law Network – Working Paper Series 1/2013.

this link between labor law and corporate law, employees obtain the opportunity to express the employees' interests in the shareholders' decision-making. Naturally, employees receive the right to attend to the shareholders' meetings of their company by buying its shares (*e.g.* on the basis of an employee shareholder program). However, some national systems go further and even guarantee employees' representatives a voice in the shareholders' meeting.

Thus, the French company committee [*Comité d'entreprise*] is entitled to demand the convocation of a shareholders' meeting in urgent cases. Additionally, the company committee has the right to put resolution demands on the agenda of the shareholders' meeting and to send two representatives to the shareholders' meeting.[124]

4. EMPLOYEE VOICE IN TRANSNATIONAL COMPANIES

The previous section surveyed institutions and bodies that are intended to promote employee voice and which were established by national law. Their scope is therefore limited to the borders of the Nation-State. They are all built upon the implicit assumption that management's decision-making can be influenced by employee participation in one Nation-State. This traditional assumption of industrial relations becomes, however, doubtful in the case of transnational companies. Their transnational character gives them an additional power resulting from their cross-border organization and activities that cannot be balanced by information, consultation and decision-making procedures within the Nation-State. One major problem is that employee representatives of subsidiaries outside the country where the transnational enterprise has its seat, have no real influence on managerial decisions taken at the headquarters abroad. Thus, the workforce of the remote subsidiaries has practically no collective voice to influence the decision-making process at the relevant level. Consequently, employee representatives, acting on the basis of national law, often end up merely implementing entrepreneurial decisions made at headquarters and can only try to reactively negotiate or otherwise influence the provision of social compensation (*e.g.* severance pay for dismissed employees) according to the domestic laws. Another problem is that transnational companies can often easily relocate their activities from subsidiaries in one country to those located in other countries, thereby playing off the workforces of subsidiaries in different countries against each other for reducing labor costs ('race to the bottom'). Consequently, the legal form of traditional industrial relations, particularly considering the objectives of institutions that promote employee's voice and the structure of economic decision-making in transnational companies, can become contradictious.[125]

This conflict only can be resolved if the existing industrial relations structures at local level are supplemented by cross-border representation bodies reflecting the transnational character of companies. Hence, industrial relations structures have to

[124] Cf. Art. L. 2323-67 French Labor Code.

[125] For a fuller analysis see Achim Seifert, Global Employee Information and Consultation Procedures in Worldwide Operating Enterprises, 327 *International Journal of Comparative Labour Law and Industrial Relations* 2008, p. 25.

follow the transnational geographical extension of companies' activities. There are various examples for such a trans-nationalization of employee representation.

a. The Case of EU Law

The most advanced effort to establishing a legal framework for transnational employee involvement can be found in the EU. In 1994, after a very long discussion, the EU has adopted a Directive establishing the European Works Councils (EWC) in 'Community-scale undertakings' and 'Community-scale groups of undertakings'.[126] These EWC represent the whole workforce in Europe-wide operating transnational companies or groups and detain information and consultation rights. A similar model exists for the European Company [*Societas Europaea – SE*] – a legal form for transnational companies under EU-law:[127] however, the rules regarding employee participation in the SE go beyond information and consultation, providing also a legal framework for employee board-level participation.

These two forms of transnational employee involvement in the EU differ from what has been described before in the comparison of national legislation. In the two arrangements the European legislature does not provide substantive rules for these cross-border forms of employee representation, and suffices instead with procedural rules institutionalizing negotiations between management and labor in order to reach an agreement on the establishment of an EWC or board-level employee representation in European companies.

i. European works councils

Directive 2009/38/EC only applies to 'community scale undertakings' or 'groups of undertakings' employing at least 1,000 workers in the EU and at least 150 in each of at least two EU Member States.[128] Thus, the Directive limits the scope of application through a double threshold and ensures that the scope of application is limited to transnational companies. The issues covered by the duty to inform and consult are limited to transnational questions affecting the interests of employees, thereby leaving the competence to discuss national questions to national bodies, if any. The EWC Directive is only intended to supplement, not to substitute the already existing national representation bodies (*e.g.* works councils, joint committees, etc.).

The parties to the negotiations on the establishment of an EWC are the company's or the group's Central Management and a Special Negotiating Body (SNB) representing

[126] Cf. Directive 94/45/EC of 22 September 1994 on the establishment of a European Works Council or a procedure in Community-scale undertakings and Community-scale groups of undertakings for the purposes of informing and consulting employees, O.J. 1994 L 254, p. 64. This Directive was replaced by Directive 2009/38/EC of 6 May 2009 on the establishment of a European Works Council or a procedure in Community-scale undertakings and Community-scale groups of undertakings for the purposes of informing and consulting employees (Recast), O.J. 2009 L 122, p. 28.

[127] Cf. Directive 2001/86/EC of 8 October 2001 supplementing the Statute for a European company with regard to the involvement of employees, O.J.E.C. 2001 L 294, p. 22.

[128] See Art. 2(1)(a)–(c) of Directive 2009/38/EC.

the company's or group's employees working in the EU Member States. The designation of the SNB is a very complex procedure since there are no uniform rules that apply all over the EU. Instead, the law of the Member State on whose territory a plant is located applies. Thus, the models that constitute the SNB may vary considerably. In some Member States the employees elect their representatives on the SNB directly, whereas in other Member States works councils or other elected employee representatives appoint the SNB members. On the other side, the central management is that of the Community-scale undertaking or, in the case of a Community-scale group of undertakings, the management of the controlling undertaking. In the event that the central management is not situated in an EU Member State, a 'representative agent' in a Member State, appointed by the central management, takes the responsibilities under Directive 2009/38/EC.[129] In the absence of such a representative, the management of the establishment or group undertaking employing the greatest number of employees in a Member State assumes the charge to negotiate an EWC agreement with the SNB.[130]

Central management and SNB should negotiate an agreement establishing the EWC within a period of six months from the establishment of the SNB. If they come to an agreement, this becomes the legal framework for the EWC. The parties determine, inter alia, all plants or affiliations inside and outside the EU territory which will be represented by the EWC, the composition as well as the information and consultation rights of the EWC, venue, frequency and duration of the EWC-meetings, financial resources provided for the EWC and the duration of the EWC agreement.[131] In most cases, the parties are able to reach such an EWC agreement, which constitutes the legal basis for establishing the EWC.[132] This contractual model allows the parties to tailor the EWC as well as its information and consultation rights according to their own needs. Thus, EWCs vary from company to company. It can be observed, however, that the contracting parties more or less reproduce the national models of employee representation applicable in the country where the company's headquarters/representation is located. A French transnational company would therefore prefer to extend the French Company Committee [*Comité d'entreprise*] to the European level and tends to establish a 'European Company Committee' [*Comité d'entreprise européen*] whereas a German company more commonly establishes an EWC reproducing the German *Betriebsrat* at European level.[133]

In the event that the parties are not able to reach an agreement or that the parties prefer to adopt a default arrangement, the so-called subsidiary requirements of Annex I to Directive 2008/38/EC apply. This means, inter alia, that an EWC will be established in accordance with these rules and has information and consultation rights regarding the structure, economic and financial situation, probable development and production

---

[129] Ibid., Art. 4(2), para. (1).

[130] Ibid., Art. 4(2), para. (2).

[131] Cf. ibid., Art. 6(2).

[132] A collection of EWC agreements is available at the Website of the European Trade Union Institute (ETUI) at: http://www.worker-participation.eu/.

[133] For a fuller analysis of this aspect, see Achim Seifert, Les CEE en Allemagne – vers une solidarité transnationale en cas de restructuration d'entreprise?, in: Isabelle Daugareilh (ed.), *Le dialogue social dans les instances transnationales d'entreprises européennes*, Presses Universitaires de Bordeaux, 2013, pp. 55–76.

and sales of the Community-scale undertaking or group of undertakings. The EWC has the right to meet with the central management once a year. In case of exceptional circumstances (*e.g.* in the event of relocations or collective redundancies) the EWC has an information right and may meet the central management.

For many EWCs information and consultation rights have only served as a starting point. Even though Directive 2009/38/EC provides only a framework for employee information and consultation, many EWCs have gone beyond these limits and negotiate agreements with central management. These agreements may cover questions such as employee protection in the case of corporate restructuring, health and safety at work or employee data protection.[134] It is therefore no exaggeration to say that something like transnational collective bargaining at company level is developing in Europe without a strict mandatory (European) legal framework. The European Commission is closely observing this development and inquiring whether the EU should establish a legal framework for transnational bargaining at company-level.[135]

ii. Board-level participation in the European company

The EWC is only an information and consultation body. Board-level representation within transnational companies has not been addressed by the EWC Directive. However, in the early 1970s, the European Commission had already envisaged adopting a legal framework for board-level participation. As a matter of fact, it published a proposal for a fifth Company Law Directive in 1971 aimed at harmonizing board-level representation in all Member States of the European Economic Community. However, due to the different industrial relations systems and traditions in the Member States,[136] these could not reach a consensus on the desirable form of board-level representation. Furthermore, the European Commission intended to recognize the European Company as a new legal form for companies operating in the Common Market. The German Government in particular insisted that a statute for a SE had to include rules on board-level representation, thereby reducing the incentive for German companies that

---

[134] A list of currently existing transnational company agreements is available at the website of the European Commission: http://ec.europa.eu/social/main.jsp?catId=978&langId=en. For an in-depth analysis of the different types of agreements see Stefan Rüb, Hans-Wolfgang Platzer & Torsten Müller, Transnationale Unternehmensvereinbarungen – Zur Neuordnung der Arbeitsbeziehungen in Europa, Berlin, 2011; Jeremy Waddington, Was leisten Europäische Betriebsräte? Die Perspektive der Arbeitnehmervertreter, in: WSI-Mitteilungen 2006, pp. 560 et seq; cf. also Valeria Pulignano, European Integration and Trans-national Employment Regulation: The Company-level Experience of EFAs in the Metal Sector in Europe, 1 *European Labour Law Journal* (2010), pp. 81 et seq.

[135] Edoardo Ales, Samuel Engblom, Teun Jaspers, Sylvaine Laulom, Silvana Sciarra, André Sobczak & Fernando Valdés dal Ré, *Transnational Collective Bargaining: Past, Present and Future*, Brussels, 2006 ('Ales-Report'). For a critical analysis of the proposals of the Ales-Report cf. Achim Seifert, Transnational Collective Bargaining: The Case of the European Union, in: Kitty Malherbe & Julia Sloth-Nielsen (eds), *Labour Law into the Future: Essays in Honour of D'Arcy Dutoit*, 2012, pp. 76–96.

[136] For a detailed analysis of the then existing models of employee representation within the Member States see Gérard Lyon-Caen, Contribution à l'étude des modes de représentation des intérêts des travailleurs dans le cadre des sociétés anonymes européennes, Brussels 1970 (Study realized for the European Commission).

are covered by the German *Mitbestimmung* to establish an SE without employee representation. These controversies blocked the adoption of the European Company Statute for a very long time. The impasse was resolved with the adoption of the EWC-Directive 94/45/EC in 1994. The Directive's negotiation model inspired a new debate on the SE and after the Recommendations of the so-called *Davignon Report* (1997),[137] the European legislator was able to cut the Gordian knot and adopted in 2001 the Regulation (EC) No 2157/2001 of 8 October 2001 on the Statute for a European Company[138] as well as Directive 2001/86/EC of 8 October 2001 supplementing the Statute for a European Company with regard to the involvement of employees.[139] Thus, the SE rules, as in the case of European works councils, do not provide substantive rules on concrete rights for employees' representatives (e.g. information and consultation or co-determination) but only procedural rules that define the negotiation process between management and employees' representatives on employee involvement in the SE.

Regulation (EC) No 2157/2001 on the Statute for a European Company allows companies to operate transnationally[140] under one common corporate regime governed by directly applicable EU law rather than the still different national laws. By and large, Directive 2001/86/EC transfers the EWC negotiation model to employee involvement in the SE. Thus, employees working in the European Company will form, similar to the model of the EWC-Directive, a SNB that negotiates with the management or administrative organs of the participating companies an agreement on the involvement of employees. These negotiations cover the establishment of a transnational information and consultation procedure as well as board-level participation. The management or administrative organs of the participating companies have a strong interest to negotiate in good faith with the SNB since the SE can not be registered unless negotiations have been conducted in accordance with the provisions of Directive 2001/86/EC.[141]

Following the negotiations, three different outcomes are possible. In the event that the SNB takes a decision with a majority vote of two-thirds not to conduct negotiations with management or to withdraw from negotiations that have already started, the SE will have no cross-border employee representation at all. Secondly, the negotiations may have been successful and the parties can agree upon an information and consultation procedure as well as on board-level employee participation. In this case, the parties are in principle free to design the information and consultation body and the degree to which employees are to be involved in the decision-making of the company's board. If the parties want to reduce the level of board-level participation that exists in at least one of the companies participating in the establishment of the European Company,

---

[137] Cf. Report of the High Level Group of Experts on 'European Systems of Worker's Involvement' (Davignon Group Final Report).

[138] O.J. 2001 L 294, p. 1.

[139] O.J. 2001 L 294, p. 22.

[140] EU-based companies established in more than one Member State may become SEs either by cross-border merger, creating a joint holding company or creating a subsidiary; a single based company may transform into an SE once it has had a subsidiary in another Member State for at least two years.

[141] Cf. Art. 12(2) Regulation 2157/2001/EC.

a decision of the SNB is made following a qualified majority of votes among the representatives representing the employees concerned.

The third possible outcome of the negotiation process is that the negotiations have failed. In this latter case, Directive 2001/86/EC provides the application of a set of standard reference rules. These subsidiary rules provide information and consultation rights to a specific employee representative body, replacing the function of an EWC.[142] As to the board level, the standard rules only require the establishment of employee representation in accordance with the so-called 'before-and-after' principle, which safeguards board-level participation that existed in at least one of the companies that established the European Company. This means that in the case of an SE established by transformation, all aspects of board-level participation continues to apply to the SE. In all other cases of the establishment of an SE (*e.g.* merger), 'the employees of the SE [...] shall have the right to elect, appoint, recommend or oppose the appointment of a number of members of the supervisory body of the SE equal to the highest proportion in force in the participating companies concerned before registration of the SE'. Consequently, the standard rules do not provide a compulsory employee board-level representation in the SE if none of the participating companies was governed by participation rules before registration of the SE. It results from this model that Directive 2001/86/EC does not provide an employee board-level representation for all SE but guarantees only *droits acquis* in the field of employee participation. Since the adoption of the European Company Statute in 2001, at the time of writing, over 2,000 European Companies have been registered.[143]

b. Other Forms of Employee Voice in Transnational Companies

The European experience of limited harmonization in the field of employee information and consultation procedures is very specific and has not been replicated so far by other regional institutions, such as the Northern American Free Trade Association (NAFTA), the Mercosur or the Southern African Development Community (SADC).[144] This is not surprising since institutionalized forms of employee representation are commonly not even recognized by national legislators. Nonetheless, this does not say that beyond the

---

[142] The standard rules concerning information and consultation resemble therefore those of the EWC Directive.

[143] In absolute terms, most operating SEs are registered in Germany, whereas in the Czech Republic many so-called 'shelf-companies' have been established not actively doing business but being on sale for other companies which might wish to use them. For German companies submitted to a statutory board-level participation regime, the establishing of an SE is a way to move from a statutory scheme to a negotiated employee regime which is much more flexible and susceptible to further (contractual) modifications by the parties.

[144] However, it is worthy of mention that Art. 13 of the Charter of Fundamental Social Rights, adopted by the Southern African Development Community (SADC) in 2003, obliges the Member States to promote 'industrial and workplace democracy' and to develop employee information and consultation as well as employee participation 'especially in companies or groups of companies having establishments or companies in two or more Member States in the Region'. Thus, SADC also seems to recognize the need for a cross-border employee involvement in transnational companies.

limited harmonization among the Member States of the EU there are no forms of employee voice in transnational companies at all. On the contrary, there are various mechanisms through which employees may obtain influence on the decision-making process in transnational companies. As to their legal basis, these forms of employee voice are less formalized and may appear as result of Corporate Social Responsibility (CSR) strategies.[145]

i. Codes of conduct

One instrument that can serve as the basis for employees voice in transnational companies may be a corporate code of conduct.[146] In such codes of conduct, companies declare they will comply with certain local or international labor norms. As to the latter, the main point of reference is the core labor standards as defined by the 1998 ILO Declaration on Fundamental Principles and Rights at Work. While many transnational companies declare their commitment to the ILO core labor standards, they rarely establish significant mechanisms of employee voice beyond a general recognition of the freedom of association.

ii. International framework agreements

European structures of employee involvement can promote the institutionalization of representation structures at a global level and can be the regional nucleus of employee involvement in transnational enterprises as Directive 2009/38/EC allows the voluntary extension of EWC's to represent employees from non-EU countries.[147] However, there are only a few agreements establishing EWCs that include employee representatives of third countries.[148] Important examples include the Group Global Works Council of Volkswagen (1998),[149] the World Works Council of Renault (2000) or the World Employee Committee of DaimlerChrysler (2002).[150]

---

[145] For an analysis of the European context cf. European Commission: Green Paper, Promoting a European Framework for Corporate Social Responsibility, COM (2001) 366 final, Brussels, 18 July 2001, defining CSR as integrating social and environmental concerns in business operations as well as in interactions with the company's stakeholders on a voluntary basis.

[146] For an overview with further references see Bob Hepple, Labour Laws and Global Trade, Oxford and Portland/Oregon 2005 (Hart Publishing), pp. 72 et seq.

[147] Directive 2009/38/EC, Art 6(2)(a). The same applies to Directive 2001/86/EC supplementing the Statute of the European Company with regard to the involvement of employees (Art. 4(2)(a)).

[148] See the empirical study of Hellmut Gohde, Europäische Betriebsräte – Analyse und Handlungsempfehlungen, Frankfurt/Main 2004, p. 18–19. See also Paul Marginson, Mark Gilman, Otto Jacobi & Hubert Krieger, *Negotiating European Works Councils: A Comparative Study of Article 6 and Article 13 Agreements,* Dublin, 1998, pp. 21–2 and European Commission, Soziales Europa – Vereinbarungen über Unterrichtung und Anhörung in Europäischen Multinationalen Unternehmen, 1995/Beiheft 5, p. 26.

[149] For the VOLKSWAGEN-Agreement see the case study of the European Foundation for the Improvement of Living and Working Conditions, available at: http://www.eurofound.eu.int/pubdocs/2005/7146/en/1/ef057146en.pdf.

[150] The Renault-Agreement is available at: http://www.imfmetal.org/main/index.cfm?n=47&l=2&c=9806.

Another way to establish employee representation bodies at a global level is transnational (global) collective bargaining.[151] Global union federations (GUF) – *e.g.* the International Metalworkers' Federation (IMF), the International Union of Food (IUF) and the International Federation of Chemical, Energy, Mine and General Workers' Unions (ICEM) – have concluded more than 40 so-called International Framework Agreements (IFAs) with transnational enterprises covering about 3.5 million employees worldwide. Often such agreements result from transnational collective bargaining between GUF and the central management of transnational companies.[152] Like the instruments that establish corporate social responsibility, IFAs are often concluded in view of promoting the company's public image as a socially responsible actor. As employees' interests during negotiations are represented by unions, labor rights tend to be a central element of IFAs which refer to international labor standards.[153] Many of the IFAs are concluded in the metal industry and by companies headquartered in Europe that traditionally subscribe to patterns of cooperative industrial relations. Some transnational enterprises already have concluded collective agreements providing for cross-border information and consultation procedures.

Some important examples of IFAs include the agreement concluded between the International Union of Food (IUF) and Danone in 1989, establishing a worldwide Information and Consultation Committee;[154] the IFA concluded between Statoil and the International Federation of Chemical, Energy, Mine and General Workers' Unions (ICEM) of 1998; the agreement between ENI and the International Federation of Chemical, Energy, Mine and General Workers' Unions (ICEM) in 2002; and the agreement between SKF and the International Metalworkers' Federation (IMF) that was concluded in 2003. The content of these collective agreements varies considerably. Some of the employee representation bodies, *e.g.* the SKF World Union Committee, are composed exclusively of employee representatives appointed by the representative union at the plant level and only represent the unionized workforce of the enterprise. Other transnational employee representative bodies are freely and democratically elected by the whole workforce, whether organized or not. The matters that are submitted to information and consultation essentially concern the economic and financial development of the company and operational changes that affect employees.

---

[151] See the overview of Torsten Müller, Hans-Wolfgang Platzer & Stefan Rüb, Globale Arbeitsbeziehungen in globalen Konzernen? Zur Transnationalisierung betrieblicher und gewerkschaftlicher Politik. Eine vergleichende Studie, pp. 248. Torsten Müller, Hans-Wolfgang Platzer & Stefan Rüb, Grenzübergreifende Arbeitsbeziehungen in globalen Konzernen, Hans-Böckler-Stiftung Arbeitspapier [Working Paper] No 98, Düsseldorf 2004; see also Stefan Rüb, World Works Councils and other forms of Global Employee Representation in Transnational Undertakings, Hans Böckler Stiftung Arbeitspapier [Working Paper] No 55, Düsseldorf 2002.

[152] Norbert Kluge & Isabelle Schömann, Corporate Governance, Workers' Participation and CSR: The way to a good company, Transfer (2008) pp. 3–26.

[153] As developed by the ILO declaration of Fundamental Principles and Rights at Work (1998) and reinforced by the ILO Declaration on Social Justice for a fair Globalization (2008). The IFAs adhere to the four core labor standards.

[154] The text of this agreement is available on the homepage of IUF: http://www.iufdocuments.org/cgi-bin/dbman/db.cgi?db=default&uid=default&ID=164&view_records=1&ww=1&en=1.

These employee-representation bodies need to be distinguished from world works councils that were established in about 60 transnational companies (mainly in the car manufacturing sector) during the 60s and 70s of the last century, as these committees operating on a global scale were unilaterally organized – and subsidized – by the International Trade Secretariats (ITS) and were only employee representatives' networks with marginal relevance. Most of them failed.[155]

5. EMPLOYEE VOICE IN STATE INSTITUTIONS

Employee representation does not only take place at the workplace, on company or sector level. In many countries, employees have also a voice in State institutions and can therefore influence the decision-making processes of public bodies such as public administrations or even the legislature. Forms and intensity vary, of course, considerably.

a. Representation in Administrative Bodies

The best example of representation within administrative bodies of the State, is the participation of unions in the governing bodies of social security institutions in which employees and employers are equally represented. The examples are many, including Belgium, Germany, France and Spain.[156] Moreover, in many countries, employees or self-employed persons affiliated to the social security system are entitled to elect their representatives within the social security bodies.

Thus, employees may influence the administration of their social insurance bodies even though the main decisions are mostly taken by the legislature that determines the legal framework of social security law.

b. Labor Courts

In countries that have a labor court system employee voice is also institutionalized through the participation of employee lay judges.[157] Indeed, these lay judges, just like

---

[155] See Karl Casserini, The challenge of Multi-national corporations and regional economic integration to the trade unions, their structure and their international activities, in: H. Günter (ed.), *Trans-national Industrial Relations – The Impact of Multi-national Corporations and Economic Regionalism on Industrial Relations*, Macmillan, 1972, p. 70 at 79 and 80. See also Torsten Müller, Hans-Wolfgang Platzer & Stefan Rüb, Globalisierung und gewerkschaftliche Internationalisierung – Zur Politik der Global Union Federations, in: WSI-Mitteilungen 2003, pp. 666, at 668, and Kurt P. Tudyka, Die Weltkonzernräte in der Krise – Die 'unternehmensorientierte' Strategie der Gewerkschaften gegenüber multinationalen Konzernen am Ende? – in: WSI-Mitteilungen 1986 (39), pp. 324–9.

[156] For a brief overview on the situation in European countries see Danny Pieters, *The Social Security Systems of the Member States of the European Union*, Antwerp Oxford & New York, 2002.

[157] See Thilo Ramm, Workers' Participation, the Representation of Labour and Special Labour Courts, in: Hepple, The Making of Labour Law in Europe (n 1) pp. 242, at 270 et seq.;

the career labor judges chairing the panels, have the mission to apply the law and not pursue employees' interests in a one-sided way. However, the participation of employee lay judges in labor court procedures may integrate the employee perspective in the application of labor law rules. In addition, the influence case law has in various fields of labor and employment law renders the input of that employee lay judges particularly important.

Valuable examples for a labor court model over three instances integrating lay judges from both the employee as well as the employers' side are Germany [*Arbeitsgerichte*] (established in 1926),[158] Austria [*Arbeitsgerichte*],[159] Israel,[160] Portugal [*Tribunais do trabalho*],[161] Spain [*Tribunales de lo Social*][162] and Brazil.[163]

In a number of other States, employee lay judges are only involved in one or two instances, the litigation going to the ordinary courts in the second or the last instance. This is the case for Belgium,[164] Luxembourg[165] and the UK.[166] Finally, there are labor court systems establishing an equal representation of employees and employers where a career judge only intervenes in the event of a deadlock: This is the case of the French *conseils de prud'hommes* ('*paritarisme*').[167]

c. Employee Voice in the Legislative Process

Regarding the legislative process, employees may exercise an influence on the decision-makers through the lobbying of their labor unions, acting as pressure groups. However, there is a strong tendency to integrate the employees' interests as a whole through labor unions, as well as the employers' interests that are articulated by the employers' associations in the political decision-making process. The role of law in these procedures differs considerably among the national models.

One instrument to ensure the integration of employees' and employers' interests is by promoting social dialogue at the national level and to rely on its outcomes. Examples

---

see also Jonas Malmberg, Enforcement of Labour Law, in: Hepple & Veneziani, The Transformation of Labour Law in Europe (n 1), pp. 263 et seq.

158 Section 15(2), Sec. 35(2) and Sec. 41(2) German Labor Courts Act [*Arbeitsgerichtsgesetz*].

159 Section 16(2), Sec. 35(2) and Sec. 41(2) Austrian Labor Courts Act [*Arbeitsgerichtsgesetz*].

160 Cf. Labour Court Law of Israel.

161 Articles 85 et seq Portuguese Judiciary Organization Act [*Lei de organização e funcionamento dos tribunais judiciais*].

162 See Spanish Judiciary Organization Act [*Ley Orgánica 6/1985, de 1 de julio, del Poder Judicial*].

163 See Art. 111 et seq of the Constitution of Brazil [constituição brasileira].

164 Article 81 et seq Belgian Judiciary Organization Act [Code judiciaire belge].

165 Article 56-1 et seq Lux. Judiciary Organization Act [*Loi sur l'Organisation judiciaire*].

166 In cases where a party believes the Employment Tribunal has misapplied the law or acted perversely, he or she may appeal to the Court of Appeal in England and Wales or to the Court of Session in Scotland.

167 Article L. 1421-1 et seq. French Labor Code. For an overview on the French system of *Conseils de prud'hommes* cf. Jean Pélissier, Gilles Auzero & Emmanuel Dockès, Droit du travail, 27th edition, 2013, paras. 100–124 with further references.

for systems of 'concerted action' or a cross-industry social dialogue at the national level can be found for example in France, where every government bill in the field of social policy must be submitted to a social dialogue of the representative social partners.[168] The same applies, inter alia, to Spain [*Concertación social*], to Belgium [*Conseil national du travail*], to Luxembourg [*Comité de coordination tripartite*],[169] to Italy [*Concertazione sociale*] and to Portugal [*Comissão Permanente de Concertação Social*].[170] In the Netherlands, the Labor Foundation [*Stichting van de Arbeid*] – a body equally composed of the Dutch umbrella organizations of unions and employers' federations – provides a similar forum for a social dialogue.[171] At the EU-level, a similar model for social dialogue has been institutionalized.[172]

However, there are various countries with more institutionalized forms of employees' participation within the legislative process. This is the case in the countries with an Economic and Social Council in which also unions are represented and are consulted on draft bills before the Parliament takes a decision. The examples for such councils are numerous. They exist, inter alia, in Belgium [*Conseil national du travail/Nationale Arbeidsraad*],[173] France [*Conseil économique, social et environnemental*],[174] Italy [*Consiglio nationale dell'economia e del lavoro*],[175] Luxembourg [*Conseil économique et social*],[176] Spain [*Consejo economico y social*],[177] and The Netherlands [*Sociaal-Economische Raad*];[178] at EU-level there is an Economic and Social Committee which

---

[168] Article L. 1 French Labor Code. The same applies to bills introduced by Members of Parliament or a parliamentary group. See Protocole relative à la consultation des partenaires sociaux sur les propositions de lois à caractère social relevant du champ de la négociation nationale et interprofessionnelle, adopté par la Conférence des Présidents de l'Assemblée nationale et du Sénat du 16 février 2010.

[169] Cf. Art. L.512-3 Luxembourg Labor Code.

[170] Cf. Art. 469 et seq Portugal Labor Code. For a more in-depth analysis see Antonio Monteiro Fernandes, Direito do trabalho, 16th edition (2012), paras. 52 et seq.

[171] According to Art. 4 (c) of its Statutes, the Labor Foundation gives advice to the government on demand or without being asked. Further information on the Labor Foundation is available at its website: http://www.stvda.nl/nl/home.aspx. For a more in depth analysis cf. Antoine Jacobs, Collectief arbeidsrecht, 2nd edition, 2005, pp. 60 et seq.; id., From the Belgian National Labour Council to the European Social Dialogue, in: Chris Engels & Manfred Weiss (eds), *Labour Law and Industrial Relations at the Turn of the Century – Liber Amicorum in Honour of Prof. Dr. Roger Blanpain*, The Hague, 1998, pp. 305 et seq.

[172] See Arts 154 and 155 TFEU. For a short overview on the structure, procedure and the outcomes of the European Social Dialogue see Achim Seifert, Transnational Collective Bargaining: The Case of the European Union, in: Malherbe & Sloth-Nielsen, Labour Law into the Future (n 134), pp. 76–96.

[173] Act of 29 May 1952 on the National Council of Labor [*Loi organique du Conseil national du travail/Wet tot inrichting van de Nationale Arbeidsraad*], Moniteur belge of 31 May 1952.

[174] See Decree No. 84-558 of 4 July 1984 fixing the conditions of designation of the members of the Economic, Social and Environmental Council [*Décret fixant les conditions de désignation des membres du Conseil économique, social et environnemental*].

[175] Article 99 Italian Constitution and Act No. 936 of 30 December 1986, n. 936, Gazz. Uff. 5 January 1987, No. 3.

[176] Act of 21 March 1966 establishing an Economic and Social Council [*Loi portant institution d'un Conseil économique et social*], Mémorial A n° 14 26 March 1966.

is involved in legislative procedures.[179] The composition of these councils may vary from one country to another. However, in most of these countries and in the EU, Economic and Social Councils do not only represent employees' interests but also other economic and social interests such as those of employers, consumers, etc.

Few countries have even gone beyond these forms of concerted action and have established, in analogy to the Chambers of Commerce and Industry representing the companies' interests, specific Chambers of Labor or of Employees whose task is to represent employees' interests, inter alia, vis-à-vis the legislator and to whom every employee is affiliated by law. The Chamber model reflects a corporatist [*ständestaatlich*] view of the social question and is mainly the result of social conservatism that prevailed in some countries during the 1920s.[180] The Worker Chambers [*Arbeiterkammern*] in Austria, for example, were established in 1920.[181] One of their main missions is to promote the employees' interests through advisory opinions on draft bills and to report to government and the Parliament.[182] Another example for the Labor Chamber system is the Grand-Duchy of Luxembourg where Chambers of Workers, Employees and Civil Servants were established by an Act of April 4, 1924.[183] Today there are still a Chamber of Employees [*Chambre des salariés*] and a Chamber of Civil Servants and Public Employees [*Chambre des fonctionnaires et des employés publics*], representing the employees' and civil servants interests in the legislative procedure and offering them professional training measures. Finally, in two German regions, in the Saar region[184] and in Bremen,[185] there are similar Acts on Labor Chambers, which have survived political changes for almost a century. The German

---

[177] Act 21/1991 of 17 June 1991 concerning the establishing of an Economic and Social Council [*Ley de Creación del Consejo Económico y Social*], O.J. 18 June 1991.

[178] *Wet op de bedrijfsorganisatie.*

[179] Art. 301 TFEU. For more details see Craig & de Burca, *EU-law – Text, Cases and Materials*, 4th edition, OUP, 2008, pp. 77 et seq.

[180] On the ideological background of the Chamber system see: Othmar Spann, Der Wahre Staat: Vorlesungen über Abbruch und Neubau der Gesellschaft, Leipzig 1921, pp. 187 et seq.

[181] For an assessment of their historical origin and development see Tomandl & Marhold, Die Koalitionsfreiheit des Arbeitnehmers in Österreich, in Mosler & Bernhard (eds), Die Koalitionsfreiheit des Arbeitnehmers (1980), 691 et seq.

[182] Article 4(2) No 1 Federal Act on Worker and Employee Chambers and a Federal Chamber of Workers and Employees [Bundesgesetz über die Kammern für Arbeiter und Angestellte und die Bundeskammer für Arbeiter und Angestellte, Bundesgesetzblatt für die Republik Österreich 1991/2593]. For a more indepth analysis of the Austrian Chamber system cf. Marhold & Friedrich, Österreichisches Arbeitsrecht, 2nd edition (2012), pp. 406 et seq. (*Pflichtverbandsrecht*).

[183] Act Establishing Professional Chambers based on Elections [*Loi portant création de chambres professionnelles à base élective*] (Mémorial A n° 21 of 3 May 1924).

[184] See Act No 255 of 30 June 1951 Establishing a Labor Chamber for the Saar Region [*Gesetz Nr. 255 über die Errichtung einer Arbeitskammer für das Saarland*], Official Journal of the Saar Region 1951, p. 980. This Act goes back to a Decree of the Saar Basing Governing Commission of the Saar Region of 18 September 1925 – the Government for the Saar region established by the Versailles Peace Treaty of 1919 – which has been proposed by the International Labor Office. The original Labor Chamber, however, not only represented workers but also employers. For an overview on the historical development of the Labor chamber system of the Saar Region see Jürgen Peters, Arbeitnehmerkammern in der BRD?, Munich 1973.

Federal Constitutional Court, in a decision of 18 December 1974, ruled that these two regional Labor Chamber Acts are in line with the Federal Constitution and do not violate the constitutional right to freedom of association[186] even though the unions' and the labor chambers activities are considerably overlapping.

6. EMPLOYEE VOICE THROUGH CIVIL SOCIETY ORGANIZATIONS

Employee voice can also be provided by civil society organizations. Relevant organizations can be established as membership organizations for mutual support giving advice or representation to members only. Others may advocate all relevant purposes including employment for identity groups such as elderly people or persons with a specific immigrant background. Such groups distribute information, give advice or legally represent their members; some seek to influence legislation to obtain stronger protection or better visibility for their constituency by means of publicity, lobbying or otherwise influencing public opinion.

One prominent example with relevant impact on labor relations is 'community unionism',[187] understood as unions engaged for the special concerns of their ethnic, religious or geographical communities. The focus of these community unions lies as much in working with the communities as working just on their behalf. The result is supposed to be beneficial to both the union and the community by mutually supporting each other with their respective experience for obtaining their goals. The union might access, for example, ethnic communities, who would otherwise not subscribe to traditional organizing campaigns, whereas the ethnic community might receive help in petitioning the local media or accessing people of influence. Such community organizations replace traditional occupational associations, which rarely exist in low wage sectors that lack the 'craft identification' associated with trade unions. Trade unions may not be overly attractive to workers in low wage jobs being characterized frequently by decentralized workplaces or unstable employment relationships, or in informal employment relationships. Such workers may prefer to be active in the neighborhood where they live rather than within a traditional trade union. Another form of organization, Workers Centers,[188] usually supporting specific ethnic groups or migrant workers in general, also focus mainly on workplace related causes. Their means of influence remain limited to individual advocacy, or appealing to public administration or government, but they lack the power of collective action that is

---

185 See Act on Worker Chambers in the Land of Bremen of 3 July 1956 [*Gesetz über die Arbeitnehmerkammern im Lande Bremen*], Official Journal of the Free Hanseatic City of Bremen 1956, p. 79. The Act has re-established a Chamber System being introduced after World War I by the Act on the Establishing of Blue-collar Worker Chambers and the Act on the Establishing of White-collar Worker Chambers, both of 7 July 1921.

186 Case 1 BvR 430/65 & 259/66, BVerfGE 38, pp. 281 et seq.

187 Jo McBride & Ian Greenwood (eds): *Community Unionism – A Comparative Analysis of Concepts and Contexts*, Palgrave, 2009.

188 Kim Moody: Immigrant workers and labor/community organisations in the US, in: McBride & Greenwood ibid., pp. 150–8.

exclusively granted to trade unions. By joining forces, the trade unions and workers' centers can potentially strengthen their constituencies' voice.

An example for coalition building between traditional labor unions and representatives of minority concerns can be drawn from the experience of the Japanese Community Union Federation, an umbrella organization for members organizing primarily socially marginalized workers, such as casual workers, women or ethnic minorities.[189] This was especially remarkable in an industrial environment otherwise characterized by enterprise unions[190] representing almost exclusively the core workforce. Minority unions are not easily recognized by companies, focusing instead on recruiting members in the local community. When joining forces with the central union organization, both sides benefitted: main stream unions won the chance of reaching out to non-regular workers, thereby broadening their membership base, whereas minority representatives strengthen their case for equal treatment of part-time or fixed-term contract employees and gain financial support from unions.

Totally outside the traditional work environment context, charity organizations like the UK's Citizens' Advice Bureau[191] provide workers with advice and representation. With union density in decline for decades, traditional employee representation resources vanish leaving a gap of problem solving competence especially in employment matters. The Bureau is part of an independent charity agency advising free of charge on a wide range of topics such as immigration, housing, private debt or employment. It operates from offices or other more easily accessible locations including community centers' or schools. Funding is provided not only by the state or local public authorities but also by private donors. In addition to its public campaigns the Bureau provides information concerning relevant rights to clients and represents them when dealing with employers in oral or written procedures or in hearings. Regularly the aim is reaching a settlement, preferably without a tribunal hearing, by 'bargaining in the shadow of the law' like in Alternative Dispute Resolution procedures. Unfair employment situations can be rectified once a relevant statutory right exists and is enforceable through legal procedures. Unlike trade union representatives, the Bureau cannot mobilize other employees to take strike actions for renegotiating unfair practices, but it relies on the threat of initiating legal procedures and negative publicity campaigns. While helping to give employees a voice, such organizations are not substituting union representation, as they lack additional means of enforcement.

[189] Edson Urano & Paul Stewart: Beyond organized labor in Japan – the case of the Japanese Community Union Federation in: McBride & Greenwood ibid., pp. 121–37.

[190] Tsuyoshi Tsuru & Motohiro Morishima: Non-union Employee Representation in Japan, *Journal of Labor Research* (1999) pp. 94–107.

[191] Brian Abbott: Worker Representation through the Citizens' Advice Bureaux, in: Geraldine Healy, Edmund Heery, Philip Taylor & William Brown, *The Future of Worker Representation* Palgrave Macmillan, 2004, Ch. 12, pp. 245–63.

PART III

REGIONAL COMPARISONS

12. European Union labour law and the European Social Model: A critical appraisal

Frank Hendrickx and Stefano Giubboni

INTRODUCTION

The European Union context of labour law has been a focal point of attention, debate and criticism in legal scholarship for quite a while. Labour law scholarship has been struggling with the notion of the 'European Social Model' and the role and position of labour law in the EU context. In current times, characterized by globalisation, agendas for economic competitiveness, financial market volatility and pressures on European welfare systems, the debate has only intensified.

In the EU, labour law is deeply rooted in state tradition, national policy, institutional settings and historical pathways. However, after more than half a century of European integration, the autonomy of EU states has severely diminished. It seems to put the integration process, including the European social dimension, at a crossroads. The mutually reinforcing contexts of globalization, the economic and financial crisis and the pressures on welfare states, require a higher relevancy of transnational and regional (European) action. However, due to the specific dynamics in the EU legal and policy order, there seems to be a growing gap between the respective understandings of labour law when EU and member states are offset.

On a deeper level, labour law as it has grown and evolved in European states, is under pressure. Academic labour law debate has increasingly become fundamental, questioning boundaries,[1] future[2] and goals or idea[3] of labour law, in European terms often brought under the rubric of 'modernization' of labour law.[4] It is not just a coincidence that the European Commission launched a Green Paper on Modernising Labour Law in 2006 'to meet the challenges of the 21st century'.[5] Furthermore, the issue of transnational worker mobility and the case-law of the Court of Justice (CJEU) in *Viking*[6] and *Laval*,[7] have pulled a legal problem into a debate about the economic

[1] *Cf.* G. DAVIDOV and B. LANGILLE (eds), *Boundaries and Frontiers of Labour Law*, Oxford, Hart, 2006.

[2] *Cf.* C. BARNARD, S. DEAKIN AND G. MORRIS (eds), T*he Future of Labour Law. Liber Amicorum Sir Bob Hepple QC*, Oxford, Hart Publishing, 2004; J. D. CRAIG AND S. M. LYNK (eds.), *Globalization and the Future of Labour Law*, Cambridge University Press, 2006.

[3] Cf. G. DAVIDOV AND B. LANGILLE, *The Idea of Labour Law*, Oxford University Press, 2011.

[4] *Cf.* S. SCIARRA, 'Modernization of labour law: a current European debate,' Public Lecture at the ILO, International Institute for Labour Studies, Geneva, March 2007, 4 (available at www.ilo.org).

[5] COM(2006)708final, 22 November 2006.

[6] C-438/05, CJEU 11 December 2007, E.C.R. 2007, I-10779.

and social purposes of the European project. Furthermore, the evolving European 'governance' of the financial and economic crisis, brings up the question of how far member state social and welfare policies can and will be brought in line in financial stability and economic competitiveness.

In this chapter, we aim to provide a critical analysis of EU labour law.[8] We have been assigned to show an understanding of the 'European Social Model'. Does it exist and if so, what characterizes it? Can it be qualified as a market-driven system? Looking at the interplay between the Union and the member states, does European law inhibit or advance a social model in the member states?

Taking into account European labour law's dynamic and evolving character and to improve its disclosure to a readership that may be unfamiliar with it, our methodological choice is to deliver our analysis through an examination of the development and evolution of EU labour law, referring to its origin, critical junctures and major steps. This allows us to disclose the broad field of European labour law while, going into the steps of European labour law's own development in different areas of Union action, making an attempt to find the paths and trails of a European Social Model, or just not yet.

We will start from the position that, if it exists, there is most likely no single view on the 'European Social Model'. Moreover, it probably has a unique outlook. In order to speak of a European Social Model, Blanpain has assumed the existence of a 'model' (explained as a vision, competences and actors), which is 'European' (seen at the EU level) and 'social' (explained as focused on labour issues and democracy).[9] We find this a useful approach but wish to take it a step further. We assume that, in order to be 'European', Union action would need to take account of (common) European 'state' traditions (e.g. in the field of labour law), and in order to be 'social', it would need to envisage the advancement of social rights and values, strike a balance between market-making and social progress, develop social citizenship and promote solidarity, democracy and legitimacy within a European society. We, therefore, do not only assume a balance between the economic and social dimension of European integration, but also expect a promotional 'social' goal in Union action.

---

[7] C-342/05, CJEU 18 December 2007, E.C.R. 2007, I-11767.

[8] For the purposes of this chapter, we rely on previous work, such as: F. HENDRICKX, *Labour Law for the United States of Europe*, Tilburg, Tilburg University, 2011; F. HENDRICKX, "European labour law after the Lisbon Treaty: (re-visited) Assessment of fundamental social rights" in R. BLANPAIN AND F. HENDRICKX (eds), *Labour Law Between Change and Tradition. Liber amicorum Antoine Jacobs*, Alphen aan den Rijn, Kluwer Law International, 2011, 75–89; F. HENDRICKX, 'Beyond Viking and Laval: the evolving European context', *Comp. Lab. L. & Pol'y J* (2011), afl. 4, 1055–78; F. HENDRICKX, 'The Services Directive and the alleged issue of social dumping' in J. van der Gronden (ed.), *EU and WTO Law on Services: Limits to the Realization of General Interest Policies within the Services Market?*, The Hague, Wolters Kluwer, 2008, 97–117; S. GIUBBONI, *Social Rights and Market Freedom in the European Constitution: A Labour Law Perspective*, Cambridge University Press, 2006; S. GIUBBONI, 'Social Europe after the Lisbon Treaty. Some skeptical remarks', 4 *European Journal of Social Law* (2011) 244–53; S. GIUBBONI, 'European citizenship and social rights in times of crisis', Working Paper LPF N°2, Centro Einaudi, 2013.

[9] Cf, R. Blanpain, 'The European social model (ESM): myth or reality?' (2011) 2(2) *European Labour Law Journal*, 143–4.

1. FREE MOVEMENT OF WORKERS: SOCIAL GOALS FROM EARLY MARKET MAKING

If one looks for an early social policy perspective, let alone a 'plan', it must be noted that social policy goals, such as worker protection or the creation of a social welfare regime, as an explicit objective of the EU, has been controversial since the very beginning of the European project. It is well known that the original Treaties only aimed at the creation of an 'economic community' of European states that had a rather well developed social policy model. In the European project, however, social policy initiative would come from the *spill-over* effect of economic integration.

Nevertheless, little by little, ways were paved for social policy. An important landmark was the Social Action Programme (SAP), which was adopted by the Council in a resolution of 21 January 1974.[10] It underlined the necessity to take measures towards realizing priorities such as full and better employment, the improvement and harmonization of living and working conditions, and increased involvement of management and labour in the economic and social decision-making process both at the European level as well as in undertakings. The document reflected high and broad ambitions and the SAP was seen as announcing a 'golden period of harmonisation'.[11] However, the labour law legislation that followed was important but remained limited to well-defined and specific areas.[12] Many legislative proposals failed to obtain approval in the Council, including the notorious *Vredeling* proposal regarding information and consultation of workers in undertakings, as well as proposals on part-time work, temporary work and working time. These were signs of how ideologically laden the issue of European labour law actually is.

While there remained a gap between ambition and reality, it is striking that the 1974 Social Action Programme already contained the important consideration that 'it is essential to ensure the coherence of social and other Community policies so that measures taken will achieve the objectives of social and other policies simultaneously'. The necessity of coherence between the original economic purposes of European integration and the *spill-over* fields was thus already seen.

In this early period of European integration with a perhaps limited context of social rights, an important impetus came from the Court of Justice of the European Union (CJEU). Using doctrines of direct and horizontal effect, articles in the early Treaty (i.e. Treaty of Rome of 25 March 1957) which could originally be understood as market ordering principles, became strong motors of social rights. The abundant case-law concerning the principle of equal pay (nowadays art. 157 Treaty on the Functioning of the EU (TFEU)) and the free movement of persons (nowadays art. 45 TFEU), were

---

10 'Social Action Programme. Resolution of the Council of 21 January 1974', (1974) 5 *B.C.L.R.*, 135–87.

11 R. Blanpain, *European Labour Law*, The Hague, Kluwer Law International, 2008, 208.

12 *Cf.* equal treatment, collective dismissal, transfer of undertakings, employer insolvency, health and safety.

originally seen as economic rights but became real and enforceable social rights, enshrining social citizenship and solidarity.[13]

In its free movement of persons' case-law, the CJEU has always assured the highest *effet utile* to migrant workers' entitlements to social integration within the host state. Such a guarantee of socio-economic integration served as a means for the full deployment of one of the fundamental freedoms enshrined in the Treaty and, at the same time, it was harmoniously included in a model for the construction of an integrated market based on the full preservation of the autonomy of national social protection systems. Equal access of migrant workers to the social rights laid down by the host member state, did not merely interfere with the 'social sovereignty' of the member states, but it helped to assure full territorial application of national labour law and social welfare. This explains why such a guarantee has been precociously interpreted extensively by the case-law of the Court of Justice starting from the early 60s of the last century. This well-known case-law does not need to be analyzed in this context.[14] Here, it is sufficient to recall how, on one hand and in absence of an express legal definition, the Court has adopted a very broad notion of employee, up to and encompassing in such a definition all activities, having any minimal effective economic consistency, carried out under the direction of another person. It allowed the holders of this fundamental freedom of movement, and their families, to access the whole panoply of social rights guaranteed to the citizens of the host state in conditions of full equality, even beyond situations and entitlements linked to the protection of the employment relationship.

If we read it in light of the historical evolution, starting from the leading case *Martínez Sala* to the more recent *Zambrano* judgment,[15] through which the Court has extended the principle of equal treatment in the access to social rights recognized in the host country to all economically inactive European citizens, then it seems fair to say that this case-law does nothing but generalize the status of social integration already widely acquired by EU law on the free movement of workers. By considering being a citizen of the Union as the fundamental status of a person in the supranational order,[16] this case-law undoubtedly has the merit of universalizing[17] the social integration logic hitherto anchored to the functioning of the internal market, also including people who do not carry out an economic activity in its protective reach. One may say that the

[13] *Cf.* C. Barnard, 'The future of equality law: equality and beyond' in Barnard, Deakin and Morris, note 2 above, 213–28.

[14] C. Barnard, *The Substantive Law of the EU. The Four Freedoms*, Oxford, Oxford University Press, 2010, 263 ff and S. Giubboni S. and G. Orlandini, *La libera circolazione dei lavoratori nell'Unione europea*, Bologna, Il Mulino, 2007, 11 ff.

[15] See respectively Case C-85/96, *María Martínez Sala vs. Freistaat Bayern*, and Case C-34/09, *Gerardo Ruiz Zambrano vs. Office national de l'emploi.*

[16] According to the well-known formula consolidated by the judgment of the Court of Justice in Case C-184/99, *Rudy Grzelczyk vs. Centre public d'aide sociale Ottignies-Louvain-la-Neuve.*

[17] In some cases, far beyond what a literal interpretation of secondary law, and particularly of Directive 2004/38/EC, would allow, but – obviously – still within the scope of the European membership, which requires the possession of the citizenship of a member state of the Union (and, therefore, excludes citizens of third countries).

innovation in this case-law is the universal projection of the transnational model of social solidarity already foreshadowed by the Rome Treaty in favour of migrant workers within the Community in a way that, as such, was still related to the actual functioning of the common or internal market.

In this free movement case-law some commentators have recognized a change in the legal paradigm of European social solidarity.[18] If the access to social protection systems in the member states was initially functional to the effectiveness of the common labour market, according to this case-law, it now becomes a self-constitutive element of Union citizenship. The *status* of social integration becomes separated from a market-rationale and from the original idea of *homo economicus*.[19] According to this analysis, a paradigm-shift has to be detected from a selective and category-based model of 'market solidarity'[20] to the recognition of 'a transnational personal status',[21] which establishes a general claim of social integration in the member state of the Union in which the European citizen freely decides to move to, not unlike what happens in federal-polities.

2. A 'SOCIAL POLICY CHAPTER': COUNTERBALANCING THE ECONOMIC DIMENSION

Social policy discussion received a renewed impetus under the Commission Presidency of Jacques Delors.[22] European political leaders felt that a stronger emphasis on social policy was needed and Delors had a strong ambition to realise a Europe with a human face, creating *'l'Europe sociale'*. This happened in the context of the 1980s in which a quest for more flexibility and deregulatory forces came through.[23] This setting was symptomatic of the tension between economic and social progress in EU integration policies. At the time, deregulation and in particular flexibility became important slogans in the fight against the economic and social crisis, in order to address the issues of decreasing economic growth and rising unemployment. Neo-liberal ideologies of deregulation clashed with social democratic viewpoints. Many proposals for EU labour law directives failed to obtain approval in the Council.

In a legal sense, the Single European Act of 1986 brought an important change. It originated from the opinion that Europe needed to be more than what the predominantly economic dimension of the Communities had shown so far. Its Preamble announced the wish to 'improve the economic and social situation by extending

---

18 O. GOLYNKER. *Ubiquitous Citizens of Europe: The Paradigm of Partial Migration*, Antwerp-Oxford, Intersentia, 2006.

19 C. PINELLI, 'Cittadinanza europea', in *Enciclopedia del diritto – Annali*, vol. I, Milano, Giuffrè, 2007, 186.

20 F. DE WITTE, 'Transnational solidarity and the mediation of conflicts of justice in Europe', (2012) 18(5) *European Law Journal*, 694 ff.

21 L. AZOULAI, 'La citoyenneté européenne, un statut d'intégration sociale', in *Chemins d'Europe. Mélanges en l'honneur de Jean Paul Jacqué*, Paris, Dalloz, 2010, 8.

22 President of the Commission of the European Communities (1985–95).

23 B. HEPPLE, 'European rules on dismissal law?' in ISLLSS, Proceedings of the 5th European Regional Congress for Labour Law and Social Security, 17–21 September 1996, Leiden, The Netherlands, 2.

common policies and pursuing new objectives'.[24] It left European social policy with a mixed result. On the one hand, new competences were included to take initiatives in the area of health and safety.[25] But on the other hand, it confirmed member states' national sovereignty over 'rights and interests of employed persons', which required, at European level, unanimous voting in the Council.[26]

The changes did not support the view that social policies were as important as economic and monetary matters, or that a 'common' European social policy would become a central issue. Voices in favour of a social dimension of the internal market were still heard. At the 1989 Madrid Summit, the European Council repeated the 1972 principle that as much importance must be given to the social dimension as to economic policies. But it could be questioned whether the Single European Act did not actually support the economic integration most of all. The pre-dating White Paper on the completion of the internal market (14 June 1985) addressed the issue of harmonization. It stated that unifying the European market presupposes the abolition of barriers of all kinds *and* harmonization of rules.[27] However, the document did not refer to the harmonized development of labour law or a project for a European social model. Instead, it aimed at the liberalization of the internal market and reaching the stage of a 'single European market'.

Only later in the 1980s was the social dimension somehow compensated. On 15 March 1989, the European Parliament adopted a resolution on 'the social dimension of the single market'. It called for 'the adoption at Community level of the fundamental social rights which should not be jeopardized because of the pressure of competition or the search for increased competitiveness, and could be taken as the basis for the dialogue between management and labour' and expressed the need to ensure the social dimension of the internal market by implementing a programme of concrete measures

---

[24] Single European Act, 17 February 1986.

[25] Article 21 of the Single European Act provides that: 'the EEC Treaty shall be supplemented by the following provisions: Article 118a 1. Member States shall pay particular attention to encouraging improvements, especially in the working environment, as regards the health and safety of workers, and shall set as their objective the harmonization of conditions in this area, while maintaining the improvements made.'

[26] Article 18 of the Single European Act reads:

> The EEC Treaty shall be supplemented by the following provisions: ARTICLE 100a 1. By way of derogation from Article 100 and save where otherwise provided in this Treaty, the following provisions shall apply for the achievement of the objectives set out in Article 8a. The Council shall, acting by a qualified majority on a proposal from the Commission in co-operation with the European Parliament and after consulting the Economic and Social Committee, adopt the measures for the approximation of the provisions laid down by law, regulation or administrative action in Member States which have as their object the establishment and functioning of the internal market. 2. Paragraph 1 shall not apply to fiscal provisions, to those relating to the free movement of persons nor to those relating to the rights and interests of employed persons.

[27] Completing the Internal Market: White Paper from the Commission to the European Council (Milan, 28–29 June 1985) COM(85)310final, 6: 'unifying this market (of 320 million) presupposes that Member States will agree on the abolition of barriers of all kinds, harmonization of rules, approximation of legislation and tax structures'.

comprising a timetable.[28] On 9 December 1989, at the Strasbourg Summit, the Heads of State of Government of 11 Member States (all except the U.K.) finally adopted, in the form of a declaration, the text of the Community Charter. The Charter, although not seen as a legally binding instrument, paved the way for a renewed and social rights-based view on European integration. The Charter was followed by an *Action Programme* relating to its implementation by European action.[29] It contained a number of measures proposed by the Commission to be developed in order to implement the core of the Charter. The Charter thus seemed to be an important step in the search for a more legitimate and socially driven Europe and it gained momentum for political will in favour of European social policy. But the political will was not unanimous. As is well known, only 11 of the then existing 12 member states were willing to subscribe to it. The same happened with the attempts to incorporate a 'social chapter' in the Treaty. Nevertheless, when during the Maastricht Summit in December 1991, the famous Social Protocol was agreed upon, whereby the 11 member states could pursue social policies (the U.K. opting out) on the conditions laid down in the annexed Social Policy Agreement, a start was made with a 'constitutionally' recognized role for the social partners in the Union's legislative process, and there was a major legal basis for action in the field of labour law. As is well known, the social chapter, as annexed to the Maastricht Treaty (1992)[30] was later incorporated in the EC Treaty (with the U.K. opting in) via the Amsterdam Treaty (1997)[31] and is currently found back in articles 151–161 TFEU.

It can be argued that this period, and the results it produced, marked a time in which the need was felt to address the tension between economic and social integration in Europe with treaty amendment and hard law initiative. The resulting synthesis can be described as a political view defending 'socially acceptable economic integration'. What seemed important, is that Delors' views on the involvement of management and labour in social policy-making, confirmed a European 'tradition of inclusion of unions and workers' interests in the shaping of industrial relations and political regulations in general'.[32] Likewise, the Delors' strategy accommodated a tradition of government activity and social policy intervention in the (integrating) economy in Europe. To a certain extent, these elements can be viewed as traces of an early growing 'social model' at European level.

Nevertheless, when the introductory article of the Treaty's social chapter (art. 151 TFEU, former art. 136 of the EC Treaty) is viewed, the difficult tension between economic and social integration remains apparent. It provides, first of all, that in making social policy, the Union and the member states 'will have in mind' fundamental social rights. This seems designed to align social policy intervention with the

---

28 *O.J.* 17 April 1989, C96, 61.

29 COM(89)568final.

30 Signed in Maastricht on 7 February 1992 and entering into force on 1 November 1993 (*O.J.* 29 July 1992, C191).

31 Signed in Amsterdam on 2 October 1997 and entering into force on 1 May 1999 (*O.J.* 10 November 1997, C340).

32 P. ZILTENER, 'EC social policy: the defeat of the Delorist project' in V. BORNSCHIER (ed.), *State-building in Europe: The Revitalization of Western European Integration*, Cambridge, Cambridge University Press, 2000, 165.

fundamentals of labour law, at least as it is understood in the member states. As we have indicated before, this would fit with 'social' aspirations of any European Social Model, if it were envisaged.

Article 151 TFEU (still) makes reference to the goal of harmonization, combined with a belief that the functioning of the internal market will favour (but not necessarily automatically lead to) the harmonization of social systems. While harmonization would in theory seem a sound and useful approach to labour law at the EU level, the element of harmonization is nevertheless interesting, seen in the reference above to the 'golden period of harmonization' in the 1970s, which became a name for something that did not actually come about. Harmonization would lay the ground for convergence in national policy choices and, potentially, in member states' labour law systems. It might be able to address pressures from social dumping or forces of deregulation. It would fit a 'European Social Model' idea. However, in the European social policy context, the element of diversity takes a strong place. Article 151 TFEU confirms that European measures shall 'take account of the diverse forms of national practices' and 'the need to maintain the competitiveness of the Union's economy'. European labour law initiatives are therefore understood for purposes of harmonization at a minimum level of protection (only). It might seem that a general resistance against harmonization came specifically in the second half of the 1980s. A strategy of harmonization of labour law was likely to be more realistic within the context of relatively compatible labour law and welfare systems, like those of the founding member states in the early times.[33] However, arguments *contra* harmonization seem often politically or insufficiently founded and the question remains whether European labour law harmonization has really no potential to go further than the current *status quo*.

Nevertheless, even in a system where member states remain relatively important social policy actors, a European social model remains a possible idea. Furthermore, the Treaty setting of the 'social chapter' provisions, also would suppose active steps at EU level. Article 151 TFEU expresses the belief that social development requires positive regulation as it 'will ensue not only from the functioning of the internal market', but also – and necessarily so – 'from the procedures provided for in the Treaties and from the approximation of provisions laid down by law, regulation or administrative action'. Initiatives based on the social chapter have been significant, and have produced a large variety of European labour law legislation, including subjects such as, for example, health and safety, working time, part-time work, fixed-term work, temporary work, European works councils, information and consultation. It may, however, be discussed how much social policy compared to market concern (be it the internal market, the economic market or the labour market) has been a reason for Union action.

---

[33] F. W. SCHARPF, 'The European Social Model: Coping with the Challenges of Diversity', MPIfG Working Paper 02/8, July 2002.

3. ECONOMICALLY ACCEPTABLE SOCIAL INTEGRATION IN THE RUNNING UP TO THE 'EMPLOYMENT TITLE'

The adoption of the 1989 Charter of Fundamental Rights and the introduction of the Maastricht Protocol on Social Policy in 1991, undoubtedly marked a major development for European labour law and social policy. However, three sets of policy papers would mark a new era, in which views on economic and social progress can be seen to start moving forward in a slightly, or is it a significantly, different way. It concerns the adoption of the 'Green Paper on European Social Policy – Options for the Future',[34] presented by Commissioner Flynn on 17 November 1993; the White Paper on Growth, competitiveness, and employment, adopted on 5 December 1993;[35] and the White Paper on European Social Policy, adopted on 27 July 1994.[36]

According to the 1993 Green Paper, European social policy entered a 'critical phase'. The existing social action programme was reaching its natural end; the entry into force of the Treaty on European Union opened up new possibilities for European action in the social field, and the changing socio-economic situation, reflected notably in the serious levels of unemployment, required, as the Green Paper explained, a new look at the link between economic and social policies, both at national and at European level. The Commission considered that this situation required the launching of a wide-ranging debate about the future direction of social policy (and that would include labour law).

The 1993 Green Paper was not only important for the development of European social policy in general. The reflection that it stimulated debate about the future direction of labour law also displayed a concern for the reconciliation of labour laws and labour markets with economic objectives. Although the Green Paper rejected the idea that 'social progress must go into retreat in order for economic competitiveness to recover' and that 'the Community is fully committed to ensuring that economic and social progress go hand in hand', it nevertheless indicated that Europe is characterized by 'its capacity to combine wealth creation with enhanced benefits and freedoms for its people'.[37] The Green Paper gave all the signs that the phrase that economic and social progress goes hand in hand, first seen as 'socially acceptable economic integration', could now be explained as 'economically acceptable social integration'. The White Paper on Growth, Competitiveness and Employment (1993) confirmed this new blue print view. This paper suggested that labour law as well as labour markets needed modernization, and mentioned issues such as flexibility of enterprises, training and modernized social protection systems.[38] The White Paper clearly suggested that the economic problems and the high unemployment figures throughout Europe could be

---

[34] COM(1993)551.

[35] EUROPEAN COMMISSION, 'Growth, competitiveness, and employment. The challenges and ways forward into the 21st century', COM(93)700final, Brussels, 5 December 1993.

[36] COMMISSION OF THE EUROPEAN COMMUNITIES, 'European Social Policy – A way forward for the Union', COM(1994)333final, 27 July 1994.

[37] COM(1993)551, 7.

[38] COM(93)700final, 11: 'Our employment systems have aged: by this term we mean the whole complex of issues made up nowadays by the labour market, labour legislation,

explained by the inflexibility of the labour market and specific institutional, legal (labour law and social security law) circumstances in each country.[39]

The 1994 White Paper did not conceal the real issue:

> A substantial base of labour standards has been consolidated in European law. The question of where to go from there is complex and controversial because the issue of labour standards is at the heart of the debate about the relationship between competitiveness, growth and job creation. (…) It must be said that there is no clear consensus on this point and that Member States and others remain divided in their opinions about the need for further legislative action on labour standards at European level.[40]

The development of a 'European Social Model' was not only hampered by the lack of consensus. The role of labour law in a market-making legal order, was at stake.

The issue of the role of labour law in light of an economic performance agenda was also reflected in the exercise by the Union of its hard European social policy competences. Under the rubric of 'economic issues', the conclusions of the Essen European Council (9–10 December 1994) emphasized the need to take steps to improve the employment situation, and called for measures aimed at 'increasing the employment-intensiveness of growth, in particular by more flexible organisation of work in a way which fulfils both the wishes of employees and the requirements of competition'. The Commission decided to initiate the procedure under the Maastricht Agreement on Social Policy in order to regulate fixed-term work, part-time work and temporary work, which were evolving as new and flexible forms of employment. From this, the view on 'social model' seemed to receive body. The hard law method had the advantage of improving 'social legitimacy and involvement' of the European social partners through the newly available forms of European 'bargaining' and European 'tripartism'[41] on subjects that would support the economic aspirations of the Union.

---

employment policy, the possibilities of flexibility within or outside enterprises, the opportunities provided or not provided by the education and training systems, and social protection.'

39 COM(93)700final, 16:

> In a general manner, they show that growth is not in itself the solution to unemployment, that vigorous action is needed to create jobs. However, such action must take account of national circumstances. More specifically, the inflexibility of the labour market, which is responsible for a large part of Europe's structural unemployment, can be traced back to specific institutional, legal and contractual circumstances in each country. The educational system, labour laws, work contracts, contractual negotiation systems, the social security system, and business management (including internal work management) form the pillars of the 'employment environment' in each Member State and combine to give each of them a distinctive appearance. In each case, the entire environment must be mobilized to improve the functioning of the labour market. This goes to show, once again, that there is no miracle solution; nothing short of coordinated action by the various players responsible for the components of these environments can effect the necessary transformation. Moreover, in each country the methods of social dialogue will reflect national traditions.

40 COM(1994)333final, 23.

41 *Cf.* T. Treu and M. Biagi, 'The role of a European social policy' in *Labour Law and Industrial Relations in the European Union* (1998) 32 *Bulletin of Comparative Labour Relations*, 217.

An agreement with the social partners was reached on fixed-term work[42] and part-time work.[43] As is well known, the social partners' negotiations on temporary work did not produce any agreement, the most severe problem being the concept of 'comparable worker' in the context of the principle of equal treatment. The European Commission, nevertheless, pushed further for a legislative instrument,[44] but it came about only in 2008.[45] The context of adaptability also required an instrument dealing with working time arrangements. An instrument was adopted, but the discussion on its revision is still running.[46]

The European initiatives were explained as accommodating the need for flexibility (of employers) and security (of workers).[47] Steps towards the development of a policy concept of flexicurity were enabled via the European employment policy. In adopting the 1997 Amsterdam Treaty, the title on employment was inserted in the Treaty. Considering the text of its provisions, the Employment Title conferred employment policy competences to the European level, but it did not change the basic starting point that the member states would have the sole competence for employment policies, leaving a more coordinated role for EU institutions. It would be an 'open method of coordination'. The Union would formulate guidelines. The member states would remain full actors, only sending in reports for evaluation, in a system of mutual learning and peer review. But the ambiguity of this 'new mode of governance'[48] was observed from the start:

---

42 Actually two instruments: Council Directive 91/383/EEC of 25 June 1991 supplementing the measures to encourage improvements in the safety and health at work of workers with a fixed-duration employment relationship or a temporary employment relationship (*O.J.* 29 July 1991, L206/19); Council Directive 1999/70/EC of 28 June 1999 concerning the framework agreement on fixed-term work concluded by ETUC, UNICE and CEEP (*O.J.* 10 July 1999, L175/43).

43 Council Directive 97/81/EC of 15 December 1997 concerning the Framework Agreement on part-time work concluded by UNICE, CEEP and the ETUC (*O.J.* 20 January 1998, L14/9).

44 Brussels, 20 March 2002, COM(2002)149final, 11–12.

45 Directive 2008/104/EC of the European Parliament and of the Council of 19 November 2008 on temporary agency work, *O.J.* 5. December 2008, L327.

46 Directive 93/104/EC of 23 November 1993 concerning certain aspects of the organization of working time (*O.J.* 13 December 1993, L307/18), later amended and repealed by Directive 2003/88 (*O.J.* 18 November 2003, L 299); *cf.* 'Reviewing the Working Time Directive (Second-phase consultation of the social partners at European level under Article 154 TFEU)', SEC(2010)1610final, COM(2010)801final, Brussels, 21 December 2010, 16.

47 *Cf.* EUROPEAN COMMISSION, 'Background Paper for first-stage consultations with the social partners, Flexibility in working time and security for workers', Sec(95)1540/3, 4; Y. SUWA, 'How to regulate the fixed-term work: a trade-off relationship in employment', (1999) 15(2) *Int. J. Comp. L.L.I.R.*, 175–8.

48 According to Caroline de la Porte and Philippe Pochet: 'New modes of governance can be referred to as "the range of innovation and transformation that has been and continues to occur in the instruments, methods, modes and systems of governance in contemporary polities and economies, and especially within the European Union (EU) and its member states (both current and prospective)".', C. DE LA PORTE and Ph. POCHET, 'The European Employment Strategy: Existing research and remaining questions', (2004) *Journal of European Social Policy*, 71.

> if we were to describe this new Title on employment as yet another example of proceduralisation in the field of social policies, we would say too little and too much at the same time: too little, because this matter goes beyond the domain of social policies, too much because procedures, as they are known in European labour law tradition, must disclose a legally meaning outcome.[49]

The EU strategy with regard to employment policies brings thus the issue of Europe's approach towards legal intervention in the field of social policy to the forefront. Arguing that the European Employment Strategy (EES) has contributed to a new pattern of regulation would be right, but it might as well be responsible for a degressive (hard law) intervention of the European Union in the social policy field,[50] although also that can be doubted. What has become clear is that the diversity and innovation in approaches portrayed in the EES, can be seen as a reflection of the (lack of) political will within the European institutions and the member states regarding EU social policy-making. Because it attempted to reach a synthesis of economic and social progress, some have labelled it as 'Third Way' – thinking.[51]

4. MARKET MAKING VERSUS SOCIAL PROGRESS IN HIGH CONTROVERSY

It is almost paradoxical *in se* that, when looking at the provisions on free movement of workers, internal market rights have been seen as promoting social rights, basically through European Court case-law. At the same time, the internal market provisions increasingly have been viewed as the biggest enemy of social development in Europe. The case-law of the European Court in *Viking*[52] and *Laval*[53] is often taken as a departure point of the debate. The matter shows that the 'European' social model discussion also involves a viewpoint on how to reconcile EU action with national social models in the European member states.

The potential clash of promoting internal market freedoms with nationally rooted social and labour policy authority, became clear with the adoption of the European Services Directive.[54] On 14 February 2006, when the European Parliament held its plenary session, Evelyne Gebhardt, the rapporteur of the European Parliament's Internal Market Commission, commented: 'We are dealing with the most important

---

49 S. SCIARRA, 'The Employment Title in the Amsterdam Treaty. A multi-language legal discourse' in D. O'KEEFFE and P. TWOMEY (eds), *Legal Issues of the Amsterdam Treaty*, Oxford, Portland Oregon, 1999, 169.

50 *Cf.* B. K. KELLER, 'The Employment Chapter of the Amsterdam Treaty. Towards a new European Employment policy?' in R. BLANPAIN and M. WEISS (eds.), *Changing Industrial Relations and Modernisation of Labour Law. Liber Amicorum in Honour of Professor Marco Biagi*, The Hague, Kluwer Law International, 2003, 234–5.

51 J. KENNER, 'The EC Employment Title and the 'Third Way': Making soft law work?' (1999) *Int. J. Comp. L.L.I.R.*, 33–60.

52 See note 6 above.

53 See note 7 above.

54 Directive 2006/123/EC of the European Parliament and of the Council of 12 December 2006 on services in the internal market, *O.J.* 27 December 2006, L 376.

piece of EU legislation apart from the Constitution.'[55] The Services Directive caused broad public debate on the European social model. It also made clear that the 'European model' was a matter of preserving 'national' social models.

Based on its 2002 report concerning the state of the internal market for services, on which the first proposal of the Services Directive broadly relied,[56] the European Commission proposed[57] to apply the 'country of origin principle', according to which a service provider would be subject only to the law of the country in which it is established. The country of origin principle would imply that a service provider in one member state would not need to adapt itself repeatedly to the local rules and regulations in another member state where the services are delivered.

It triggered a 'social dumping alarm'. The country of origin principle was seen as putting strong pressure on the high-level social protection systems present in various countries in the EU. It was called a radical change in EU labour law.[58] Clearly, from a traditional labour law point of view, the services directive was 'unsolicited' and undesirable. The Services Directive, therefore, now underlines that its provisions do "not affect labour law",[59] but this is not a technique of exclusion of labour law, which remains not immune from internal market principles.

The cases of *Viking*[60] and *Laval*[61] similarly represent the key issue of reconciling labour law (and social policy goals) with European internal market freedoms. However, both cases are as much about European 'internal market law' as about trade union and strike law. Both cases deal with the right to collective action under member state law, which is a matter of national jurisdiction and excluded from the Treaty's social chapter.[62] This has left member states with relative respect to their national traditions guided by the principles of the International Labour Organisation and the European Social Charter, two frameworks that recognize the fundamental right to strike, vested under the supervision of authoritative expert bodies.[63]

In the two cases the Court did not provide for immunity of the right to take collective action from the operation of the fundamental Treaty freedoms reflecting the internal market objectives; the Court took the view that trade union rights cannot be excluded from article 49 TFEU (free establishment) and article 56 TFEU (free services). This implies that, if an exceptional position of collective labour rights is to be granted at all, it will be given only within the scope of application of the Treaty itself.[64] The Court, nevertheless, established the fundamental character of the right to collective action by recognizing it as a fundamental right under EU law, without avoiding the application of

---

[55] Press note of the EP, n° 20060210/IPR05172.

[56] COM(2002)441final.

[57] COM(2004)2,final/2.

[58] N. Bruun, 'The proposed directive on services and labour law', 58 *B.C.L.R.* (2006), 24.

[59] *Cf.* arts 1, 6 Services Directive.

[60] See note 6 above.

[61] See note 7 above.

[62] *Cf.* art. 153, 5 TFEU.

[63] *Cf.* The ILO's Committee on Freedom of Association and the Council of Europe's European Committee of Social Rights.

[64] *Cf.* C-309/99 *Wouters*, CJEU 19 February 2002, *E.C.R.* 2002, I-1577; E. Szyszczak, 'Competition and sport', (2006) *E.L.R.*, 94–110.

the internal market provisions. On the contrary, fundamental rights and internal market principles have to be reconciled in light of the *Schmidberger* case-law.[65]

In *Viking*, the Court found that the right to take collective action for the protection of workers is a legitimate interest, which, in principle, justifies a restriction of one of the fundamental freedoms safeguarded by the Treaty.[66] To assess this further, the Court looked into the purpose of the collective action and held that collective action aimed at protecting the jobs and conditions of employment of the union members affected by the reflagging plan, would qualify as an acceptable purpose of collective action, namely 'collective action for the protection of workers'. But this would not be the case, according to the Court, if it were established that the jobs or conditions of employment at issue were not jeopardized or under serious threat.[67] Furthermore, the Court found it difficult to maintain that a policy of combating outflagging would be pursued through collective action, irrespective of whether or not the employer's exercise of his right to free establishment is liable to have a harmful effect on the work or conditions of employment of its employees.[68] With regard to 'the appropriateness of the action'[69] and its proportionality, the Court held that a national court must examine whether unions would be able to revert to means that are less restrictive to the freedom of establishment.

The manner in which the Court has examined the right to strike in light of legitimacy and proportionality has raised a lot of criticism.[70] The European Committee of Social Rights, operating in the framework of the Council of Europe, only allows a proportionality test in so far as the essence of the right to strike is not touched.[71] This obviously leaves room for interpretation,[72] but it is clear that the way the internal market principles were applied went straight to the core of a sensitive labour law debate. Also the *Laval* case has put national labour law in a difficult relationship with the European internal market principles. This case must, at least partly, be seen in the specific light of the European Posting Directive (Directive 96/71/EC).[73] In the leading case of the

---

65 C-112/00, *Eugen Schmidberger*, CJEU 12 June 2003, *E.C.R.* 2003, I-5659.

66 *Viking*, (note 6 above) para. 77.

67 Ibid., para. 81.

68 Ibid., para. 88.

69 Ibid., para. 86.

70 *Cf.* A. Davies, 'One step forward, two steps nack? The *Viking* and *Laval* cases in the ECJ' (2008) 37(2) *I.L.J.*, 147:

> The decisions in *Viking* and *Laval* are not surprising, but they are disappointing. Although the CJEU has recognized the existence of a right to strike in EU law, it has subordinated that right to the free movement rights contained in Articles 43 and 49 EC. This reflects the fact that the ECJ regards its own role as one of protecting and promoting the fundamental principles of Community law.

71 European Committee of Social Rights, *Conclusions*, XVIII-1, 2006, Germany, 304–5.

72 *Cf*: N. Hös, 'The principle of proportionality in Viking and Laval: an appropriate standard of judical review?' (2010) 1 *E.L.L.J.*, 236–53.

73 Directive 96/71/EC of the European Parliament and of the Council of 16 December 1996 concerning the posting of workers in the framework of the provision of services, *O.J.* 21 January 1997, L 18.

CJEU, *Rush Portuguesa*,[74] it was accepted that EU law would not prevent member states from applying their own legislation or collective bargaining agreements to employers and their workers, when these employers are foreign service providers and their workers are only temporarily employed on their territory. However, in *Laval*, the Court held that article 3(7) of the Posting Directive cannot be interpreted as allowing a host member state to make the provision of services in its territory conditional on the observance of terms and conditions of employment which go beyond the mandatory rules for minimum protection listed in this Posting Directive.[75] The Court, in other words, brought the country-of-origin principle, so much discussed in light of the draft Services Directive, back into the labour law arena. The Court went further in securing internal market principles in the cases *Rüffert*[76] and *Commission vs. Luxembourg*.[77]

The matter makes us reflect on how the role of the CJEU could be reflected with (national) constitutional traditions in the member states. In evaluating the Court's reasoning in *Viking* and *Laval* in light of the notion of balancing of rights that is prevalent within highly-developed national constitutional cultures, as well as in the most reliable European theoretical thinking,[78] we cannot find any proper kind of balancing exercise in the two judgments, as the Court's *modus operandi* did not deviate from the classical logical framework of application of a fundamental economic freedom in (any of) the situations where the national measure that is obstructing its exercise is properly related to (any) interests worthy of protection within the legal order of the member state. In spite of the declared reallocation of the right to strike and to take collective action within the circle of EU fundamental rights, 'what the Court has accomplished is not a balancing-act between two equally footed rights, but a much more traditional scrutiny of compatibility between national rules and Community law'.[79] And in this logic, the aim is not to carry out a balancing between equally standing rights but, rather, to reaffirm a principle of hierarchy among legal systems according to the classical view of the primacy of Union law affirmed by the CJEU.[80] Some progress on this point could be expected from the new legal framework offered by the Lisbon Treaty.

---

[74] *Rush Portuguesa*, C-113/89, *E.C.R.* 1990, I-1417.

[75] Ibid., para. 80.

[76] C-346/06 *Rüffert*, 3 April 2008.

[77] C-319/06 *Commission vs. Luxembourg*, 19 June 2008.

[78] See: A. ALEXY, *A Theory of Constitutional Rights*, Oxford, Oxford University Press, 2010; 100 ff.

[79] LO FARO, 'Diritto al conflitto e conflitto di diritti nel mercato unico: lo sciopero al tempo della libera circolazione', *Rassegna di diritto pubblico europeo*, 2010; No. 1, 54.

[80] See: LO FARO, 2010, ibid; N. ALIPRANTIS, 'What remedies for social derivatives and expansionism of the Court of Justice of the European Union?', in M.-A. Moreau (ed.), *Before and After the Economic Crisis. What Implications for the 'European Social Model'?*, Cheltenham & Northampton, Massachusetts, Edward Elgar, 2011, 89–98.

5. THE IMPACT OF LISBON

When the Lisbon Treaty entered into force on 1 December 2009, the European legislative framework received a new Treaty on the European Union (TEU) and the TFEU. Although the first impression is that with this Lisbon Treaty the main outlook of European labour law remained unaltered, its framework has provided for a new set of general clauses and a strong legal basis for the protection of fundamental (social) rights. The EU Charter on Fundamental Rights has now received 'the same legal value as the Treaties'.

Article 2 of the TEU imbues the Union's new array of values with a strong social connotation where it states that the Union is founded, above all, on the values of respect for human dignity, freedom, democracy, equality and the safeguard of human rights. This is also true where it recognizes its participation in the values – common to all member states – of pluralism, non-discrimination, tolerance, justice, solidarity and equality between men and women. Article 3, paragraph 3 innovates the Union's objectives with the much-debated and politically challenging formula of a 'highly competitive social market economy, aiming at full employment and social progress'. This formula, virtually capable of rearticulating the very foundations of European social policies seen in close connection with economic policies, is also endowed with a new operational potential in the no less innovative, all encompassing provision of article 9 TFEU. According to this broad horizontal clause, in the definition and enforcement of its policies and actions, the Union is bound to take into account the fundamental objectives of promoting a high level of employment, the guarantee of adequate social protection, and the fight against exclusion.[81] An analogous horizontal clause in the Treaty endows the Union with a similar duty to mainstream the complex range of anti-discriminatory policies across the entire sphere of supranational social action (art. 10 TFEU).

At the same time, the principle of an 'open market economy with free competition', once at the core of the European economic constitution,[82] has been formally expunged from the heart of the values, objectives and general principles of the Union and relegated to an ancillary role in article 119 TFEU (which opens Title VIII on economic and monetary policy) and Protocol No 27 attached to the Lisbon Treaty. The formula of an 'open market economy with free competition' would thus seem to be normatively weakened, and practically declassed, from a major finalistic principle to a secondary and instrumental objective: it now merely characterizes the sphere of legislative competences and action to which it specifically refers. Moreover, a new emphasis on the social dimension of the internal market is added in the reformulation of the provision now contained in article 14 TFEU stressing the central place occupied by

---

[81] The importance of the horizontal social clause and its close connection with the objective of the 'social market economy' is acknowledged in the Communication from the Commission, Towards a Single Market Act for a Highly Competitive Social Market Economy, COM(2010)608 final.

[82] *Cf, e.g.* J. BAQUERO CRUZ, *Between Competition and Free Movement. The Economic Constitutional Law of the European Communities*, Oxford & Portland, Oregon, Hart Publishing, 2002.

services of general economic interest in the shared values of the Union as well as their role in promoting territorial and social cohesion (see also Protocol No 26). In short, the general provisions of the new Treaties reformulated at Lisbon disclose, *in abstracto*, 'great potential for inverting the relationship between economic and social Europe'.[83] A new set of values, objectives and principles profoundly innovated by the Treaties trace a new trajectory for the Union beyond the functional dimension of market integration towards the recognition of a coessential *finalité sociale* of the European political project.

Furthermore, article 152 TFEU should be mentioned, as it obliges the Union to recognize and promote the role of social partners at its level by facilitating their dialogue, with due respect for their autonomy, while taking into consideration the diversity of national systems of industrial relations and collective labour law. In agreement with article 11 of the TEU and the instruments of participatory democracy set out therein, article 152 TFEU carries out the function of strengthening the legitimacy of the institutions of social pluralism at the Union level.[84] In this perspective, it increases the relevance of collective 'involvement' and bargaining as a method of governance and regulation both at the supranational and transnational level (see art. 155 TFEU),[85] potentially envisaging forms of 'auxiliary' legislation at the EU level.

In this sense, article 152 TFEU should be read in close connection with the new provisions of the TEU that, in reshaping the values and objectives of the Union, undoubtedly strengthen the European social dimension endowing it with a relevance unknown to the text of the (former) European Community Treaty. The increased weight of social values and objectives easily emerges from a quick comparison between the text previously in force and the current one set out in articles 2 and 3 of the TEU. It emerges even more clearly still from the comparison between the corresponding provisions regarding the sphere of market integration and what might be called the hard core of the European economic constitution.[86]

The Lisbon Treaty marks a major step in the development of fundamental social rights in the EU. A first important step was made after the adoption of the Amsterdam Treaty. After a long process of preparation, the Charter of Fundamental Rights of the European Union was solemnly proclaimed on 7 December 2000 at the occasion of the Intergovernmental Conference (IGC) held at Nice. It was assumed that the Charter had political rather than legal meaning, but the IGC committed itself to consider its future status after a year as part of a constitutional reform of the Union. The Charter provided a broad range of fundamental rights. It is divided into different chapters, entitled dignity, freedoms, equality, solidarity, citizen's rights and justice, and takes an

---

83 D. GOTTARDI, 'Tutela del lavoro e concorrenza tra imprese nell'ordinamento dell'Unione europea'(2010) *Giornale di Diritto del Lavoro e di Relazioni Industriali*, 521.

84 *Cf* B. CARUSO, *I diritti sociali fondamentali dopo il Trattato di Lisbona (tanto tuonò che piovve)*, Working Paper C.S.D.L.E. 'Massimo D'Antona', INT.-81/2010.

85 See on this S. SCIARRA, 'Collective exit strategies: New ideas in transnational labour law', Jean Monnet Working Paper, NYU School of Law, 04/10.

86 *Cf* C. PINELLI, 'Il Preambolo, i valori, gli obiettivi' in F. BASSANINI and G. TIBERI (eds), *Le nuove istituzioni europee. Commento al Trattato di Lisbona*, Bologna, Il Mulino, 2010, 67 ff; A. WILLIAMS, *The Ethos of Europe. Values, Law and Justice in the EU*, Cambridge, Cambridge University Press, 2010, 283 ff.

integrated approach, including civil, political, economic and social rights all together. Most, but not all, labour law and social policy provisions are concentrated in the fourth chapter on 'solidarity'. The legally non-binding character of the Charter was seen to have only a limited effect in the labour law discourse. As a consequence, labour law scholarship seemed to be cautious and avoided overestimating the Charter's impact.[87] With the adoption of the Lisbon Treaty on 13 December 2007 and its entry into force on 1 December 2009, however, the EU Charter of Fundamental Rights received binding 'Treaty status' in the EU legal order.

Fundamental social rights can be seen as conditional for a more complete view of labour law in Europe and as constitutive to a 'European social model'. Fundamental rights approaches have limitations,[88] but can be perceived as having a proactive and promotional function.[89] There may be an influence on the discussion (and thus also the Court's case-law) concerning the balance between social rights and market freedoms and there is room for a stronger connection of the EU legal order with traditional European social values, seen the as the EU Charter provides that it needs to be interpreted in accordance with the European Convention on Human Rights (1950).[90] That would, arguably, require that the interpretation of the European Court on Human Rights cannot be neglected by the CJEU,[91] when for example dealing with right to strike issues.

6. ECONOMIC GOVERNANCE

We cannot analyze in detail here the complex measures by which the member states of the Union, particularly those that are part of the Eurozone, have tried to emerge from the financial crisis by reforming the European economic and monetary governance along with the introduction of instruments of financial aid for the countries that are exposed the most, in some cases up to the risk of default. From the initial measures

---

[87] L. BETTEN, 'The EU Charter on Fundamental Rights: a Trojan horse or a mouse?'(2001) *Int. J. Comp. L.L.I.R.*, 157.

[88] *Cf.* A.T.J.M. JACOBS, 'The fences surrounding the charter of fundamental rights in the new European constitution' in D. RYLAND (ed.), *An Era of Human Rights International legal Essays in Honour of Jo Carby-Hall*, Manchester, Barmarick, 2006, 341–60; *Cf.* B. BERCUSSON, 'Episodes on the path towards the European social model' in BARNARD, DEAKIN and MORRIS, note 2 above, 179–99.

[89] Cf. O. DE SCHUTTER, 'Introduction: fundamental rights and the transformation of governance in the European Union' in O. De SCHUTTER and V. MORENO LAX, *Human Rights in the Web of Governance: Towards a Learning-based Fundamental Rights Policy for the European Union*, Brussels, Bruylant, 2010, 13; see earlier work: F. HENDRICKX, 'Fundamental social rights in pre-constitutional and post-constitutional terms' (2006) 22 *Int. J. Comp. L.L.I.R.*, 407–33; F. HENDRICKX, 'European labour law after the Lisbon Treaty: (Re-visited) assessment of fundamental social rights' in R. BLANPAIN & F. HENDRICKX (eds), *Liber Amicorum Antoine Jacobs*, (2011) 78 *B.C.L.R.*, 75–87.

[90] Article 52 of the Charter of Fundamental Rights of the European Union of 7 December 2000.

[91] W. WEISS, 'Human rights and EU anti-trust enforcement: news from Lisbon' (2011) 32(4) *Eur. Comp. Law Rev.*, 190.

taken in 2010 to face up to the crisis of the Greek debt, until the adoption of the Treaty on the European Stability Mechanism (ESM) and the entry into force of the so-called *Fiscal Compact*, the Union has undoubtedly made a considerable effort to provide appropriate instruments to counter an unprecedented crisis that has put at risk the survival of the single currency project.[92]

These reforms – both those implemented within the institutional framework of the Union, and those adopted through recourse to the intergovernmental method and to the subtly revised instruments of international law present a common trait[93], which can be described as the radicalization of the trend to compress the autonomy of the member states (especially those whose common currency is the Euro) in respect of the management of their social policies. This trend is intensified, in particular within the new rules of the Stability Pact and of the *Fiscal Compact*, for it assumes the shape of a creeping de-politicization of the issues of social and distributive justice that are central in the definition of the very identity of the different welfare systems of the member states.

The importance of fundamental (social) rights for the European labour law debate, considered in their development as well as in light of the Lisbon Treaty, is discussed below. The single currency project, as conceived by the framers of the Maastricht Treaty, was built on a model opposite to one with a solidaristic nature *sensu lato*, which generally characterizes federal systems, although according to very different variations. The single currency, the stability of which is ensured by the establishment of a European Central Bank, was not based on a partial centralization of competencies regarding fiscal and budget policies at Union level, as in federal entities, nor on a federal budget, as instead was suggested in the 70s by the McDougall Report.[94] The Union is also completely devoid of automatic stability mechanisms that are necessary to cope with asymmetric shocks.[95]

A first type of corrective measure, introduced as part of the so-called *Stability Compact*,[96] is designed to support the instruments outlined by the Maastricht Treaty, with the purpose of providing the Union with the ability to prevent systemic crisis of

---

92 Which has become an essential part of the political project of an ever closer Union among the European people since the nineties: *cf.* G. MORO (ed.), *The Single Currency and European Citizenship. Unveiling the Other Side of the Coin*, New York, London, New Delhi & Sydney, Bloomsbury, 2013.

93 See F.W. SCHARPF, 'Monetary union, fiscal crisis and the pre-emption of democracy', LEQS Paper No. 35, May, London School of Economics and Political Science, 2011; A. SOMEK, 'The social question in a transnational context', LEQS Paper No. 39, London School of Economics and Political Science, June 2011; K. TUORI, 'The European Financial Crisis – Constitutional aspects and implications', EUI Working Papers Law No. 28, 2012; F. DE WITTE, 'EU law, politics and the social question' (2013) 14(5) *German Law Journal*, 581–612.

94 That in designing a possible path of monetary integration among EEC countries, had suggested a gradual construction of a federal budget in stages that should have been completed, in the final stage, with the allocation of 25 per cent of the European GDP to the Community budget.

95 J.-V. LOUIS, 'Solidarité budgétaire et financière dans l'Union européenne' in C. BOUTAYEB (ed.), *La solidarité dans l'Union européenne*, Paris, Dalloz, 2011, 110.

96 See the so-called Six Pack (consisting of Regulations 1173, 1174, 1175, 1176, 1177 of 2011 and of Directive 2011/85) and the Fiscal Compact. In November 2011 the European

the Eurozone by strengthening the rules on budgetary constraints and fiscal austerity. The new legislation – partly of a EU law nature, partly of international law character – introduces significant innovations, aimed first at making the limits on deficit and public debt, provided for by the Maastricht Treaty and the Stability and Growth Pact, effectively liable to be sanctioned. On the other hand, the states signatory of the *Fiscal Compact* are bound to insert the new rigorous golden rule of budgetary balance in their respective legal orders, preferably through rules of constitutional status.[97] On the other hand, the procedure concerning excessive deficits – which can be activated also in the event of exceeding the limits of public debt – is decisively strengthened through the introduction of a reverse majority rule. Therefore, a qualified majority in the Council becomes necessary in order to reject a proposal from the Commission, by inverting the voting rule traditionally provided for by Union law and contemplated by the Stability Pact. Thus, once initiated by the Commission, the sanctioning procedure assumes a semi-automatic course of action, making it much more difficult to form blocking minorities for the member state concerned. In addition to the procedure referred to in article 126 TFEU, on the basis of article 121, the 2011 EU law reform also introduces a new procedure for the prevention and correction of macro-economic imbalances. This procedure broadens the power of the Commission to intervene far beyond the borders of fiscal policy, by extending it to the whole range of economic policies of national governments. And even in this case, any failure to comply with the corrective actions planned by the member state, according to the recommendations made by the Commission and the Council, is liable to be sanctioned by a procedure marked by a reverse majority voting.[98]

By the same token, the *Euro Plus Pact*,[99] although having the nature of a political intergovernmental agreement, essentially ends up integrating those new supranational constraints, given the close bond with the new legislation on macroeconomic surveillance. The *Euro Plus Pact* intends, inter alia, to have a direct impact on the wage-setting systems that operate at member state level, which are per se excluded from the sphere of legislative competencies of the Union in the field of social policy (art. 153.5 TFEU). In the chapter on productivity, which is central in regard to the general objectives aimed at promoting the increase of competitiveness and employment within the Union, the *Euro Plus Pact* – while promising to preserve the different national traditions in the field of social dialogue and industrial relations – indicates which are the precise measures that member states should apply in relation to wage-setting arrangements, both in the public and private sectors. Particularly important is the recommendation made to align wages to productivity by proceeding, if

Commission made two further proposals for regulation in jargon known as Two-Pack: see COM(2011)819 and COM(2011)821.

97 See art. 3 of the Treaty on stability, coordination and governance of the economic and monetary Union, to which Italy has proceeded to adapt by modifying art. 81 of the Constitution with the constitutional law No. 1 of 2012. Germany had already introduced the so-called Schuldenbremse in 2009, by modifying arts 109 and 115 of its Fundamental Law.

98 TUORI, The European Financial Crisis, see note 93 above, 17 ff.

99 C. BARNARD, 'The financial crisis and the Euro Plus Pact: A labour lawyer's perspective' (2012) 41(1) *Ind. L.J.*, 98 ff.

necessary, to a decentralization of the systems of collective bargaining and, if appropriate, by reviewing the mechanisms for automatic indexation.

A second and more creative type of legal innovations, totally absent in the structure of the Maastricht Treaty and therefore subject to bitter controversy, concerns the introduction of suitable tools in order to provide the Union, and in particular the Eurozone, with the effective ability for the management of financial crises, through variously devised mechanisms of financial aid to countries in difficulty. Besides the first modest measures adopted within the *European Financial Stabilisation Mechanism* (EFSM), established with Council Regulation No. 407/2010 according to article 122 TFEU, these instruments of financial assistance all operate outside the institutional framework of the Union. The *European Financial Stability Facility* (EFSF), precursor of the ESM, lies evidently outside the legal framework of the founding Treaties as it was actually established as a limited company registered in Luxembourg, according to a very inventive and uneven combination between contract and financial-market law and public international law rules.[100] On its part, by providing Eurozone States with a fairly strong permanent instrument of financial aid, the ESM was established as a body of public international law, expressly subtracted to the application of EU law.

In the strongly debated *Pringle* judgment,[101] delivered by the Court of Justice after the authorization given by the German Constitutional Court (under specific conditions), regarding the ratification of the ESM by Germany,[102] the Luxembourg judges basically dismissed all the objections raised by the plaintiff in the main proceedings, an independent deputy of the Irish Parliament, regarding the compatibility of ESM with EU law. The most problematic issue – among the several raised by the Irish Supreme Court in its request for a preliminary ruling – concerned the very suspicious compatibility of the ESM with the prohibition to bailout laid down by article 125 TFEU. With an elaborate motivation, the Court of Justice excluded a violation of article 125 of the Treaty thanks to an innovative and restrictive interpretation of the no-bail-out-clause, stating that the (not yet operational) amendment of article 136 TFEU[103] has a merely confirmation value of the competencies of member states in this field. In the Court's interpretation, article 125 is only intended to prevent member states from relying on a redemption of their public debt by other members of the Eurozone, in

---

100 TUORI, The European Financial Crisis, note 93 above, 13–14.

101 See the judgment delivered by the Court in plenary session on 27 November 2012 in the case C-370/12, *Thomas Pringle vs. Government of Ireland.* See e.g. the critical comments by Tomkin (J. TOMKIN, 'Contradiction, circumvention and conceptual gymnastics: The impact of the adoption of the ESM Treaty on the state of European democracy' (2013) 14(1) *German Law Journal*, 169 ff.) and Van Malleghem (P.-A. VAN MALLEGHEM (2013), 'Pringle: A paradigm shift in the European Union's Monetary Constitution' (2013) 14(1) *German Law Journal*, 141 ff.).

102 BVerfG, 2 BVR 1390/12, of 12 September 2012. See also S.K. SCHMIDT, 'A Sense of Déjà Vu? The FCC's Preliminary European Stability Mechanism Verdict', 14(1) *German Law Journal* (2013), 1 ff; M. WENDEL, 'Judicial Restraint and the Return to Openness: The Decision of the German Federal Constitutional Court on the ESM and the Fiscal Treaty of 12 September 2012', 14(1) *German Law Journal* (2013), 21 ff.

103 Article 136 of TFEU was modified according to Decision 2011/99, not yet in force, using the simplified revision procedure introduced by the Lisbon Treaty for the first time. The amendment was intended to clarify the competence of the member states to adopt an instrument of the type of ESM.

this way, leading them to maintain a sound fiscal policy and, especially, a moderate budget policy. In the terms in which it is set, the ESM does not contradict the rationale and substance of this prohibition, since the financial solidarity that the member states ensure through it to the fellow countries whose difficulties jeopardize the stability of the whole Eurozone, is subordinate to a strict conditionality requirement, as specified by the same reformulation of article 136 TFEU. On one hand, the ESM is fundamentally committed to assuring the European collective interest of protecting the stability of the Eurozone as a whole, without definitely bearing itself with the public debt of the subsidized member states, which will remain individually liable anyhow; on the other hand, the strict conditionality-requirement for acceding to ESM financial aid gives adequate guarantees that this does not result in disincentives to pursue sound fiscal and budget policies, avoiding the temptation of moral hazard by the assisted countries.

From the review carried out here, although briefly, it is evident that the reforms introduced within and (especially) outside the structure of the founding Treaties to cope with the financial crisis of the Eurozone, contribute to determine a significant compression of the autonomy of the member states in the field of social and labour law and policy. The new supranational constitutional constraints to fiscal and budget policies of the member states of the Eurozone limit the redistributive options available to the national democratic process, with strong repercussions on the national welfare state arrangements.[104] Overall, the new rigid neo-liberal structure of the European economic and monetary constitution can be characterized as a monumental exercise undertaken by 'the economic' to rule 'the political', which is unprecedented in the history of democracies, at least for the pervasiveness of its ramifications. Having pushed itself to this point, the Union – as has been critically remarked – is not far from the Hayekian ideal of a 'limited democracy' based on dethroning politics in the name of market-discipline as the supreme arbiter.[105]

However, the doubt that such a design is resting on fragile assumptions of democratic legitimacy is dangerously powered by the dramatically ineffective measures adopted by the Union to overcome the economic and financial crisis. The austerity policies, adopted under the pervasive guise of the new European economic and fiscal governance,[106] have so far produced prolonged recession and mass unemployment (especially among young people) in the countries in which they have been more or less mechanically adopted, starting from Greece, while in some cases they have even worsened the ratio between gross domestic product and public debt (as in Italy). In the words of one of the most lucid critics of that disquieting state of affairs, if compared to a fully-fledged, federal-state regime or even with the 'European Monetary System' in force until the introduction of the single currency, 'Member States in the reformed

---

[104] See the first comparative analysis by Heise and Lierse (A. HEISE and H. LIERSE, *Budget Consolidation and the European Social Model. The Effects of European Austerity Programmes on Social Security Systems*, Friedrich Ebert Stiftung Study, 2011) and by Hinrichs and Jessoula (K. HINRICHS and M. JESSOULA (eds), *Labour Market Flexibility and Pensions Reforms*, Houndmills, Basingstoke, Palgrave-Macmillan, 2012).

[105] A. SUPIOT, *L'esprit de Philadelphie. La justice sociale face au marché total*, Paris, Seuil, 2010, 33.

[106] For an effective definition of the Fiscal Compact as a form of constitutionalisation of austerity see DE WITTE, note 93 above.

Monetary Union will indeed find themselves in the worst of these three world'.[107] While the EMU does not have the ability to undertake the economic and fiscal manoeuvres that only a truly federal budget allows to draw unto, the Union does not even let its member states autonomously use such residual macroeconomic levers – especially those in the Eurozone, that have lost any competency related to monetary policy. And while the new instruments of economic governance accentuate its institutional fragmentation, the Union is faced with a double deficit of democratic legitimacy, as a direct consequence of such an asymmetry between (poor) ability to give political answers (i.e. positive integration) and (strong) constraints to the autonomy of the member states in the name of the stability of the market's (negative) integration. The already thin Union's input-oriented legitimacy (utterly weakened by the marginalization of the European Parliament's role within the structure of the new economic governance) is further aggravated by a dramatic, and perhaps more serious, crisis of output-oriented democratic legitimacy, as demonstrated by the widespread anti-European resentment shown by the national public opinion of the countries most affected by the crisis.

7. EUROPEAN UNION LABOUR LAW AND THE EUROPEAN SOCIAL MODEL: AN APPRAISAL

Let us refer back to our starting position. The concept of the European Social Model is problematic. There is a broad range of Union interventions in the area of labour law and social policy, but they cannot be seen as unequivocally advancing social rights or social citizenship. As can be understood from our overview of policy areas, the European Social Model seems more an attempt than a realization and, to the extent that it is evolving, being based as a market model, it is very vulnerable. Trails of a European Social Model come down to a combination of (a limited range of) hard law, soft law and governance measures, with market making, corrective and minimum harmonization objectives, causing tensions between negative (de-regulation) and positive (regulation) regulatory strategies, a growing relevance of fundamental social rights, and, in general, attempts to reconcile economic objectives with European (but often mainly national) social policies.

The search for a balance between economic and social progress is a *fil rouge* in European labour law and social policy development. However, striking a balance seems to be more difficult than ever. Alan Neal concludes that;

> the declaration in the Presidency Conclusions to the 1989 Madrid Summit, that 'in the course of the construction of the single European market, social aspects should be given the same importance as economic aspects and should accordingly be developed in a balanced fashion' now suffers from a fundamental disequilibrium in favour of the 'economic dimension'.[108]

---

[107] SCHARPF, note 93 above.

[108] A. NEAL, 'Freedom of movement for employers and employees in the European Union. Some Observations from the Perspective of a High-Wage Economy' (2013) 4(1) *European Labour Law Journal*, 66.

Our analysis confirms this scepticism. It also confirms that legitimacy remains problematic, as well as the ability of European policies to connect well with traditional labour law and social policy understanding *and* development in the member states, knowing that, despite common traits, differences in state traditions are quite apparent.

After more than half a century of European integration, there are great achievements. European states have never cooperated before in such an intense and peaceful manner, and we agree with Fritz Sharpf that:

> in their own terms, the efforts to complete the internal market and monetary union have succeeded beyond expectations. At the same time, however, the advance of economic integration has greatly reduced the capacity of member states to influence the course of their own economies and to realize self-defined socio-political goals.[109]

Not only the internal market provisions challenge the capability of the member states to maintain adequate levels of social protection and distributive justice within their borders. At the same time the new economic and monetary constitution of the Union, in responding to the financial crisis, imposes increasingly severe and pervasive supranational constraints on the national democratic welfare state systems. Union law deprives member states of decisive levers of political-democratic control over their welfare systems, without being able to compensate for such a partial loss in delivering distributive social justice at a supranational level. The asymmetry between negative and positive integration has never been thus evident in the history of the integration process. And with the deepening of this asymmetry, the European integration social deficit risks converting into a crucial factor of crisis for the Union's democratic legitimacy.

There are nevertheless signs that the European Social Model might take more effect and legitimacy in the future. It may be argued that, in the setting of the Lisbon Treaty, the market loses its sovereignty within the EU political horizon and competition is no longer purposefully protected as an end in itself, thereby becoming an instrument for pursuing the overarching objective of a 'social market economy'. Within this new normative framework, such a general constitutional rebalancing and such a specific strengthening of social values and objectives receive their definitive constitutional consecration by the Charter of Fundamental Rights of the European Union (art. 6, para. 1, TEU). It is in fact in the fully achieved constitutionalization of fundamental social rights and principles as enshrined in the Nice Charter that it is possible for the EU legal order to enter its full constitutional maturity, enhancing and transposing at the supranational level a dimension which is historically typical, in Europe, to the constitutional democratic nation state.

---

109 F.W. SCHARPF, 'The European Social Model: Coping with the challenges of diversity' (2001) 40(4) *J.C.M.S.*, 648.

13. Labor law in transition: From a centrally planned to a free market economy in Central and Eastern Europe

Erika Kovács, Nikita Lyutov and Leszek Mitrus

INTRODUCTION

This chapter covers the specifics of countries in Eastern Europe,[1] all of which had been governed by a socialist political system some 20 years ago.[2] A whole generation has grown up since the time of the socialists. However, the labor law systems of these countries were so much affected by the socialist political structure, that even now they retain important features of the past, making them significantly different from the models of 'capitalist' labor law. At the same time, all countries of the region have undergone more or less radical neo-liberal economic reforms that have influenced the economy generally,[3] and the systems of labor relations and labor law in particular. The shifts in the labor law started from rather similar socialist starting points.[4] In many ways they moved in the same direction. However, the different path taken in some areas seem to be the most interesting for comparative analysis. This chapter covers three countries – Russia, Poland and Hungary, demonstrating both common points of departure and changes, but also revealing differences that emerged during the years of transition.

To fully understand the specifics of the labor law systems in the countries of the region, that is – not just to know *what* is written in this or other labor law act, but also *why* is it written and *how does it work* in practice, it is important to have a basic idea about the socialist origins of the three systems. This will be described in Part 1.

[1] The study covers Hungary, Poland and Russia not only because of the nationality of authors but mainly because these countries are quite representative in demonstrating the development of labor law within Eastern Europe. Obviously other countries' systems are not identical, but the general direction of change from a centrally planned economy to market economy in the field of labor law may be well observed based on the examples of these three countries.

[2] The frequently used terms 'communist' and 'post-communist' seem to be misleading because, despite the slogans that were used in the official ideology, there was neither communism in Marx's vision, or even a real trend to move in the direction of Marxist communism in those countries. It was a socialist system.

[3] The consequences of these reforms were different in the various countries, ranging from relatively mild in the shift to a market economy in Poland and Hungary, to catastrophic, as it was in Russia.

[4] The now independent countries of the region that were initially parties of the Soviet Union had almost identical labor legislation, while the socialist countries outside USSR had their own separately drafted law. Nevertheless, the basic philosophy was the same.

Following an account of the origins, the subsequent parts of the chapter explain how and why the labor law systems of the three countries changed during the last 20 years, leading up to the current regulatory regimes. Part 2 observes the various sources of labor law, leading to the discussion of individual employment law in Part 3, collective labor law in Part 4, and the concluding comments in Part 5.

1. THE ORIGINS OF TRANSITION

The commonplace Western writing about the socialist system usually does not go further than stating that political freedoms and human rights were severely limited and no real human rights were respected. The same is usually said about their labor law systems. But such a bald description cannot explain why several features of socialist labor law were adopted and imitated by the capitalist countries,[5] and why such important bodies as the International Labor Organization (ILO) were established to counterbalance the socialist system while accepting its notions of social protection.[6] The political motivation in the creation of the welfare state system in the capitalist countries of Europe sought to prove, to an extent, that workers can live well without overthrowing the capitalist system itself, thus posing a kind of competition with the socialist bloc.

Indeed the workers of the socialist countries could not strike or negotiate the terms of their labor contracts. However, at the same time, the right to work was treated not just as a state obligation to help people to find the job, but as an absolute state guarantee to provide everyone able to work with a job.[7]

Socialist trade unions were quasi-governmental structures and therefore could not act in conformity with market-economy principles of freedom of association. Trade unions were not acting as real collective bargaining agents of the capitalist state and therefore were strongly criticized by the market economy countries and the ILO.[8] This, however, does not mean that socialist trade unions were useless. They played a different role from that of unions in the capitalist countries. Instead of being a representative of

---

[5] E.g. the post-War constitutions of some capitalist states included notions of a right to work, inspired by the communist parties of these countries, which were quite influential at that time. See: Art. 4 of the Italian Constitution (La Costituzione della Repubblica Italiana: http://www.governo.it/Governo/Costituzione/principi.html). Moreover, the Preamble to the French Constitution, still in force, states not just a right to work but a notion of obligation to work '*le devoir de travailler*' (Préambule de la Constitution du 27 octobre 1946: http://www.conseil-constitutionnel.fr/conseil-constitutionnel/francais/la-constitution/la-constitution-du-4-octobre-1958/preambule-de-la-constitution-du-27-octobre-1946.5077.html).

[6] The fact the ILO was established by the Versailles Treaty mainly as a means of protection of western political structures against the world communist revolution is sometimes concealed but it is no secret to researchers of the ILO's history. See, for example: Kaufman B. The global evolution of industrial relations: events, ideas and the IIRA. Geneva, ILO, 2004. pp. 79–80; Standing G. The ILO: An Agency for Globalization? (2008) 39(3) *Development* and *Change*, p. 380.

[7] At the same time, 'the right' to work was an obligation. See more about this further.

[8] See: Hepple B. *Labour Laws and Global Trade*. Hart Publishing, Oxford and Portland, Oregon. 2005. p. 33.

workers, which is the tradition of the western trade unions, socialist trade unions were rather an amalgam of intermediates between the state and the employees, and a kind of social ministry. This distinct role will be described in greater detail later in this chapter, although it is clear to state that it previews a complex system, that requires careful reading, particularly for those who seek to understand it 'from the outside'. For example, officially there was collective bargaining in the socialist countries.[9] But as long as the right to bargain collectively was not accompanied with a right to strike, it was actually an imitation of bargaining. According to the official Soviet labor law doctrine, unlike their capitalist colleagues, workers in the socialist country did not need the right to strike. This was explained by the fact that the socialist state officially belonged to the proletariat, i.e. the workers, and all entities ('employers') were state-owned, and therefore belonged to the workers themselves, rendering any conflict of interests pointless.[10]

In addition to being, in Lenin's terms,[11] a 'transmission gear' connecting the communist party with the 'masses' (i.e. workers), the trade unions were a significant social institution. The first major function of trade unions was to control the social security, healthcare, leisure and tourism institutions, controlling vast resources such as social security funds, funds, hospitals, sanatoriums, and sports stadiums. The control of this property was assigned to the trade unions by the socialist state. For instance, in the Soviet Union a People's Commissariat (Ministry) on Labor was liquidated in 1933, and all its functions and property was assigned to the USSR Council of Trade Unions (VCSPS).[12] The trade union members could, for example, travel on a 'trade union trip ticket' to an annual vacation at a quite affordable price. The principles of distribution guiding these trade union benefits were connected to the employee merits in their professional activities. So, trade unions in this field were a kind of employer's disciplinary body – a role unthinkable for the market economy system of industrial relations. Trade union membership was not universal, but it was steadily growing throughout the socialist period until trade unions had united almost all workers.[13]

Another function of trade unions was to *negotiate* with the employers for collective agreements at plant level. The word 'bargaining' would not be appropriate in this context; 'consultation' better describes the process. The object of negotiations was not the wages (which were determined at the centralized level, by the state) but a limited range of additional benefits.

---

[9] In Russia, collective agreements existed at only at the plant level. In Hungary and Poland agreements were concluded at several levels, but most collective agreements were concluded at the plant level. See in more detail, Part 4, infra.

[10] For more details on this doctrine see: Aleksandrov N.G. Trudovoe pravootnoshenie [Labor legal relations], Moscow, 1948, pp. 129–63.

[11] Lenin V.I. Polnoe sobranie sochineniy [Complete works], 5th ed., Vol. 44, Moscow, Izdatelstvo politicheskoy literatury [Political literature editors], 1967. p. 349.

[12] Sovetskoye trudovoye pravo [Soviet Labor Law] N.G. Alexandrov (ed.), Moscow, 1972, p. 185.

[13] For the USSR see the dynamics of VCSPS membership in Bolshaya Sovetskaya Encyclopedia [Big Soviet Encyclopaedia] (Moscow, 1977, available at: http://bse.sci-lib.com/article093699.html).

As long as there was no right to strike, there were no collective labor disputes or disputes of interest envisaged by the law. The totally different role of trade unions can be well illustrated by the fact that for certain period they were a pre-court instance for resolution of (individual) labor disputes, i.e. grievances. This meant that the 'workers' representative' was at the same time akin to a judge in a dispute between a worker and an employer. In fact, the trade unions were mainly representing the employer's needs, but were also supposed to be 'close to workers'. A good example of this situation may be found in the latest Soviet labor law history: the first collective labor dispute in mining sector in Kuzbass region of the USSR was settled by signing of an agreement between the miners' *strike committee as one party*, and joint commission of local Communist party authority, employer and the representative of *Soviet trade union Committee – as another party*.[14]

An exceptional case in the socialist countries was the trade union *Solidarity* (Solidarność), established in Poland in 1980, at the time of heavy economic crisis and social tensions. The new organization was an 'independent and self-governing trade union' and was meant to become a real representative of workers' interests. It constituted an alternative for the communist party and the trade unions connected to it. 'Solidarity' soon became a massive social movement and an organization that was active at national level. 'Solidarity' fought for workers' rights. At the same time it formulated political and social demands, such as the freedom of expression, access to mass media (entirely controlled at the time by the communist party), recognition of right to strike and stopping repression based on political opinions.

After a series of strikes in 1980 in various regions of Poland, 'Solidarity' concluded a 'social pact' with the government concerning workers' rights and the recognition of 'Solidarity' as a legal trade union. For the first time in the post-war history of Poland, a conflict between the communist party and the 'working class' was settled in a peaceful way. It is estimated that in 1980–81, approximately 10 million Poles were 'Solidarity' members. After introducing martial law on 13 December 1981 'Solidarity' became an illegal organization. It acted as an opposition until the end of the decade. In 1983 the 'Solidarity' leader, Lech Walesa, was awarded the Nobel Prize.

In 1988 the next wave of strikes took place. At that time the economic situation of Poland was even worse than in 1980. Following the strikes, a dialogue between the communist party and the political opposition was initiated and led to 'the round table' negotiations in 1989. As a result, new parliamentary elections took place and 'Solidarity' formed the government that started significant economic reforms. Thus, it should be underlined that the trade union movement's fight for human dignity and workers' rights was a very important factor in overcoming the communist system in Central and Eastern Europe. 'Solidarity' played, in Poland, a crucial role in the process of peaceful transformation from socialist to democratic country.

The idealistic part of the socialist labor law doctrine was that there was no inherent 'antagonist' conflict of interests between the employer and the employee, which is

[14] Protocol on agreed measures between the regional strike committee and commission of ZK KPSS, Council of Ministers of the USSR and VCSPS of July 19, 1989 (quoted by Lopatin L.N. Istoriya rabochego dvijeniya Kuzbassa [The History of Kuzbass Labor Movement], Kemerovo, 1995, p. 66.

inherent in privately owned business in market economies. Despite the now popular 'win-win' concepts concerning collective bargaining in a market economy, its fundamental tradeoff, recognized for centuries, remains: the more the employee gets, the less will be left as the employer's profit. By contrast, the socialist entity (employer) was remote from its formal 'owners' – the people, but in the same manner it was not controlled by anyone whose direct interest was to get the immediate profit from its economic activity. Being a part of socialist economic machine, any entity's goal was twofold: a) to fulfill an economic plan that was assigned to it by the governmental institution; and b) to solve the social tasks – provide employment to the population of the region, finance the social infrastructure, etc.

The managers of the socialist entities were not motivated to economize the company resources, spending less on the employees. Instead, they were interested in lowering the production plan to make their own life easier. In monetary terms workers were getting much lower wages than the employees in the richest capitalist countries, but this was in some way compensated by many goods and services in-kind: free or cheap housing, free medicine, free education of all levels, cheap transport services, cheap prices on basic foods, etc. From a social point of view this system was in some way more humane than the capitalist system.[15]

An important feature of labor legislation of that time was that the goal of law was not to set up the 'rules of the game' between the independent players, but rather to issue technical instructions for the subordinated actors – employees and employers. A good example of this legislative approach was the limited list of dismissal grounds that was used in the Soviet Union. Employers had a right to dismiss an employee not on 'just cause' or 'at will' (as the western countries frame the legal alternatives) but only according to one of the permitted grounds, established by law.[16]

When analyzing the recent labor law systems of the Eastern European countries we should always bear in mind that they developed in different ways after the fall of the Iron Curtain. Labor law is closely connected with, and indeed dependent on, the political and economic situation of each country. Eastern European labor law systems have similarities – especially concerning industrial relations – rooted in the socialist time, but they have serious differences which are – at least partly – the consequences of the various political and economic developments of the last 20 years. These recent political changes strongly influenced the labor regulation, the role of unions, and also the present attitude towards the socialist labor law. Another important factor is the membership in the European Union, which leads to more similarity between Eastern European states that are currently members.

---

[15] This is all the more true for the late period of socialism when there was no brutal totalitarian rule and no economic-military mobilization.

[16] See further in Part 3.

2. SOURCES OF LABOR LAW

a. Introductory Remarks

The scheme of labor law's sources seems to be more complicated than sources of other laws. In principle, although statutes play an important role, it is not only the legislature that is competent to enact provisions of labor law. Social partners have an important role in establishing labor law's provisions, and employers have the right to enact work regulations, which regulate day-to-day activities at the establishment. Thus, one of the distinguishing features of labor law is the fact that state institutions do not have a monopoly in setting its provisions. Legal and political norms, specific to each region, produce a specific 'cocktail' of these sources. The new democracies of Central and Eastern Europe had to find a new balance between different sources and norms, while introducing a new 'labor deal'. Characteristic to these countries are new labor codes. In most countries, including the countries surveyed here – Poland, Hungary and Russia, they remained the most important sources of individual labor law. On the other hand, the shift from rigid statutory law to more flexible labor law sources, which was enacted to a large extent by the social partners, is one of the most important features of change in the last two decades.

There are certainly many differences among various countries as far as sources of labor law are concerned. There are many points for comparison, including the role of state institutions and social partners, the interactions between them, the strength of trade unions, degree of flexibility, and legal tradition. Statutes and collective labor agreements may play different roles in the different countries. Generally speaking, the system of sources of labor law is strongly embedded in the industrial relations and collective bargaining system in each country. Countries that overcame the socialist system had to change the network of sources of labor law, which generally became more complex, but also more flexible at the same time.

On the other hand, there are some common features that may be indicated with regard to Hungary, Poland and Russia. *First*, there is the principle of employees' privilege (Ger. – *das Günstigkeitprinzip*). According to this principle, the provisions of collective agreements, employer's regulations (Ger. *die Arbeitsordnung*) and statutes may not disadvantage employees more than provisions of the Labor Code and other statutes.[17] In other words: statutory law provides the minimum standard of employee protection. Social partners are free to establish a higher level of protection. *Second*, the government and state institutions are the strong actors of industrial relations. The state not only lays down provisions of labor law, but also introduces a detailed framework for collective bargaining and acts as a member of tripartite commission.[18] *Third*, the

[17] In Hungary this principle was applied between 1992 and 2012. The new Labor Code in 2012 introduced the new general rule, according to which social partners are allowed to deviate from the Labor Code even to the detriment of workers in collective agreements and works council agreements.

[18] See e.g. Świątkowski A.M. The Role of the State and Trade Unions During the Polish Process of Transformation (in:) A.M. Świątkowski (ed.) *Yearbook of Polish Labor Law and Social Policy*, Volume 8, Krakow 1998, pp. 27 and following.

development of collective labor law in the Central and Eastern European countries has not been a spontaneous development, because in the communist era state institutions dominated, and there were no 'real' social partners. After the collapse of the old political system, the establishment of collective labor law was settled by statutes. Thus, the creation of industrial relations and collective labor law has been more political than legal. It was the state, through legislation, and not the continuous development of cooperation between employers and employees, which formed the basis of collective industrial relations. *Fourth*, the development of labor law has been, to some extent, influenced by international standards, as established by the ILO and the Council of Europe. However, since Hungary and Poland joined as members of the EU, their national legislation has been much more affected by the standards imposed by the Union law. While there are regional instruments that affect labor law in Russia, but not Poland and Hungary, until now they were of negligible importance to the legal practice.[19] There is however a possibility that this kind of regional integration will be more important for Russia and several neighboring states, once the Eurasian Economic Union mechanisms is developed.[20]

Hungary, Poland and Russia have rather similar provisions in their Labor Codes (*hereon*: HLC, PLC and RLC – designating each code respectively) concerning the system and sources of labor law.[21] As a starting point for the comparison, all three countries share a fundamental feature. Labor law is regulated both by state legislator and social partners. Our countries make a division between 'state-made' labor law (LC, other statutes, subordinate legislation) and provisions that are negotiated by the social partners (various collective agreements, works council agreements and regulations (*die Arbeitsordnung*) issued unilaterally by an employer). The degree of regulation by these actors may vary, but generally it seems that statutory law still plays primary and dominant role.

b. Statutory Law

Poland

In Poland the Labor Code is of primary importance for individual labor law. This Labor Code is very detailed and has a significant influence on day-to-day practices. The current PLC was enacted on June 26, 1974, and took effect on January 1, 1975.[22] This statute regulates the principles of labor law, the rights and duties of employees and employers, the types and content of an employment contract, protection against dismissal and employees' claims in case of unfair dismissal, remuneration for work, ban on discrimination, employee's liability, working time, holiday leave, employee rights connected with parenthood, protection of minor workers, collective labor

---

[19] Some treaties and model labor legislation are adopted within a framework of the Commonwealth of Independent States and the Eurasian Economic Community.

[20] It is planned to establish the Eurasian Economic Union in 2015, which will include Belarus, Kazakhstan, Russia and probably several other former USSR states, as a kind of a confederative structure in some aspects analogous to the EU unification process. Since the beginning of 2012 the single labor market for the three countries has been established.

[21] Article 13 of the HLC, Art. 9 of the PLC, Art. 5 of the RLC.

[22] Compiled text Journal of Laws 2014, pos. 1502 with further amendments.

agreements, health and safety issues. The original PLC was enacted in other political, economic, and social circumstances. It was designed to regulate employment relations in large, state-owned enterprises. Since that time there have been more than 100 amendments, which were introduced to take into account the nature of the market economy, as well as the requirements of EU law.[23] Consequently, the provisions of old PLC are very detailed, but not clear, and difficult to interpret. The process of so-called 're-codification of labor law' (i.e. enacting a new labor code) commenced in the 90s, and has been elaborated since then, but there is still no new Labor Code in Poland.

Given the numerous legislative changes, the PLC gradually became more market-oriented. For example, the chapter on working time became much more flexible than the old version in the socialist period. The very new chapter on equal treatment in employment was introduced while implementing the Directives of the EU. The rules regarding prohibition on competition tend to safeguard employer's interests. The new chapter on telework introduced the legal framework for this kind of atypical employment.

The PLC does not regulate all the issues that are part of labor law. There are many other statutes that are applicable, for example – on collective dismissals, or the protection of employees' claims in case of their employer's insolvency. Both phenomena came into effect after the transition in 1989. Other statutes regulate collective labor relations, such as the laws on trade unions, employers' organizations, collective labor disputes, and information and consultation rights of employee councils. Particular statutes concern situations pertaining to specific professional groups, such as civil servants, self-government officials, teachers and judges. There is still competence of government to introduce subordinate legislation, but these possibilities are currently much more limited in comparison with socialist period.

Russia

The current Russian Labor Code is a federal law and was enacted ten years after the dissolution of the USSR – in 2001 – and came into force in early 2002. Its adoption had been preceded with very long and tense disputes of a political nature. About 12 draft labor codes were under discussion in the Russian Duma (Parliament), four of them simultaneously, before the current text was adopted. The current RLC is a difficult social compromise. Although it is much younger than the Polish one, it has also undergone lots of amendments.

The RLC, like the PLC, is also the central act of labor legislation. It covers most, but not all, the labor law issues. The main 'separate' federal laws on labor include the Act on employment,[24] Act on trade unions,[25] Act on employers' associations, and several

---

[23] See. Mitrus L. The influence of Community regulations on Polish labor law, 'Archivum Iuridicum Cracoviense', Vol. XVI, Krakow 2008, pp. 107 and following.

[24] Zakon o zanyatostu naseleniya v Rossiyskoy Federazii [The Law on population employment in Russian Federation], 1991.

[25] Federalniy Zakon o professionalnih soyuzah, ih pravah i garantiyah deyatelnosti [Federal Act on Trade Unions, their Rights and the Guarantees of their Activity], January 12th, 1996.

others.[26] The issues of collective bargaining, collective agreements, and collective consultation rights are included in the Code itself. Other distinctive features of the RLC are the inclusion of particular norms for distinct categories of workers.[27] Unlike the PLC, the newer RLC does not include provisions on non-competition which is currently a matter that is still limited to academic debates.[28] A specific chapter on telework was introduced to the RLC in 2013.

Hungary

In the early 1990s it was necessary to adopt a completely new Labor Code in Hungary, as the old one was no longer suitable for regulating the new issues associated with the market economy. When the HLC entered into force in 1992, all the important statutes of the new capitalist system had already been adopted. The HLC contributed regulations on nearly all individual and collective labor issues. During the last 20 years the HLC has been amended more than 50 times. In 2011 the conservative Government decided to adopt a new Labor Code[29] (the 'new HLC'), which entered into force in July 2012. The main aim of the new HLC is to make the regulation more flexible and employer-friendly; in order to enhance the competitiveness of the Hungarian economy. This idea influences the whole new HLC. It emphasizes the significance of individual and collective agreements and gives both the partners of the employment contract and of the collective agreement stronger rights to regulate the employment relationship.[30] This principle is in line with the lessening protection of individual workers and trade union officials.[31] The new HLC contains very little protection against dismissal, increases the liability of workers for damages relating to the employment relationship, introduces the possibility of employers limiting worker's privacy[32] and makes the rules on working time as flexible as possible within the confines of the EU Directive

---

[26] Federalniy Zakon ob objedineniyah rabotodateley [Federal Act on Employers' Associations], November, 27, 2002. Sobraniye Zakonodatelstva Rossiyskoy Federazii.

[27] In Russia, an interesting feature of the past was that beside the Code of Laws on Labor most labor acts of technical character (certain types of working time for specific categories of workers, etc.) were adopted as joint acts of Government and Trade Unions Union (VCSPS). This demonstrates the particular role of unions in Russia that is discussed in Part 1, supra.

[28] See, for example: Stepanova E.A. Soglasheniya kak sredstva individualno-dogovornogo regulirovaniya otnosheniy v sfere nayomnogo truda [Agreements as means of individual regulation of employment relations] Sochetaniye gosudarstvennogo i dogovornogo regulirovaniya v sfere nayomnogo truda i sotsialnogo obespecheniya [The combination of statutory and contractual regulation in the field of employment and social security] Conference proceedings. Moscow, 2012. p. 424.

[29] 2012. évi. I. törvény a Munka Törvénykönyvéről [Act I. of 2012. on Labor Code].

[30] For example, collective agreements, and where there is no union – also works council agreements, can deviate from the Labor Code to the detriment of workers.

[31] Union officials enjoyed great protection from dismissal during the socialist regime and the 1992 HLC maintained this system. However, the new HLC limits the number of people protected and the scope of the protection. Union officials also had significant paid leave of absence for representing workers, the length of which has been reduced.

[32] Workers' privacy can be limited at work, if it is absolutely necessary for the aim of the employment relationship and is proportional with the aim. Workers have to be informed on the nature, conditions and probable length of the limitation.

2003/88/EC on working time. The new HLC, like the old one, regulates all rights and obligations relating to the employment relationship (even atypical employment) and all collective labor issues (trade unions, collective agreements, works councils, collective dispute resolution issues), excluding only the strike. Like in Poland, particular statutes regulate the relationship of some professional groups, e.g. civil servants, public-sector employees, armed employees, judges.

Common situation

Thus, in Hungary, Poland and Russia labor codes constitute the main sources of labor law.[33] They cover a broad range of issues, but they do not regulate the entire subject matter of labor law and the codes are supplemented by other statutes. However, the borderline between labor codes and other statutes may be different. For example in Poland and Hungary separate statutes concern the situation of some particular groups of employees (e.g. teachers, some categories of public officials), while in Russia they are partly covered by the Labor Code. In Poland many issues are regulated by separate statutes, such as collective dismissals and employer's insolvency. The same applies for collective labor law issues, including the legal situation of trade unions, employers' organizations, employee councils and collective disputes.[34] In Hungary all of these topics are covered by the HLC. In Russia the situation is between the Hungarian and Polish systems: there are separate laws on trade unions, employers' organizations and tripartite commission of social-labor matters[35] but the collective bargaining and collective conflicts are set up by the RLC.

It may be stated that labor codes are a dominant characteristic of the labor law systems in Central and Eastern Europe. There is tremendous difference between these countries and, for example, the USA, the UK or the Scandinavian countries.[36] In the countries studied here, there is continuity in regulating employment relations, but at the same time there are also changes which took place. Common to all three national labor law systems is the move away from an absolutely paternalistic system of regulation in the socialist time towards a more and more flexible labor market with less protection of workers. There are new codes (Hungary, Russia) or the old one that was substantially amended (Poland). It seems that adoption of the totally new labor code is a sign of significant change in the social policy of the country in question. However, in all the three countries the labor law regulations are amended very often. Obviously this reflects social tensions and problems in establishing the appropriate level of employee protection. The need to implement the EU directives in Poland and Hungary constitutes a very important factor in explaining patterns of change. It seems that labor regulation in these countries has not yet reached the level of stability and is subject to constant changes.

---

[33] In terms of everyday use, not the formal hierarchy of acts.

[34] Strangely enough, the Labor Code regulates collective labor agreements, which can be seen as inconsequence of the legislator.

[35] Federalniy Zakon o rossiyskoy trekhstoronney komissi po regulirovaniyu sozialno-trudovih otnosheniy [Federal Act on Russian Social-Labor Relations Tripartite Commission] No. 92-FZ of May, 1, 1999.

[36] Countries that do not have uniform Labor Codes, are usually common law countries or countries with a very long, organic development of labor law (like Germany and Austria).

c. Collective Agreements

Poland

Industrial relations were affected to a large extent by the transformation. In the socialist period there was no room for free and effective collective bargaining.[37] Since the radical changes of the political and economic system in 1989, Poland has been introducing the new labor deal. The development of collective labor relations since 1989 has not been a spontaneous process. The basic principles and legal basis for the activities of trade unions and employers' organizations as well as the procedure for settling collective disputes were introduced by the Parliament in 1991.

The regulation of collective labor agreements in Poland is the subject of chapter XI of the PLC (Arts 238–241). Amendments to the PLC of 1994 created the legal framework for free collective bargaining with a very broad scope of application. The only restrictions on the collective agreement's contents are that the agreement may not interfere with those matters which are regulated by mandatory rules and shall not infringe the rights of third parties. It is possible to conclude agreements at the plant level, as well as on sectoral, regional or national levels. There are no restrictions on the autonomy of the social partners in this respect. In practice, sectoral and other higher levels agreements are not common in Poland. Most agreements are concluded at the plant level. All employees are covered by an agreement, regardless of whether they are unionized or not.

The distinctive feature of Polish labor law seems to be the so-called 'social pacts'. They constitute another kind of collective agreements which causes particular concerns. They are concluded during the privatization of state-owned enterprises or other kinds of structural transformations in an establishment. Such agreements govern the situation of employees in such an establishment. Typically they introduce a ban on dismissal for a certain period of time and the right to financial compensation in case of terminating an employment contract. There is no clear statutory basis to making such an agreement. However, according to the well-established case-law of the Supreme Court they constitute a source of labor law and may serve as the basis for an enforceable claim.[38]

Hungary

The Hungarian regulation on collective agreements is very similar to the Polish. The extensive personal and content scopes of collective agreements have to be highlighted. As in Poland the vast majority of collective agreements are concluded for a particular establishment. Sectoral agreements are characterized by their poor quality, which means that their norms tend to replicate those of the HLC. Unlike Poland, the procedure of negotiations is hardly regulated. Consequently, the social partners have much freedom to determine the process by themselves. Social pacts do not exist in Hungary.

---

[37] However, to a limited extent, it was possible to conclude collective labor agreements for certain branches of industry, e.g. mining or steel industry.

[38] See also Mitrus L, *The Relationship Between Statutory Law, Collective Agreement and Employment Contract. The Case of Poland*, (w:) G. Kiss (ed.), *Recent Developments in Labour Law*, Budapest 2013, pp. 63–76.

Russia

In Russia, the procedure of collective bargaining is similar to the Polish and Hungarian with some immaterial differences. For example, collective agreements are always concluded for a fixed term (up to three years) with one possible extension of the term.[39] In Russia, like in Poland and Hungary, collective agreements add something substantial to the workers' rights only in exceptional cases.

d. Internal Regulations

Poland

In Poland an employer is competent to issue unilaterally an internal work regulation.[40] Work regulations set out the organization and order in the work process, along with the related rights and duties of the employer and employees (Art. $104–104^3$ PLC). They may regulate such matters as working time schedules, night-time hours, the method of confirming the arrival and presence at work as well as the procedure for justifying absence from work. Work regulations are not introduced if the provisions of collective labor agreement apply, or when an employer employs less than 20 employees.

An employer who employs at least 20 employees who are not covered by a collective labor agreement must determine the conditions of remuneration for work in the remuneration regulations. Other employment-related benefits may be determined as well (Art. 77^2 PLC).

Hungary

In Hungary every employer can establish unilateral work regulations to regulate such matters as working time, or data protection in the workplace. However, unilateral work regulation always has to remain within the framework of the HLC and the employment contract.

Russia

The same system of internal regulations is applicable in Russia, but it is not dependent on the size of the company and the existence of collective agreements. Certain types of work regulations are to be adopted 'taking into account of the company trade union's opinion' and some by the employer unilaterally. The procedure for 'taking into account' the trade union's opinion is established in the RLC (Art. 372). The procedure is quite convenient for the employer and at most may postpone the employer's decision up to ten days. Moreover, the procedure is only applicable when there is a trade union at the workplace. It therefore represents a very weak imitation of the EU's information and consultation system.[41] Nevertheless, these internal work regulations may be of crucial

[39] Article 43, paras 1 and 2; Art. 48, para. 2 of the RLC.

[40] Consultation with trade unions is necessary. If regulations are not agreed upon with the trade union within a period specified by the parties, or when there is no trade union at the establishment, the regulations are determined by the employer.

[41] In Poland and Hungary there are legal acts on the information and consultation of employees, see Part 4, infra.

importance for the substance of employment relations. For example, according to Article 101 of the RLC, an employer may establish a list of work positions with 'un-normalized working-day regime', which means that workers to whom such a regime is applied may 'episodically' be obliged by the employer to work beyond their ordinary working time. Such work is not considered as overtime.[42]

3. INDIVIDUAL LABOR LAW

a. Freedom of Employment Contract

It is often stressed by researchers that Western labor law was very much focused on collective issues from the end of nineteenth century and through much of twentieth.[43] The emphasis on collective bargaining and trade unions provoked the discussions about crisis or even 'the death of labor law' in the market-economy countries where trade unions have lost much of their membership and influence.[44] Paradoxically, unlike Western individualized society that relied on collective labor law extensively, the socialist system, despite its collectivist ideology, relied predominantly on detailed statutory regulation and individual mechanisms of workers' legal protection. Although Central and Eastern Europe countries' trade unions are facing very significant difficulties (see Part 4, infra), this does not lead to a wholesale discussion about the crisis of the labor law. The individual aspects of labor law that were established in the socialist times retain many of their features until now.

In the socialist era, work was an obligation on the citizens and there was almost no choice whether to work or not.[45] Failure to work was a criminal offence called (in Russian) *tuneyadstvo* (parasitism, literally – wasteful eating).[46] This norm was applied

---

[42] From the practical point of view, the actual meaning of 'episodically' remains unknown.

[43] See, for example: Arthurs H. Labour law after labour, in G. Davidov, B. Langille (eds.) *The Idea of Labour Law*. Oxford University Press, 2011. pp. 14 ff.

[44] See: C. Barnard, S. Deakin, G.S. Morris (eds.) *The Future of Labour Law. Liber Amicorum Sir Bob Hepple QC*. Hart Publishing, Oxford and Portland, Oregon, 2004; R. Blanpain, M. Weiss (eds) *Changing Industrial Relations and Modernisation of Labour Law. Liber Amicorum in Honour of Professor Marco Biagi*. Kluwer Law International, 2003; G. Davidov, B. Langille (eds.) *The Boundaries and Frontiers of Labour Law*. Hart Publishing, Oxford and Portland, Oregon, 2006; and many others.

[45] Article 9, para. (2) of the Hungarian Constitution of 1949 stated: 'Every employable citizen has the right, the obligation and the honor to work according to his capabilities.' The same provisions existed in the constitutions and legislation of all socialist countries. Ironically, the first Russian Constitution of 1918 that was adopted in the time of fierce anti-religious state campaign quoted the Bible with a passage, noting that the socialist system adheres to the principle 'who does not work, does not eat' (Art. 18 of the Constitution of 1918). Compare with: 'If a man will not work, he shall not eat' from the second epistle of Paul the Apostle to the Thessalonians.

[46] Article 209 of Russian Criminal Code of 1960 (Vedomosti Verhovnogo Soveta RSFSR, No. 40, Art. 591, 1960) stipulated punishment up to two years of imprisonment for 'systematic vagabondism or beggary or performance of other parasitic way of life which is being continued after repeated warning made by the administrative bodies'. Article 266 of the former Hungarian

rather rarely, either in political cases – to punish the dissidents;[47] or to 'anti-social elements' living on 'non-labor income'. Although the obligation to work was not applied to housewives with children, a vast majority of them were also working.

Given the obligation to work, the contractual nature of the employment relationship was in fact limited to the possibility of choosing the employer.[48] The terms of employment, such as wages, were set up in centralized manner according to huge lists of occupations and job positions – separate for manual workers and specialists.[49] Even if the company was willing to pay higher wages to an employee who was particularly desirable for its operations, there was no legal ground for this.

With the transition, the freedom of work has led to significant modifications of the law concerning all aspects of employment contract. Two examples demonstrate the way in which new norms address market-related issues, as opposed to the regulations of the socialist period.

In the socialist period, Article 101 of the PLC held that a full-time employee was not allowed to take up an additional job without the consent of an employer. Thus, the possibilities of entering into parallel employment with several employers were limited during socialist period. The abovementioned provision was abolished in 1989. But the freedom to work for several employers may in practice lead to infringing the rules on working time in all three countries. The problem at stake at present is to prevent an employer from establishing a company, hiring an employee to perform an 'additional' job, in what is in essence the entity (even if legally a different company). This arrangement enables the circumvention of working time restrictions. Considering that the employer may establish several additional companies, the actual working time may in fact become limitless.

Another indicator of changes is the growing interest on the regulation of competition in the context of the employment relationship. All three countries are concerned with the question, but each takes a different path. Polish law introduces the possibility of concluding a separate agreement on prohibition of competition.[50] In general, under such a contract an employee may not perform an activity that competes with his or her employer or perform work. In Russia the non-competition clause is not established by law and is held to contradict the freedom to work established by the Constitution. Employers are only protected by the law of commercial secrets. In Hungary the parties to an employment contract can conclude a non-competition agreement. The maximum length of such a prohibition was three years pursuant to the old HLC and was reduced

Criminal Code (Law IV. of 1978. 1978. évi IV. törvény a Büntető Törvénykönyvről, 266 §) regulated the crime of 'work deviation bearing danger for the public'. In Poland there was a special statute of 26 October 1982 on proceedings against persons avoiding work.

[47] The most notorious case was the accusation in 'tuneyadstvo' and imprisonment in 1964 of famous poet J. Brodskiy, later a Nobel Prize laureate in literature, because he could not prove that he was a poet as long as he did not belong to an official writers' organization.

[48] Even this was not always possible. For example the graduate of a university in a big city could be obligated to work in certain provincial entity for several years after the graduation.

[49] E.g. in Hungary the basic wage of the worker, the wage scale and the conditions of classification were determined by the Secretary of State for Labor Affairs. Art. 61 par. 1. of the Government Regulation Nr. 34/1967. (X.8.) on the implementation of the Labor Code.

[50] Arts 101^1–101^4 of the PLC.

to two years in the new HLC. If the employer does not provide an appropriate reward for the ban on employment, the agreement will be null and void.[51]

b. Equal Treatment in Employment

Socialist legislation did not use the very term 'discrimination'. However, workplace discrimination, as it appeared in the Western countries, was not a major problem as long as the employers were totally state-owned, and negotiations over placements and terms of work were very limited. The situation has changed after the transition, but the state of the law in this area is at different levels of development in the three countries studied here.

Russia

Currently although Russia ratified both ILO fundamental Conventions on discrimination[52] and other international treaties on the matter, and also introduced an article on prohibition of discrimination in the RLC,[53] case-law in discrimination issues is not well developed. While workers often win in labor law cases, their success in discrimination cases lags behind.[54] These outcomes may be attributed to problems with the high burden of proof that is required, or to a persisting administrative approach to the employment relationship that leads courts to a substantive misunderstanding regarding the very notion of non-discrimination.[55]

Hungary

As in Russia, workplace discrimination in Hungary was not widespread during the socialist period. After the change in the political regime, discriminatory practices developed in tandem with growth in unemployment.[56] Article 5 of the 1992 HLC clearly prohibited any kind of discrimination concerning the employment relationship. It shifted the burden of proof to the employer. In 2003 the Act on Equal Treatment and

---

51 Article 3(6) of the 1992 HLC and Art. 228 of the new HLC.

52 ILO Conventions No. 100 and 111.

53 Article 3 of the RLC.

54 There are no reliable statistics on this matter, but this opinion is shared by practicing labor lawyers.

55 For more details see the ILO discussion on the matter: International Labour Conference, 100th Session, 2011. Report of the Committee of Experts on the Application of Conventions and Recommendations (CEACR). Report III (Part 1A). P. 496. Or in Russian: Lyutov N. Rossiyskoye trudovoe zakonodatelstvo i mejdunarodniye trudoviye standarty: sootvetstvie i perspectivy sovershenstovaniya. Moscow, 2012. (Russian labor legislation and international labor standards: the issues of compliance and perspectives for modification) pp. 48–59. Available at 'Center for social and labour rights' website: http://trudprava.ru/files/pub/rostrudzak.pdf.

56 There are serious problems with discrimination related to the extremely low level of employment of Roma people in Hungary. See: Kertesi G.: Roma foglalkoztatás az ezredfordulón – A rendszerváltás maradandó sokkja, [Employment of Roma at the turn of the millenium – Long-lasting shock of the change of the regime] Szociológiai Szemle, 2005/2. p. 59, Kertesi G., 'The Employment of the Roma – Evidence from Hungary', pp. 12–13. Budapest Working Papers on the Labor Market, 2004/1.

Promotion of Equal Opportunities has been enacted, which regulates and prohibits discrimination uniformly and in a comprehensive way with regard to all fields of law.[57] The Act is applied, inter alia, to the employment relationship, broadly defined.[58] Any direct and indirect discrimination, harassment and retaliation is prohibited in the employment relationship.[59]

In 2004, the government established the Equal Treatment Authority, an independent organization for guaranteeing the implementation of the equal treatment principle.[60] Until early 2012 the Equal Treatment Authority had the right to make inquiries, whether on request or on its own initiative, to state whether the principle of equal treatment was violated. Every person, natural or legal, had the right to bring a complaint to the authority alleging that she or he was discriminated against. On the basis of its inquiry the authority adopted a resolution, in which it could impose a fine on the employer for violating the principle of equal treatment.[61] A considerable majority of the complaints received by the Authority were related to employment.[62]

In 2012 the Hungarian legislation seriously cut the power of the Authority, changing the procedural rules regarding the filing and investigation of complaints regarding violations of the equal treatment principle. Currently the Equal Protection Authority has limited public rights.[63] Similarly, until 2012 the labor inspectors had the right to review whether employers complied with the principle of equal treatment.[64] This right to review was also extended to the preparation of the employment relationship, that is – the hiring stage. However, since 2012 the labor inspectors no longer have the right. With the withdrawal of the rights and powers granted to the Equal Treatment Authority and the labor inspectors, workers who are discriminated against only have the

---

57 2003. évi CXXV. törvény az egyenlő bánásmódról és az esélyegyenlőség előmozdításáról [Act Nr. CXXV of 2003. on equal treatment and promotion of equal possibilities].

58 The Act has to be applied to all forms of employment in both public and private sectors. Furthermore, it applies for other legal relationships, which are intended to provide labor, e.g. contract for work.

59 Article 22.(1) contains two exemptions from the general principle specified for the employment relationship. Difference in treatment does not constitute discrimination, if a) it is a proportional, different treatment based on important and lawful conditions, justified by the feature or nature of the work, or b) the different treatment is based on religious or other beliefs, national or ethnic affiliations, and it directly arises from the special nature of the employer's organization and it is a proportional and real different treatment, justified by the content or nature of the activity concerned.

60 Egyenlő Bánásmód Hatóság [Equal Treatment Authority]. See its homepage, also in English: www.egyenlobanasmod.hu.

61 To get compensation for the discrimination the victim has to sue the violator at court. The Authority only imposes a fine.

62 See: Report of the activity of the Equal Treatment Authority in 2010 and on application of Act CXXV of 2003 on Equal Treatment and the Promotion of Equal Opportunities

http://www.egyenlobanasmod.hu/data/2010report.pdf., p. 4.

63 It can bring an action to the court to protect the right of a violated group of people. Furthermore, it has some information and consultation rights and the right to make a proposal for an Act.

64 1995. évi LXXV. törvény a munkaügyi ellenőrzésről 3. § (1) d) [Art. 3. § (1) d) Act Nr. LXXV. of 1996 on Labor Control].

possibility of suing their employers, which is obviously a lengthy and expensive procedure.

Poland

In Poland, the PLC of 1975 established (and continues to do so at present) the principle of equality of employees. According to Article 11 PLC employees have equal rights in respect of the same performance of the same duties. In an amendment to the PLC, the new chapter IIa – entitled 'Equal treatment in employment'[65] was added, with a view to implement Directives of the EU. Currently Polish labor law expressly states that there may be no differentiation between employees, on the basis of, in particular, sex, age, disability, race, religion, nationality, political beliefs, trade union membership, ethnic origin, belief, sexual orientation as well as type of an employment contract or full time or part time employment. The burden of proof of absence of discrimination lies upon employer.

To sum up, in all three countries there is a new approach to bans on discrimination and rules on equal treatment have been introduced with substantial practical importance. Consequently, equality in the workplace constitutes a new and important factor of labor law systems in the post-socialist countries. At the same time, the three countries are not uniform in their approach. Hungarian and Polish regulations have been influenced to a large extent by the detailed standards of EU law, while Russia has mainly adapted the more general ILO norms in the field without considerable implementation of anti-discrimination practices.

c. Trends in Regulating Working Conditions

The provisions of socialist labor law were relatively rigid. The statutory regulations introduced a tight framework for the employment relationship. For example, the original (1975) Article 18 § 1 PLC, required that employment contracts should be fully compatible with labor law's provisions. This article was amended and now states that the employment contract shall not be less favorable to employees than provisions of legislation.[66] A similar development can be seen in the Russian labor law. Similarly, Article 43(1) of the new HLC stipulates that the employment contract can derogate from the second part of the HLC (which regulates the employment relationship) and other sources of labor law, namely – the collective agreement and works council agreement, only in favor of the employees. The abovementioned provisions constitute a fundamental change in the status of labor law. Currently, the margin of discretion accorded to both the social partners and the parties to an employment relationship is much broader. To demonstrate this, we will indicate two examples of areas in which change is apparent.

i. Working time

Provisions on working time constitute a good example of changes that have taken place in all three countries. In the socialist period, the regulation of working time in all

---

65 Article 18^{3a} –Art. 18^{3e} of the PLC.

66 The amendment was introduced by the Law of 02.02.1996.

countries of the region were quite rigid. For example, the PLC of 1975 introduced eight hours per day and 46 hours per week, with possibilities for shorter arrangements. The corresponding norms for USSR were seven hours per day and 41 hours per week,[67] with shorter schedules for certain categories of work (harmful and dangerous work, juvenile work, etc.).

Following the political transformation, provisions on working time gradually became more flexible. Current Russian legislation on working time is established on a weekly basis – 40 hours with daily limitation only for juvenile workers.[68] Alongside the common regulatory provision, there are special possibilities for employers to introduce other arrangements, such as the 'unnormalized working-day regime' (see part. 2.d, supra).

In Hungary and Poland the developments on working time were strongly influenced by the law of the EU. In Poland the main amendments were introduced in 2003 with a view to implementing the requirements of the EU. The general amount of working time is eight hours per day and 40 hours per week, thus reducing working time in comparison to the past.

While the European Directive is considered a protective measure to guarantee against employing workers overtime, it also has many discretionary components to accommodate the employers' needs of flexibility. In Hungary, one of the main objectives in drafting the new HLC in 2011 was to take advantage of all the options provided for by the European Directive 2003/88/EC on working time in order to make the provisions in this field as flexible as possible.[69] On the whole, in both Hungary and Poland the reference periods for calculating work time have been extended, giving the employer broad discretion in the organization of work. Employers with continuous operations, in shift work, seasonal work, in so-called 'stand-by positions', as well as in certain positions in the air, road, rail and traffic sector can even unilaterally adopt a reference period of six months for calculating time.[70] The new HLC further provides for the

---

[67] Zakon SSSR of May, 7th, 1960 'O zavershenii perevoda v 1960 godu vseh rabochih I slujashih na semi- i shestichasovoy rabochiy den' [The USSR Law 'On finalization of transfer of all workers and employees in 1960 to six and seven hours working day'].

[68] Article 91 of RLC.

[69] See the government's declaration in: Széll Kálmán Terv – Magyar Munka Terv, [Plan of Széll Kálmán – Hungarian Work Plan, 2011.05.19. p. 47–48. Available: http://www.kormany.hu/download/e/a7/40000/Magyar_Munka_Terv.pdf.

[70] The so-called 'stand-by position' is a special institution in Hungarian labor law, which probably violates the provisions of Directive 2003/88/EC. Pursuant to § 91 of the new HLC 'stand-by position' shall mean where: a) due to the nature of the job, no work is performed in at least one-third of the employee's regular working time based on a longer period, during which – however – the employee is at the employer's disposal; or b) in light of the characteristics of the job and of the working conditions, the work performed is significantly less strenuous and less demanding than commonly required for a regular job. To those employed in a 'stand-by position' different rules apply. Their normal daily working time can be 12 hours, the scheduled normal (!) working time can be 24 hours and scheduled weekly working time can last up to 72 hours. Within these extended time brackets, the stand-by workers do not receive a supplement for overtime, therefore composing a segment of an extremely cheap workforce. It was a political decision to maintain this institution in the new HLC, as thousands of people work in such positions, e.g. in the railway, doorkeepers, firemen, repairmen, technicians, etc.

possibility of setting a reference period of one year in collective agreements and the conditions it imposes are quite loose – 'technical reasons or reasons related to work organization' (§ 94 (3) new HLC). Another sign of the far-reaching flexibilization of measuring working time is the introduction of the so-called 'payroll period' which is in fact a rolling reference period, meaning that the reference period starts every week from the beginning. This provides another possibility to the employer to schedule the employees' working time very flexibly.

In addition to the flexibility in framing the reference period for calculating working time, the law in Hungary extends broad possibilities of introducing specific working schedules at a particular branch or an establishment, depending on the kind of economic activity and the employers' needs. The law also recognizes the possibility of concluding individual agreements on working time for a particular employee.

ii. Payment of wages

The regulation of wages is another example of change. In the centrally planned socialist economy the conditions of remuneration were largely determined by the state authorities, with possibilities of introducing changes according to the branch, industry or type of an undertaking. However, the employment contracts, or the preferences of the employee or the employing entity, were irrelevant as far as determination of remuneration was concerned. Following the transition, the determination of wages and benefits reflects the differences in the relative weight of labor law's sources in the three countries (statutory provisions, collective agreements, internal regulations and individual contracts).

A common feature of all three countries is that statutory law determines the minimum remuneration, the amount of which is adjusted annually. However, when looking at the statutory provisions in the broader context of the law's sources, there are also important differences.

In Poland the conditions of remuneration for work and other work-related benefits are currently regulated primarily by collective labor agreements, as well as by remuneration regulations that are issued by an employer. The conditions of remuneration in state-owned entities are specified by an executive regulation issued by a particular Minister, provided that employees are not covered by collective labor agreements. It is certainly permitted to stipulate conditions of remuneration in employment contracts, although such contractual provisions usually reflect the rules accepted at the particular establishment. Generally speaking, there is a broad margin of discretion to determine remuneration. It should be indicated that other work-related 'fringe benefits' have become a common component in remuneration schemes, including such benefits as health or dental care for employees and their families. The same is true for Hungary where employers often provide vouchers for meals, holidays, health care, etc. This method is widespread due to the advantageous tax provisions of such vouchers.

Unlike Poland, in Hungary and in Russia collective agreements play a minor role in determining remuneration. It is a special characteristic of the Hungarian situation that many collective agreements do not prescribe the levels of, and rules on, remuneration; or even if they do, the remuneration set in the collective agreement is only slightly higher than the statutory minimum wage that is set in a government's decree.[71] Therefore two factors are dominant in the determination of remuneration, namely statutory law and the employment contract. Exemplary case for the significance of statutory regulation is that both the old and the new HLCs include detailed regulations on wage supplements and prescribe their levels. In this way the state overtakes the role of social partners.

In Russia wages are also currently regulated in much more flexible way. Instead of the Soviet 'unified tariff and qualifications net' that established wages for any specific type of work by statutory norms, now privately-owned employers are generally bound only by minimum wage requirements and provisions on form and periods of payment. One of the serious problems in this respect is that the minimum wages' payment is currently much less[72] in Russia than in the EU member states with comparable GDP per capita level.[73] The payment of wages in state-budgetary institutions is now also much more flexible. Since 2008 state-financed employers have been covered by so-called 'new system of wages payment';[74] the system of wage payment in state institutions is now established by their director, so management is completely free to establish the wage levels. This broad discretion in public institutions obviously leads to corruption.

d. Modification of the Employment Contract

The freedom to modify the employment contract in the socialist times was very much connected with the general limitation of freedom to negotiate its terms. In Russia the modification of contract was (and in certain situations is now) called 'a transfer of worker'. Such an approach is rooted in the 1920s, and supposes an administrative regulation of labor: if the worker systematically did not perform his/her task in a proper way, he or she could be 'transferred' to a less-qualified (and paid) job by the employer without the consent of worker. In the socialist Hungarian labor law, 'transfer of the worker' to another employer was only possible with his/her consent, but 'transfer' to another position was one of the disciplinary measures.[75]

In all three countries, employment contracts may be amended by the mutual consent of the employer and the worker. However, in Hungary the employer can unilaterally order employees to temporarily work in another position, in another workplace or for

---

[71] There are two kinds of minimum wage in Hungary, namely – minimum wage and guaranteed wage minimum. The latter is be applied to those employees who are required to have a secondary school qualification. These categories of minimum wage are applied to all employees in Hungary without exception.

[72] Since 2015 it has been 5965 rubles per month, i.e. about 100 US dollars. Federalniy Zakon 'O vnesenii izmeneniy v statyu 1 Federalnogo zakona o minimalnom razmere oplaty truda' [Federal Law 'On amending article 1 of Federal Law 'On minimum wage level'] of December 1st 2014 No. 408-FZ.

[73] See the minimum wage data at World Bank, The International Finance Corporation. Doing Business Report, 2014. GDP data may be seen at International Monetary Fund World Economic Outlook Database.

[74] The system is established by the Government Resolution of August 5, 2008, No. 583.

[75] Article 55 of the 1967 HLC.

another employer.[76] The maximum duration of this cannot exceed 44 working days a year, but collective agreements can prolong this period. In practice the permissible maximum length of the reassignment is controversial; the new HLC maintained this rule unaltered.[77] Similarly, in Poland an employer can assign new tasks for a period no longer than three months in any calendar year. It may not result in the reduction of employee's remuneration and must correspond to employee's qualifications. In Russia it is permitted to assign tasks outside the ordinary duties of the employee without his or her consent in cases of catastrophes or the necessity to prevent the stoppage of the operation of the entity or for the replacement of an absent worker.[78] Except for the catastrophe case the transfer to the lower qualified job is only permitted with the written consent of worker.

In Poland an employer may also unilaterally issue a changing notice.[79] A notice of termination of work or remuneration conditions is considered made when an employer proposes other conditions of employment. If the employee rejects the proposed work, the employment contract is terminated at the end of notice period. This conditional termination – which is called in German '*Änderungskündigung*' – does not exist in Hungary, as it is considered a violation of the freedom of contract. In Russia there is a possibility for the employer to offer the amendment of the employment contract to the employee on 'technological or organizational reasons applicable to work' with two months' notice.[80] If the employee does not agree to the amendment, the employer is entitled to dismiss him/her with two weeks' severance pay.

e. New Trends in the Termination of an Employment Contract

Socialist era – protection and control

There are several ways to terminate an employment contract. Generally speaking, the contract can be terminated by the mutual consent of the parties, upon a declaration of one of the parties with or without notice, after the expiry of the period for which a contract has been concluded or upon the date of completion of the task it was concluded for. A contract can also automatically expire in cases determined in the Labor Code and other statutes (e.g. the death of an employee). Protection against dismissal is one of the basic issues of individual labor law. The economic and social transformation has led to legal amendments in this area, although in particular countries of Central and Eastern Europe different developments took place.

The employer in the socialist time was not always free to hire and dismiss workers. In some situations, such as an educational institution's direction of a graduate 'young specialist' to a particular employer by an administrative authority, the employer was obligated to hire the specific worker. In most situations the employer had to fill the specified number of vacancies with workers having certain qualifications. The employment contract was therefore a document that fixed and reflected the commencement of

---

76 Articles 83/A. and 105–106. of the 1992 HLC.

77 Articles 53 and 58 of the new HLC.

78 Paragraphs 2 and 3, Art. of the 72^2 RLC.

79 Article 42 of the PLC.

80 Article 74 of the RLC.

the employment relationship. The employment relationship could not be terminated by the employer without cause, as was directly indicated in law. For example, in Russia, Article 33 of the last Soviet Code of Laws on Labor (KZoT)[81] permitted dismissal of an employee only in certain situations,[82] including the employee's non-conformity with the job due to lack of qualification or health condition; systematic non-fulfillment of working duties if an employee has previously been disciplined; absence from work for three hours or more during one working day without justifiable cause; attendance of work in a state of alcoholic, drug or toxic intoxication.

To some categories of employees, this list was applied in limited way, to others it was more extensive. For example, a pregnant woman could (and can even now) only be dismissed on her own initiative, or in a case of company's winding up: such a regulation, on one hand, protected the employees from the employers' abuse. On the other hand, it was also a tool of control over the employees themselves. This control was achieved by the use of 'labor booklets'[83] – a kind of 'career passport' that was issued to the employee by his first employer and was subsequently kept and filled by all employers throughout his career. These booklets contained (and in Russia still contain) information about changes of the worker's job positions, disciplinary awards (but not penalties, except for the dismissal ground), the dates and grounds of dismissals. Although it was not permitted to note in the booklet penalties against the employee, the notification that an employee was dismissed on 'shameful' grounds from the statutory list, restricted his chances of finding a decent job in the future.

In the market economy the booklet system became less effective because of the multiplicity of employees who are not employed by state-owned establishments, and whose employers do not share information with each other. This system is therefore expected to be abandoned soon even where it still persists, namely – in Russia.

In Hungary labor booklets existed in the communist time, but were abolished after the change in the political regime. Instead, the 1992 HLC requires the employer to give the worker a 'work certificate' within one year after the termination of the employment relationship. The certificate contains the scope of the employee's activities, and upon the explicit request of the worker also an assessment of his activities. Recently, Article 81 new HLC ruled out that at the worker's request the employer was obliged to give him a written assessment of his work.

In Poland there was (and still is) an employer's obligation to issue a special work certificate, which should be handed out at the end of an employment relationship (Arts 97–99 PLC). This document states the information about conditions of employment, its duration, as well as information on the way of the contract's termination. Before 1989 there was also an obligation to issue an opinion about an employee if he so wished.

---

81 Kodeks Zakonov o Trude Rossiyskoy Federatsii, Art. 33.

82 There were special dismissal grounds for certain categories of workers (directors, etc.) but these grounds were still exhaustively listed in legislation.

83 Labor booklets are not a Soviet invention. Initially they were issued in Western Europe. Recently, many people have had problems, if they have to prove their earlier employment relationships when claiming entitlement to pension, because they cannot easily provide proof of their earlier employment phases.

This obligation has been set aside, and currently an employer is not obliged to issue such an opinion, although he certainly may issue such a document.

Following transition, the three countries experienced change in the law on dismissals, although some remained more stable than others. Moreover, the three countries maintain distinct approaches to the regulation of dismissals.

Russia

The Russian system, in which there is a limited list of grounds for dismissal, has outlasted the socialist regime. At present, Russian legislation provides such a list, which has been adapted to a certain extent, so as conform to market economy principles.[84] In fact, such a system represents the different model of employment protection legislation that prevails in Russia, compared to the EU countries. While in the latter the workers are protected in the case of dismissal mainly by the system of dismissal notices, which terms are usually dependent on the tenure and with monetary compensation, Russian legislation protects employees from the very fact of dismissal. While in most EU countries the employer may dismiss an employee for economic reasons (with significant compensation, notice in advance and severance payment), in Russia economic dismissal is more strictly defined as the liquidation of a certain position within the company. This means that if employer dismisses an employee from a particular position, e.g. a junior accountant, it may not hire anyone to this liquidated position for a certain period, which is not identified in law. The dismissal notice in modern Russian legislation is also applied, but only for several grounds of dismissal, such as collective redundancy[85] or expiration of temporary employment contract[86] and this term is not dependent on tenure. Such rules are in clear contradiction with the requirements of Article 4, paragraph 4 the European Social Charter, as it is interpreted by the European Committee on Social Rights.[87] But it must be borne in mind that these requirements are elaborated with respect to different systems of dismissal protection that prevail in other CE countries that do not have the limited list of dismissal grounds established by law. This system of dismissal protection is understood by trade unions and civil society as one of the basic pillars of Russian labor law and it is unlikely that it can be changed significantly in the near future.

Hungary

The exceptional nature of the Russian system was not universally applied in all of the socialist countries. For example, in Hungary there was no single list of permissible grounds of dismissal. The law permitted various grounds for dismissal, but the real and clear ground for dismissal always had to be given. Even so, there were several rules that rendered dismissals more difficult. Only in exceptionally justified cases was it permitted to dismiss a worker employed for a long time by the same company, who had

---

[84] The grounds for dismissal are now contained in Arts 77, 81 and some others articles of RLC and separate laws that relate to specific categories of workers.

[85] Two months' notice – Art. 180, para. 2 of the RLC.

[86] Three days – Art. 79, para. 2 of the RLC.

[87] Council of Europe. Digest of the Case Law of the European Committee of Social Rights, 2008. pp. 46–47.

an outstanding work performance and exemplary behavior. There was also a detailed list of periods during which dismissal was prohibited. It was not permitted to dismiss a worker during illness, pregnancy, child-care leave, or during military service, etc.[88] Also in some instances in which workers were bearing familial responsibilities the employer needed an extraordinary ground to dismiss the worker, like in case of a single parent until the child reached the age of 18.[89]

The 1992 HLC differentiated between ordinary and extraordinary dismissal. An employer or employee could terminate an employment relationship by extraordinary dismissal in case the other party: a) deliberately or by gross negligence committed a grave violation of any substantive obligation arising from the employment relationship, or b) otherwise engaged in conduct rendering further existence of the employment relationship impossible.[90] The HLC provided three possible vague grounds of ordinary dismissal. According to Article 89.(3) HLC an employee could be dismissed only for reasons in connection with his/her ability, his/her behavior in relation to the employment relationship or with the employers' operations. The employer had to specify one concrete reason of dismissal on one of the three broadly defined grounds. Specific reasons can include, for example, restructuring, personnel reduction (employer's operation), replacement of the worker with a more qualified one, a driver losing his/her driving license, etc., (ability of workers), or if the worker violates his obligations (behavior in relation with the employment relationship). Specifying the reason of dismissal is more of an administrative obligation, rather than a real protection. Protection is constituted by the fact that during certain periods the employer is prohibited to dismiss workers (e.g. illness; sick, maternity or pregnancy leaves, etc.). The 2012 new HLC did not bring great changes in this system. It maintained the three groups of grounds of ordinary dismissal described above. The most important protected periods remain in force, except the protection during illness, which was often abused by workers. When a worker learned that he/she would probably be dismissed he/she went to the doctor, who signed him/her off work. The new HLC is intended to put an end to this practice.[91]

A similar path of change can be observed in the Hungarian law regarding remedies for wrongful dismissal. While originally, under socialist labor law, the prevailing norm was that of an absolute right for reinstatement, the law has gradually been transformed to the compensation principle in the 2012 HLC. The socialist HLC stated that in cases where the employer wrongfully dismissed the worker, the latter has to be set in a situation as if nothing had happened; i.e. he had to be reinstated and his or her damages

88 Art. 22. of 48/1979. XII.1., Order on the Enforcement of the Labor Code.

89 34/1967. (X.8.) kormányrendelet a Munka Törvénykönyve végrehajtásáról, 25–28. § [Arts. 25–28. of the Government Regulation Nr. 34/1967. (X.8.) on the Implementation of the Labor Code].

90 Article 96.(1) of the 1992 HLC.

91 In Russia this problem is solved in a more worker-friendly way: although the prohibition to dismiss during illness is left intact, the Supreme Court has explained that the employee who informed his employer about his sickness only at the actual time of dismissal, is violating the general principle of good faith. Para. 27 of Supreme Court of Russian Federation Ruling No. 2 of March 17, 2004.

had to be compensated.[92] The 1992 HLC maintained the reinstatement as the main principle. In some cases the employer could ask the court for the omission of a reinstatement order. In 1999 the regulation was changed and the employer was, as a rule, no longer obliged to reinstate the worker. Nevertheless, reinstatement continued to be obligatory if the dismissal violated the principle of due process, the principle of equal treatment, particular dismissal prohibition rules, or the special rules protecting union officials. The main principle of the 2012 HLC is the remedy of compensation for wrongful dismissal. An employer has a reinstatement obligation only in limited and clearly defined situations, such as the violation of the principle of equal treatment, the employee being a workers' representative, termination taking place during a prohibited period[93] and some other strictly defined situations.[94]

Poland

A different legislative technique was used in Poland, where, generally speaking, there is a continuity of legislation on termination of an employment contract. For the extent of protection, the type of employment contract was, and remains, of primary importance. The highest level of protection against dismissal is guaranteed for workers employed by a contract for an indefinite period. In such a situation, a termination with notice has to be justified.[95] An employer must inform a plant-level trade union about the intention to terminate the contract and must provide grounds justifying the termination. The abovementioned employer's duty concerns those employees who are trade union members and those non-unionized employees that asked trade union for a representation. A trade union may present its objections within five days.[96] The employer must consider the objections presented by a trade union, although the final decision is for the employer to make. A dismissed employee may challenge a termination of a contract in the labor court (see below).

The Polish labor law does not introduce the list of grounds that may constitute a reason for dismissal. Instead, the concept of 'justified' termination is broad and flexible. There is an extensive amount of judicial decisions of Polish courts, including the Supreme Court, on the notion of justified dismissal. Thus, both reasons lying on either the employer's or employee's side may be reason for dismissal.

An employer should observe some procedural requirements with regard to termination of an employment contract.[97] A notice of termination must provide grounds which justify the termination and must include information on employee's right of appeal to the labor court. With regard to a contract for indefinite period, the period of notice depends on the employment period within a given employer and amounts to two weeks,

---

92 1967. évi II. törvény a Munka Törvénykönyvéről, 31.§ [Art 31. Act II. of 1967 on Labor Code] and 48/1979. (XII. 1.) MT rendelet a Munka Törvénykönyve végrehajtásáról, 29. § [Art. 29 of the 48/1979. (XII. 1.) Order on the Enforcement of the Labor Code].

93 The employer is not allowed to dismiss a worker during her pregnancy, during child-birth leave, unpaid leave for caring a child, voluntary army service and during the time participating in reproductions treatment for a maximum period of six months. Art. 65 (3) Labor Code.

94 See Art. 83 of the new HLC.

95 Article 45, PLC.

96 Article 38, PLC.

97 Article 30, PLC.

one month or three months. As far as other types of employment contract is concerned – the period of notice is shorter and amounts from three days to two weeks.

The fixed-term contracts theoretically should not be terminated upon notice before the expected time of its termination (e.g. the specified day). However, upon the conclusion of a contract for more than six months, the parties may provide for the possibility of early termination with a two-week notice period.[98] Polish law does not stipulate a maximum duration of a contract for a fixed term. It is open to too many abuses by employers, especially in periods of high unemployment.

Each termination of an employment contract is effective, even when an employer violates the labor law provisions on dismissal. An employee is entitled to challenge a termination of an employment contract before the labor court. The court can declare the notice of termination ineffective. An employee can claim reinstatement or financial compensation.

There are many categories of employees who enjoy broader protection and who should not be dismissed in 'regular way', i.e. their contract should not be ended upon the termination with notice.[99] This principle applies to e.g. employees who are four years or less from retirement age and will be entitled to an old age pension, employees during a justified absence from work (e.g. during illness), female employees during pregnancy and maternity leave, and trade union officers during their term of office and one year after it elapses. In some cases a termination is allowed provided there has been consent from a body representing the employee.

Each type of employment contract can be exceptionally terminated without notice. An employer may terminate an employment contract without notice due to employee's fault in three situations: an employee's serious disciplinary fault; committing a crime, which prevents the further employment; an employee liable losing a license required to perform the work (e.g. a driver loses a driving license).[100]

Over time, in Poland there were no substantial amendments with regard to rules on dismissal protection. The only major legislative change was the introduction of a special procedure for collective dismissals in 1989 by a separate statute. This regulation was replaced by the statute of 2003 that concerns termination of a contract for reasons not related to employees.[101] This so-called law on collective dismissal covers all terminations based on the reasons connected with an establishment, both individual and collective. The statute introduces particular conditions for collective dismissals, mainly a requirement for concluding an agreement between the employer and a trade union, and provides special rights for dismissed employees, i.e. severance pay, and possibility of entering into a new employment contract with the same employer when the new staff are recruited.

In sum, the legislative technique in Poland, which describes the reason of termination in a general way that is 'universal', was effective both under socialist period and after transition. However, some important changes took place in the judiciary's approach.

---

98 Article 33, PLC.

99 At the same time they may be terminated without notice, especially in the event of a grave violation of the employee's basic duties.

100 Article 52, PLC.

101 Journal of Laws 2015, item 192.

Whereas before 1989 labor courts were very protective of employees, they have come to be more 'employer-friendly' and currently they take into account needs of an establishment to a greater extent than before. Exactly the same change in the attitude of the labor law judges can be noticed in Hungary and Russia, as well.

The abovementioned analysis certainly does not exhaust all changes of individual labor law that occurred after the collapse of socialism.[102] Certainly, different solutions have been introduced as far as particular institutions are concerned. However, in general it can be stated that in post-communist countries the regulations on employment contract became much more flexible than before. Certainly, statutory provisions still provide the minimum level of employee protection and limit the will of the parties. However, employers and employees (as well as social partners) enjoy broader margin of discretion with regard to determining the content of an employment relationship. Some new phenomena are connected with universal trends on labor markets (especially introducing new forms of employment, e.g. telework, temporary agency work) but majority of them constitute a result of a transformation to market economy.

4. COLLECTIVE LABOR LAW

a. The System of Collective Employee Representation

The system of collective employee representation is different in the Eastern European countries depending on whether or not they are member states of the EU. In the EU countries works councils exist as a second channel of employee representation. In some states works councils were introduced shortly after the political transition, (e.g. in Hungary – 1992); in others countries they were introduced later, under the influence of the EU (e.g. in Poland – 2006, implementing the European Directive 2002/14/EC). By contrast, in Russia only unions represent workers. The Russian law sometimes mentions 'other representatives of the employees' but there is almost no practice of non-union representation.[103]

Hungary introduced works councils in 1992 as a second channel of workers' representation, side by side with the trade unions. Trade unions felt jeopardized by the new rival organ and insisted on preserving their exclusive right to conclude collective agreements at the company level and their participation rights. A works council is elected by the workers in every workplace with more than 50 employees. At workplaces with 16–50 workers, a representative of the workforce (shop steward) is elected, who has the same status and rights as the works council.[104] There are no

[102] For example: provisions on holidays leave became more flexible in Poland.

[103] For more details see respective authors' contributions in: Workers' Representation in Central and Eastern Europe: Challenges and Opportunities for the Works Councils' System, *Bulletin of Comparative Labour Relations* No. 85, R. Blanpain, N. Lyutov (eds.). Aspen: Wolters Kluwer, 2014.

[104] Article 236. (1) new HLC. The number of employees is counted at the employer or at the employer's independent establishment or division.

sanctions for neglecting this rule and no guarantees in place to enforce its application. Thus, in only 13–18 percent of the companies do works councils operate.[105]

Theoretically, works councils are intended to be the instrument of cooperation with the employers, whereas trade unions are rather the instrument of bargaining. The main function of Hungarian and Polish works councils are to take part in information and consultation procedures. The rights of works councils in Poland and Hungary are rather weak compared with their German counterparts. In Hungary works councils have the right to co-decision only in one clearly described and very limited social welfare issue.[106] In Poland they do not have any co-decision rights. Works councils have to be informed on the financial and employment situation of the company and on planned decisions, which can bring significant changes in the organization of the company.

In both Poland and Hungary there is an unclear division of responsibility between the trade unions and works councils, as well as overlapping information and consultation rights. It is a difficult problem in practice: with whom an employer should co-operate and what would be the consequence of disregarding employee representation? The problem is augmented by the fact that the majority of collective agreements are concluded at the enterprise level. Both trade unions and works councils operate at the same level, namely at the workplace. Therefore they can be seen as a duplication of workplace-level representation rather than dualism of different employee representation systems. In reality, works councils play a minor role in the protection of the employees' interests.

The division of responsibility between the works councils and trade unions is not static. In Hungary, the new HLC 2012 accorded works councils a new competence. In companies where a trade union does not have 10 percent membership of the workforce and the employer is not covered by a collective agreement, the works council has the right to conclude with the employer an agreement with normative power.[107] In this case the works council agreement can regulate all terms and conditions of employment relationship, except for wages, and it applies to all the workers of the company.

Unlike Hungary and Poland, Russia does not have a similar institutionalized system of works councils. However, the 'taking into account' procedure (see Part 2.d., supra; requiring the employer to take into account the trade union's position) can be viewed as an imitation of the EU works councils system, although it is far from being effective in protecting the workers' interests. In 2013 the provision about 'works councils' was introduced in the RLC,[108] but this body is chosen by the *employer* in order to give

[105] See the empirical survey of Neumann: Neumann L. Szakszervezet? Üzemi tanács? Egyik se? [Trade unions? Works Councils? Neither of them?] Munkaügyi Szemle, February 2011. p. 1. The proportion is higher in cases of employers with more than 50 employees. Pursuant to the survey of the Hungarian Central Statistical Office [Központi Statisztikai Hivatal] in 2009 32.7 percent of the employees – working for an undertaking with more than 50 employees – answered that there were works councils at their workplace. See: Statisztikai Adatok, [Statistical Data] Bálint M. (ed.) available: http://econ.core.hu/file/download/mt09/hu/statisztika.pdf p. 298. (last visited 8. May 2012.)

[106] Pursuant to § 263. new HLC the employer and the works council shall collectively decide on the administration of welfare funds.

[107] Article 268.(1) new HLC.

[108] Article 22 of the RLC as amended by Federal Law No.95-FZ of May 7, 2013.

advice concerning the company development. It therefore has nothing in common with usual notion of the term 'works council' and is aimed only at imitation of social policy in this field.

b. The State of Trade Unions

The transition of former socialist trade unions into democratic organizations and the formation of new trade unions created a difficult challenge in Eastern Europe. As former supporters of the socialist regime, the legitimacy and reliability of the 'old' trade unions as real representatives of workers had been questionable for a long time. New trade unions that were founded after the transition face similar difficulties as their counterparts in Western Europe, particularly the small number of members and the problem of obtaining democratic legitimacy and status of representation. When examining two factors that demonstrate the power of trade unions, namely the number of members and the number of strikes they have carried out, it becomes obvious, that in Poland and Hungary only some trade unions are powerful, in sectors which were previously owned by the state and where the earlier structures have changed the least, for example – the Hungarian railway sector. In Russia, the most active and ready to initiate strikes are the 'new' trade unions – mainly those representing workers in manufacturing companies with foreign investment.

Most trade unions in Hungary are not powerful enough to negotiate with the employer as an equal bargaining partner. This was clearly demonstrated by the impact of the trade unions' reaction to the draft of the new HLC, which was presented by the government in 2011. Although the proposed change was to the detriment of workers, trade unions were not able to demonstrate their power, articulate their interests or organize significant strikes. Demonstrations gathered only hundreds of people. Unions were fragmented and the government used this fragmentation to negotiate only with certain trade union federations.[109] These trade unions were criticized for having government-friendly policy and supporting the government's politics for particular advantages.

The successor to the earlier union that had the state-endorsed monopoly, is still the dominating union – the Federation of Independent Trade Unions of Russia (FNPR). According to the FNPR's statement, it unites more than 95 percent of total union members in Russia.[110] FNPR is frequently criticized for being more interested in close relations with state authorities than in defending the interests of the employees. After the change in the regime, new trade union federations were formed but they are incomparably smaller and are much weaker at the political level.[111]

---

[109] Ten days before the adoption of the new HLC the government concluded a one-and-a-half page long agreement with four trade unions' representatives. In this agreement the trade unions' rights have been slightly extended and therefore the unions declared that they mainly support the adoption of the new act.

[110] FNPR official site: http://fnpr.ru/n/252/4890.html.

[111] The main 'alternative' trade union federation is Russian Labor Confederation (Konfederatsiya Truda Rossii, KTR). See its official site: http://www.ktr.su/.

In Poland trade unions are very powerful in large enterprises, but practically do not exist in small workplaces. This fact affects the Polish system of industrial relations to a large extent, because only trade unions are competent to conclude a collective labor agreement or declare a strike. In large enterprises there are usually several trade unions, which more often compete among each other than cooperate. The small trade unions quite often raise many demands as a way of justifying their existence. This situation is very similar to Russia. On the other hand, there are trade unions that are representative at the national level. This requirement is fulfilled in Poland by those organizations that have at least 300 000 members and are active in various branches of the economy. They enjoy the right to be consulted on drafts regarding labor law and social security. They can also suggest the relevant bodies to enact a new legislative act although they do not enjoy independent legislative initiative. In general it should be said that trade unions have more competences than employers' organizations, which act according to legislation from 1991. These associations can be seen as a new institution in industrial relations, introduced at times of transition.

c. Unionization Rate and Protection of Trade Unionists

It is difficult to determine the exact number of trade union members, since there are no reliable statistics on this data. In Hungary and Poland the rate of unionization is fairly low and trade union membership has been continuously declining in recent years. This trend started in tandem with the change of the regime. It is estimated that in Hungary approximately 12 percent of the employees are union members.[112] In Poland it may be estimated that approximately 10–12 percent of all workers are trade union members. The level of trade union membership in Russia is higher, ranging at approximately 45 percent of the total number of employees.[113] Although this level is rather high compared to many other countries, the figures should not be overestimated, as many of the unions can hardly be considered independent. There is a sharp division between the dominant majority 'old' trade unions and the 'new' or 'independent' trade unions. The former often do not act as real collective bargaining agents. They are affiliated to the company's management and are in fact not independent. Due to the system of collective bargaining that is established by the RLC, they can effectively block the attempts of minority unions to perform real collective bargaining (see infra).

Trade union membership is not evenly distributed. In Hungary, trade union density differs strongly between economic sectors. Union membership level is relatively high only in the public sector, the public utilities sector and in branches that belonged to the state in the past, like the energy sector, transportation, post, public administration,

---

[112] See: survey of the Hungarian Central Statistical Office [Központi Statisztikai Hivatal] from 2009, In: Statisztikai Adatok, [Statistical Data] M. Bálint (ed.) available: http://econ.core.hu/file/download/mt09/hu/statisztika.pdf p. 295. In 2001 19.7 percent and in 2004 16.9 percent of all workers were members of trade unions. This data clearly show the decreasing tendency.

[113] Calculated by the authors on the basis of the total workforce in Russia and the number of members announced by the biggest trade-union associations.

education and healthcare.[114] By contrast, in small- and medium-sized companies trade unions are rarely present. Altogether, trade unions represent workers in only 12–15 percent of the economic enterprises.[115]

Coverage rate is slightly higher in Hungary than union density due to the extended scope of collective agreements.[116] The difference results from the fact that coverage of collective agreements is determined by the employer's status. If an employer is covered by a collective agreement then all of his workers are covered, independent of their union affiliation. Another factor that determines the level of coverage is the extension of some collective agreements. Despite these rules of coverage, the prevailing decentralized structure of bargaining resists broader coverage. In more centralized systems – where collective bargaining takes place at branch level – the coverage rate is higher than in the decentralized systems of collective bargaining, like Hungary or Poland.

There is a clear tendency in Eastern European countries to loosen the protection of trade union representatives. In Russia and Hungary the guarantees were previously much stronger.[117] In these states the earlier protection (limitations on dismissal) were applied to any worker who was elected to the trade union body, and the protection was extended not only to dismissals but also to the transfer of the employee to another position and to any disciplinary sanction. Moreover, in Russia the protection was applicable to any ground of dismissal. Currently the rules are more refined and offer a lesser blanket of protection (see Part 3.e., supra on the changing law of dismissals).

d. The Right to Conclude Collective Agreements

At the company level

Trade unions are the main representatives of workers in all three states and they enjoy a broad range of rights, the most significant being the right to collective bargaining and to negotiate collective agreements. There is no uniform system for the right to conclude collective agreements. Every state has its own system. A common feature of collective bargaining in Hungary, Poland and Russia is that it can take place at several levels. It is permitted to conclude agreements at the level of a particular establishment, as well as at the branch of industry, region or the entire country. Still, the structure of collective bargaining in Poland and Hungary is strongly decentralized. Collective bargaining usually takes place at the company level and collective agreements are in most cases single-employer (company) agreements.

---

114 Ibid. p. 295. In certain sectors, like construction, trade, catering and communication unionization rate is under 3 percent.

115 See: the empirical survey of Neumann note 105 above, p. 1. In about 78 percent of the undertakings there are no kinds of employees' representatives, neither unions, nor works councils.

116 Last available data is from 2007, which states that 37 percent of the employees have been covered by collective agreements. See: Statisztikai Adatok, [Statistical Data] Bálint M. (ed.) available: http://econ.core.hu/file/download/mt09/hu/statisztika.pdf p. 292.

117 For more details see: Chernyaeva D.V. 'Trade union rights in Russia: past and present'. Report submitted to 15th World Congress of the International Industrial Relations Association 'The New World of Work, Employment and Organizations' Sydney, Australia, August, 2009.

In Poland and Hungary, on the workers' side, only trade unions have the right to conclude collective agreements. As noted earlier, in Hungary, since July 2012, this situation has changed. The new HLC provides the possibility of concluding an agreement with the works council, under specific conditions, as explained above (see Part 4.a., supra). This works council agreement can regulate all rights and obligations of the employment relationship, except for wages, with normative force.[118] In Russia, the collective agreement at the company level is signed between the company and workers. For collective bargaining purposes workers are usually represented by the union.[119]

All three legal systems share in common the requirement that only one collective agreement can be concluded at the company level.[120] This collective agreement covers all workers irrespective of their trade union membership. In all three countries, if the employer is under the scope of a more general collective agreement, then it has to be applied to all of his workers, regardless of trade union membership.

The advantage of this system is that every worker is covered, and working conditions in the company are uniform, which is beneficiary for social peace. At the same time, a closer look on the reasons for the 'one company one collective agreement' principle raises some doubts regarding its objective. It obviously prefers the big trade unions, and in general adversely affects the smaller trade unions and demotivates workers from participating in any union.

In Poland, if trade unions do not cooperate with each other, it is necessary to indicate the 'representative' trade union (chapter XI of the PLC), which is generally the strongest union. Where employees who are covered by a company agreement are represented by more than one trade union, the agreement should be negotiated by a committee of joint representation, or by the respective trade unions acting jointly. At least one representative trade union should participate in negotiations. A representative trade union is a union that is an organizational unit or a membership organization of a multi-enterprise trade union, union covering at least 10 percent of employees. Should a particular union not participate in negotiations, it has no possibility of blocking the collective labor agreement.

In Hungary trade unions have to agree with each other during the collective bargaining and they have to conclude the collective agreement together. According to the new HLC only a union can participate in bargaining and conclude collective agreement, which has 10 percent members among the workers in the company.[121]

[118] The works council agreement will be terminated: a) upon the collective agreement concluded by the employer entering into force; or b) upon the trade union notifying the employer of its entitlement to conclude a collective agreement. § 268. new HLC.

[119] If there is no union within a company, then the 'other representative' may be elected by the employees.

[120] In Russia collective agreements may also be concluded at the plant level, i.e. there may be separate agreements in the company generally and in its subdivisions. But there may be no two collective agreements at the same level. The same principle applies to Poland.

[121] The old HLC of 1992 made the capability of collective bargaining dependent on the results of the works council elections, which actually made the two collective employee representations mutually dependent on each other.

In Russia, if there are several unions acting within a company, they have to elect a joint bargaining unit, representing all the relevant trade unions.[122] If a trade union unites more than half of the employees, it is entitled to start collective bargaining without prior creation of the joint body. Smaller unions have difficulties to participate in collective bargaining. A minority union has no right to conclude a separate agreement on behalf of its members; and its special demands within the joint bargaining unit may be easily blocked by the majority union. This system of collective bargaining, which could be effective in a situation where there is no dominant trade union and all trade union organizations are more or less equal in power, also greatly undermines the possibility for the newly formed trade unions to take part.

Above the company level

Sectoral collective bargaining in Hungary, Russia and Poland is the most typical among the agreements that are concluded above the company level.

Sectoral bargaining is a weak element of the Hungarian collective bargaining system and it exists mainly in industries where only a few employers are present, for example in electricity, the chemical industry and in major public utility companies (such as public transport, energy and water utilities, postal services).[123] In 2009 a new statute on sectoral social dialogue committees was enacted with the intention of strengthening bargaining at the sector level. According to the new law social partners can create bipartite social dialogue committees at the sector level, including employers' organizations and trade union federations. The Act provides a detailed 'points system', which determines which trade unions federation and employers' organizations have the right to participate in the social dialogue committees and to conclude collective agreement. Recently, in every important sector a social dialogue committee has been created. This development is easy to understand, because sectoral committees receive financial and administrative support from the state. However, upon a closer look the efficacy of these committees, can be questioned. Until the end of 2012 only one collective agreement at the sector level was concluded in these committees.

In Poland sectoral agreements cover only those employers who are a party to a particular agreement and to their employees, regardless of their membership status in the trade unions.

Russia has been criticized by the ILO in that trade unions organized by certain professions (sailors, air dispatchers and others) are not allowed to conclude collective agreements at the occupational, or professional, level.[124] This situation is due to the position of the main trade unions organization (FNPR), which is organized on the basis of branch of industry, and tries to avoid competition. While territorial collective agreements exist in Russia, there are no such agreements in Hungary and Poland. In Hungary some collective agreements are concluded by several employers, who belong to the same branch or have the same owner.

---

[122] Article 37, RLC.

[123] In 2010 there were 19 sectoral collective agreements of national scope in force.

[124] This situation was a matter of complaint made by the Russian Seafarers' Union (RPSM) to ILO Committee on Freedom of Association: Case No. 2216, ILO ref. No. GB.288/7.

National tripartite bargaining

The state and the government play a crucial role in industrial relations in Eastern Europe. A Tripartite Socio-Economic Commission usually exists in these countries, composed of representatives from government, trade unions and federations, and employers' organizations. These bodies are entitled to participate in information and consultation processes (e.g. discussing legislative proposals in the field of labor law and social security and establishing the level of minimum remuneration). The composition and thus the legitimacy of these tripartite commissions are in some cases controversial. Hungary and Poland have such commissions.

In Hungary, until 2009 there was no regulation on the composition of this commission, casting doubt upon its legitimacy. Especially controversial was the commission's competence, because the commission had the right of co-decision with the government to determine the minimum wage. The Hungarian Constitutional Court declared that the Commission did not have legal authority and legitimacy to take part in the legislative process, and subsequently the law was changed. The tripartite commission was abolished by the new Conservative Government in 2011 and was replaced by the National Economic and Social Council, which is composed of representatives from the economic sphere, unions, churches, civil society and sciences, so the significance of the social partners has clearly decreased.[125]

A Tripartite Socio-Economic Commission also exists in Poland. It acts on the basis of the law of 2001 (although it was created in the mid 90s), and its main goal is to facilitate information and consultation processes.[126] It constitutes a forum of social dialogue to reconcile employee and employers' interests as well as the public good. Its main goal is to keep social peace. All the matters connected with labor law and social policy may be a subject of discussion. The Commission can propose an amount of minimum remuneration, which is updated every year.

Content and quality of collective agreements

The only restriction concerning the contents of collective agreements is that their provisions may not contradict statutory rules.

In Poland, the procedure to negotiate and conclude collective agreements is regulated with much detail in legislation. The dense regulation can be attributed to the fact that before 1989 there was no free bargaining. At present, both employer and trade union are entitled to initiate negotiations. A collective agreement can be concluded for an unfixed or a fixed term. A register of collective agreements is kept by the Minister for Labor (for collective agreements that apply to several establishments) or by a regional labor inspector (for collective agreements that apply to a single establishment). Should the terms of the collective labor agreement be better than those of employment contract, they *ex lege* replace provisions of individual contract.

---

[125] 2011. évi XCIII. törvény a Nemzeti Gazdasági és Társadalmi Tanácsról [Act XCIII of 2011 on the National Economic and Social Council].

[126] Świątkowski A. The role of the state and trade unions during the Polish process of transformation (especially regarding the area of industrial relations and employment politics, *Yearbook of Polish Labour Law and Social Policy*, Vol. 8, 1996, Cracow 1996, pp. 28 and following.

The Hungarian legislation on procedure is much the same as the Polish one, with the only difference that collective agreements are registered only by the Minister for Labor.

In Poland social partners can conclude other agreements in addition to collective agreement. For example, in the case of collective dismissals, they can indicate the groups of employees to be dismissed, or establish employee benefits. Similarly, it is common when state companies are privatized, to conclude the so-called 'social agreements', which regulate the parties' rights and obligations during the privatization process.

Across the different states in Eastern European, provisions in collective agreements often reproduce the rules of the Labor Code. Employers are often not willing to undertake additional obligations towards the employees in the collective agreements. The reason for this could be twofold. First, Labor Codes contain very detailed regulation on the terms of the employment relationship, and at the same time, the weakness of trade unions, as described earlier, makes bargaining for additional benefits more difficult.

e. Collective Action – Strike

In all three countries, the right to strike is accepted as a fundamental right.[127] Nevertheless, regulation of the strike is quite different; whereas in Hungary the regulation is rather liberal, in Poland and Russia it is not easy to organize a legal strike.

In Poland the law on collective disputes settlement was enacted in 1991. It provides a complicated procedure, which set stages in the process of a labor dispute. Negotiations and conciliation are obligatory, and mediation is optional. Only after passing these stages may a strike be organized. A trade union is the only entity that is entitled to initiate a strike. A referendum at the company needs to be organized. At least 50 percent of staff should participate in a referendum. As a result, majority of strikes organized in Poland are illegal.

In Russia only the employees themselves can take a decision to strike. The strike can be declared if no less than half of the employees present at the employees' meeting or conference have voted in favor of a strike. The meeting quorum is half and conference quorum is two-thirds of the employees of the employer. This procedure makes it rather difficult in practice to call a strike.

In Hungary, workers have the right to initiate a strike, and even a small group of workers can call a strike. However, the majority of strikes are organized by unions and only 15 percent by groups of workers.[128] Trade unions are not required to hold a ballot prior to the strike, but there is a cool-off period. During this seven-day period, workers or the union and employer are required to negotiate, and if negotiations end without an

---

[127] In Poland the right to strike is proclaimed in Art. 59. Constitution of 1997, available: http://www.sejm.gov.pl/prawo/konst/angielski/kon1.htm (in English). In Russia, Art. 37. para. 4 of the Constitution sets up the right to strike 'in a way provided by law', i.e. it is not an unconditional right. The right to strike is stated in the Constitution in Hungary, as well (see: Art. XVII. para. 2 of the Constitution of 2012).

[128] Berki E., A sztrájkok hazai gyakorlata. Mit mutatnak a számok? [The practice of strikes – What do the numbers show?] Pécsi Munkajogi Közlemények, 2008./II. 117-128. 122.

agreement, workers can strike. Despite the general leniency of the law on strikes in Hungary, there are growing pressures on strike activity. For example, since 2010 there is a new regulation on strikes in public utility companies.[129] Prior to this amendment unions and employers were required to come to an agreement on the minimum level of service that should be maintained during the strike. Even if they could not agree on the minimum level, the strike was lawful. According to the new law, the strike cannot start without the agreement. If the parties cannot agree, the union can call the labor court to determine the level of minimum service. However, the experience of the last years clearly demonstrates that this system makes it more difficult for the trade unions to call a lawful strike.

A different way of limiting strike activity is by restricting the issues over which workers and unions can declare a lawful strike. In Hungary, all forms of strikes are allowed, insofar as their aim is to exert pressure on the employer in order to protect the workers' interests. In Russia the scope of collective labor disputes is limited, and must address demands that are listed in law: 'the establishment and modification of working conditions (including the wages), conclusion, modification and execution of collective accords and agreements, and the refusal of the employer to take into account the employees' representatives' opinion in the process of adoption of employer's acts'.[130] Consequently, solidarity strikes are not allowed in Russia, but are lawful in Hungary and Poland.

Frequency of strikes can be a good indication for the real power of trade unions. The official strike statistics of Russia shows a very low number of strikes.[131] The explanation for these low figures is the fact that only legal strikes are counted by the official statistics. The rules governing strikes in Russia, as shortly explained here, render the legitimate performance of strikes practically impossible. Most conflict situations are resolved outside the scope of law. Illegal protests that fall outside the official statistics happen much more frequently than legitimate strikes.[132] This is a very dangerous sign from a social and political point of view. In Hungary, the number of strikes has been constantly low over the last ten years.[133] Even after the transition, in the 90's there were not more than 20 strikes a year. Most effective strikes happen in the traffic sector.

---

[129] § 4 (3), 1989. évi VII. törvény a sztrájkról [Art. 4 (3) Act VII. of 1989 on strike].

[130] Art. 398 RLC.

[131] Only four strikes in 2008, one in 2009 and zero (!) in 2010. Federalnaya Slujba Gosudarstvennoy Statistiki (Rosstat Rossii) [Federal Service on State Statics (Rosstat of Russia)] Rossiysky Statisticheskiy Ejegodnik, 2011. Moscow, 2011. [Russian statistical annual, 2011] http://www.gks.ru/bgd/regl/b11_13/IssWWW.exe/Stg/d1/05-26.htm.

[132] See: Bizyukov P. Trudovye protesty v Rossii v 2008-2011 gg. Analiticheskiy otchet [Labor Protests in Russia in 2008-2011 – analytical research] Zentr socialno-trudovih prav [Centre for Social and Labor Rights] website, 2012: http://trudprava.ru/index.php?id=2112.

[133] See: Berki E. Op. Cit, P. 117–128.

5. GENERAL CONCLUSIONS

The examples of legal change throughout this chapter indicate that labor law of Central and Eastern European countries has changed substantially during and following the political transformation. The main changes can be summarized as follows: a renewed system of labor law and the acceptable sources of law, especially strengthening the role of collective agreements (see Part 2, supra); a new approach to the individual freedom of work; much more flexibility in the field of individual labor law and freedom of the parties to shape the content of an employment relationship; different approach to equality at workplace and ban on discrimination (see Part 3, supra); and a radically different notion of collective labor law and the growing independence of trade unions (Part 4, supra).

Labor law did not pave the way for political transformation and did not create a 'new reality', but rather reacted to the political, economic and social changes. Labor law always tried to respond to current needs and consequently quite often there was ad hoc legislation to settle a particular issue at the particular moment. This reactive approach resulted in the fact that there was no general or far-reaching vision concerning the development and future of labor law.

Current problems in the countries studied here, after more than two decades of transformation, are often similar to problems faced by the western countries. The logic of the communist system is gradually becoming less significant, although it is not wholly irrelevant. Future changes will be even more remote from the previous system, and will respond to new forms of employment and changing market conditions.

The prevailing economic and political situations equally dominate the trajectory of change. Their effect is twofold. On the one hand global competitiveness requires more flexible working conditions, which appears for example in the loosening of the working time regulations. On the other hand, many aspects of labor law in these countries are purely populist and there are several sensitive issues that have not been changed because of social concerns, for example – the dismissal protection in Russia (see Part 3.d, supra).

In Hungary and Poland, the necessity to approximate internal regulations to the requirements of the EU also plays a decisive role in the legislation of the last decades. Although the directives and regulations of the EU do not create a comprehensive labor law system comparable with national law, they touch on many questions in the social sphere and significantly influence the labor laws of the member states.

Throughout the chapter we indicated a gap between the legal changes and their translation into practice. For example, there is a general tendency to strengthen the role of the social partners, side by side with more flexible regulations, in both individual and collective labor law. However, in reality social partners are rather weak in representing the workers' interests. As long as this is the case, the flexible space that is open for negotiations is tilted to the employers' advantage. The chapter therefore reminds us that in all legal systems it is important to observe how the law is implemented in fact, but that understanding the ever-changing effects of labor law in Eastern Europe, as well as its political context, such awareness is particularly important.

14. Building BRICS of success?

Sean Cooney, Darcy du Toit, Roberto Fragale, Roger Ronnie and Kamala Sankaran

INTRODUCTION

This chapter explores the current regulatory challenges in four major countries whose economies have a very significant impact internationally. These countries are China, India, Brazil and South Africa – four of the so-called BRICS, the 2010 rephrased acronym used to refer to the emerging market economies of these four countries plus Russia, after South Africa joined in at its III Summit. The original group, named at the time BRIC,[1] had gathered together in 2006 in order to have some common foreign policy guidelines.[2] Unlike many countries in the developing world, these nations have the expertise, and the political and economic capacity, to determine the orientation of their labour laws. In the case of South Africa and China, in particular, they have made use of these circumstances to embark on many significant labour law reforms; unlike the recent experience of southern Europe, these have not been 'deregulatory'.

Despite the fact that the BRICS constitute a formal grouping, the first response of many readers may be that this discussion involves a comparison of apples and oranges.[3] Undoubtedly their economies are very differently structured; their political trajectories vary enormously; and their legal frameworks have evolved from very different origins. Still, their growing importance in a globalised environment draws everyone's consideration and stimulates a consideration of the nations as a group.

Thus, for all their evident dissimilarities, we set out to investigate whether there is a cluster of similar problems relating to labour and employment law among four of the BRICS states.[4] The underlying assumption is that fundamental labour problems are present in these countries. Although they are hardly unique to the BRICS states, the question that arises is whether the fact that these are powerful emerging economies,

---

1 The acronym BRIC was first used in 2001 by Jim O'Neill in Global Economics Paper nº 66 of the Goldman Sachs Economic Research Group. O'Neill discussed the then state of the world economy with particular emphasis on the emerging market economies of four countries: Brazil, Russia, India and China. Cf. O'Neill (2001).

2 The group trajectory can be retraced at specific webpages for the 2012 and 2013 Summits: Fourth BRICS Summit, http://www.bricsindia.in/india.html and Fifth BRICS Summit, http://www.brics5.co.za/site/about-brics/, both last accessed February 4, 2013.

3 A Chinese equivalent is 风马牛不相及 ('the lost horse and cow will not meet'); a Portuguese one is *misturando alhos com bugalhos* ('mixing nutgalls and garlic'). This is to say taking one thing for another or just establishing confusion.

4 Excluding Russia, which is covered in Chapter 13 of this volume, see: Erika Kovács, Nikita Lyutov, Leszek Mitrus, 'Labor law in transition: From a centrally planned to a free market economy in Central and Eastern Europe'.

whose models are attracting worldwide attention, entail similar regulatory strategies or outcomes.[5] Otherwise stated, can the comparison help in identifying whether the powerful emerging economies share some kind of a common regulatory trajectory, or whether there are many paths and logics to becoming a member of this newly privileged group?

Moreover, examining the BRICS countries might enable us to scrutinise possible relations between labour law and economic development, a correlation that has been mostly forwarded by economists.[6] Legal scholars are resistant to this kind of approach as it may demand an important amount of empirical work which is usually conceived as something unrelated to legal thinking. Indeed, although legal teaching should no longer be just 'legal' and compartmentalised by isolated units and should instead incorporate an impressive amount of economical, sociological, political and management contents, this required openness has not been able to create a friendly environment for empirical legal analysis. This has remained an open field for the work of economists and, every now and then, sociologists and anthropologists. But the reader may be reassured: we do not postulate an economic analysis for our comparison. We do not intend to drown our reader in numbers. Our object remains the legal environment of the four compared countries and our focus will still be on their corresponding law. What may then be different is the effort to overcome the simple contrast in legal regulation and the attempt to relate it to economic development.

It is clearly not possible in a single chapter to embark on a comprehensive analysis of the labour law framework in each country. We have therefore concentrated on issues that have featured in law reform efforts. There is a significant degree of commonality in relation to these issues – especially concerning regulatory responses to informality and the breakdown of the standard employment relationship. The chapter examines these issues first in South Africa, then India, China, and Brazil. These discussions are followed by a general conclusion, noting that these states have actively and creatively sought to use legal measures to address the consequences of fragmenting employment forms.

---

[5] Some related initiatives in the academic world can be found at the BRICS Policy Center, a conjoint initiative of Pontíficia Universidade Católica do Rio de Janeiro (PUC-RIO) and Rio de Janeiro City Hall (available at http://bricspolicycenter.org/homolog/, last accessed February 4, 2013), and BRICLAB, a forum animated by the School of International and Public Affairs in Columbia University, USA (available at http://www.sipa.columbia.edu/briclab/index.html, last accessed February 4, 2013). For a related examination of China, India and Indonesia (a potential BRICS member), see Sean Cooney, Peter Gahan, Petra Mahy and Richard Mitchell, The evolution of labour law in three Asian Nations: An introductory comparative study, (2014) 36 *Comparative Labor Law and Policy Journal* 23–68.

[6] Edward L. Glaeser, Rafael La Porta, Florencio Lopez-de-Silanes, and Andrei Shleifer, 'Do institutions cause growth?' (2004) 9(3) *Journal of Economic Growth* 271, available at http://www.economics.harvard.edu/faculty/shleifer/files/do_institutions_cause_growth.pdf, last accessed February 6, 2013; Nicola Gennaioli, Rafael La Porta, Florencio Lopez-de-Silanes, and Andrei Shleifer, 'Growth in regions' (2013) 19(3) *Journal of Economic Growth* 259.

1. SOUTH AFRICA

South Africa is a constitutional state with an entrenched Bill of Rights, including extensive labour rights.[7] Most of these rights are given legislative expression in the Labour Relations Act (LRA)[8] and the Basic Conditions of Employment Act (BCEA).[9] This framework was the outcome of lengthy and at times acrimonious negotiations between the social partners.

The LRA, representing a complete overhaul of its predecessor,[10] was drafted by a team of experts with technical support from the ILO and international labour law experts. Replacing the judge-made 'duty to bargain' with a system of voluntary collective bargaining based on majoritarian principles, the new Act recognised that South Africa's re-entry into the global economy presented challenges relating to productivity, flexibility and (as promised by the new Government of National Unity)[11] workplace empowerment. To this end the concept of workplace forums, which promoted a form of consultation and joint decision-making resembling that of German works councils, was introduced.[12] The final product was supported by organised labour as being consistent with the promises made in the 1994 election manifesto of the ANC.[13]

The South African labour market has undergone extensive changes since then, with growing numbers of workers performing what is termed 'non-standard' work[14] and over 30 per cent of all working South Africans estimated to be earning a livelihood through informal types of work.[15] Yet the labour relations system, Theron argues, has remained informed by 'social and economic assumptions that prevailed when the primary and

---

[7] Chapter Two, Constitution of the Republic of South Africa, 1996. Section 23 is the 'labour clause', which includes a right to 'fair labour practices' as well as the right to join and form a trade union or employers' organisation, to engage in collective bargaining and to strike.

[8] Act 66 of 1995.

[9] Act 55 of 1998.

[10] I.e., the Labour Relations Act 28 of 1956. See Explanatory Memorandum (1995) *Industrial Law Journal (South Africa)* 278 at 279–80.

[11] A coalition of the African National Congress (ANC) which had led the liberation struggle, the National Party which had ruled apartheid South Africa, and the Zulu-based Inkatha Freedom Party (IFP), which governed South Africa from 1994 to 1997. The IFP retained a presence in the cabinet until 2004.

[12] Due to the antagonistic labour relations climate inherited from the apartheid past, however, very few workplace forums were established and adversarial collective bargaining remained the rule.

[13] The ANC has since the early 1990s operated in an extra-parliamentary 'Triple Alliance' with the Congress of South African Trade Unions (COSATU) and the South African Communist Party, with some robust debate among the partners around policy choices.

[14] I.e., temporary, part-time and agency work (or 'triangular employment') in particular: see note 16 below. In general, see Paul Benjamin, 'Decent work and non-standard employees: Options for legislative reform in South Africa: A discussion document' (2010) 31 *Industrial Law Journal (South Africa)* 845.

[15] Paul Benjamin, 'Informal work and labour rights in South Africa' (2008) 29 *Industrial Law Journal (South Africa)* 1579.

secondary sectors were seen as the engines of the economy.'[16] This refers in particular to the assumptions that: (a) the workplace is the place where workers actually work; (b) employment is a binary relationship between employer and employee, with a clear distinction between employment and self-employment; (c) the centrality of industrial bargaining; and (d) the employment relationship is indefinite or of long-term duration. Indeed, unlike in Europe and elsewhere, virtually no provision was made in labour legislation for non-standard forms of employment; as discussed below, amendments to this end were enacted only in 2014. The effect is that an increasing number of South African workers have up to the present performed work that largely fell beyond the reach of labour law[17] and, in the process, new tensions accumulated.

The South African Labour Market

The transformation of South Africa between 1990 and 1994, from a racist state hovering on the edge of civil war to a turbulent but vibrant constitutional democracy, is regarded as one of the greatest political success stories of the late twentieth century.

On the surface much has changed. In terms of numbers the black middle class had overtaken the white middle class by 2006.[18] Yet the gap between rich and poor has widened. The Gini coefficient[19] for South Africa, reaching 63.1 in 2009, is the highest among the BRICS countries and one of the highest in the world.[20]

This stark statistic reflects a volatile combination of factors. Although South Africa is classified as an upper middle income country, this is not based on the living standards of the majority of workers. In line with trends across both advanced and developing economies, the share of wages in GDP in South Africa dropped from 57 per cent to 51 per cent between 1994 and 2012[21] while both pre-tax and post-tax profits increased over the same period.[22] In addition, the labour market is skewed by high and rapidly growing income levels at the top while 'less skilled workers continue to earn more or

---

16 Jan Theron, 'The shift to services and triangular employment: Implications for labour market reform' (2008) 29 *Industrial Law Journal (South Africa)* 1 at 4. 'Triangular employment' means work done by employees for a third party to whom their employer provides their labour or services, also referred to as 'agency work'. The LRA uses the term 'temporary employment services' while trade unions and employers often speak of 'labour brokers'.

17 Benjamin (note 15 above) at 1583.

18 Statistics South Africa *Profiling South African middle-class households, 1998–2006* (2009) http://www.statssa.gov.za/publications/Report-03-03-01/Report-03-03-01.pdf (accessed 3 February 2014) Figures 11, 12.

19 The Gini coefficient is a ratio between 1 and 0, where 0 shows perfect equality and 100 shows perfect inequality.

20 World Bank *Data: Gini Index* at http://data.worldbank.org/indicator/SI.POV.GINI?order=wbapi_data_value_2012+wbapi_data_value+wbapi_data_value-last&sort=asc (accessed 19 January 2014). The figures for Brazil, Russia, China and India were 54.7, 40.1, 42.1 and 33.9 respectively (ibid.).

21 Niall Reddy, 'Wages, profits and unemployment in post-apartheid South Africa 2014' (Alternative Information Development Centre (AIDC) 2014) at 24–6.

22 Ibid. at 17–18.

less the same wages that they earned towards the end of Apartheid'.[23] The historical 'apartheid wage gap' thus remains firmly in place.

It is also relevant to note that, while some 63 per cent of the total work force are employed on a 'permanent' or indefinite basis,[24] only 29 per cent have their wage increments determined by means of collective bargaining, either directly between an employer and a trade union or at sectoral level.[25] As in many countries, sectoral agreements may be extended to non-parties, although provision is made for non-party employers to apply for exemption from extended agreements. In fact, only 2.9 per cent of the total work force are covered by extended agreements.[26] In addition, some 34 per cent of the total workforce are covered by sectoral determinations.[27] These figures suggest that over a third of all workers are not in 'permanent' employment, while about the same percentage fall beyond the coverage of collective wage regulatory mechanisms. As for the formal/informal divide, a 2007 study indicated that informal (i.e., unregulated) jobs represented 22.8 per cent of total employment.[28] While this may reflect a lower rate of informality than countries such as Brazil, Mexico, Indonesia or the Philippines, where informal employment is above 50 per cent,[29] it is nevertheless substantial enough to exert downward pressure on wages and working conditions in a number of sectors.

The second major feature of the South African labour market is the exceptionally high rate of unemployment. The official figure (including discouraged work-seekers) stood at 36.7 per cent in the third quarter of 2013[30] while, according to the ILO, more than 50 per cent of youths aged between 15 and 24 are unemployed.[31] Government initiatives to relieve unemployment include interventions aimed at promoting job

---

[23] Ibid at 16. The mean wage of 'highly skilled workers', over the same period, increased by 67 per cent.

[24] Statistics South Africa *Quarterly Labour Force Survey* (Quarter 3, 2013) (hereafter 'LFS') at 38.

[25] Ibid at 39. Sectoral bargaining council agreements covered 20.3 per cent of the total work force in 2004: Shane Godfrey et al, *Collective Bargaining in South Africa* (Juta, 2010), 114.

[26] Godfrey et al., ibid.

[27] I.e., issued by the Minister of Labour in terms of Chapter 8 of the BCEA to set minimum wages and conditions for workers in unorganised sectors. For statistics, see Development Policy Research Unit *Minimum Wages, Employment and Household Poverty: Investigating the Impact of Sectoral Determinations* (University of Cape Town, 2008) Table 1 at http://www.labour.gov.za/DOL/downloads/documents/research-documents/Sectoral%20determinations%20POLICY%20VERSION%20v4.pdf (accessed 6 February 2014).

[28] Benjamin (note 15 above) at 1583.

[29] Ibid. The LFS records that 15.56 per cent of the total employed population fell within its definition of 'informal' employment in the third quarter of 2013: LFS iv Table A.

[30] LFS Table 2.

[31] This is more than double the youth unemployment rate in North African countries and four times that in sub-Saharan Africa as a whole; on a global scale, only Greece and Spain record worse figures: see International Labour Organisation, *Global Employment Trends for Youth 2013: A generation at risk* (ILO, Geneva 2013) 19–20, 10; available at http://www.ilo.org/wcmsp5/groups/public/ – dgreports/dcomm/documents/publication/ wcms_212423.pdf (accessed 3 February 2013). According to Statistics South Africa the number of youths not in employment, education or training was 31.7 per cent: LFS xiii.

creation,[32] improvements in education and skills development[33] and, more controversially, the Employment Tax Incentive Act[34] whereby employers will be encouraged to employ young people by means of tax incentives for up to two years.

Updating Labour Legislation

These themes – extreme inequality, the plight of the most vulnerable workers, mass unemployment – and the conflict generated by these conditions have dominated the discourse on labour law in South Africa for some time. Pressure from trade unions, on the one hand, for labour market reform and greater protection for workers has been sharpened by pressure on union leaders by their members and intensive debate about the economic policies of the ANC Government, described by critics on the left as 'neo-liberal'. Particular opposition was aroused by the growing use of agency workers at the expense of secure employment, resulting in widespread union demands for the prohibition of 'labour broking'. Employers, employers' organisations and lobby groups such as the Free Market Foundation (FMF),[35] on the other hand, have persistently argued that 'over-regulation' and 'rigidity' of the labour market, exacerbated by increasing industrial unrest, are at the root of the country's inability to create sufficient jobs.

In the aftermath of the global economic crisis of 2008, with slow and uncertain recovery on a global scale and high-growth economies like India, China and Brazil performing below expectations,[36] these debates became more intractable than ever. Faced with these pressures government in 2010 – for the second time in a decade[37] – proposed significant amendments to the country's main labour statutes.[38] A central objective was to regulate non-standard employment and agency work in particular. Another objective was to address the problem of non-compliance by employers with minimum employment standards. The government also set out to clarify the law relating to dismissals and to curb unprocedural industrial action.

---

[32] In particular, through the Expanded Public Works Programme for creating temporary jobs in the public sector and non-profit organisations: see http://www.epwp.gov.za/ (accessed 3 February 2013).

[33] Medium Term Budget Policy Statement 2013, National Treasury Republic of South Africa, October 2013 at 9.

[34] Act 26 of 2013. Trade unions fear that it will encourage employers to replace workers in indefinite employment with 'cheap youth labour'. Section 5 of the Act sets out to penalise this.

[35] According to its website, the Free Market Foundation is an '(i)ndependent public benefit organisation founded in 1975 to promote and foster an open society, the rule of law, personal liberty, and economic and press freedom as fundamental components of its advocacy of human rights and democracy based on classical liberal principles. It is financed by membership subscriptions, donations and sponsorships': http://www.freemarketfoundation.com/about/who-we-are (accessed 4 February 2014).

[36] Medium Term Expenditure Framework Guidelines, National Treasury, August 2012 at 2.

[37] The previous amendments, enacted in 2002, had on balance been favourable to labour: Darcy du Toit et al, *Labour Relations Law: A Comprehensive Guide* (LexisNexis, 2015), 38–41.

[38] I.e., the Labour Relations Amendment Bill, the Basic Conditions of Employment Amendment Bill, the Employment Equity Amendment Bill and the Employment Services Bill.

The draft Bills were met with considerable criticism from employers and others, not least because of their technical shortcomings, and were withdrawn. In 2012 the redrafted Bills were submitted to the Cabinet and, after extensive deliberations and further amendment, completed their passage through Parliament by early 2014.[39] The debate surrounding these Bills largely encapsulated the contestation of the previous decade and a half, and the final text is a good measure of government's policy stance as well as the compromise reached between organised business and labour.

Is the South African Labour Market Over-regulated?

Employers have consistently argued for greater flexibility as a pre-condition for economic growth in South Africa, in the context of a world order characterised by growing trade liberalisation.[40] Andrew Kenny, a zealous exponent of employers' interests, expresses the free market view in perhaps its purest form:

> Between our catastrophic levels of unemployment and the prospect of an economy with full employment stands the impenetrable barrier of our labour laws. These wicked laws are not only throwing millions of our people into the dustbin of joblessness, not only crippling our economy, not only the cause of hideous poverty and humiliation, not only a primary reason for SA being about the most unequal society on the planet, but they are a violation of human rights. Our labour laws deny South Africans a fundamental human right: the right to work.[41]

Evidence to substantiate this view, however, is elusive. In essence it represents an assumption that '[o]ur onerous labour laws make the cost of employment so high and the difficulties of getting rid of lazy or delinquent workers … so great that employers are loathe to employ',[42] based on episodic examples of difficulties experienced by employers allegedly due to inflexible legal requirements, combined with a zero-sum theory that job creation depends on lower wages.[43] In fact, a study commissioned by the Organisation for Economic Co-operation and Development (OECD) found minimal evidence of the restrictiveness of South African labour law and, on the contrary, rated South Africa fifth in a scale of 39 countries with the most liberal employment protection legislation.[44] Russia, Brazil, India and China (in that order) were all rated as

---

[39] The Basic Conditions of Employment Amendment Act of 2013, the Employment Equity Amendment Act of 2013 and the Employment Services Act of 2014 were promulgated during 2014 and the more controversial Labour Relations Amendment Act of 2014 took effect on 1 January 2015.

[40] Jan Theron, 'The shifts to services and triangular employment: Implications for labour market reform' (2008) 29 *Industrial Law Journal (South Africa)* 1 at 1.

[41] A Kenny, 'Wicked' labour laws deny basic human right to work' *Business Day* 19 April 2011; republished at http://www.bdlive.co.za/articles/2011/04/19/andrew-kenny-employment;jsessionid=2624B8DD4C5ABFEEC370D579EBCD44FF.present1.bdfm (accessed 4 February 2014).

[42] Ibid.

[43] For more in-depth discussion, see Maree in Godfrey et al. (note 25 above) at 25–32.

[44] OECD (2013), OECD Economic Surveys: South Africa 2013, OECD Publishing, 32 Figure 18 at http://www.treasury.gov.za/publications/other/OECD%20Economic%20Surveys%20South%20Africa%202013.pdf (accessed 4 February 2013). See Bob Hepple, 'Is South African

having more restrictive laws than South Africa. From a trade union perspective, various areas remained where regulation was inadequate and needed to be tightened.

The Current Amendments

Inevitably, the long process of amending the LRA and BCEA from 2010 to 2014 reignited the debate about the alleged over-regulation of the South African labour market.[45] In its submissions to Parliament, Business Unity South Africa (BUSA)[46] declared that the amendments, viewed as a whole, would 'increase both the cost and complexity of doing business' and, while tackling 'the abuse of vulnerable workers employed in atypical employment', did so 'in an overly complex legalistic manner'. If enacted, it was claimed, the Bills would 'destroy a very significant number of jobs' and undermine the objectives of the National Development Plan.[47] For their part the trade unions concentrated largely on the demand for the prohibition of agency work.[48]

Against this background the new provisions for the protection of non-standard workers are of special interest. While no detailed discussion is possible within the scope of this chapter, the measures in many ways resemble those found in other jurisdictions in Europe and elsewhere.[49] However, two provisions which perhaps aroused the strongest opposition deserve to be looked at more closely.

The first is a provision seeking to ensure that the 'temporary' employment of agency workers by clients is indeed temporary and does not serve as a disguise for indefinite employment under unacceptable conditions (as alluded to in the BUSA submission, cited above).[50] It does this by placing a three-month limit on the placement of agency workers with clients, after which the worker is deemed to be employed by the client.[51] However, it excludes workers earning above a prescribed income threshold[52] as well as

---

labour law fit for the global economy?' in Rochelle Le Roux and Alan Rycroft (eds) *Reinventing labour Law – Reflecting on the first 15 years of the Labour Relations Act and future challenges* (Juta, 2012) at 2–3. Hepple goes on to conclude that, on an analysis of World Bank indicators, it is 'no more difficult or expensive on the whole for an employer in South Africa to make a worker redundant' than in the United Kingdom, China or South Korea: ibid 3–7.

[45] For an index to the debate from 2010 to 2013 plus government statements and articles on line, see SabinetLaw *Labour Relations Amendment 2012* at http://www.sabinetlaw.co.za/labour/legislation/labour-relations-amendment-2012 (accessed 4 February 2014).

[46] BUSA is the principal confederation of employers' organisations in South Africa.

[47] Submission by BUSA to the Parliamentary Portfolio Committee on Labour regarding the Labour Relations Amendment Bill and the Basic Conditions of Employment Amendment Bill, 28 June 2012; at www.pmg.org.za/files/docs/120725busa.doc (accessed 4 February 2014).

[48] See Paul Benjamin, 'To regulate or to ban? Controversies over temporary employment agencies in South Africa and Namibia' in K. Malherbe and J. Sloth-Nielsen (eds) *Labour Law into the Future* (Juta, 2013) 189.

[49] See Craig Bosch, 'The proposed 2012 amendments relating to non-standard employment: What will the new regime be?' (2013) 34 *Industrial Law Journal (South Africa)* 1631, who concludes that the new protection is 'arguably no more than is fairly obviously due' (at 1644).

[50] LRA, s 198A read with s 198.

[51] LRA, s 198A(1) and (3).

[52] Currently set at R205,433 (approximately US$17,000) per year. With the median earnings of South African workers in formal employment at R3,683 in 2010, the effect is to

those working as substitutes for employees who are temporarily absent, regardless of the length of their placement. The three-month limit and the application of the provision may also be varied by sectoral collective agreement or by ministerial notice, on which the Minister must invite public comment and consult with organised business and labour.[53]

The second provision is aimed at the practice of evading the consequences of indefinite employment by appointing workers on a series of temporary contracts. It places a three-month limit on all temporary employment contracts, but proceeds to exclude all cases where an employer may have a legitimate reason for entering into a temporary contract.[54]

The provision also does not apply to workers earning above the aforesaid income threshold or to employers with fewer than ten employees, or with fewer than 50 employees who have been in business for less than two years, or to contracts permitted by collective agreement, or to any other situation where a fixed-term contract is 'justified'.[55]

In the context of South African labour relations, it is submitted, it is inappropriate to describe the careful attention to detail reflected in the above provisions as 'overly legalistic'. Rather, it may be seen as illustrative of the finely-balanced negotiations which led to their adoption and were necessary in seeking a sustainable balance between the highly polarised positions of business and labour.

The Attack on the Extension of Sectoral Agreements

The collective bargaining provisions of the LRA and, more specifically, the power vested in the Minister of Labour to extend bargaining council collective agreements to non-party employers and workers in the sector,[56] have been a bone of contention for a decade and a half[57] and are currently the subject of a constitutional challenge by the Free Market Foundation.[58]

---

exclude approximately the top 10 per cent of wage and salary-earners: Statistics SA *Monthly earnings of South Africans, 2010* Table 5 at http://www.statssa.gov.za/publications2/P02112/P021122010.pdf (accessed 7 February 2014).

53 That is, in the tripartite National Economic Development and Labour Council: LRA, s 198A(1), (6) and (7).

54 LRA, s 198B.

55 LRA, s 198B(2), (3). Section 198B(4) lists nine specific cases where temporary contracts will be justified which, for practical purposes, cover every situation where an employer's operational requirements may call for a temporary appointment.

56 LRA, s 32.

57 The time scale is significant, given that the system for extending sectoral agreements to non-parties has been in place since 1924 when it was established by South Africa's first national labour statute, In Industrial Conciliation Act 11 of 1924. Opposition to centralised bargaining only started emerging in the era of globalisation: Du Toit et al. (note 37 above), 20–21.

58 See note 35 above. The case is *Free Market Foundation v Minister of Labour and others* (Gauteng North High Court, Case No 13762/2013). Fifty bargaining councils are cited as respondents. For comment by a constitutional lawyer, see Pierre de Vos, 'The Free Market Foundation's quixotic venture' *Constitutionally Speaking* (7 March 2013) at http://constitutionallyspeaking.co.za/2013/03/07/ (accessed 5 February 2014).

There are two principal legal grounds for the challenge. The first is that the parties to bargaining councils are private actors to whom, in effect, the power of legislation which is vested in the state has improperly been delegated by permitting the extension of their agreement to non-parties. The second is that the technical prerequisites for extension do not guarantee that the process will necessarily be supported by unions and employers respectively organising and employing a majority of workers in the sector.

Space does not allow any detailed discussion of the merits of these arguments.[59] In summary it may be said that the sectoral bargaining model adopted in South Africa is essentially no more inclusive or restrictive than those existing in many other countries and less so than the *erga omnes* systems found in certain countries. The legitimacy of centralised bargaining as a form of collective bargaining, and the case for the extension of collective agreements as a necessary component of centralised bargaining, have long been argued[60] and are reflected in the relevant ILO Conventions.[61] De Vos is no doubt accurate in his conclusion that, in essence, the Free Market Foundation is 'aggrieved by the policy choices made by the legislature [for] protecting collective bargaining agreements' rather than seriously asserting the unconstitutionality of those choices.[62]

If this is so, it is the broader political context of the issue rather than its legal merits that is significant for present purposes. The action by the FMF has certainly had a polarising effect. The Congress of South African Trade Unions (COSATU)[63] has condemned it as part of a 'coherent, deliberately orchestrated and socio-economically and politically right-wing funded campaign to weaken and ultimately dismantle our democratically legislated labour relations dispensation, especially its collective bargaining machinery',[64] which will serve to 'deepen poverty amongst the employed and further worsen income inequalities whilst bosses will even make more obscene profits'.[65] For its part, the government has responded by including no fewer than six amendments to the provisions for the extension of collective agreements that are aimed at facilitating the process of applying for exemption.[66]

This, too, may be seen as part of the ongoing process of crafting and recasting the legal framework in response to the volatile and ever-shifting relations between South African business and labour, without reflecting any particular policy trend.

---

59 For discussion, see D. du Toit 'The extension of bargaining council agreements: Do the amendments address the constitutional challenge?' (2014) 35 *ILJ* 2637.

60 See, for example, L. Hamburger, 'The extension of collective agreements to cover entire trades and industries' (1939) XL(2) *International Labour Review,* 153 at 156–7.

61 That is, ILO Conventions 98 (on Right to Organise and Collective Bargaining, 1949) and 154 (on Collective Bargaining, 1981), read with Recommendation 163 of 1981.

62 Indeed, as an alternative remedy the FMF asks that the Minister of Labour be required to exercise discretion in extending an agreement rather than being bound to do so if certain conditions (which the FMF also seeks to amend) are met. See De Vos (note 58 above).

63 COSATU is the country's largest trade federation, with more than 2 million members.

64 Special Declaration adopted by the 2013 COSATU Collective Bargaining, Organising and Campaigns Conference.

65 Ibid.

66 See LRA, s 32 subsections (3)(dA) and (e), (3A), (5)(c) and (d), and (11). Significantly, s 32(5) requires the Minister to call for public comment and consider it before extending an agreement, thus building in an element of discretion as called for by the FMF.

Turmoil in the Trade Union Movement

As noted above, increasing industrial militancy among workers is seen by employers as yet another factor inhibiting economic growth. There has undoubtedly been an upturn in strike action since 2009. A recent summary by the Department of Labour reads as follows:

> A total of 99 strike incidents were recorded in 2012 as compared to 67 in 2011, 74 in 2010, 51 in 2009 and 57 in 2008. Working days lost were during 2012 amounted to 3.3 million … (involving 241 391 employees) as compared to 2.8 million … in 2011 (involving 203 138 employees).[67]

At the same time, there has been a long-term decline in the number of strikes from 1 324 in 1997 to 51 in 2009 before rising again to 99 in 2012.[68] The overall picture has thus been one of fewer but bigger strikes, many of them in the public sector.

2012 is seen as a watershed year. 58 per cent of the workers taking part in industrial action in 2012 were in the mining sector, which was racked by violent and often unprocedural strikes, brought to a macabre climax on 16 August 2012 when police opened fire on striking workers at the Marikana platinum mine,[69] killing 34 and wounding 78.[70] Industrial action continued at high levels in 2013, with the number of workdays lost rising from 1.6 million in January–September 2012 to 4.7 million in January–September 2013[71] – almost 50 per cent up on the total for 2012 – although the intensity and duration of the strikes levelled off in comparison with 2012 and unprocedural ('wildcat') action declined.[72] But, with economic growth remaining sluggish,[73] industrial action was inevitably identified from the side of business and the media as a key reason for poor economic performance.

---

[67] Department of Labour *Industrial action report 2012* at http://www.labour.gov.za/DOL/media-desk/media-statements/2013/industrial-action-report-2012 (accessed 5 February 2014).

[68] Darcy du Toit and Roger Ronnie 'The necessary evolution of strike law' in le Roux and Rycroft (eds), note 44 above; also published in (2012) *Acta Juridica* 195. The figure of 99 strikes in 2012 marks a return to the level of 2006.

[69] The mine is owned by the British multinational Lonmin plc.

[70] See Mark Anstey, 'Marikana – and the push for a new South African pact' (2013) 37 *South African Journal of Labour Relations* 133; Tembeka Ngcukaitobi, 'Strike law, structural violence and inequality in the Platinum Hills of Marikana' (2013) 34 *Industrial Law Journal (South Africa)* 836; Gavin Hartford 'The mining industry strike wave: what are the causes and what are the solutions?' (*Groundup*, 10 October 2012) http://groundup.org.za/content/mining-industry-strike-wave-what-are-causes-and-what-are-solutions (accessed 5 February 2014).

[71] South African Reserve Bank (SARB) *Quarterly Bulletin* (December 2013) 19 at http://www.resbank.co.za/Lists/News%20and%20Publications/Attachments/6007/01Full%20Quarterly%20Bulletin%20%E2%80%93%20December%202013.pdf (accessed 5 February 2014).

[72] See, in general, Department of Labour *Annual Labour Market Bulletin 2012/13* at http://www.gov.za/documents/index.php?term=labour+market&dfrom=&dto=&yr=0&subjs%5B%5D=0 (accessed 5 February 2013).

[73] Growth slowed from 3.2 per cent year-on-year in the second quarter of 2013 to 0.7 per cent in the third quarter: SARB *Quarterly Bulletin* (note 71 above) 5.

Notably, the Department of Labour responded by seeking to introduce a number of direct and indirect limitations on the right to strike in the amendments to the LRA.[74] These were, however, progressively abandoned in the course of negotiations in the face of questions about the practicality of some restrictions and the constitutionality of others. It could also not be denied that economic performance was negatively affected by a range of factors other than industrial action, ranging from poor harvests caused by drought to 'lustreless export markets and domestic supply-side constraints'.[75] Most importantly, of course, it may also have reflected some understanding that industrial conflict is not caused solely by trade unions but is also influenced by employer conduct and by broader social conditions.

The Marikana massacre offered a tragic but salutary object lesson. It prompted national soul-searching about 'what had gone wrong', why the machinery created by the LRA had failed to resolve the dispute and, above all, the underlying causes of the disaster.[76] Hartford observes that '[t]here is no doubt that the gross poverty and inequality in SA … provides the social and economic context to heightened expectations of wage increases', but also that the explanation for the breakdown in the LRA processes at Marikana must be sought in more specific causes.[77] These, he argues, can be found in the persistence of the migrant labour system, dire living conditions experienced by workers with no improvement in sight and, above all, neglect of the rock-drill operators' demands by the majority union, the National Union of Mineworkers (NUM), accompanied by what was perceived an excessively cosy relationship between NUM full-time shop stewards and mine management. Aggravating factors were the considerable privileges enjoyed by full-time shop stewards and the exclusion, due to the majoritarian system embodied by the LRA, of the rival Association of Mining and Construction Union (AMCU) from the collective bargaining process. The result, after a long period of deepening frustration, was a spontaneous rebellion by rock-drill operators, led by an informal workers' committee.

At a legal level, the amendments to the LRA include some relaxation of its majoritarian bias by opening more space for non-majority unions to obtain organisational rights.[78] Many have recognised, however, that the real challenges lie deeper, on the one hand in the extreme contrast between poverty and wealth in South Africa and, on the other, in the need for greater political will on the part of all key role-players to seek durable solutions in the tradition of the mid-1990s.[79]

Since Marikana disaffection has spread further through COSATU and, to a less visible extent, the ANC. Although finding expression in conflicts among leaders of

---

[74] Including the requirement of a compulsory strike ballot, the power of the Commission for Conciliation, Mediation and Arbitration (the Department of Labour's national labour dispute resolution agency) to suspend a strike 'in the public interest', and the power of the Labour Court to prohibit a strike under certain circumstances.

[75] SARB *Quarterly Bulletin* (note 71 above) 2, 5.

[76] A commission of inquiry headed by a retired judge of the Supreme Court of Appeal, Mr Justice Farlam, to investigate legal accountability for the police action is due to submit its report and recommendations to President Zuma by the end of March 2015.

[77] Hartford, (note 70 above).

[78] See the new sections 21(8A)–(8D), LRA.

[79] See the articles cited in note 70 above.

different schools of thought in the movement, there can be little doubt that dissatisfaction with the economic policies of the current ANC administration, seen by many as favouring employers and the new black elite at the expense of workers and the poor, is a major driving force. There can be equally little doubt that the incoming administration, following the April 2014 elections,[80] is having to face the challenge of reconciling these differences.

The Outlook: South Africa

To sum up: inequality and mass unemployment cast their shadow over every facet of South African society and the labour market. In a sense, the endemic strife between employers and labour can be explained by conflicting responses to these realities. From a free market perspective the answer must be of a deregulatory nature, liberating employers from legal constraints on the assumption that this will enable them to create jobs and new wealth. From a trade union perspective the way forward lies in more inclusive policies and a more egalitarian distribution of social wealth. However, nothing remains static. The question is how these differences will evolve.

Some improvement is expected globally and South Africa's growth rate is expected to rise over the next two years.[81] The National Development Plan, seen by government as being consistent with South Africa's membership of BRICS,[82] was described in 2013 as a framework for accelerated growth and the reduction of inequality.[83] But, against the background sketched above, this in itself is highly unlikely to offer a solution. Growth would need to take place at unprecedented rates over a prolonged period to overcome the social chasm. Moreover, the proceeds of growth would need to be applied towards social need rather than private enrichment. These challenges go well beyond the traditional terrain of labour law, raising issues relating to the realisation of workers' basic rights both inside and outside the workplace and creating conditions under which they can be met. But, from a labour law perspective, the workplace is where the process must begin.

It seems likely that Department of Labour's regulatory philosophy of 'regulated flexibility' will be tested to the utmost. Based on the ILO's approach to flexibility, which factors in employers' interest in flexibility as well as employee interest in job

---

[80] The elections saw a reduction in support for the ANC from 66 per cent to 62 per cent and 6 per cent of the vote going to the Economic Freedom Fighters, a radical populist group expressing frustration among the youth and the poor. In addition, some 23 per cent of potential voters did not register to vote and, of those who did, some 27 per cent did not vote.

[81] United Nations 'World situation and economic prospects 2014' at 2.

[82] President Jacob Zuma was quoted on the eve of the 5th BRICS Summit held in Durban in March 2013 as saying that being a BRICS member 'fits in well with our NDP objectives of raising employment through faster economic growth, improving quality of education, skills development and innovation, as well as building the capacity of the state to play a developmental, transformative role': http://www.sanews.gov.za/world/brics-fits-well-sa%E2%80%99s-national-development-plan-zuma (accessed 6 February 2013).

[83] At http://www.npconline.co.za/MediaLib/Downloads/Downloads/Executive%20Summary-NDP%202030%20-%20Our%20future%20-%20make%20it%20work.pdf (accessed 3 February 2013).

security, this concept has informed the drafting of the post-1994 labour law dispensation.[84] Going beyond a simple balance between competing interests, the object has been to create a framework within which a balance can be struck and constantly adjusted.[85] But 'flexibility' has thus far been 'narrowly circumscribed, aimed at enabling employers to vary minimum employment standards rather than addressing the divergent conditions prevailing in different sectors, and non-industrial sectors in particular'.[86] It is arguable that a broader concept of flexibility, not confined to employers' operational requirements but seeking to address the needs of workers as well as employers in different sectors, will need to be developed if sustainable solutions are to be found.[87] This, in turn, is seen by some as key to unlocking the growth and productive potential of the South African economy.

2. INDIA

India, billed as one of the 'emerging' economies of the South, has enjoyed a rate of growth of over 8 per cent in the first decade of this century. Maintaining a high growth rate has been a matter of critical concern given the sheer enormity of the population and the work force in India. The growth rate for 2013 however fell to around 5 per cent. This slow-down has been accompanied by a decrease in investments, casting doubts on the sustainability of the higher rates of growth experienced over the past couple of decades, a period that coincided with the 'opening up' of the economy. The new government elected in 2014 has projected a growth rate of 8% for 2015–16.

Official unemployment figures in India have always been relatively low, at around 10.8 million in 2011–12. Employment, which was 457 million in 2004–05, reached 472.9 million in 2011–12. The bulk of this employment has been in the informal economy, which accounts for over 80 per cent of all employment in India. The quality of work available in the informal economy and the need to formalise the informal in

---

[84] Halton Cheadle, 'Regulated flexibility: Revisiting the LRA and the BCEA' (2006) 27 *Industrial Law Journal (South Africa)* 663 at 668. Cheadle provides a comprehensive review of the origins of the LRA and why the objectives of regulated flexibility have not come to fruition.

[85] Ibid at 668.

[86] Darcy Du Toit and Roger Ronnie, 'Regulating the informal economy: Unpacking the oxymoron – From worker protection to worker empowerment' (2014) 35 *Industrial Law Journal (South Africa)* 1802. See, for example, sections 14 and 15 of the BCEA providing for variations of daily or weekly working hours. Flexibility in such forms addresses the needs of large employers rather than seeking to promote more appropriate forms of protection for workers in non-standard jobs.

[87] See Ian Ayres and John Braithwaite, *Responsive Regulation: Transcending the Deregulation Debate* (Oxford University Press, 1992). In response to the programme of deregulation associated with the 'Washington consensus' the authors proposed that regulation should be capable of responding to the realities of different sectors, workplaces and work processes. The implication is that regulatory processes should be decentralised in order to allow workers and employers to formulate the rules by which their relationship is governed in their specific environment, whether by means of collective bargaining or other appropriate mechanisms. See also Hepple's analysis of 'meaningful engagement' in Bob Hepple, 'Negotiating social change in the shadow of the law' (2012) *South African Law Journal* 248.

order to achieve decent work goals and to enable enterprises to become more productive is currently a matter of much discussion within the ILO and India.

According to the ILO, 'The informal economy is marked by acute decent work deficits and a disproportionate share of the working poor.'[88] The International Labour Conference in 2002 had characterised the informal economy as covering:

> all economic activities by workers and economic units that are – in law or in practice – not covered or insufficiently covered by formal arrangements. Their activities are not included in the law, which means that they are operating outside the formal reach of the law; or they are not covered in practice, which means that – although they are operating within the formal reach of the law, the law is not applied or not enforced; or the law discourages compliance because it is inappropriate, burdensome, or imposes excessive costs.

Informality, thus, is inextricably linked to how the law, and therefore the right to social security/decent work, is structured and enforced.

This part of this four-country chapter examines some aspects of the informal economy in India and highlights the case of those employed through intermediaries (contract labour), which is a growing segment of employment in India, to understand the key challenges that informality in employment poses to labour law and the trajectory of development in this region.

The Informal Economy in India

India perhaps has the largest numbers of persons employed in the informal economy.[89] Despite conventional wisdom, the high rates of growth experienced by India during the past decade or so have not resulted in any reduction in the proportion of persons working in the informal economy. On the contrary, the informal economy has emerged as a 'shock absorber' for creating bare livelihood options during the periodic downturns and crises in the formal sector, as well as regularly providing a 'safety net' for those who are unemployed and under employed.

In terms of the nature of employment, the share of regular wage and salaried workers has been just 17.9 per cent of total employment, and the figures for women workers is far lower at 12.7 per cent in 2011–12. In terms of the sector where persons were employed, in 2011–12 around 82.2 per cent of those working were in the informal sector. There has been a gradual increase in the share of workers employed in the formal sector in the last decade, growing from 13.7 per cent in 2004–05 to 17.8 per cent in 2011–12. A substantial part of this increase has been in informal jobs in the formal sector.[90]

---

[88] ILO, *Transitioning from the Informal to the Formal Economy*, Report V(1), International Labour Conference, 2014 (2013).

[89] The terms 'unorganized'/'organised' rather than 'informal'/'formal' are used in official India documents.

[90] Figures mentioned here are drawn from the ILO, *India Labour Market Update,* (December 2013, ILO Country Office for India). The terms 'organised/unorganised' used in India have been replaced with 'formal/informal'.

Far from dying out, the informal economy has been thriving and growing in India. The formal and informal parts of the economy appear to be inextricably entwined.[91] Further, the contribution of the informal economy to the GDP is significant. A government appointed commission in India assessed its contribution to be around 55 per cent of India's GDP in 2008.[92] Many of the economic activities of the enterprises in the informal economy i.e., enterprises not covered by the regulatory framework, are often economically linked to the formal part of the economy. Home-based workers who carry out part of the manufacture within their homes are one example of such linkages. The manufacturer saves on the costs associated with employing workers and supervising their work on his/her premises. Workers working on a casual basis, without regular jobs, are a large category of informal workers. Self-employment has emerged as the largest segment within informality in India, and this consists mainly of own-account workers carrying out economic activities; these household enterprises as well as those who work there often fall outside the scope of legal regulation. Often, such own-account workers rely on family members to eke out a living, and such contributing family workers are not recognised as workers under labour law. Street vendors, waste-pickers, individual landholders working on their piece of land, fish workers, village artisans, etc. are examples of such survival activities carried on by such households.[93] Whether these tiny, household-based 'enterprises' can scale up to become enterprises subject to various regulations or are a 'cushion' to allow households to eke out a livelihood is a matter of discussion at the ILO which is slated to adopt a Recommendation pertaining to the transition from the informal to the formal economy at the International Labour Conference in 2015.[94]

Another example of informal employment arises where the workers are employed in an enterprise which is otherwise covered by the labour law but where the duration of employment is irregular or intermittent or else is mediated through a contractor/intermediary and the eventual employer/user enterprise/principal employer is not treated as the employer of such workers.

Indian law considers the informal economy as comprising all those working in the informal sector (broadly speaking, enterprises below a certain employment threshold where most of the labour laws relating to regulation of work or social security do not apply) as well as those working in large enterprises where such protection exists but

---

[91] Dibyendu Maiti and Kunal Sen, 'The informal sector in India: A means of exploitation or accumulation?' (2010) 5(1) *Journal of South Asian Development*, 1–13.

[92] NCEUS, *Report on Conditions of Work and Promotion of Livelihoods in the Unorganised Sector*, (Government of India, 2007); K. P. Kannan and T. S. Papola, 'Workers in the informal sector: Initiatives by India's National Commission for Enterprises in the Unorganized Sector (NCEUS)' (2007) 146(3–4) *International Labour Review*.

[93] Although traditionally considered to be part of the informal economy, India has recently enacted a new law that provides for the regulation of street vending and protects street vendors from harassment, eviction and confiscation of their property. The Street Vendors (Protection of Livelihood and Regulation of Street Vending) Act, 2014.

[94] See for instance, ILO, Sixth Supplementary Report: *Report of the Tripartite Meeting of Experts on Facilitating Transitions from the Informal Economy to the Formal Economy* (16–20 September 2013), and the Text of Resolutions adopted at the International Labour Conference, 2014.

where the nature of employment of informal workers is such that they are excluded from social security protection. This latter limb captures a process of *informalisation* where, due to reasons such as the short duration of their contract of employment, or nature of work, or mode of employment such as via intermediaries, such employees fall outside protection. The Unorganised Workers Social Security Act (UWSSA) enacted in 2008 captures this broad-based method of defining the sector and the workers involved.

S. 2 (l) states: 'unorganised sector' means an enterprise owned by individuals or self-employed workers and engaged in the production or sale of goods or providing service of any kind whatsoever, and where the enterprise employs workers, the number of such workers is less than ten.

S. 2 (m) states: 'unorganised worker' means a home-based worker, self-employed worker or a wage worker in the unorganised sector and includes a worker in the organised sector who is not covered by any of the Acts mentioned in Schedule II to this Act.

In short, informality can occur in both the formal and informal sectors, as the focus is worker-centric and not enterprise-centric. The size of the enterprise, the nature of work performed as well as the coverage under social security benefits determine if a worker is working in conditions of informality. I examine below one example of informality dealing with contractualisation, i.e., the employment of informal workers engaged through an intermediary/contractor in formal enterprises that has been steadily growing in recent years in India and how this impacts the development of the Indian economy.

'Contractualisation' as a Growing Form of Informality in Employment

In 1997, the ILO considered a draft instrument dealing with contract labour. It was perhaps the only instance where an instrument that was proposed at the International Labour Conference was not adopted for lack of the necessary consensus.[95] One of the reasons for this was a bitter debate over the role of intermediaries, and their role and liability in the employment relationship. The expression contract labour used by the ILO[96] was already familiar to Indian law. The Industrial Disputes Act, 1947 that largely

---

[95] See for instance, Leah F Vosko, 'Gender, precarious work, and the International Labour Code: The ghost in the ILO Closet' in Judy Fudge and Rosemary Owens (eds), *Precarious Work, Women, and the New Economy: The Challenge to Legal Norms* (Hart Publishing, 2006).

[96]

a. The proposed instrument defined the terms 'contract labour', 'sub-contractor' and intermediary' as follows (Article 1) the term 'contract labour' means work performed for a natural or legal person (referred to as a 'user enterprise') by a person (referred to as a 'contract worker') where the work is performed by the contract worker personally under actual conditions of dependency on or subordination to the user enterprise and these conditions are similar to those that characterize an employment relationship under national law and practice and where either:

   i. the work is performed pursuant to a direct contractual arrangement other than a contract of employment between the contract worker and the user enterprise; or
   ii. the contract worker is provided for the user enterprise by a subcontractor or an intermediary;

covers employment relations within the formal sector has grappled with whether the employment relationship traditionally envisaged as a bilateral relationship between employer and employee could also extend to triangular relations, and whether such contract labour (i.e., a person engaged via a contractor, rather than a person employed on a fixed-term contract) could correctly be treated to be an employee of the user enterprise.[97] The question whether the term 'employee' should cover such workers engaged through an intermediary has been a vexed question in India. The employment relations for such 'contract labour' engaged through an intermediary is regulated through the Contract Labour (Regulation and Abolition) Act, 1970. This law holds the principal employer (the user enterprise in ILO parlance) as ultimately responsible for payment of wages and other social security benefits but in the first instance such liability is cast upon the contractor or the intermediary who actually employs such workers to work on the premises of the principal employer.

India has seen a tremendous spurt in the use of contract labour in recent times. Some estimates suggest that around 30 per cent of all employment in the manufacturing sector could be such contract labour. Contract labour is not only used for 'low end' activities such as cleaning services, security services, but is also to be found on the shop floor working alongside regular workers, but earning a fraction of that earned by permanent regular workers directly employed by the user enterprise. The biggest Indian auto manufacturer, for instance, employs 70 per cent of its workers not directly, but through a contractor and who work along-side regular workers. The lack of a uniform set of labour regulations governing workers performing same or similar work within an enterprise has been a cause of social unrest across India.

Formalising the Informal

The current ILO focus has been on 'formalising' the 'informal'. The strategy has been to formalise enterprises by bringing them under legal frameworks that regulate their business, financial and property rights aspects. The effects of the over-regulation of enterprises in the informal sector have been highlighted, such as, for instance, a reduction in their capacity to absorb surplus labour, which would result in enormous social exclusion with its related social and political costs. The need to 'manage' regulation in a manner such that such enterprises serve as sites for skill development, incubating entrepreneurship, employment generation or livelihood creation is often

---

b. the term 'subcontractor' means a natural or legal person who undertakes by a contractual arrangement with a user enterprise to have work performed for that enterprise;
c. the term 'intermediary' means a natural or legal person who makes contract workers available to a user enterprise without becoming formally the employer of these workers.

[97] See for instance, the judgment of the Indian Supreme Court in *Hussainbhai, Calicut v Alath Factory Thozhilali Union, Kozhikode* (1978) 2 LLJ 397 which debated whether workers employed by an intermediary could be treated as workers of the main enterprise, and held that upon lifting the veil in some cases, the user enterprise could be shown to be the true employer and the use of an intermediary or contractor, a mere paper arrangement.

underscored.[98] What is interesting is that the debates, at least in countries such as India, around the regulation of the informal enterprises, seek to pay attention to the viability of the enterprise alongside their financial capacity to deliver decent work goals.[99] Thus, laws relating to regulating conditions of work or inspection services do not extend to such enterprises for fear of causing harassment or adding to their transaction costs. This is somewhat in contrast to the debates that have surrounded the 'labour law regulation versus economic development' debates of the last century in India where the inability to pay the minimum wages or bear the costs of regulation has not been a ground for stake holders to permit any flexibility or dilution of such standards in the formal enterprises.[100]

The focus of formalising the informal in India has been largely worker-centric, and aimed at ensuring that informal workers get some modicum of social protection, even if it be at levels lower than formal workers, either in the same enterprise or in informal enterprises. The strategy has been for the labour law to 'formalise' such an informal worker by providing limited social security benefits (albeit at levels different and lower than those enjoyed by formal sector workers). Labour law has chosen a trajectory of reform different from that traditionally used in the formal sector. For instance, under the UWSSA, the employer is not a contributor to the new social security schemes covering informal workers. This marks a shift from traditional social security schemes in India which are usually either exclusively employer-liability schemes or jointly contributory schemes. In the case of the UWSSA, the government has set up a new social security fund where the burden of formalisation of informal workers through their access to social security benefits is mainly borne by the government. Recent estimates indicate that the expenditure of central and state governments on social security (this includes contributions to the above fund as well as ongoing social assistance schemes) were about 5.25 per cent of the GDP in 2010–11 and had increased from 4.42 per cent in 1995–96.[101] Increasing the coverage of social security schemes and including greater numbers within a social security net appears to be the chief method by which India seeks to formalise the informal workers. The new government has proposed a slew of social security/social assistance schemes that are to be available to all citizens and not just those in informal employment. Given the enormous scale of the informal employment in India, universal social security options may fare better than traditional social insurance schemes.

The challenge of formalising the informal *enterprises* rather than the informal worker has been more contentious. A government-appointed commission (the NCEUS) chose a worker-centric strategy and focused on providing a social security net instead as

---

[98] See for instance ILO, *Transitioning from the Informal to the Formal Economy* Report V(1) (2013).

[99] See National Commission for Enterprises in the Unorganised Sector, *The Challenge of Employment in India: An Informal Economy Perspective*, vol 1 (New Delhi, Government of India, 2009); also see the position of the Government of India in ILO, *Transitioning from the Informal to the Formal Economy* Report V(2) (2014).

[100] For a useful summary of these debates see, Errol D'Souza, 'Labour market institutions in India: Their impact on growth and employment', ILO Asia-Pacific Working Paper Series (2008).

[101] Institute for Human Development, *India Labour and Employment Report 2014* (Academic Foundation, New Delhi 2014).

regulating other conditions of work within such enterprises could adversely affect their sustainability. The trade-off between the sustainability of such enterprises post-regulation and their usefulness in providing social inclusion and viable options for those outside the formal sector is a matter that can only be determined on a case-by-case basis as the Indian example indicates. The challenge of providing for a uniform set of labour laws for all those working *within* an enterprise, whether they are directly employed or engaged through a contractor, remains to be addressed.

Recent legislative changes introduced by the new government in India, simplify the documents and registers that need to be maintained by small enterprises (defined as employing between ten and 40 persons) through an amendment of the Labour Laws (Exemption from Furnishing Returns and Maintaining Registers by Certain Establishments) Act, 1988, in an effort to expand the compliance of labour laws by such enterprises. The government is also considering a special law for small factories (employing up to 40 persons), and amendments to other labour laws. The new proposals, aimed at formalising the informal, move away from a 'one size fits all' approach towards customising labour laws based on the employment thresholds of enterprises. The coming period is expected to see more of such size-specific labour legislation targetting enterprises currently operating outside the labour law framework.

The Outlook: India

This part of the chapter has focused on one aspect of the Indian economy, namely – the informal economy, to demonstrate the kinds of challenges labour law and development face in emerging economies such as India. A trajectory of development and, in turn, the future of labour law in countries such as India has necessarily to address key concerns of a post-Fordist economy and manage the challenges to the formal and informal economy simultaneously.

3. CHINA

Regulating the Chinese Labour Market

Over the last 30 years, China has grown to become the world's second largest economy, and has overtaken the United States as the world's largest manufacturing power.[102] It has the world's largest workforce[103] and plays a pivotal role in the global trading regime. Unlike several of the other BRICS, China's high economic growth rate has not

[102] 'The End of Cheap China'. *The Economist*, 10th March 2012.

[103] At the end of 2012, according to official Chinese statistics from the Ministry of Human Resources and Social Security, the total workforce was 767 million. 371 million or 48 per cent were defined as being in the urban workforce (working in cities and townships); this proportion has been steadily increasing. 33.6 per cent of the workforce was engaged in primary production, 30.3 per cent in secondary industry (including manufacturing) and 36.1 per cent in tertiary industry (including the service sector): 2012 年度人力资源和社会保障事业发展统计公报.

as yet faltered – for more than 20 years it has continued to attain annual GDP growth in excess of 7 per cent.[104]

This high rate of growth has coincided with a massive influx of labour from agriculture into the industry and service sectors, although migrating rural workers continue to encounter discriminatory treatment in relation to benefits enjoyed by many urban workers.[105] In contrast to the experience of South Africa, unemployment has remained quite low in China, even in the wake of the global financial crisis.[106] Indeed, several parts of the country, especially along the coast, have experienced labour shortages in recent years.[107] China's low birth rate, which is partly a function of the one child policy, means that as long as the economy continues its rapid expansion, these shortages are likely to continue.

Unlike India, South Africa and Brazil, China is an authoritarian, one-party state in which constitutional rights cannot be enforced by judicial review.[108] Freedom of association – and in particular the right to organise – is curtailed in that the only legitimate trade unions are those which are controlled by the Chinese Communist Party.[109] The state also has a pervasive role in the economy; although foreign invested and private enterprises now account for the majority of output and employment in the manufacturing sector, state enterprises continue to dominate in strategic sectors ranging from energy to telecommunications and banking.[110]

The Chinese party-state continues to maintain features of central planning, including overarching economic strategies and industry policies. The current Five Year Plan (2011–2015) proposes to rebalance the economy, which has hitherto been dependent on export-led growth and state investment, by promoting consumption and the service

---

[104] See World Bank historical data on GDP growth (annual).

[105] This is a consequence of the internal migration controls known as hukou (household registration).

[106] According to the government's Xinhua news agency, the official urban rate of unemployment in early 2014 was 4.1 per cent: China's 2013 urban unemployment rate at 4.1 per cent, available at http://news.xinhuanet.com/english/china/2014-01/24/c_133071541.htm. See also 2012 年度人力资源和社会保障事业发展统计公报.

[107] 'Dangerous curve ahead, the IMF warns China', *Wall Street Journal*, 31 January, 2013.

[108] Jianfu Chen, *Chinese Law: Context and Transformation* (Martinus Nijhoff, 2008).

[109] See, e.g., Tim Pringle and Simon Clarke, *The Challenge of Transition: Trade Unions in Russia, China and Vietnam*, (Palgrave McMillan, 2011); Eli Friedman and Ching Kwan Lee, 'Remaking the world of Chinese labour: A 30 year retrospective', (2010) 48 *British Journal of Industrial Relations*, 507–33.

[110] Around 65 million urban workers are engaged in state-owned enterprises; this figure has remained static in recent years but as a proportion of total urban employment, employment in state owned enterprises has fallen from 90 per cent in the 1990s to less than one-quarter. Around 60 million are engaged in urban large private enterprises (such as domestic corporation and foreign firms), a figure which has been rapidly increasing. Around 100 million are self-employed or engaged in small firms. China Labour Statistical Yearbook 2011 Table 1.7. It should be noted that the ownership status of employers engaging some 100 million urban workers is not accounted for in official statistics.

sector.[111] One aspect of this has been a shift from a policy of containing wage growth to attract investment to one of encouraging rapid wage rises. Minimum wages, which are locally determined, have risen extraordinarily in recent years, well in excess of 10 per cent annually in many cases.[112]

Collective contracting has also been heavily promoted as a means of driving up wage growth for workers already above the minimum wage.[113] Most of the resulting agreements are concluded by enterprise heads and state-controlled union officials with little real bargaining. However, there are increasing instances of multi-firm and regional negotiation with the support of the state-sanctioned trade union movement. There are also many reported cases of workers taking industrial action in support of wage claims; such strikes are usually illegal but are often tolerated if they make no political demands or attempt to set up rival unions.[114]

Apart from these initiatives around remuneration, China has undertaken a number of significant reforms to labour laws since the mid-2000s. In contrast to the stagnation of federal labour law in the United States[115] or (until very recently) India, China's law-makers have been prompted to fundamentally reshape key labour statutes by both economic drivers (as mentioned, raising consumption) and – perhaps more significantly – fear of social instability.[116] The new statutes, which have included the Labour Contract Law, the Labour Disputes Mediation and Arbitration Law, and the Social Security Law have been developed after very extensive consideration and debate about appropriate forms of work regulation in the contemporary Chinese economy.[117] These laws have been directed at issues of formalisation, agency work, wage protection, access to arbitration and the courts, social security payments and anti-discrimination. Initial empirical work has suggested that these measures have had significant impact on workplaces.

At first glance, then, China appears to be moving along quite a positive trajectory as far as work regulation is concerned. In marked contrast to the position in the 1990s and early 2000s, there is a reasonably effective and comprehensive regulatory framework in place. This operates in a context of relatively low unemployment in international terms, and rapidly rising wages.

---

[111] The original Chinese version is available at http://news.sina.com.cn/c/2011-03-17/055622129864.shtml. For an English translation of the Plan, see http://www.britishchamber.cn/content/chinas-twelfth-five-year-plan-2011-2015-full-english-version.

[112] 'China pushes minimum wage rises', *Financial Times*, 4 January, 2012.

[113] Sarah Biddulph, 'Responding to industrial unrest in China: Prospects for strengthening the role of collective bargaining', (2012) 34(1) *Sydney University Law Review*, 35–63.

[114] See, e.g., Chris King-Chi Chan and Elaine Sio-Ieng Hui, 'The Dynamics and Dilemma of Workplace Trade Union Reform in China: The Case of the Honda Workers' Strike' (2012) 54(5) *Journal of Industrial Relations*, 653–68.

[115] Cynthia Estlund, 'The ossification of American labor law' (2002) 102 *Columbia Law Review*, 1527–612.

[116] Sarah Biddulph and Sean Cooney, 'Rule of law with Chinese characteristics: The role of campaigns in law-making and enforcement' (2012) 34(4) *Law and Policy*, 373–401.

[117] See, e.g., Mary E. Gallagher and Baohua Dong, 'Legislating harmony: Law reform in contemporary China' in Sarosh. Kuruvilla, Ching Kwan Lee and Mary E. Gallagher, *From Iron Rice Bowl to Informalization: Markets, Workers and the State in a Changing China* (Cornell University Press, 2011) 36–60.

There are, however, serious doubts as to whether this growth pattern is economically and environmentally sustainable.[118] There is increasing concern that this growth reflects unsustainable debt levels, particularly in relation to construction projects in the provinces and municipalities. Furthermore, the regulatory strategies China uses to deal with economic and social difficulties are highly party-state dependent.[119] This seriously constrains the mechanisms for responding to crisis – there is little scope for private and community sector organisations to contribute to governance. Nonetheless, for the moment, the conditions of work for many Chinese are steadily improving, without the obvious problems of high unemployment (as is the case of South Africa), pervasive informality (as is the case in India) or the cost of living (as is the case in Brazil).

On the other hand, Chinese work regulation does face some similar challenges to counterparts in India and South Africa. We can focus on two here: precarious work and agency work (which is often seen as a form of precarious work, but which will be treated in particular detail here).

Precarious Work

The 1990s and early 2000s saw rising informality, in the sense of precarious work with little or no effective regulation by labour statutes.[120] Until the late 1980s, the core of the industrial workforce in China's socialised economy had enjoyed extensive job security and a privileged economic position.[121] However, factors such as the restructuring of the state-owned sector, the rapid expansion of the private sector and the replacement of administrative regulation by contracting saw increasing numbers of workers placed in a precarious situation. Three different instances of precarious work can be mentioned. First, there were a large number of people who lacked written evidence of a labour relationship (even though they were in one). They were unable to claim entitlements they had been denied by means of legal proceedings.[122]

Second, the rapid introduction of the contract system across the Chinese economy meant that by the early 2000s, a large majority of the employed workforce was engaged on rolling fixed term contracts, of increasingly short duration.[123] Not only could these employees be terminated readily – including in the event of a dispute about entitlements – but they also faced obstacles in accruing employment benefits under labour and social security laws.

---

[118] China's exports plunge as fears of credit crisis grow, *The Telegraph,* 8 March 2014; Most Chinese cities fail minimum air quality standards, study says, *New York Times,* 27 March 2014.

[119] Kenneth Lieberthal, *Governing China: From Revolution Through Reform* (2nd ed,: W.W. Norton, 2004).

[120] Albert Park and Fang Cai, 'The Informalization of the Chinese Labor Market' (2011) in Kuruvilla, Lee and Gallagher (note 117 above) 17–35.

[121] It should be emphasised that the vast majority of the workforce at that time enjoyed the much less privileged conditions of rural and village areas.

[122] See, in particular Aaron Halegua, 'Getting paid: processing the labor disputes of China's migrant workers' (2008) 26 *Berkeley Journal of International Law*, 254–322.

[123] Mary E. Gallagher, *Contagious Capitalism: Globalization and the Politics of Labor in China* (Princeton University Press, 2007), 76–82.

Third, there were – and are – many workers beyond the scope of labour regulation. This is generally the case if the nature of their work relationship means that they are not 'labourers' engaged by a 'work unit'. Such people cannot invoke labour law standards law or labour dispute resolution institutions. Where they attempt to do so, those institutions will deny jurisdiction. For example, interns, dependent contractors, people employed by individuals rather than registered entities and domestic workers have not been covered by Chinese labour law.[124]

The Labour Contract Law and allied reforms made significant inroads in addressing the first two of these problems.[125] Labour contracts, other than casual contracts, must now be in writing, with very significant penalties (such as a doubling of pay obligations) for employers who fail to comply. Again, modifications to the rules of fixed-term contracting have attempted to reverse the trend towards ever shorter periods of engagement. There are two important aspects to Labour Contract Law rules. On the one hand, substantial severance payments must be made upon the termination of a fixed term contract (arts 46(4) and 47). As these severance entitlements are payable each time a contract is terminated, but are not payable if the contract is renewed on equal or better terms, they constitute a significant financial penalty for engaging workers on a short-term basis. On the other hand, to curb rolling contracts, there is now a provision (art. 14(3)) stipulating that where a worker has been twice engaged on fixed-term contracts, the third engagement must be ongoing. Empirical research since the passage of the law has tended to suggest that these measures have been effective in increasing the proportion of the workforce covered by written contracts, and in lengthening contract terms.[126]

Despite these measures, there are still important categories of disadvantaged workers. First, the provisions in the Labour Contract Law dealing with casual workers are mostly concerned with denying them entitlements enjoyed by workers on permanent or fixed-term contracts. Contracts with casual workers (who are defined as 'part-time' workers engaged on average for less than 24 hours per week and four hours per day) do not have to be in writing (art. 69), their engagement can be terminated at will (art. 71) and they are not entitled to termination payments (art. 71). Because of the nature of

---

124 Sean Cooney, Sarah Biddulph and Ying Zhu, *Law and Fair Work in China,* (Routledge, London, 2013), 53–4; Ye J. (叶静漪) (2007) 劳动合同法十二讲 (Twelve Lectures on the Labour Contract Law), Beijing, 中国法制出版社 (China Legal Publishing); S. Zheng and K. Li (郑尚元，李坤刚)(2010) 劳动和社会保障法学 (*Labour and Social Security Law*) Beijing, 北京师范大学出版集团 (Beijing Normal University Publishing Group), 53–5; B. Dong (董保华) (ed.) (2005) 劳动合同研究 (*Research on Labour Contracts*), Beijing: 中国劳动社会保障出版社 (China Labour and Social Security Publishing), 54–77.

125 Cooney et al, Id 86–107.

126 See, e.g., Mary E. Gallagher; John Giles; Albert Park; Meiyan Wang, 'China's 2008 labor contract law: implementation and implications for China's workers' *World Bank Policy Research Paper* 6542, (2013); Zhiming Cheng, Russell Smyth and Fei Guo, 'The impact of China's New Labour Contract Law on socioeconomic outcomes for migrant and urban worker', *Monash University Department of Economics, Discussion Paper* 51/13; Richard Freeman and Xiaoying Li, (2013). 'How Does China's New Labor Contract Law affect floating workers?' *NBER Working Paper* 19254. Official Chinese statistics put the rate of written contracts in enterprises at 88.4 per cent, without explaining how this figure is derived: 2012 年度人力资源和社会保障事业发展统计公报.

their engagement, casual workers are unlikely to receive pay for overtime, or premium rates for work at unsociable hours, or paid leave (although work statutes are silent on whether there is at least an in-principle entitlement).[127]

Failure to create clear limits around casual workers risks undermining the legal entitlements of more secure forms of employment by encouraging employers to resort to casualisation in order to escape the obligations associated with fixed and ongoing positions. Moreover, overuse of casual category detracts from the formalization of labour relations that the Labour Contract Law was intended to achieve.

Furthermore, the Labour Contract Law did not expand the scope of work regulation to cover categories such as domestic workers dependent contractors and interns. This means that as much as half the workforce lies outside formal labour law. While coverage compares favourably to countries such as India, there are still many vulnerable workers without recourse to labour standards and labour dispute resolution mechanisms.

Agency Work

As is clear from the other contributions to this chapter, agency work (also called labour hire or dispatch work) has become widespread in many labour markets, not least because the costs to the end user of using hired labour are often less than those of direct employment.

Agency work creates a legal division between the entity which uses the workers and the entity which is their formal employer for the purposes of work regulation.[128] The end user can, in some cases, deny responsibility for the employment entitlements of the hired labour notwithstanding the fact that that the hired labour may be quite integrated into the end user's business, working with directly employed workers for lengthy periods. As is the case with South Africa and India, agency work has posed a major challenge to traditional work law in China;[129] on some estimates there are as many as 60 million agency workers, three times the number recorded in the 1990s.[130]

While agency workers in China are likely to be engaged under worse conditions than their direct counterparts, Chinese work law has attempted to ensure some baseline protections. In 2008, the Labour Contract Law[131] introduced minimum capitalisation requirements for labour hire firms. It attempted to provide for equal treatment between the hired labour and an end user's direct employee (art. 63). The law also required labour hire firms to engage agency workers on fixed term contracts of at least two years' duration (art. 58). Finally, the law specified that agency workers should be engaged 'generally for temporary, auxiliary or substitute jobs' (art. 66).

---

127 On the other hand, they do have some legal rights. They are entitled to be paid at least the hourly rate of the minimum wage applicable in the location in which they work. They must be paid within 15 days and they are entitled to access the labour dispute resolution system.

128 See David Weil's discussion of fissuring in: 'A strategic approach to labour inspection' (2008) 147 *International Labour Review*, 349–75.

129 C. Zhou (周长征) (ed, 2007) 劳动派遣的发展与法律规制 (*The Development and Legal Regulation of Labor Dispatch*), Beijing: 中国劳动社会保障出版社 (China Labour and Social Security Publishing).

130 Baohua Dong, 董保华 论劳务派遣立法中的思维定势.

131 Chapter 5 Section 2.

These measures encountered legal and practical obstacles and must be counted among the less successful initiatives in the Labour Contract Law.[132] Judges found the 'equal treatment' provision difficult to apply because the reference point to determine equal treatment was unclear. The attempt to confine agency workers to temporary positions was widely ignored. The number of agency workers both in absolute terms and as a proportion of the total workforce has dramatically risen over the last decade[133] and the 2008 Labour Contract Law provisions appears to have had little impact on this. Accordingly, the central government has enacted further restrictions to prevent agency workers from becoming the dominant form of contracting, undermining direct employment.

In late 2012, the Standing Committee of the National People's Congress amended the Labour Contract Law[134] to strengthen the limits on agency work. The minimum capital requirement for labour hire agencies was quadrupled to two million yuan (amended art. 57) and a licensing requirement stipulating. The equal treatment provision was clarified to require employers to use the system of payment distribution methods for its own employees and for agency workers (amended art. 63). Further, article 66, which as indicated above, originally provided that agency work would be used 'generally for temporary, auxiliary or substitute jobs' was amended to provide as follows:

> The employment contract is the basic form through which Chinese enterprises engage workers. 'Labour dispatch (agency work) is a supplementary form and may only be used for temporary, auxiliary or substitutive positions'.

Each of the three kinds of positions is now clearly defined in the same article.

The most far-reaching innovation was a provision (also in art. 66) that enabled the relevant ministry (the Ministry of Human Resources and Social Security) to cap the number of agency workers at a certain proportion of a firm's total employers. This cap was implemented in 2014 in the Interim Provisions on Labour Dispatch issued by the Ministry.[135] They stipulate that the number of agency workers shall not exceed 10 per cent of the total number of a firm's workers (art. 4). There is a two-year phase in period, but firms cannot engage new agency workers unless they reduce the number of previously engaged agency workers below the requisite percentage (art. 28).[136]

Whether these new measures will be strictly enforced is unclear. Many local governments may be resistant to implementing them, as they control entities which frequently engage agency workers, including public sector entities such as hospitals.[137]

---

132 L. Zhu (2011) (朱丽君)《劳动合同法》实施中遇到的困境：以未签书面劳动合同问题和劳务派遣问题为例, 22 法治论坛 68–73.

133 In many Chinese firms, between one-third and one-half of the workforce are agency workers: 'China tightens loophole on hiring temporary workers', *Reuters*, Friday, 28 December 2012: http://www.reuters.com/article/2012/12/28/us-china-labor-idUSBRE8BR04120121228.

134 全国人大常委会关于修改《中华人民共和国劳动合同法》的贵定, promulgated 28 December 2012.

135 劳务派遣暂行规定 issued 24 January 2014.

136 Another significant provision is art. 18, which is directed at ensuring that agency workers sent into a different locality are not denied social security benefits.

137 Gallagher at al, (note 126 above).

However, since the enactment of the Labour Contract Law and the Labour Disputes Mediation and Arbitration Law, Chinese workers' consciousness of their legal entitlements has grown and they have proved quite litigious. This may mean they create ongoing pressure for enforcement.[138]

The Outlook: China

In comparative terms, China is remarkable for its preparedness to resort to increasingly strict labour market regulation, combined with improved dispute resolution structures, to deal with erosion of the 'standard employment relationship', attempting to curb undocumented, short-term and agency work. It has had some success so far. As the South African experience shows, such measures are, in many countries, strongly opposed by business groups and some governmental organisations as limiting labour market flexibility. There is certainly contestation around the new initiatives in China.[139] Indeed, one prominent labour law professor critical of the wave of new laws has complained of a 'vicious cycle' in which tighter government rules encourage employer evasion which then leads to further tighter rules.[140] He suggests that business will now shift from agency work to contractors.

However such criticisms have not, as yet, provided much of a brake on the direction of regulatory reform. There are a number of factors that may account for this. Until recently, the reforms have been instituted from a comparatively low regulatory base, with minimal restraint on non-standard work forms. Further, the preparedness of workers to protest through both legitimate and illegitimate channels places the government (which still, at least rhetorically, adheres to socialist ideology) under continual pressure to provide solutions to labour market problems. And unlike in the democratic states, the Chinese Central Government has a relatively free hand in implementing reforms, although local governments can notoriously resist central measures, not least because they have an important degree of control enforcement and dispute resolution bodies. Perhaps even more significantly, macroeconomic circumstances have been favourable over the recent reform period, so that unemployment has remained low. This has so far helped to deflect a critique that the measures are pricing people out of jobs. Whether this current approach to labour market regulation is sustainable may depend on China avoiding a major economic crisis, which is by no means assured.

---

[138] Data on labour disputes is available in the China Labour Statistics Yearbooks at Table 9.1 (中国劳动统计年鉴).

[139] See, e.g., Liisi Karindi, 'The making of China's new Labour Contract Law', (2008) 66 *China Analysis*, Trier University, Germany, November 2008.

[140] See B. Dong, 董保华 论劳务派遣立法中的思维定势 2013 (3) 苏州大学学报 *Suzhou Daxue Xuebao* 50–60. Compare, in the same issue of the journal, Q. Wang and H. Yang 王全兴 杨浩楠 试论劳务派遣中的同工同酬 – 兼评2012年《劳动合同法修正案》 and T. Shen 沈同仙, 论我国劳务派遣适用范围的法律规制 at 61 and 70 respectively.

4. BRAZIL

Although the rhythm has slowed down in the last few years, since 2004 Brazil has known a period of unprecedented economic growth that, combined with a strong policy of direct money transfer to the poorest people, has contributed to a reshaping of the country. Brazilian economic figures are well under these presented by China and India, but do not differ greatly from those presented by Russia and South Africa. Formal employment has been on the rise and wages have increased as a real gain over inflation has been accorded to the national minimum wage as a governmental policy.[141] For a country that three decades ago was struggling with hyperinflation,[142] uncontrolled public expenditures, IMF negotiations, a gigantic external debt and very low international credibility, things have definitely changed. This positive economic environment has contributed to the emergence of a new middle class which is the basis for the growing mass of new consumers that suggests a possible link between consumption and citizenship.

Nevertheless, social rights remain at the core of Brazilian citizenship.[143] Of course, civil and political rights also constitute an important dimension of citizenship[144] and this is not different in the Brazilian context. Yet, although the electoral body has grown over the years and is now composed of almost 141 million voters, the building of a democratic society in which equal opportunity is available to everyone remains a challenge for the country. Likewise, the question of property remains as an overwhelming challenge to civil rights. As Brazilian citizenship has thus strongly relied on social rights for its development, labour rights gained much weight, which is reflected in the *Consolidação das Leis do Trabalho* (CLT) [labor code]'s prominence. Since its edition in 1943, Brazil has undergone an authoritarian military period (1964–85) and has known three different constitutions (1946, 1967 and 1988), the last one being a symbol of the country's redemocratisation. As if it was immune to all these transformations, the labour code has resisted and remained almost unchanged. Even more, whenever talks about its need to be reformed and adapted to the country new economic circumstances arise, especially forwarding the urge of according preference to parties' negotiations

---

141 José Dari Krein, Anselmo Luis dos Santos, 'La formalización del trabajo en Brasil. El crecimiento económico y los efectos de las políticas laborales'. (2012) 239 *Nueva Sociedad* 90–101 (available at http://www.nuso.org/upload/articulos/3849_1.pdf, last accessed May 16, 2014). For the Portuguese version, see 'A formalização do trabalho: crescimento econômico e efeitos da política laboral no Brasil'. (2012) *Nueva Sociedad especial em português* 60–73 (available at http://www.nuso.org/upload/articulos/3860_1.pdf, last accessed May 16, 2014).

142 By March 1990, the monthly inflation rate had reached 84.32 per cent. See Luis Carlos Bresser-Pereira, 'Da Inflação à Hiperinflação: uma abordagem estruturalista', in *Inflação e Hiperinflação – Interpretações e Retórica* 7–28 (J. M. Rego ed. 1990) (available at http://www.bresserpereira.org.br/papers/1990/86.DaInflacaoAHiperinflacao.pdf, last accessed May 16, 2014); Luis Carlos Bresser-Pereira, Yoshiaki Nakano, 'Hiperinflação e Estabilização no Brasil: o primeiro Plano Collor', (1991) 11 *Revista de Economia Política* 89–114 (available at http://www.rep.org.br/PDF/44-6.PDF, last accessed May 16, 2014).

143 Wanderley Guilherme dos Santos, *Cidadania e Justiça: a política social na ordem brasileira* (1979); José Murilo de Carvalho, *Cidadania no Brasil: o longo caminho* (2001).

144 T. H. Marshall, *Cidadania, classe social e status* (1967).

over legislative settings, resistance steps up and blocks the debate.[145] Still, such preference for a legislative approach does not eliminate the quest for social rights' effectiveness.[146] Engraving social (and labour) rights in the constitution (as well as in the labor code) is not enough to inscribe them in the workplace, which remains an extremely conflictive space. Labour courts have therefore an important role in implementing labour rights and making formal statutory guarantees effective.[147]

Although Brazilian labour regulation does not have a specific statute that sets a minimum for employment conditions, it is all about statutes. As it has already been said, the Brazilian labour world is drowning in laws.[148] Labour regulation spreads out from the constitution to administrative ordinances issued by the Labour Ministry and it includes the labour code and several federal acts. Following what can be described as a 'legislative inflation' labour regulation has become a real normative labyrinth that is continuously growing.[149] As it is almost impossible to sum up this wide legal setting, one might concentrate the examination to the labour code (hereinafter, CLT).

CLT dates back to 1943 and remains valid in every aspect which is not contrary to the constitutional regulation. Back in the 1940s João Dirceu Mota, founder and president of the construction workers union of Quaraí in the State of Rio Grande do Sul, used to refer to it as 'my bible'. He used to wander around carrying his CLT booklet as a bulwark against employers' abuses, suggesting that all do's and dont's of the execution of a labour contract would be inscribed in it. Exploring workers' legal consciousness, French argues that the workers looked at it simultaneously as fraud and as hope.[150] Indeed, on one hand, reality on the working floor seemed not to correspond to what was inscribed into the law, while, on other hand, the law's prescriptions seemed to establish a desired scenario in which workers' rights would be fully respected. Thus labour law was not just a simple instrument of domination as ideological and institutional analysis usually points out but it was mobilised by workers to transform an ideal situation into a real setting. In other words, CLT reached the workers' imagination as the inevitable framework for a better circumstance on labour relations. A struggle for better working conditions would therefore also be a quest for labour law effectiveness and so it remains despite the new constitutional status of social rights.

This almost septuagenarian body of labour law remains a controversial one. Uncritically and mostly perceived as a 'mythical gift' of authoritarian President Getúlio

---

145 Entidades repudiam acordo coletivo como base das relações trabalhistas, in Senado Federal, http://www12.senado.gov.br/noticias/materias/2012/11/22/entidades-repudiam-acordo-coletivo-como-base-das-relacoes-trabalhistas, last accessed November 28, 2012.

146 Roberto Fragale Filho, 'Cidadania & Trabalho: fios de uma mesma fibra, constitucional?', in Fernando Facury Scaff (ed), *Constitucionalizando direitos: 15 anos da constituição brasileira de 1988* (2001) 443–75.

147 This and the following three paragraphs have been previously published in Roberto Fragale Filho, 'Resolving disputes over employment rights in Brazil' (2013) 34 *Comparative Labor Law & Policy Journal* 929–48.

148 John French, *Drowning in Laws: Labor Law and Brazilian Political Culture* (Univ. of N. Carolina Press, 2004).

149 José Eduardo Faria, *Direito e Conjuntura* (2009).

150 See note 148 above.

Vargas despite of other also available interpretations,[151] discussions over its reform have been on the public and legislative agenda almost permanently. Back in the 1960s, the core of the debate was related to the stability system of employment protection that assured tenure for employees after ten years working for the same employer.[152] Then, in the late 1970s during the military authoritarian period, unions' organisation became the central issue of dispute.[153] More recently, throughout the 1990s, in tune with international debate, flexibility came to be the main question as opposed to CLT's rigidity.[154] As Luiz Inácio Lula da Silva, a former union leader in São Paulo, became Brazil's President in 2003, expectations over a new turn on this debate were on its highest point.[155] Yet, despite some fragmented and circumstantial changes, one may say that CLT succeeded to resist most of its reform attempts. It persists as the main framework to regulate labour relations and its dispositions might be enhanced through negotiation.

Always a Matter of Flexibility

Notwithstanding CLT's durability, the debate over its impact on Brazilian economy has always cleaved between rigidity and flexibility. One may actually claim that flexibility has been a major issue in Brazilian labour relations over the last 50 years. Dispute over its pertinence as a tool for competitiveness has certainly grown in recent years. Yet this is definitely not a new debate. Actually, it is not hard to postulate it is an old debate over flexibility that has been repaginated under new economic circumstances mostly related to global competition. Back in the 1960s, when the law provided for tenure after ten years of work in a single labour contract, employers used to argue that such circumstances deeply affected employees' productivity and encouraged employers to circumvent the law as the cost of employee discharge increased enormously. Put differently, employers would maintain that they were economically incentivised (or compelled) to break the law so as to reduce expenses because employees would become lazy and unproductive after tenure. Such a never-proved argument was forwarded to justify the approval of Federal Act 5,107/1966 creating the *Fundo de Garantia de Tempo de Serviço* (FGTS), a time service fund made available to every employee in the case of an unfair dismissal that in practice ended up with the tenure regime that would be completely revoked only by the Federal Constitution in 1988.

Back in the 1970s, when the new syndicalism from where later to be President Lula emerged, the union structure forwarded by CLT was criticised by union leaders such as he, allegedly because its rigidity would not allow them freely to organise and to adequately represent employees. A new turnaround came by in the 1990s, when

---

[151] Luis Werneck Vianna, *Liberalismo e Sindicato no Brasil* (1976); Adalberto Paranhos, *O Roubo da Fala* (1999).

[152] Vera Lúcia Ferrante, *FGTS: Ideologia e Repressão* (1978).

[153] Iram Jácome Rodrigues, *O Novo Sindicalismo: Vinte Anos Depois* (1999).

[154] José Márcio Camargo (ed.), *Flexibilidade do Mercado de Trabalho no Brasil* (1999); Adalberto Moreira Cardoso, *Sindicatos, Trabalhadores e a Coqueluche Neoliberal. A era Vargas acabou?* (1999).

[155] Cf. Roberto Fragale Filho, 'Flexibilização e reforma da CLT: mais do mesmo?' (2004) 10 *Revista Trabalhista* 221–32.

Brazil's political and economic agendas were closer to the hegemonic neo-liberal perspective and labor regulation was mainly criticised as being an obstacle to the country's economic development. Flexibility was then praised as a tool to improve the country's economic figures and employability was in the order of the day. Criticism over CLT's allegedly rigidity echoed in law reform proposals concerning unemployment benefits and the access to FGTS. Alongside this debate focused on individual labour relations, flexibility pushed the discussion over outsourcing to the front of the scene. No one wanted to be an employer any longer: workers were then hired to work through contractors, temporary agencies and even cooperatives.

Flexibility and Labour Courts

Outsourcing in the beginning of the 1990s became a critical problem for labour relations. As flexibility and employability became the order of the day, long before David Weil's description of the fissured workplace,[156] Brazil became an intense laboratory for this kind of fragmented work environment. Lack of legislative response was then circumvented by labour courts, especially the highest one, the *Tribunal Superior do Trabalho* (TST), whose jurisprudence on the matter dated from September 1986. This prior jurisprudence was inscribed in *súmula* 256 which only admitted outsourcing in the restricted cases of temporary work and private security, which were both regulated by statute, respectively Federal Act 6,019/1974 and Federal Act 7,102/1983).[157] Clearly, the court's jurisprudence embraced a very restricted vision of outsourcing which required legal authorisation and, in the case of temporary work, was limited to two circumstances (momentary replacement and exceptional increase of work) and to a period of three months.

As economic conditions changed in the beginning of the 1990s and outsourcing became a major phenomenon in Brazilian labour relations, hundreds of thousands of cases came to the labour judicial system: between 1988 and 1994, the annual amount of new cases doubled as it went from 1,044,469 to 2,048,944.[158] As labour courts were then offering a wide set of different decisions concerning this supposedly new labour relations reality, in December 1993, TST finally reviewed its *súmula* 256 and edited its *súmula* 331 setting the new jurisprudence on the matter. The newly edited *súmula* reaffirmed outsourcing possibilities related to temporary work and private security and extended it to maintenance and cleaning services as well as establishing that it would

---

[156] David Weil, *The Fissured Workplace. Why Work Became So Bad for So Many and What Can Be Done to Improve It* (Harvard Univ. Press, 2014).

[157] 'In Portuguese, the word 'súmula' comes from the Latin word *summula*, which means brief, restricted, abstract. It is a synthesis of all similar cases, decided in the same way, put through a direct and clear proposition.' See Supremo Tribunal Federal, *Legal Glossary*, available at http://www2.stf.jus.br/portalStfInternacional/cms/verGlossario.php?sigla=portalStfGlossario_en_us&indice=S&verbete=196031, last accessed May 16, 2014.

[158] For 2013, the annual amount of new cases has reached 3,643,885. Actually, exception made to the first five years of the 2000s, when the number of new cases stabilised around 2,200.000, statistics indicate continuous growth. See Tribunal Superior do Trabalho, *Série Histórica da Movimentação Processual 1941–2014*, available at http://www.tst.jus.br/justica-do-trabalho2, last accessed May 16, 2014.

be legal for the end user to outsource the jobs related to its activities-means, as long as personal identity and subordination are not present. This newly introduced part created an unlikely and undefined conceptual distinction between activities-end and activities-means assuming that the former is related to the core activity of the end user and the latter does not have such characteristic.[159] A good example for such a conceptual distinction would be the call-centre of an automobile company: apparently, it would undoubtedly correspond to an activities-mean. Yet, this is a very subtle and difficult distinction that does not necessarily solve the problem. Another important innovation created by the *súmula* was the subsidiary responsibility of the end user in case of lack of compliance of labour standards by the labour supplier provided that the end user simultaneously has taken part in the judicial claim and appears in the judicial executive title.

Legislative response to this labour jurisprudence resulted in the Federal Act 8,494/1994 which established that 'whatever the field of activity of a cooperative society, there is no employment relationship between it and its members or between them and the end user of the labour services provided by the cooperative society'. This response was an attempt to make outsourcing easier whenever it was done with a cooperative society. Once again, the problem remained as CLT establishes that all acts aiming to undermine, prevent or circumvent the application of its precepts are full-fledged null. The dispute remained therefore over the conceptual matter of activities-end and activities-means.[160]

Differently from South Africa, India and China, in Brazil labour courts became the arena where flexibility gained legal recognition. But the court's jurisprudence was not intended to give outsourcing a free pass as it introduced a conceptual difference between activities-end and activities-means and invented a subsidiary responsibility unknown to the law. Controversy, still framed by the ideological criticism of a rigid regulation and its impact on economic development, has then moved to the legislative field.

Reforming the Law

As the debate moved to Congress, Bill Proposition 4,330 which was introduced originally in 2004, regained the scene. The bill aimed to regulate outsourcing practices arguing that it has become a reality that can be no longer ignored: 'trying, in a myopic way, to protect workers simply ignoring outsourcing, Brazilian legislation managed to leave Brazilian workers under such type of contract more vulnerable'. The bill acknowledges the non-existence of an employment relationship between the end user and the workers hired by the provider or its partners. Basically, the bill allows

---

[159] Karen Artur, *O TST e os doutrinadores jurídicos como agentes de novas noções contratuais do trabalho: um estudo sobre a terceirização* (2004).

[160] Later on, as the *Supremo Tribunal Federal* (STF), the Brazilian Supreme Court, held the constitutionality of article 71 of Federal Act 8,666/1993 that exempts Public Administration from any responsibility on labour, social security, tax and business duties of contractors hired through a public bidding, TST reviewed *súmula* 331 to indicate that the Public Administration's subsidiary responsibility can be recognized whenever it can be proved that it has failed to supervise that the labour provider complies with all the required labour standards.

outsourcing of any activity eliminating the court distinction between activities-end and activities-means. Textually, it establishes that 'the contract for the provision of services may relate to the development of activities inherent, ancillary or complementary to the economic activity of the user end'.[161] Needless to say that TST clearly reacted against the bill as 19 of its 26 members signed a public petition stating that its approval would result in a severe harm to labour and the social security rights of Brazilian workers.[162] The reaction was not limited to TST but also came from the *Associação Nacional dos Magistrados do Trabalho* (ANAMATRA), the national labour judge's association, which released an open letter urging congressmen and political parties to refuse its adoption[163] and released together with the NGO *Movimento Humanos Direitos* a series of videos casting well-known TV actors speaking against outsourcing.[164] Although the bill was not voted upon, the debate has not come to an end and outsourcing still is mainly regulated by the jurisprudence of labour courts.

Reforming the law seems to be extremely difficult in the Brazilian context where social rights are perceived as central to citizenship and most of the recent legal reform comes mostly to incorporate new rights or new workers to the labour standards provided by CLT. Evidence of such circumstance may be found in the debate over the incorporation of CLT provisions to domestic workers, which became a reality with Constitutional Amendment 72, approved in April 2013. Labour rights such as extra payment for overtime, indemnities due to unfair dismissal, FGTS, unemployment benefits then extended to domestic workers, are pending the adoption of implementing regulations.

The Outlook: Brazil

Brazil's labour regulation as expressed in CLT dates back to 1943. Ever since the debate has always revolved around its rigidity and how it slows down economic development, although no consistent empirical evidence of such has been provided. Unlike South Africa, India and China, labour courts and judges have played a critical role in Brazil both enhancing flexibility (as to make possible outsourcing of activities-means) and resisting a complete labour market flexibility (as to condemn outsourcing of activities-end). The debate is far from an end and it has recently turned to in a more

---

161 The bill is available at http://www.camara.gov.br/proposicoesWeb/prop_mostrarintegra;jsessionid=FC16E50E8BBCA91A5B71ABDF6C1BD820.proposicoesWeb1?codteor=246979&filename=PL+4330/2004, last accessed May 16, 2014.

162 See *'Ministros do TST condenam PL da terceirização'*, in *Consultor Jurídico*, http://www.conjur.com.br/2013-set-03/maioria-ministros-tst-condena-pl-libera-terceirizacao. The petition is available at http://s.conjur.com.br/dl/oficio-tst-terceirizacao.pdf, both last accessed May 16, 2014.

163 The open letter is available at http://s.conjur.com.br/dl/carta-aberta-anamatra.pdf, last accessed May 16, 2004.

164 Associação Nacional dos Magistrados do Trabalho, *Todos Contra a Terceirização*, available at http://www.youtube.com/watch?v=ajDjKK2Q9kA&list=UUBkzIMln4tENJ71oPcHCTdw (video 1), http://www.youtube.com/watch?v=tybXNwLfMco&list=UUBkzIMln4tENJ71oPcHCTdw (video 2), and http://www.youtube.com/watch?v=QfHdC0d1ZTg&list=UUBkzIMln4tENJ71oPcHCTdw (video 3), last accessed May 16, 2014.

expressive way to law reform. Even though most of the recent legal reform has mostly been done to enhance labour rights (and social rights) and to include a greater amount of workers under its application, general claims from the business world ask for greater flexibility in labour relations. Relating lesser costs to competitiveness, they cry out for flexibility.

This scenario does not seem to be unknown to the other BRICS, but similarities do not translate into common answers. For that matter, Brazil does not seem to draw any policy from its BRICS partners but relies essentially on its legal history and on the general perception that whatever flexibility may be provided it will always remain a matter of incorporating more and more workers to the ideal conditions provided for the minimum labour standards.

5. GENERAL CONCLUSIONS

The recent experience of the developed world, especially in several of the member states of the European Union, may create a general impression that labour law is in a phase of retrenchment. Whether this is in fact a correct impression may be debatable, but it is clear that, as far as the BRICS are concerned, no such simple conclusion can be drawn. We have in this chapter seen examples of major recent initiatives from each of the countries studied. There are striking similaries between law reforms in South Africa and China which have been implemented in 2013 and 2014. Amendments to the Labour Relations Act and the Basic Conditions of Employment Act in South Africa and the Labour Contract Law in China have targeted agency work in particular. While India has not taken similar measures as yet, there has been the important development of the Unorganised Workers Social Security Act in 2008.

These measures have been controversial, with opponents criticising their alleged rigidity. Whether these criticisms are well founded may soon become apparent – although earlier initiatives in China's Labour Contract Law have not, on current empirical evidence, led to widespread counterproductive effects.

We conclude this chapter by raising the issue of the influence of the BRICS countries on regional and indeed global labour law. During the twentieth century, the international study of labour law was overwhelmingly directed to the advanced economies of Europe, North America, Australia and Japan. These countries constituted the 'core' of labour law, with other nations, despite their huge workforces, relegated to neglect at the periphery. With many of the advanced systems sclerotic, in the process of being dismantled, or at least in gradual decline, it may be that the edge has moved to the centre, and vitality, innovation and experimentation are more likely to be located in Asia, South America and Africa.

Index